A Nation
of Nations

A Nation of Nations

Harper & Row, Publishers
New York, Hagerstown,
San Francisco, London

The People Who Came to America
as Seen Through Objects and
Documents Exhibited at the
Smithsonian Institution

Edited by Peter C. Marzio

FIRST EDITION

Designed by Chermayeff & Geismar Associates

Library of Congress Cataloging in Publication Data

Main entry under title:

A Nation of nations.

   Includes bibliographical references and index.

   1. United States—Civilization—Addresses, essays, lectures. I. Marzio, Peter C. I. Smithsonian Institution.

| E169.1.N3742   1976 | 973 | 75–25051 |

ISBN 0–06–012834–8 pbk.

76 77 78 79 10 9 8 7 6 5 4 3 2 1

Contents

Foreword

A Nation of Nations is a pretentious title for almost any exhibition or single publication. No one is more conscious of this than the historians, curators, and technicians who have been working on the Bicentennial salute to America here at the Smithsonian Institution. They are all aware of the obvious fact that every immigrant group has contributed in innumerable ways to American life. From the most pragmatic solutions of Samuel Slater to the most abstract theories of Albert Einstein, foreign-born citizens have given America its special place in the world. But the nation of nations has also been a place of turmoil among red men, white men, black men, and yellow men; it has been a caldron which has refused to melt the antagonistic elements into a new, single race of composite men. Rather, the American has come to be a multiple man, with allegiances here and sympathies to a past which somehow seems essential to his quest for personal identity.

Where were your parents from? And your grandparents? Your great-grandparents? Eventually, if the questioner persists, he will find a transplanted root. The 100 percent American is, after all, 100 percent something else. This book and the exhibition upon which it is based point out that simple theme: America is a nation of nations. In its laws, its foods, its arts, and its life styles, it represents a unique blend of Old World forms in New World conditions.

This book is unusual in several ways. First of all, its emphasis is on three-dimensional objects that reflect the theme of the settling of America. From Indian arrowheads to shortwave television, the range of objects reflects the varieties of people who make up our nation. Secondly, instead of focusing on the standard themes of immigration history, the work attempts to illuminate some of the ignored areas—the Old World contributions to America: from comic strips to handcrafts. And finally, *A Nation of Nations* touches both the masses of newcomers who built America and those special individuals who shone like stars in a turbulent galaxy of people on the move.

A Nation of Nations is a book to look at, to browse in, and to read. It is one of the Smithsonian's tributes to the American past.

S. DILLON RIPLEY
Secretary, Smithsonian Institution

Introduction

The transfer of peoples and cultures to America is one of the great themes of American history and, indeed, of the history of man. Migrations take place everywhere, but there has never been anything like the movement that produced the United States of America and generated continuing complexes of change. It yielded a nation unintentionally based upon the tensions of pluralism. The new nation ultimately reflected aspects of the best and the worst of many of the nations of the world—and yet differed remarkably from all nations that had previously existed: a land of hope and a land of trial to its own people and to people throughout the world.

Historians have not been unmindful of the drama of the transfer of peoples and cultures, but they have seen only selected aspects of the phenomenon. One pioneering student, Edward Eggleston, wrote a book called *The Transfer of Civilization,* in which he established the major questions that have dominated subsequent historical writing. He focused upon the "mental outfit" of the migrants because he believed their ideas, their attitudes, and their concepts constituted the essence of this transfer. Eggleston's concern was with the seventeenth century and primarily with English colonists. Historians who followed him have continued to be largely bound by the written word, and most of them have emphasized the transfer of ideas. Even recent scholars who attend to the elements of social history or who incorporate careful statistical analysis show limited interest in the material world.

This book, in contrast, is concerned primarily with the three-dimensional, nonverbal world, with the dwellings, clothing, food, means of transportation, arts, tools, and the homely accouterments of daily living. These objects do not suggest new theories about the migrations, about differential variation, or about conflict and consensus. They offer the opportunity to see some of the material aspects of these lost worlds and thereby to understand them a little better.

When this nation was proclaimed in 1776, it was already a nation of nations, set upon its remarkable course of receiving more and more diverse peoples and cultures, seeking usually to assimilate them, but succeeding often only in accommodating them in sometimes creative, occasionally destructive relationships. The Revolution itself and the character of the War for Independence can never be understood unless the cultural diversity of the English colonies is perceived.

By the time the Declaration of Independence was adopted, many of the characteristics of later migrations to the United States had already been demonstrated. This was surely not a melting pot but more of a tossed salad, with a very strong English dressing to carry it. Those who were not English or of English derivation and who did not belong to the dominant, established churches (the Anglican Church in the South and in New York, and the Congregational Church in Massachusetts and in Connecticut) suffered obvious disadvantages. There was consistent pressure to conform, to be assimilated into the culture of the majority. These pressures had very real force and effect, but at the same time all sizable minorities, except for the suppressed blacks, celebrated—often exuberantly—their cultural background and differences.

The prologue had already been stated. The almost impossible problems of bringing together under a single nation the great diversity of conflicting groups had already been experienced. Similarly, cultural creativity, based upon national and religious diversity, had been demonstrated in the flowering of Newport and especially in the achievements of the great city of the Revolution, Philadelphia. The two hundred years of national history that followed can now be seen as already forecast. The Revolution and the resulting War for Independence united many of the divergent and conflicting groups in a common cause which they called "The American Cause."

New dimensions of understanding arise from an examination of the three-dimensional world of those who participated in the great drama. What did immigrants bring with them? What did they quickly abandon? To what extent did they alter the objects and techniques they used in America? What was their physical world like?

The written record, even diaries and census and tax returns, leaves out many of the most obvious characteristics of history. Much that was taken for granted is especially hard to recover from the past. A traveler might comment upon the clothing, furnishings, tools, and buildings he encountered, but usually only when he found them unfamiliar. Diarists and other commentators had no need to describe what was known and understood by everyone.

Even when they did, their descriptions must be interpreted today by those who know intimately the objects mentioned. It is especially difficult to visualize the material world encountered by the earliest immigrants and their descendants. The objects assembled for the Nation of Nations exhibition and pictured in this book offer a wonderfully direct access to the period prior to the effective use of photography. When creative photography was applied by such men as Jacob Riis to the development of a visual archive of the immigrant's life, we were provided with a further dimension of the past.

Objects do not speak for themselves, or at best they speak very softly. Some parts of the messages are immediately apparent—for example, the scale of a windmill and the lightness of its construction, the care given to making a wedding dress. The similarity of spinning wheels of different derivations tells of the almost universal importance of that device.

Deeper levels of meaning are often contained in objects, but reaching them requires the same intensity of study that is devoted to the written word. The authors of this book have given their careers to acquiring this sort of expertise. They can effectively marshal products of English culture in America so that they may be easily and meaningfully compared with products of the non-English cultures. Beyond this, their experience reveals that even non-English artisans tended to follow English models. Thus, a Dutch silversmith in New York made silver objects similar to the English, and yet not entirely like them.

How is the peddler's wagon related to wagons found in Britain or on the Continent? The Pennsylvania farm wagon of 1860 is a descendant of the Conestoga wagon, which is assumed to have derived from a German market wagon abetted by English influences. Another descendant was the prairie schooner used in the westward movement. However, the record preserved in surviving examples and in writing is so defective that no clear genealogy can be constructed. Moreover, like the spinning wheel, the covered wagon was an experience shared by most of the parts of Europe from which immigrants began to move to America.

A similar complexity surrounds the story of the Pennsylvania or Kentucky rifle. It played a dramatic but severely limited role in the War for Independence, and it probably did derive from the German Jaeger rifle brought to America. On the other hand, the sort of evolution that converted the clumsy German prototype into the remarkably accurate Pennsylvania rifle was also taking place in Europe. The American development was probably not isolated from European influence, but that cannot yet be documented. The surviving examples on both sides of the Atlantic illustrate a fascinating but incomplete story.

Agriculture was the concern of most Americans and of most immigrants until well into the twentieth century, but the nature of the transfer of agricultural techniques does not fit neatly the expected model. Seventeenth-century settlers, more frequently than previously suspected, came from town rather than rural backgrounds. Even many of those with farming experience made little use of the plow in America and followed a type of agriculture that looked much like that of the Indians. By the nineteenth century, agricultural tools had evolved in a manner that differentiated them from what was familiar to the immigrants; the tools and techniques they had known were seldom applicable to the new scene. When Justus Liebig's study of soil chemistry opened new opportunities for improving yield, it was not the immigrants who brought the new knowledge. This was transferred by the scientific and scholarly community, primarily by Americans who went back to Europe to learn.

The industrial revolution, on the other hand, was transferred from England by immigrant mechanics who brought almost no actual machines with them. Following the classic example of Samuel Slater, they carried knowledge of devices and techniques and reproduced them here. This movement is demonstrable primarily in textiles, but it prevailed in the introduction of coke smelting, rolling, and puddling in iron production, and, in a more circuitous way, in the introduction of steam power. In the early nineteenth century, most American machine shops employed at least one English mechanic, a visible agent of transfer. There are many examples of the bodily transfer of discrete techniques, as in the case of the Bohemians who brought over the mother-of-pearl industry; Czech descendants still dominate it.

A continuing tension arose between the demands of American nationality for conformity and the desire of the immigrant and his descendants to preserve something of their old world. This social process has been more broadly a part of most Americans' experience than the transfer and adaptation of techniques. It can be significantly illuminated by examining surviving artifacts on still another level. From an early date most immigrants could move into or maintain ties with communities that preserved familiar cultural and religious patterns. In the eighteenth century, Philadelphia was the great port of entry, and immigrants were often met there by representatives of national societies who offered help. In the nineteenth and twentieth centuries, New York became the great magnet, with Castle Garden and then Ellis Island serving as the initial receiving centers. Voluntary groups were still active, but the government had taken a much larger responsibility for indoctrinating and assisting, and the nationalization process had become more formalized. For the earlier period, very little of either documentary or material sources remain; for the later, the photographic record is good and many helpful artifacts survive.

After the first shock of entry, the immigrant joined the rest of the ceaselessly striving Americans, although often in company with those who spoke his language and shared his values. The material life he experienced was only a variant of those prevailing at the time. In traveling, for example, he went by wagon, rail, canal boat, or steamboat, or he walked. Indeed, more than we have realized, most Americans in the nineteenth century walked. In the cities, they walked to work and they even walked from the settled areas out to the frontiers.

The institution most consciously dedicated to the inculcation of American values was the public school. Nothing could better demonstrate the ideal of equality and advancement through hard work than the physical appearance of the traditional classroom, in which every desk was exactly the same and every book was used by all. Differences would depend not upon background but upon effort and talent. The overarching community was emphasized by the flag, the prime symbol of the American nation, and by the pledge of allegiance.

On the whole, the immigrant accepted the American dream, the dream of equality under the law and of personal effort as the great engine of advancement. We know now that some were more concerned with security than with advancement; we also know that the stereotype of the docile, politically conservative immigrant is only partially correct. There also were radical immigrants who sought to improve life through large changes. Immigrants were pulled in differing directions into American political life. Their own leaders as well as native politicians played both noble and ignoble roles in reaching for the immigrant vote. In the large view, the political process did serve the American system while also serving the cultural identity of many immigrant groups. Something of the complexities of this process can be perceived in the physical trappings that have survived. They capture the flavor in a way words often miss. Even less verbal were other areas of endeavor that embraced divergent peoples within comprehensive American enthusiasms. These include the military life, sports, entertainment, and, perhaps most of all, work.

Not only immigrants and their descendants, but other Americans were prevailed upon to submerge their differences during wartime in a great national effort. As in the case of the classroom, the barracks is a symbol of the irrelevance of background in the face of an urgent task. Prejudices, of course, often surfaced, reflecting patterns of civilian life. Still, barriers were frequently broken in military life—as in the case of integrating blacks, beginning in World War II—before comparable progress was made outside.

Sports have always been great levelers. Questions of national, religious, or racial background truly become irrelevant to performance. Thus, immigrants and representatives of ethnic minorities have fulfilled the American dream by gaining fame and fortune in sports, while their brothers in other fields remained unknown. From Jim Thorpe, the Indian football hero, through Roberto Clemente, the Puerto Rican big league player, to Muhammad Ali, the black heavyweight champion, American sports have recognized individual performance. Here, despite the plethora of existing photographs, one can gain an almost mystical sense of returning to the past by contemplating the Yankee Stadium ticket booth and bench.

Even more than athletes, foreign-born entertainers and artists have succeeded in America. Such names as Jenny Lind, Enrico Caruso, and Harry Lauder recall performers of the past who helped transfer arts or traditions from abroad. Whether actors, musicians, playwrights, or composers, the objects associated with them serve as fundamental source materials and remarkably evoke the era in which they flourished.

Despite the importance of these activities, schooling and the military are temporary occupations for most people, and sports and entertainment are pastimes. The normal state of man, and increasingly of woman, in America is work or gainful employment. Here, as in other exposures, immigrants did not always encounter equal justice. Early foreign-born mechanics complained that they were valued only for their skills and that as soon as these were transferred, they were fired. Labor unions and American law have sometimes established restrictions or preferential patterns to limit incoming workers. Yet the work experience of the immigrant was nearly universal, and this was always a deeply important dimension of his indoctrination or acculturation. On the whole, immigrants entered existing trades or fields, and frequently they were very much impressed by the intensity of the American work effort. Although most immigrants did not come from a leisured background, they knew leisure as an ideal, yet they accepted the American standard of hard work and often exceeded other Americans in drive and application.

Among the technological and social changes that the United States, in common with much of the rest of the world, is still seeking to assimilate is the problem of instant, mass communication. It may well be that this will prove the greatest sandpaper of all. Television has already made inroads on regional accents and speech patterns, and it provides a nearly universal leveling device. Cultural diversity must relax in the face of instant news from everywhere. It is too early to know whether the result will be a culturally broader nation and one more responsive to social need. The institutions that have served a similar cause in the past have their weaknesses, but they have functioned well. It is reasonable to assume that present and future technologies will join proven institutions in further developing this pluralistic society within the nation.

Throughout most of the course of our history, the American people have seen themselves as a nation with a mission. From the Puritans who sought to plant their "City upon a hill" as a beacon to the world we received the sense of being a chosen people. Abraham Lincoln, with all his humility, saw us as "the last, best hope of earth." Americans have truly believed themselves superior to the evils and immorality that afflict the rest of the world. Immigrants have added some of the most impassioned statements supporting these views.

Yet today the picture is less clear and progress less certain. We recognize that the melting pot did not really melt, and it has taken some time to discover that the balance of diversity and conformity that has resulted may be vastly more desirable. America's role as the greatest peace-loving nation in the world has seemed sadly challenged in recent years, and the recognition of our true achievements has not sufficiently surfaced. We have even come to realize that our vaunted standard of living can be exceeded elsewhere and is almost certainly in jeopardy in the future.

Our present problems are primarily a result of our being the first to encounter the negative side effects of forward movement in the modern age, for example, in the new technologies and systems developments pioneered chiefly by the United States. It may still be as Gertrude Stein asserted that Americans were the oldest people in the world because they were the first to enter the twentieth century.

The United States has descended from the lonely pedestal on which it enjoyed a sense of unique virtue. It has entered the world of men and women from which it came and of which it has always been a part, but without always recognizing that it, too, may make the mistakes of Nineveh and suffer the misfortunes of Tyre. More than ever, we share the fortunes of the rest of the world, bound not only by instant communication and exceedingly rapid transportation but by culture, economy, technology, and science.

America today is part of an intricate fabric; we have been knitted into the daily life of the rest of the world. Often the United States has taken basic concepts from abroad, developed them, and exported them. Then, some of them have been further altered and developed and sent back to us as valued products. This has been the history of the automobile, the revolver, the sewing machine, instant photography, and the typewriter. Even institutions of popular culture, such as the comic book and the motel, have been thrown off and have taken root in unlikely places. These processes can be described in words, but they can be fully apprehended only through familiarity with the objects involved.

The networks of change and interchange that relate the United States to the rest of the world transcend nationality, and yet they have within them the spirit that made this country a nation of nations. The United States may find the years of its maturity the most difficult of all; they are surely the most challenging. But because much has been given to this nation, given by the peoples of all the world, much is still expected.

BROOKE HINDLE
Director
National Museum of History and Technology

For most illustrations of three dimensional objects at least one measurement is provided to give the reader a sense of scale:

D = diameter
L = length—left to right across the page
H = height— top to bottom of the page
R = radius
OAL = overall length

Part One

People
for a New Nation

These States are the amplest poem,
Here is not merely a nation,
but a teeming nation of nations.

Walt Whitman

Chapter 1

The First Americans

America was discovered about 22000 B.C. by a band of hunters from Siberia, crossing into Alaska at a time when the Ice Age glaciers trapped so much water that the sea was lowered and the Bering Strait was dry land. The New World was the last of the continents to be settled, quite recently in the perspective of the four-million-year age of the human family. On a scale of one hour per thousand years, that happened only yesterday, and Leif Ericson rediscovered America only an hour ago. Columbus, the third discoverer, arrived only half an hour ago, and the American Revolution was twelve minutes ago.

Those first arrivals were not aware of the vastness and richness of the new lands awaiting them south of the narrow glacier-free corridors that led east of the Rockies. We know they had reached southern South America by 9400 B.C. The hunting must have been good, for there were tremendous herds of large game animals which had not learned to fear this new predator, man. The human population expanded very rapidly. The fossil record shows that in a few centuries after man arrived, many species of large animals became extinct; it may be that this timing is no coincidence, that the southward-moving frontier of hunters, whose tools and weapons are sometimes found with the bones of these mammals, was responsible for their extinction [1]. Once the big game was gone, about 6000 B.C., the Paleo-Indian cultural period ended. The successor cultures, adapted to hunting smaller game, to fishing, and to the gathering of wild plants, differed more from region to region than had the Paleo-Indians.

Sometime around 5000 B.C. a cultural revolution began, probably in southern Mexico but also, very early, in the region of the Andes: agriculture was invented, independently of its earlier invention in the Old World and based on different crops. The most important plant brought into cultivation was the wild grass that was domesticated as maize, or Indian corn. From agriculture flowed settled village life, with a whole train of consequences in material inventions, including (in a few places) metallurgy and writing, in the increase of population, and in the development of new social and political institutions culminating in states and even empires. But the Indians in North America were on the peripheries of these developments. To the Mexican civilizations they were the northern barbarians, the Chichimecs, just as the inhabitants of Germany, Scandinavia, and the British Isles were for thousands of years the barbarians on the fringes of the Mediterranean centers of civilization.

From Mexico, agriculture based on corn, beans, and squash spread into the American Southwest, up the Mississippi Valley and throughout the forested East, up to about the present Canadian border. It never reached California, the Great Basin, and the far Northwest. Nevertheless, in some regions without agriculture, other food resources were sufficiently rich to allow the development of permanent villages and some of the cultural complexity that normally goes with agriculture. This was true in the central valley of California (dependent mainly on acorns) and in the coastal settlements living on the resources of the sea from northern California to the beginnings of the Aleutian chain [2–5].

Not only domesticated plants spread north from Mexico. Particularly on the lower Mississippi Valley and to the east, temples were constructed on mounds in a very Mexican manner, and Mexican concepts in art and perhaps in religion and sociopolitical organization were present. By the beginning of the sixteenth century there seem to have been small Indian states—with political organizations more complex than tribes—along the Gulf coast, across Florida, and up the Atlantic coast as far as Virginia. Here and elsewhere local agricultural innovations were added. Special varieties of corn were developed to grow in the desert and others were specialized for the short northern growing season. The sunflower was a North American addition to the Indian repertoire of cultivated plants. A local turkey was domesticated in the American Southwest (the only other animals domesticated in America were the llama and guinea pig of South America and turkeys and the "Muscovy" duck in Mexico; dogs came from Asia with their human masters).

By the time of Columbus there may have been about a million people living within the present boundaries of the United States. There were in this region many different kinds of native economies and tremendous cultural variety in other respects: for example, there were over two hundred different languages belonging to several unrelated linguistic families. There were certainly several hundred separate societies—small but distinct nationalities, some organized only as simple family bands of nomads, others as villages of a few score or a few hundred, others probably as small states or sets of affiliated towns totaling a few thousand citizens [6, 7].

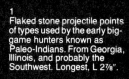

1
Flaked stone projectile points
of types used by the early big-
game hunters known as
Paleo-Indians. From Georgia,
Illinois, and probably the
Southwest. Longest, L 2⅞″.

2

3

4

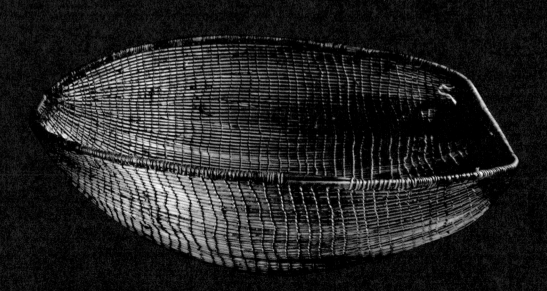

5

2
Prehistoric New Mexico
Pueblo Indian ax head of
basalt, grooved for hafting.
H 3½″.

3
Stone mortar and pestle used
by prehistoric Indians in New
Mexico to grind corn into flour
This Indian device was
named a *metate* and *mano*
(hand) by the Spaniards.
many of whom adopted its
use by 1600. Metate L 22′

4
Mortar and pestle used by
the Luiseño Indians of
southern California c 1900 to
grind acorns. The coiled
basketry hopper is attached
to the stone mortar with
asphaltum

5
Twined basket used by the
Yokuts Indians of California
for winnowing wild seeds.
collected in 1898. L 24′

One result of the arrival of Europeans was an increase in political complexity. The invaders, used to European concepts of political organization, wanted single leaders with authority to speak for scattered individuals and for several settlements at once. In response to this demand, many Indian communities developed more centralized authority. Isolated and independent bands united as tribes for the purpose of negotiating with Europeans. Similarly, independent tribes found it expedient to form or to strengthen already existing confederations.

Even in advance of the Indian-white frontiers the effects of the conquest were felt. Economic realignments, new movements of Indian populations, the arrival of horses on the plains, the spread of guns everywhere—all these were unsettling changes that must often have resulted in new social, political, and religious inventions even before literate observers could record them.

Disease was the major early gift from the Old World. The Puritans could not explain why it struck the Indians but not the English who mingled with them. They concluded, with self-interest or naïveté, that God was thus preparing the cleared fields of the Indians for the English to occupy. The real cause was the Indians' lack of immunity to diseases common in Europe but previously unknown in America. Smallpox was a major killer, and in the earliest periods so were respiratory infections, measles, and other diseases of European children. Epidemics started from brief and casual contacts: for example, with fishermen on the New England coast before the Puritans arrived and, surely, with de Soto's large force that walked from Florida across the South to Mexico in 1539–1543. In many places sudden deaths from disease cut populations by half or more in a matter of weeks, and the same societies were hit repeatedly by epidemics every few years. The effects can hardly be imagined; since there were no sympathetic literate observers, we can only estimate the number of deaths and guess at the disastrous social and cultural consequences that are indicated in some places by a rapid deterioration in the number and complexity of archaeological sites dating from this period. The Indians often suspected that they were being poisoned, but they never understood why this was happening to them.

There is much debate about the actual figures, but it is known that the total Indian population went from a high point at the time of Columbus to a low point about 1890. Since that time, much to the surprise of non-Indians who still think of them as the "vanishing Americans," Indians have become the most rapidly growing American minority. The total is now up to about one million—approximately the total population at the time of Columbus—from a low of about half a million. Of course, the population is differently distributed: for example, today the largest tribe is the Navajo, whereas in 1492 there were large populations in areas of the East Coast where there are now no survivors at all.

Although the effects of military campaigns on population decline are often exaggerated, they cannot be discounted. It may be true, as has recently been claimed, that in the period of the Indian wars the Indians actually killed more whites, both soldiers and civilians, than the Army killed Indians in the course of open hostilities. In guerrilla warfare the irregulars probably do have lower losses. But the non-Indian population rose rapidly through immigration as well as by natural increase, so even though they were perhaps losing more people in warfare than were the Indians, the effects were less serious. But body counts of direct battle deaths do not give the whole picture, especially when the counts are almost all recorded by one side. There was also a tremendous loss among the Indians due to forced movements and disruption of community life: people on the run have difficulty feeding themselves and recovering from illnesses. We know that during the forced removals of eastern tribes to the west of the Mississippi, mortality was great among the weaker elements of the populations.

In California during and after the Gold Rush, casual hunting and killing of Indians amounted to genocide. It surely was not national policy, but there it was unofficial local policy and went unpunished. Elsewhere, too, Indian communities had more to fear from the local and state authorities (and still have), as well as from individual white frontiersmen, than they had from the policies of the more remote central government at first in London and then in Washington.

The interaction between the native Americans and the later arrivals resulted in warfare and destruction and also in the evolution of legal concepts to define the rights of the discoverers and of those discovered. According to the traditional rhetoric of American history, Columbus, or maybe Leif Ericson, discovered America, and the Pilgrims, or the Jamestown settlers, first settled it; the prior discoverers and the prior settlers tend to be ignored in the popular view of American history. Yet the priority of Indian occupation and the nature of the interaction between Indians and whites in the New World help to explain why the Indians achieved their unique separate legal status in the United States. That special status—as contrasted, for example, with the much weaker position of the aborigines vis-à-vis the European invaders in Australia—owes much to the way Indians developed strong military and political organizations in the centuries of contact with Europeans.

But the preservation of some autonomy (internal sovereignty might be a better expression) by American Indian societies owes something to European religious and legal assumptions as well as to the effort of American Indian nations to maintain their cultural and political identity. Christianity recognized in principle the equal worth of every human being. Although it took many centuries for that principle to reach its present state of observance, the root concept did save important Indian minorities from being erased. Similarly, the practical-expedient strain in English legal thought encouraged colonial officials to recognize the independent status of Indian nations with resulting treaties binding on both parties.

Although treaty making came increasingly under attack by Americans like Andrew Jackson (who felt that the growing weakness of the tribes made it unnecessary to deal with them as equals), the process continued until 1871. Even after the treaty form of negotiation was abolished, agreements continued to be made with Indian tribes that have proved to be as legally binding as the treaties that preceded them. Though it is a commonplace among Indians to remark that none of the treaties has been kept by the whites, in fact the record is less grim. But because fraud was widespread in both treaty and nontreaty relationships, Congress in 1946 established the Indian Claims Commission to examine the record and reimburse (in money, not in land) Indian tribes that had been victims of "fraud, duress, unconscionable consideration, mutual or unilateral mistake, or dealings less than fair and honorable, whether or not the claims might be recognized by existing rules of law or equity." Over half a billion dollars in awards have been made by the commission.

The treaty relationship by which American Indian societies are tied to the federal government is perhaps the most fundamental legal evidence of the special position of the Indian in American life. The most visible physical evidence of that special status is the reservation. A map of the United States will show the country (in particular the western half) dotted with reservations, some the size of smaller eastern states. It is not generally known that a reservation boundary has some of the characteristics of an international boundary. The taxing power of the state, for example, cannot extend within the reservation except in a restricted fashion, and lands held in trust for the Indian tribes are not subject to taxation. This exemption is part of the special arrangement by which the Indians ceded most of their land in return for certain rights. An Indian nation, by its treaty with the government, sometimes has the right to exclude all except approved government officials from its territory; it may have the right to refuse to turn over fugitives unless appropriate extradition agreements are in effect. Indeed, some Indian reservations are experimenting with separate automobile license plates, as a highly visible symbol of tribal jurisdiction.

Instead of the amalgamation and assimilation that many theorists hoped for, or the extermination and destruction that others sought, the Indian has been able to retain his tribal identity at the same time that he has obtained the option to function as an individual American citizen. Some Indians became citizens in the early years of the Republic, largely under the provisions of treaties which authorized individual allotment of lands and integration into the surrounding white community. In World War I many noncitizen Indians loyally served their country without enjoying full rights and privileges. This injustice was corrected by Congress in 1924 with a blanket grant of citizenship to all Indians. Even after the passage of the act, Indians could not vote in a number of states which required additional qualifications beyond citizenship. The act of 1924—at the height of the concern over mass immigration from Europe—marked the full legal acceptance of American Indians into the multinational United States. At the same time it did not invalidate the special legal status of the Indian tribes and hence of the individual tribal member.

In the seventeenth and eighteenth centuries it was usual to refer to Indian ''nations'' rather than ''tribes.'' But there has never been a single ''American Indian'' nationality: there are hundreds of different groups of native Americans who speak (or did speak) different languages, with different customs and different histories. But just as the term *European* describes the geographical and cultural links that bind the different European ethnic groups together, so does the term *Indian* (based on Columbus's mistaken notion that he had reached India) bind together the varied ethnic strains of the Americas (also inappropriately named, for the traveler Amerigo Vespucci).

The unity implied in the phrase *American Indian* has over the years taken on real meaning. The reasons are many. Whites traditionally have thought of Indians as basically similar, and so they were in comparison with European man if not in comparison with each other. European (and later American) policy with regard to the Indian has emphasized unity rather than diversity among Indian groups. Indians from different tribes have shared experiences in dealing with non-Indians and increasingly have shared elements of the general American culture they have learned from these experiences. Intertribal contacts increased steadily, with forced and voluntary removals, more efficient means of transportation, shared knowledge of English; with this increase has come borrowing of cultural traits between different tribes and also increased understanding of each other's home communities.

Today for many Indians identity as Indian, as Native American, is at least as important as membership in any specific tribe. Pan-tribal organizations such as the National Congress of American Indians and, more recently, the American Indian Movement (AIM) have been formed by Indians to speak with a more powerful and unified voice in influencing legislation and other matters affecting Indian status. The existence of pan-Indian groups has helped define a new Indian identity which is distinct both from individual tribes and from the larger society with which the new organizations are grappling. Pan-Indianism tends to be especially strong in the urban areas, where Indian people increasingly reside—more than half of them by latest estimate—although their individual tribal roots go back to the various reservations and rural communities from which they came (and with which they tend to maintain stronger contacts than do most rural migrants to American cities).

The cultural contributions of Indians to the American nation were most important in the earliest period of European settlement. It is strange that American tradition holds that the Indians were wandering savage hunters who had to be taught settled civilized farming, while at the same time Americans remember that the first European colonies would not have survived without the help of neighboring Indian farmers, from whose stocks came the corn, beans, and squash to carry the helpless English over the first hard winters. Quickly the new settlers learned Indian methods of growing these crops and of harvesting, storing, and eating them. Cornbread, grits, hominy, roasting ears, and succotash are all based on Indian recipes. North Americans have also adopted Mexican Indian foods—avocados, chocolate, tomatoes, chilis, tortillas—which have spread either via the Southwest or indirectly via Europe.

From the Indians the Old World invaders also learned how to get along in the new land. They borrowed Indian names for many animals, plants, and places; they followed Indian trails (at first with Indian guides) on land—using Indian moccasins, snowshoes, and pack baskets—and on streams and rivers in Indian-made or Indian-style birchbark and dugout canoes. They learned Indian uses of wild plants for medicine and food, and they even adopted military tactics from Indian enemies and allies (and later turned them with advantage against European-trained armies). Beyond the frontiers individual Europeans lived in many ways like Indians. In the high Arctic until quite recently, explorers and travelers survived only by copying Eskimo methods of dress, shelter, and travel, and by using Eskimo guides and hunters. Similarly, in the first centuries of settlement in the more temperate regions, frontiersmen, trappers, explorers, and mountain men, in order to survive, copied Indian clothing, hunting techniques, food, and shelter, followed Indian routes, and participated in Indian trade.

Cultural borrowing—what anthropologists call diffusion and acculturation—is, of course, a two-way street. In North America, Indian societies have in the long run been overwhelmed by European cultural traits; the exchange has by no means been a balanced one. The disparity in the sizes of the populations ensured that. Borrowings began with the very first meetings, and soon items of European origin became typically Indian: not only the Indian pony, but glass beads (and floral beadwork designs), metal tomahawks and other tools and weapons, wood-splint basketry, cloth clothing, vermilion face and body paint, Navajo sheep, weaving, and silver jewelry, and much more [8–14].

6
Cliff Palace, Mesa Verde, Colorado, occupied by Pueblo Indians around 1200 A.D. Dwelling and ceremonial rooms have thick stone walls, some rising to a height of four stories under the sheltering face of the cliff. Indians grew corn and squash in the fields below and hunted game elsewhere.

7
The branch-supported grass lodge of Papago Indians in southern Arizona extends a traditional type of domestic architecture from prehistoric America into the late nineteenth century. Photographed in 1894.

8
After receiving the horse from Spanish settlements about 1700, the tribes on the Great Plains became nomadic hunters of bison, living in mobile homes of tanned hides supported by a cone of poles much larger than those dogs could pull. However, the dog travois continued in use to transport household goods, as shown in this engraving of an Assiniboin camp after an 1833 drawing by Carl Bodmer.

8

9
9
A Hopi village in Arizona,
photographed in 1876. The
apartment-house archi-
tecture retains its prehistoric
forms and construction techniques, except that roof-hole
entries have been replaced
by Spanish-derived door-
ways. The woman wears a
blanket woven by Indians of
wool from Spanish-introduced
sheep, while a purely native
rabbitskin blanket hangs on
a wall.

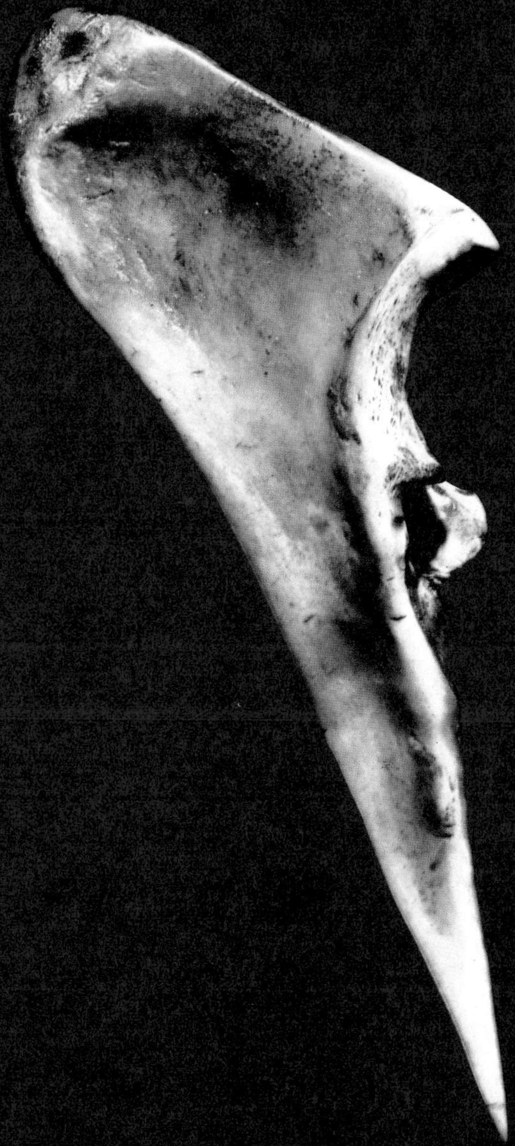

10
Eskimo awl of shaped bone
from St. Lawrence Island,
Alaska: late 1800s. Generally
used for punching holes in
hides. L 6″.

11
Triple-envelope Algonquin Indian pouch made of hide, porcupine quills, brass, and hair in the late 1700s. The art style is traditional Indian, especially in the manner of depicting the human figures and the two turtles, but the house or chapel and the ship with its rigging and flag are European. European brass is integrated with native materials and dyes. H 20½".

12
American Indians were a great curiosity to Europeans throughout colonial times. This trio of Cherokees was invited to London in 1762 and presented with silver gorgets, elegant robes, a clay pipe, and a metal hatchet. While the heads may be Cherokee portraits, the remaining parts of the figures were copied from engravings of Mohawks who visited England in 1710, exemplifying the European tendency to stereotype the American Indian.

11

12

The Three Cherokees, came over from the head of the River Savanna to London 1762.
1 Their Interpreter that was Poisoned.

13
This dignified portrait of
Hodjiage-de (born c. 1816), a
Cayuga Iroquois of the eastern woodlands, displays native traditions in the roach
head ornament (made of deer
hair), shell jewelry, and
decorated buckskin garment.
European influence is demonstrated by the imported
beads, lace, and ribbons, and
by the cut of the velvet jacket
and its floral decorative patterns. The metal pipe tomahawk is a product of the
welding of Indian and European cultures.

14
This engraving of a 1791
Creek house demonstrates
how Indians adopted the use
of the metal hoe, the gun, and
horizontal notched log
houses from Europeans be-
fore 1800. Western Euro-
peans had begun to meet
eastern American Indians on
a regular basis for trade before 1550.

15
Wooden food bowl used for
ceremonies by the Haida
Indians, carved c. 1870. L 11″.

14

15

16
Dance mask made of local wood, fiber, leather, and paint and imported copper by the Tlingit Indians of Alaska c. 1880. With his head covered by this mask and his shoulders by a large cape, the dancer dissolved into the spirit of the bird represented. L 23″.

17
Iroquois wooden mask, with non-Indian white paint and tin eye plates, and horsehair attachment. Made on the Six Nations Reserve, Ontario, c. 1900, but of a type still used for curing by New York Iroquois. H (including hair) 31″.

By now, acculturation has proceeded to the point where members of many Indian communities share practically the entire cultural inventory of non-Indian Americans, including language, attitudes, and values. But it must be emphasized repeatedly that such acculturation does not necessarily mean assimilation of Indian individuals and Indian societies into the larger society; Indian social identity and distinctness still persists, along with their special legal status. None of us practices unchanged the customs of our grandparents; yet that has not broken our continuity with our past. What is significant is the continuity of communities, of social groups. If such communities maintain separateness to some degree, if their distinct identity continues to be recognized, then a very few special customs, cultural traits, or forms of behavior will suffice to symbolize and label that separate identity. In some Indian communities today the special culture amounts to little more than sharing a group name. In others, of course, a great deal of distinctive culture survives from the past. Especially in the Southwest are traditional Indian cultures strong: Indian languages, religions, arts, and distinctive behavior can readily be observed [15–17].

Biological contributions of Indians to America are a separate issue. Interbreeding and intermarriage have been going on for about 475 years in North America. If one could ask all Americans whether they have any Indian ancestors, a large proportion of both whites and blacks would reply that they do (no one knows how large a proportion). On the other hand, most Indians have some European ancestry, and a smaller percentage have some African ancestry. Many people who are socially and legally entirely Indian are biologically nearly wholly European. The point is that biology—"race"—is different from both social identity and cultural tradition. Evidently it is easier for modern Americans to recognize that this is true of Indians (and Orientals) than it is for them to realize that the same applies to whites and blacks.

For most of the time that there has been an "Indian policy" in America—official and popular—that policy has been assimilationist. The idea has been that Indians as individuals and as communities should merge with the rest of the population, that they should disappear as Indians. But the policy has not worked. Many individual Indians have indeed vanished through assimilation, but hardly any community or tribe has wholly disappeared since the end of the days of conquest by warfare, genocide, or disease.

There are many reasons Indians have not disappeared into the general population as have several larger minorities of European origin. Prejudice and discrimination have always existed (though perhaps applying less to Indians than to other non-Europeans), and, while assimilation was the stated goal and policy, those who had to implement it erected barriers to prevent or impede the process. Furthermore, the social theorists, the politicians and statesmen, the missionaries, administrators, schoolteachers, have until very recently had little idea of how difficult an act they were expecting of the Indian people. Assimilation of immigrants from Europe and elsewhere has not been easy, but that it happened with Europeans and not with Indians is partly because the cultural distance was much less and partly because individuals or families were involved, not whole villages or entire societies. For the Indian to be fully assimilated, entire social organizations had to be shattered and totally eliminated.

All other elements in the American population either decided to leave their native country (which implies some dissatisfaction and thus readiness to adjust to a new environment) or else were violently wrenched from their homes and sent into slavery across the ocean, leaving no choice but adjustment and assimilation. But Indians are not like this at all. They are members of societies that remained in their native country, where they were invaded, conquered, and overwhelmed by foreigners. How much more difficult it has been, then, for them to give up all that remains of the ancient homeland, the old ways, and their original identity in order to join the society of the invaders.

The schools of the Bureau of Indian Affairs no longer forbid the use of Indian languages; overt coercion to an ideal of dress or behavior is a thing of the past. The path to assimilation is easier than it ever was, if Indians wish to follow it. Many Indians continue to seek to retain both the ways of their fathers and the ways of their non-Indian friends. Over ten thousand Indians are now in the nation's colleges and over five hundred are pursuing graduate work. These figures represent a tenfold increase over ten years. Indians have made rapid strides economically: income has risen from a tiny fraction of the white average to half that average and is on the way up. While still subject to manipulation by Bureau of Indian Affairs administrators (many of them Indians themselves) by virtue of the trust relationship, Indian tribal governments have established a widening area of political and cultural autonomy by means of judicial decrees, presidential initiative, and legislative enactments. Yet many thorny issues continue to bedevil Indian-white relations, particularly issues of fishing and hunting rights as guaranteed in treaties, water rights of western tribes, and problems of the constitutional rights of individual Indians against their tribal authorities.

Although immigrant Americans have often appropriated Indian traits and the Indian past to symbolize their own distinctness from their overseas origins—the Mohawk dress donned for the Boston Tea Party is not an isolated example—still, what D. H. Lawrence called the "ghost of the Indian" continues to infuse the white American's psyche, disturbing his conscience, continually recalling to him the manner of America's birth. For the red minority was originally on the other side of a cultural and political barrier. When the European immigrant advanced, the native American retreated. Although whites and Indians frequently joined hands in trade, often in alliance, and occasionally in love, most often their relationship was one of conflict. Each side developed a psychic antagonism toward the other. These attitudes were expressed in the customary Indian denunciation of the white man who spoke with a forked tongue, while the white stereotype, incorporated in a hundred captivity narratives, was of a savage and merciless fiend who tortured for the love of it. Included in the European attitude toward the Indian were elements of physical fear, of sexual attraction, and of personal admiration for the Indian's apparent freedom from civilization's restraints.

More recently the qualities of strength, endurance, bravery, and oneness with nature have come to supplant the negative aspects of cruelty, ferociousness, and anger in the image of the Indian. Both Indians and non-Indians can at last join in a dialogue about what represents the Indian heritage, and both sides can claim to cherish and honor that heritage. If Americans agree on what the Indian stands for in American life, there is hope that the most painful of the divisions in America's multiethnic society can finally be bridged.

Chapter 2

The Letter to Santángel

In [Española], there are many havens on the seacoast, incomparable with any others that I know in Christendom, and plenty of rivers so good and great that it is a marvel. The lands thereof are high, and in it are very many ranges of hills, and most lofty mountains incomparably beyond the island of Tenerife, all most beautiful in a thousand shapes, and all accessible, and full of trees of a thousand kinds, so lofty that they seem to reach the sky. And I am assured that they never lose their foliage; as may be imagined, since I saw them as green and as beautiful as they are in Spain during May. And some of them were in flower, some in fruit, some in another stage according to their kind. And the nightingale was singing, and other birds of a thousand sorts, in the month of November, there where I was going.

So wrote Christopher Columbus in 1493 to Luis de Santángel, who had helped finance his voyage. Columbus's letter, soon published, informed Europeans for the first time of his momentous discoveries. It recorded the epic moment of contact between Western civilization and a virgin continent of breathtaking wonder.

Had the conquest of the New World been motivated only by the desire to colonize side by side with the Indians, it might have had a less sanguinary history. The lure of gold and obsessive fantasies about America's riches, together with a compulsion to Christianize, determined that it should be otherwise.

It was primarily the search for wealth that inspired the exploration of the New World. One of the marks of Europe's emergence from the Middle Ages and feudalism was a new urban middle class of aggressive traders which promoted adventurous, seaborne commerce and the growth of merchant states like Venice and Genoa. Among the earliest stimuli to maritime enterprise were Marco Polo's travels to China in the thirteenth century. First by word and then by print in 1477—after the invention of movable type—Marco Polo's account spread wide its wonders and stirred breathtaking projects in the minds of a new generation of men. The world of the Renaissance had arrived and ideas were bubbling like champagne, providing inspiration for princes and merchants to make profitable contacts with the distant eastern trade routes.

So it was that the Portuguese in the fifteenth century sponsored voyages of daring length along the African coast for slaves, ivory, and spices. By this time practical navigators and scientific philosophers alike were accepting the fact that the world was a sphere. One of these was Christopher Columbus, about whose youth we know little, only that he was a well-read Genoese. A learned Florentine named Toscanelli stirred Columbus with the assertion that the shortest and most direct route to China and the Indies was due west from Europe—indeed, it was a matter of a mere five thousand miles or less.

Columbus, obsessed with the idea that a voyage of only a few weeks would bring the fabled cities of Cathay within reach of western Europe, solicited the king of Portugal's support for an expedition. He failed because the king's scientific advisers could not accept Toscanelli's theory of a world smaller in circumference than was generally believed. Columbus then approached the royal family of Spain. After years of delay, but with support both substantial and political from the Lord Privy Purse, Luis de Santángel, Queen Isabella finally authorized Columbus's unprecedented expedition.

Once achieved, his voyage was to have immediate renown. The evidence of his well-kept journal, the display of six Indians whom he brought back, and his belief, shared by most contemporaries, that he had reached the Indies confirmed his achievement. Despite the Vikings and other possible explorers, Columbus was, for the European nations, the discoverer of the New World.

Of course, Columbus himself was convinced that Hispaniola, Cuba, and whatever land he saw were offshore Asian islands. He had, he thought, succeeded in reaching India, and just beyond lay the mainland. Columbus's delusion was his frustration. Although convinced that he would reach cities of gold, he found only simple villages of primitive Indians. When he returned to Spain he was able to show scarcely a handful of gold. Yet he felt compelled to write to Santángel, as though it were a fact, about "many and great rivers and excellent waters, most of which contain gold."

Columbus made three more voyages. Although he failed each time to produce the riches of the Indies (his credibility was at such a low ebb during his third voyage that his detractors put him in irons), he nevertheless established Santo Domingo and other European settlements and his son Diego built a Renaissance palace, Isabela, that still stands. Thus, while searching for what was not there, Columbus, before 1500, succeeded in initiating the historical reality of America. After Columbus— and indeed before his death in 1506—there was a great burst of exploration and discovery.

It was Spain that invested its resources most heavily in the search for the myth, legend, and fact of great riches. A Portuguese under Spanish auspices, Ferdinand Magellan, confirmed that the new lands consisted of independent continents—by sailing around one of them through the straits that bear his name and across the "South Sea" that Balboa called "Pacific." In the early sixteenth century Spain found the wealth it had been seeking—not in the Indies, but in the two new continents.

In 1519 Hernando Cortés began his dramatic demolition of the Aztec empire, which led to the establishment of New Spain. Landing at the seacoast near the site of Vera Cruz, he was met by emissaries of the Aztec emperor Montezuma. Overwhelmed with presentiments of his own doom that Cortés's arrival inspired, Montezuma was unsure whether Cortés was a foreign enemy or the predicted reincarnation of the white god Quetzalcoatl. With submission seemingly inevitable in either case, Montezuma fended off Cortés by sending lavish gifts of gold and jewels from Mexico City, but rejected Cortés's wish to visit him.

Cortés, with real proof now of the existence of treasure, ignored Montezuma's rejection a.. ' set off with his army, fighting hostile Indians along the mountainous way to Mexico City. Arriving peaceably, he was met by Montezuma, bearing more gifts. After a period of nervous coexistence in the city, Cortés forced the great surrender and detention of Montezuma and plundered his treasure. When the people realized what had happened, they killed Montezuma and rose in rebellion against Cortés, driving him and his army back to the sea in retreat.

In 1521 Cortés returned for a horrendous, blood-drenched reconquest. With Cortés securely in control, Mexico City now rose from its ruins with Spanish-style churches and palaces to become the capital of New Spain. From here ruled the government which explored and populated a vast area of the present United States, establishing a Spanish culture that continues to enrich this nation. Cortés himself, however, aroused the resentment of his superiors and was refused the office of viceroy of New Spain. Although granted land and estates and the nobleman's title Marquess of the Valley of Oaxaca, he was never given back a power that had threatened to exceed that of the emperor himself.

Meanwhile, the position of New Spain was consolidated and the unknown lands to the north were eyed. In 1528 Pánfilo de Narváez, the grand constable of New Spain, titular governor of Florida, and a defeated enemy of Cortés, led a seaborne expedition from Cuba to explore the Gulf of Mexico. Landing in Florida, he divided his forces of about four hundred men between ships and land. His plan was to move his soldiers along the Gulf Coast and explore the adjacent territory, while one of the ships would find a vaguely rumored port in which to anchor, keeping in contact with the men on shore. Failing this, the ships would go back to Havana and return with more ships. Narváez's treasurer and second in command was the able and valiant Cabeza de Vaca, who vehemently opposed such a plan as disastrous. The pilot, he pointed out, not only did not know where the alleged port was, he did not even know where he was at that moment. Once parted, reunion was forever unlikely.

Narváez was adamant; de Vaca, whose predictions proved to be terrifyingly correct, bowed to his superior. Thus began an expedition of such tribulation and death, of such prolonged suffering, as few men in history have endured. When the journey ended for the survivors after eight years and two thousand leagues, only four in Narváez's original overland company remained alive—de Vaca, a black Moorish slave named Estévan or Estevanico, and two Spaniards.

De Vaca's account, written as a report to the viceroy of New Spain, is an epic of Indian fights, impenetrable swamps and forests, starvation, thirst, enslavement, and disease. At the start in Florida, the Indians told Narváez that there was gold in the town of Apalachen, located in the Florida panhandle. With this as an objective, the company started off. Having rapidly consumed the two pounds of hardtack and the pound of bacon that Narváez had allotted each man, they struggled against hunger in addition to hostile Indians and dangerous river crossings. They arrived at last in Apalachen, a town of forty huts with no gold in sight but a welcome supply of corn. Narváez seized the corn, took custody of the chief, and captured the women. The male Indians, not surprisingly, attacked.

Finally Narváez decided to build boats and take to the Gulf Coast waters, even though skills and tools were lacking. Relying on their ingenuity, their single carpenter, and a Greek named Theo, who made caulking out of pine tree resin, they built a forge, made nails and hardware from spurs and stirrups, and completed five boats. Loaded to the gunwales, the boats set sail, but they soon became separated. At one point, de Vaca's men, stripped to the skin, pushed their boat into deep water, having first tossed their bundles of clothes inside. A wave capsized the boat, their clothes sank from sight, and for the rest of their eight-year journey they were as naked as the Indians.

In order to survive, de Vaca and his companions dispersed to live with Texas Indian tribes. Six years went by, until their number diminished to only four. Reduced finally to slavery, they were subjected to savage abuse, belabored past endurance, and almost starved to death. Yet they shared the misery of these Indians and came to understand their ways. Finally they escaped and came to another Indian village, where they were commanded to cure some inhabitants of their headaches. With the consequences of refusal overbalancing religious scruples and fears of failure, they prayed and commended the Indians to God. The Indians "instantly said that all pain had left, and went to the houses bringing us prickly pears, with a piece of venison."

Word flashed ahead. "As through all the country they talked only of the wonders which God our Lord worked through us, persons came from many parts to seek us that we might cure them." Joined by an increasing following of Indians, de Vaca's little group were met with awe and gifts wherever they went, praying over sick Indians, in whose eyes they caused miraculous cures. Eventually they reached the regions of New Mexico, Arizona, and northern Sonora, curing, healing, and by benevolent example converting whole populations to Christianity.

One day they heard that Christians had arrived from a westerly direction. The evidence of hundreds of fleeing Indians was confirmation that "Christians" of a different sort were indeed nearby. For these men, de Vaca and his companions, naked and gaunt, were an astonishing sight. These were Spanish slave hunters, who pillaged Indian villages and seized the inhabitants.

There was an angry confrontation between the two groups, but despite their differences, some of the slave hunters set off to guide the four men to San Miguel de Culiacan, the northern outpost of New Spain.

"They took us through forests and solitudes, to hinder us from intercourse with the natives," wrote de Vaca, "that we might neither witness nor have knowledge of the act they would commit. It is but an instance of how frequently men are mistaken in their aims; we set about to preserve the liberty of the Indians and thought we had secured it, but the contrary appeared; for the Christians had arranged to go and spring upon those we had sent away in peace and confidence." Nevertheless, de Vaca's influence with the Indians was so great that after his arrival in San Miguel he prevailed over the slave hunters. The captain "made a covenant with God, not to invade nor consent to invasion, nor to enslave any of that country and people, to whom we had guaranteed safety."

The importance of de Vaca's and his companions' incredible wanderings of more than five thousand miles was many-sided. Western man's first North American journey from coast to coast established a geographic sense of the vast continent as well as the true character of the country. Also, de Vaca's meticulous and uniquely objective descriptions revealed the nature of the Indians and their ways of life, while displaying a compassionate understanding which years of shared hardship had doubtless generated. In many ways de Vaca exemplified basic Christianity in his naked poverty and sympathetic powers of faith healing. Preceding the military cruelties of de Soto and Coronado, he apparently left among countless Indians the impression of Christianity as a benevolent religion.

Notwithstanding de Vaca's reports that earthen jars, straw mats, deerskin, and bone implements—not gold or silver or emeralds—were the normal equipment of the Indians, the belief in golden cities held firm. To be sure, de Vaca had reported gifts of copper, cotton, coral, turquoise, and arrowheads supposedly made from emeralds. He himself thought these were evidence that rich cities might lie to the north. It was these fragile illusions, not the reports of simple poverty, that impressed the minds of the *conquistadores*.

One of these was the viceroy of New Spain, who tried to persuade de Vaca's companions to head an expedition to the seven fabled cities of Cibola. In the end, only the black slave, Estévan, was willing to go. Assigned to guide a company of Franciscans led by the French Friar Marcos of Nice, Estévan proceeded ahead with a large scouting party of Indians. He sent back word of finding Cibola, a town of stone-and-lime houses, as rumored. But alas, Estévan angered the Zuñi governors of the pueblo, with the result that they murdered him. Friar Marcos, far behind when he learned this news, ascended a high place and was able to see distantly the pueblo identified as Cibola. In the morning sunshine of the desert, its bare sandstone walls shone with a golden glow. This was proof enough for Friar Marcos, who reported finding one of the promised cities of gold.

His word fed ambitions in Mexico City to send a full-scale expedition into the north, but not until 1540 did this take place. Less than a year before, however, another expedition was under way in Florida. Both of them evoke the aura of the word *conquistadores;* both contributed to the assembling of factual data about the North American interior. They came, unwittingly, within but two hundred miles of each other.

The first of these was the expedition of Hernando de Soto, formerly second in command under Pizarro during the bloody conquest of the Incas in Peru. Now he was governor of Cuba and *adelantado* of Florida. Able and dashing, de Soto was also, according to a contemporary, "very fond of this sport of killing Indians." De Soto had read de Vaca's account and seems to have been convinced that there was an untold part which de Vaca had reserved for the ears of the emperor alone—a message that "the richest country in the world" could be found to the north.

De Soto sought to have de Vaca accompany him, but de Vaca declined. Many others, however, joined the expedition, selling their estates and turning over their resources. Among them were a group of Portuguese, including the "Gentleman of Elvas," who wrote the account of the expedition. In 1539, with seven ships, 720 men, and great numbers of horses, de Soto arrived in Florida from Havana. Almost immediately upon landing, his army was attacked by Indians. During the battle there was a startling cry in Spanish: "Do not kill me, cavalier, I am a Christian! Do not slay these people; they have given me my life!"

This was Juan Ortiz, who had remained with Narváez's ships when they sailed back to Havana in 1528. Ortiz had then returned to Florida in search of Narváez and his missing army. Indians soon seized him, spread-eagled him from stakes, and began to burn him alive. At the life-or-death moment, in a prototypal enactment of the John Smith–Pocahantas story, the chief's daughter intervened to save his life. Now, after having lived with the Indians for twelve years, Ortiz joined de Soto as interpreter and guide.

De Soto followed in Narváez's footsteps to Apalachen. En route there occurred a sequence of kidnappings of Indian chiefs, seizures of women, and enslavement of the males. At Palache (perhaps the town of Apalachen, visited by Narváez) "a hundred men and women were taken," wrote the Gentleman of Elvas, "one or two of whom were chosen for the Governor, as was always customary for officers to do after successful inroads, dividing the others among themselves and companions. They were led off in chains, with collars about the neck, to carry luggage and grind corn, doing the labor proper to servants." Small wonder that the Indians kept retaliating.

Small wonder, too, that having been so preoccupied with bloody subjugation, de Soto never discovered the gold the Indians had told Narváez existed in Apalachen. That they had spoken the truth was apparently borne out twenty-five years later by French traders from Fort Caroline, who reportedly found both the source and products of gold. They, however, approached the Indians as friends.

De Soto moved north from present-day Florida, through Georgia, the Carolinas, Tennessee, Alabama, and Mississippi. He and his army crossed the Mississippi River (the first white men to do so) and explored parts of Arkansas, Kansas, Texas, and Oklahoma. He went everywhere as a conqueror—scourging, massacring, burning, and enslaving.

At Nilco, in Arkansas, at the sight of the Spaniards,

. . . the Indians ran from one to another habitation, numbers collecting in all parts, so that there was not a man on horseback who did not find himself amidst many; and when the captain ordered that the life of no male should be spared, the surprise was such, that there was not a man among them in readiness to draw a bow. The cries of the women and children were such as to deafen those who pursued them. About one hundred men were slain; many were allowed to get away badly wounded, that they might strike terror into those who were absent.

De Soto died at the conclusion of this episode and was succeeded by Luys de Moscoso. Moscoso, a man less driven to glory, carried out brief explorations in Arkansas, then headed back to the Mississippi. Determined to end the bloody expedition and return to New Spain, he ordered the building of seven brigantines. The company was better prepared for shipbuilding than Narváez's had been. It included representatives of several nations other than Spain, adding to the evidence that even in that closed society of conquerors many countries were contributing to the initial occupation of America. There was a Portuguese sawyer to cut the planks. The only trained shipwright was a Genoese, who was helped by five Biscayan carpenters. One of the caulkers was Genoese, the other a Sardinian.

Moscoso and the remainder of de Soto's army arrived at Pánuco on the Gulf of Mexico, where the *alcade* received them. The description of Pánuco by the Gentleman of Elvas might have applied to all the places visited by the de Soto expedition in its fruitless search for gold: "The country is poor. No gold or silver is to be found."

Eleven months after de Soto left Havana, Francisco Vásques de Coronado left the northern frontier of New Spain, accompanied by Franciscan missionaries and a following of some three hundred Spaniards and eight hundred Mexican Indians. The objective was Cibola and its gold. In the three-year expedition nothing was found that coincided with their wishful preconceptions. When Cibola was revealed as a stark stone Indian village, Coronado decided to go in search of another mythical city of gold, Quivira, hundreds of miles to the northeast. He marched day after day across the plains, but Quivira was in fact Kansas, and there was no gold there, only Indians in grass huts.

Like de Soto's but in lesser degree, Coronado's way was marked by death and bloodshed and treachery on both sides. A Pawnee Indian named by the Spaniards "the Turk" because of his appearance, gave lurid descriptions of future riches and so became a guide. He encouraged Coronado to extend his supply lines dangerously far by promises of much gold at Quivira. When the Turk, at one point, tricked Coronado's captain Alvarado into demanding certain pieces of gold of two friendly Indians, the Indians denied having any and said with equal truth that the Turk was lying. With that, Alvarado seized them and put them in chains. "Thus," wrote the chronicler of the expedition, Pedro de Castañeda, "began the want of confidence in the word of the Spaniards whenever there was talk of peace from this time on."

Coronado, injured by a fall from his horse and depressed by the inevitable failure of his objectives, retreated from Quivira and its false hopes and ordered his army back toward Mexico. There were mutinous reactions among the more adventurous. Discipline broke down, men wandered away, and Coronado arrived in Culiacan with less than one hundred men. "His reputation was gone from this time on," wrote Castañeda.

Coronado's real contribution went unrecognized. For all his seeming failure, he had acquainted his countrymen with the fertile plains, river valleys, and mountains of the future United States heartland, from the Gulf of California to Taos, New Mexico, and to central Texas, Oklahoma, and Kansas. A half century was to pass, however, before the true wealth of the land would be appreciated and colonization would take place.

Spain during all this time felt secure in her right of possession of most of the New World. In 1493 the papal line of demarcation had assigned spheres of discovery to Portugal east of the line and to Spain west of it. There were mutually agreed upon adjustments in the following years, so that what is now Brazil lay to the east and was colonized by Portugal. Since the northern part of North America was still unknown to the Spanish, they paid little heed to the voyage that John Cabot, an Italian like Columbus, made in 1497 on behalf of Henry VII of England. Barely of sufficient scale to be called an expedition, it consisted of Cabot and eighteen men. They landed on Cape Breton and explored the North American coast from Newfoundland possibly as far south as the Chesapeake Bay. The purpose was information, not settlement, however.

The French in their rising power also felt the urge to investigate America. As early as 1534 Jacques Cartier, seeking a northwest passage to the Orient, sailed to Labrador, the Gulf of St. Lawrence, and Gaspé Bay. He took possession of the country for France. Like Columbus, he returned home with Indians. He went back to Canada the following year, sailed up the St. Lawrence as far as the site of Montreal, and six years later attempted unsuccessfully to settle a colony at Quebec. As usual, there was no gold, and King Francis I lost interest in giving further support.

Although there was little about these far northern voyages to alarm the Spanish, the arrival of a party of French Huguenots in so thoroughly anointed a Spanish Catholic territory as Florida was something else. The first effort under Jean Ribaut in 1562 to establish a Protestant religious refuge was unsuccessful. Two years later René de Laudonnière arrived at the mouth of St. John's River in Florida, where he established a colony and built Fort Caroline. The history of this enterprise was one of poor leadership, near starvation, and mutiny.

Again Jean Ribaut arrived from France, with supplies in seven ships. Only three of the ships could enter the river and sail to the fort, and within a week they were pursued by eight Spanish ships. The Spaniards landed a few miles from Fort Caroline and put ashore Negroes with picks and mattocks. There they began to dig the foundations of St. Augustine. Ribaut decided to attack the Spaniards while they were on shore, but a violent storm blew his ships for fifty miles, eventually destroying them as well as the Spanish ships.

The Spaniards then moved overland, attacked Fort Caroline, and massacred all but the few who escaped, among whom was the artist Jacques le Moyne. His drawings, recording the Indians and natural life around Fort Caroline, still evoke for us, through Theodore de Bry's engravings, the exotic and ominous environment he found. Ribaut and his shipwrecked company were later betrayed and murdered by the Spaniards at Fort Caroline. The French did not return to Florida for two centuries.

It was not until the ascent of Elizabeth to the throne that England developed an active interest in America. This arose largely out of Elizabeth's Protestantism and her fear of dominance by a wealthy, Catholic Spain in alliance with the rest of Catholic Europe. Her interest in the New World was at first secondary to the more attractive and attainable goal of plundering Spanish treasure ships—a fast and reasonably sure way of enlarging her treasury and countering the wealth of Spain. The royal, if unstated, purpose of the nautical wanderings of the adventurous Sir Francis Drake was, in essence, piracy; the riches he thus accumulated won him a knighthood and the queen's personal gratitude.

That Drake sailed into the Pacific, a hitherto unchallenged Spanish ocean, is a mark of his daring. Although plunder was the primary objective, he did land in Calfornia north of San Francisco and, while repairing his ship, the *Golden Hind*, obtained the fealty of the reigning Indian king. He nailed up a brass plate which proclaimed the taking of "New Albion" in the name of the Queen. (What is purportedly this plate was discovered in 1936; now preserved in the University of California's Bancroft Library, its authenticity has been the subject of continuous debate.)

Daring, imaginative, enterprising, and thoroughly at home on the sea, the English saw mercantile advantages in establishing colonies overseas. In that view lay the seeds of their success in America where others had failed.

Sir Walter Raleigh, the archetypical enterprising Elizabethan courtier, dispatched an expedition which focused on Roanoke Island off the North Carolina coast. In honor of the Virgin Queen, the land was name Virginia. In 1585 a second expedition, commanded by Raleigh's cousin Sir Richard Grenville, set forth to establish a settlement. Raleigh envisioned a miniature England that would, with future colonies, help to take care of England's expanding population of unemployed.

The next year Grenville returned to England for supplies. Due back by Easter, he had not arrived by June, and the colonists found themselves beleaguered by Indians and faced with famine. On June 8 sails appeared on the horizon—not of one ship but of twenty-three. It was soon clear that they were not Grenville's but the fleet of Sir Francis Drake, en route to England from the West Indies. Drake made several offers of ships, supplies, and men, but in the end, fearful that Grenville would never appear, the Roanoke colony returned to England with Drake. Only two weeks later Grenville arrived to find his colony gone. He put fifteen men on the island, equipped them with two years' supplies, then he too returned to England.

Raleigh assembled more colonists, appointed John White as governor, and gave instructions to settle at a new site on the Chesapeake Bay. But when the colony of 150 arrived in July 1587, their plans were thwarted by an insubordinate ship's master, who wanted to return to England without delay, and they got no farther than Roanoke. There they searched for the fifteen, but found only the original colony's houses and razed fort, all "overgrown with melons of divers sorts and deer within them, feeding on those melons; so we returned to our company without hope of ever seeing any of the fifteen men living."

The same day White ordered his men to repair the houses, and the colonists settled in. On August 18 Governor White's daughter, wife of Ananias Dare, gave birth to a daughter, the first English child born in America. She was appropriately named Virginia. Four days later the colonists came to the governor to express their unanimous wish that he should return to England with the ship to obtain supplies. Although White protested, he finally, at the last possible moment, agreed.

By the time he arrived in England, he found the whole country in alarm: invasion by Spain was considered imminent, and every large ship and every mariner was being pressed into service. In 1588, however, White was allowed to set out with two small ships for Roanoke, but Spanish pirates forced them back. Later that year the Spanish Armada moved toward the English Channel, was soundly defeated by the seamanship and modern naval tactics of Drake and hundreds of his fellow Elizabethans, and England now ruled the seas.

Eventually White reached Roanoke once more, with three ships. Not a person nor a trace of one was found. The houses had been dismantled and surrounding their site was a heavily constructed fortresslike palisade. One post bore the carved letters CRO, another the entire word CROATOAN. Croatoan was an island south of Roanoke; it was also the name of an Indian tribe. In 1587 White had arranged for the colonists to indicate their destination should they move from the island, and if there was trouble, to accompany the word with a cross. There was no cross, so apparently they had not moved under duress.

White planned to sail directly to Croatoan island, but a storm forced the search to be postponed. The plan was now to spend the winter in the West Indies and return in the spring, but the winds drove the ships straight for England via the Azores. The "lost colony" remained lost, as it has to this day. White never returned.

Elizabethans were now reading Richard Hakluyt's multivolumed *Voyages,* and at the same time Hakluyt's uncle Richard the elder was spelling out with missionary zeal the significance for England of colonization. Attempting to counter the failure of earlier settlements, he described (in *Purposes and Policies to Be Observed in Colonization*) details of situating a colony. Here and in another essay (*Reasons for Colonization*) Hakluyt emphasized the necessity for fair dealings with the Indians, so that they would

. . . be drawn by all courtesy into love with our nation, that we become not hateful unto them as the Spaniard is in Italy and in the West Indies and elsewhere by their manner of usage; for a gentle course without cruelty and tyranny best answereth the profession of a Christian, best planteth Christian religion, maketh our seating most void of blood, most profitable in trade of merchandise, most firm and stable, and least subject to remove by practice of enemies.

Although the English did not unfailingly observe these admonitions, their relations with the Indians were usually more successful than those of the Spanish.

Hakluyt made it clear that the main objective was to supply crops and raw materials needed in England, and that labor to produce them was one of the reasons for the settlements. The goal was to develop a busy commercial exchange between natural products of the New World and manufactured goods from England. It remained for the seventeenth century to see the fruits of Hakluyt's persuasive prose. For that matter, it was not until that century that the Spaniards recognized the true wealth of their northern lands and established permanent settlements in New Mexico.

The great drama that had been enacted since 1492, for all its vain sacrifices and romantic obsessions, its cruelties, its greed, and its tests of human endurance and valor, was a period of magnificent achievement. It remains unique in the history of mankind.

Maps drawn from 1500 to 1700 [18–21] show the changing concept of America and the growth of knowledge about the shape and size of the continent. This information was supplied by men of many nations, by the Spaniards, Portuguese, Italians, black Africans, Germans, Frenchmen, Greeks, Sardinians, Belgians, Swiss, Englishmen, and Irishmen who poured into America from the very beginning.

1513—Ptolemy's European Coastline Combined with the New Lands. The impetus that Claudius Ptolemy, an Egyptian astronomer and geographer of the second century A.D., gave to the infant science of cartography was considerable. The twenty-seven maps contained in his most noted work, *Geography,* were not only remarkably extensive, although inaccurate, but so influential after their introduction in Europe around 1400 that they were translated, redrawn, revised, and frequently reproduced in various countries over the next two centuries.

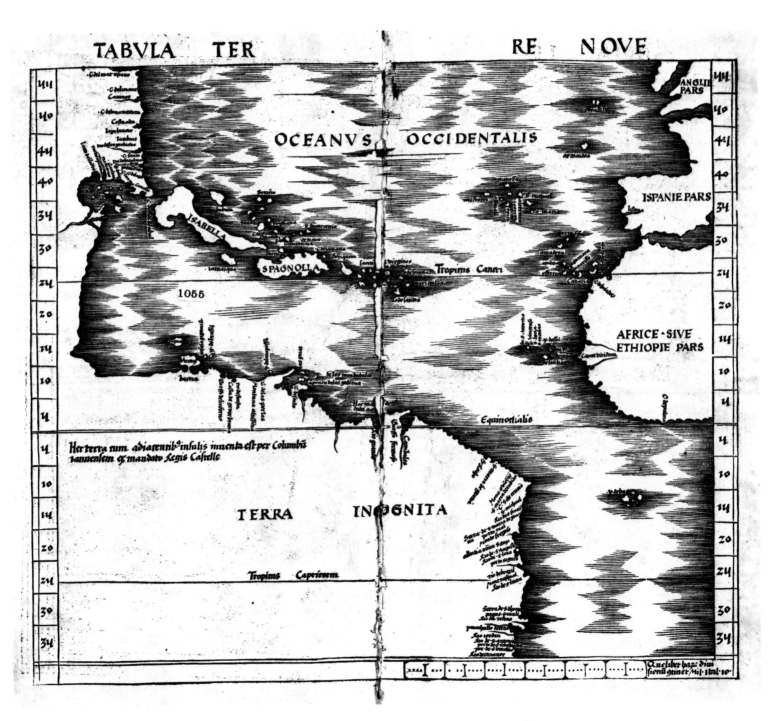

19
1671—Plate from Ogilby's America. Ogilby is known chiefly for his surveying and mapping of the British countryside. His most important contributions were the adoption of the statute mile of 1,760 yards and the introduction of roads on county maps. In addition to crossings, bridges, and boundary lines, his road atlases contained legends such as "The Porcupine Inn" and "Enter a moore" to better define the area for the traveler.

Ogilby published accounts of Africa, America, and Asia from 1670 to 1673. On this plate of New England and parts of Virginia are represented not only the terrain and wildlife of the region, but the areas inhabited by various native tribes.

20
1688—Coronelli's America Settentrionale. The form of California is generally helpful in dating maps of the North American continent. Although earlier maps showed California as a peninsula, it appeared as an island from approximately 1622 to 1730 as a result of a misinterpretation of reports from Spanish explorers. The Spanish had in fact penetrated and "conquered" much of the region as early as 1520. The Spanish conquests resulted in enticing but exaggerated accounts of New World wealth.

Italian cartographer, geographer, and theologian Vincenzo Coronelli produced this fine copper-plate engraving, characteristic of Italian maps of the sixteenth century.

19

20

33

21

1700—De L'Isle's l'Amerique Septentrionale. Nearly a century of settlement along the Atlantic coast of the New World by various European groups provided the Old World with an increasingly enlightened view of both positive and negative aspects of life in America, as well as a more realistic picture of the land.

Guillaume De L'Isle (or Delisle) was a French mapmaker whose chief contribution to cartography was a genuine attempt to be scientific in his drawing. Specifically, he preferred to leave unknown areas blank rather than compensate with guesswork, as was often the custom.

Chapter 3

The English Heritage

. . . whence came all these people? They are a mixture of English, Scotch, Irish, French, Dutch, Germans, and Swedes. From this promiscuous breed, that race now called Americans have arisen. The eastern provinces must indeed be accepted, as being the unmixed descendants of Englishmen. I have heard many wish that they had been more intermixed also: for my part, I am no wisher, and think it much better as it has happened. They exhibit a most conspicuous figure in this great and variegated picture; they too enter for a great share in the pleasing perspective displayed in these thirteen colonies. I know it is fashionable to reflect on them [i.e., hold a poor opinion of them], but I respect them for what they have done; for the accuracy and wisdom with which they have settled their territory; for the decency of their manners; for their early love of letters; their ancient college, the first in this hemisphere; for their industry, which to me who am but a farmer, is the criterion of everything.

J. HECTOR ST. JOHN CRÈVECOEUR
Letters from an American Farmer, 1782

As the seventeenth century unfolded, the English gained predominance in the Atlantic colonies. This was a result in part of their recent mastery of the seas, in part of their colonial policy of stable settlement and trade. Overpopulation in Britain also provided an abundance of settlers. There were in addition large numbers of non-Englishmen who were allowed a wide latitude to preserve their separate cultural identities within a common English political system, law, and language.

Although the English maintained this tolerance for cultural diversity, inevitably English standards became prevalent. With commerce restricted to trade with Britain, British goods were almost the only imports, and London became the arbiter of fashion. Since English models prevailed, most American craftsmen, regardless of their previous traditions, emulated them. This was especially true when the patrons were wealthy members of the mercantile governing classes; typical provincials, they often wanted to be more English than the English. Yet in the work of the colonial craftsmen there emerged qualities that were both regional and distinctly American. The elegant restraint and attenuation of Puritan New England forms in silver and pewter and furniture, for instance, are quite unlike the greater opulence of those objects made in Philadelphia or the sturdier products of Manhattan Dutch craftsmen trying to imitate English prototypes.

When they first came, the English were simply one nation among the many settling in America. After the disaster of Roanoke, as well as minor colonizing failures elsewhere, it took them seventeen years to plant a successful colony. This was Jamestown, established in 1607 on a swampy, mosquito-ridden island on the James River in Virginia, under the auspices of the Virginia Company in London. The early history of Jamestown resembles that of other beginning colonies. There were the usual Indian troubles, periods of starvation, and internal dissent. Although the colony almost failed when its starving survivors gave up and embarked for England in 1610, their timely interception by Lord de la Warr's arrival with supply ships saved the day. From then on, craftsmen poured in, as did the necessities and luxuries that eventually turned Jamestown and the surrounding settlements of Virginia into Sir Walter Raleigh's earlier vision of a miniature England.

Even before the "starving time" that almost ended the English effort, an ambitious program of craft enterprise was inaugurated by the Virginia Company. Their objective was the profitable exploitation of New World resources. It began with the building of America's first glass factory in 1608, only a year after the colony was founded. This extraordinary and unrealistic undertaking broke the exclusively English nature of Jamestown's population by the introduction of German and Polish glassworkers. The colony's struggle simply to survive, plus inadequate raw materials for making glass, meant failure for the enterprise the following year. Notwithstanding the demonstrated difficulties of making glass in that remote situation, an English entrepreneur in 1621 brought a group of Italian glassblowers to revive the abandoned glassworks. The Italians were intractable and doubtless miserable in that harsh, Anglo-Saxon outpost. George Sandys, the colony's secretary, wrote of them: "A more damned crew hell never vomited." The effort was finally abandoned in 1624.

Excavation of the site by the National Park Service in 1948 revealed a nine-foot furnace, annealing ovens, and a fritting furnace, all made of local stones, as well as fragments of ceramic melting pots, crucibles, and working holes. Small drippings and trimmings of glass and a coating of glass on the furnace floor and on melting-pot shards are proof that glass was actually made there.

On the list of tradesmen to be sent to Virginia in 1611 were four "potters of earth." The uncovering of kiln remains and the presence of kiln "furniture" and potters' wasters prove that pottery was another industry at Jamestown, more successful than the glassworks. A pitcher, eloquent of surviving English medieval ceramic shapes, probably made in Jamestown before 1650, is shown in **22**. Later, between 1660 and 1680, Governor William Berkeley established a pottery on his nearby plantation. Excavation of the kiln site revealed a wide variety of forms. One, a wine cup, relates Berkeley's potter to the Dutch and English delftware potters of the London Thames-side [**23**].

Several miles up the James River from Jamestown, at Falling Creek, an ironworks was established in 1619 with 150 trained English ironworkers. The Indians brought it to an untimely end in 1622, however, by massacring twenty-seven of the ironworkers and destroying the works. The furnaces were never revived, and it is not known where the survivors went. At least one may have remained in the neighborhood, for a resident of the area some thirty years ago unearthed on her property an anvil bearing the date 1645.

The extensive archaeological excavations of Jamestown and nearby sites by the National Park Service and others have revealed early Virginia's cultural richness. Often archaeology provides the only tangible evidence of what people used and what their dwellings were like. Pottery, which survives below ground when other materials do not, remains the best cultural indicator. London and Bristol tin-glazed wares and West-of-England slip-decorated earthenwares occur abundantly among the Jamestown finds. A reconstructed sgraffito-decorated dish made in North Devon appears in **24**. More astonishing is the range of exotic ceramics, from Chinese porcelain to German stoneware and Spanish, Portuguese, and Italian earthenwares. Although most of these were shipped first to England and then to America, luxurious Chinese porcelains such as a Ming wine cup excavated at King's Mill plantation below Jamestown may be the product of one of England's repeated raids on Spanish treasure ships [**25**].

The rich variety of materials from many parts of the world reflects the intensity of English maritime commerce and the cosmopolitanism that has traditionally run hand in hand with British insularity. At Jamestown and other seventeenth-century sites, archaeologists have found, for instance, several examples of Italian sgraffito-decorated pottery dating from about 1650. This red-bodied earthenware was coated with opaque white "slip" through which designs of birds and flowers were scratched to reveal the red body below. Added liveliness was supplied by dashes of green, orange, and yellow under the transparent lead glaze. A Hispanic wine bottle of buff earthenware with two characteristically Mediterranean high-shouldered handles and a simple brushed-on dark-red asterisk-like decoration on each side was excavated from a well dating from about 1630–1650 [**26**]. Exotic variety was also revealed in Dutch and Flemish majolica, while great majolica chargers made in Portugal and recovered at Jamestown explain references to "Lisbon" ware found in mid-seventeenth-century inventories. German stoneware was represented by a salt-glazed stoneware "bearded-man" jug made in Cologne or Frechen and collected in New England [**27A, 27B**].

Not only had England become accustomed to an international mercantile outreach; it had also become, during the religious wars of the sixteenth century, a haven for Protestant refugees from Holland, France, and Germany. In the census of 1567, for example, 2,030 out of a total of 2,730 aliens in England were "Dutch"—usually meaning German. There were great numbers of Flemish immigrants, while so many Genoese and French carpenters were employed that there was resentment among native craftsmen. The English acceptance of ethnic pluralism was a fact before the settling of the first English colony in America.

These first colonies sometimes differed from each other as much as they did from those of other nationalities. The Plymouth colony in New England was comprised of English Puritan Separatists who, as believers in self-governing congregationalism, had moved outside the established Anglican Church. Many members of this small sect, mostly yeoman farmers of small means, fled persecution in England to the safety and tolerance of Holland. Fearing erosion of their culture and beliefs if they remained there, they eventually obtained financial backing in England to settle in America. Calling themselves Pilgrims, the contingent from Holland joined co-religionists from England at Plymouth and set sail in the *Mayflower*. The ordeal of a crowded, stormy Atlantic crossing ended when they touched land at the end of Cape Cod. After exploring the shore, they sailed into a harbor on Massachusetts Bay and in December 1620 established their settlement, also named Plymouth. They signed among themselves the Mayflower Compact, which assured the continuation of traditional English guarantees of human justice and self-government.

Every schoolchild knows the story of the *Mayflower*, the landing at Plymouth Rock, the Indian Squanto, Miles Standish, John Alden, Priscilla, and the "first" Thanksgiving. There are, too, many legends of family heirlooms alleged to have "come over on the *Mayflower*." A cartoon from the turn of the twentieth century, poking fun at such snobbish claims, depicts the *Mayflower* with her decks piled high with miscellaneous furniture. Yet obviously the colonists brought with them a few cherished small possessions—reminders of the civilized world they were leaving behind. Some have survived. An octagonal looking glass with a tooled wooden frame stained black to imitate ebony was an elegant personal possession of Edward Winslow, which according to substantial family tradition he did indeed bring with him on the *Mayflower* [28].

Eight years after the founding of Plymouth, a vanguard of Puritans under the leadership of John Endicott settled at Salem, about sixty miles away on the north shore of Massachusetts Bay. In 1630, after a reorganization of the company's charter, the main body of the Massachusetts Bay Company's settlers arrived at Boston.

The Puritans were dissident members of the Church of England who, while remaining within the church, disagreed with it. Since the time of Henry VIII these Protestant critics had opposed the formalism and ceremony of the Anglican service and church organization as symptomatic of a return to Roman Catholicism. They sought instead to strip away—to "purify"—the accretions of ritual and to revive the directness and simplicity of the early Christians. They looked to the Bible as God's Holy Word and sought direct communion with Him by means of it [29]. They opposed the intervening presence of authoritative bishops and a hierarchical priesthood and regarded the Mass and the Holy Sacrament as abominations. Their intense personal seeking to learn God's will meant that the affairs of daily life and government were inseparable from religion.

The early-seventeenth-century English Puritan leaders were not, like many of the Pilgrims, poor yeomen whom the establishment could harass with impunity. They were men of substance and influence, essentially conservative despite the radicalism of their search for an honest relationship with God. They were tolerated if not enjoyed for many years in England, but when Charles I dissolved Parliament in 1629 they feared loss of their freedoms, and certain groups of them decided to emigrate to America. Organized as the Massachusetts Bay Company, with John Winthrop elected as their governor, it was they who came to Boston in 1630. They brought with them their own charter—an unprecedented procedure that protected their rights from being nullified by the king. The colony, which was simultaneously the chartered company, thus became a self-governing community dedicated to a godly life. Church and state were inseparable and the religiously elect males were the electorate. Although far from constituting a democracy, they annually elected a governor, his deputy and assistants, and members to a general court.

Massachusetts Bay was organized in a series of towns, each with its own meeting house and self-governing congregation, led by a minister whom the congregation appointed. Its local civil affairs were conducted in town meetings, which still remain today as indispensable elements in the New England political system and reminders of the old English traditions of responsibility to people and their liberties.

Although strong religious motivation was a cohesive basis for permanent settlement and community, there were tributary reasons for the Puritans' colonial success. In common with most Christians of their time, they believed that the devil finds work for idle hands; it therefore followed that honest hard work was a virtue. When financial gain resulted, that was viewed as the measure of God's munificence and a recognition of holy zeal on His behalf. To be sure, wealth was not permitted to be the means for excessive display, arrogance, or overstepping the rights of others; with it went rules of responsibility to support church, government, and those less fortunate.

Closely related to these interwoven religious and practical aims was the Puritan belief in education. Prerequisite was the ability to read—above all to read the Bible, a central possession of every family. The King James version was generally used, as it was among the Anglicans.

A teaching device, used then and throughout the colonial period, was the English hornbook [30]. Paddle-shaped, this bore a pasted sheet of paper with the alphabet, the exorcism, and the Lord's Prayer printed on it. A sheet of transparent horn covered the paper. Not only in New England but also in other English colonies schoolmasters taught basic reading from hornbooks. In Virginia, where private tutors instructed children on the great plantations of the Tidewater, John Mercer of Marlborough plantation recorded the purchase of one as late as 1747.

The Puritans, driven by religious principles and aided by education, which extended to the founding of Harvard College in 1636, were vigorously and productively energetic. Located on a coast well lined with good harbors and navigable streams, they followed English traditions of maritime commerce and carried on aggressive trading. Limited in their agriculture by a rocky landscape, they supplemented it by craft industries everywhere.

The enormous energy of this self-disciplined society was reinforced by a steady stream of new Puritan arrivals. These were people like themselves, mostly middle class, always respectful of manual as well as intellectual work. In a brief few years they spread into the interior, setting up the Connecticut and New Haven colonies, which together with Plymouth and Massachusetts Bay formed the New England Confederation in 1643. (Rhode Island, established in 1644 by Roger Williams and others who believed in religious toleration, as the orthodox Puritans did not, was excluded.)

"So great was the diligence and industry of the New-England planters," wrote Hannah Adams in 1805, "that they had already settled [by 1642] fifty towns and villages, erected between thirty and forty churches, and a larger number of parsonage houses. They had built a castle, forts, prisons, &c. and had founded a college, all at their own expense. They had furnished themselves with comfortable dwelling-houses, had laid out gardens, orchards, cornfields, pastures, and meadows, and lived under the regular administration of their own government and laws."

After the first generation of settlers, Puritan fervor diminished markedly, but the lasting vigor and prosperity of their enterprises served to draw large numbers of new colonists less motivated by extremes of piety. Toleration, abhorred at first, became a necessity with the revocation of the Massachusetts charter and the appointment of a royal governor for the whole of New England in 1684, as well as with the establishment of Anglican churches. Thousands of indentured servants and tradesmen also diluted Puritanism after 1700. Nevertheless, the old Puritans' initial motivations and beliefs set a pattern that determined the essential character of New England for centuries to follow. They did, indeed, cradle the ethos that governs the actions and views of many Americans today.

In the realm of the crafts, the Puritans' moral criterion of conscientious work related directly to integrity in what they made. Ingrained attitudes were responsible for the way things looked: reticence in ornament was an expression of Puritan culture. Yet a pine Bible box from Massachusetts sported an intricate pattern of geometric gouge carving on its front surface [31].

The survivals of furniture and other crafts that emerged from New England tradesmen's shops at the turn of the eighteenth century reflect the transition from Elizabethan massiveness to lighter and more mobile American furniture. The ladder-back armchair that belonged to Jonathan Copp of Stonington, Connecticut, designated "my great chair" in his will, is one example [32]. Despite its unusually large proportions, it shows both New England character and changing tastes in its turnings and slender posts and back splats. Reflected in some of his possessions was the cosmopolitan character of English America; an example is a covered drinking bowl of blue-decorated Frankfurt faïence [33].

The English relationship with the sea continued in New England. Fishing was an important part of colonial life on Massachusetts Bay, and oil from fish and whales was essential for artificial light. As early as 1621 Edward Winslow, owner of the mirror mentioned earlier, advised new settlers to bring "cotton yarn for your lamps," and in 1630 Francis Higginson wrote that "By the abundance of fish thereof [New England] can afford oil for lamps." In 1704 French and Indians captured a New England ship bearing "30 Tons of Lamp Oyl." One kind of lamp from the seventeenth century looked like an open iron pan with a long "beak" or slanting channel for the yarn wick; it burned fish or whale oil. One pictured in 34 was used in Dedham, Massachusetts, and is the counterpart of a lamp excavated from a seventeenth-century house site in Plymouth.

Clocks, too, played a part in the lives of the upper-class colonists. The English shelf or bracket clock of the seventeenth century was made of brass with an ornate crest above the dial and a crownlike structure on the top encompassing a bell. It is known as a "lantern" clock. An unusual miniature version of it [35], made about 1680 by Joseph Hall of London, was taken to Bermuda by an English emigrant shortly after that date. When this settler's children decided to move to Massachusetts early in the eighteenth century, they again brought the clock with them. It remained in the possession of his descendants until it was given to the Smithsonian Institution in 1974.

The houses of the English colonists in the seventeenth century owed their styles and technology of construction to English prototypes. There are only meager descriptions of the first, immediate shelters that the earliest colonists flung up when they arrived. In a remarkably short time, however, they built more substantial houses, recreating within the differing limits of climate, available materials, and skills that they remembered from England. Many of their houses survive today.

Plentiful timber led to a strengthening in America of the timber-frame tradition that had flourished in late medieval England but began to wane in the seventeenth century as timber became scarce. The New England Puritans developed a regional architecture whose roots seem to lie in certain forms of the late sixteenth and early seventeenth centuries found in Essex County in England. The basic timber-frame structure was a system of interlocking posts and beams, hewn square to remarkable smoothness by a broad ax. The ends were cut into complex mortise joints, so that tongues called tenons fitted into slots, or mortises, and wooden pins driven through holes where the timbers came together locked the elements into a tight frame. Studs or planks were placed vertically within the frame to support, on the inside, split-oak laths to which shell-lime plaster was applied. Joists or crossbeams lay horizontally to support wide pine floorboards. The exterior coverings of the walls were heavy, wide horizontal planks, beveled top and bottom to shed rain water. Windows were swinging casements with small diamond-shaped panes set in strips of lead. In New England second stories often projected out over the first, as in medieval English houses, with decorative pendants or brackets under the overhangs. Roofs were usually steeply pitched and in large houses often had transverse gables at right angles to the main longitudinal ridge.

The interiors of seventeenth-century houses unabashedly displayed their wooden structural elements, which were integral with the design. Corner posts, beams, and ceilings were undisguised. Plaster covered the inside surfaces of the outer walls, while the interior partition wall where the fireplace was located was made of vertical boards, or wainscot, interrupted by the brickwork of the fireplace. One or two batten doors of wide vertical planks nailed to cleats or battens opened into entryways or other rooms.

Brick, recently introduced from Holland, was popular in England during the seventeenth century. Prosperous Virginians anxious to live up to the latest fashion soon found that suitable clay underlying their properties made it easy to provide brick houses. In Jamestown brick kilns were established before 1625, and in an effort to recreate an urban European environment the colonists actually built brick row houses there, as archaeological excavations have revealed.

Most brick structures for domestic use in Virginia came into being in the prosperous period of the later seventeenth century. In 1624 Charles I had dissolved the Virginia Company on the grounds that it had failed its objectives, as indeed it had. From then on until the Revolution, Virginia was a crown colony with a governor and council. Five years before that date, representative government had been introduced with the establishment of the House of Burgesses in 1619. Under the new colonial government this legislative body continued, assuring the rights and protection of English common law in the colony. Like New England, where the seeds of liberty were planted early, Virginia helped to build the foundations for freedom and self-government.

The economic base for Virginia was tobacco, a very popular commodity in Europe. Copying Indian pipes, the English and Dutch made their own versions out of white kaolin fired in kilns. Early-seventeenth-century pipes had tiny ovate bowls to hold the strong tobacco and rather heavy tubular stems through which to draw the smoke. As time went by, the bowls grew larger and the stems finer and longer; archaeologists have found that the approximate ages of colonial pipestems can be determined by the diminishing diameters of pipestem bores as time progressed.

Virginia granted ''head rights'' of fifty acres to each settler and fifty more for each person he brought to America. Indentured servants, after serving their time, were entitled to the same rights. With tobacco planting their usual objective, the Virginians spread out for miles along the rivers.

The tobacco was purchased in such centers as London or Bristol or Bideford by a merchant who paid for it in bills of credit. Against these bills he furnished supplies for the planter. The planter could also use the bills of credit as paper currency to make purchases and pay debts in the colonies. In the eighteenth century, as wealthier planters bought up lands of the less successful, great estates evolved, with large mansions and many dependencies, reliant upon a rapidly increasing population of black slaves.

Unlike the New Englander, who commonly made things for himself and others, the Virginia planter, concentrating on his tobacco crop, was more likely to rely on English materials, particularly in the seventeenth century. Yet several examples of seventeenth-century Virginia-made furniture have survived, and a pewterer, Joseph Copeland, left a single example of his work that was found buried at Jamestown—a spoon bearing his mark and the date 1675.

The Virginians, while sharing similar basic attitudes about freedoms and the Protestant belief, were different from the New Englanders in the details of their political, religious, and economic ways. Tobacco culture and the head rights system in Virginia determined a geographic spread contrasting with the close-knit village organization of New England. While the Puritans were English dissidents, the Virginians were ''cavaliers,'' meaning that they were loyal subjects to the crown, adhering to the status quo (not all noblemen, as nineteenth-century romanticists would have it). Plantations were isolated from each other, with few special centers other than churches and courthouses to draw them together. They were therefore partly self-sufficient social and economic units, with the master and his family at the top of the hierarchy and the slaves at the bottom. The Virginian identified himself more closely with the English country squire than with his merchant or farmer counterpart in New England. He accepted the established church, although his religious practice was as informal and stripped of ceremony as most Puritans could wish. Unlike New England, however, religion was not central to the lives of Virginians.

Maryland was also a tobacco-producing colony, with both economic and architectural patterns resembling those of Virginia. In other respects there were wide differences. Maryland's origin was Charles I's grant to Sir George Calvert, Lord Baltimore, making him proprietor of a new province of Maryland. His son soon inherited the proprietorship and his title. The younger Lord Baltimore sent his brother Leonard to settle St. Mary's City in 1634. What was unique was the fact that the Calverts were Roman Catholics, while most of their colonists were Protestants, a situation necessitating skill and tact on the part of the Calverts. They measured up to it by passing a Toleration Act, which assured freedom of religion for all inhabitants. With a representative legislature and a governor and council appointed by the proprietor, Maryland was yet another example of the traditions of English self-government and human liberties in America.

22

23

22
Lead-glazed earthenware pitcher excavated at Jamestown, Virginia. The lingering influence of the English medieval traditions is well expressed in this simple form probably made at Jamestown during the mid-seventeenth century. H 12″.

23
Earthenware wine cup (restored) made at the pottery on Virginia Governor William Berkeley's Green Spring plantation. The influence of the Dutch and English potters working on the banks of the Thames in London is evident in this American piece probably made between 1660 and 1680. H 4⅜″.

24
English ceramics such as this sgraffito dish (restored) made in North Devon were imported to the colonies in great quantity during the seventeenth century. D 7⅜″.

25
Chinese blue-decorated porcelain cup excavated at King's Mill plantation in James City County, Virginia. A product of the Ming dynasty datable to the first half of the seventeenth century, it is an example of the exotic variety of ceramics used on American sites during that century. Actual size.

24

25

26
Spanish or Portuguese bottle (restored) of lead-glazed buff earthenware decorated in dark-red iron oxide slip. Made in the first half of the seventeenth century, this bottle is but one example of the great variety of materials that came to the colonies via English ships from all over the world. H 9″.

27A
German salt-glazed stoneware Bellarmine or "bearded-man" jug. Made in Cologne or Frechen during the seventeenth century, the jug is typical of those found on many American sites of the period. H 12¾″.

27B
Detail: Bearded-man jug.

26

27B

27A

28

29

30

28
Looking glass which according to tradition was brought to Plymouth on the *Mayflower* in 1620 by Edward Winslow, who was later governor of Plymouth colony. H 15¼".

29
King James version of the Bible printed in 1613 by Robert Barker. H 16¼".

30
Hornbooks, such as this one made in the eighteenth century, were used in the English colonies to teach basic reading. A piece of transparent horn covers the sheet of paper upon which the alphabet and Lord's prayer are printed. L 4⅛".

31

32

31
Pine Bible box made in New
England about 1700. L 16¼″.

32
Ladder-back armchair, which
according to family tradition
was used by Jonathan Copp
in Stonington, Connecticut.
Measuring approximately 51″
high by 27″ wide by 25″ deep,
it was known as his "great
chair."

33
Tin-glazed earthenware cov-
ered bowl, probably made in
Frankfurt, Germany, c. 1700.
This piece was used in the
Stonington, Connecticut,
home of Jonathan Copp. H
6¼″.

34
Wrought-iron lamp made in
Dedham, Massachusetts, in
the seventeenth century and
probably used in the
Jonathan Fairbanks house
there. The lamp would have
burned fish or whale oil, with a
cotton yarn wick resting in the
wick channel. H 4″.

33

34

35
This English lantern clock (c.
1680) was brought to Mas-
sachusetts about 1700 from
New Providence (Bermuda).
The maker, Joseph Hall, was
at work in London in 1684.
The clock was originally made
with a balance: the conversion to a pendulum was made
years later. H 47½".

The coming of the eighteenth century brought many changes in the material surroundings of the colonies. The changes arose partly from growth in population and increases in wealth. They originated also in the style trends of England. These influences did not rush into the colonies but rather crept in, slowly modifying what had become traditional modes.

In New England architecture the seventeenth-century center-chimney plan lasted through the Revolutionary period, but houses became larger; double-sash sliding windows with wooden-mounted rectangular panes took the place of leaded casements. Before the middle of the century builders' handbooks provided classical Roman designs for doorways and moldings. No longer acceptable to the upper classes were the medieval interiors of hand-hewn beams and corner posts and open ceilings comprised of joists and boards of the floors above. Instead, molded cornices and paneling combined with elaborate carved mantels and overmantels; plaster covered portions of the walls and the ceilings.

While certain forms of furniture that originated in the seventeenth century continued through the eighteenth and into the nineteenth, such as the ladder-back chair, their details reflected change. Jonathan Copp's "great chair," mentioned earlier, displays the trend toward greater refinement in this form at the turn of the century. Most radical were New England adaptations of new styles that began to come from England in the 1720s. The walnut side chair of the mid-eighteenth century contrasts strikingly with its seventeenth-century predecessors made in Rhode Island or Massachusetts [36]. The smooth rhythmic lines, the cyma curve of the front legs, and the tone and texture of finished natural wood add up to a new standard of comfort, elegance, and craftsmanship. Nonetheless, the uprightness of the shape, the restraint in ornament, and the verticality of proportions reflect the Puritan environment in which such chairs were made and used. Compared to contemporary high-style English chairs in this so-called Queen Anne mode, this is a restrained counterpart.

Perhaps the most American interpretation of a European form is the Windsor chair. It was an entirely different version of the original English Windsor chair and represented the tendency toward economy of material and mass production that led American craftsmen to try to get more out of less. The late-eighteenth-century American Windsor chair demonstrates the use of a light, tough bentwood bow to form the back, its ends securely anchored in a sculptured pine slab seat, the intervening space filled with supporting, equally light and tough spindles. Elegantly turned legs, strengthened by stretchers joined in an H, and splayed to keep the chair from tipping, provide a strong but light support. Short curved arms are securely bracketed out from the bow back [37]. The various elements were turned out in numbers and then assembled.

Among New England's superlative colonial craftsmen were its pewterers who, throughout the colonial period, made well-proportioned tableware for daily use, though wooden plates, or trenchers, were more commonplace. Less severe than wood or metal was the tin-enameled earthenware shipped from potteries in London, Bristol, and Liverpool. Known generically as delft ware because of its similarity to the ceramic products of Delft, Holland, this ware imitated in its opaque white glaze the appearance but not the substance of porcelain. Decorated by hand in blue or polychrome with designs from Chinese porcelain, English delft responded to an avid taste for "Chinoiserie." Wallpaper, furniture, and silks all reflected this. With Dutch origins for its ceramic technology and Chinese inspiration for its designs, English delft symbolized a continuing English interest in and acceptance of the exotic and the cosmopolitan.

From about 1720 until the Revolution, potteries in Buckley, north Wales, shipped to America a hard red earthenware, usually glazed a lustrous black. While most utilitarian ceramics came from England in the seventeenth century, Buckley ware is unusual for its occurrence here in the next century, no doubt attributable to its durability. Meanwhile the growth of American potteries succeeded in assuming much of the market. Handsome lead-glazed red earthenwares emerged especially from the potteries of New England, New York, New Jersey, and Pennsylvania. At least 230 potters worked in New England between 1635 and 1800.

All influences on colonial New England pottery were not purely Anglo-Saxon, even at the outset. Of the first three Massachusetts potters who arrived in 1635, William Vincent from Kent in southeast England was probably of French Huguenot descent, perhaps having come from the Low Countries, where many French Protestants sought refuge in the sixteenth century. He called himself a "pot baker," a term applied to potters in Holland and Germany.

Colonial potters shipped their wares along the coast. Shards of seventeenth-century pottery of the type made in the Salem area have been found in Pemaquid, Maine. In the late eighteenth century Joseph Procter of Gloucester shipped his pottery from Maine to Virginia, while William Rogers of Yorktown, Virginia, appears to have shipped his stoneware to Boston.

Of all material used for making things, wood was most widespread. It was everywhere available, and craftsmen at home and in shops became skilled at shaping it. In addition to household furnishings, they made mortars and pestles, cheese ladders, toys, and hardware such as strap hinges, locks, and keys—all of wood.

The textile arts were essentials in all the colonies. Women were not considered accomplished unless they could perform intricate feats of stitchery. There were schools in the larger towns where young ladies could learn such genteel skills. Ruth Hern advertised in the Boston *News-Letter* on March 9, 1775, her intention to open school and "Teach young Misses all the various Arts and Branches of Needle-Work: Namely, Needle-Lace-Work, Needle-work on Lawns and Muslins, flowering with Crewel-working Pocket-Books. . . ."

The making of cloth as a home industry still prevailed in England during the seventeenth century, so inevitably many emigrants skilled in textile crafts arrived in the colonies, particularly during the great migration to New England in the 1630s. English traditions of family textile production were perpetuated. Nearly everyone grew flax; many raised sheep. In 1708 E. Bridger, an agent of the king, reported to the Board of Trade in London: "there is scarce a Country man comes to town or woman but are clothed with their own Spinning. Every one Incourages the Growth and Manufacture of this Country and not one person but discourages the Trade from home, and says 'tis pitty any goods should be brought from England, they can live without them."

Spinning and weaving were ubiquitous, as was blacksmithing. The production of bar iron for blacksmiths was one of the reasons for establishing the first colonial iron foundries, such as the ill-fated Falls Creek ironworks in Virginia and those established at Saugus and Braintree in Massachusetts during the seventeenth century. Horse-shoes and hand-forged nails were probably in highest demand and required much of the blacksmith's time. Beyond these, however, the blacksmith was usually a craftsman of varied talents. A 1732 advertisement in the Boston *News-Letter* states that the blacksmith William Bryant "mends Glazier's Vises, Cloather's Screws, and worsted Combs, and makes, grinds and setts Cloather's Shears; he also makes and mends Smiths' Vises, Ship Carpenters', Blockmakers', Tanners', Glovers' and Coopers' Tools, Braziers', and Tinsmen's Shears, and makes House work [house hardware]."

In brief, practicality and usefulness were essential qualities in the colonial crafts. The colonial Englishman marked his material culture with straightforward integrity. If the lines that separated English colonists from those of other nationalities began to blur as the Revolution approached, the century preceding 1776 was one of variety in both style and skill. The non-English colonists, as we shall see, can also be known by their work.

36

37

36
Side chair in the Queen Anne style. Probably made in Massachusetts or Rhode Island, c. 1740–1760. Outer breadth, front legs 21¾″.

37
Brace-and-bow Windsor side chair, probably made in New England. H 39½″.

Chapter 4

A Plantation of Differences— People from Everywhere

What then is the American, this new man? He is either an European, or the descendant of an European, hence that strange mixture of blood, which you will find in no other country. I could point out to you a family whose grandfather was an Englishman, whose wife was Dutch, whose son married a French woman, and whose present four sons have now four wives of different nations. He is an American, who, leaving behind him all his ancient prejudices and manners, receives new ones from the new mode of life he has embraced, the new government he obeys, and the new rank he holds. He becomes an American by being received in the broad lap of our great Alma Mater. *Here individuals of all nations are melted into a new race of men, whose labours and posterity will one day cause great changes in the world. Americans are the western pilgrims, who are carrying along with them that great mass of arts, sciences, vigour, and industry which began long since in the east; they will finish the great circle.*

J. HECTOR ST. JOHN CRÈVECOEUR
Letters from an American Farmer, 1782

Before the founding of Jamestown, the French explorer Samuel de Champlain had reconnoitered the shores of New England. Where Maine and Canada now meet he started a settlement at St. Croix. Soon after, in 1608, he established a trading post at Quebec out of which grew the French Canadian nation that still flourishes north of New England. The French in the ensuing 150 years moved inland along the St. Lawrence River, southward west of the Appalachians, and down the Mississippi Valley, planting fur-trading posts, forts, Jesuit missions, and villages, finally arriving at the Gulf of Mexico. As in the case of the Spanish, riches and Christian conversions were their goals, while alliances with Indian tribes were important means of achieving them. Some of their towns in the Mississippi Valley—St. Louis and New Orleans, for example—became permanent cities. For the most part, the French hold on the Middle West was a series of outposts bound together by alliances with friendly Indian tribes.

Archaeological evidence reveals that even in those remote places French luxuries such as decorated faïence and pewter, and civilized utensils such as copper and iron cooking ware found their way. Numerous survivals of eighteenth-century French architecture can also still be seen in the Mississippi Valley, although most of these date from the days of English or American dominion. For example, a house built at Cahokia in Illinois during the French period in 1752 and later used as a courthouse is still standing. Its palisade construction of vertical timbers infilled with clay, grass, and rubble is characteristically French.

The conflicting interests of French and English, the pitting of Indian tribe against Indian tribe, the hardening knot of French encirclement cutting across western lands claimed by the English colonies, and the secondary effects of Anglo-French hostilities in Europe led to sporadic fights and then all-out war. It ended with British victory in Quebec in 1759, when all of continental New France was surrendered.

The French presence has remained in the United States, nevertheless, most conspicuously in Louisiana. Louisiana was ceded to Spain after the final British victory, but prior to that it became a refuge for several thousand French Acadians whom the British exiled from Nova Scotia in 1755. Numbers of these exiles sought refuge in the English colonies, some even in Puritan New England. Joseph B. Felt, the historian of Ipswich, Massachusetts, in 1834 noted under the heading "Neutral French": "1757, Nov. 21st. Voted £ 20 for their assistance—1762. A Plan is to be devised for supporting them at less expense. The number of them was about twenty. There was a priest among them, who used to bring along wooden ladles for sale. They were industrious. Both sexes of them wore shoes of wood. They left Ipswich in 1766." The vast majority of Acadians went to Louisiana, where their descendants, who form a part of the present population, are called Cajuns.

Bordering the French in the earliest days of settlement and competing with them in the fur trade were the Dutch. Before their permanent arrival the Dutch hired the English navigator Henry Hudson to explore the American coast. Ever hopeful of finding the elusive northwest passage to the Orient, Hudson sailed along the shores of New England southward to probe the Delaware Bay and then up the river that now bears his name as far as present-day Albany. By making contact with the Mohawks, Hudson discovered the potential for fur trading, which the Dutch tested with further exploration. They founded the Dutch West India Company in 1621, then settled small numbers of colonists at Fort Nassau, near the site of Philadelphia, and at Fort Orange, where Albany now stands. In 1626 they founded New Amsterdam on Manhattan Island, which they purchased from the Indians in a legendary deal for the modern equivalent of about fifty dollars' worth of trinkets. The Dutch called the large territory surrounding these settlements New Netherland.

The settlements began essentially as trading posts, but the need for greater self-sufficiency to assure a permanent colony resulted in the establishment of the patroon system in 1629. Anyone who would bring over fifty persons was entitled to be a patroon—proprietor of a large feudal domain on the Hudson, with civil and criminal jurisdiction over many tenants and slaves and other exclusive privileges. The most notable of the few who took advantage of patroonships were the Van Rensselaers, whose rights were supported not only by the Dutch, but also by the succeeding British and American regimes until as late as 1840, when the tenants at Rensselaerswyck rose up in arms in the Rent War against the last reigning patroon.

Unlike England in the seventeenth century, Holland was not overpopulated, nor were its citizens suffering from civil or religious repression. To augment the few emigrating Dutchmen, the Dutch West India Company recruited Walloons—Protestant Belgians—as well as Germans, French Protestants, and others. New Englanders also spilled over into Long Island and Westchester, where the Dutch granted them settlement and religious privileges. New Netherland was thus from the outset an ethnic mix. In 1643 a French Jesuit, Father Isaac Joques, who had fled captivity by the Mohawks, found refuge in New Netherland. He reported that in the environs of Manhattan, as told him by Director General Kieft, "there were persons there of eighteen different languages."

As early as 1630 New Amsterdam was a village of brick houses with steep roofs and stepped gables facing the streets, as in seventeenth-century old Amsterdam. The village included a fort and a brick church. Fort Orange and later settlements displayed similar architecture. Paintings of Albany from the early nineteenth century, now in the Albany Institute of History and Art, show many Dutch houses still lining the streets.

In 1638 the Swedish West India Company under Peter Minuit took possession of the lower Delaware Bay, establishing Fort Christina on the site of Wilmington and occupying both the Delaware and south Jersey shores. The Swedish colony included Finns as well as Swedes, men used to cutting wood and hewing logs to build houses in their native tradition. Log houses built in New Sweden still exist in Delaware, though little else of the Swedish colony's material culture remains.

The Dutch, whose access to Fort Nassau up the Delaware was by Swedish sufferance only, were annoyed by this foreign intrusion into their claimed territory. They solved the problem in 1655 by moving soldiers into New Sweden and annexing it. Less than nine years later, the English arrived at New Amsterdam in four well-manned armed frigates. Peter Stuyvesant, the ill-tempered autocrat who governed New Netherland, sought to inspire his people to resist. But he commanded so little respect that they refused, and the colony surrendered without a shot. Charles II, who had declared war against Holland, made his brother, the Duke of York, a present of the Dutch colony. New York was now the name for both New Netherland and New Amsterdam [38]. Fort Orange became Albany, and the former Swedish Fort Casimir on the Delaware became Newcastle.

The English brought change gradually, and life went on among the Dutch much as it had before. The English confirmed the patroonships and gave strength to these feudal anachronisms by granting enormous tracts, now called manors, to well-established English and Scottish families. Such names as Pell, Livingston, and Gardiner were added to those of Philipse, Van Rensselaer, and Van der Donck to establish an Anglo-Dutch aristocracy that still remains influential in New York.

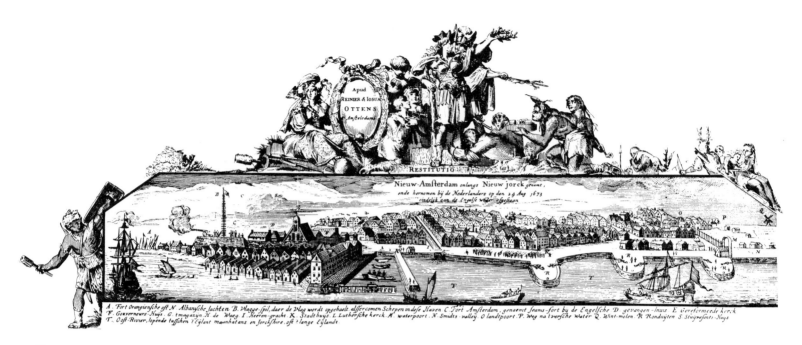

A. Fort Orangienfche oft N Albanfche Iachten B. Vlagge-fpil, daer de Vlag wordt opgehaelt alffercomen Schepen in defe Haven C Fort Amfterdam, genaemt feams-fort by de Engelfche D. gevangen-huis E. Gereformeede kerck F. Gouverneurs-Huys G. tmagazyn H. de Wreg. I. Heeren-gracht. K. Stadthuys. L Lutherfche kerck. M. waterpoort. N. Smidts-valley O landtpoort P. Weg na t'verfche water Q. Wint-molen R Ronduiten S Stuyvefants-Huys T. Ooft-River, lopende tuffchen t'eylant maunhatans en Jorckfhire, oft t'lange Eylandt

The Dutch left their stamp, not only in their distinctive architecture, but in their furniture, silver, pewter, and ironwork. The large number of wealthy families—both merchants and patroons—accounts for the high degree of luxury expressed in many of these objects and for the surprising amount of surviving works of art and decoration. Even after the English takeover, Dutch craftsmen continued to incorporate characteristic Dutch forms.

Early in the eighteenth century, New York silverwork had a character of its own, not to be found in Holland or England or the other colonies. Around the turn of the century various New York silversmiths made a unique series of splendid two-handled silver presentation bowls. These have a lobed or scalloped form and are elaborately embossed with repoussé work. One of these, made by Benjamin Wynkoop of New York City for Nicholas and Helletje Roosevelt on the occasion of their twenty-fifth wedding anniversary in 1707, features cast foliated handles which emphasize the baroque quality of the overall form and decoration [39]. Similar bowls in Holland were used to serve brandy and raisins. They were passed from guest to guest, each of whom dipped out his share with a silver spoon. This custom very likely prevailed in New York as well.

New York pewter reflected Dutch tastes to a less noticeable degree. A flat-top tankard by Cornelius Bradford of New York City follows the form of contemporary silver tankards, but lacks the adornment of applied cutwork bands or elaborate engraving found only on silver [40A, 40B]. Bradford, whose father was English and mother Dutch, was one of those emerging "Americans" of mixed blood described by Crèvecoeur. Like Paul Revere, he was an active Revolutionary, serving as dispatch bearer between the committees of correspondence in Philadelphia, New York, and Boston.

As the paintings of Jan Steen tell us, the Dutch loved and indulged their children. Affluent Hudson Valley Dutch families had their children depicted in such engaging portraits as that of Magdalena Veder painted by an anonymous artist [41]. A provincial version of eighteenth-century Dutch portrait style, this naïve painting is quite different in style from New England naïve portraiture of the same period.

The population of neighboring New Jersey was as mixed as New York's. Connecticut Puritans had migrated to eastern New Jersey and left their architectural stamp on the Dutch colony. In south Jersey, Swedes and Finns remained in evidence, while in the eighteenth century Germans from Philadelphia spilled across the Delaware. Essentially agricultural, New Jersey was characterized by pleasant farms and small towns. An early industrial effort was an attempt in 1688 to make delft ware in Burlington, but American clays were unsuitable and the project failed. More successful was the later glassworks of Casper Wistar at Allowaystown, begun in 1740. Until it was engulfed by the Revolutionary War, this factory, manned by German glassworkers, made bottles and window glass, the first successful glassmaking effort in the colonies.

39

40B 40A

38
Detail from a map published in 1673 with a view of New Amsterdam shortly after it was captured by the English from the Dutch and renamed New York.

39
The continuing Dutch influence in the former New Netherland is strongly felt in this silver drinking bowl made by Benjamin Wynkoop in New York about 1707. L (approx.) 11″.

40A
Pewter tankard made by Cornelius Bradford (1729–1786), who worked in Philadelphia and New York. H 7″.

40B
Bradford's maker's mark, which appears on the base of the tankard.

41
Portrait of Magdalena Veder
by an unknown artist. Mid-
eighteenth century. L 37½″.

The most significant colonization under English auspices, after New England, Virginia, and Maryland, was William Penn's settlement of Pennsylvania. Granted a proprietorship of the new colony by Charles II in 1681, Penn, a Quaker, published the next year *Some Account of the Province of Pennsylvania* in English, German, French, and Dutch. Offering complete religious toleration, liberal head rights, and other inducements, he opened Pennsylvania as a haven not only for his fellow Quakers, but for those of other religious beliefs, including Catholics, who were seeking a refuge.

Penn laid out Philadelphia in 1683 and provided for an elected assembly for Pennsylvania. In 1683 a group of Mennonites settled Germantown—the vanguard of German immigrants who were to flow in continuously and profoundly affect the character of America. The Germans established a genuine folk culture in Pennsylvania, while the English Quakers controlled mercantile trade, wealth, and upper-class social structure. The English imported their fashions and some of their furnishings from England and established standards in the eighteenth century for Philadelphia craftsmen to create magnificent furniture.

To the south of Virginia, the proprietary province of Carolina was established in 1663, at least on paper. Not until 1670 did a group of poor white laborers from Barbados land at the site of Charleston as colonists under the proprietary leadership of Lord Ashley. Their ineffectual start was not given momentum until 1680, when a group of Huguenots—French Protestants—settled near Charleston. When, five years later, Louis XIV revoked the Edict of Nantes, which had granted toleration to Huguenots, Charleston became a refuge for large numbers of them. Skilled in agriculture and in the crafts, the Huguenots established rice plantations along the rivers and built Charleston into a flourishing town and a center of culture and fine craftsmanship.

North Carolina became a separate province with particular political and economic provisions which favored small landholders and thus attracted farmers and planters from Virginia who were unable to compete against the large landowners there. Democratic in government and in the social structure of a small landholding society, North Carolina's largely Anglo-Saxon population always has had a distinctly regional flavor.

Georgia, not established as a colony until 1732, began under the leadership of James Edward Oglethorpe. Oglethorpe was a humanitarian, interested in providing a better life for English prisoners by releasing them to colonize; he was also a soldier, concerned with providing a defensive buffer against Spanish or French incursions from Florida and Louisiana. A benevolent, paternalistic government was set up under an English-based trusteeship. It prescribed a system of small farms, exclusion of Negro slavery, screening of prospective colonists to eliminate undesirables, prohibition of rum as a commodity in the fur trade, exclusive inheritance of property by eldest sons, laws against resale of property, and religious tolerance for all Protestants. The populace, however, became restive under these restrictions, and the result was a total failure of the original system and the ultimate conversion of the trusteeship in 1751 to a royal colony that allowed slavery and large plantations.

While all the coastal colonies were English after 1664, all had non-English settlers. Some colonies or towns were more receptive to foreigners than others. While sections of Pennsylvania were open and welcoming, Ipswich, Massachusetts, in 1673 ordered that "Any one who let houses of lands to those, whom the town disapprove of, shall be fined, or any who entertain strangers, shall pay 20s. a week, unless security be given for their honesty and ability." As late as 1789, "Persons, recently moved hither, are warned away, without any respect to their character, profession, or condition."

Probably the first large importation of non-English in New England were the 150 Scottish Royalist prisoners of war taken by Oliver Cromwell's Puritan forces and shipped to Boston in 1650. About fifty of these were put to work at the Saugus ironworks; the remainder were sold off as bond servants. Many Scots settled in the new town of Alexandria, Virginia, after 1748. Some became prosperous merchants whose comfortable town houses are still to be seen. Nicholas Cresswell, the young loyal Englishman who unhappily found himself stranded in Virginia at the start of the Revolution, reported that Scots had settled throughout the colony. On November 30, 1774, when he was in Leesburg, he noted: "This being the Anniversary of St. Andrew, the titular Saint of the Scotch, was invited to spend the evening with Captn. William Douglas and a number of other Scotch guests. Have been genteelly treated and am now going to bed drunk."

He spent another evening in Alexandria with William Ramsay's son Dennis and a friend. "Two conceited ignorant fops," he wrote, a remark possibly engendered by Dennis's enthusiasm for the cause of liberty.

In addition to the Scots were the Irish and the so-called Scotch-Irish, one of the most numerous of immigrant groups in the colonial period. The Scotch-Irish, mostly Presbyterians, were more Scottish than Irish, the English having moved them into Ulster to displace dissident native Irish there. A shipload of "Protestant Servants" from Ireland arrived in Boston in 1716, part of a vanguard of fifty-five shiploads of Scotch-Irish who were sent to New England between 1714 and 1720, before their later migrations through New York and Pennsylvania. This group represented such trades as anchor and ships' smiths, house carpenters, joiners, locksmiths, tailors, and silversmiths. Among the women there were "Ribband & Lace Weavers," a buttonmaker, and an "Earthen Ware Potter Maker."

The Scotch-Irish found New England generally inimical, although a group of Ulster weavers settled the towns of Derry and Londonderry, New Hampshire, in the eighteenth century. In about 1770 they comprised at least one-third of Pennsylvania's population, mostly in the mountainous western regions. Some of the descendants of the colonial Scotch-Irish have survived with little change as Appalachian mountain people from Pennsylvania to Tennessee.

There were doubtless many indigenous Irish Catholics who came to America, but unless they went to Maryland or Pennsylvania, where they could worship freely, they conformed to local Protestantism. Early accounts and records refer frequently to Irish, but it is not always clear whether Scotch-Irish is meant. Cresswell recorded in Alexandria on March 17, 1775, that he "Went to a Ball made by the Irish Gentry in commemoration of St. Patrick," clearly indicating a sizable number of Catholic Irish there. Runaway Irish servants were frequently advertised: "Charles Daly, an Irish boy," "an Irish man servant named Florence Carty." Occasional Irish tradesmen appeared in the newspapers, their names usually distinguishing them from Ulstermen: Hercules Mulligan, a New York tailor; John Hickey, a "Silk Dyer and Scowerer, from Dublin." As early as 1683 the royal governor of New York was an Irishman, Colonel Thomas Dongan.

42

By far the most influential and numerous people to come to America aside from the English were Germans. William Penn's appeal to the persecuted to settle in his province brought a response of enormous proportions. Wars, almost uninterrupted since the Protestant Reformation, had brought much of Germany into poverty, internal conflict, and suppression. Martin Luther's original Protestantism split off into many new religious sects, among them the so-called Pietists, themselves fragmented into groups such as Mennonites, Amish, Dunkers, and Moravians. The unending warfare that swirled around these people and forced male members into military service doubtless strengthened the pacifism of their religious philosophies. There was thus an affinity between them and the English Quakers that made Pennsylvania especially appealing as a refuge from the persecution that had become their lot in German states governed by Catholic rulers.

Although "Dutchmen" (usually meaning Germans) are mentioned sporadically in the colonies, beginning with the Jamestown glass-workers of 1608, it was not much after the establishment of Pennsylvania that Francis Daniel Pastorius brought his group of Mennonites to settle Germantown in 1683. This was the real beginning of the German cultural impact on American society; it was also the prototype for communities that have maintained German culture in distinctive enclaves to the present day.

In 1710 the English Board of Trade, in an effort to develop naval stores in America, sent to New York three thousand Palatine German refugees who were among the thousands that had fled to London at the invitation of Queen Anne. The intention of the project was to have the Germans make tar and turpentine from pine trees. This bureaucratically inspired mass movement resulted in the deaths of one-quarter of the passengers in a terrible voyage that epitomized the horrendous conditions aboard vessels bearing indentured servants. Once landed, their children were sent to other colonies as apprentices. The naval stores project came to an untimely end after a period of militarily enforced labor for the refugees. They subsequently spread over New York State but suffered deprivation and abuse. A few evidences of their stay in New York remain, among them a pair of wrought-iron hinges with cut-out hearts. [42]. One large group finally moved south into the Pennsylvania piedmont, where they became the first inland farmers of the "Dutch" country. They spread south into Maryland, and some of them formed the vanguard of German settlers in Virginia.

Of all the Germans who came to America, the Moravians managed to bring and maintain the most wholly intact communities of German culture. These transplanted German islands owed their origins to early Protestant followers of the Bohemian martyr Jan Hus. Formed as the Unity of Brethren, the sect had been intermittently persecuted in Europe. Early in the eighteenth century a group of them gathered at Herrnhut in Saxony, seat of Count von Zinzendorf, a wealthy adherent of the sect. Organized in a communal pattern, the Brethren decided to emigrate to America and plant new communal settlements. A small advance party went to Georgia in 1741, but fearing war with the Spanish, they moved to Bethlehem, Pennsylvania. Reinforcements arrived from Herrnhut and a highly organized community developed, with craft industries, farming, education, and especially music—all conducted as an integral enterprise for the greater glory of God. Later the Moravians built communities at Nazareth and Lititz.

Wholly German, the Moravians continued to live and work as they had done before leaving Germany. Their German peasant-style plank chairs were made and used in the Nazareth community [43]. Distinguishable in no significant way from German prototypes, they are totally distinct from English colonial furniture. Equally Germanic is the pewter communion flagon [44] made by Johann Christopher Heyne in molds that he quite clearly brought with him to America. The flagon differs from other American pewter as much as the Moravian chair does from American furniture. The spreading base, the angel's-head feet, the pouring spout, and the lid could only be German.

In 1753 the Moravians planted a new community in distant North Carolina. Named Wachovia, it eventually included three settlements, the chief of which was Salem, now well preserved in the city of Winston-Salem. Among the most important craft industries of the community were potteries. The first potter was Gottfried Aust, from Herrnhut. Quite uninfluenced by anything American, he continued to make elaborate slip-decorated red earthenware at Wachovia just as he had done in Germany. Aust's principal apprentice and successor was Rudolf Christ, who came in 1764, at age fourteen, to Wachovia from Wurtenberg. Well into the nineteenth century Christ continued to make the same types of German folk pottery as his master.

43

42
Pair of wrought-iron side hinges made in New York in the eighteenth century illustrates the strong influence of German culture. L 7".

43
Plank chair possibly made in Pennsylvania. An ink inscription under the seat reads: "Old chair from the Moravian Church of Nazareth, Pa./was one of the original chairs in use when Nazareth was first settled." H 37¼".

44

Outside the organized communities of Moravians were individual representatives of the other Pietist sects, as well as German Lutherans. By the midcentury they were pouring into Philadelphia and elsewhere by the thousands. Many of them, desperate to start new lives in America, but without funds, were victimized by unscrupulous agents and conniving ship captains who crowded them together on vessels little different from slave ships. In return for their passage, the captain sold their labor for terms of five years or more. The unspeakable conditions aboard ship prompted a committee of the Pennsylvania Assembly, of which Benjamin Franklin was a member, to write to the governor in 1755:

... the melancholy Spectacle of the Distress of so many of our Fellow creatures perishing for Want of Change of Apparel, Room, and other Necessaries, on board the Ships, and after their being landed among us, the extreme Danger the Benevolent and the Charitable exposed themselves to in approaching those unhappy Sufferers ... Many ... have frequently been afflicted with such secret and loathsome Diseases ... as have rendered them altogether unfit for the Services they had contracted to Perform.

Notwithstanding, those who survived and worked out their indentures usually ended as thrifty and industrious contributors to America. Many of the great barns and sturdy farmhouses seen today in the Pennsylvania "Dutch" country were built by colonial descendants of these first German settlers. Here and there an original example from the earliest period has survived, sometimes as a log house concealed under a clapboard covering.

The log house as an architectural form was native to Germany as well as to Scandinavia. While the Swedes and Finns were the first to introduce it, the Germans were influential in establishing the log house as a model for others. Neighborhood participation in house raisings was customary in the colonies, and in Pennsylvania's ethnically mixed settlements the Germans, skilled in building technology peculiarly adapted to the timber resources of newly cleared woodlands, inevitably taught newcomers as they helped them build their houses. Crèvecoeur recounts an instance in describing the happy evolution of the "honest Scotch Hebridean" Andrew's settlement in America:

... I told him that the time had come to build his house; and that for that purpose I would myself invite the neighborhood to a frolic; that thus he would have a large dwelling erected, some upland cleared in one day. Mr. P. R., his old friend, came at the time appointed, with all his hands, and brought victuals in plenty: I did the same. About forty people repaired to the spot; the songs, and merry stories, went round the woods from cluster to cluster, as the people had gathered to their different works; trees fell on all sides, bushes were cut up and heaped, and while many were thus employed, others with their teams hauled the big logs to the spot which Andrew had pitched upon for the erection of his new dwelling. We all dined in the woods: in the afternoon the logs were placed with skids, and the usual contrivances: thus the rude house was raised ... though this new dwelling, erected in the midst of the woods, was nothing more than a square inclosure, composed of twenty-four large clumsy logs, let in at the ends....

Soon after he hired a carpenter, who put on a roof and laid the floors, in a week more the house was properly plastered, and the chimney finished.

In towns like York and Lancaster, a medieval German flavor was given by half-timbered or *Fachwerk* houses consisting of mortise-and-tenon frames infilled with brick. Small stone houses no larger than log houses are believed to be derived from Rhenish prototypes. As the Revolutionary years approached, the English Georgian style of the Philadelphia area began to influence the character of German houses of the interior, but as with many other aspects, the influence was superficial, and the nuances of proportion and detail distinguish them from purely Anglo-American dwellings.

Even more distinctly German were the furnishings of colonial homes in the Pennsylvania interior. The most vivid illustrations occur in the dower chests. Unlike the plain wooden chests for ordinary household use, these were painted with folk symbols of ancient German significance. Young girls filled them with utensils and clothes, anticipating married life [45].

44
Pewter communion flagon made by Johann Christopher Heyne, eighteenth century. H 13½".

45
Pine dower chest made by Christian Selzer, Jonestown, Dauphin County, Pennsylvania, 1777. L 52".

45

46

With furniture as with architecture, the proximity of Philadelphia and its elegantly designed and furnished houses led to a gradual adoption and adaptation of prevailing English styles among the more affluent Germans. This occurred even while such expressions of German folk life as the dower chests were vigorously continuing. An example of Anglo-German furniture is a ladder-back side chair inspired by Philadelphia Chippendale design of about 1760, but made in the vicinity of Lancaster [46]. Its massive lines, thick decorative brackets, and squat and staunch proportions relate it to the "Dutch" culture of Pennsylvania.

In Philadelphia the German population grew by leaps and bounds as the "redemptioners"—bonded immigrants—moved in. A Germantown printer, Christopher Sauer, and his son responded to the need for German publications and established a German-language newspaper that was read throughout the colonies. They printed many books, pamphlets, almanacs, and Bibles. The extent to which German was spoken in the city is suggested by a Philadelphia apprenticeship agreement of 1746, which stipulated that one Mathias Keable would be bound for a period of twelve years to the potter Jacob Udery, who was to teach Keable the trade of potter and to read and write the German language.

The compulsive industriousness of the Germans, their skilled craftsmanship, and their mechanical ability led to important contributions in the arts and in industry. Ironwork of a high order emerged from numerous foundries in Lancaster County. The Germans' liking for stoves (as opposed to the conservative English taste for wood-burning fireplaces) led to a large production of cast-iron stove plates. In keeping with the religious tone of the households in which they were used, these embody Biblical quotations in German and folk decorative devices that relate them to the Frakturs and dower-chest decorations derived from medieval illuminated manuscripts and long-standing cultural symbols. One stove plate made at Redding Furnace and dated 1748 is inscribed in German: "God's well has water in plenty," a passage excerpted from Psalm 65 in the Lutheran Bible.

Of the German iron founders, one of the most flamboyant was Heinrich Wilhelm Stiegel, who came to America in 1750 from the Palatinate. He learned the iron business from Jacob Huber, whose furnace in Lancaster County was a prosperous one, and he married Huber's daughter Elizabeth, who died in 1758. He became the owner of the Huber furnace, remarried, to another Elizabeth, and renamed the ironworks Elizabeth Furnace. In 1759 he cast there a tubular stove, made in three sections, which looks like a cannon [47]. The father of the donor of this stove to the Smithsonian found it on a dump in London in the late nineteenth century. At the time he heard the traditional story that the stove was one of several that Stiegel took to England before the Revolution to sell in order to defray his passage. Since he was there about 1764, presumably investigating English glassmaking, the story is plausible. Stiegel shipped iron to the West Indies, however, so it is possible that he also shipped stoves to England.

47

46
Chippendale-style ladder-back side chair probably made in the Lancaster, Pennsylvania, area, c. 1780–1800. H 38″.

47
Cannon stove made at Heinrich Wilhelm Stiegel's Elizabeth Furnace in Lancaster, Pennsylvania, in 1759. It is copied from eighteenth-century examples called *Pommerofen,* probably after Wolfgang Pommer, a sixteenth-century Nuremberg inventor of stoves. H 56″.

Stiegel became affluent and designated himself "Baron." With Parliament's increasing burden of taxation on the Americans, there was a growing reliance in the colonies on domestic manufactures. Stiegel therefore decided to enter the glass business, opening a modest factory for window glass and bottles at Elizabeth Furnace in 1763. In 1765 Stiegel built a new factory called the American Flint Glass Works. There he set out to make tableware for the Anglo-colonial and German-colonial markets. Importing blowers, cutters, ironworkers, and engravers from the Continent and England, he made glass in many current styles and established retail agencies from Baltimore to Boston. At one point he employed 130 workmen. Unfortunately, the colonies' resources diminished as Stiegel's production increased. In 1773 he went bankrupt and into debtors' prison.

Most of the colonial glass factories were, like Stiegel's, dependent upon German technology and workmen. In 1752 the Boston *Evening Post* announced that

Tuesday last [September 19] a ship arrived with about 300 Germans, Men, Women and Children, some of whom are going to settle in Germantown [part of Braintree, Massachusetts] and the others in the Eastern Parts of this Province . . . among the artificers come over in this Ship, there are a number of Men skilled in making of Glass, of various Sorts, and a House proper for carrying on that useful Manufacture, will be erected at Germantown as soon as possible.

The glassworks was built in 1753 and became so much an object of curiosity that the Boston *Gazette* on September 4 carried a notice:

. . . none will be admitted to see the new manufactory at Germantown, unless they pay at least one shilling lawfull money; and they are desired not to ask above three or four Questions, and not to be offended if they have not a satisfactory answer to all or any of them. Note. The manufactory has received considerable Damage, and been very much retarded by the great Number of People which are constantly resorting to the House.

The most spectacular and romantic glassmaking venture occurred in Maryland after the war. In 1784 Johann Friedrich Amelung, scion of a long-established family of German glass manufacturers, arrived in Baltimore from Bremen with sixty-eight German glassworkers. He built a furnace at the foot of Sugar Loaf Mountain in Frederick County, enlarged his staff, and proceeded to make bottle and window glass while struggling with unfamiliar raw materials to produce clear table glass. He did so in 1788 when he produced a covered pokal, or ceremonial goblet, exquisitely engraved with the arms of the city of Bremen and the inscriptions "Old Bremen Success and the New Progress" and "New Bremen Glassmanufactory—1788—North America, State of Maryland." This he sent to his backers in Bremen, the only return they ever received on their investment.

Amelung's engraving was Germanic, in the high style, and skillfully executed; the glass itself was never quite able to match the quality of the engraving, however [48]. Yet, like Stiegel, Amelung expanded his enterprise, built a village for his workers and a mansion for himself. He established schools to teach English, German, and music. Reportedly there were five hundred persons at New Bremen at the height of his operation. But Amelung's enterprise collapsed in 1795, and he too went bankrupt, though without the ignominy of being committed to debtors' prison. Despite his financial failure, he succeeded in producing fine quality glass, and from his huge reservoir of skilled German workmen the American glass industry developed, spreading to small factories as far west as Ohio.

As in other efforts of manufacture, the Germans made significant contributions to ceramics. In Pennsylvania, Virginia, and North Carolina they produced the colorful slip-decorated red earthenwares already mentioned, as well as plain utilitarian pottery. In Philadelphia they merged their own traditions of earthenware with those of the English. This amalgamation resulted in an American-style product emulated by potters from New England to Virginia, who advertised that they made "Philadelphia earthenware" or pottery that was "equal to any made in Philadelphia."

The familiar American blue-decorated gray salt-glazed stoneware of the nineteenth century, so much sought after by collectors today, owes its origins to potters trained in the Rhine Valley region of Germany [49A–49D]. In 1718 Johann Wilhelm Crolius came to New York from Neuwied, the German county that included the Westerwald centers for the manufacture of blue-and purple-decorated gray salt-glazed stoneware. By 1724 he was listed as a potter in New York, almost certainly making stoneware, as did succeeding generations of Croliuses until 1849. Related by marriage to the first Crolius was the founder of another dynasty of stoneware makers, Johannes Remi (soon to be Remmey), also from Neuwied. Although we can surmise that Crolius introduced the German stoneware tradition to America, the earliest proof of its manufacture is the 1730 petition of a Huguenot potter in Philadelphia, Anthony Duché, for the sole right to make stoneware in Pennsylvania, which asserted that he and his three sons had been making stoneware "for several years past." Proof of his work has been found in archaeological excavations.

48
Glass bowl made in 1789 by
Johann Friedrich Amelung, a
German who established a
glassworks near Frederick,
Maryland, in 1784. H 4⅛″.

49A

49B

The influence of the German stoneware tradition is strongly felt in these pieces made in the New York and New Jersey areas where potters were working as early as the first half of the eighteenth century.

Salt-glazed stoneware jug marked "Rum." Made in New York or New Jersey, c. 1790. H 12½".

49B
Salt-glazed stoneware jar with cobalt decoration. New York, c. 1790. H 9¾".

49C
Salt-glazed stoneware jar with incised and cobalt-infilled decoration. Late eighteenth century, New York. H 10¼".

49D
Salt-glazed stoneware jug made by Thomas Commereau, New York City, 1796–1810. H 11".

49C

49D

There were certain nationalities and ethnic groups that, while maintaining their identities, remained in the cities and were assimilated in the prevailing society. Among these were the French Huguenots—the Calvinist Protestants outlawed by the government of Louis XIV. They were most evident in South Carolina, Virginia, and Pennsylvania, but they were also in New York and Boston and smaller cities as well. Some came in groups and settled in enclaves, such as New Paltz in the Hudson Valley, founded in 1677. Much of its domestic architecture is still intact today: small stone houses, some dating from the seventeenth century, line the tree-shaded main street. Another community was New Rochelle, settled at the end of the century.

The first Huguenot arrivals in Charleston, as well as many subsequent refugees, specialized in cultivating the silkworm. A late as 1767 the *New-York Gazette and Weekly Post Boy* carried a dispatch from South Carolina (May 28): "We have the pleasure to acquaint the public, that the successful introduction of the Silk Manufacture in this province bears a promising aspect, as we hear there are great quantities of Silk-worms raised in almost every family in Purrysburg Parish, and some by the French of Hillsborough, and the English and Germans near Long Canes." On September 23, 1773, the New York *Journal* printed a news item from London: "It is said that a considerable number of French refugees, well skilled in the management of silk worms, and making of wines, have within these few days, engaged themselves on very advantageous terms to go to New-York, and South-Carolina."

For the most part, the Huguenots were scattered as individuals throughout the colonies, practicing fine crafts, particularly those of the jeweler, goldsmith, watchmaker, miniaturist, engraver, carver, and gilder. Goldsmiths—in reality silversmiths—were prevalent among them. Even though he was not trained in France before arriving in America, it was natural for the young Apollos Rivoire, for example, to be apprenticed to the Boston goldsmith John Coney. By Anglicizing his name to Paul Revere and marrying a native Boston girl, he was easily assimilated into the New England populace. His better-known namesake son learned the silversmith's trade and became famous in the Revolution.

Also well known as gold- and silversmiths were Simeon Soumaine of New York and his erstwhile apprentice Elias Pelletreau, who worked in Southampton, Long Island, and Salisbury, Connecticut. Another Soumaine, Samuel, made silver in Annapolis and Philadelphia. Pelletreau, by 1773, appears to have attempted to give up silversmithing. He advertised that he had set up "at his House on Golden-Hill, at the Sign of the Dish of Fry'd Oysters, a place for cutting of Whale Bone . . . N.B. He has for sale a parcel of Silver Smith's Tools, which he will sell cheap for cash." Nevertheless, Pelletreau continued as a silversmith even after the Revolution [50]. As for other goldsmiths, Elias Boudinot, John Hastier, Daniel du Puy, William Ghiselin, and John le Telier are a few of the many Huguenot names.

Prominent Huguenot merchants of the midcentury were Gilbert and Lewis Deblois, of Boston. A musical family in a community as yet unsophisticated in music, the Debloises built the Boston Concert Hall and introduced serious secular music, thus establishing a musical tradition in Boston. The Faneuils and Sigourneys and Bowdoins in Boston, like the De Lanceys, Gallaudets, and de la Noyes (later Delano) in New York, similarly became affluent and prominent.

As the Huguenots did, the Jews participated in the society in which they settled. The first Jews admitted to America were a small handful who came to New Amsterdam in 1654. At a time when toleration of dissident or non-Christian religious beliefs was limited, this was a significant step on the part of the Dutch. It was taken, in fact, a year before Jews were allowed in England. Most of those who came to New York were Sephardic Jews of Spanish and Portuguese descent, some of whom had lived in Holland and the Dutch West Indies as refugees from the Inquisition. Others were Ashkenazim from Germany and eastern Europe. Although the Dutch did not allow Jews to worship in public or to have a synagogue, the Jews nevertheless soon participated in local business and maritime trade. The New York Jewish colony finally succeeded in establishing Congregation Shearith Israel and opened their synagogue in 1730.

All through the colonial period there were problems of Jewish citizenship and rights, but these rested much more on legal technicalities than on anti-Semitism, which was virtually nonexistent in the colonies. Some Jews remained aliens, some were naturalized, some had an intermediate status of "denizens," and in New York City some gained full recognition as freemen of the city. Among those freemen between 1688 and 1770 were twenty-two merchants, a butcher, a baker, two tailors, six shopkeepers, a chandler, a tallow chandler, two distillers (one of whom was also a tobacconist), three goldsmiths, two perukemakers (one of whom was also a barber), a snuffmaker, a brazier, a cordwainer, a saddler, and a watchmaker. The majority of colonial Jews were merchants; some engaging in overseas trade became wealthy and influential. Jacob Franks, Nathan Simson, and Rodrigo Pacheco were typical of the prosperous merchants who dealt in all sorts of goods and maintained retail shops and warehouses as well as ships.

Philadelphia was an important colonial center of Jews, as were Rhode Island and South Carolina. A noted example of colonial architecture is the so-called Touro synagogue of the Jewish congregation in Newport, Rhode Island. This was designed by the accomplished gentleman architect Peter Harrison and completed in 1763.

Numerous craftsmen bearing Jewish names appear in colonial newspapers. Lazarus Isaac, for example, announced in the *Pennsylvania Packet* for May 17, 1773, that he had just arrived from London and that he "undertakes to cut and engrave on glass of every kind, in any figure whatsoever." Stiegel, the glass manufacturer, evidently saw this advertisement, for less than three weeks later Isaac had contracted to work for him as a "Cutter and Flowerer." In Philadelphia in 1785 were Michael and Isaac Levy, "Watch and Clock Makers, Late from London." Jeremiah Levi, who lived in Charles County, Maryland, in 1750, "makes and mends all Sorts of Jeweller's and Silversmith's work." In New York, in 1758, Levi Simons was an "Embroiderer from London . . . to be heard of at I. Abrahams near the King's Arms." Abrahams was a Jewish distiller.

Perhaps the outstanding Jewish craftsman of the colonial period was the New York goldsmith Myer Myers, who flourished in the mid-eighteenth century. Myers made elegant silver inspired by English models in the current style. In a rare instance of literal copying, he even cast a pair of candlesticks, now in the Garvan Collection at Yale University, from a mold shaped around an English candlestick. But Myers's work usually represents original, fine interpretations of the prevailing Georgian style that mark them as American. Like other silversmiths, Myers was catering to the sophisticated tastes of fashionable New Yorkers, including members of the Jewish community. When Isaac Seixas's house was burglarized in 1754, he advertised that among "sundry Things stolen" were "two large Silver Table Spoons, mark'd with the Cypher I R S. Maker's Name M M." The last could only have stood for Myer Myers.

The crowning achievements of his art as a goldsmith were dedicated to his own religion and they remain as splendid tributes to Jewish ceremonial traditions as well as superb expressions of his craft. These are the *Rinomin*—Torah scroll ends and bells—that he made for Temple Shearith Israel in New York, Mikveh Israel in Philadelphia, and Touro synagogue in Newport.

Like many prominent Jews, Myers was an active supporter of the American Revolution. He and his family left New York ahead of the British in 1776, moving to Norwalk, Connecticut, where he made bullets for the colonial troops. Driven away again by the Dutch, he and his family moved to Philadelphia. He was one of three signers of a letter to Governor Clinton, representing "the Ancient Congregation of Israelites," stating that "Though the Society, we Belong to, is but small, when Compared with other Religious Societies, Yet, we flatter ourselves that none has Manifested a more Zealous Attachment to the Sacred Cause of America, in the late War with Great Britain." Not all shared these feelings, and indeed the Jewish community was riven in two by the war. There were many loyalists who felt that Jewish freedoms were best served by an English government which had already nurtured Jewish emancipation. For most, however, both individual liberty and financial interest led them to side with independence.

There were several other nationalities among the colonial Americans. Two Italians were numbered among Oglethorpe's Georgia-colonists, for example. In 1774 "Nicholas Biferi . . . Musician of Naples" advertised as a music teacher in New York. There were numerous Swiss, some coming in groups, such as the hundred Swiss (plus fifty Germans) who came with Baron de Graffenried to North Carolina to establish New Bern. In 1767 Lewis Turtaz "from Lausanne in Switzerland" advertised as a limner and miniature painter in Charleston. There was also the very English-sounding John Ingram, who, in 1757, advertised himself in Boston as the "Original Flower of Mustard Maker, from Lisbon." Both in Wilmington, Delaware, and Philadelphia in the eighteenth century there were residual communities of Swedes.

Although such national minorities added flavor to America's diversity, their numbers were sparse in contrast to the most widespread non-English group of all—black Africans. Silent, held to submission, placed at the bottom of the English and continental Europeans' unquestioned scale of social and natural order, Africans supplied the strength for much of the colonial achievement and introduced cultural elements that only recently have begun to be fully recognized.

As early as 1512 the Spaniards were sending Negro slaves to Hispaniola. They accompanied Cortés to conquer Mexico; they went with Pizarro to Peru. Between 1570 and 1580 blacks in Mexico numbered 18,569, compared with 14,711 Spaniards. England entered the slave trade with Sir John Hawkins's efforts to sell Negroes to the Spanish in the 1560s. His successors in the sordid business fared well for two centuries and more. The English colonies in continental North America were at first slow to acquire Africans as slaves, however. Negroes arrived in 1619 at Jamestown, where, in the words of Robert Beverley (*The History and Present State of Virginia*, published in 1722), "In *August* . . . a Dutch Man of War landed Twenty *Negroes* for Sale; which were the First of that kind that were carried into the Country."

For some years Virginians looked upon blacks as indentured servants. Like white bond servants, when Negroes worked out their periods of indenture they became free. There are even recorded instances of blacks in Virginia owning slaves during the first half of the century. With small landholdings the rule at that time, the black population grew slowly there: twenty-five years after the first twenty blacks arrived, there were only three hundred in the whole colony. The white man was still doing his own work in the fields.

This situation, both in Maryland and Virginia, changed as unsuccessful small planters sold out to larger ones. The scale of tobacco growing then enlarged, and the demand increased for regimented mass labor in the fields. By midcentury the underlying distinctions engraved upon the European mind between white Christians and black pagans apparently were brought to the surface to serve practical ends. It was decided in Maryland in 1664 that Negroes, as distinct from white servants, would henceforth be slaves for life. Thus, the white planter would reign supreme and the steady operation of his plantation would be assured. In 1671 Virginia passed a law similar to Maryland's.

From then on the slave population in the southern colonies increased as a constant supply came in the packed holds of the slave ships from West Africa. The tobacco and rice plantations required their labor; the slave traders supplied it at a rich profit. In time only those whites at the lowest social levels were without slaves in the plantation South, for a gentleman did not work with his hands.

Slaves were held in the North as well. In establishing the patroon system in New Netherland the Dutch promised black servants for each patroon after 1629; the big Hudson Valley estates employed many blacks. The needs and economic system of the northern colonies, however, did not demand slavery in large degree and therefore most northern blacks were house servants, porters, and individual workers who labored alongside their masters in farming. Nevertheless, by 1764, the number of Negroes in Essex County, Massachusetts, for example, was 1,049—over 2 percent of the population.

Until recently it has been one of the verities among historians that slaves, uprooted from their tribal communities and mixed with blacks from other parts of Africa, were so disassociated from their native backgrounds that they became deculturated. It follows in this view that the white master became the center of a new culture along with Christian religion. It is true that the transmission of material culture was virtually impossible on slave ships and the circumstances of slaves in the colonies did not allow re-creation of their former environments, yet there is a growing body of evidence that the social isolation of blacks may have strengthened memories and encouraged the handing down of cultural traits.

Of all the contributions that Afro-Americans have made to America's complex of cultures, music and dance have been among the most influential. For blacks herded into the slave ships, disease, depression, suicide, and revolt were threats to their survival. And for the captain, deaths among his cargo could produce staggering financial losses. It was to his practical interest, even if it was not an expression of his humanity, that he should offer his unwilling passengers exercise, fresh air, and even rudimentary entertainment during the voyage. There are numerous records of encouragement and even enforcement of dancing on deck, according to the ethno-musicologist Dena J. Epstein. She quotes *Chambers's Encyclopaedia*, first published in 1728: "As soon as the Ship has its Complement, it immediately takes off, the poor Wretches, while yet in sight of their country, fall into Sickness, and die. . . . The only sure means to preserve 'em, is to have some Musical Instrument to play to 'em, be it ever so mean." Epstein quotes the observation of a West Indian traveler in 1793: "In the intervals between their meals they [the slaves] are encouraged to divert themselves with music and dancing, for which purpose such rude and uncouth instruments as are used in Africa, are collected before their departure."

Thus it is clear that on occasion blacks brought native African musical instruments along on the slave ships when no other possessions were allowed. Even when they did not, they brought their memories of a highly complex system of music and of the instruments needed to play it. At least until the period of the Revolution, African music and dances continued on the large plantations in the South, as in the West Indies. Musical instruments were made by the slaves, and on Sundays there were customarily large gatherings, with dancing that continued all night. The *kalenda,* or *la calinda,* a dance described by more than one observer as "lascivious," was the usual form. It was accompanied by drums made from hollow tree trunks with skin stretched across one end, held between the legs and strummed with the fingers. A primitive banjo, or *banza,* made of a gourd or calabash, was also used. The *kalenda* continued to be danced by blacks in New Orleans as late as the mid-nineteenth century, but Anglo-American clergymen saw it as a heathen custom to be extirpated, and it disappeared as Christianity and revivalist music began to take its place. Nevertheless, the rhythms, the calls and refrains of the black field hands, and the musical structure of the spirituals were living continuations of basic African musical traditions. The emergence of jazz and its widespread adoption in the Western world speak for the vitality of African musical forms that passed through the acculturation process and endured.

Very seldom, however, have the instruments used by African slaves in America survived. A notable exception is an Akan-type drum reportedly made of American materials and collected in Virginia in the eighteenth century [51]. It is part of the collection of Sir Hans Sloane, founder of the British Museum, to which he bequeathed it in 1753. Sir Hans lived in Jamaica from 1687 to 1689 and became interested in slave music there. The drum is an extraordinary and probably unique survival of African material culture in colonial America.

Despite frowning moralists, African customs persisted. Nicholas Cresswell, when he first landed in Maryland in 1774, observed:

Mr. Bayley and I went to see a Negro Ball. Sundays being the only days these poor creatures have to themselves, they generally meet together and amuse themselves with Dancing to the Banjo. This musical instrument (if it may be so called) is made of a Gourd something in the imitation of a guitar, with only four strings and played with the fingers in the same manner. Some of them sing to it, which is very droll music indeed. In their songs they generally relate the usage they have received from their Masters or Mistresses in a very satirical stile and manner. Their poetry is like the Music—Rude and uncultivated. Their Dancing is most violent exercise, but so irregular and grotesque. I am not able to describe it.

Afro-American banjos have occasionally survived, notably the one preserved at Monticello, home of Thomas Jefferson. Another is depicted in a late-eighteenth-century painting, "The Old Plantation," showing slaves of Yoruba and Hausa descent dancing and playing musical instruments on a South Carolina plantation. The painting is in the Abby Aldrich Rockefeller Folk Art Museum in Williamsburg, Virginia.

Eileen Southern, in *The Music of Black Americans,* quotes and discusses an account of the Pinkster Day (Pentecost Sunday) festivities in Albany, New York. For thirty years or more in the late eighteenth century, blacks annually paid homage to "Old King Charley," an ancient slave from Angola. For days there was dancing to African music, the principal instrument being an eel pot covered with sheepskin. Other instances of such celebrations are on record.

51
Akan-type drum, reportedly
fashioned from American
cedar and deerskin by an
unknown slave in Virginia or
Carolina. H (approx.) 18″.

52
Iron figure sculpted by an unknown Afro-American,
eighteenth century. The figure was excavated at the
site of a forge in plantation
slave quarters in Virginia. H
15″.

The evidence of specialized skills among slaves is repeatedly apparent. On well-organized plantations they were trained in many trades. As early as 1649, Captain Mathews, who lived in Virginia on the James River, kept spinners and weavers, tanners, shoemakers, and brewers among his forty Negroes. The Dublin traveler Isaac Weld noted in 1795 that among Virginia slaves were "taylors, shoemakers, carpenters, smiths, turners, wheelwrights, tanners, &c." Blacksmithing is repeatedly referred to. A remarkable example of African artistic expression in ironwork was revealed by the excavation of a slave-quarter forge site in Alexandria, Virginia. Under the baked red earth of the forge a small figure of a man was found, made of bar iron in a sculpture of extraordinary power and sensitivity [52].

Some plantation owners kept careful records of their slaves, as the account book of David Minge illustrates. Isaac Weld was impressed that the "slaves on the large plantations are in general very well provided for, and treated with mildness. During three months, nearly, that I was in Virginia, but two or three instances of ill treatment towards them came under my observation." Weld described their quarters and small gardens and yards for poultry. "Many of these little huts are comfortably furnished, and they are themselves, in general, extremely well clothed." He nevertheless had second thoughts: "Still, however, let the condition of a slave be made ever so comfortable, as long as he is conscious of being the property of another man, . . . it is not supposed that he can feel equally happy with the freeman. It is immaterial under what form slavery presents itself: whenever it appears, there is ample cause for humanity to weep at the sight."

Weld had not read the earlier runaway slave advertisement in Boston of "Cyrus . . . Had on when he went off, an iron collar riveted round his neck, and a chain fastened to it." Neither could he have seen what Cresswell saw—"the quarter of a Negro man chained to a tree for murdering his overseer." Brissot de Warville, writing in 1794, a year earlier than Weld, also saw a different view: "In the South, the Blacks are in a state of abjection difficult to describe; many of them are naked, ill fed, lodged in miserable huts, on straw." He went on to draw a depressing picture of their ignorance and brutalization, especially in the case of field hands. Then he described examples of achievement among blacks to prove their capacity if given the chance. One slave, John Kearsley, learned surgery and was eventually freed to live successfully in New Orleans as a doctor. Another was Thomas Fuller of Alexandria, an illiterate slave with a genius for mathematics. De Warville was doubtless unaware of such prominent black personages of the eighteenth century as the surveyor and mathematician Benjamin Banneker, the poet Phillis Wheatley, and the physician James Derham.

By the end of the century the northern states had begun to free their slaves by law. There were individuals in the South, also, who felt the burden of guilt and set free their slaves. De Warville observed:

The free Blacks in the Eastern States are either hired servants, or they keep little shops, or they cultivate the land. . . . Those who keep shops live moderately, and never augment their affairs beyond a certain point.

The reason is obvious; the Whites, though they treat them with humanity, like not to give them credit to enable them to undertake an extensive commerce. . . . If, then, the Blacks are confined to the retails of trade, let us not accuse their capacity, but the prejudices of the Whites, which lay obstacles in their way.

The Christianizing of Negroes during the colonial period did not bring them equality in church participation. Not that it did to anybody, since it was customary for rank in society to determine the order in which one was seated in church. For blacks the gallery was always the last of the seating. It was inevitable that in the cities, at least, they should eventually have their own places of worship.

Twenty-one years before the first blacks landed at Jamestown, the Spanish, thousands of miles to the west, were renewing their efforts to control New Mexico. As usual with the Spanish, gold and silver were the main objectives for the laity; Christian souls were the goals of the Franciscan missionaries. An expedition under Don Juan de Oñate arrived at the Rio Grande in July 1598 and attempted to convert the Indians to Spanish rule and Christian belief. When a detachment of eighteen soldiers attempted to obtain food at Acoma pueblo, the Indians attacked them, killing thirteen. Oñate, in time-honored Spanish fashion, retaliated. Storming the pueblo high up on its fortified mesa, his troops massacred between six and eight hundred Indians. Having failed to find gold, having expended enormous sums of money, and having shocked even his superiors by the devastating cruelty of his attack on Acoma, Oñate was later put on trial for his crimes.

But eventually several missions were established and Spaniards settled in New Mexico. In 1609 Don Pedro de Peralta went there as governor, founding in 1610 a new provincial capital at Santa Fe. For the next seventy years the history of New Mexico was one of constant conflict between the clergy and missionaries on the one hand and the governors on the other. The governors, notable for their corruption, considered the Indians exploitable for personal enrichment. The Indians saw in the weakness and divided authority of the Spaniards an opportunity to rise from their long submission. In 1680 a San Juan medicine man named Popé rose to organize them, claiming his authority from three infernal spirits; pueblos simultaneously revolted, besieged the thousand or so Spaniards inside Santa Fe, laid waste to villages and haciendas, and killed some four hundred. The Spanish governor Otermín broke out of Sante Fe with his people, joined refugees at Isleta, and retreated to the Rio Grande at El Paso, thus abandoning New Mexico.

But the Spanish investment in colonization and Christian conversions was too great, and in 1692 the brilliant Don Diego de Vargas marched north from El Paso. For a year he successfully persuaded the Indians to return to the Christian fold and accept Spanish rule. In 1693 some eight hundred settlers arrived at Santa Fe, but it was another three years before sporadic Indian uprisings were put down and a peaceful existence became possible.

A dual culture developed, with each part drawing heavily from the other. The Indians continued to live in their pueblos, but with the Spanish-Christian presence always evident alongside them. Mission churches of plastered adobe rose above the pueblos as impressive monuments. The Spaniards established their own towns with Spanish names—Cordova, Santa Rosa, Albuquerque, Española. In the villages and mission churches an indigenous religious folk art developed that owed its iconography and forms to the Catholic Church and Mexico, but its simplicity to deeply felt religious folkways [53]. With imported supplies at a minimum and natural resources limited to the earth itself and to sparse supplies of timber, the New Mexicans devised their own architecture, borrowed from that of the Indian pueblos. Though unfailingly Spanish, the New Mexicans expressed their individual character in a movingly strong and somber series of art forms, ranging from religious sculpture to textiles, silverwork, carved furniture, and architecture.

During the eighteenth century there were still Spanish-born pioneers in the New Mexican community. One of these was Captain Bernardo Miera y Pacheco, a native of Burgos, who lived first in El Paso, then settled at Santa Fe in 1754. He was a professional soldier who served as military captain and *alcalde* (mayor) at several pueblos, a mapmaker who was the first in New Mexico to draw maps from firsthand observation, a rancher, and a skilled wood-carver and painter who sold statues and *retablos* to the Indians for their churches. A *bulto* (or saint in the round) by his hand, representing the Archangel Michael, was salvaged from the ruins of the church at Zuñi by Smithsonian ethnologists in 1880 [54].

Farther from Mexico City but more accessible by ship was California. The establishment of the Franciscan missions, and presidios and pueblos to complement the missions, is an epic in itself. Like the conquering of New Mexico, it represented Spain's final efforts to secure the far reaches of its empire in North America [55]. Only because of the determined zeal of the Franciscan Fray Junípero Serra was the mission of San Diego de Alcalá established in 1769, while San Carlos Borromeo was built at Monterey the next year and rebuilt at Carmel the year following. Then Juan Bautista de Anza opened the ''land bridge'' across Arizona and in 1775 led thirty-four families overland to establish Mission San Francisco de Asís near the bay that bears its name. Before 1880 there were other missions and pueblos, including El Pueblo de Nuestra Señora de la Reina de los Angeles del Rio de Porciúncula—now simply Los Angeles. Many Indians were converted and lived at the missions, but California slumbered on in pastoral indolence. As late as 1820 there were only 3,750 non-Indians in all of California.

53
St. Anthony and the Infant
Jesus painted in natural colors on tanned buffalo hide.
This unique artifact was made
by a Spanish Franciscan
priest working in New Mexico
sometime between 1700 and
1725. H 47".

54
Bulto of Archangel Michael by the multitalented Bernardo Miera y Pacheco. H 41″.

55
Leather shields of this indented oval shape, *adarga,* appeared with Spanish soldiers in Mexico by 1520. Two and a half centuries later, this shield—made of four layers of oxhide and stitched together and painted to portray the coat of arms of Spain—was serving the presidios of the Southwest. L 20¾″.

56
This chain-mail shirt was worn by the Russian governor of Alaska during 1799–1818, Alexander Baranov. He presented it to a Sitka Indian chief; later, a Tlingit chief gave it to a czar's interpreter, who offered it to this country through President Theodore Roosevelt. H 31″.

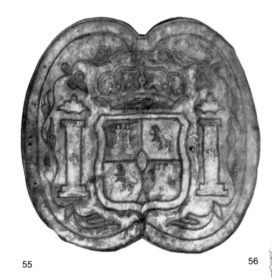

55   56

North of California during our colonial period were the Russians. In a series of incredibly difficult voyages, Vitus Bering discovered the strait that separates Asia from America and in 1741 landed in Alaska. Not until 1783, under the Siberian fur merchant Gregory Schelikov, were colonies and factories established along the Alaskan coast. Schelikov set the pattern for Russian relations with the Indians for years to follow. According to Robert Greenhow (*The History of Oregon and California*, 1845), "He and his followers are said to have exhibited the most barbarous dispositions in their treatment of the natives on the coasts, whole tribes of whom were put to death upon the slightest prospect of advantage from their destruction, and often through mere wantonness of cruelty."

Accompanying Schelikov was Alexander Baranov, who became chief agent for the Directory of Russian America, endowed with despotic powers. "He was a shrewd, bold, enterprising, and unfeeling man, of iron frame and nerves, and the coarsest habits and manners," wrote Greenhow. Baranov was indomitable in subjugating the Indians—invulnerable, in fact, from the Indian viewpoint. In 1799, when Alaska became a full-fledged Russian colony, Baranov became its governor. In 1906 George Kostrometinov, of a Russian Alaskan family, included the following description in a letter to President Theodore Roosevelt, which is now preserved in the Smithsonian Institution.

Head and shoulders above the men of other days stands out the striking character of Alexander Baranoff, the first Russian Governor of Alaska. His dauntless courage and indomitable energy made the settlement of Alaska by the Russians possible. In spite of the cunning of the bold and cruel Kaloshi [Indians] he founded and maintained his settlements among them. . . . Time and time again they tried in vain to kill him until at last they looked upon him as a great shaman or conjuror and sought his friendship. It was said that weapons refused to penetrate his body and it had always been supposed that he must have worn a suit of armor under his clothing.

Kostrometinov, the letter continued, set out to establish the truth of this belief. After an extensive search he found a Tlingit chief, Sha-ke-too, who brought to him a bundle neatly tied in calico. Baranov, said the chief, at a farewell celebration on the eve of his final departure in 1818, presented to Na-oosh-Katl, chief of the Sitkas, the chain-mail shirt that he had worn constantly since his arrival in Alaska. The armor, kept wrapped in calico, descended through the intervening generations to Sha-ke-too, who told Kostrometinov to take it in memory of one whom his ancestors had called friend. Concluding his letter, Kostrometinov wrote: "It is my desire Mr. President to present through you to the United States Government this interesting relic." The armored shirt has been in the Smithsonian Institution since that time [56]. The Russians also left their mark during the eighteenth century on territories later acquired by the United States. Like the Indians and the Spanish, they were there as America expanded its dominion to include them.

As immigrants poured in to settle the eastern seaboard colonies, the more restless and the more adventurous pressed westward. The stable ones settled in the new land; the misfits gambled with their luck, fought or traded with the Indians or with each other. They came from everywhere. "A man in that country [the American West]," wrote Brissot de Warville, "works scarcely two hours in a day, for the support of himself and family; he passes most of his time in idleness, hunting, or drinking."

Nicholas Cresswell, in his journey to the Ohio country to trade with the Indians for furs, joined a group on its way down the Ohio River. "Our company is increased to 14 persons and almost as many different nations, two Englishmen, two Irishmen, one Welshman, two Dutchmen, two Virginians, two Marylanders, one Swede, one African Negro, and a Mulatto. With the motley, rascally, and ragged crew I have to travel six hundred miles." He forgot to list a Frenchman named Boassiers. On the way he stopped to eat at "a plantation belonging to one Rous a Dutchman." As he prepared to move into Indian territory, he "Employed an Indian Woman to make me a pair of Mockeysons and Leggings." Later, as he left to return to Virginia, a friend "gave me an Indian tobacco pouch made of a Mink Skin adorned with porcupine quills." Commenting on the Indians, he observed: "In all their trades with the Europeans they are imposed on in the greatest manner." Then he concluded: "They are beings endowed with reason and common sense and I make not the least doubt but they are as valuable in the eyes of their Maker as we are, our fellow creatures, and in general above our level in many virtues that give real preeminence, however despicably we think of or injuriously we treat them."

Crèvecoeur, a pacifist about to flee the Revolution, planned with his family to join the Indians and to be adopted by them. "I rely more securely on their strong hospitality," he wrote, "than on the witnessed compacts of many Europeans."

The recognition by these sensitive men of the Indians' ennobling qualities was not a prevailing one. The dynamisms of a whole new society, comprising the American whom Crèvecoeur defined so well, moved irresistibly westward, its most belligerent and least orderly members in the vanguard, striking down whatever stood in their way. But a new culture was planted firmly behind them. Some of the material expressions of this culture remain, providing an insight into the American character before the advent of Independence.

Chapter 5

"We the People"—
The Emergence of
the American Nation

Early in July 1776, representatives from the "Thirteen United States of America," meeting at the Second Continental Congress in Philadelphia and acting in behalf of "*the good People of these Colonies*," adopted a "Unanimous Declaration" in which they proclaimed the colonies to be "Free and Independent States . . . Absolved from all Allegiance to the British Crown" [**57, 58A–58E**]. While still other agents of those same "good People" were striving—on the battlefield and in the sea lane, in the political arena and at the diplomatic table, on the farm and in the manufactory—to ensure that these claims would become a reality, the members of the Congress, after four years of painful negotiations, finally succeeded in obtaining ratification of thirteen "Articles of Confederation and perpetual Union between the States." But the parties to this transaction in 1781 were the states, not the people; political independence was not immediately accompanied by the establishment of an American nation.

Within four short years after the successful conclusion of the War for Independence in 1783, however, another group of delegates, also meeting in Philadelphia, during the summer of 1787, fashioned a Constitution that provided a suitable political framework for the creation of precisely such a nation. No less important, perhaps, by beginning with the phrase "*We the People*," the Constitution announced that that nation had already come into being. Within a dozen years "the good People of these Colonies" in the Declaration of Independence had been transformed into "We the People of the United States" in the federal Constitution. This extremely rapid and comparatively easy transformation raises a series of interesting questions. Who were the "People" in whose name the Constitutional Convention acted? How had they been converted into a single nation in such a short time? What was the broad meaning of the achievements that underlay that transformation?

Although they differed about the character of the American people, British and other foreign observers were unanimous in the opinion that Americans were comparatively well off economically, remarkably heterogeneous, and extraordinarily fecund. Indeed, population growth in the colonies was without precedent within the recent annals of the Western world. During the sixty years from 1710 to 1770, the white population increased almost six times, from just under 300,000 to nearly 1,700,000. This phenomenal rate of growth—reaching as high as 40 percent per decade and never dipping under 30 percent—was at least three times as high as that of contemporary Europe at any time during the eighteenth century, and it provided the basis for the pessimistic theories of the English economist T. R. Malthus, who predicted that population growth would eventually outstrip food production in the world. Over three-fourths of this total growth of over 1,400,000 was the result of natural increase, as the population reproduced at the rate of nearly 30 percent per decade.

This extraordinary population surge had never been adequately explained. Contemporaries such as Benjamin Franklin attributed it to unusually early marriages for women. In his pioneering "Observations Concerning the Increase of Mankind and the Peopling of Countries" (1751), Franklin said that people "increase in proportion to the number of marriages, and that is greater in proportion to the ease and convenience of supporting a family. When families can be easily supported, more persons marry, and earlier in life." According to Franklin, what made it so easy to support a family was the plentifulness and cheapness of land, which enabled any "laboring man, that understands husbandry" to save money enough "in a short time . . . to purchase a piece of new land sufficient for a plantation, whereon he may subsist a family." By uncovering the fact that the age of marriage was not significantly different in the colonies than in Britain, recent scholarship has cast doubt on Franklin's explanation, pointing instead to a combination of moderately high fertility, an "astonishingly low infant mortality," and a relatively low incidence of contagious diseases. Behind this combination of favorable conditions lay an abundant food supply.

Something of the expansive response to the colonial environment, the sense of boundlessness felt by so many colonists, was suggested in 1729 by Colonel William Byrd of Westover, Virginia, a planter and famous colonial diarist and humorist. ''Mrs. Byrd will hardly be in a Travelling condition 'till she's towards 50,'' he wrote to a friend in London in explaining why he could not visit England. ''I know nothing but a Rabit that breeds faster. It would [be] ungallant in a Husband to dissuade her from it, but it would be kind in you, to preach her upon that Chapter as a Friend. She was dilivered of a huge Boy in September last an[d] is so unconsionable as to be breeding again, Nay the learned say she is some months gone. The truth of it is, she has her reasons for procreating so fast. She lives in an Infant country which wants nothing but people.''

A similar response drew thousands of people from Britain and Europe to the colonies: immigrants accounted for between one-fifth and one-fourth of the total increase in the white population between 1710 and 1770. Most of the roughly 330,000 immigrants who arrived during these years, perhaps as many as 75 percent, were British. Of these, at least three-fifths were from England and Wales, but significant numbers came as well from Ireland and Scotland. Although there was always a smattering of Anglo-Irish and native Irish immigrants from the south of Ireland—itself little more than a colony of Great Britain during the eighteenth century—the vast majority of immigrants from Ireland were Ulster Scots. Starting in 1718, a series of natural calamities, along with rising rents, a volatile linen industry, and long-standing Presbyterian fears of Episcopal persecution, combined to drive significant numbers of these descendants of seventeenth-century Scottish colonists to the American colonies. From then until 1770 as many as 75,000 Ulster Scots migrated in successive waves that correlated closely with periods of adverse economic conditions in Ulster. Fewer people, probably only between 30,000 and 35,000, came directly from Scotland over the same period, largely, as in the case of Ulster, as a result of economic difficulties in Scotland. Both the Scots and the Ulster Scots were heavily represented in all the colonies south of New England.

But the appeal of the colonies was not limited to Great Britain. From at least the middle decades of the seventeenth century, there had been a few continental Europeans in the colonies. The English had inherited from 5,000 to 7,000 Dutch settlers and from 1,000 to 3,000 Swedes and other Scandinavians with the conquest of New Netherland in 1664. During the twenty years following the ending of toleration for Protestants in France by the revocation of the Edict of Nantes in 1685, about 15,000 French Huguenots, excluded because of their Protestantism from the orthodox Catholic French colonies in Canada and the West Indies, fled to the British colonies, especially to South Carolina, New York, and Rhode Island. The largest single national group of Europeans to migrate to the colonies were Germans. A few German Pietists had settled at Germantown, Pennsylvania, in 1683, and a heavy German emigration began early in the next century. By 1770, over 90,000 people from the German states and from Switzerland had settled primarily in Pennsylvania and the colonies to the south. Finally, after 1740, from 1,000 to 1,500 Sephardic Jews emigrated from Spain and Portugal to join a few hundred of their countrymen who had scattered themselves throughout the colonies during earlier decades. Together, these non-British white settlers and their descendants probably constituted between one-fifth and one-fourth of the total white population.

57
Portable writing desk on
which Thomas Jefferson
drafted the Declaration of Independence. Made to Jefferson's own design sometime in
1775 or 1776 by Benjamin
Randolph, a prominent
Philadelphia cabinetmaker,
the desk is approximately 9¾"
long by 14⅜" wide by 3¼"
deep, with a folding writing
board hinged to the top which
opens to give a surface 19¾"
long.

58A–58D
Four views of the portable
writing desk on which
Thomas Jefferson drafted the
Declaration of Independence.

57

58A

58B

58C

58D

58E

Under the writing board of the Declaration of Independence desk, Thomas Jefferson placed the following affidavit in his own handwriting:

Th. Jefferson gives this Writing Desk to Joseph Coolidge, junr. [the husband of Jefferson's granddaughter] as a memorial of affection. It was made from a drawing of his own, by Ben Randall, cabinet maker of Philadelphia, with whom he first lodged on his arrival in that city in May 1776 and is the identical one on which he wrote the Declaration of Independence. Politics as well as Religion has its superstitions, these gaining strength with time, may, one day, give imaginary value to this relic, for its association with the birth of the Great Charter of our Independence, Monticello. Nov. 18, 1825.

About a quarter of the people living in the colonies on the eve of the American Revolution were neither European nor British, of course. Within the bounds of white settlement there were only a few thousand Indians, but there were over 450,000 people of African origin, a tenfold increase over the roughly 45,000 blacks in the colonies in 1710. Indeed, the black population expanded even more rapidly than the white, especially after 1730, growing by 65 percent during the 1730s and never falling below 40 percent in any decade prior to 1770. Because the vast majority of blacks were slaves, this dramatic increase reflected a major expansion of the institution of slave labor, especially in the plantation colonies from Maryland south to Georgia. But the black population also grew steadily in the colonies north of Maryland. In 1770 slavery was still an expanding, rather than a contracting, institution everywhere except in New Hampshire, albeit the proportion of the black population living in the northern colonies was declining continuously. The southern plantation colonies contained just over 80 percent of the black inhabitants in 1710 and almost 90 percent in 1770.

In contrast to the white population, a much smaller proportion of the growth of the black population can be assigned to natural increase. Whereas only one-fifth to one-fourth of the total rise in the white population between 1710 and 1770 can be attributed to emigration, over three-fifths—nearly 250,000—of the roughly 400,000 increase in blacks over the same period was the result of heavy importations of new slaves from Africa and the West Indies. As these numbers suggest, the rate of natural increase was substantially lower for blacks

than for whites, probably below 20 percent per decade as opposed to almost 30 percent for whites. This reflected the operation of a series of conditions that are thought to have retarded the natural growth of the African populations in all the slave societies of the Americas: the heavy preponderance of males in the slave labor force, at least during the early years; the impermanency and instability of many slave families; high mortality rates, especially among infants; harsh working conditions; poor or inadequate diet; and a general lack of incentive for reproduction within a group that had been forcibly torn from its roots and was condemned along with its posterity to perpetual bondage. But the thirteen colonies reflected these conditions to a far lesser degree than did any of the other slave societies of the Americas, including the British Caribbean colonies. For nowhere else was the African population able even to sustain itself, much less to show any natural growth, prior to the abolition of slavery. As was the case with whites, better diet and fewer diseases were probably responsible for this remarkably strong—in comparative terms—growth among colonial American blacks.

The ethnic origins of colonials of African descent are much more difficult to trace than the sources of the white population. That they were considerably more diverse, however, is beyond dispute. Recent research has shown that the blacks were drawn largely from eight different regions in Africa stretching over a territory much larger and culturally and linguistically more varied than the small area of Western Europe and Britain from which the white settlers were drawn. The largest number came from Angola and the Bight of Biafra, each of which contributed around 25 percent of the total. The Gold Coast, Senegambia, and the Windward Coast each contributed between 10 and 15 percent, while Sierra Leone, the Bight of Benin, and Mozambique-Madagascar each supplied 5 percent or under. But even this breakdown does not adequately reflect the diverse character of the population, for each of these regions was in turn composed of several different ethnic groups, with the result that the composition of the black population was extraordinarily complex.

The forced migration of Africans to work in the fields and urban centers of the colonies and the massive movement of British and European settlers to North America shared one important characteristic: they were both undertaken primarily in the hope of securing a better life—for the whites. In the 1760s the colonies were still almost as rustic and culturally underdeveloped as they had been in 1710, when the South Carolina Indian trader Thomas Nairne wrote that they did ''not abound so much with those gay and noisy Amusements, which generally the great and the rich'' affected in Britain. But ''for such who have experienc'd the Frowns of Fortune, and have yet something left to make a handsome Retreat from the World; for those who affect Solitude, Contemplation, Gardening, Groves, Woods, and the like innocent Delights of plain simple Nature, and who, with a small Fortune, would provide some competent fix'd Settlement for themselves and Children,'' the colonies could scarcely have been any better suited to ''answer their Expectation.'' With ''no Beggars'' and none who were ''vastly rich,'' most of the colonies enjoyed that ''state of Life which many People reckon the happiest, a moderate Subsistence, *without the Vexation of Dependence*. . . . How much better is it for those who have but a small Subsistence at home, to retire to a Place where they may with moderate Industry be supplied with all the necessaries of Life . . . ? How much better for Men to improve their own Lands, for the Use of themselves, and Posterity; to sit under their own Vine, and eat the Fruits of their Labour . . . ?''

Of course, many people were cruelly disappointed in their hopes. Some failed to survive the sea crossing or died shortly after they arrived. Others were cheated out of their possessions or otherwise ruined by the unscrupulous "traffickers in human souls" who arranged passage to America or received immigrants in the ports. Still others never managed to acquire even the small amount necessary to secure their own lands, and they spent the rest of their lives as dependent laborers. But the generous land policies of the several colonies, each eager to attract settlers who would contribute to their development by settling uninhabited areas, meant that many more would in fact eventually "live in great Affluence of most things necessary for life," while a few managed to convert a modest fortune, a set of professional skills, or mercantile enterprise into considerable wealth.

But the prospect that "People of Sobriety and Industry" could secure economic independence, "live plentiful, and in a few Years become of good Substance and Worth" was not the only reason that animated men and women to pull up their roots, undertake an extremely hazardous sea voyage, risk the dangers of a new disease environment, and commit themselves to the hard labor necessary to wrest a subsistence from an often harsh wilderness. Equally important were the promises that their property would be protected by mild laws and light taxes and that they, by the standards of the day, would be exceptionally free in the exercise of their religion under a government in which they would have, as property owners, some significant voice. For not only did the colonies have a remarkable amount of self-government, but an unusual number of men could expect to participate in it. Even servants, once their terms had expired and they had acquired their own land, could anticipate being "as free in all Respects, and as much entitled to the Privileges of the Country, as any other Inhabitants whatsoever."

So eager, in fact, were the colonies to attract new settlers that colonial legislatures made the naturalization of foreigners exceptionally easy. "All possible encouragement," said Virginia statutes of 1680 and 1705, "should be given to persons of different nations to transport themselves hither with their families and stocks, to settle, plant or reside, by investing them with all the rights and privileges of his majesty's natural free born subjects." In the spirit of this law, most of the colonies passed measures giving foreigners who had resided in the colonies for a short time full civil rights, including the right to hold land and, in most cases, the right to vote. Seven colonies even enabled naturalized subjects to hold office. Religious qualifications effectively excluded foreign Catholics from naturalization following the establishment of the Protestant Succession in England in 1689, but foreign Jews could be naturalized and were deliberately encouraged to do so by Rhode Island, New York, and Georgia, albeit by British custom they were usually excluded from the rights to vote and hold office.

In the colonies the naturalization of foreigners was thus "not an incidental affair but a well-established public practice" by the time the British Parliament got around to passing a comprehensive law in 1740. Unlike colonial laws, which could not extend rights to aliens beyond the bounds of a particular colony, the parliamentary statute of 1740 granted the naturalized subjects rights that extended throughout the realm. In all other respects, it simply gave imperial recognition to colonial practices by providing for the naturalization of Protestants and Jews after residence of seven years and payment of a small fee and for the absolute exclusion of Roman Catholics. These naturalization practices in the colonies stood in sharp contrast to customs in Britain and elsewhere in the Old World, where aliens were forbidden either to hold or to bequeath real property in the form of land and buildings, and naturalization was rare, expensive, and difficult.

But the heterogeneous population that had been pulled to the colonies by the promise of economic independence, mild government, and full civil rights did not always live in a state of blissful coexistence. Ancient ethnic animosities accompanied immigrants and were often intensified by firsthand contact. In New England, descendants of the old Puritan settlers were especially suspicious of non-English immigrants, and traditional hostility between Scots and Englishmen often flared wherever the two groups came together. That naturalization did not automatically mean assimilation was strongly manifest in the reaction of British Pennsylvanians to the heavy influx of Germans through the middle of the eighteenth century. Offended by the "disonant Manners" of these "Dutch" settlers, many English colonists were beginning "to quit particular Neighbourhoods surrounded by Dutch ... and in Time, Numbers will probably quit the Province for the same Reason," Benjamin Franklin reported in 1751. "Why should the Palatine Boors be suffered to swarm into our Settlements, and by herding together establish their Language and Manners to the Exclusion of ours?" "Why should Pennsylvania, founded by the English, become a Colony of *Aliens,* who will shortly be so numerous as to Germanize us instead of our Anglifying them, and will never adopt our Language or Customs, any more than they can acquire our Complexion?" The aversion felt toward the Germans was weak compared with that directed against that much larger and far more "disonant" segment of colonial society: the "outlandish" African slaves.

Yet if white Americans often found that they could live together more harmoniously by setting themselves apart, there was an inevitable flow back and forth across ethnic boundaries as "individuals of all nations melted into a new race of men," as Crèvecoeur, the Frenchman who came with the French army to America during the Seven Years' War and subsequently settled in New York, had said. But what mattered even more than this random intermixing was the common experience among whites of all ethnic groups. "*He* is an American," declared Crèvecoeur, "who, leaving behind him all his ancient prejudices and manners, receives new ones from the new mode of life he has embraced, the new government he obeys, and the new rank he holds. He becomes an American by being received in the broad lap of our great *Alma Mater,*" Crèvecoeur continued:

In this great American asylum the poor of Europe have by some means met together.... Every thing has tended to regenerate them; new laws, a new mode of living, a new social system; here they become men: in Europe they were as so many useless plants, wanting vegetative mould, and refreshing showers.... Formerly they were not numbered in any civil lists of their country, except those of the poor; here they rank as citizens.

This "surprising metamorphosis" was the result of the "ample rewards" Americans received for their labors, rewards that enabled them to procure lands, which in turn conferred "on them the title of freemen, and to that title every benefit is affixed which men can possibly require."

Crèvecoeur's identification of manhood with citizenship and the economic independence that came with property in this idealized portrait of American society penetrated to the very essence of American life. Crèvecoeur himself took enormous pride in the "pleasing equality" of American society, and the Declaration of Independence trumpeted the American commitment to the principle "all men are created equal." But the actual commitment to equality was far from universal; it was in fact deeply qualified. Americans had no illusions that all men were equal by nature. Nor did they believe in equality of social condition. American society might not have the same extremes of wealth and poverty or the hereditary privileges and exclusions that characterized most Old World societies, but it obviously

still had deep social inequalities, even among the free population. "Was there, or will there ever be," John Adams once asked, "a nation, whose individuals were all equal in natural and acquired qualities, in virtues, talents, and riches?"

What they were committed to was equality of opportunity for *free men of British and European descent* "to reap the benefit of honest industry." Of course, this kind of equality implied social differences and distinctions. In the aphorism of James Harrington, the seventeenth-century English political philosopher: "Industry of all things is the most accumulative, and accumulation of all things hates leveling." Equality of opportunity thus signified to the Revolutionary generation the preservation of the individual's equal—and unrestrained—right to acquire as much as he could, to achieve the best life possible. A society based upon such a belief "could not only tolerate great economic inequalities but required them as a safeguard" for the property acquired.

Equality of opportunity thus did not in any way imply social leveling; it did, however, require that no legal impediments be placed in the way of individuals. The deep American hostility to all of the many forms of legal, economic, social, and political privilege that sustained the Privileged orders of Europe was revealed in the constitutional prohibitions of such privileges adopted by most of the states during the Revolution. In America, social, economic, and political distinctions were to be "fairly earned," the legitimate fruits of "superior industry, talent and virtue." Political office, social status, economic benefits—all were to be equally accessible.

But accessible to whom? The answer to this question requires an examination of still another and much more prevalent meaning applied to the concept of equality by the men of the Revolution: the idea that all men were "equal in respect to their rights; or rather that nature has given to them a common and an equal right to liberty, to property, and to safety; to justice, government, laws, religion, and freedom." But there was a problem with this meaning of equality. As the great British legal theorist Sir William Blackstone had pointed out to Americans in the 1760s in his *Commentaries on the Laws of England,* to say that men were "equal in respect to their rights" amounted "to nothing more than to the identical proposition, that all men have *equal rights to their rights*; for when different men have perfect and absolute rights to unequal things, they are certainly equal with regard to the perfection of their rights, or the justice that is due to their respective claims." This, Blackstone argued, "is the only sense in which equality can be applied to mankind. In the most perfect republic unequal industry and virtues of men must necessarily create unequal rights," and various categories of people must therefore be "eternally unequal, and have unequal rights." Thus, *all* men were not entitled to "equal liberty and equal privileges" in political society, but only those who possessed the right to such equality. "A popular government," one American political writer said, ought to provide "equal liberty and equal privileges" to "its citizens." But who were—and were not—deemed citizens?

As the most basic right in Anglo-American political society, the right to vote may be taken as the essential index to citizenship, to full membership in American society, and to the legitimate claim to equality of opportunity and equality of rights. In colonial America, no less than in contemporary Britain, property requirements for the suffrage were universal. Part of the logic behind these property requirements for voting was spelled out with great clarity by the Virginia legislature when it prefaced a law of 1670 with the statement that the "laws of England grant a voice in such election only to such as by their estates real or personal have interest enough to tie them to the endeavours of the public good." Just as it was widely assumed in English and colonial law that membership in a corporation should be restricted to those with a full legal share, so citizenship—as symbolized by the right to vote—was limited to those with a permanent attachment to society in the form of property. But lack of sufficient property was not the only cause for exclusion from the franchise. Women, minors, aliens, Catholics, Jews, and nonwhites were all subject to exclusion, as were slaves, servants, short-term tenants, the poor, and even sons over twenty-one still living with their parents. Most members of these categories could be excluded for lack of sufficient property. For unmarried women and any other member of these groups who did meet the property requirements, however, the grounds for exclusion had to lie elsewhere.

What precisely these grounds were and what defined the boundaries of full citizenship and determined access to equal opportunity in colonial America may be surmised from an analysis of British legal and political theory of the seventeenth and eighteenth centuries. "If there be anything at all that is a foundation of liberty," said one writer, "it is this, that those who shall choose the lawmakers shall be men"—and this is the crucial clause—"freed from *dependence upon others.*" Not property per se, but the independence property conveyed was the most essential component of liberty and the *sine qua non* of citizenship. Blackstone explained the logic behind this emphasis more fully:

If it were probable that every man would give his vote freely and without influence of any kind, then upon the true theory and genuine principles of liberty, every member of the community, however poor, should have a vote in electing those delagates, to whose charge is committed the disposal of his property, his liberty, and his life. But, since that can hardly be expected in persons of indigent fortunes, or such as are under the immediate dominion of others, all popular states have been obliged to establish certain qualifications; whereby some, who are suspected to have no will of their own, are excluded from voting, in order to set other individuals, whose wills may be supposed independent, more thoroughly upon a level with each other.

What most categories of people who were deprived of citizenship in early modern England and the American colonies had in common was their dependence upon the wills of others; wives were dependent upon husbands, minors and sons still living at home upon their fathers, servants and slaves upon their masters, short-term tenants and renters upon their landlords, aliens upon their native countries, Catholics upon Rome, soldiers and sailors upon their commanders, debtors upon their creditors, and the poor and insane upon the community.

But there were other categories who, however free they might be from external control, were considered to lack the capacity for self-control. People who were thus "slaves to their lusts" could "never be free" and could not be accorded full civil status in society. The conventional attitude toward women was elaborated by one of Locke's associates, James Tyrrell, when he wrote toward the end of the seventeenth century that there "never was any government where all the promiscuous rabble of women and children had votes, as not being capable of it." The same lack of capacity was used as an excuse for the exclusion of nonwhites in the colonies. They could never be given citizenship, said Lieutenant Governor William Gooch of Virginia in the 1730s, "until time and education has changed the Indication of their spurious Extraction, and made some Alteration in their Morals." They lacked, in other words, the moral capacity for citizenship. The specific rationale for the exclusion of Jews is less clear, but the inherited stereotype of Jews as people who could not control their peculiarly strong passion of avarice probably served to mark them off as still another category of people who could not be trusted with a full civic role.

The American Revolution thus took place within a society in which whole groups of people—slaves, servants, women, minors, Catholics, Jews, and free people of African descent—were systematically excluded from the suffrage and from the full exercise of equality of opportunity. It was a society as well in which, as in Britain, the lower and middle segments of the voting population of independent adult white men customarily deferred to the leadership of the successful members: In short, American society was not in principle very different from British society: standards for full membership were roughly the same on both sides of the Atlantic. What made American society unique and what in practice seemed to make it far more egalitarian than any society in Europe was the broad diffusion of property and the absence of a privileged order. As Crèvecoeur appreciated so clearly, the wide extent and easy availability of land in America made it possible for a much larger proportion of the population to gain the economic independence required for citizenship; so that, to a far greater degree than in Europe, ''Industry'' might indeed be the ''Criterion of everything''—at least among white adult males.

Unavoidably, however, the Revolution had a liberalizing effect upon American society. The ideology of the Revolution with its emphasis upon liberty of the citizen, equal rights, and the sovereignty of the people inevitably affected the ways men thought about their society. Most important, it reinforced the traditional American antagonism to legal privilege, stimulated a thorough reconsideration of the custom of having a state-established church, and injected increased vigor into a growing movement against slavery. As a result, many states severed formal connections between church and state and enunciated broad principles of religious toleration, at least for Christians; many states prohibited the slave trade; and all those states in which the black population was small and slavery not of central economic importance took steps toward eventual abolition of the institution. Some abolitionism was manifest even in those states with large and economically viable slave populations.

The exigencies of war and independence, moreover, produced a dramatic increase in popular participation in public life. The long movement of opposition to British attempts to tax and to tighten controls over the colonies beginning in 1765 focused the attention of large numbers of people upon politics and drew many previously politically inert segments of the population, including tradesmen and seamen in the towns, into an active role in public life. The intense crisis of 1774–1776 that witnessed the outbreak of military conflict and the decision for Independence furthered this process of political mobilization. Voters turned out in larger numbers than ever before, while thousands of ordinary citizens attended public protest meetings, served on local committees to enforce the measures of the Continental Congress or on the new state legislatures, and participated in the activities of the militia [**59**].

59

An army flag used by a unit of the Continental forces during the American Revolution. According to tradition, it was carried by Francis Headman, a Pennsylvanian. The revolting colonies are symbolized by thirteen hands holding aloft a liberty pole, atop of which is the traditional liberty cap. "Old 76" was probably painted on the flag after the war. H 70¼".

With independence and the establishment of new state governments came an enormous expansion in the number of representatives in the state legislatures and of elected officeholders at both state and local levels. An increasing number of less wealthy citizens held office, and the voting public exercised a much wider voice in the selection of their leaders. In addition, the war itself operated to politicize large segments of the American public: the movements of the British army and universal military service for Americans made it impossible for most people not to be involved in the war. The need for soldiers forced the American governments to turn to all kinds of people who had formerly had no role in public life: indentured servants, transported convicts, short-term tenants, poor laborers, and former slaves.

Indeed, it was this extensive participation in the war that as much as anything else made possible the emergence of an American nation during the short period from 1776 to 1787. For by giving "each member of a large majority" of free adult white males a feeling that he had a "concrete share in the creation of the United States," it nurtured a kind of hothouse nationalism. Not all Americans, of course, responded to the emerging American nation with enthusiasm. Perhaps as many as 500,000, a fifth of the total white population, took sides with Britain. Nearly 20,000 American men served in the British army, and during the war at least 60,000 fled the United States to Britain, Nova Scotia, Canada, or the British Caribbean colonies. Lacking confidence in the ability of the new United States to maintain effective government and unable to break the deep emotional ties that had bound them to Britain for the previous century and a half, these "Loyalists" found the prospects of life under the independent American republic far more frightening than anything they had experienced under the British prior to 1776.

For a vastly larger number of Americans, their common involvement in a successful war and revolution had precisely the opposite effect: it fostered a belief in the future of an independent United States. Yet it was not only the common bonds forged in the furnace of war and revolution that enabled such a heterogeneous group organized into thirteen separate states with many conflicting interests and divergent experiences and orientations to come together to form a nation. Equally, perhaps more, important was the deep commitment among the property-owning adult white males to that most essential of the many benefits they and their ancestors had wrested out of the

American environment: economic independence and the sense of worth, autonomy, and manhood that derived from it.

How deep that commitment ran can be surmised from a brief analysis of the limited achievements of the American Revolution in the area of the suffrage. During the Revolution almost all the states either lowered or made more flexible the property requirements for voting, and it may even be true, as one noted scholar argued a half century ago, that the term "We the People of the United States" in the Constitution of 1787 included "much larger" numbers than had the expression "the good People of these Colonies" in the Declaration of Independence in 1776. The abolition of religious tests for voting during the Revolution resulted in the extension, in most states, of the suffrage to Catholics and Jews. But these were the only new categories of people to gain citizenship, for the traditional logic of political exclusion remained essentially unchallenged. A more precise rendering of the phrase "we the People" in the Constitution would have been "we the economically independent adult white males."

The record of the states on the suffrage during the Revolution thus makes it clear that the men of the Revolution were fighting quite as much for independence as for Independence, for a right to government by independent men as well as for separation from Britain. As one scholar has recently pointed out, the specific kind of freedom they fought and died for was "not a gift to be conferred by governments" but "a freedom that sprang from the independence of the individual." The American commitment to this conception of freedom and citizenship necessarily meant that the spirit of '76 could not generate a very sweeping movement in the direction of a more inclusive political society. Given their racial attitudes, the men of the American Revolution stretched their definition of an independent man as far as they could in an attempt to bring political practice into conformity with social fact, continuing to exclude, among property-owning men, only those of African or Indian ancestry. But they showed no disposition to abandon the traditional British insistence upon independence and self-mastery for citizenship.

Of course, these men did enunciate a body of principles to which the excluded could later appeal in their quest for incorporation as full members of the American nation. For each generation the phrase "all men are created equal" has served as an imposing reminder of what might be achieved, and much of the American experience from the Revolution to the present can be viewed as a continuing expansion of the conception of citizenship.

However limited in character the American Revolution was, the proportion of independent property-owning men in the population was so much larger than that of any other Western society that it appeared to be an extraordinarily radical event. By "disseminating just sentiments of the rights of mankind, and the nature of legitimate government; by exciting a spirit of resistance to tyranny . . . ; and by occasioning the establishment in *America* of forms of government more equitable and more liberal than any that the world has yet known," the Revolution seemed to social radicals such as the Englishman Dr. Richard Price to have opened up "a new prospect in human affairs" and to have begun "a new aera in the history of mankind," perhaps, "next to the introduction of Christianity among mankind," the "most important step in the progressive course of human improvement." Men such as Price looked to the new United States as "the seat of liberty, science and virtue . . . from whence there is reason to hope these sacred blessings will spread, till they have become universal, and the time arrives when kings and priests shall have no more power to oppress, and that ignominious slavery which has hitherto debased the world is exterminated." Of course, such expectations proved to be much too sanguine. But the American Revolution did provide inspiration for the attack on privilege that began with the French Revolution in 1789 and spread through much of the rest of Europe and into the Americas over the following half century. Defenders of the old order in Europe correctly perceived that the United States was "the real school and nursery of all these revolutionary principles." Revolution became the first export of the new American nation.

Chapter 6

Objects of the Revolution— A Pictorial Essay

Wars are great mixers of people, and the Revolution was no exception. What began as a dispute between Great Britain and its North American colonies became a world war that eventually embraced the French, Spanish, Dutch, Germans, as well as North American Indians and blacks both slave and free. Peoples of other nations, while not directly involved in the fighting, were inspired and affected by the outcome.

The contributions of foreign volunteers such as Pulaski, Kosciusko, de Grasse, Rochambeau, Lafayette, and von Steuben have long been recorded in the annals of history. Yet there were many others less famous whose deeds have been largely forgotten. For both the celebrated and the unsung, the number of surviving objects associated with their service in the Revolution are very few. Assembled here is a collection that reflects in a small way the contributions of ethnic groups to the winning of Independence.

60

61

60
British soldier's shoes, c. 1760. These shoes, found in the ruins of Fort Ligonier, Pennsylvania, represent the footwear used by both British and American soldiers during the American Revolution. Eighteenth-century shoes were designed to be worn on either foot and thus had no lefts or rights. British army regulations stated that a shoe should not be worn on the same foot for more than three days. The buckles are modern reproductions.

61
Field drum. Drums were used by eighteenth-century armies to transmit signals to troops in the field and with fifes for marching. This German drum is dated 1734. D 18½".

62
British Atlas of the American Colonies, 1776. The title page of an atlas of the British Colonies in North America published in London in 1776. It was designed to meet the needs of British officers assigned to America during the Revolution.

63
Military commission issued by the colony of Massachusetts for the preservation of "*American* Liberty" being threatened by England. Despite the great ethnic and racial diversity in America, the symbols and the substance of unity were apparent from the start of the Revolution.

THE

AMERICAN

Military Pocket Atlas;

BEING

An approved Collection of Correct MAPS,

BOTH GENERAL AND PARTICULAR,

OF

THE BRITISH COLONIES;

Especially those which now are, or probably may be

THE THEATRE OF WAR:

Taken principally from the actual Surveys and judicious Observations of Engineers DE BRAHM and ROMANS; COOK, JACKSON, and COLLET; Maj. HOLLAND, and other Officers,

EMPLOYED IN

HIS MAJESTY'S FLEETS AND ARMIES.

LONDON:

Printed for R. SAYER and J. BENNET, Map and Print-Sellers, (No. 53) Fleet-street.

Cambridge, April 24, 1775.

WHEREAS you have this Day received Orders for inlisting 56 Soldiers, including Serjeants, for the Massachusetts Service, for the Preservation of the Liberties of America: You are hereby acquainted that the Commission of a Captain in said Service shall be made out for you as soon as you have compleated the said Inlistment, and you will also be allowed to nominate 2 Subalterns to serve under you, who will receive Commissions accordingly, if the Committee shall approve of them.

By Order of the Committee of Safety,

Jos Warren Chairman.

In Committee of Safety, Cambridge, Apl 24 1775.

To Mr Joseph Guild

SIR,

YOU are hereby empowered immediately to inlist a Company, to consist of 56 able-bodied and effective Men, including Serjeants, as Soldiers in the *Massachusetts* Service, for the Preservation of *American* Liberty; and cause them to pass Muster as soon as possible.

Jos Warren Chairman.

64

64
French cannon, 1751. During the winter of 1777–1778, the first of the French volunteers made their way to General Washington's headquarters at Valley Forge. One of the most famous was a young nobleman, the Marquis de Lafayette. With him he brought ordnance stores for the American army. Shown here is one of the cannons he delivered, cast in 1751 and designed to fire a 16-pound shot. The carriage and wheels are modern reproductions. H 4′.

65
British accompanying gun, 1775, rear view. A light field gun, cast in the royal foundry at Woolich by the Verbruggen gun founders in 1775, it fired a 3-pound shot. It was designed to be easily disassembled for transporting. The carriage and wheels are modern reproductions. The gun itself was among the arms surrendered by the British at Saratoga, the turning point of the Revolutionary War. L 7′.

65

66
American keg mine, 1777. H 15″. After the British forces had occupied Philadelphia, the Americans who lived upstream devised an ingenious method of harassment. Joseph Plowman of Bordentown, New Jersey, designed a floating mine that resembled a butter keg. Members of the community made a number of these kegs and filled them with black powder. The top of the keg was fitted with a wooden tripping arm, which was connected to an iron pin that activated a flintlock detonating device. These waterproof kegs were then probably tied in pairs before being placed in the water at ebb tide. The plan was that the mines would float against a ship or wharf, which would activate the exploding mechanism. Evidently the nature of the devices was discovered before any damage was done, but the knowledge of their existence led British sentries to fire at everything in the river—to the great amusement of the Americans. The incident was commemorated by Francis Hopkinson in his humorous poem, "The Battle of the Kegs," one stanza of which declares:

The kegs, 'tis said, though strongly made
Of rebel staves and hoops, sir,
Could not oppose their powerful foes,
The conquering British troops, sir.

67

67
Model of the American ship *Bon Homme Richard,* 1779. In February 1779, King Louis XVI of France gave the United States the former French East Indiaman *Duc de Duras* for use against the British. Captain John Paul Jones converted the fourteen-year-old merchant vessel into a raiding ship, and renamed it *Bon Homme Richard,* in honor of Benjamin Franklin's pen name, "Poor Richard." It served as the flagship of Jones's squadron, which raided the British Isles that autumn and captured sixteen merchant ships. Jones's ship won a dramatic victory over H.M.S. *Serapis,* but it suffered so much damage that it sank soon afterward. The ship was 152' long, had a beam of 40', and carried 42 guns. (This is a ¼"=12" scale model.)

68
American swivel gun, 1775. This cast-iron swivel gun was mounted on the rail of the Continental gondola, or gunboat, *Philadelphia* and was used in the naval battle fought near Valcour Island in Lake Champlain on October 11, 1776. The Americans under General Benedict Arnold built a flotilla of three schooners, a sloop, five galleys, and eight gondolas to challenge the passage of a British fleet down the lake. Each of the gondolas was fitted with one of these swivel guns, which fired a ¾-pound shot and was used as an antipersonnel weapon. Although the Americans lost the battle, they delayed the British long enough so that it was not prudent for them, with winter approaching, to continue their campaign to split the colonies. The British withdrew their forces to Canada, and the Americans gained a year in which to prepare for the next British attack. The original yoke or swivel mount on this gun was broken in the battle. The yoke shown here is a reconstruction. L 51".

69A
English sword, hanger, and
baldric, c. 1751. This sword
was encased in a leather
scabbard and suspended
from the shoulder by a wide
leather strap. The brass lion's
head and spiral grip are of a
pattern adopted between
1742 and 1751. The counter
guard bears the inscription of
the 16th Regiment of Foot,
which adopted that name in
1751. L 31".

69B
Detail: Sword, hanger, and
baldric.

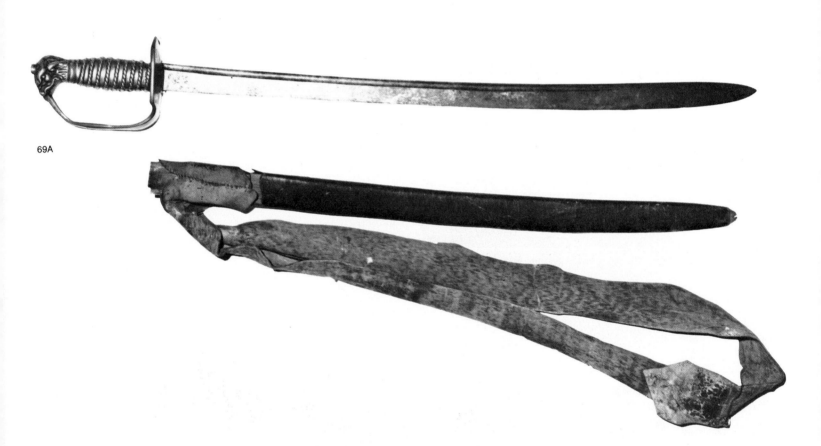

69A

102

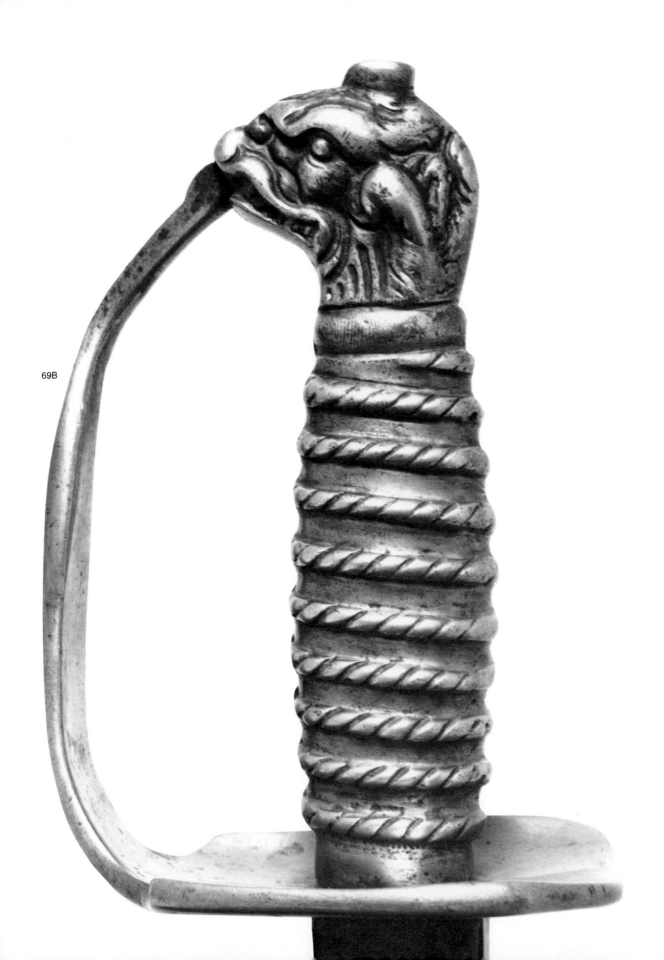

69B

70A
American officer's short
saber, c. 1760. A lighter and
less cumbersome version of
the saber and an important
weapon of cavalry and dragoon units. This specimen
has a bronze pommel shaped
like a lion's head, a cherry-
wood grip, and an iron blade
34¼" long. It has the name
"Bowers" engraved on the
underside of the knuckle bow
and is believed to have belonged to Captain Jonathan
Bowers of the Connecticut
militia, who was wounded in
the battle of Stillwater, September 19, 1777.

70B
Detail: short saber.

70A

70B

71
American horseman's saber.
Between 1776 and 1787
American swordsmiths made
distinctive heavy sabers such
as this. Its slightly curved
blade measures 35⅞". Made
by James Potter, this saber
had wrappings of steel and
black leather on the handle.
The specimen shown here belonged to Major Benjamin
Tallmadge of the 2nd Continental Dragoons.

72
British dragoon saber, c.
1780. This long, plain, slightly
tapered blade measures
37⅛". An iron knuckle bow extends into an oval-shaped
counter guard with a rectangular opening. The iron pommel is somewhat ball-shaped.
Both sides of the blade are
marked with a crown over the
letters GR/IEF/RIS. The
wooden grip is covered with
leather and wrapped with six
turns of brass wire.

73
Detail: Dragoon saber.

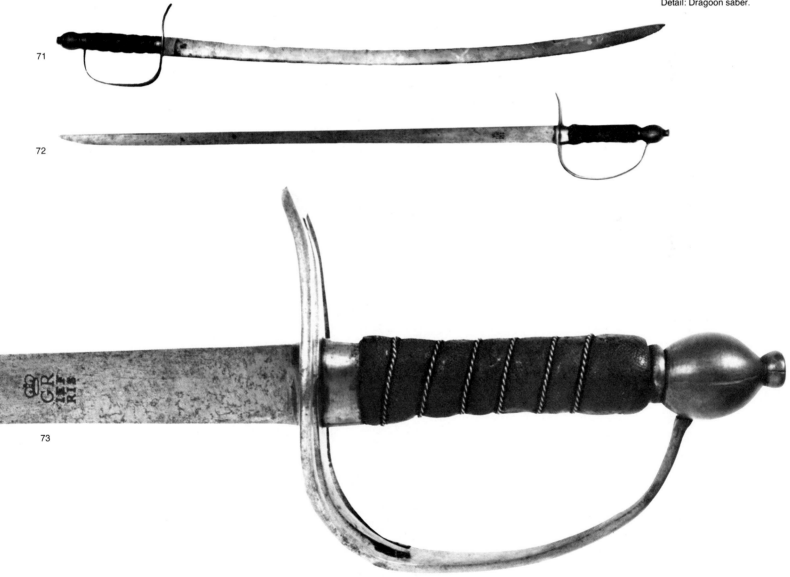

71

72

73

74
French musket, model 1763.
The standard weapon of the
French infantry and various
Continental soldiers. This
model, bearing the stamp of
the Charleville armory, has
the letters "U.S." engraved on
the breech. Subsequently the
Charleville became the prototype of the standard musket
of the United States army.
OAL 59½".

75
British "Brown Bess" musket.
An example of the standard
weapon of the British infantry.
This musket, made after
1764, is stamped "29th Regiment," which is the unit that
was stationed in Boston at the
time of the Boston Massacre.
OAL 61¾".

76
German flintlock musket, c.
1775. This .68-caliber musket
is one of a pattern used in
America during the Rev-
olutionary War. Barrel 44".

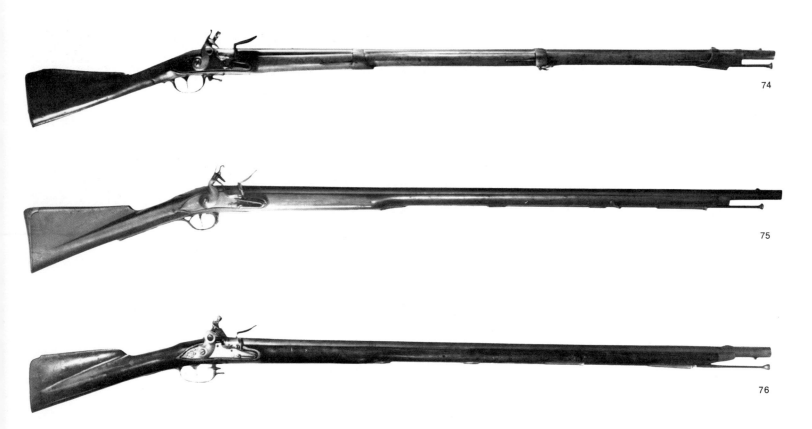

74

75

76

Indian pipe tomahawk. Axes
designed to serve as both
pipe and tomahawk were
made by Europeans for
trading with the Indians.
Shown here is a brass version made by the French in
the eighteenth century which
came into the possession of
a Seneca Indian. The wooden
stem is a reproduction. The
Senecas were one of the
Iroquois Six Nations, a powerful confederacy that had
strong ties to the British. The
Continental Congress urged
the Iroquois to remain neutral
in the war, and for a time they
did. In the summer of 1777
the British commander at Fort
Niagara induced the Senecas
to take up arms against the
Americans. The unity and
neutrality of the Six Nations
was weakened. Two of the
other nations, the Oneida and
the Tuscaroras, served with
the colonial forces. H 17⅞".

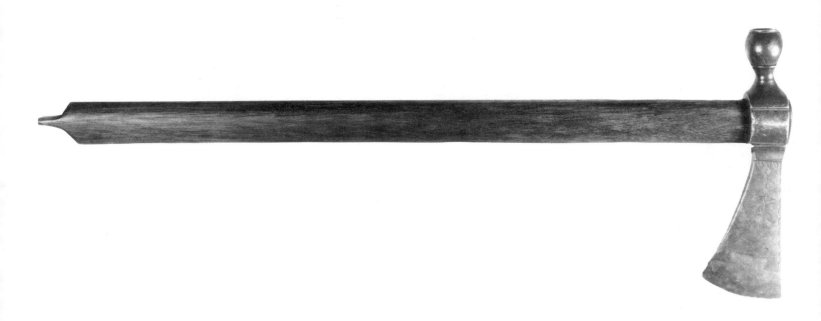

78A, 78B
German fusilier cap worn by a
Hessian soldier during the
American Revolution is said
to have been captured at the
battle of Trenton. H (approx.)
12".

78A

78B

79

79
German regimental flag. Some twenty thousand soldiers hired from various German states served with the British in the Revolution. Americans referred to these troops as "Hessians," although only a part of them came from the state of Hesse-Cassel. Illustrated here is the white silk damask flag of the Ansbach-Bayreuth Regiment that was used during the Revolution and surrendered at Yorktown. The first four letters of the initials SETCA stand for *Sincere et Constanter,* the motto of the Prussian order of the Red Eagle and the Margrave of Brandenburg Ansbach-Bayreuth. The fifth letter, A, honors Alexander, the reigning prince. The prince's full monogram appears on the brass spearhead as CFCA, for Christian Friedrich Carl Alexander. The crown, wreath, and letters MZB represent the Margraf zur Brandenburg, the ruler of the German principality from which the regiment was drawn. L 50″.

81
French officer's saddle. This saddle belonged to Baron de Kalb, an experienced soldier who came to America with Lafayette. The Continental Congress gave de Kalb a commission as a major general. A huge man who was always in the thick of a fight, he lost his life at the battle of Camden, South Carolina, in August 1780, after being wounded eleven times. L 27".

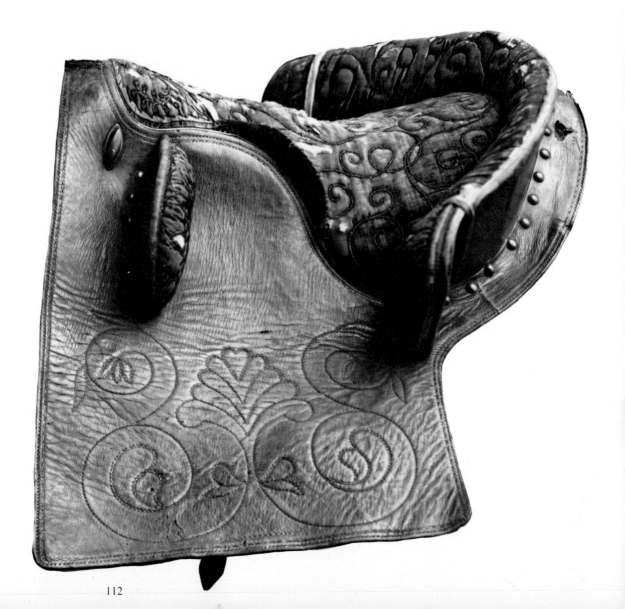

George Washington's mess chest. An unknown craftsman made this mess chest used by George Washington in the field during the Revolution. It contained tin plates and platters, tin pots with detachable wooden handles, glass containers for condiments, as well as knives and forks. The chest is similar to other traveling kits used by British and American officers in the eighteenth century. L 21¼″.

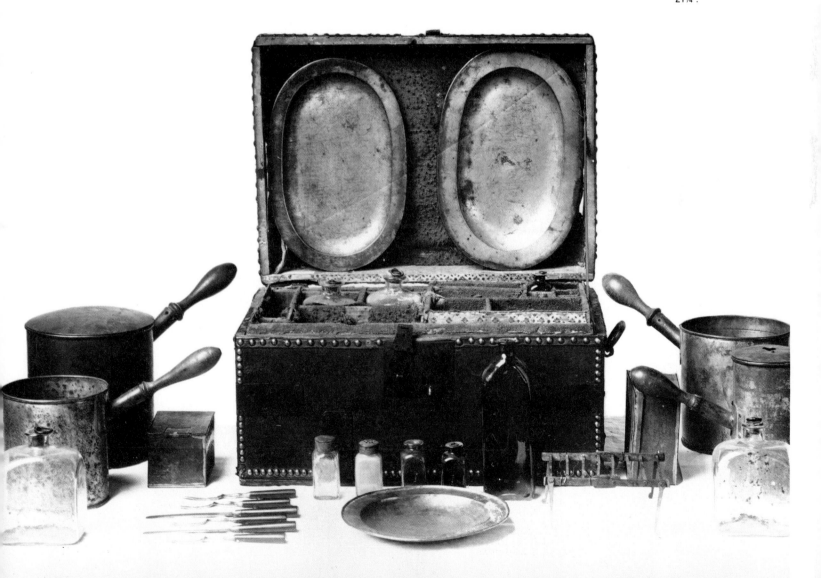

Part Two

Old Ways,
New World

*America does not repel the past
or what it has produced.*

Walt Whitman

Chapter 7

The Ocean Voyage

Transatlantic Travel

To appreciate what the earliest emigrant to America faced in being transported across the Atlantic Ocean, it must first be realized that the wind system that controlled the movement of his ship was predominantly westerly; that is, the wind blew directly against the course his vessel had to make. To avoid this wind system the earliest voyagers to America from England took a southerly course to pick up the northeast trade winds, shaped their routes westward to the Antilles, and made a port of call at the English islands (with a possible deviation for a little privateering against the enemy). Then they would follow the Gulf Stream around Cuba, or proceed via the Windward Passage, north to their landfall. Such a voyage, fraught with dangers from French or Spanish enemies or the dreaded lawless sea marauders, might consume the better part of three months.

Experience gained from the sailing of reconstructions of seventeenth-century ships, such as *Mayflower II,* leads us to believe that the general run of deep-sea merchant vessels were cranky, ill-natured beasts. An improperly ballasted one could be brutal to the men who sailed in her. A bluff-bowed, high-pooped vessel like the *Mayflower* was quite poor to windward and could tack only under the most ideal conditions of wind and sea. For the most part, such a vessel resorted to wearing (to come about with the stern to windward) in order to change tacks, a maneuver that could prove to be dangerous. Accounts of crews exhausted to the point of helplessness working against the raging winds and seas of a North Atlantic gale are many. One can only surmise the terror of passengers utterly ignorant of the working of a ship, unaccustomed to the rigors of sea life, battened below hatches in a stinking atmosphere of excrement and vomit, soaked by water seeping through the working decks of a violently rolling, laboring vessel. As inured to hardship ashore as the passenger might have been, this would have marked a new dimension in misery.

By the middle of the seventeenth century, most vessels bound for North America struck out directly across the North Atlantic. The navigation season for the American trade was confined largely to the months between the spring and autumn equinoxes. Until the end of the eighteenth century, the merchant fleet for North America set sail in early April, and the close of navigation came between September and November. Yet the summer season was also the season of hurricanes in the Caribbean, many of which annually vent their fury in the middle latitudes of the North Atlantic. Even with pleasant weather prevailing over the North Atlantic, the westerlies and summer calms could make a voyage to America a long one—of working incessantly to windward or rolling helplessly in a sweltering calm.

As for navigation, the only check on the vessel's position was afforded by observations for latitude carried out at local apparent noon with cross-staff, back staff, or the later reflecting quadrant. While calculations from lunar positions were possible by the late eighteenth century, they were beyond the capability of most merchant masters [83]. Generally, a master of a westbound vessel would take his departure from a charted point as close as possible to the latitude of his destination and try to maintain that latitude throughout his voyage. Each noon, weather permitting, he would ascertain his latitude and alter his course north or south to regain his landfall latitude. To calculate his divergence from his base course he would employ traverse tables. His movement in longitude could be estimated only from the speed of his vessel through the water, which he measured by means of a log chip tied to a long knotted line which was streamed over the stern and timed with the aid of a sandglass generally gauged to fourteen seconds.

Given a gale of a week's duration, the reckoning of even the most experienced navigator could become hopelessly confused as far as his longitudinal distance from America was concerned. In effect he would sail on blindly with the sole comfort being the knowledge that as long as he sailed west he would, if food and water held out, raise up the American continent. At this point the final success of the voyage drew on the master's skill, intuition, and luck, for the coastline was for the most part uncharted and without lighthouses or buoys until the nineteenth century.

As the days at sea wore on, the tension aboard the vessel grew and even the greenest landlubber could not help but be affected. To sail at night or in thick weather became a nerve-racking experience; every ear was bent to catch the roar of breakers. As the voyage neared its end, a prudent shipmaster would lay his vessel to at night rather than risk running it ashore. A vessel making a sudden landfall on low-lying Sable Island or the terrifying shoals off Cape Hatteras was more than likely to be violently destroyed. While closing the North American coast, the only warning signal aboard ship was the lead line. When closing the New Jersey coast, where a definite relationship exists between the depth of the sea and the distance off the coast, the droning of the leadsman telling the depth of water was somewhat reassuring, but for the master approaching the foggy coast of Maine, the lead was small comfort, for the water is deep close to the rockbound coast.

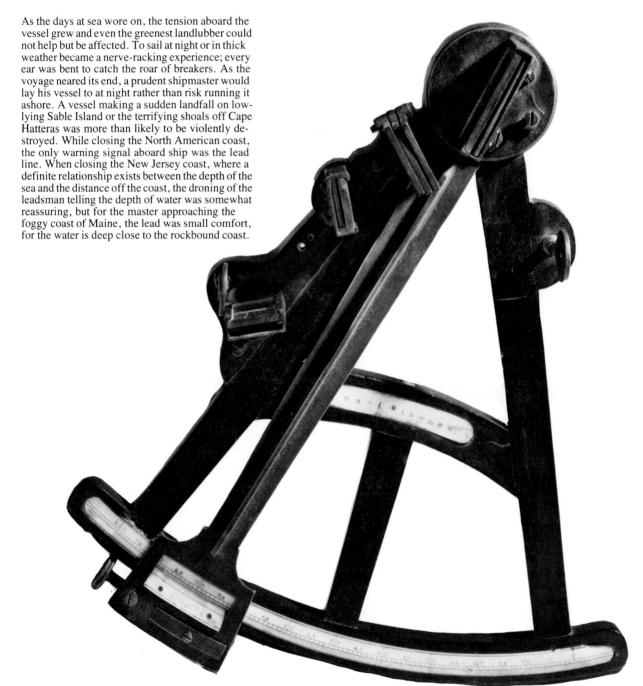

83
Reflecting quadrant made in England during the first half of the nineteenth century. One of the instruments used in navigation to find a ship's position. R: 10″.

Few vessels in the early days afforded anything that might be called accommodations for the emigrant passenger. While some cabins were available to those able to afford them, it was not until well into the nineteenth century that vessels were fitted out with large-scale steerage accommodations. In the early ships a few planks knocked together in the hold to cover the cargo would give the passenger a place to stretch out in. Food was generally the concern of the passenger, who might be allowed access to the galley stove for cooking. Sanitation was no better than that enjoyed by the ship's company. Those with the stomach for it might repair to the ship's head, located between the bowsprit and the gracefully flowing rails. In a howling North Atlantic gale, that wind-swept, spindrift-soaked, plunging seat could be a rare experience. The ship's bilges were more often than not resorted to.

During the migrations of the eighteenth century, overcrowding was the general rule. No regulations protected passengers, whose accommodations were at the discretion of the owners and masters. The 1731 passage of an emigrant-laden vessel bound from Rotterdam to Philadelphia via Falmouth, England, might be an extreme case but one worth noting. The vessel was provisioned for twelve weeks when its passengers boarded. However, as was so often the case even into the nineteenth century, waiting for cargoes and for adverse winds to change consumed six weeks of provisions, which the owners refused to replace with fresh supplies before the ocean passage. After eight weeks at sea the passengers were on short rations, and for the last four weeks they did without bread or biscuit. The going rate for a mouse was sixpence and a rat brought twelve pence. Finally the passengers, convinced that the captain was starving them for the money, revolted and seized the ship. After a voyage of twenty-five weeks, the vessel arrived in Rhode Island with forty-eight of the 156 passengers alive.

On the great majority of emigrant vessels, which carried from 100 to 150 passengers, conditions did not approach those cited above. The larger the scale of emigrant movement, especially that promoted by land developers, the more likely was overcrowding. A harbinger of things to come was the German Palatine emigration, refugees from the War of Spanish Succession sent to the Hudson Valley by the English government in 1710. Of the 3,000 emigrants, 470 died en route and 250 soon after their arrival.

From 1756, the outbreak of the Seven Years' War, until 1817, the Atlantic community knew only wars or threats of wars, with two decades of respite. For the most part, the wars were of a maritime nature, and passage over the seas was perilous. Furthermore, warring nations, pressed to build armies and navies, were reluctant to release their populations for emigration. The steady stream of migrants to America that marked the seventeenth and early eighteenth centuries was reduced to a trickle. The Treaty of Ghent, which ended the War of 1812 and saw an exhausted Western world at peace, marked the beginning of the first swell of the tidal wave of emigrants to come to American ports seeking a refuge from the social and economic dislocation of the Old World.

The sailing ship continued to be the main vehicle of sea transport well beyond the middle of the nineteenth century, in spite of the rapid rise of steam navigation. Sailing ships had made steady progress in tonnage and size, but ocean passages continued to be lengthy, and sailing ships still used a twelve-week North Atlantic passage as a standard by which to stock food supplies. Navigation was greatly aided by the introduction of the chronometer and the general acceptance of the prime meridian at Greenwich for nautical purposes. The gradual improvement of charts due to the survey of the British and French hydrographic offices and the work of such pioneer oceanographers as the American Matthew Fontaine Maury, as well as the efforts of governments to provide sufficient lighthouses and other navigational aids along their coastlines, contributed to more accurate position finding. Britain's licensing of shipmasters led the way in improving the quality of seagoing personnel.

It must be noted that there were no generally agreed upon rules of the road designed to reduce the risk of collision at sea until those drafted in 1855 by Britain's Board of Trade. However, the United States did not see fit to recognize these rules until 1863. The goal of safety at sea on an international scale can only be dated from 1889, when the International Marine Conference was called at Washington. The resolutions adopted there included recommendations for determining the seaworthiness of vessels. The conference, however, failed to set up any international agency to coordinate the national action. This had to await the twentieth century and the shock of the *Titanic* disaster.

The phenomenal growth of the emigrant traffic in the first half of the nineteenth century brought with it problems of shipboard overcrowding beyond any experience. The fine fleet of packet ships—those square-riggers that sailed on definite schedules serving England and the Continent under the American flag—was only interested in high-value cargo and the luxury cabin passenger trade [**84A– 84D**]. The steamers that swept the great American sailing packets from the hegemony of the North Atlantic trade were also primarily interested in the deluxe trade. The Cunard Line, established in 1840, did not carry steerage passengers until 1862. Consequently, the emigrant trade was confined to sailing vessels, more often than not inferior in seaworthiness and in passenger accommodations. As the demand for passage to North America began to exceed the supply of ships, an industry arose marked by rapaciousness and disregard for human suffering that equaled or surpassed that of the slave trade. The emigrant, preyed upon ashore, defrauded by ship owners, masters, and emigrant agents, and brutalized by the ship's crew, was jammed into cargo vessels like so much beam filling.

It was Great Britain, the prime exporter of emigrants, that made the first significant move to bring about an amelioration of conditions aboard the ships. The attack against overcrowding began with a formula, long in existence, that governed the ratio of crew to the tonnage of the vessel. The passenger-tonnage ratio of the British law of 1803 prescribed that one passenger (including crew) would be allowed for every two tons (100 cubic feet = 1 ton of ship) of the unladen part of the ship. Foreign flagships clearing out of British ports could carry two persons for every five tons. In addition, the act called for a vessel to be victualed (stocked with food) for twelve weeks, with a daily food allowance of one-half pound of meat, one and one-half pounds of biscuit or oatmeal, one-half pint of molasses, and one gallon of water per passenger. A surety bond was to be posted by which the owner and the master guaranteed the seaworthiness of the vessel and the delivery of passengers to their destined ports. A surgeon was to be shipped on vessels carrying fifty or more passengers, and both master and surgeon were to give bond of £100 each to keep a true journal of the voyage, to be delivered upon the return of the vessel and verified by oath. If there had been some means of enforcement, the guidelines set forth in the 1803 act might have created tolerable conditions aboard the emigrant ships.

In the succeeding years, amendment followed amendment as authorities attempted to define the amount of space to be devoted to the steerage passenger. The passenger-tonnage ratio was juggled, minimum vertical clearance between decks was defined, the area to be allowed for each passenger was laid down, and computation of children's requirements was made (in 1817, three children under age fourteen were equal to one adult; in 1823 it was two children under fourteen). The penalties for overloading ships were set as high as £50 per passenger.

However, so fierce was the opposition from shipping enterpreneurs to government regulation in Britain that in May 1827 all passenger legislation was repealed and the trade was left utterly uncontrolled by law. But the reign of unfettered laissez faire lasted only one year. On May 23, 1828, new restrictions on the passenger trade were imposed. From that time the lawmakers of Great Britain sought to render the emigrant trade safer and more humane and to put the responsibilities for it on shipowners, shipmasters, and passenger agents.

While Britain was pioneering regulation of the emigrant trade, the United States remained passive. It was not until 1819 that the American Congress enacted its first passenger law. Its intent was praiseworthy—"to give to those who come in passenger vessels a security of comfort and convenience"—even though the provisions of the act governed only vessels leaving U.S. ports. Between the years 1819 and 1847 no further regulations were enacted by Congress relating to the carriage of passengers by sea. Britain, in a series of acts dated 1828, 1835, 1842, 1847, and 1848, doggedly persisted in its humanitarian efforts.

84C

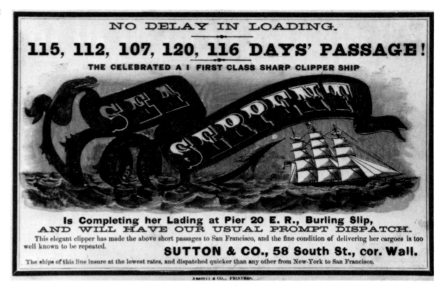

NO DELAY IN LOADING.

115, 112, 107, 120, 116 DAYS' PASSAGE!

THE CELEBRATED A I FIRST CLASS SHARP CLIPPER SHIP

SEA SERPENT

Is Completing her Lading at Pier 20 E. R., Burling Slip,
AND WILL HAVE OUR USUAL PROMPT DISPATCH.

This elegant clipper has made the above short passages to San Francisco, and the fine condition of delivering her cargoes is too well known to be repeated.

SUTTON & CO., 58 South St., cor. Wall.

The ships of this line insure at the lowest rates, and dispatched quicker than any other from New-York to San Francisco.

ABBOTT & CO., PRINTERS.

84A–84D
The great Yankee Clipper ships that circled the globe in the 1840s and 1850s also developed a brisk business in transporting immigrants from New York to San Francisco. The advertising trade cards pictured here reflect the popular image that the ships themselves created.

84D

GLIDDEN & WILLIAMS LINE

FOR SAN FRANCISCO

FROM LEWIS WHARF.

THE SPLENDID NEW A I CLIPPER SHIP

Pharos

JAMES COLLIER, Commander,

Is now receiving cargo for the above port, and will be promptly despatched. Shippers will oblige by the early delivery of their engagements.

For Freight or Passage apply at the California Packet Office, 114 State Street, Boston.

Agents at San Francisco, Messrs. Williams, Blanchard & Co.

Watson & Clark, Prs., 21 Franklin St.

84B

NO DELAY THE EVER-POPULAR A I FIRST CLASS MYSTIC-BUILT CLIPPER SHIP **IN LOADING!**

GARIBALDI

EMERY, Master,
IS RECEIVING HER CARGO AT PIER 20 EAST RIVER, BURLING SLIP.

Shippers are respectfully notified that this Favorite Clipper is again taking Cargo

FOR SAN FRANCISCO!!!

The extraordinary good order in which the "Garibaldi" delivers her cargoes is too well-known to be repeated, which, with her uniform good passages, makes her the most desirable Clipper up.

SUTTON & CO., 58 South St., corner of Wall.

The ships of this line insure at the lowest rates, and dispatched quicker than any other from New-York to San Francisco.

ABBOTT & CO., PRINTERS, N. Y.

84A

COLEMAN'S CALIFORNIA LINE for SAN FRANCISCO.

THE EXTREME CLIPPER SHIP

"FLYING SCUD,"

P. HARDING, Commander, is now rapidly loading at Pier 11 East River.

This superb vessel is one of the **SHARPEST** and **FASTEST** Ships in the world, and has all the modern improvements of ventilation, &c. Parties will please examine her, and complete their shipments without delay. She will have **QUICK DISPATCH.**
For balance of Freight, apply to

Agents in San Francisco: Messrs. WM. T. COLEMAN & Co.

WM. T. COLEMAN & CO., 88 Wall-st., Tontine Building

NESBITT & CO., PRINTERS.

As the flow of emigrants from Europe increased [85], continental ports began to adopt regulations governing not only the ocean carrier but the problems posed by transient populations awaiting passage. Holland, in 1837, set up regulations holding those responsible for transporting passengers to be answerable for shipboard conditions and the seaworthiness of vessels, and a passenger-tonnage ratio of four to five was prescribed. Antwerp, early in the forefront of the European emigrant trade, set up a board of maritime commissioners in 1843 to ascertain the seaworthiness of passenger ships, and a two-to-five ratio was established. Hamburg and Bremen, two cities that began to vie for the emigrant trade and that were to become leaders in social legislation for the accommodation and protection of emigrants, both while awaiting passage and afloat, passed significant regulations in 1845, and 1847, on the very eve of the second great German migration [86A-86C].

It was not until 1847, when the Irish migration started, that the United States once again stirred itself to mitigate overcrowding. Again a passenger-tonnage ratio—this time one to two—was adopted; it was reinforced, however, with a prescription of fourteen cubic feet of deck area per passenger. But the American regulations were too little and too late to counter the overcrowding occasioned by the unprecedented demand for transatlantic passage.

Dr. John A. Griscom visited the emigrant ship *Ceylon* in 1847, shortly after the vessel came to anchor in New York Harbor. His description illustrates the gulf between the statute book and reality.

. . . a considerable number had died upon the voyage, and 115 were then ill with the fever, and were preparing to be removed to the hospital. Before any had yet left the ship, we passed through the steerage, making a more or less minute examination of the place and its inhabitants; but the indescribable filth, the emaciated, half nude figures, many with the petechial eruption disfiguring their faces, crouching in the bunks, or strewed over the decks, and cumbering the gangways; broken utensils and debris of food spread recklessly about, presented a picture of which neither pen nor pencil can convey the full idea. Some were just rising from their berths for the first time since leaving Liverpool, having been suffered to lie there all the voyage, wallowing in their own filth. It was no wonder to us that with such total neglect of sanitary supervision, and an entire absence of ventilation, so many of such wretched beings had perished, or were then ill of fever; it was only surprising that so many had escaped.

In the Canadian trade, where overcrowding was infamous, conditions were even worse. The Quebec board of health reported on August 12, 1847:

The Larch, *reported this morning from Sligo, sailed with 400 passengers, of whom 108 died on the passage and 150 were sick. The* Virginius *sailed with 496; 158 died on the passage, 186 were sick, and the remainder landed feeble and tottering; the captain, mates and crew were all sick. The Black Hole of Calcutta was a mercy compared to the holds of these vessels.*

The U.S. passenger law of 1847 was superseded fifteen months later. American shipowners had clamored for removal of the passenger-tonnage ratio reinforced by the area provisions, which, they claimed, worked to the disadvantage of American-built vessels, generally narrower and deeper than their British counterparts. With those restrictions eliminated by the law of 1848, sailing passenger vessels began rapidly to assume new conformations—new cabins, compartments, and deck-houses. For example, the cabin accommodations, originally under the raised poop, spilled over and crept forward over the main deck until in some vessels more than 65 percent of main deck area was encumbered. Vessels under 1,200 tons, which might accommodate 400 passengers under the old act, could now take in double that number. In such vessels no more than a fourth of the passengers could be on the open deck at one time.

As late as the 1855 U.S. Passenger Act—which on the surface seemed quite enlightened with its specifications for increased air space, better ventilation, cooking facilities, improved berthing, and open deck space—there remained almost a complete lack of enforcement procedure. Indeed, under this act there was no penalty provided for overloading inbound to the United States. The law applied only to the outbound vessels.

In the unending struggle for legislation, the steamship played an anomalous role. The main concern of the steamship owner was to wrest control of the North Atlantic luxury trade and cabin class passengers from the sailing packets. The displaced sailing vessels sought the less desirable trades, one of which was that of carrying emigrants.

85
Advertisement for passage to
America from Gothenburg,
Sweden (1870).

86A
Norddeutscher Lloyd poster
(printed on two sides) complete with rates, schedules,
and a cutaway view.

86B
This detail shows a transatlantic vessel employing both
sail and steam to power it across the sea. This drawing
was printed in 1878. Within
ten years the sails would be
gone.

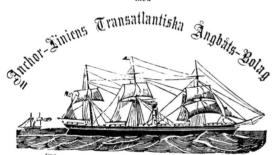

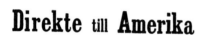

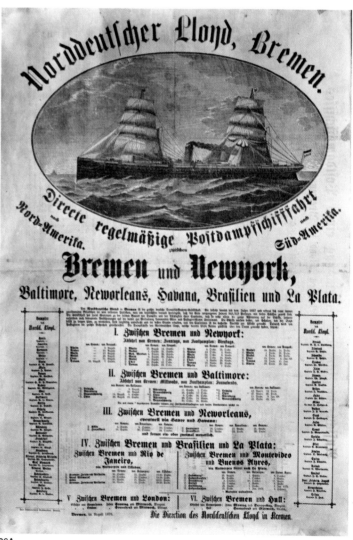

85

86A

86B

86C
Cutaway view of a
Norddeutscher Lloyd vessel,
complete with rates. (Reverse side of 86A.)

Ansicht der inneren Einri...
des Norddeutsche...

A Hinterer Salon oder I. Cajüte. B Vorderer Salon oder II. Cajüte. C Zwischendeck. D Räume für Ladung. E Kohlenräume. F Proviantraum G Kesselraum. H Maschinenraum. J Schornstein. K Masten. f Raderhaus. g Gangspille. h Oberlichter. i Navigationszimmer. k Commandobrücke. l Damp...

Ueberfahrts-Bedingungen für die Passagiere der ...

I. Linie Bremen—Newyork.

Die Schiffe dieser Linie haben 3 Classen und beträgt das Ueberfahrtsgeld:

1. für einfache Fahrt.

	I. Cajüte.	II. Cajüte.	Zwischendeck.
Von Bremen nach Newyork	ℳ 500	ℳ 300	ℳ 120
Bremen nach Southampton	75	50	35
Southampton nach Newyork	470	270	
Havre nach Newyork	485	290	126
Paris nach Newyork	500	300	126
Newyork nach Southampton, London, Havre und Bremen ...	Golds 100	Golds 60	Cu.s 30
Newyork nach Paris	105	63	31.50

2. für Retourbillets.
(mit unbeschränkter Gültigkeitsdauer.)

	I. Cajüte.	II. Cajüte.	Zwischendeck.
Von Bremen nach Newyork und zurück ..	ℳ 780	ℳ 460	ℳ 200
Southampton n. Newyork und zurück	750	430	
Havre nach Newyork und zurück	765	450	200
Paris nach Newyork und zurück	780	460	210
Newyork nach Southampton, London, Havre, Bremen und zurück	Golds 185	Golds 110	Cu.s 50.00
Newyork nach Paris und zurück ..	195	115	53.00

Vorstehende Preise verstehen sich für eine erwachsene Person. Für Kinder von 1 bis 10 Jahren wird die Hälfte berechnet, wenn zwei derselben erforderlichenfalls ein Bett benutzen. Für Kinder unter 1 Jahr sind 9 Mark zu entrichten. Passagiere I. Classe können sich durch Bezahlung der 1½-fachen Passage das Recht der alleinigen Benutzung eines Zimmers sichern.

Dienstboten werden in I. Cajüte für ⅔ des tarifmäßigen Passagepreises befördert, wenn sie bei ihren Herrschaften in den Schlafkammern logiren. Sie haben daselbst auch ihre Mahlzeiten einzunehmen und dürfen den Salon nicht als Aufenthalt benutzen.

In den Passagepreisen ist volle Beköstigung exl. Wein, Bier und dergleichen Getränke inbegriffen. Cajütspassagiere erhalten außerdem vollständige Betten, Bettwäsche und Handtücher; Zwischendeckspassagiere haben sich dagegen mit Betten, Eß-, Trink- und Waschgeschirr selbst zu versehen.

Auf jedem Schiffe ist ein promovirter Arzt angestellt, derselbe ist verpflichtet, denjenigen Passagieren, die während der Reise erkranken, unentgeltlich Beistand zu leisten. Die verabreichten Arzneien sind ebenfalls frei. Der an Bord befindliche Barbier kann für geleistete Dienste eine Vergütung beanspruchen.

Die Mitnahme von Reibzündhölzern, Pulver oder sonstigen feuergefährlichen Gegenständen ist streng verboten. Schießwaffen sind dem Capitain zur Aufbewahrung während der Reise abzuliefern.

Das Rauchen ist in keinem Theile des Schiffes, ausgenommen in den Rauchzimmern und auf Deck, erlaubt.

Keinem Passagier ist es gestattet, Wein, Bier oder sonstige geistige Getränke mitzunehmen. Dieselben sind an Bord zu festgesetzten Tarifpreisen zu erhalten.

Packete, geschlossene Briefe oder Documente dürfen von keinem Passagier zur Beförderung angenommen werden, sondern sind gleich am Bord dem Zahlmeister abzugeben.

Gelder, Werthpapiere oder sonstige werthvolle Gegenstände können versiegelt und mit dem vollständig und deutlich geschriebenen Namen des Eigenthümers versehen dem Zahlmeister während der Fahrt, jedoch ohne Gewährleistung der Gesellschaft, eingehändigt werden.

Jeder Passagier ist verpflichtet, sich an Bord nach den Bestimmungen des Schiffsreglements zu richten und den Weisungen des Capitains überall nachzukommen.

Die Direction behält sich vor, die Passagiere an Stelle des im Ueberfahrts-Vertrage bemerkten Dampfers, mit einem anderen zur nämlichen Zeit abgehenden Dampfschiffe ihrer Linie zu befördern.

Die Passagiere werden an den festgelegten Expeditionstagen unentgeltlich von Bremen nach Bremerhaven auf das Postdampfschiff befördert. Ihre Beköstigung fängt jedoch erst an Bord desselben an.

Sollte irgend ein Umstand das zur Ueberfahrt zu benutzende Schiff unterwegs an der Weiterreise verhindern, so werden die Passagiere nebst Gepäck dennoch an den bedungenen Preis an den Bestimmungsort gebracht, zu welchem Ende der Betrag der Passage- und Verwendungsgelder gesetzmäßig verichert wird.

Zur Sicherung eines Platzes auf den Dampfschiffen ist die Einzahlung eines Handgeldes von ℳ 150 für jeden Platz in der Ersten Cajüte, von ℳ 60 für jeden Platz in Zweiter Cajüte und im Zwischendeck erforderlich.

Nur nach Bezahlung dieses Handgeldes, welches später bei Entrichtung des Passagegeldes in Abzug gebracht wird, sind Plätze als fest belegt zu betrachten, voraufgesetzt, daß solche beim Eintreffen der Anmeldung für die gewünschte Fahrt noch frei sind. Auf Bestellung ohne Beifügung des Handgeldes werden

keine Plätze reservirt. — Jeder abgeschlossene Ueberfahrtsvertrag ist nur für die darin namhaft gem... Personen gültig.

Bei Bestellung von Plätzen für Cajüte ist aufzugeben, ob solche für Herren oder ... gewünscht werden.

Reisegepäck.

An Reisegepäck hat jeder erwachsene Passagier ½ Cubikmeter frei, Dienstboten und jedes ... von 1—10 Jahren die Hälfte.

Das Gepäck muß in Koffern, Kisten, Reisesäcken gut verpackt und jedes Stück mit ... vollen Namen des Eigenthümers und des Bestimmungsortes versehen sein. Passag... können dasselbe unter der Adresse „Norddeutscher Lloyd", Bremen im Vo... absenden.

Jeder Passagier hat sein Reisegepäck an der von der Direction bezeichneten Verladestelle zur bestimmten Zeit ordnungsmäßig aufzuliefern, um, nachdem das Gepäck gemessen und etwaige Ueber... 50 Mark per Cubikmeter bezahlt ist, den Uebernahmschein abgestempelt in Empfang zu nehmen, ... ohne solchen Uebernahmschein kein Stück Gepäck an Bord genommen wird.

Die Cajütspassagiere können nur Mäntel- oder Reisesäcke bei sich behalten; alles größere ... wird im Bagageraum verstaut.

Jeder Passagier hat darauf zu achten, daß er bei Ankunft am Bestimmungsorte sein Gepäck ... richtig empfange, da spätere Reclamationen nicht berücksichtigt werden können.

Im Falle der Beschädigung oder des Verlustes von Gepäckstücken oder darin enthaltenen Gegen... ist die Gesellschaft höchstens bis zum Betrage von 300 Mark für jedes beschädigte oder verlorene Stück ... verantwortlich und haftbar, es sei denn, daß nachweislich der Verlust oder die Beschädigung von der Gesells... oder deren Angestellten absichtlich herbeigeführt wäre, oder daß ein Connoissement oder Empfangschein ... ausgestellt ist, in welchem Inhalt und Werth der Gepäckstücke specificirt sind.

Gelder, Juwelen, Uhren und sonstige Werthsachen werden nur für eigene Gefahr der Pass... befördert, wenn sie nicht in Verwahrsam der Gesellschaft gegeben und Connoissemente oder Empfangs... darüber gezeichnet und ausgehändigt sind.

Für die Folgen unvermeidlichen Aufenthalts des Gepäcks haftet die Gesellschaft nicht.

Waaren, deren Kaufmannsgüter dürfen unter keinerlei Vorwand sich unter dem Gepäck bef... Diese müssen besonders verpackt und Connoissemente darüber gezeichnet werden. Stellt sich bei der ... suchung durch die Zollofficianten in Amerika dennoch heraus, daß dieser Bestimmung zuwider gehandel... so haben die Eigenthümer nicht allein Confiscation und Defraudationsstrafe zu gewärtigen, sondern ha... außerdem für die dem Schiffe daraus entstehende Strafe am Betrage von 400 Dollars verantwo... Zollfrei sind nur wirklich gebrauchte Passagier-Effecten; sämmtliche neuen Gegenstände unterlieg... gewöhnlichen Eingangszoll, und müssen diese vor Ankunft in Amerika dem Capitain aufgegeben w... damit er sie im Manifeste nachfügen läßt.

Directe Billets.

Passagiere, welche von Newyork weiter nach dem Westen zu re... beabsichtigen, können in Bremen directe Billets nach allen größ... Plätzen der Vereinigten Staaten erhalten.

Nach Japan, China, Australien und Neuseeland werden directe Bill... via Newyork und San Francisco zu ermäßigten Preisen ausgegeb...

II. Linie Bremen—Baltimore.

Das Ueberfahrtsgeld beträgt:

1. für einfache Fahrt.

	Cajüte.	Zwischendeck.
Von Bremen nach Baltimore	ℳ 400	ℳ 120
Bremen nach Southampton	75	
Southampton nach Baltimore	370	
Havre nach Baltimore	385	126
Paris nach Baltimore	400	126
Baltimore nach Southampton, London, Havre und Bremen	Golds 90	Cu.s 3...
Baltimore nach Paris	95	

ng eines Postdampfschiffes

loyd in Bremen.

ruber. N Maschine. O Wellenleitung. a Decksalon und Eingang zur I. Cajüte. b Eingang zur II. Cajüte. Eingänge zum Zwischendeck. d Eingang zu den Räumen für die Mannschaft. e Logis für die Mannschaft.
Windfänge. o Erste Küche. p Zweite Küche. q Rauchzimmer für II. Cajüte. r Gemüsekammer.

ampfschiffe des Norddeutschen Lloyd in Bremen.

II. für Retourbillets. (mit unbeschränkter Gültigkeitsdauer.)	Cajüte.	Zwischendeck.
remen nach Baltimore und zurück	ℳ 725	ℳ 200
outhampton „ „ „ „	„ 695	„ —
avre „ „ „ „	„ 710	„ 200
aris „ „ „ „	„ 725	„ 210
altimore nach Southampton, London, Havre, remen und zurück..................	Gld.$ 180	Cy.$ 50.00
altimore nach Paris und zurück...............	„ 190	„ 53.00

Die allgemeinen Bestimmungen sind im Uebrigen genau dieselben, wie für Passagiere auf den n zwischen Bremen und Newyork.

I. Linie Bremen — Havana — New-Orleans.

Die Schiffe sind nur für Passagiere in I. Cajüte und im Zwischendeck eingerichtet. Zwischendecks- iere nach dem Staate Texas können Billets bis nach Galveston oder Indianola erhalten.

Passage-Preise.	in Cajüte.	im Zwischendeck.
remen nach Havana und New-Orleans	ℳ 630	ℳ 150
remen nach Galveston..........................	„ —	„ 175
remen nach Indianola..........................	„ —	„ 190
avre nach Havana und New-Orleans..........	„ 615	„ 140
aris nach Havana und New-Orleans..........	„ 630	„ 146
outhampton nach Havana und New-Orleans ..	„ 630	„ 150
ew-Orleans nach Bremen, Southampton, London und Havre............................	Gold.$ 150	Gold.$ 45
avana nach Bremen, Southampton, London und Havre..................................	„ 150	„ 45

Bei Entnahme von Retourbillets wird der Passagepreis für die Rückreise um 10 Procent ermäßigt. Im Uebrigen sind die Ueberfahrtsbedingungen dieselben wie für Passagiere der Linie Bremen-Newyork; schließt der Passagepreis nach Galveston und Indianola nicht die Beköstigung auf den Dampfern ein, elchen die Weiterreise von New-Orleans nach diesen Plätzen erfolgt.

V. Linie Bremen — Brasilien und La Plata.

Passage-Preise für Cajüte.

Nach	Von Bremen	Von Antwerpen	Von Lissabon	Von Bahia	Von Rio de Janeiro	Von Montevideo	Von Buenos Ayres
	£	£	£	£	£	£	£
aen	—	3	13	33	33	38	38
verpen	3	—	10	30	30	35	35
nouth	—	—	9	30	30	35	35
bon	13	10	—	25	25	30	30
eira	23	20	6	—	—	—	—
ia	33	30	25	—	5	11	12
de Janeiro .	33	30	25	5	—	8	9
atevideo.....	38	35	30	11	8	—	1.14
uos Ayres ..	38	35	30	12	9	1.14	—

Vorstehende Passagepreise verstehen sich für eine erwachsene Person und begreifen vollständige igung excl. Wein, jedoch incl. Betten, Bettwäsche, Handtücher, überhaupt Alles, was zur Bequemlichkeit assagiere dient, in sich. Kinder von 6—12 Jahren zahlen den halben Preis, von 1—6 Jahren ¼ en. Säuglinge unter 1 Jahr werden frei befördert.

Sämmtliche Zimmer liegen auf dem Haupt-Deck und haben alle Passagiere gleiche Berechtigung zur gung des Salons.

Passagiere, die eine Cabine zu alleiniger Benutzung wünschen, bezahlen außer dem für 1. Platz den einfachen Fahrpreise für jeden weiter darin befindlichen Platz ½ Passage.

Familien erhalten besondere Ermäßigungen, wenn das tarifmäßige Passagegeld mindestens 4 volle Passagen beträgt. Für männliche Dienstboten, welche bei der Schiffsbesatzung untergebracht werden, ist der halbe Fahrpreis, für weibliche Dienstboten, welche ihre Schlafstelle in der Damenkajüte erhalten, ⅔ desselben zu entrichten. Bei Entnahme von Retourbillets tritt eine Ermäßigung von 25 % auf den tarifmäßigen Fahrpreis für die Aus- und Rückreise ein, mit Ausnahme von Madeira.

Zur Sicherung eines Platzes ist eine Anzahlung von ⅓ des Passagegeldes erforderlich; der Rest ist wenigstens 24 Stunden vor Abgang des Schiffes zu entrichten. Versäumt der Reisende aus irgend welchem Grunde die Abfahrt des Dampfers, so ist das Handgeld der Gesellschaft verfallen.

... ein Inhaber eines Retourbillets auf dem Dampfer, mit welchem er die Rückreise zu machen wünscht, bei Anmeldung keinen Platz mehr frei findet, so kann er die Rückzahlung des Passagegeldes (nach Abzug des tarifmäßigen Preises für die einfache Reise) beanspruchen.

Passagiere, welche sich an einem Zwischenhafen angemeldet haben, können nur Anspruch auf Beförderung machen, soweit Platz vorhanden. Können nicht alle angemeldeten Passagiere Beförderung finden, so haben diejenigen das Vorrecht, welche vor Anderen durch Zahlung des Handgeldes Plätze belegt haben. Denen, die nicht aufgenommen werden können, wird der gezahlte Betrag ohne Abzug erstattet.

Die Passagiere können ihre Reise in einem Zwischenhafen unterbrechen, haben jedoch auf dem Dampfer, mit welchem sie ihre Reise fortsetzen, nur Anspruch auf die noch unbesetzten Plätze. Der Aufenthalt in dem Zwischenhafen darf 2 Monat nicht übersteigen.

Personen, die mit einer ansteckenden Krankheit behaftet sind, können an Bord der Schiffe keine Aufnahme finden. Stellt sich nach Antritt der Reise heraus, daß ein Passagier mit einer solchen Krankheit behaftet ist, so hat er es sich gefallen zu lassen, von den übrigen Passagieren und der Mannschaft abgesondert, und in dem nächsten Hafen zur Wiederherstellung der Gesundheit auf seine Kosten gelandet zu werden. Nach vollständiger Wiederherstellung steht dem Passagier das Recht zu, mit dem nächstabgehenden Dampfer der Gesellschaft weiter befördert zu werden.

Getränke, als Wein, Bier, Spirituosen und Mineralwasser sind an Bord zu mäßigen Preisen zu erhalten und ist es deshalb keinem Passagier gestattet, dergleichen bei sich zu führen.

Der an Bord befindliche Arzt ist verpflichtet, Jedermann, der an Bord erkrankt, unentgeltlich Beistand zu leisten. Für gereichte Medicamente darf keine Zahlung verlangt werden.

Es befindet sich ein Barbier an Bord, welcher für geleistete Dienste eine Vergütung zu beanspruchen berechtigt ist.

Die an Bord befindlichen Badezimmer können von den Passagieren gratis benutzt werden.

Das Rauchen ist nur in dem dazu hergerichteten Rauchzimmer und auf dem Deck gestattet.

Jeder Passagier hat sich nach den bestehenden Schiffs-Reglements zu richten und in besonderen Fällen den Anordnungen des Capitains Folge zu leisten.

Der Norddeutsche Lloyd übernimmt keine Verantwortlichkeit, weder für eine verspätete Ankunft oder Abfahrt in, resp. von irgend einem Hafen, und für den dadurch entstehenden Aufenthalt der Passagiere, noch für Verzögerungen, welche durch irgend einen Unfall entstehen mögen, oder für irgend welche Verluste, welche durch die Gefahren der Schifffahrt, durch Unglücksfälle an den Kesseln oder der Maschine veranlaßt sind; auch nicht für die Folgen von Sanitäts-Maßregeln, welche von den Behörden an irgend einem Hafenplatz getroffen werden. Wenn in Folge des letztgenannten Umstandes die Passagiere auf einem andern als dem im Fahrplane festgestellten Wege nach ihrem Bestimmungsplatze befördert werden, oder mit Zustimmung der Agenten oder Capitaine der Gesellschaft an Bord der Schiffe bleiben müssen, so haben die Passagiere in dem einen Falle die Kosten der Weiterbeförderung, oder, falls sie an Bord der Dampfer bleiben, eine Vergütung für Beköstigung und Aufenthalt an Bord von 10 Shilling per Tag außer dem festgesetzten Passagegelde zu entrichten.

Reisegepäck. Jeder Passagier hat auf den Dampfern des Norddeutschen Lloyd 20 Cubicfuß Gepäck frei; Kinder und Dienstboten die Hälfte. Bei Ueberfracht kommt der Fracht-Tarif für Maaßgut in Anwendung.

Das Gepäck muß in starken Kisten, Koffern oder Säcken fest und gut verpackt, und jedes Collo **deutlich und in haltbarer Weise mit dem Namen des Eigenthümers und des Bestimmungsortes** versehen sein.

Waaren und Kaufmannsgüter dürfen nicht als Passagiergepäck aufgeliefert werden. Bei etwaiger Zuwiderhandlung wird die doppelte höchste tarifmäßige Fracht für Maaßgut berechnet.

Unter dem Reisegepäck dürfen keine feuergefährliche, explodirende oder sonstige gefährliche Gegenstände verpackt sein; jeder Passagier, welcher dawider handelt, hat nicht nur eine Strafe bis zu Pfd. Sterl. 100 zu entrichten, sondern ist auch außerdem der Gesellschaft für jeden daraus erwachsenden Schaden verantwortlich.

Für Beschädigung, Verlust oder Folgen unvermeidlichen Aufenthalts des Gepäcks haftet die Gesellschaft nicht, ebensowenig für Verlust von Geld und Werthsachen, wenn sie nicht zu den bestehenden Frachtsätzen als Frachtgut aufgegeben und Connoissemente oder Empfangsscheine dafür gezeichnet sind.

Packete, versiegelte Briefe oder Documente dürfen von keinem Passagier zur Beförderung angenommen werden.

Bremen, im August 1878.

Die Direction des Norddeutschen Lloyd.

The years between 1819 and 1885 marked the transition between sail and steam. Those years saw vast technological accomplishments in ocean steam navigation. The improvement in propulsion machinery was impressive. Nineteen years elapsed between the twenty-nine-day, eleven-hour crossing of the United States's *Savannah*, aided by her intermittently operating, wheezing, fuel-gobbling machinery, and the voyage of the British steamer *Sirius*, whose seventeen-day westward passage, entirely under power, between London and New York in 1838 demonstrated the practicability of transatlantic steam navigation. Two years later the first regular transatlantic service subsidized by the British government was inaugurated by Samuel Cunard.

The exuberance of growth and engineering advances in the steamship can best be appreciated in I. K. Brunel's 1843 masterpiece, the *Great Britain*. She was the first ocean-going steamer built entirely of iron and propelled by a screw rather than paddle wheels. A marvel of advanced technology, she boasted a double bottom and watertight compartments. She still endures today as a great monument to British naval engineering. Brunel's *Great Eastern*, built in 1857, was fifty years ahead of her time in size, speed, and accommodations. She was not to be surpassed until 1906, when Cunard launched a vessel called the *Lusitania*.

For the emigrant the sailing ship remained the main mode of transatlantic travel until William Inman organized the New York & Philadelphia Steamship Line in 1850, with fortnightly service from Liverpool to Philadelphia and New York [**87, 88**]. Gradually he enlarged his steerage accommodations and within ten years practically cornered the trade. The prosperity of the company was based on offering more economical and rapid transportation. Between 1856 and 1857 the company is reported to have carried some 85,000 passengers, a figure representing about one-third of all those crossing the Atlantic (west and east). The following table compiled for the year 1870 illustrates the status of the Inman Line as compared with other steamship lines then operating. Note particularly the incidence of deaths to total steerage passengers carried. (It is interesting to observe that only the Guion Line was under American ownership.)

Official return on emigrants landed in N.Y. 1870 from U.K.

	Trips	Cabin	Steerage	Total	Deaths
Inman	68	3,635	40,465	44,100	22
National	56	2,442	33,494	35,736	35
Guion	55	1,115	27,054	28,569	18
Anchor	74	1,637	23,404	25,041	19
Cunard	70	7,638	16,871	24,509	10

Two further tables illustrate the relative mortality in sailing vessels as against steam vessels for the years 1867 and 1872.

	Voyages	Av. length of voyages (days)	Total pass.	Total deaths	No. of pass. to 1 death	No. of deaths on sail to 1 on steam
1867						
Steam	222	13.84	97,703	100	977	1
Sail	128	44.24	22,090	259	93	3.46
1872						
Steam	295	13.19	183,337	63	2,195	1
Sail	41	44.18	6,456	35	184	3.52

87
Steerage tickets for the Inman Line of the 1870s.

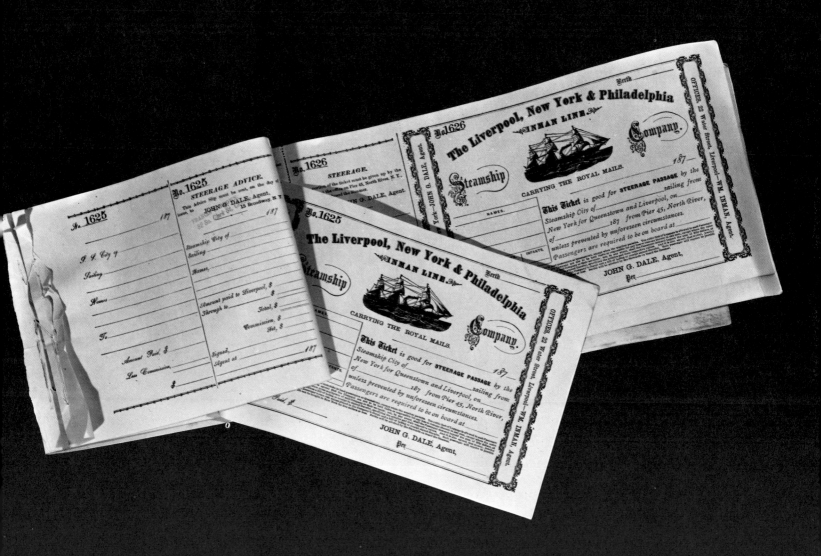

88
German emigrants boarding
an America-bound steamer in
Hamburg. (*Harper's Weekly*,
November 7, 1874.)

The sailing packets held on the longest in the Liverpool to New Orleans trade, but in 1870 steam took over that route as well, with the formation of the Mississippi & Dominion S/S Co. Primarily cotton carriers, the company, like the Guion Line, was principally owned and operated by Americans. Its ships connected Liverpool and New Orleans during the winter months and Liverpool and Canada during the summer. On its New Orleans run the company's vessels called at Bordeaux, Coruña, Lisbon, and Havana. The Mississippi & Dominion was one of the first to provide service to the emigrants who found their way from the southern areas of Europe to settle in the southern and southwestern regions of the United States via the Mississippi River steamboats.

With effective competition among steamship lines, and the steady pressure of passenger regulations, conditions in steerage made a slow but steady improvement. The certainty and regularity of service and the reduction of time at sea cut deeply into passenger mortality, as did effective medical examinations at ports of embarkation. Improved sanitary conditions and increasingly stringent regulations on the scale and quality of provisions and its service reduced physical hardship drastically.

However, as the century drew to a close, a reinforced wave of emigrants from Eastern and Southern Europe [89] again made overcrowding an issue. In the United States, an 1873 report strongly criticized overcrowded conditions and laid the groundwork for the first modern comprehensive act applicable to the steamship. But most significantly, the U.S. Passenger Act of 1882, which finally defined the steerage passenger as any passenger other than a cabin passenger, legislated the inspection of arriving vessels not only at quarantine but also when the ship was at its berth. It was finally realized that the old passenger-tonnage ratio had become meaningless when a vessel might have five or six or more decks as compared with the sailing vessel of three or four decks. The 1855 Passenger Act, which made no distinction as to which deck might be assigned to steerage passengers, was corrected in the 1882 act, which specifically stated which deck could accommodate steerage passengers and specified the cubic footage to be allotted to each passenger.

But the provisions of the 1882 law were rapidly rendered obsolete as the size of the ships increased. Vessels built of steel—a lighter material than the iron it replaced—grew in height to eight or nine decks. This meant the main deck (the uppermost continuous deck) might be two or three decks below the weather deck, and the application of the 1882 law would push steerage well below the water line, making ventilation a serious problem even in the age of power, not to mention the situation that might arise in the event of a collision. In 1908, a year that marked a movement toward achieving a degree of uniformity in British and American passenger legislation, the "lowest passenger deck" was defined as the deck next below the water line. This was a regulation that persisted to the end of the days of the emigrant trade.

The crest of the great tidal wave of emigration to America came between the years 1905 and 1914, when a staggering 10,121,940 emigrants arrived. Almost a century's experience was at hand in the legislating of regulations concerning the carriage of passengers by sea. The vagaries of wind and weather that could make the transatlantic passage a hideous nightmare were long gone. Even the slowest of steamers could negotiate an eight-day passage. The handling of passengers at ports of embarkation was accomplished with remarkable efficiency. In some instances, such as that of the Italian government, humaneness and concern for the welfare and well-being of their emigrants was particularly noteworthy. Yet the sea continued to claim its victims. In the case of the *Titanic,* then the world's largest ship at 46,382 tons, 1,635 passengers and crewmen were lost in 1912 in a collision with an iceberg. That 732 were saved was largely due to the *Titanic*'s wireless; otherwise those who made the lifeboats certainly would have perished.

89
Cartoon expressing the popular notion that special-interest
groups supported the flow of
poor immigrants to America.
(*Judge*, 1898.)

Castle Garden

As emigration to the New World gathered momentum in the first half of the nineteenth century and hundreds of thousands of strangers poured undirected into American ports, the plight of the arriving immigrant worsened, as *Harper's Weekly* of June 26, 1858, describes:

. . . his condition at this stage in his fortunes was truly pitiable. Federal, State, and municipal authorities regarded him with as much indifference as if he had been a bale of cheap goods. Scoundrels of the very lowest calibre—emigrant runners— seized him, and made him their own. If he had any money, they robbed him of it. If he had a pretty wife or daughters, they stole them too, if they could. If he had neither money nor daughters, they merely took his luggage. It was well for him if, after having been robbed of all he had, he was not beaten to death, or entrapped into committing crimes which transferred him almost directly from the emigrant vessel to Blackwell's Island or the State Prison.

New York was the port of entry for the majority of immigrants and was consequently most pressed to do something to alleviate these distressing conditions. During the 1840s the efforts of the Irish and German emigrant societies in arousing public concern resulted in the establishment of a Board of Commissioners of Emigration by the State of New York in 1847. This board, in 1855, set up the nation's first formal immigrant receiving station.

Originally a fort called the West Battery, it was built between 1807 and 1811 on an artificial island about two hundred feet off Manhattan's Battery, to serve as a defense against British invasion during the Napoleonic Wars and the War of 1812. Renamed Castle Clinton for New York's first governor, George Clinton, it continued in military use until 1822, when it was ceded to the city by the federal government. Under the city's control, Castle Clinton was rented and quickly converted into an amusement park, where concerts, fireworks, wrestling, and other entertainment were held. Along with the transformation came a new name: Castle Garden.

In 1839 two entrepreneurs, Philip French and Christopher Heiser, leased Castle Garden and gave it a place in the sun. They added a stage and six thousand seats and eventually roofed the circular auditorium. They transformed a simple, somewhat tawdry amusement area into an elegant resort and fashionable center for cultural, social, and sometimes political events. Lola Montez, the Italian Opera Company of Havana, and an 1842 demonstration of Morse's telegraph were attractions, as were Presidents Tyler and Polk in 1847 and 1848. But the moment most remembered in many years of performances was the American premier of the "Swedish Nightingale," Jenny Lind, in 1850. Her debut was a triumph. Publicized by no one less than Phineas Taylor Barnum, her Castle Garden appearance netted the management the then great sum of $87,000.

In 1855 Castle Garden, the theater, was selected by the Commissioners of Emigration, with the authorization of the New York State Legislature, to become Castle Garden, the immigrant receiving station. The pressing need for an immigrant depot precluded the building of a new structure, and Castle Garden, with its great size and waterfront location, was considered adequate for the purpose. The decision brought immediate criticism. Residents in the ward adjacent to Castle Garden, the runners profiting from the vulnerability of immigrants who had previously been dropped at random points of debarkation, and even the City of New York, violently disapproved. It was suggested that immigrants would threaten the health of the neighborhood, property values would decline, residents would move away because of "pestilential and disagreeable odors," merchants would suffer, and shoppers would be inconvenienced by the crowds. The transfer of the Castle Garden lease to the state was unsuccessfully challenged in the courts in an effort to stop the opening of the depot.

In the forefront of the opposition were the so-called runners who cheated immigrants by selling them bogus train tickets or charging them inflated prices for lodging and food. They were not permitted inside the depot and were thereby deprived of what they considered their ''vested interest'' in the business potential of the unwary immigrant. The New York *Daily Tribune* (August 6, 1855) reported that ''The foul brood of villains who have so long fattened upon the plunder of emigrants, don't relish the landing of passengers at Castle Garden. Indeed their exasperation breaks out in absolute violence'' [90].

Castle Garden as an immigrant depot bore a great deal of criticism over many years, some warranted and some not. While not a perfect halfway house, it did for a time answer many of the immigrants' needs. Officials registered immigrants and helped them to change money, buy railroad tickets, transport their luggage, and find a job or a place to stay [91, 92]. Additionally, the newcomers were given some protection from the preying runners and swindlers. An article that appeared in *The New York Times* in the 1870s indicated the immigrants' reaction: ''Castle Garden is so well known in Europe that few emigrants can be induced to sail for any other destination. Their friends in this country write to those who are intending to emigrate to come to Castle Garden where they will be safe, and, if out of money, they can remain until it is sent them.''

Throughout the Civil War and the era of Reconstruction, Castle Garden boomed with life, but beginning in 1875, it was beset by a string of ills which eventually led to its closing. In that year, an unfavorable Supreme Court decision declared the New York State law that required a bond or head tax on immigrants unconstitutional and a matter for Congress to regulate. The absence of these funds, crucial to the operation of the depot, produced a financial crisis at Castle Garden, which was only partially alleviated by state assistance. And on July 9, 1876, a devastating fire caused $40,000 worth of damage and destroyed about a thousand pieces of luggage. These problems were aggravated by the city's repeated attempts to close the center. By the 1880s the New York *World* was reporting the ''wholesale robbery'' of immigrants at Castle Garden and calling for the abolition of the Board of Commissioners of Emigration. A federal investigation revealed that various interests, such as the railroads and the baggage handlers, were making huge profits at the immigrant's expense, that the center's management was generally poor and inept, and that the facilities were ''hopelessly inadequate.'' Castle Garden was doomed.

On February 15, 1890, the Secretary of the Treasury revoked the contract with the Commissioners of Emigration, giving them sixty days notice. New York State, angered by this action, refused to allow the Treasury to continue the operation at Castle Garden while a new site was being prepared. So, on April 18, 1890, Castle Garden received immigrants for the last time. The depot was moved to the Barge Office, a little-used structure built in 1883 by the Treasury Department as a receiving lounge for the privileged cabin-class passengers. Meanwhile a new site in New York Harbor, Ellis Island, had been selected and construction was soon under way. From 1855 until 1889 Castle Garden had processed a total of 8,280,917 immigrants.

Castle Garden remained closed for six years. In 1896 it was reopened as a municipal aquarium. Closed again in 1940 to make room for construction of the Brooklyn-Battery Tunnel, it is now being restored by the National Park Service to its fortified appearance during and after the War of 1812 and will be called Castle Clinton National Monument.

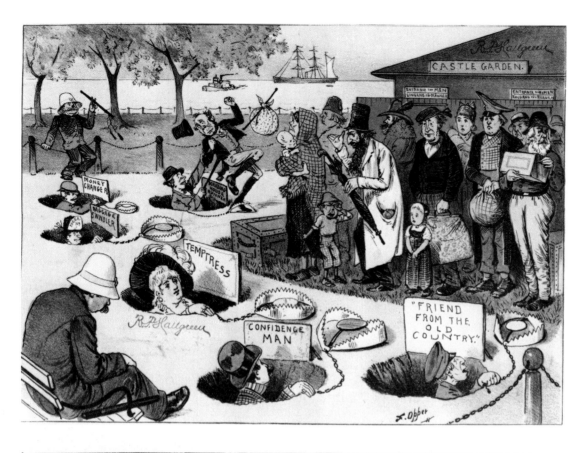

90
The horrors awaiting immigrants leaving Castle Garden were represented by Frederick Burr Opper, a brilliant humorist, late in the nineteenth century.

91
Interior of Castle Garden, the great hall where immigrants were processed (*Harper's Monthly,* April 1871).

92
Immigrant transfer barge carrying people from Castle Garden to train depots in New York and New Jersey (May 28, 1874). Notice the German lettering on the barge offering to take immigrants to the Erie Railroad and points west.

Ellis Island

On January 1, 1892, a new federal immigration station was opened at Ellis Island in New York Harbor. This small island in shallow waters had witnessed Dutch oyster fishing in the seventeenth century and public hangings of pirates in the eighteenth (when it was named Gibbet Island); it had been fortified during the War of 1812 and accommodated a naval powder magazine as early as 1835. At one point, at the end of the eighteenth century, it was owned by Samuel Ellis, a Manhattan merchant.

Ellis Island was considered a logical site for the new immigration station: it was uninhabited, was already owned by the government, and its selection solved the problem of what to do with the old powder magazine, which had for decades been a subject of concern among newspapers and local residents who thought it dangerously close to New York and New Jersey [93]. In 1890 a law was passed authorizing $75,000 for the removal of the powder magazine and $75,000 "to improve said Ellis Island for immigration purposes."

In spite of its advantages, the small island required a great deal of preparation. Because of the shallow waters, a channel 12 feet deep, 1,250 feet long, and 200 feet wide had to be dredged; new docks were constructed to receive barges bringing immigrants to the station; and it was necessary to double the area of the low island with landfill and 860 feet of cribwork to hold it in place.

The immigration depot that opened in 1892 was constructed primarily of Georgia pine. A two-story structure costing about $500,000, it housed baggage rooms on the ground level and the inspection hall on the floor above. Five years later, in June 1897, it was completely destroyed by fire. As in the months following the closing of Castle Garden, immigrants were received at the Barge Office and its annex on the tip of Manhattan. The New York *Tribune* in 1900 called the Barge Office "grimy, gloomy . . . more suggestive of an enclosure for animals than a receiving station for prospective citizens of the United States."

Replacement of the destroyed facilities was soon authorized and a contract awarded in August 1898 to the architectural firm Boring and Tilton. The new—fireproof—building opened on December 17, 1900. It was constructed of brick with limestone trim and was three stories high in the central section with a two-story wing on each end. The center was accented by a tower at each of its four corners. The architectural quality of the new Ellis Island facility was highly praised, though no one, then or now, has been quite sure how to define its style [94].

The novelty of the design could not hide the building's practical inadequacies. Immigration officials, believing the influx of aliens to American shores was diminishing, had estimated that a maximum of half a million immigrants would enter New York in any coming year. This estimate was drastically low: the greatest period in American immigration was about to begin and Ellis Island was to be plagued by a constant struggle for space to accommodate the incoming thousands. The new depot failed in other ways to bring about the improvements in immigrant reception that were hoped for. The administration of the depot soon proved corrupt, and the unwary immigrant again was the victim of poor treatment and exploitation.

Theodore Roosevelt, a great advocate of reform, was quick to see the critical situation at Ellis Island, and soon after becoming President, in September 1901, he set to work to improve conditions. He replaced many of the old officials with new appointments, among them William Williams, commissioner of immigration, who proved effective in uncovering and correcting corrupt practices. Under Williams's direction, old contracts for concessions at the immigration depot were canceled and new contracts let, dishonesty was severely punished, and favors to employees were no longer permitted. He even put up large signs at Ellis Island directing employees to use "kindness and consideration" in dealing with immigrants; punishment was forthcoming for violators. Conditions were greatly changed by these measures, fortunately in time for the peak immigration years beginning in 1903 and ending with the outbreak of World War I.

93
Protest from *Judge* magazine in 1890 against the use of New York harbor as a "dumping area" for immigrants.

94
Ellis Island, early 1900s, with the New Jersey docks in background, right.

93

94

During these years millions of immigrants were processed through Ellis Island; 1,004,756 entered in 1907 alone [**95**], and on one day—April 17, 1907—there were 11,745 arrivals. But not all immigrants arriving in New York went through Ellis Island. Second- and first-cabin passengers received only a simple examination on board by an inspector and a doctor from the Public Health Service and then disembarked directly to the city without setting foot on Ellis Island. A more lengthy examination awaited the steerage passengers, and it could result in deportation for those who did not meet the requirements. Some immigrants bought cabin-class tickets for members of their family who might be unable to pass the physical examination at the depot.

After the privileged travelers disembarked, remaining ship passengers were herded into ferries to Ellis Island. Edward Corsi, who became commissioner of Ellis Island in 1931, described his impressions in 1907 when, as a ten-year-old boy, he was ferried to the island from the ship that had brought him from Italy: "During this ride across the bay, as I watched the faces of the people milling about me, I realized that Ellis Island could inspire both hope and fear. Some of the passengers were afraid and obviously dreading the events of the next few hours; others were impatient, anxious to get through the inspection and be off to their destinations." And indeed, over its many years, it was called both "Isle of Tears" and "Island of Hope."

Admittance procedure began in the Registry Hall with a medical examination, which isolated those with suspicious health, usually amounting to about two out of ten or eleven. These people were marked with a white letter indicating their supposed condition: L for lameness; a circled X for possible mental defects, H for heart condition; and F for a rash on the face. Those bearing such a mark were separated out for more extensive examination and possible deportation.

Others went next to be questioned by an inspector with the aid of an interpreter. They were asked, among other questions, what type of work they did, where they were going, how much money they had, who had paid for their ticket, whether they had been in prison. Most passed this without difficulty, though the answers could reveal a violation of the Contract Labor Law or show that the immigrant was a pauper and potential public charge, either of which could be grounds for rejection.

Though the number of immigrants deported was not great, it was a fearful prospect to new arrivals, who had in most cases nothing to return to and occasionally were fleeing political persecution. Deportation also caused a great problem for the constantly overstrained facilities at Ellis Island, where immigrants were detained until they could be returned. Though the cost for their maintenance during this period and for the return passage was absorbed by the shipping companies, who were thus obligated to screen their passengers carefully, this did little to alleviate intolerable crowding. In one extreme case, 1,700 people were forced to sleep in a room with beds for only 600.

Those who passed all the examinations were free to leave Ellis Island; if they had encountered no difficulties, they had probably spent only three or four hours there [**96, 97A–97C**]. Railroad tickets could be bought at Ellis Island for points outside New York City, an often confusing business for both immigrant and railroad representative. Communication of such destinations as "Pringvilliamas" (Springfield, Massachusetts) could occasionally end badly, as it did for a group of immigrants who wanted to go to Amsterdam Avenue in New York City but wound up in Amsterdam, New York.

Ellis Island's period of greatest activity was over by 1914. During both world wars it was used for detention of known and suspected enemy aliens, and in World War I its hospitals cared for wounded soldiers. By the end of World War II its function as an immigrant receiving station had virtually come to an end, and most processing was done through American consulates. Until its closing in 1954, aliens awaiting deportation were held there, especially after the Internal Security Act of 1950, when Ellis Island had a short-lived period of reactivation, housing as many as 1,500 suspected "subversive aliens" arriving in New York.

Ellis Island was declared "surplus property" by the government on March 4, 1955, and the unused immigration depot fell into disrepair. In 1965, it was added to the Statue of Liberty National Monument under the administration of the National Park Service.

Several years before Ellis Island was opened, the Statue of Liberty was erected in New York Harbor. The idea was proposed by the French historian and social commentator Édouard de Laboulaye shortly after the Civil War. It was to symbolize the alliance of friendship between France and the United States during the Revolutionary War. Designed by the French sculptor Frédéric Auguste Bartholdi, the proposed statue was to be constructed and paid for by the French and erected by the Americans.

For ten difficult years, from 1876 to 1886, numerous American businessmen devised a series of fund-raising schemes to accumulate money for the pedestal. Little by little they reached their goal, but public spirit ran below high tide. For one fund-raising effort the poet Emma Lazarus produced a sonnet about the statue, which was sold with some paintings for $1,500. Miss Lazarus was descended from an old New York Jewish family. Although she had deserted Judaism in her youth, the anti-Jewish pogroms in Russia fired a new dedication to her ancestral faith, and from the early 1880s until her death she championed the cause of the Jews. To her, the Statue of Liberty would symbolize America as a refuge for the uprooted. Her poem went as follows:

The New Colossus

Not like the brazen giant of Greek fame,
With conquering limbs astride from land to land;
Here at our sea-washed, sunset gates shall stand
A mighty woman with a torch, whose flame
Is the imprisoned lightning, and her name
Mother of exiles. From her beacon-hand
Glows world-wide welcome; her mild eyes
    command
The air-bridged harbor that twin cities frame.

"Keep, ancient lands, your storied pomp!" cries
    she
With silent lips. "Give me your tired, your poor,
Your huddled masses yearning to breathe free,
The wretched refuse of your teeming shore.
Send these, the homeless, tempest-tossed, to me:
I lift my lamp beside the golden door!"

Miss Lazarus died four years after the poem was sold. Her obituaries failed to make note of it.

95

95
Immigrant women and children at the Battery in New York City, c. 1907.

96
Immigrants at South Ferry, New York City, with a cart of trunks and bundles, c. 1901.

97A
Oval-shaped trunk (1850–1870) with metal button decoration. Although many of the emigrant trunks were factory-made and therefore reflected little of their owners' cultural origin, the contents often documented ethnic, social, religious, and occupational status. Typical articles were hand embroideries, ceremonial dress, cooking utensils, religious images or writings, and craft tools. L 23¾".

97B
French trunk made of wood, metal straps, and horsehair. Brought from France by the Dominican nuns who established the Monastery of St. Dominic at Newark, N.J., in 1881. L 44".

96

97A

97B

97C
North German chest (1740 or
1749) brought to Charleston,
South Carolina, by Hans
Jager in the 1820s. Jager was
a fabric merchant who applied
for citizenship in 1831. L
62½".

On July 4, 1884, the 152-foot statue was completed in France and presented to the United States. Two more years elapsed before it was disassembled, brought to New York, and reassembled on its 225-ton pedestal which stood as high again as the statue. By this time the man who had conceived the whole idea, Édouard de Laboulaye, had died, but the sculptor, Bartholdi, saw President Grover Cleveland dedicate the statue on October 28, 1886. Representing Liberty with the broken shackles of tyranny at her feet, the statue's official name is "Liberty, Enlightening the World." She holds in one hand a tablet which symbolizes the Declaration of Independence, guaranteeing that all men are created equal.

At the time of its dedication, the statue meant to Bartholdi and the French liberals a sign of republican stability. The idea that Liberty would mean "welcome" did not occur to the French, and only one newspaper, the New York *Herald,* commented on this role for the statue. It was the immigrants who arrived after 1886 who transformed the statue's original symbolic message. For the great majority who debarked at Ellis Island in New York Harbor, this passive, majestic woman was the welcoming gatekeeper to a land of promise.

At the high tide of immigration to the United States, on the twentieth anniversary of Emma Lazarus's "The New Colossus" (1903), the entire poem was engraved in bronze and placed on an interior wall of the pedestal. Yet it remained there for three decades virtually unnoticed. Ironically, at that time for many Americans the "huddled masses" and "wretched refuse" who came by the hundred thousands were more to be feared than welcomed. This mood of unease crystallized in the restrictive immigration quota acts of the 1920s. But as the fear subsided along with the mass immigration, the message of Emma Lazarus came at last to be *the* meaning of the Statue of Liberty. By the late 1920s, according to historian John Higham, young schoolchildren in Missouri were being instructed that Bartholdi's lady was a dame of hospitality. Indeed, the stereotypical photograph became one of immigrant families looking in awe of the colossus, Liberty.

Chapter 8

Agriculture and the Movement West

The Yankee and the Immigrant

The word "Yankee" appears repeatedly in the immigrant guidebooks, letters, newspapers, and diaries of the nineteenth century. Its origin is unknown, but it certainly dates as early as the 1750s, when British soldiers pinned it on New Englanders as a term of contempt. By 1819 "Yankee" was still considered derogatory by the Jesuit scholar and president of Georgetown College, Giovanni Antonio Grassi, who wrote in his book *Notizie varie sullo stato presente della repubblica degli Stati Uniti dell' America:*

Among the inhabitants of the United States, those from New England, called the Yankees, are regarded as the most knavish and capable of the most ingenious impositions. The large volume of business that they carry on in all the other states, and the tricks they resort to for profits have fixed this conception on them. It is certain that to deal with such people one needs much sagacity and an exact knowledge of their laws of trade.

Father Grassi undoubtedly reflected the bias of many newcomers, but "Yankee" did not mean danger to everyone. Indeed, the word was used repeatedly as a compliment, and for many of the foreign-born, "Yankee" was synonymous with "American." James Fenimore Cooper observed in 1828 that at home "the native of even New York, though of English origin, will tell you he is not a Yankee. . . . But, out of the United States, even the Georgian does not hesitate to call himself a 'Yankee.' " The *Congressional Record* of May 7, 1874, quoted one member of the House of Representatives, who stated unequivocally: "When I say a Yankee, I mean an American."

It was used sometimes as a reference to Americans of English heritage and sometimes by southerners who lumped all northerners together. It referred to commerce, to styles, to manners, to speech, and even to foods. Rich in a variety of meanings, it was used as a noun, an adjective, a verb, and even an adverb. Untranslatable, it was a word that millions of immigrants heard or saw before they arrived. In C. L. Fleischmann's *Nordamerikanische Landwirth* (1848), it appears typically: "*Sie werden von verschiedener Grösse, Schwere und Form gemacht; die sogenannte Kentucky-Axt . . . und die "Yankee Heavy-Ax" sind die besten und gesuchtesten.*"*

At times encompassing too much, "Yankee" implied a past history of pioneering, of colonial settlement, and of revolution. For the immigrant, it implied "them," not "me." But then the word "immigrant" was invented in America, too.

Jedidiah Morse's *American Geography* of 1789 is credited with being one of the earliest printed works to use the word: "There are in this state [New York] many immigrants from Scotland, Ireland, Germany, and some few from France." By 1809, an English traveler could write that "*Immigrant* is perhaps the only new word, of which the circumstances of the United States has in any degree demanded the addition to the English language."

Throughout the early colonial era, the settlers, who had moved *out* of their homes in Europe and Africa, were called "emigrants." But the notion that they were moving *into* someplace new demanded another word—"immigrant." So by the start of the nineteenth century there were words to distinguish those who were here from those who were on their way.

Throughout the nineteenth century, as millions of newcomers, the "ragged regiments of Europe" (as described by one journalist), poured into American ports, a second migration was taking place in America itself. An army of settlers was advancing across the continent in pursuit of a new and better life. This western expansion together with the western migration from Europe make up two of the persistent themes in our history. While each has been studied in itself, little has been done to interpret their relationship.

What did the immigrant do when he landed in America? Did he join the pioneer in the relentless advancement of civilization? [98] It is difficult to determine how many found themselves on the frontier before the Civil War, because not until 1850 did census reports distinguish between native Americans and those of foreign birth.

*They are made in different size, weight, and shape; the so-called Kentucky ax . . . and the "Yankee heavy ax" are the best and most wanted.

This much, however, seems clear. Between 1790 and 1860, relatively few immigrants joined the vanguard of the westward movement. The professional trapper and the Indian trader, whose exploits created some of the popular literature in both America and Europe, were seldom foreign-born. Even the frontiersman, who followed in the second wave of western expansion, was more apt to be ''Yankee'' than German or Irish. Renowned for his skill with the ''American ax'' and the ''American rifle,'' the Yankee had a reputation for knowing, almost innately, the ways of gathering food, clearing land, building shelter, and surviving the haunting solitude of frontier life. One observer wrote in 1844:

English agriculturists will do better by settling in the eastern states, upon land partly brought into cultivation, though the price of this land be higher, than they will in travelling to the far west. There are large tracts of good land to be had in New York, New Jersey, Pennsylvania, and other eastern states. The Yankees are leaving these states and these lands in shoals, and stretching themselves out to the farthest west, to Wisconsin, Iowa, and even the Oregon territory; let them go, they are the best pioneers for settling that country.

Ten years later, an English writer concurred: ''The west may be best settled by American pioneers, with constitutions and habits adapted to the new regions. . . .''

The Yankee frontiersman, according to the general pattern of western settlement, was followed in the third stage of expansion by the pioneer farmer, who was, more often than not, a native son. As the dean of immigration history, Marcus Lee Hansen, has noted, the pioneer farmer was still a backwoodsman who used an ax as often as a plow. His lifestyle was simply a repetition of that practiced by his ancestors, the early colonial settlers.

98
Title page illustration from Frederick Goddard, *Where to Emigrate and Why* (1869).

The Immigrant Farmer

The fields of Europe had been cleared for centuries. How different was the land in America! The art of clearing and preparing the soil demanded skills that were not a part of the immigrant's European experience. The tall, thick forests that abounded on the east coast were both a treasure and an obstacle: the trees provided a rich raw resource for building fences, tools, and homes; they also served as a natural blockade to any would-be farmer. From the Indians the European colonists learned the techniques of destroying trees by burning and by girdling—cutting through the bark all the way around the trunk.

Along the tidewater were swampland and marshes which had to be drained, an often defeating task for the novice. In New England the farmer fought against the glacial residue of earlier epochs. Stone after stone was removed and stacked to make fences. Today the picturesque remains of the farmer's drudgery can be seen snaking through the forests of New England.

All this work—clearing forests, draining swamps, and removing stones—was only the first, rudimentary step toward long-term survival. From north to south in the seventeenth century the new Americans pursued a subsistence agriculture which supported some other major economic activity. Pennsylvania developed possibly the most flourishing subsistence farming. The commercial production of tobacco, an American crop with American methods and uses, began early in Virginia and Maryland and developed commercially almost exclusively in the upper South. The lower South had hesitantly begun rice culture, but as the seventeenth century ended, men in the Carolinas still found hides and furs the most rewarding commodities. Meanwhile, the rapid increases in population in Europe and in the West Indies were creating consumers for American foods as the eighteenth century got under way.

Europeans wanted primarily European foods rather than exotic Indian crops; comparatively non-perishable and easily transported, grains—particularly wheat [**99**]—and processed meat such as hams and salt pork met European preferences. In the commercial production of these commodities American farmers embraced the best European technology that was compatible with the American scene. Contrary to a European view common at the time, the immigrants did not bring the worst available methods to the New World. Nor did the Americans allow any deterioration of stock or plants without practical reasons.

Most European criticism about American farming centered on practices of no consequence to American farmers selling in a world market. True, Americans tended toward slovenly cultivation, but niceness of method mattered little if the land yielded an abundant exportable surplus. Americans paid less attention than Europeans to fertilizer, but they at first had less need for it. Livestock, in spite of nearly continual importation from Europe, tended to decline from a European standpoint. Still, the animals yielded meat of a quality suitable for export, and the hardy American animals could survive in spite of casual care and the absence of barns and sheds. American dairy cows yielded ridiculously low volumes of milk, butter, and cheese, but dairy products then served only the resident Americans. The corn-and mast-fed hogs of America provided ham that was equal to any in Europe.

New Englanders tended to concentrate on animals, the middle Atlantic on grains, the upper South on tobacco, and the lower South on rice and indigo. The Revolutionary War disrupted the marketing from the farmers' view, but the major commercial commodities remained largely unchanged in the years immediately after the war. Indigo declined and then disappeared as a major export commodity, but cotton almost at once replaced it.

The fact that by the end of the eighteenth century the once little villages that dotted the bays and inlets of the east coast had joined a belt of populated areas extending to the Appalachian Mountains is a success story with few parallels. Moreover, it became part of the Yankee heritage. Early in the nineteenth century, as the Yankee pioneer left the family farm in New York State or Massachusetts and made his way into the Ohio Valley or farther west, he went to battle the wilderness and become self-sufficient as his forebears had been [**100A–100D**].

99
Winnowing basket made of
woven wood and fibers with
leather patches. New York, c.
1775–1800. Since antiquity,
winnowing baskets have
been used to separate chaff
from grain. D 40½″.

100A

100B

100C

100D

100A–100D
The dream of pioneer settlers throughout America was to build an agricultural kingdom. It was pictured in O. Turner's *History of the Holland Purchase*, published in Buffalo, New York, in 1850. The four scenes cover a period of forty years, and they show the evolution of a New York farm from a simple log cabin with a few acres of cleared land to an enterprise that extends to the horizon. Success of this magnitude eluded most immigrants, but it was the life force of their dreams. It made their labor and sacrifices, as well as their expenditures on essential equipment, seem worthwhile. Reverend D. R. Thomason noted the sacrifice in his *Hints to Emigrants* (1848):

Alas, for you my friend, a new settler! You will have little to do now with poetry or song, with flowers or birds. For a while, at least, you will be employed only with the stern realities of a struggle for subsistence. In encountering the forests, you will be, in a certain sense, at war with nature; and the fabled deities of the woods—Diana and her nymphs—will mediate signal vengeance for the profanation of which you will be guilty. The havoc which your axe will commit in their sylvan shades, they will carry amid the finer feelings of your cultivated nature. Happy for you, if by the time you might gather about you a portion of the refinement and embellishment of your past existence, the habit of living without them has not destroyed their relish, and indisposed you for the effort necessary to procure them.

147

As the Yankee moved out, the immigrant moved in. The immigrant farmer first appeared in appreciable numbers in the fourth stage of western expansion—following in the footsteps of the trapper, the frontiersman, and the pioneer farmer. His timetable for occupying cleared farmland was very regular: Ohio, Pennsylvania, and western New York in the 1820s; Missouri, Illinois, and southern Wisconsin in the 1840s; eastern Iowa and Minnesota in the 1850s and 1860s, and the prairies in the 1870s.

The farmer who found himself knee-deep in the black soil of Ohio or Indiana may have been spared the backache of clearing the forest, but he encountered equally demanding and unique conditions. Most had been raised in traditional agriculture, intensively farming only a few acres of land, raising a variety of fruits and vegetables, and generally consuming everything produced. The farming experience in America was different beyond belief. Once the immigrant farmer moved across the Appalachians, he found it most profitable to raise many acres of a single crop. The switch from intensive farming with variety to extensive, one-crop agriculture made the farmer an entrepreneur, subject to the rise and fall of prices in a freewheeling market economy.

Throughout the nineteenth century the immigrant farmer had to deal with a variety of unfamiliar soils, weather conditions, terrains, and vegetation. While a Pennsylvania farmer might use a wooden pitchfork [101] to stack his hay and a Spanish-American farmer would borrow tools from Europe [102, 103A, 103B] for some of his chores, most immigrants learned to use a new agricultural technology: these tools were the product of American ingenuity, symbolized by the American plow [104A–104D, 105] but including disk harrows, seeding machines, automatic planters, expanding cultivators, cradle scythes [106A, 106B], reapers [107A, 107B], and windmills [108].

These new tools were factory made. From having virtually no industry in 1801, America rose to be a leading industrial power in 1900, with more railroads and more manufactured goods per capita than any other nation. The farm implement and machinery industry was an important part of this industrialization.

In these years the cities of the East grew fantastically, and wilderness outposts became gigantic metropolises. Within one man's lifetime Chicago increased from 350 people in 1830 to 112,000 in 1860 to 1,099,000 in 1890. The rich cities provided even greater markets for the farmers' produce, and the rapidly developing transportation system made farming profitable in remote regions. Farmers also felt the advantages of the return flow of goods and services: city people made a countless range of devices for the country farmer.

Industrialization and urbanization were accompanied by a dramatic burst of activity in invention and discovery, which had a delayed but considerable impact on farm methods and technology. Included were such diverse elements as the invention of the cotton gin by Eli Whitney in 1793, the introduction of Mexican Upland cotton in 1805, the discovery of the cause of Texas fever in cattle in 1889, and the invention of the internal combustion tractor in 1892. These and many other achievements substantially changed the farm enterprise in two major directions: advances in technology allowed farmers to do more in less time; discoveries in science allowed farmers to increase the yield from the land [109].

Instead of enjoying greater leisure, the farmer usually used the saved time for more work. On occasion he found outside employment, a practice that became even more common in the next century. Greater man-hour efficiency gave the farmer more time to devote to managing his enterprise, to keeping records, and to studying his business.

Technological efficiency also allowed farmers to use more land and more animals, and the size of farms increased steadily across the century. The expenses of the new machines and the purebred livestock could most profitably be absorbed if the farmer specialized in one or at most two types of enterprise. So the greater efficiency created specialization, and with specialization came even greater efficiency. For the consumers, foreign and domestic, greater farming efficiencies resulted in abundant food at comparatively low cost.

Not only did the immigrant bring with him a willingness to farm an alien land; he made specific contributions to American agriculture by bringing with him plants and animals that proved especially successful under the often hostile conditions of the New World. Turkey Red wheat, introduced in 1873 by Mennonites from Russia, not only survived drought and yielded well, but provided the genetic elements for new breeds of wheat. Even earlier, in 1857, Wendelin Grimm, an immigrant from Külsheim, Germany, brought some twenty pounds of alfalfa seed to Carver County, Minnesota. Over a number of years the alfalfa acclimatized, and winter-kill was no longer a problem. (While it was known locally, it was not until the turn of this century that Grimm alfalfa was accepted as a hardy and a superior general feed crop for the Northwest.)

The empty lands of America were in themselves a splendid resource in aiding national growth. They were the distant magnets that attracted millions. The railroads, which eventually crossed the land, were financed in part by huge land grants from the federal government. And much of the food, minerals, and other natural resources were produced from the land by people who were lured with the promise of a better life. Advertising posters, booster pamphlets, real estate plans, guidebooks, and general promotional literature were published by railroad companies, midwestern states, and private land developers—each competing for the westward-bound Yankee and the recently transplanted immigrant. The literature was often printed in German script, in Norwegian, Swedish, and even Finnish [110]. It called for muscles, determination, and cash—in return, it offered economic freedom, even wealth. One enthusiastic newspaper, writing about the Minnesota territory, promised:

Every man who is desirous of possessing a home of his own in a healthy and prosperous country . . . who wishes to earn a comfortable maintenance for himself and family, and in a few years attain independence and wealth, is earnestly invited to come forward at once. Let such come and be convinced that as choice farming lands as are to be found "under the sun" are here offered for sale. Information will be furnished on application in person, or by letter, in English, German, Dutch, or Scandinavian languages.

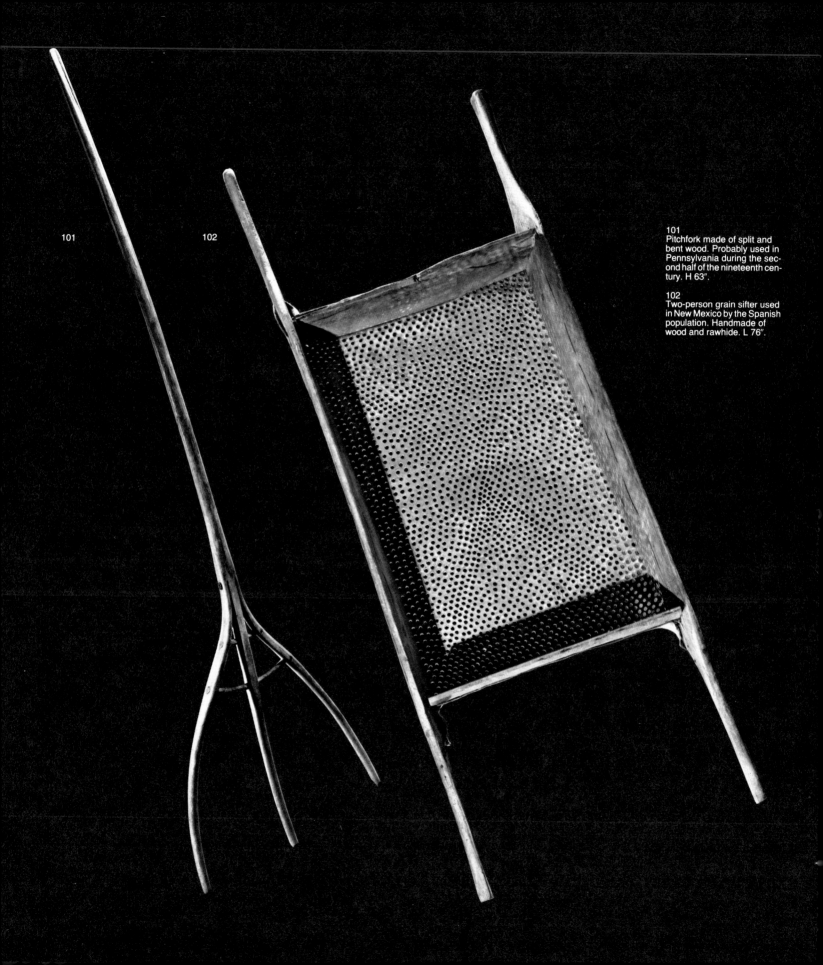

101
102

101
Pitchfork made of split and bent wood. Probably used in Pennsylvania during the second half of the nineteenth century. H 63".

102
Two-person grain sifter used in New Mexico by the Spanish population. Handmade of wood and rawhide. L 76".

103A

03B

103A
Molino, nineteenth century. In this notched-log building, set directly over a channeled raceway, the father of Maximiano Cruz ground wheat and corn and chili for Spanish families near Trampas, a village in the Sangre de Cristo mountains of New Mexico.

103B
This wooden hopper, in the Cruz grist mill (*molino*) at Trampas, held grain which the miller fed into a pair of hand-cut volcanic stones, housed in a drum and turned by a shaft rising through the floor timbers from an ancient, horizontal type of water wheel.

104A
"Old Colony Strong" plow, late eighteenth to early nineteenth century. The moldboard is made of wood and covered with thick straps of iron. It was the first important stage in the evolution of the metal plow. L 101″.

104B
The Mahlon Smith plow. By the mid-nineteenth century, both the Eagle and the Smith plows were the standard types used throughout the North. Though exceptionally functional in northern soils, they would not have been effective in the prairie sod. Both were mass-produced and made of iron; their parts were interchangeable. On the Eagle plow, note the moldboard, which follows a design conceived by Thomas Jefferson. L 92″.

104C
Eagle plow (cast iron). Made in Massachusetts in the late 1840s to early 1850s. L 90″.

104D
A replica of John Deere's plow, used to farm the soils of the prairie. It was a special tool made of a steel share jointed with a wrought-iron moldboard. More than ten thousand a year were being produced by 1857. It answered the peculiar needs of the farmers who wrestled with the new environment of the Midwest. On the prairie, the sod roots ran deep and they intertwined to form a subterranean mat which defied penetration. The conventional plows often broke in the tangle.

Generally, the first crop was corn. The mechanical action of the corn roots broke up the soil, but with the second plowing the heavy soil stuck on the moldboard and the farmer had to carry a paddle to clean the plow repeatedly. In 1833 John Lane tried to overcome this problem with a highly polished moldboard made of steel, but the John Deere design proved most effective. L 76½″.

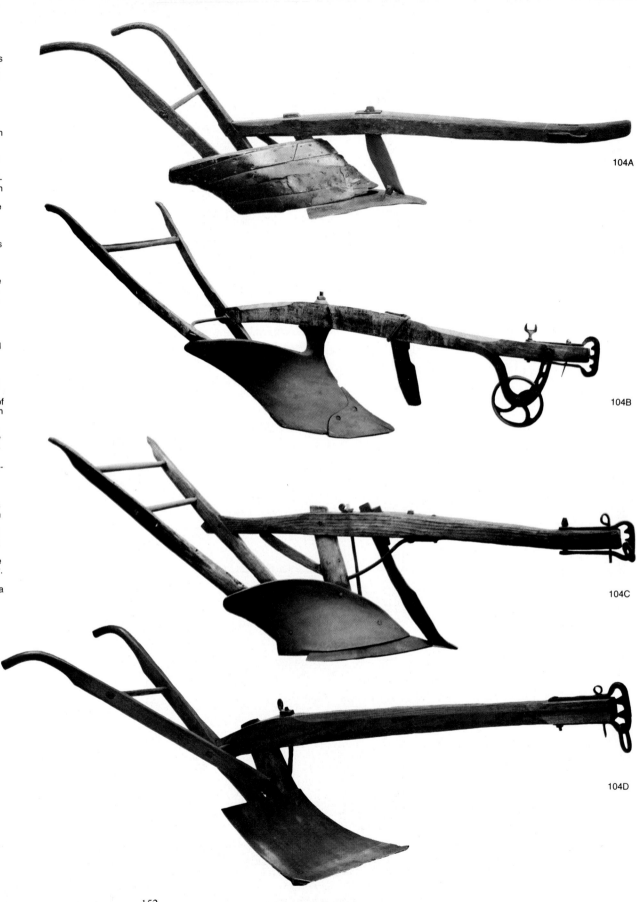

104A

104B

104C

104D

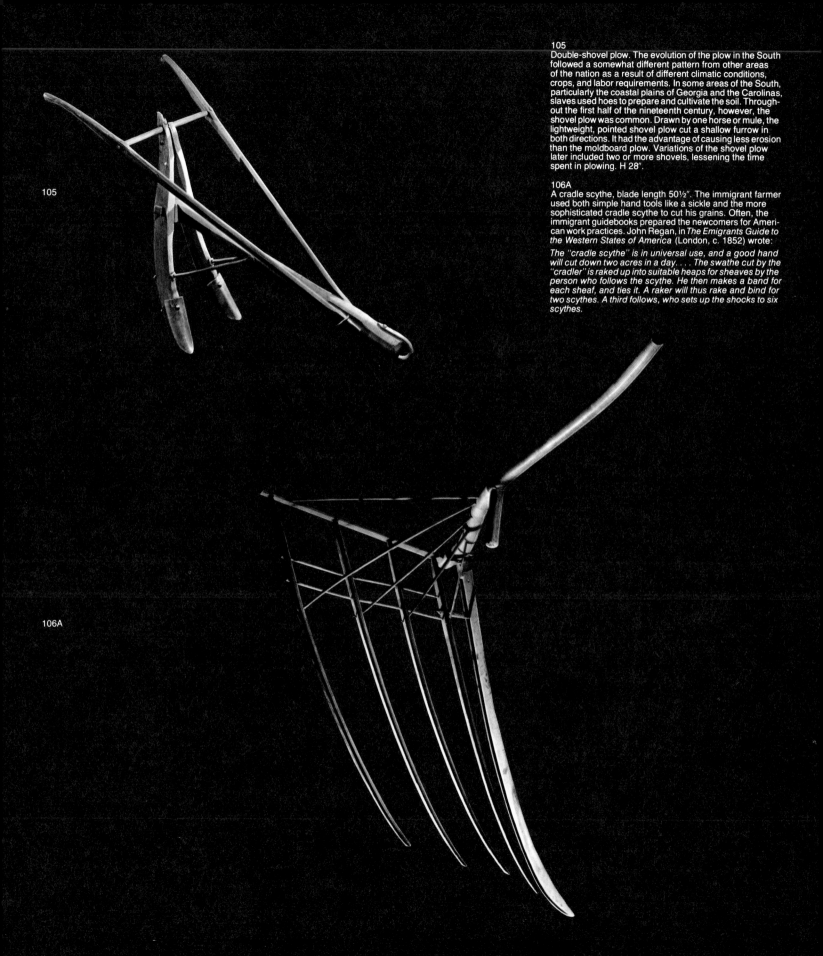

105

105

Double-shovel plow. The evolution of the plow in the South followed a somewhat different pattern from other areas of the nation as a result of different climatic conditions, crops, and labor requirements. In some areas of the South, particularly the coastal plains of Georgia and the Carolinas, slaves used hoes to prepare and cultivate the soil. Throughout the first half of the nineteenth century, however, the shovel plow was common. Drawn by one horse or mule, the lightweight, pointed shovel plow cut a shallow furrow in both directions. It had the advantage of causing less erosion than the moldboard plow. Variations of the shovel plow later included two or more shovels, lessening the time spent in plowing. H 28″.

106A

A cradle scythe, blade length 50½″. The immigrant farmer used both simple hand tools like a sickle and the more sophisticated cradle scythe to cut his grains. Often, the immigrant guidebooks prepared the newcomers for American work practices. John Regan, in *The Emigrants Guide to the Western States of America* (London, c. 1852) wrote:

The "cradle scythe" is in universal use, and a good hand will cut down two acres in a day. . . . The swathe cut by the "cradler" is raked up into suitable heaps for sheaves by the person who follows the scythe. He then makes a band for each sheaf, and ties it. A raker will thus rake and bind for two scythes. A third follows, who sets up the shocks to six scythes.

106A

106B
Curved-blade grain sickle.
L 16″.

107A
McCormick reaper, Model of
1834. In 1833, Obed Hussey
patented a reaper which he
began to manufacture on a
small scale for the American
farmer. Cyrus Hall McCormick
patented his reaper in 1834,
but not until the 1840s was it
improved to be commercially
produced. In 1848, foresee-
ing the Midwest as the great
grain-growing center of the
country, McCormick estab-
lished a factory at Chicago.
Before long he completely
overshadowed Hussey, his
first major rival. H 14¾″.

107B
A McCormick reaper in the
field.

106B

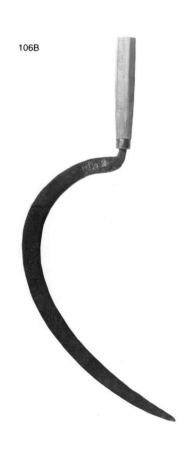

107A

108

108
1880-type Eclipse windmill, rescued from its original packing crate and erected in Stinett, Texas, by J. B. Buchanan
and J. Laubhan. Thin wooden sails form a 12-foot-diameter
windmill with a rudder extending back 14 feet to catch the
wind. Perhaps the supreme symbol of our ability to survive
on the Great Plains of North America is the windmill, which
punctuates prairies from North Dakota to southern Texas
and powers pumps that draw up subsurface water for ranch
and farm. The principle of a wind-powered engine came to
America from Europe in the seventeenth century. The Dutch
windmills often had four broad sails and a larger, enclosed
pump house, in comparison to those developed for the
Midwest in the 1860s. In that decade, dislocation after the
Civil War, extension of the railroad, and the Homestead Act
opened millions of acres to American farmers. Early innovations on the wooden windmill were developed by Connecticut inventor John Burnham and machinist Daniel Halladay,
and by L. H. Wheeler. Halladay moved his production to
Batavia, Illinois, while Wheeler's Eclipse Wind Engine
Company operated from Beloit, Wisconsin. To avoid racing
in high winds, alterations were made with weights, pivots,
and hinges that resulted in practical windmills which sold by
the thousands each year. In the 1870s iron windmills began
to be patented. They became popular after an engineer
working for Halladay, Thomas O. Perry, developed
adjustable-pitch sheet-steel sails and back-gearing wheels
to protect the pump in heavy wind. In 1892 alone, the
Chicago-Noyes firm sold 20,000 windmills. Except for the
initial investment, many American farmers believed their
mills provided power that was "as free as the wind." H 30'.

109
Cover of Winona and St.
Peter Railroad Co. pamphlet,
c. 1879.

110
In 1843, commercial fertilizer was introduced to the United
States with the importation of Peruvian guano, a sea-bird
manure high in nitrogen. Around one million tons were imported in the 1850s. At the same time the United States
began to manufacture its own mixed fertilizers at a few
hundred tons per year, and superphosphates from bones
and nitrophosphates also became available commercially.
Better soil management through the use of manure and
commercial fertilizers dramatically increased agricultural
production. By 1900, in the north central states alone, farmers were spending $7,274,000 on commercial fertilizers
a year.

109

Wegweiser

— nach —

Süd-Minnesota und Ost-Dakota.

Die

Winona und St. Peter Eisenbahn

öffnet dem Landwirth eine Gegend, die für Ackerbau ihres Gleichen sucht.

1,160,000 Acres Vorzügliches Land

unter den liberalsten Bedingungen und zu äußerst billigen Preisen zu verkaufen.

Preise von 2 bis 8 Dollars pr. Acre, auf lange Frist.

12½ Prozent Nachlaß bei Bar-Kauf.

Auf den Ländereien haften keinerlei Schulden oder sonstige Verbindlichkeiten.

Grundstücke, groß oder klein, nach Belieben des Käufers, verkauft die

Winona und St. Peter Eisenbahn-Gesellschaft.

Chas. E. Simmons,
Land-Commissär,
im Geschäfts-Gebäude der Chicago und North-Western Eisenbahn-Gesellschaft zu Chicago in Illinois.

H. M. Burchard,
Land-Agent
zu Marshall in Minnesota.

Dampfpressen-Druck von John Anderson & Co., 87 und 89 Franklin Str., Chicago.

110

The most dramatic of all the real estate programs in the story of America's foreign-born was sponsored by the federal government itself. This was the Homestead Law of 1862. It offered 160 acres of land free to any adult American, or to any immigrant who promised to become an American citizen (for whom a small legal fee was required), if he would live on the land and farm a part of it for at least five years. That was all! The most popular tracts of land were located approximately in the northern triangle bordered by Canada, the Mississippi and the Missouri rivers. The area would eventually become the portions of the states of Minnesota, Iowa, and the Dakotas. To the west lay the plains and the mountains. To the south were public lands generally considered to be of poor quality. Those immigrants who took up agriculture in the 1870s and 1880s found themselves within the triangle. The dominant groups came from Scandinavia, supported by numerous colonies of Germans and Englishmen.

The Scandinavians—mainly the Swedes—had flirted with the New World for several centuries; their colony on the Delaware River even antedated the experiment of William Penn to the north. Their New Sweden prospered for several decades in the seventeenth century, and during that time they introduced the log cabin. In 1655 New Sweden was conquered by the Dutch, who in time surrendered it to the English. In the eighteenth century Swedish scientists, including Carolus Linnaeus, the father of systematic botany, studied the vegetation of North America, thus maintaining an intellectual link with the future homeland of thousands of Scandinavians.

During the nineteenth century the sturdy nations on the Baltic Sea experienced a population explosion as the birth rate rose and the death rate declined. Crop failures, dislocations brought about by the industrial revolution and the mechanization of agriculture, and prejudice by and against the state religion—Lutheranism—all contributed to the rise of "American fever" in these northern lands.

At first a trickle, then a flood: 10,000 a year in 1860 to 105,326 in 1882. To the Homestead lands they went, first to Iowa and Wisconsin and Illinois, then to Minnesota and the Dakotas. Of the Swedes, 25 percent retained their role as farmer—dairy farming being a specialty—while others quarried or mined or cut down trees, all overwhelmingly directed to the riches of the land.

The Swedes were accompanied by the Norwegians, so many that only Ireland could claim a greater percentage of manpower lost to America. Their pilgrimage to and their lives in America were captured in the cold realism of Ole Rölvaag's novels. In one, *Giants in the Earth*, the all-important minutiae of everyday life are vividly described. The scene is a caravan of Norwegians migrating from Minnesota to the Dakota Territory:

A stocky, broad shouldered man walked at the head of the caravan. He seemed shorter than he really was, because of the tall grass around him and the broad-brimmed hat of coarse straw which he wore. A few steps behind him followed a boy of about nine years of age. The boy's blond hair was clearly marked against his brown sunburnt neck; but the man's hair and neck were of exactly the same shade of brown. From the looks of these two, and still more from their gait, it was easy to guess that here walked father and son.

Behind them a team of oxen jogged along; the oxen were drawing a vehicle which once upon a time might have been a wagon, but which now on account of its many and grave infirmities, ought long since to have been consigned to the scrap heap– . . . . The rear of the wagon was stowed full of numberless articles, all the way up to the top. A large immigrant chest at the bottom of the pile, very long and high, devoured a big share of the space; around and above it were piled household utensils, tools, implements, and all their clothing.

Hitched to this wagon and trailing behind was another vehicle, homemade and very curious-looking, so solidly and quaintly constructed that it might easily have won a place in any museum. Indeed, it appeared strong enough to stand all the jolting from the Atlantic to the Pacific . . . It, too, was a wagon, after a fashion; at least, it had been intended for such. The wheels were made from pieces of plank fitting roughly together; the box, considerably wider than that of the first wagon, was also loaded full of provisions and house-hold gear, covered over with canvas and lashed down securely. Both wagons creaked and groaned loudly every time they bounced over a tussock or hove out of a hollow. . . . "Squeak, squeak!" said the one . . . "Squeak, squeak!" answered the other . . . The strident sound broke the silence of centuries.

Even more immediate in impact than novels were letters home from Finns, Danes, Swedes, and Norwegians living in America. They wrote about everyday life, the joys, the disappointments, the rewards. They wrestled with the sod and devised schemes for cutting through it. They faced the problem of getting water to their livestock and crops. They searched for lumber in an area where lumber was scarce. They tolerated living in a house built of sod and endured long winters of wind and frigid temperatures which were all too reminiscent of home. For some, the struggle was too much; for others, including the following, the sacrifice was worth it.

Letter from Johannes Nordboe, at Ottawa, LaSalle County, Illinois, to Hans L. Rudi:

April 30, 1837

If God grants my children life and strength, and if they themselves are willing to work, they will be far more fortunate here than in Norway. It is very easy to raise cattle here and also to till the soil. This year as well as last we have had nothing with which to feed the cattle except what my two sons have cut on the prairie, amounting to about thirty tons. . . .

The summers are extremely beautiful. Then the whole country, both woodland and prairies, is bedecked with grass and flowers of all colors, which bloom from earliest spring to late autumn. When some fall, others come up. Some big, yellow ones in the autumn have stalks ten feet high. The summer may be compared to an earthly paradise, but the winter, on the contrary, may be likened to a mountain climate.

From Gjert G. Hovland, at Middle Point, Illinois, to a friend:

July 6, 1838

Anyone who wants to make good here has to work, just as in all other places in the world. But here everything is better rewarded. . . .

We who are accustomed to work since childhood feel that this is Canaan when we consider the fertile soil that without manuring brings forth such rich crops of everything. Norway cannot be compared to America any more than a desert can be compared to a garden in full bloom.

From Hans Barlien, at St. Francisville on the Des Moines River, Missouri, to the Reverend Jens Rynning:

April 23, 1839

All kinds of people from all nations of the world live together here like brothers and sisters; and in spite of the fact that there are no garrisons of soldiers, police, and the like, you never hear anything about theft, begging or any noticeable ill will between neighbors.

When such letters were published in the local newspapers of European towns and villages, they reached hundreds or maybe thousands of eyes. Of course, the letters of praise were countered by notes of doom and discouragement, but in the long run the positive recommendations were triumphant. Phrases such as "here nobody has to be poor" or "everything has something new, something distinctive about it" were tempered by the truth that work in America was "very hard, as you have to accomplish in one day here what you get three days to do in Norway." These letters sailed across the oceans in growing numbers, reaching over five million pounds in 1900. They symbolized the simple fact that a nation of nations was a transatlantic phenomenon.

Chapter 9

Transportation in Early Nineteenth-Century America

Moving On

Americans are always moving on.
It's an old Spanish custom gone astray,
A sort of English fever, I believe,
Or just a mere desire to take French leave,
I couldn't say. I couldn't really say.
But, when the whistle blows, they go away.
Sometimes there never was a whistle blown,
But they don't care, for they can blow their own
Whistles of willow-stick and rabbit-bone,
Quail-calling through the rain
A dozen tunes but only one refrain,
"We don't know where we're going, but
we're on our way!"

STEPHEN VINCENT BENÉT
"Prelude," *Western Star*

Recent statistics show that the average American family moves to another home every three or four years. Some observers believe that this mobility is distinctly American and is a symptom of a society still seeking its cultural roots. When the nineteenth-century Scandinavian critic Knut Hamsun wrote that in America "every day is a moving day . . . the population is only half-settled," he was not being complimentary. After our break from Europe, Africa, Asia, or wherever, we have been accused of failing to construct a true homeland or, at the least, communities with strong family and cultural ties. Surely we can reply that in an open society the love of mobility and a search for stability are not mutually exclusive.

American society is far too complex to be completely characterized by an insatiable urge to be "moving on." But we can share the fascination of a mid-nineteenth century English traveler who concluded that, for Americans:

Attachment to locality is scarcely known; and shifting from place to place, a thousand miles at a stretch, with a view to bettering the condition, seems to be an ordinary occurrence. There is, in fact, an immense internal migration. New England is continually throwing off swarms towards the newly opened territories and states in the far West; the latest manifestation of this kind being the movement of a colony of settlers from Massachusetts to the newly organized state of Nebraska.

Throughout our prehistory and the shorter colonial era, travel received recognition as a viable, if not an ideal, way of life. The attitude persisted into the last century and helped to promote the settlement of lands made available by the westward movement of the frontier. In the two generations that grew up between the explorations of Lewis and Clark (1804–1806) and our military entry into California and New Mexico (1846–1848), the boundaries of our contiguous states were largely established. And the vast territories between Washington and Sacramento continued to entice the adventurous, the desperate, and the hopeful.

The early vehicles were as diverse as the people themselves. From Indian bullboats and sleds [**111, 112**] to solid-wheel Mexican oxcarts [**113**], the Americans spread out in a diversity of ways. Trails and paths crisscrossed ranges of plateaus, leading on prospectors and trappers, sheep drovers and cowboys, scouts and early topographical engineers committed to geographic description. Better roads provided a way for itinerant preachers and peddlers, for gamblers and highwaymen, for draymen and traders alike. Rivers and streams, under the eye of pilots and canalmen, guided settlers into the Middle West and beyond. And in villages and towns, streets served as display counters for foodstuffs, clothing, and hardware, and as workshops for patrolmen, hucksters, and beggars.

Indeed, as Stephen Vincent Benét sang in *Western Star,* the source of the pattern of American mobility may be too complex to unravel, but it certainly persists today. New means of transportation have made the majority of Americans into commuting workers. The medieval arrangement of combined living and working quarters survives almost entirely in economically depressed sections of our cities, but most of us leave home and travel to work. Moreover, hundreds of thousands of Americans travel as a routine part of earning a living.

Reliability, speed, and standardized technologies have evolved to accommodate this peculiar American desire to keep on moving. But early in the nineteenth century the forms were diverse and unpredictable. The stagecoach and the canal boat slowly became the standard means of travel, only to be replaced in importance by the railroad. Nevertheless, the diversity of forms persisted as each group of Americans pursued its own life style.

As popular as sagas of the covered wagon have become in movie westerns, the truth about western migration in nineteenth-century America is somewhat less picturesque. Countless emigrating travelers—the majority, according to some historians—walked the entire distance to their destinations [**114–116**]. If slightly more fortunate, the traveler could purchase a horse, enabling members of the family to ride alternately, but more likely the horse carried the family belongings [**117, 118**]. Occasionally walking emigrants, such as Mormons on their way to Utah, would be seen with a hand-pushed cart or even with a wheelbarrow [**119**].

Overland travel was accomplished in a number of other ways by those who could afford it. During the early years of the century the stage wagon was used [**120**]. This was a sophisticated form of covered wagon that was going through the evolutionary process of becoming a stagecoach. It contained three or four benches, all facing forward, with the driver sharing the foremost bench with one or two passengers. The seats had no backs, except for the rear bench, and the only attempt toward comfort was the suspension of the body on heavy leather straps, or thorough braces. The cost of stage travel during the first half of the century often ran from five to seven dollars per hundred miles, and the daily travel rate was about fifty miles, or up to eighty with ideal conditions and a hard-pushing driver. Conditions, however, were sometimes so far from ideal that even the smaller figure could not be reached, and passengers occasionally walked over portions of the journey, either by choice or through necessity.

The famous Troy and Concord stagecoaches came into common use after 1830 [**121, 122, 123**]. They had side doors for easy access, seats with backs, a raised driving seat on the front of the coach, and, like the stage wagons, thorough brace suspension. While this suspension system was an improvement over dead-axle vehicles, it was not the most comfortable type available; it was used simply because of its serviceability and ease of maintenance. One traveler of the late 1820s remarked that if his sketch of an American stagecoach did "not recall to persons who have travelled in America the idea of aching bones, they must be more or less than mortal!" [**124, 125**].

Many of the wagons were hired to carry the belongings of several families and were operated by a commercial wagoner. The cost varied from one to two dollars per hundredweight per hundred miles, with a daily travel rate of fifteen to twenty miles, though road and weather conditions as well as mechanical failure often reduced the distance to a few miles a day. Eastern wagons might have been Conestoga or Pitt wagons [**126**], while western types were sometimes Murphy or Gibson wagons [**127**]. Varying in size, all were of a similar construction, with a box body and a cloth cover supported by wooden bows. Since many migrants were farmers, the ordinary farm wagon was often seen moving west. If the traveler was capable of purchasing a wagon expressly for his migration, he paid anywhere from $75 to $150 for it. Besides these heavier wagons, a large number of light wagons and carts were put to use, with or without covers, drawn by one or two horses, mules, or oxen.

In the eastern section of the country accommodations for the emigrants, or "movers," as they were frequently known, were furnished by the numerous taverns. Too often, however, the emigrants were treated badly by the tavern keeper, who gave preferential treatment to those he expected to see again, such as wagoners and others traveling on business. The mover was sometimes refused service, or perhaps given shelter in a rude unfurnished hut or cabin adjacent to the tavern. Even when allowed in the tavern, he might have to yield his chair to a teamster or other regular customer. He was on occasion ill fed, if indeed he was given any food, and at times was even deprived of the warmth of a fire. Sleeping accommodations were frequently filthy and inadequate, if they were available at all. Women and children reportedly spent many nights crying from hunger and discomfort. The movers were frequently forced to push on in search of acceptable accommodations—or any accommodations. If they were unable to find a tavern or other shelter, they would have to camp out. Later in the century, the western emigrants knew in advance, through advice received from earlier travelers either by word of mouth or in publications directed at those intending to move on, if there were no taverns or other accommodations on their route, and they went prepared for living on the road, carrying with them the necessary equipment and provisions.

111
Bullboats were used by Indians of the Great Plains to float possessions across deep streams to new campsites. They were made of lightweight frameworks of branches covered by pieces of buffalo rawhide. D 66".

112
Mandan Indians on the upper Missouri River in 1833–1834 traveling in winter with a sled drawn by dogs in a manner that survived from prehistoric times. The woman carries a load in a pack basket.

111

Bodmer pinx ad nat.

Imp. de Bougeard.

Lasterer R. Hutter.

163

We know too little about those who walked; they have become a faceless infantry of settlers who left only faint traces for historians to study. One reason for their invisibility is that they seldom wrote about their migrating experiences. The written records that do survive were usually produced by those who rode west—first on wagons and canal boats, later on trains. The riders, compared with the walkers, were more prosperous and better educated, and they had the time and often the inclination to reflect about their moving.

If the riders disagreed with one another about the quality of their lodgings, the edibility of the food, and the social contact with the Yankees, they were almost unanimous in decrying the inadequacy of the roads. Road conditions of the nineteenth century were as varied as the travelers and vehicles; yet, generally speaking, they were bad. Delays of several days were not uncommon when traffic was backed up at the often bridgeless streams while travelers waited for high waters to recede before they could attempt a crossing. The badly rutted and potholed roads frequently were studded with tree stumps which had not been removed when the roads were built. Since they were not properly graded or drained and were seldom surfaced, the roads were often seas of mud. A so-called road might in actuality be merely a right of way.

During the 1790s the Philadelphia and Lancaster Turnpike Road was constructed in Pennsylvania, the first notable example of an American road surfaced with broken stone. The stone was not broken to a uniform size nor laid with any system; the result was a firm but rough road. In 1803 the federal government became involved in road financing; it set aside 2 percent from the sale of public lands in Ohio to be applied to the building of roads to and through that state. Initial work took place between 1811 and 1818, when it reached Wheeling, Virginia. In 1823 the road between Hagerstown and Boonsboro, Maryland, was surfaced with broken stone according to the macadam system, developed by the Scottish engineer John MacAdam and introduced into England a few years earlier. Macadam pavement, consisting of small, angular stone fragments, tightly compacted (without the bituminous binders later used), offered a firm, smooth surface; yet it was used during those early years on only a few of the leading highways. Briefly in the 1840s and 1850s a number of plank road surfaces, used earlier in Russia and introduced to this country from Canada, were laid on the main routes leading into some of the larger cities, but the perishable nature of wood gave them a short life. The city streets of nineteenth-century America were paved largely with cobblestones and, after mid-century, stone. After 1850, the rapid spread of rail service across the country, offering greater speed and economy of transport, led to a serious and general deterioration of roads that was not corrected until the twentieth century.

Thus, all through the nineteenth century the traveler was likely to encounter poor road conditions, to the extent that he not only had to leave his stage or wagon and walk at times, but even found it necessary to assist, in the muddy ruts or on a hill, by putting his shoulder to the wheel.

113
Massive, medieval carts entered New Mexico with Spanish settlers before 1600. The sound of the solid wheels turning on the stationary axle could be heard for miles. The specimen pictured probably dates from the 1800s. L 16′.

114
Prehistoric southwestern Indian sandals of braided fibers,
dating from A.D. 100–600.
Smallest, L 8½″.

115
Pointed and square-toe
snowshoes made of wood,
sinew, and cotton by Indians
of northwestern North
America between 1865 and
1900. The large snowshoe is
from the Northwest Territory,
Canada, and the small size is
from the Kutchin Indians.
Smaller, L 29″.

115

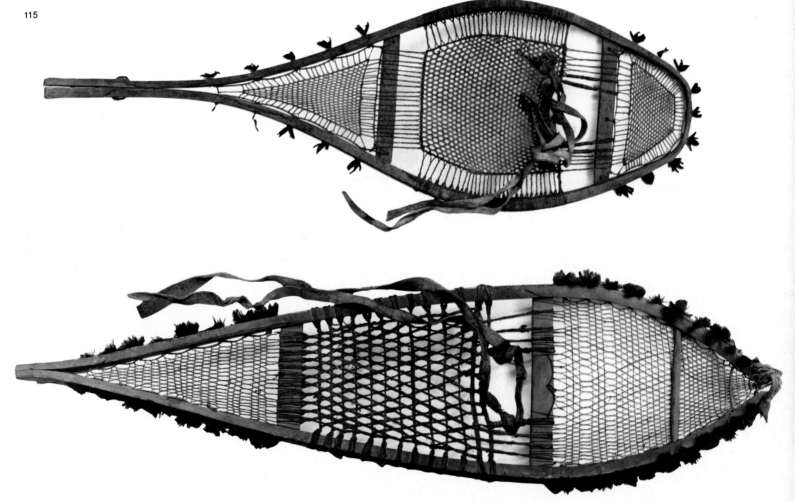

116
Sturdy work shoes of the type
used by workmen and sol-
diers during the period from
the Civil War to near the end
of the century. These were extremely durable if not comfortable. They are made in
rights and lefts, which was not
usual until after the Civil War.

117
Sketch (early nineteenth century) by artist Joshua Shaw
showing a traveler, on foot,
heading west with a pack
horse.

118
This early-nineteenth-century
eyewitness illustration by artist Joshua Shaw shows a
traveling family cooking over
a campfire. They are all wearing moccasins.

117

116

118

119
Wheelbarrow, probably
nineteenth century. Numerous observers noted that
emigrants used wheelbar-
rows to carry their belongings
west. L 75″.

120
A typical stage wagon of the
late eighteenth to early
nineteenth century pulling
away from a tavern.

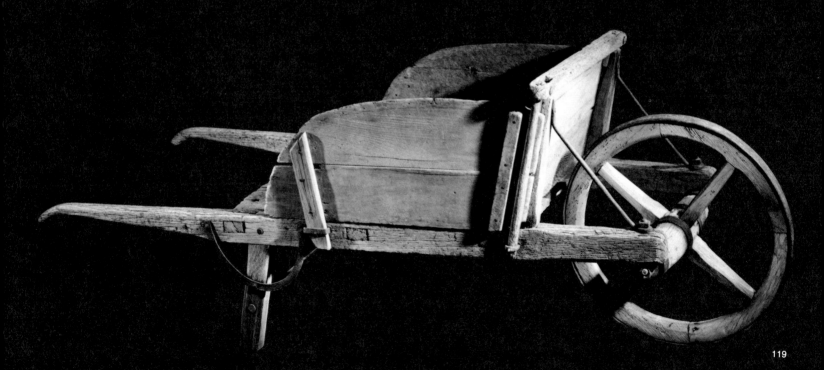

120

121
Predecessor of the Troy or
Concord coach. This drawing
was produced by the British
visitor Captain Basil Hall in
1827–1828. By the late 1820s
the vehicle was refined to include a luggage rack and
passenger seat on the roof.
Compare to 122.

122
This is a lighter version of the
Concord coach, also known
as a hotel coach, which usually carried six passengers. It
served travelers by meeting
trains at the depot and transporting them to hotels. This
illustration is from an original
Abbot, Downing Co. pencil
drawing in the collections of
the New Hampshire Historical
Society.

123
Hack passenger wagon, often
called a mud wagon. This was
a principal means of transportation in the first half of the
nineteenth century. With the
spread of the railroads by
midcentury, its use for long
journeys was reduced, but it
continued to supplement rail
service. In 1880 a six-
passenger model cost almost
$550, half as much as the
more elegant Concord coach.
It was a rugged vehicle, as its
name implies, yet it was valued for its comparative comfort. L 13′3″.

121

122

123

124
Stage advertisement (1821).

125
Stage receipt (1839).

126
The Conestoga wagon developed during the second quarter of the eighteenth century in southeastern Pennsylvania, and took its name from the Conestoga Creek area of Lancaster County. Initially these wagons carried produce to the market in Philadelphia, but eventually they became the general freight carriers in Pennsylvania, Maryland, Virginia, and Ohio. Evolving from a small version of the eighteenth century, large examples such as this 18-foot-long wagon reached a peak of activity between 1810 and 1850 on the Pennsylvania Road and the National Road. In the mid-1850s the growth of the railroads brought an abrupt end to wagon freight in the East. L 18'.

127
Photograph supposedly representing an emigrant wagon train of the post–Civil War era. It is unidentified. It may be authentic or, more probably, it may be a scene from an early motion picture. Wagon trains did attract the notice of foreign observers. T. H. Gladstone in *The Englishman in Kansas* (1857) wrote:

The distance from Leavenworth to Santa Fé is between 800 and 900 miles. In the winter months, when the journey is accompanied by great hardship and peril, the mail is the only communication, which is transported once a month by means of mules. With Oregon the trade on the plains has almost ceased in favour of the route by the Pacific; but the Government has still occasion to use the Oregon track as far as Fort Kearney and Fort Laramie, a distance of 600 miles. The great traffic, however, is to Fort Riley, Fort Munn, and thus to Sante Fé. Independence in Missouri, Kansas City on the border, and Leavenworth, are all made use of as the entrepôts of this trade; and few things can be imagined more strangely picturesque than the sight which these cities present when, in the spring or early summer, their streets are filled with scores of long, cumbrous-looking covered waggons, and hundreds of oxen and mules; while a noisy crew of light-hearted adventurers—Missourian, Spanish, half-breed, and Indian—dressed in every variety of romantic costume, are busied in fitting out their train for its many weeks' journeying over the rolling grassy plains of the Western prairies.

The commerce of the plains, which during more than thirty years, has been rising in importance, has become, since the war with New Mexico, and the removal of commercial restrictions which has followed the war, a most valuable feature in the Kansas trade. Setting aside the very numerous trains in the service of the Government, which maintains communication between Fort Leavenworth and the outposts on the Santa Fé and Oregon routes, the annual value of the regular commerce amounts to from $2,000,000 to $3,000,000. This employs many hundreds of waggons, and a still larger number of men, and tends materially to keep up the price of labour in the territory. Each waggon, again, requires twelve or more oxen, and a great number of mules are also employed on the expeditions. This makes the rearing of stock a very profitable employment for the farm lands in Kansas and Missouri. The trains go almost exclusively during the spring and summer months, when the prairie grass furnishes the necessary food for the animals. According to the season, they get over from ten to twenty miles in the day. A waggon is estimated to carry about 5,500 lb. The expense of transport varies with the season.

NEW LINE OF
STAGES.

Winter Establishment.

This Line will commence running on the 16th inst. from Providence to Worcester, through Smithfield and Uxbridge, twice a week, Viz:

LEAVES Providence Tuesdays and Fridays, at 7 o'clock, A. M. and arrives in Worcester same Evenings.......RETURNING......Leaves Worcester Wednesdays and Saturdays, and arrives in Providence the same Evenings.

N. B.—This Line will connect with the Keene, New-Hampshire, Mail Coaches, leaving Worcester on Wednesdays for the same place.

Books kept at Wesson's, Providence, R. I. at Farnham's, Smithfield, Slatersville, and at Howe and White's, Worcester, Mass.

FARE THREE DOLLARS.....CUSTOMARY WEIGHT OF BAGGAGE ALLOWED.

A. WESSON & SONS.
JOB N. TUTTLE.

Providence, Oct. 9, 1821.

124

125

$ Philadelphia, Feby 7 1839

Received of Mr. *Rockhold*

Eighteen Dollars — Cents, for *one*

Seat in the GOOD INTENT MAIL LINE, by Harrisburg and Chambersburg, to *Pittsburg*

C. A. Malborn

☞ **50 Pounds of Baggage allowed to each Passenger.**

126

127

It had long been the dream of a few farsighted individuals to connect America's natural waterways, for water was the cheapest and easiest way to move large freight shipments. In the 1780s the construction of a few canals was begun, but it was not until 1817, when work on New York's Erie Canal started, that America's canal era commenced. The Erie, connecting the Hudson River (at Albany) with Lake Erie (at Buffalo), spanned 364 miles at an average cost of $20,000 per mile, and was completed by 1825. Originally intended for freight movement, the Erie, and the more than four thousand miles of canals that were built during the next several decades, were soon found to be well suited to passenger travel.

Canals were variously financed by stock companies, lotteries, and state and federal governments. Many made a poor financial showing, and in some cases revenues could not match the operating costs and interest on the original debt. Yet they were of tremendous economic importance. Not only did they move large quantities of goods and passengers, but they also provided employment for the thousands who labored to build them and for the many thousands more who maintained and operated the canals and boats. Unskilled workers, such as Irish and German immigrants, labored for thirty to fifty cents a day, in an era when all work was accomplished by manpower and animal power, assisted by primitive blasting methods. Cities such as Chicago, Akron, and Louisville grew rapidly under the influence of canal traffic, and numerous smaller towns developed along the way.

The canals of nineteenth-century America were generally about forty feet wide at the top, twenty-six feet wide at the bottom, and four feet deep, although the dimensions of both old and new work were often increased as the years progressed. Since the canals frequently traversed terrain of different elevations, it was necessary to construct locks, with gates at both ends, so that a boat could be transferred from one level to another by raising or lowering the water level with the lock. In a few instances, such as the Pennsylvania Canal, it was necessary to use railway cars on inclined planes to raise the boats over an unusually high elevation.

Passengers had a choice of taking either a line boat or a packet boat. The line boat, drawn by two or three mules or occasionally oxen, moved at a rate of one and one-half to two and one-half miles per hour, for a passenger cost of one and one-half to three cents a mile. This low price often did not include food or bedding, so that travelers had to provide for their own needs, or perhaps procure food at taverns or inns along the way. The line boat was commonly used by immigrants for whom cost, not time, was of consequence.

Packet boats traveled about one mile per hour faster than line boats, at a cost of one or two cents more per mile. They were drawn by better stock—usually horses, which accounted for their greater speed—and by the end of a week of travel had covered about 150 miles more than a line boat. The furnishings and accommodations were also better, with meals and bedding provided and in many instances even games, reading material, and music (some boats had an organ on board). Packet boats were used by the more affluent immigrants, and by people on business journeys who wished to save time rather than money.

The canal boat was sixty to eighty feet in length and ten to twelve feet wide. It was more or less a barge with a cabin stretching nearly the entire length, its roof serving as a deck where some luggage could be stored and passengers could sit in fair weather, though they would have to duck frequently as they passed under a low bridge. The forward part of the boat comprised the crew's quarters, followed by a washroom and dressing room for women. Behind this was the women's cabin, the men's cabin, and finally the cook's cabin. Sometimes there was a permanent partition between the men's and women's cabins, but more often only a curtain. The men's cabin was the largest, about forty-five feet long, and during the day it served as the lounge and dining room for all. For meals the crew set up collapsible tables, which could be removed later, or left standing for letter writing, games, or extra beds at night.

Charles Dickens, who took a canal boat trip in 1842, reported that a great variety of food was available. Other travelers complained that captains gave disapproving looks if they helped themselves too freely. Since travelers paid by the mile, an interesting custom developed among some thrifty folk who walked the towpath during the day. As meals were usually served at regular times, these freeloading hikers called for the boat to touch shore for them just about mealtime, paid for one mile, ate a satisfying meal, then went ashore again to continue the journey on foot, sleeping in the woods, or at nearby taverns if the weather turned bad. The practice was eventually overcome by charging a minimum fare of around twenty-five cents, regardless of the distance traveled.

In the evening, folding bunks were let down from the cabin walls. There were usually seven rows of bunks on each side, arranged in three tiers. This allowed twenty-one men to a side, or forty-two in all, plus large numbers of "extras" who slept on the tables and floor. The smaller women's cabin was similarly arranged. The lower row of bunks was often constructed to serve as benches for the passengers during the day. A scanty quantity of bedding was provided for each passenger. Conditions in the cabin were crowded, foul-smelling, often hot, and generally uncomfortable. At night many could not sleep, being bothered by swarms of mosquitoes in summer and by fellow travelers who snored, stirred, or—according to Dickens—spat, all night long ("either . . . they never sleep at all; or they expectorate in dreams. All night long, and every night, on this canal, there was a perfect storm and tempest of spitting . . .").

Arising early in the morning (5 or 6 A.M.), the male passengers went on deck, where they ladled the somewhat polluted canal water into a basin for washing, though Dickens remarked that "many were superior to this weakness." A person who desired to primp a bit could find the public comb and hairbrush hanging near the bar, situated next to the cook's cabin and tended by the cook. A few claimed to have enjoyed the leisurely cross-country trip by canal boat, but most found it a dreadful experience. Wrote Horace Greeley: "I say nothing about the good old times; but if anyone would recall the good old line boats, I object."

Crews for the boats consisted of the captain, a cook, two steersmen, and two animal drivers, the latter four men serving as day and night crews. The two not steering and driving at meal and bed times assisted in preparing the main cabin for the ensuing activity. Any one of the crew or passengers, depending on ability or inclination, might entertain with the organ, fiddle, or accordion. The animals pulling the canal boat were changed at intervals. Relief animals were either kept at relay stations along the canal or carried on board.

Winter brought a halt to all canal traffic. Depending on the severity of the weather, canals were closed down for three to five months of the year. Boats caught in an early freeze were abandoned until spring.

In the mid-nineteenth century the American canal system totaled nearly 4,500 miles, covering much of the Northeast from the Mississippi to the Atlantic as well as parts of the South. The Erie Canal and the Pennsylvania Canal were of national importance, while others were primarily of local significance. Canal passenger travel peaked in the mid-1850s then declined as the railroads spread across the continent. Canal freighting also fell off, but at a slower rate. By 1880 nearly 2,000 miles of canals had been abandoned and the revenues of many surviving canals were not even meeting expenses. The greater speed and comfort or railroads, combined with such negative aspects as high canal construction costs and the impracticality of building canals in some areas, led to the demise of canals. The canal era, begun in 1817, effectively ended in the 1850s, though canals continued to operate throughout the rest of the century.

Canals stimulated the growth of cities and entire states; and in fact, the Erie has been given much credit for helping New York become the Empire State through early industrialization. Canals provided employment for immigrants and native Americans, in building, maintenance, and operation. They helped the farmer get his produce to market and took the products of industry, both in bulk lots by way of freight boats and individually by way of peddler's boats, to the canal communities and beyond. They moved huge freight shipments at a fraction of the cost of wagon transport and carried countless migrants westward.

Chapter 10

Railroads and the Westward-Bound Immigrant

In 1829 the steam railroad came to North America from England. It was clearly an imported technology, but it became an American passion. By 1855 the northeastern United States was operating a dense network of lines [128]. The South and Midwest were developing similar systems, and by 1869 steam cars reached the Pacific coast. By the end of the century half the world's railways were in the United States.

Before we can understand why and in what form the railway came to America, something must be said of its origins. Its ancient beginnings were in the mines of Europe. It was many centuries before the railway's ability to move heavy loads with minimum power suggested the general carriage of goods and passengers. The public railway as we know it today was a late development, essentially a manifestation of the nineteenth century. We are indebted to the British for advancing the primitive industrial tramway into a sophisticated conveyance.

It is not surprising that the railway should emerge in Britain, which, by the mid-eighteenth century, was the dominant industrial power of the world. At this time the British were busy perfecting steam engines, textile machinery, iron bridges, and in general causing the mechanical arts to flourish as they did nowhere else. As the Italians are given to working stone, the English have always shown a facility for shaping iron; they have been described as a "ferruginous race."

To make the railway suitable for speedy long-distance travel, two basic reforms were necessary: a faultless track and mechanical power. Existing civil engineering techniques aided in the construction of level, straight lines. Iron rails, in use since the mid-1700s, offered a smooth, substantial path. And the steam engine, a reasonably compact, powerful machine, by 1800 was easily converted into a self-propelling vehicle. In 1825 these ingredients were brought together: mechanical land transport was at last realized on a commercial scale and easily outran its competition—the canal and the highway. England's railway revolution was under way.

Young America watched these developments with considerable interest. A vast, unsettled inland empire needed some form of communication, and to suit the temper of the energetic population, it had to be developed quickly. Arguments for a national system of highways, canals, and river improvements had been voiced since the beginning of the Republic, but little had been accomplished. Upstart advocates of the new British invention were received with considerable sympathy. They argued that canals were painfully slow and subject to spring floods and winter freezes, highways were equally slow and were the most expensive form of freight haulage, but railroads were fast, cheap, and not subject to seasonal vicissitudes. The partisans mustered enough support so that some railway construction was under way by 1830. The first steam locomotive had been landed here a year before and others followed [129].

America was the first country outside Great Britain to give the steam railway a considered trial. Within two years we were not merely convinced, we were fanatical converts. We speak glibly today of America's love affair with the automobile, but we forget our earlier romance with the railroad. And it was no mere infatuation; it was a burning passion. We built railroads faster than anyone in the world. By 1850 we had outbuilt the British by 1,500 miles. The pace quickened to 2,000 to 10,000 miles a year thereafter. The system developed, as might be expected, from the settled east coast westward. The New England network was finished by 1850, and the Appalachian barrier was crossed a few years later. An east-west connection was made with the midwestern lines previously built. As the Civil War began, the northern states east of the Mississippi River were crisscrossed by rail lines and the South had a comprehensive system which lacked only a few important connections. West of the Mississippi, however, steam cars were almost unknown.

The technology was borrowed directly and unashamedly from Britain. American engineers went overseas to copy what had been so painfully developed. William Strickland was sent over in 1825 by a group of Philadelphia worthies interested in bolstering their city's trade position against New York's recently opened Erie Canal. Horatio Allen went abroad three years later, and the Baltimore and Ohio sent their chief engineer and several assistants. The observations and reports of these men, together with several general texts on the subject, were all that was known of the railway in America. Moreover, the locomotives, rails, wheels, axles, and other necessary hardware were imported directly from Britain. That our pioneer lines were thus facsimiles of the British is not surprising. What is, is how fast the British plan was abandoned and a uniquely American style of construction and rolling stock came into being.

First to go was the method of roadway construction. The English conceived of a railway as a monumental civil engineering feat. Enormous cuts and fills, masonry viaducts, and lengthy tunnels produced level, direct roadbeds. Tracks were constructed with massive stone blocks as ties; iron chairs mounted on the blocks held wrought-iron rails. It was a railway intended to last for the ages, as indicated by the British term ''Permanent Way.'' Such excellence, however, cost $179,000 a mile, a price Britain could afford but America could not.

America was looking for a provisional form of transit. We needed a cheap, easy-to-build railway. We had great distances to cover: centers of population were not only widely separated, but the land between was sparsely settled and traffic density was thus low. There was also a chronic shortage of both capital and labor.

The most obvious way to lower costs and hasten construction was to lower standards of construction. The elimination of extensive grading was the first economy: railroads would follow the natural rise and fall of the land. Tracks would go around hills rather than tunneling through. Wooden trestles took the place of masonry viaducts, and the track was fabricated from local timber, with only a thin iron strap for the running surface. The result was a decidedly inferior railroad. It was makeshift, dangerous, and expensive to operate and maintain. But it was wonderfully cheap to build; our costs were only one-sixth of the British plan.

Such economies were apparent to most American engineers after building only a few miles of track. Converts to the thrifty American plan were legion by the early 1830s. But a few stubbornly held to the old pattern, notably the Boston and Lowell Railroad. Financed by the Boston textile barons Nathan Appleton and Patrick Tracy Jackson, it could afford to build on the best plan. It was decided to copy exactly the finest railway in England, the Liverpool and Manchester. Grades were held to ten feet per mile; only broad curves were tolerated. The best wrought-iron edge rail was imported from England, and local quarries were pressed hard to produce some 82,000 stone-block ties. For all this, the project proved a failure.

After the first hard frost the stone-block ties were heaved up, throwing the track out of alignment. Similar derangements were noted as far south as Delaware (the Newcastle and Frenchtown Railway). Stone-block ties were not suitable to the North American climate.

The American strap rail presented numerous problems too. It was admittedly an expedient: it was weak and could sustain slow speeds only; even conservative operating practice did not prevent its rapid deterioration. After only four years of service, the strap rails on the Philadelphia and Columbia Railroad were so dilapidated that they were reported ''a fruitful source of injury to cars and engines.'' Passengers were wary of travel on strap-rail lines lest a ''snake head'' pierce the bottom of the car's floor. To reassure its passengers, one midwestern line advertised that the undersides of their cars were sheathed in iron to guard against loose bars. The defects of strap rail were recognized from the beginning, and most roads converted to some form of solid rolled rails as soon as they could afford to rebuild. This process was hastened in at least one instance by legislation when New York State passed a public law in 1847 requiring the elimination of strap rail. Most strap rail tracks were gone by the beginning of the Civil War.

From the 1830s, when steam railroads first became an important part of inland transport in America, provision was made to carry emigrating settlers westward. The service provided was economical but spartan, as might be expected. Some railroads used convertible boxcars outfitted with bench seats that could be removed for the eastward trip, when the cars carried merchandise. Such elementary comforts as lighting, heating, and toilet facilities were unknown in such boxcars. Even windows were considered a luxury.

As late as 1867 the Grand Trunk Railway of Canada was carrying immigrants in ordinary boxcars without seats. Some eight hundred to nine hundred German travelers were jammed at one time into a ten-car train, provoking a local newspaper reporter to state that he had never before witnessed such an inhumane or shameful scene. Within the folklore of railroading it is claimed that immigrant families would hire a freight car for the family members, their possessions, clothing, furniture, and, on occasion, livestock. Such caravans were called Zulu cars by contemptuous trainmen.

Overall statistics for immigrant traffic by rail are not available, but some indication of its volume can be gained from the operations of the Baltimore and Ohio in June 1881. Baltimore was far from the largest port of entry, yet in the first two weeks of that month nine thousand immigrants arrived. To accommodate this horde, the railroad ran as many as eight special trains a day. A similar B. & O. train loading at the Locust Point pier is shown in **130A** and **130B.**

In the early years of the ''immigrant cars'' confusion appeared to be a part of the newcomers' journey inland. There were long delays in switching trains. Inevitably, the immigrants lost their tickets, their baggage, and even their children. They boarded the wrong trains or stood in horror of what to do next. In Cincinnati, at midcentury, one observer described the scene at the train depot: ''Some hundreds of Germans and Irish of both sexes were seen bivouacked beside vast piles of trunks and bags. Some had lost sight of their baggage, and ran frantically about looking for it everywhere, at the risk of being run over by locomotives.''

128
Front cover of *Phelps's Travellers Guide through the United States containing Upwards of Seven Hundred Rail-Road, Canal, and Stage and Steam-Boat Routes* (New York, 1847). This is one of hundreds of guidebooks published in America during the nineteenth century. H 5¾".

129
The *John Bull,* 1831. Imported from England, this and similar locomotives opened a new era of land transportation. The *John Bull* ran regularly from 1831 to 1865 for the Camden and Amboy Railroad Company of New Jersey. L 39'.

129

To reduce the confusion, numerous companies attempted to issue tickets that could be used for passage from start to final destination. Whether the newcomer was riding a canal boat or a railroad car, the single fare was supposed to take him all the way [**131, 132**]. Ole Munch Raeder, a visitor from Norway, described this system in 1847:

The trip on the Erie Canal, from Albany to Buffalo, costs only $7.50, including meals, and lasts a day longer than the journey by rail. This price, however, is only for ordinary travelers. The spirit of speculation has led to a rather material reduction in the price for immigrants. Some canal boats, I believe, transport them and their belongings for $2.00, but they have to provide their own food.

The railroads, too, in their case have made an exception to the general rule of having only one class. Sometimes a large boxcar labeled in huge letters "IMMIGRANT CAR," is added to the train, and here the immigrants are piled together in grand confusion, with all their trunks and other belongings. In New York there are companies which arrange the entire journey for immigrants, making their profits through the large masses they transport, as well as whatever they can make through cheating—by dropping them off half way, and so on.

The consul general at New York has made a splendid arrangement for the immigrants whereby they deposit a sum of $6.00 and are then transported to Wisconsin by one of the most dependable companies, which is paid by the consulate upon notification from the immigrant that the company has faithfully discharged its obligation. This plan is announced to the immigrants upon their arrival in New York, but they are so suspicious—or perhaps so unsuspecting when it comes to the Yankees and their agents—that they seldom make use of this splendid means of securing a journey that is both safe and cheap. They cannot resist the temptation of an offer to transport them for a few cents less. The immigrant companies have in their service Norwegians and Swedes who carry on a very profitable business.

Profit, not humanitarianism, was the guiding force of the transportation systems. Yet a few railroad managers felt immigrants deserved better conveyances, especially as the railroad network expanded westward in the 1850s and 1860s and journeys increased from jaunts of a few hours into three-thousand-mile treks that might occupy seven days. Even the hardiest Polish peasant looked longingly for a berth, a toilet, and a warm meal. For the aged, children and expectant mothers, a week-long cross-country rail trip under primitive conditions was nearly unendurable.

A modicum of comfort—even for the poor—did appear in the late 1870s when the Central Pacific Railroad introduced the immigrant sleeping car. While plain in finish, it provided the basic comforts necessary for overnight travel. Berths were offered, but the traveler was expected to furnish his own bedding. A common kitchen at one end of the car provided a place to prepare a warm meal, and provisions could be picked up along the line if the initial stock of food was insufficient. Station restaurants and dining cars, the latter common after 1885, were too expensive for immigrants. Even the ordinary coach traveler depended on a box lunch. The immigrant cars evolved into tourist sleepers as the great European migration began to ebb after 1915 [**133, 134**]. They remained a popular fixture on western railroads until about 1950.

130B   130A

131

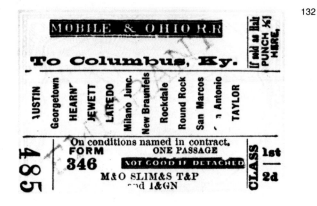

132

133
A Palace Sleeping Car
(1897) of the Pullman Company.

134
An immigrant sleeping car
(1897). Although it did not
begin to match the Palace
sleepers for elegance, it did
provide clean and comfortable quarters compared to the
Zulu cars of midcentury.

133

134

The railroad's relationship to the immigrant extended beyond the one-way trip to the West. Like the European trading companies which, two hundred years before, had been granted vast tracts of real estate in the New World, the railroads were given millions of acres of western lands as an inducement to cross the continent with iron and steel. Railroads were thus also land companies, eager to sell a bit of the virgin territory to the hopeful newcomers [135–138]. The St. Paul, Minneapolis, and Manitoba Railway nicknamed itself "The Nile of the American Continent"; not only could it transport you, as could the Egyptian Nile, but it terminated in a land rich as a delta—of "2,500,000 acres of the best wheat."

Western lands were nearly worthless when given to the railroad companies, but the opening of the railroads provided the catalyst of cheap transport that encouraged rapid settlement and a remarkable escalation in property values. Land began to sell rapidly. Six months after the Transcontinental Railroad opened, the Kansas Pacific R.R. alone sold nearly half a million acres. In 1870 the Burlington organized a land development office to sell 600,000 acres in Nebraska and Iowa. One hundred agents pushed for sales to American buyers, ten offices were opened in the British Isles, and literature was published and distributed in German, French, Bohemian, and Scandinavian. Prospective buyers, invited to inspect the land, were given a rebate on their tickets and provided with shelter in immigrant hotels specially built by the railroad. Credit was easy: ten years to pay at 6 percent interest and interest only payable during the first two years. Not many could resist such an attractive deal. In less than three years the Burlington sold half its land, some 300,000 acres, at a net profit of $7.50 per acre.

The railroad as a transporter and as a colonizer did not exhaust the relationship with the foreign-born. Access to market was essential for every immigrant farmer, and year after year, the railroads' ever-growing feeder lines penetrated the lives of the foreigners on the land.

The railroad was also a major employer in nineteenth-century America. The skilled and unskilled found work—managers, executives, and financiers, as well as track workers, firemen, and brakemen. It is common to think only of the lowest working ranks being filled by the immigrant, but some of the highest offices were held by foreign-born Americans, such as Albert Fink (1827–1897).

Fink began life with many advantages. He was distinguished in appearance, with a noble head and a tall, well-proportioned body. His manner was calm and thoughtful, he spoke clearly and to the point, and he was intelligent and carefully educated. He was not destined to be a failure.

He was born in Lauterbach, Germany, in 1827, and received a private school education. He studied architecture and engineering at Darmstadt Polytechnic School, graduating in 1848. The political revolution of that year, in which the democratic forces were defeated, prompted Fink's decision to emigrate to the United States, and in a typically methodical manner he began a rigorous study of the English language. In 1849 he found work with the Baltimore and Ohio Railroad's engineering department in Baltimore. The railroad was then pushing its main line over the Allegheny Mountains and required designs for countless new bridges and shop buildings. Fink showed great facility—particularly in preparing plans for iron bridges—and was soon advanced to a more responsible position.

In 1857 he left Baltimore to become an assistant engineer for the Louisville and Nashville R.R. Again Fink's skill and capacity earned him a promotion, and after two years he was made chief engineer. In 1865 he became general superintendent of the line and five years later was appointed vice-president. Fink's talents as an administrator equaled or exceeded his engineering abilities. His overview and understanding of railroad economics made him the logical choice to head the Southern Railway and Steamship Association, established in 1875 to coordinate rates and traffic between connecting and competing lines. The administration of such a complicated and potentially explosive arrangement called for tact, judgment, and a thorough knowledge of the transportation industry. Fink was so successful in dealing with the problems of the Southern Association that he was asked to supervise similar negotiations between the major northern trunk lines. He was a central figure in railroad traffic pooling operations until the Interstate Commerce Commission put an end to such arrangements. He retired from business in 1889 and spent his remaining years in the study of art, history, and philosophy, together with extensive travels abroad.

But Fink was the exception. The ordinary immigrant came with less education and fewer skills, prepared to handle a shovel but not a drafting pen. There was a middle echelon of locomotive engineers, machinists, and car painters who as skilled and semiskilled professionals earned good wages and sometimes rose to management positions. The greater number of railway workers, however, continued an unremitting grind of manual labor. The locomotive fireman not only stoked the firebox but worked long hours before and after the run, cleaning the engine. In the old South he was often a Negro, who had no hope, as was true elsewhere in America, of eventually taking the throttle as a locomotive engineer. The brakeman faced an even harder and certainly a more dangerous day than the fireman. He was expected to jump from car to car to wind up the hand wheels when the engineer whistled "Down brakes." A careless step and he was under the wheels. Between stops, he tended the heating stoves, refilled the lamps, and called the station names. Few men wanted this thankless job, and it was said that only the poor Irish could readily be signed on.

The trackworker did the heaviest, roughest work. From early in the morning to sunset he was lifting ties and rails, shoveling ballast, and rebuilding culverts and embankments. He would carry his weighty tools and supplies on a hand-pumped car, perhaps ten miles from his home station. It was an exhausting routine which continued winter and summer, fair weather and foul, and which only a strong, able-bodied man could endure. Many of the early lines were built and maintained by Irish day laborers.

In the Midwest in the 1850s, however, the Irish fell into disfavor. The Illinois Central Railroad, for example, found them too troublesome. Their excessive drinking and constant fistfights, which at times appeared to constitute minor riots, led the Illinois Central's labor agents to look for sober men with families who sought employment and hoped to buy a homestead—from the railroad, of course. The German immigrants filled the bill.

According to company records, the Germans were poor, less accustomed to the work, but more docile and reliable. The agents combed the eastern ports, promising high pay, cheap land, and good climate; they even arranged to transport German workers from New York City to Illinois for $4.75. One historian has estimated that between 1852 and 1856 the Illinois Central induced between five thousand and ten thousand immigrant workers to join the road gangs. Many of these did eventually settle on company lands, becoming successful farmers.

In the Far West the Central Pacific, desperate for construction crews, imported hands from China. Their efficient work is legendary. In the South before the Civil War, Negroes worked as slaves on the lines in Dixie, and after the war they continued the same labor as free men.

Indeed, members of every immigrant group rode on trains, worked on track crews, purchased lands, and shipped goods with the railroads. For many newcomers, the railroad played a direct and continuing role in their American lives.

SOUTHERN KANSAS RY.

Emigrant ❖ Movables!

To Parties emigrating to Points on the Line of the

Southern Kansas Railway

The following articles are enumerated under the head of

❖ EMIGRANT OUTFIT ❖

Household Goods, Second-hand Farm Implements, Second-hand Wagons, Second-hand Miners' Tools, and Live Stock to the extent of Six Head in a Car, when loaded with the above-mentioned articles.

☞ Groceries or mixed goods of any kind must not be loaded in with above-mentioned articles, as they are subject to regular merchandise tariff.

In car-load lots, when any live stock is included in the car, one man will be passed free on the contract to take care of the stock. If over six head of stock are loaded in one car, freight will be charged, as per regular tariff, at Class B rates.

☞ All freight must be prepaid. Trunks and wearing apparel will not be taken as freight unless boxed.

☞ For further information, write to or call on

S. B. HYNES, General Freight Agent, Lawrence, Kas.
G. L. McDONAUGH, General Traveling Agent, 320 Chestnut Street, St. Louis, Mo.
W. D. HYNES, Southeastern Traveling Agent, Indianapolis, Ind.
D. E. McCLELLAND, Northern Traveling Agent, 54 Clark St., Chicago, Ill.
W. T. HAYES, Western Traveling Agent, Room 9, West End of Union Depot, Kansas City, Mo.

SOUTHERN KANSAS RY.

Special Emigrant Freight Tariff —FROM— KANSAS CITY —TO—		In Cents per 100 pounds, Boxed, Released and Prepaid.	In Dollars per Car of 20,000 pounds.
Olathe	Kansas	20	14.00
Morse	"	22	15.00
Stanley	"	23	15.00
Belton	"	24	16.00
Raymore	"	25	18.00
Pleasant Hill	"	25	19.00
Gardner	"	25	16.00
Edgerton	"	25	18.00
Wellsville	"	25	20.00
Le Loup	"	30	22.00
LAWRENCE	"	25	16.00
Vinland	"	32	22.00
Baldwin	"	32	22.00
Norwood	"	32	22.00
OTTAWA	"	32	22.00
Homewood	"	40	25.00
Ransomville	"	40	25.00
Williamsburg	"	40	25.00
Agricola	"	45	25.00
Waverly	"	45	25.00
Hall's Summit	"	45	25.00
BURLINGTON	"	50	25.00
Princeton	"	35	24.00
Richmond	"	35	25.00
GARNETT	"	40	25.00
Welda	"	40	25.00
Colony	"	40	25.00
Carlyle	"	40	25.00
IOLA	"	40	25.00
HUMBOLDT	"	50	25.00
CHANUTE	"	50	25.00
Eastern Junction	"	50	25.00
North Erie	"	50	25.00
Walnut	"	50	30.00
Brazilton	"	50	30.00
Girard	"	50	30.00
Earlton	"	50	30.00
Thayer	"	50	30.00
Morehead	"	50	30.00
CHERRYVALE	"	50	30.00
Liberty	"	50	30.00
Kalloch	"	50	30.00
Coffeyville	"	50	30.00
Independence	"	50	30.00
Crane	"	50	35.00
Elk City	"	50	35.00
Oak Valley	"	50	35.00
Longton	"	50	35.00
Elk Falls	"	50	35.00
Moline	"	50	35.00
Grenola	"	50	35.00
Grandview	"	50	40.00
Cambridge	"	50	40.00
Burden	"	50	40.00
New Salem	"	50	40.00
WINFIELD	"	50	40.00
Oxford	"	50	40.00
WELLINGTON	"	50	40.00
Rome	"	60	40.00
South Haven	"	60	40.00
Hunnewell	"	60	40.00
Mayfield	"	60	40.00
Milan	"	60	40.00
Argonia	"	60	40.00
Albion	"	60	40.00
Danville	"	60	40.00
Harper	"	60	40.00

UNION DEPOT KANSAS CITY.

— ALL TRAINS OF THE —

SOUTHERN KANSAS RY.

Arrive at and depart from this depot, where connections are made with all trains

❋ EAST AND WEST ❋

136

CHEAP
RAILROAD LANDS
OF
WISCONSIN
AND
NORTHERN MICHIGAN
OVER
HALF A MILLION
ACRES
OF GRAND FORESTS

Of the most highly prized varieties of hard and soft woods, pine, hemlock, spruce, cedar, birch, maple, elm, basswood, and many other valuable woods in almost limitless variety and abundance.

LARGE QUANTITIES OF

Cleared Lands

From which the pine timber has been cut, making SPLENDID FARMING LANDS, the valuable timber still remaining, securing to the industrious an excellent livelihood from the beginning. Ready markets at good prices for ties, posts, wood, hay, grain, vegetables, and all products of this land.

These Lands are for sale by the Chicago & North-Western Railway Company at prices that make them sure and profitable investments.

A. A. Shepherd, of Fond du Lac, Wis., will personally conduct Excursions to the Minnesota Lands, on the 1st and 3d Tuesday of each month, and to the Wisconsin and Michigan Lands, on the 2d and 4th Tuesday of each month.

For prices, terms, and specific locations, address any of the following:

A. A. SHEPHERD, Land Agent C. & N.-W. Ry., - **FOND DU LAC, WIS.**
P. C. PETERSON, Land Agent C. & N.-W. Ry., 206 Clark St., **CHICAGO, ILL.**
F. H. VAN CLEVE, Land Agent C. & N. W. Ry., - **ESCANABA, MICH.**
Or **C. E. SIMMONS,** Land Commissioner C. & N.-W. Ry., - **CHICAGO, ILL.**

P. B. Haber Printing House, Fond du Lac, Wis. OVER.

From the Original by MIDWEST RAILWAY HISTORICAL SOCIETY – Chicago, Illinois 60647

4

135
Broadside advertising special immigrant freight rates on the Southern Kansas Railway.

136
Broadside advertising land for sale by the Chicago & North-Western Railway Company. It also offers excursions to the sites for the prospective buyer.

137
Broadside used by the Burlington Lines c. 1875. The exaggeration in posters of this type was noted in *American Railways* by E. A. Pratt (London, 1903), who wrote that the successful railroad promoter "must cast his eye over the older settled portions of the country and see where he is likely to find people who would succeed in the new country, and once having determined on his hunting ground he must begin to set his traps."

138
Santa Fe Railway land poster in German, 1876.

137

LOW PRICES! LONG TIME!

THE GREAT MIDDLE FARMING AND STOCK REGION

THE BEST FOR WHEAT, CORN, HOGS, CATTLE AND SHEEP.

VIRGIN AND PROLIFIC SOIL.

HO! FOR
THE WEST!
NEBRASKA AHEAD!

THE TRUTH WILL OUT!

THE BEST FARMING AND STOCK RAISING COUNTRY IN THE WORLD!

THE GREAT CENTRAL REGION, NOT TOO HOT NOR TOO COLD

The facts about Western Iowa and Southern Nebraska, are being slowly but surely discovered by all intelligent men. The large population now pouring into this region, consists of shrewd and well-informed farmers, who know what is good, and are taking advantage of the opportunities offered.

The crops of Southern Nebraska are as fine as can be; a large wheat and barley crop has been harvested; corn is in splendid condition, and all other crops are equally fine. The opportunities now offered to buy

B. & M. R. R. LANDS

On long credit, low interest, twenty per cent. rebate for improvements, low freights and fares, free passes to those who buy, &c., &c., can never again be found.

There are plenty of lands elsewhere, but they are in regions which can never be largely prosperous. Southern Nebraska, with its fine soil, pure water, and moderate climate, is the right country for a new home.

Go and see for yourself. You will be convinced as thousands have been before you.

Low Round Trip Rates to all points and return, and the amount paid is refunded to those who buy.

I am now prepared to sell Round Trip Tickets to Nebraska and return. The General Office of the B. & M. R. R. is at Lincoln, the Capital of the State. I will sell tickets from Grinnell to Lincoln and return for $12.75, and the fare is refunded to those who buy.

Write to me or call, for a circular and for full information, or for tickets to Lincoln or other points.

E. R. POTTER, Grinnell, Iowa,
Agent for B. & M. R. R. in Poweshiek County

138

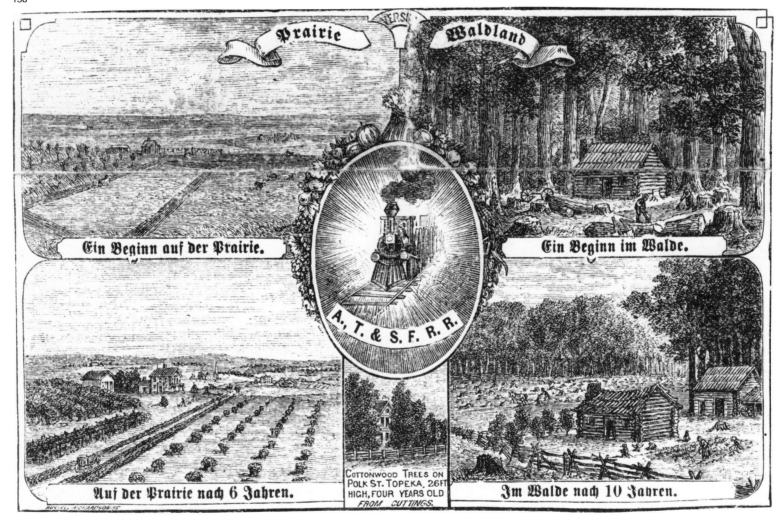

Prairie   Waldland

Ein Beginn auf der Prairie.   Ein Beginn im Walde.

A. T. & S. F. R. R.

Auf der Prairie nach 6 Jahren.   Im Walde nach 10 Jahren.

COTTONWOOD TREES ON POLK ST. TOPEKA, 26 FT HIGH, FOUR YEARS OLD *FROM CUTTINGS.*

Chapter 11

The Immigrant Bridge Builder

The expanding American transportation systems—wagon roads, railroads, canals—created and shared a crucial need: bridges. Across the continent a host of impressive and troublesome natural barriers needed to be crossed, and railroads and waterways themselves required spanning, before the links could be joined into a sound travel network. The bridge was essential to America, and the greatest of America's bridge builders was an immigrant named John Roebling (1806–1869).

Bridges were Roebling's passion. The master bridge builder of his era, he constructed suspension bridges whose designs have influenced builders for the century since his death. The German-born Roebling offered more to his adopted nation, however, than a genius for bridges. His inventive mind, boundless ambition, and limitless confidence in his own capabilities enabled him to make far-reaching contributions in engineering, manufacturing, and business. The America Roebling embraced in the 1830s was ripe for his gifts.

Roebling's decision to emigrate had been carefully thought out and had come as a climax to years of personal growth and dedication to his field. Raised in a Germany buffeted by military, political, and philosophical upheavals, Roebling, along with his contemporaries, had a feeling of participation in history and a longing for change very different from the outlook of their tradition-bound predecessors. These sentiments were encouraged in him by his ambitious, determined mother, whose self-denial and fanatical devotion enabled John to attend the best schools.

At the world's foremost engineering school, the Royal Polytechnic Institute in Berlin, Roebling was first introduced to the principles and unknowns of building suspension bridges, a technique then in its infancy. Immediately fascinated by such a logical, efficient concept, he spent his senior-year vacation at Bamberg analyzing the newly constructed suspension bridge over the Regnitz.

As important as his technical training at the institute was Roebling's friendship with the philosopher Georg Wilhelm Friedrich Hegel. Through Hegel's influence, Roebling's interest in the humanities was awakened and his personal philosophy crystallized. Schooled for so many years in engineering, mathematics, and science, Roebling immediately responded to his professor's belief in logical thinking and the necessity of relying on one's own conclusions. The elderly philosopher also instilled in him a desire for freedom and a vein of idealism. "One thing remember," Hegel told him. "Nothing in the world has been accomplished without passion!" Most important for American history, Hegel's lectures on the philosophy of history started Roebling thinking of the United States as the land of freedom and hope for the future.

Once he had his engineering degree, Roebling discovered that the sole market for his talents was in government service. There, however, the rigidity of thought coupled with bureaucratic ossification thwarted his ambition. He was naturally intrigued when a boyhood friend returned from the United States in 1830 and reported that men there were not restrained by tradition. Simultaneously, a wave of repression spread through Prussia in reaction to the spirit of libertarianism fostered by the July Revolution in nearby France and the birth of free Belgium. A friend was jailed for encouraging emigration, and all skilled workmen and technicians were forbidden to leave the country without a permit.

Finding the situation intolerable, Roebling and his brother Carl secretly planned the organization of a colonizing party. As in all things he attempted, Roebling studied every book he could locate on the subject—in this case, the new country. His rational approach tempered his youthful idealism and ambition: "We are not going with exaggerated hopes. . . . The decision to settle in America must come from a man's own power of will and deed; otherwise he is not suited for America."

Niagara R.R. Susp.ⁿ Bridge.   Completed — 1855   John A. Roebling, Engineer.

M.H. Traubel & Co.'s Lithographic Institute, 46¾ Walnut Street. Philadelphia

Manufacture of
Patent Wire Rope
by

JOHN A. ROEBLING,

Civil Engineer

TRENTON N.J.

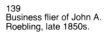

139
Business flier of John A.
Roebling, late 1850s.

Upon his arrival in Philadelphia in August 1831, Roebling, then twenty-five, was immediately struck with the possibilities: "Whence has the multitude of splendid steamboats, mailboats, highways, steam cars, canals, and stages sprung up in so short a time? . . . it is principally the result of unrestricted enterprise and the concerted action of an enlightened, self-governing people."

For the first six years in the new country, John and his brother labored to make their colony, at Saxonburg, Pennsylvania, a success. They concentrated on taming the rugged terrain, farming, and raising families. It was a period that gave Roebling a chance to study and to develop skills which later proved invaluable. He became the struggling colony's promoter, writing to friends about the area's opportunities. He surveyed the land, planned roads, and designed and built houses. At night he studied all the new technical and engineering books and periodicals he could find. In these early years he also produced a remarkable outflow of inventions: a boiler for steamships, a steam tractor, a safety valve, a radial engine, a spark arrester for locomotives, and a "submarine" propeller. (In later years he continued this passion for inventing and promoted an iron railway passenger car, the concept of a transatlantic telegraph cable, and a wire-rope system of transmitting power.)

By 1837 Roebling was restless with the limited horizons of Saxonburg, and as a first step toward getting beyond the small community he received his American citizenship. Devoted to his new country, he named his first son Washington, after his favorite American patriot. Also in 1837, Roebling revived his engineering career, and his past ambition reasserted itself. Henceforth, he was frenetically devoted to his profession, working inhuman hours on projects while simultaneously preparing papers on engineering and economic subjects.

His first major contribution to his field was the development of a wire rope which was recognized for its strength and durability. Orders for the rope began trickling in from railways and shipowners and canal companies. After his colonizing experience, Roebling recognized the need for salesmanship and initiative; he actively promoted and found users for the product, and soon his expanding wire rope factory gave new impetus to Saxonburg. His son Washington later wrote: "My father always held it as a necessity that a Civil Engineer . . . should always, when possible, interest himself in a manufacturing proposition."

By 1848 the industry had outgrown Saxonburg, and Roebling moved the mills to Trenton, New Jersey, which was more accessible to its customers and had a larger pool of skilled labor. He personally designed the new mills, ropewalks, shops, and machines for the enlarged production. By the next year the factory's annual sales were $40,000; twenty years later, at his death, they had reached $250,000. Under his sons, the firm's sales ran far into the millions, and its products were used in elevators, logging, quarrying, oil drilling, dredging, and cableways.

In World War I, Roebling cables were used in the North Sea mine barrage, which bottled up German U-boats and reduced the effectiveness of their submarine warfare. Roebling's German biographer, Wilhelm Auener, noted the irony in this event: "To us it appears tragic fate that this emigrant's cleavage of nationality exerts its effect long after his time. With Roebling the Fatherland not only lost an engineering genius and a great industrialist; but that which he created has worked damagingly against Germany. . . ."

Simultaneous with his success in the wire rope business, Roebling commenced his career in bridge building. By this time his Hegelian idealism had been supplemented with the more practical philosophy of Ralph Waldo Emerson. The value of time and the importance of hard work became the dominant precepts of his life. Later, during the Civil War, when he was kept waiting to see General Frémont, Roebling declared, at the general's tardy appearance, "Sir, I am happy to do any work you want. But waiting in idleness is a luxury I never permit myself." Roebling's devotion to work and his belief in mind over matter were so great that during a cholera epidemic in 1854, while building the Niagara Bridge, he determined not to have the sickness, declaring, "Keep off fear—this is the great secret."

Driven by such single-minded purpose, Roebling by 1850 had completed six suspension bridges, five of which were canal aqueducts. In this relatively new field, he constantly had to battle ignorance and doubts fostered by the proliferation of inferior bridges built by unskilled promoters. Often Roebling would resort to appealing to the American spirit of enterprise and courage. As he had discovered with his wire rope, once his first bridges were successfully built, backers were easier to find: "Whenever anything new is proposed the first question is always—'Has it been tried:' or 'Where can I see it in operation?' When such questions can once be met satisfactorily, then the further introduction of any article is simply a question of time and of individual enterprise."

Because of the infancy of the field, Roebling had to fight political battles, vested interests, and financial difficulties in addition to justifying the economy, efficiency, and durability of each structure. He had to design most of the construction machinery himself, as well as try out new theories with each bridge. Even in his initial structure he used totally new anchorage designs and employed the method of spinning cable in place, so that each strand of wire in the cable carried its share of the weight load. For protection against corrosion, each cable was then wrapped with wire and painted.

Upon completion in 1855 of the Niagara Bridge—the first successful railway suspension bridge—Roebling's reputation was established [139]. His design of stiffened suspension spans introduced a new stability and durability to suspension bridge construction. In his remaining three master-works—the bridge across the Allegheny River in Pittsburgh, another across the Ohio River in Cincinnati, and the Brooklyn Bridge—he continued to make innovations and improvements. On the Ohio, he used diagonal stays to provide additional support and to stiffen the floor. In designing the Allegheny River Bridge, he employed four short spans instead of one long main one, as in his other major constructions.

The climax of his career was his appointment as chief engineer of the Brooklyn Bridge. To him the assignment embodied more than ordinary construction:

The contemplated work, when constructed in accordance with my designs, will not only be the greatest bridge in existence, but it will be the great engineering work of this Continent and of the age. Its most conspicuous feature—the great towers—will serve as landmarks to the adjoining cities, and they will be entitled to be ranked as national monuments; as a great work of art, and as a successful specimen of advanced bridge engineering, this structure will forever testify to the energy, enterprise, and wealth of that community which shall secure its erection.

As always, Roebling's design was revolutionary: it called for a span 50 percent longer than the longest to date and required steel instead of iron cables. Sadly, during the first year of construction, 1869, John Roebling was killed in an accident at the bridge site. His son Washington, a talented engineer in his own right, took over construction of the 1,595-foot bridge and saw his father's ideas through to completion in 1883.

The marvel of the age, the Brooklyn Bridge, proved to be a lasting tribute to the skill of its designer. It aptly symbolizes his background of German technical training combined with American opportunity and ingenuity. Its design, massive and unadorned, recalls the medieval architecture of Roebling's native Mulhausen. The innovations in the bridge's structure bear witness to his belief in himself and his abilities.

Chapter 12

Importing a Revolution

Work!—WORK!!—WORK!!! must be the order of the day with all who emigrate to better their fortunes. To honest and prudent industry every thing will be conceded, to indolence and imprudent movements–NOTHING BUT DISAPPOINTMENT. The roughest of first appearances must not be minded, but a vigorous and resolute hand put forth, and all discouraging appearances will melt as the mists of the morning before the rising sun.

JOHN REGAN
The Emigrant's Guide to the Western States of America, c. 1852

In his propagandist essay *Common Sense,* Tom Paine argued for independence by noting that "Europe, and not England, is the parent country of America." Indeed, as we have seen, peoples from many nations helped to build the thirteen colonies. This polyglot amalgamation continued to grow after the adoption of the federal Constitution. From 1790 to 1815, approximately 250,000 immigrants arrived. During the 1830s, 500,000 appeared, and by the 1850s the figure stood at more than 2.5 million. The *Democratic Review* (July 1852) described this as one of the wonders of modern times: "There has been nothing like it in appearance since the encampment of the Roman empire, or the tents of the Crusaders."

By 1860 there were almost 31,500,000 people living in the United States and of these 4,136,000 were foreign-born. Most had come from rural villages in Europe, and while a few left their homelands for religious or ideological reasons, the majority were prodded by the hope of improving their economic status. A Belgian observer wrote in 1846 that immigrants "did not leave their native villages to seek political rights in another hemisphere. The time of the Puritans and of William Penn is past. Theories of social reform have given way to a practical desire for immediate well being."

The bulk of the foreign-born lived north of the Mason-Dixon line and east of the Mississippi in cities in New York State, which contained the greatest number, followed by Pennsylvania, Ohio, Illinois, Wisconsin, and Massachusetts. In New York City, Cincinnati, Chicago, Milwaukee, and Detroit, close to one-half the population came from Western Europe. The Irish were the most numerous: between 1830 and 1860 almost two million landed in eastern ports. Driven from their rural villages by the potato famines of the 1840s, they settled in city slums. More than one observer noted "this strange contradictory result, that a people who hungered and thirsted for land in Ireland should have been content when they reached the New World . . . to sink into the condition of a miserable town tenantry, to whose squalors even a European seaport could hardly present a parallel" (1855).

The Germans, 1,301,000 of them, spread across America from 1830 to 1860. Few found their way into New England, preferring instead to put their energy into Ohio, Illinois, Wisconsin, and Missouri, where they built farms and cities. The newcomers from England, Scotland, and Wales amounted to 587,775 in 1860. They moved about easily and quickly assimilated themselves into the social fabric. There were small groups of Norwegians and even a few Dutch.

Regardless of their nationality, most immigrants generally arrived penniless and ready to work, usually settling in areas where they could practice the skilled or semiskilled crafts they had learned in their homeland. Welsh miners made their way to the hard-coal fields of eastern Pennsylvania, while pottery makers of Staffordshire found employment in Trenton, New Jersey, or East Liverpool, Ohio. German craftsmen settled in numerous areas, including Cincinnati, where furniture was factory-made. British textile workers appeared in the mill towns where woolen or cotton goods were produced. It turned out that one of these English immigrants, Samuel Slater, was to have a share in starting the industrial revolution in America.

The industrial revolution had begun in England in the eighteenth century, and one of the earliest crafts to be affected was the spinning of cotton. Samuel Slater, who was eventually to be known as the father of cotton manufacturing in America, was born at Holly House, near Belper, England, in 1768. He was apprenticed to Jedediah Strutt after the death of his father in 1782, spending over six years learning how to operate the machines and oversee the mills at Milford, England. This was more than a routine apprenticeship, for Strutt was a family friend who treated Slater as a son.

Strutt was a partner of Richard Arkwright, who had given an early impetus to the industrial revolution by improving the machine spinning of cotton through an invention that used rollers traveling at increasing rates of speed to draw out the fibers. This dynamic period in England saw many mechanical inventions and improvements (and lawsuits over patent rights), and Slater was exposed to the best of the new high-speed, labor-saving machines. He served his apprenticeship faithfully, proving to be an excellent machinist as well as an efficient factory manager. Indeed, at this early period in the history of manufacturing, an industrialist had to be a man with a mechanic's sense of the practical and an entrepreneur's organizing prowess. Slater was learning both.

While Slater was serving his apprenticeship in England, several attempts were being made at Beverly, Massachusetts, and in other places throughout America to erect cotton carding and spinning mills. Time and again they failed. Americans, apparently, lacked the skills to start their own industrial revolution. More than one newspaper carried employment advertisements similar to this one appearing in the New York *Journal* of January 5, 1789:

A person to act as manager and superintendent of the business of the society, whose office it shall be to devote his whole time and services to overseeing the different branches of the linen and cotton manufactures that may be established, take charge of the raw and manufactured articles, and fulfill the orders of the Director.

Almost every state sponsored societies for the encouragement of manufacturing and the useful arts, and many offered premiums for the introduction of efficient cotton machinery. As late as 1832, Calvin Colton's *Manual for Emigrants to America* was emphatic: "manufacturers *especially* will find employment."

This was surely the thrust of Alexander Hamilton's *Report on Manufactures,* which appeared in 1791. The foreign-born secretary of the treasury believed in the "promoting of emigration from foreign countries" because America needed the muscle power to build factories and the brain power to organize and automate the work. The introduction of "new inventions and discoveries . . . as may have been made in other countries; particularly, those which relate to machinery" was thought by Hamilton and his advisers to be a basic need.

The difficulty of learning the art of cotton manufacturing was compounded by the laws of England, which forbade the export of models or plans of any machines. The laws, however, were circumvented when Samuel Slater departed for America in 1789, carrying neither models nor drawings, but with all the essential information in his brain.

Historians are at a loss to explain why this twenty-two-year-old Englishman, who had acquired some property and seemed to have a bright future in England, would leave. None of the explanations is sound. Just before his ship sailed, he posted a letter to his mother: he was beginning his New World adventure.

Slater arrived in New York in November 1789. He inspected the cotton products and mills of the area and quickly discovered what many already knew—the industrial revolution was still across the sea. Then he learned of Moses Brown and of the spinning mills he was attempting to build in Rhode Island. After a polite exchange of several letters, Slater found himself in Pawtucket.

The cotton business started by Moses Brown was operated by William Almy, his son-in-law, and Smith Brown, a kinsman. Impressed by Slater's obvious knowledge of the new cotton machines, Almy and Brown entered into a partnership with him, giving Slater half ownership and half the profits in exchange for erecting the Arkwright system in Pawtucket [**140A–140C, 141–144**].

Slater not only built the machines from memory but made or supervised the making of the tools and parts as well. He also trained machinists according to English standards and instilled in these workmen a sense of professionalism and organizing skills. It was Slater's students who erected the first successful cotton mills in various parts of the country. George S. White wrote in 1836: "most of the establishments erected from 1790 to 1809, were built by men who had, either directly or indirectly, drawn their knowledge from Pawtucket, the cradle of the cotton business."

140A
Carder built by the English-born Samuel Slater in 1790. Powered by water, this "finisher" carder, as it was called, consisted of a rotating drum covered with "card clothing" (leather to which wire teeth were attached). As the drum turned it picked up the cotton and pulled it against the "top card" (the series of wooden slats on which "card clothing" was attached), thus aligning the mass of cotton fibers. Simple in design, this machine replaced the laborious process of carding by hand and, together with the powered spinning frames and looms of English immigrants several decades later, revolutionized the manufacture of cloth in America. H 50″.

140B
Detail: Samuel Slater's finisher carder. The cotton is fed through the small rollers onto the drum for carding.

140C
Detail: One of the slats forming the top card from Samuel Slater's finisher carder.

140A

140C   140B

141
Hand cards for short fibers
used by slaves on a plantation
in Nelson County, Virginia
(1856–1865). The raw, tan-
gled cotton or wool was
placed between the cards and
straightened by rubbing one
card across the other. The
carding surface was 5″ by 8″,
and the operation was
painstakingly slow.

142
Illustration from George S.
White's *Memoir of Samuel
Slater* (1836) representing a
row of carders and spinning
frames on the left and drawing
machines for reducing the
diameter of the carded yarn
on the right. Before the
carded yarn could be spun, it
had to be pulled into narrower
widths. Early in the nineteenth
century this was done by
hand, but as this view of Slater's factory shows, machines
were used for this inter-
mediate operation by the
1830s.

143
The legacy of Samuel Slater.
Taken around 1910, this
Lewis Hine photograph
shows a girl in a cotton mill
operating a drawing machine,
which reduced the diameter
of carded yarn and prepared it
for the spinning frame.

141

142

144
The spinning frame of Samuel Slater, 1790. The carded and drawn cotton was placed on the bobbins at the top and fed through three sets of rollers in the middle of the machine. The first set of rollers turned at a slow speed; the second and third sets traveled progressively faster. This reduced the diameter of the roving (a drawn-out, slightly twisted fiber) to the thickness of yarn. Leaving the final set of rollers, the cotton was fed to the spindles near the bottom of the frame. These fliers, similar to those on hand-operated flax-spinning wheels, rotated and twisted the yarn into strong strands, thus readying them to be made into textiles. H 61″.

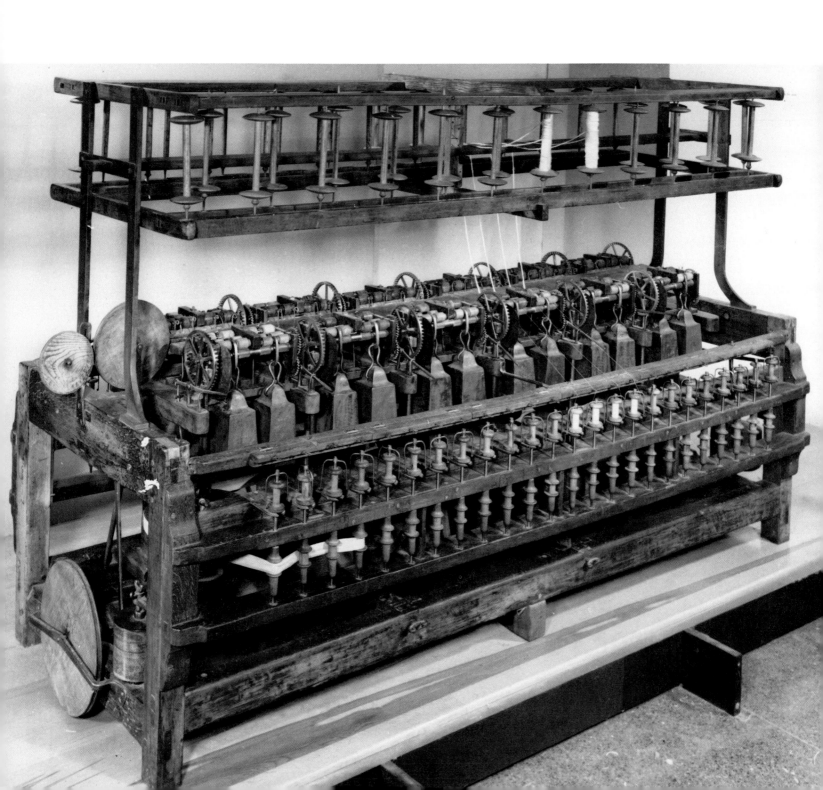

The Cromptons

The Englishman William Crompton, born in Preston, Lancashire, left his family behind the first time he came to America at the age of thirty in 1836. He was already an accomplished weaver and mechanic with a thorough understanding of the pattern-weaving looms used in England's cotton manufacture. Crompton found a job with a Taunton, Massachusetts, textile mill. It is said he was asked to weave a certain type of patterned cloth, but, unable to do so with the looms available, he adapted one to produce the desired cloth. A patent was issued for his loom November 25, 1837. When the mill failed that same year, he returned to England, continued in cotton manufacture, and took out a British patent on his loom in the name of John Rostran, his English partner.

Perhaps American business opportunities seemed brighter to Crompton in 1839, for he once again moved to Taunton, this time emigrating with his family. To promote his looms, he launched a series of visits to New England cotton mills. This met with little success until Samuel Lawrence, who was in charge of the Middlesex Mills of Lowell, Massachusetts, asked Crompton to adapt his fancy cotton loom to weaving woolens. A fashionable French patterned wool fabric called cassimere had attracted Lawrence and motivated his suggestion. Crompton completed his adaptation by 1840, and his subsequent success in developing and distributing the loom for weaving fancy woolens put America in a newly competitive position in this field.

Although patterned woolens had been power-woven before Crompton's time, the cams that controlled the looms limited the complexity of patterns; also, changing patterns was very complicated. Both these drawbacks were eliminated by Crompton's system, in which series of pegged bars, or lags, held together by links, controlled the weaving of patterns. These lags were capable of activating up to thirty loom harnesses and could easily be changed to accommodate new patterns.

William Crompton was naturalized an American citizen in the police court in Lowell, Massachusetts, on November 5, 1842, just three years after he had settled in this country. In 1849, an illness cut short his business career, which had been very active throughout the 1840s. Fortunately, his son George, though only twenty years old at the time, was willing and able to become involved in his father's business, which he subsequently took over completely [145].

George was ten years old when his father decided to move the family to America. William's business activities enabled him to provide his son with a good private education, which George supplemented with practical training in his father's mills and in the Colt pistol factory in Hartford. Once he took charge, George Crompton obtained more than thirty patents for improvements which increased the Crompton fancy loom's efficiency and speed. Over the years he also improved the quality of the loom's workmanship.

He began the manufacture of fancy looms in Worcester, Massachusetts, but in 1861, when the Civil War caused a reduction in the demand for looms, George turned to manufacturing gun-making machinery. In 1863–1864, when the need for soldiers' blankets and other textile supplies increased, he resumed the manufacture of plain and fancy looms for weaving woolens. He had to enlarge his works, and soon employed four hundred hands [146].

Crompton looms won awards at both the Paris Exposition of 1867 and at the Centennial held in Philadelphia in 1876. Their use was widespread in Europe as well as in America.

Abetted by such technological advancements as Slater and the Cromptons provided, factories spread inexorably, for good and evil, throughout the nineteenth century [147]. The many water sites in America provided abundant power, and the economics of the factory system lent itself to increasingly larger factories and machines requiring more and more semiskilled labor. The masses of immigrants filled this need. A government-sponsored report on the "condition of the Industrial Classes in the United States" observed in 1869:

. . . foreign is every day replacing native skilled labour. . . . Indeed, the great number of foreign workmen employed in all the branches of American industries is very remarkable. . . . Nearly all the hands at present in American cotton, woolen, and worsted mills, and in the foundries and rolling-mills of the country, are of recent foreign extraction.

Factory life was better in America than in England, but it was far from ideal. In a letter written in 1827 from South Leicester, Massachusetts, to England, Jabez Hollingworth said:

. . . this state is better calculated for manufacturing than farming. This causes it to be more like England, because where manufacturing flourishes Tyranny, Oppression, and Slavery will follow. . . . As to the manner of living there is not a King on earth that can live better. We have everything to eat that a reasonable man can wish for. We have beef or pork three times a day, potatoes, cheese, butter, tea and coffee and sometimes milk. . . .

But many immigrants, even before 1860, who worked in American factories and mill towns would not have compared their living standard to that of a king. The social statistics concerning crime, disease, and pauperism are far from precise for this period, but they frequently point to the immigrants' disadvantage. In Boston more than half the paupers between 1845 and 1860 were immigrants; at least 86 percent of the names on New York's relief rolls for 1860 appear to belong to immigrants.

The problems were most trying and most visible in the eastern cities. When the aristocratic New Yorker Phillip Hone wrote in his *Diary*: "All Europe is coming across the ocean; all that part at least who cannot make a living at home; and what shall we do with them? They increase our taxes, eat our bread and encumber our streets, and not one in twenty is competent to keep himself," he was expressing the thoughts of many who had found a comfortable spot in society.

GEORGE CROMPTON,

FANCY COTTON AND WOOLLEN

LOOM BUILDER,

GREEN STREET,

WORCESTER, ... MASS.

146
Illustration of the Crompton
Loom Works from its 1860s
letterhead.

147
The legacy of the Cromptons.
In this photograph by Lewis
Hine a mill girl (c. 1910) is
beaming—unwinding yarn
from spools and winding it on
a warp beam. Once the
proper amount of yarn is on
the beam, it is transferred to
a power loom, to be made
into textiles.

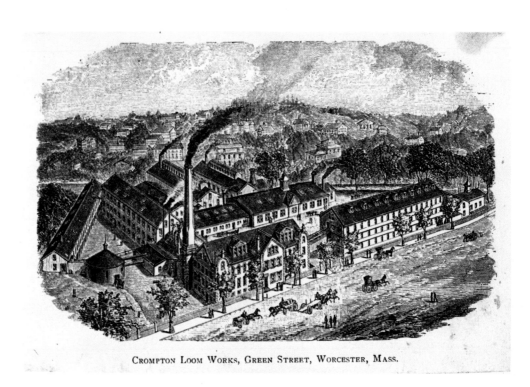

CROMPTON LOOM WORKS, GREEN STREET, WORCESTER, MASS.

146

147

Chapter 13

Crafts, Trades, and Technologies

Contract Labor

Henry Bradshaw Fearon, a British traveler in America during the early years of the nineteenth century, witnessed and wrote about some of the ugly facets of immigration, such as the abuses suffered by contract laborers. Contract laborers were penniless immigrants who paid for their ocean voyage by binding themselves to American masters. The masters paid the price of the passage to ship captains and received a human being in return. It was a modified form of temporary enslavement which was common in America until the Civil War and finally outlawed by Congress in 1885. It affected both whites and Negroes.

There were two classes of contract laborers. The luckier *indentured servant* signed, in his homeland, a labor contract that often read like apprenticeship papers, specifying the number of years he would serve an American master and sometimes the minimum conditions under which he was to be employed. The *redemptioner* was less fortunate. He signed nothing when he boarded ship and became the rightful property of a ship captain, who sold him to an American master for an indenture of three to fourteen years.

In one newspaper advertisement Fearon read of a new supply of foreign tradesmen:

The Passengers on board the brig "Bubona," from Amsterdam, and who are willing to engage themselves for a limited time, to defray the expenses of their passage, consist of persons of the following occupations . . . 13 farmers, 2 bakers, 2 butchers, 8 weavers, 3 taylors, 1 gardener, 3 masons, 1 mill-sawyer, 1 white smith, 2 shoemakers, 3 cabinet-makers, 1 coal-burner, 1 barber, 1 carpenter, 1 stocking weaver, 1 cooper, 1 wheelwright, 1 brewer, 1 locksmith.

The advertisement was a guide to the essential Old World crafts practiced in America. Traveler Fearon, "no lover of America," condemned the practice of selling human cargo, and he reported the scene upon the *Bubona* with revulsion:

As we ascended the side of this hulk, a most revolting scene of want and misery presented itself. The eye involuntarily turned for some relief from the horrible picture of human suffering, which this living sepulchre afforded. Mr. —— enquired if there were any shoe-makers on board. The captain advanced; his appearance bespoke his office; he is an American, tall, determined, and with an eye that flashes with Algerine cruelty. He called in the Dutch language for shoe-makers, and never can I forget the scene which followed. The poor fellows came running up with unspeakable delight, no doubt anticipating a relief from their loathsome dungeon. Their clothes, if rags deserve that denomination, actually perfumed the air. Some were without shirts, others had this article of dress, but a quality as coarse as the worst packing cloth. I enquired of several if they could speak English. They smiled, and gabbled, "No Engly, no Engly . . . ." The deck was filthy. The cooking, washing, and necessary departments were close together. Such is the mercenary barbarity of the Americans who engaged in this trade, that they crammed into one of those vessels 500 passengers, 80 of whom died on the passage. The price for women is about 70 dollars, men 80 dollars, boys 60 dollars. When they saw at our departure that we had not purchased, their countenances fell to that standard of stupid gloom which seemed to place them a link below rational beings. From my heart I execrated the European cause of their removal, which is thus daily compelling them to quit the land of their fathers, to become voluntary exiles in a foreign clime. . . .

The poor of Germany, Ireland, Scotland, and England were numerous in the ranks of the indentured servants and redemptioners. From England, in particular, craftsmen willingly submitted to servitude in order to start their lives again in the United States. Despite reports in works such as Isaac Holmes's *An Account of the United States of America* (1823) that some departed mechanics were unhappy in America, having "been much dissatisfied, and . . . [having] deplored the circumstance of their quitting England," official records of the Select Committee on Emigration from the United Kingdom contain notices to the contrary. One, published in 1827, observed that there "is undoubtedly a very great tendency to emigrate, produced by the utter inability of the weaver to obtain adequate wages" in England. One letter from an English weaver in Philadelphia claimed the unheard-of wages of 4½ to 6 dollars per week . . . for weaving a striped calico." In England, observed a contemporary, "he would not earn much more than the same number in shillings."

Little historical research has been done to evaluate the skills brought to America under the system of contract labor. It is evident, however, that many free craftsmen, who sailed to America on their own economic power, felt that the contract labor had caused native Americans to stereotype all foreign tradesmen as slovenly and poor. A British observer, E. Howitt, wrote in 1820: "The old American (or Yankee) looks with the most sovereign contempt upon the emigrant: he considers him a wretch, driven out of a wretched country, and seeking a subsistence in his glorious land."

The truth was not so simple. The supply and demand for skilled craftsmen ebbed and flowed throughout the nineteenth and early twentieth centuries. In boom periods, the cities seemed to swell with skills, often of intense specialization and artistry. And in times of economic depression, these very same hands could be seen moving west. This accounts, in part, for the plethora of contradictions in the immigrant literature that guided the skilled newcomers to fruitful areas of settlement.

A resounding chorus chanted against settling in eastern cities; from a restrained word of advice in 1800 to a high-pitched scream in the 1880s, cautions were voiced about overcrowding and intense competition. There were also dissenting voices. The Swedish writer Theodore Schytte (*Guidance for Immigrants*) contended as late as 1849 that the "good craftsman can earn his bread anywhere" in America and went so far as to suggest the craft centers of New York and Philadelphia as cities of opportunity. In agreement was Thomas Mooney, who wrote in *Nine Years in America* (1850):

There are classes of mechanics for whom New York and other Atlantic cities may afford the most certain employment, such as watch and timepiece makers of the highest capacities, carvers and gilders, house decorators, fine stucco men . . . silver workers, gold workers, upholsterers. . . . All these can probably do better in New York, Philadelphia, and other Atlantic cities north, as far as Portland in the state of Maine and southward, as far as Norfolk, Virginia, than in the western interior. . . . Mechanics of second and third rate abilities will do far better a thousand miles westward.

The Steinways

William Steinway (1836–1896) came to New York City in 1850 with his family, under the name Steinweg. They had come from Seesen, Germany, where Henry Engelhard Steinweg, William's father, had made a reputation as a master piano builder, winning prizes at the 1839 Brunswick Fair. William's brother Charles had arrived in New York in 1849 after a hasty retreat from Germany following his involvement in the unsuccessful 1848 revolution. When the family business became paralyzed by the political upheaval, and letters from Charles promised that opportunities in America were greater than in Germany, Henry and his wife, Juliane, took fourteen-year-old William, two of their three other sons, and two daughters and moved to the new land. There Henry and his sons worked for three years with established American piano builders, learning the language and the customs of the Americans. In March 1853 the sons joined their father to form Steinway & Sons, a firm that within decades became known as the aristocrat of the piano industry.

Before William left Germany, he had excelled in languages and music, and his family offered him the chance of studying music in America. Instead, he chose piano-making and was apprenticed with William Nunns & Company. After joining the family firm, he worked at the bench for several years, gradually devoting more time to the financial and commercial aspects of the business, while his father and brothers concentrated upon technical improvements and the supervision of a well-run factory. In March 1865, two brothers died: Charles at thirty-six; Henry, Jr., at thirty-four. With this blow, the eldest son, C. F. Theodore, who had remained in Germany, emigrated to join the firm and to provide, following Henry, Jr., some of the most important technical developments for the piano in the second half of the nineteenth century.

The members of the family signed a new, legal partnership agreement in 1866 with the Americanized form of the name: Steinway.* For William, especially, the Americanization was more than nominal. Without neglecting his business, he threw himself into the task of improving life in the city of New York. He supported many musical groups, the Metropolitan Opera, and also the noted conductor Theodore Thomas, whose musicians set orchestral standards for the country. William sang tenor in the Liederkranz, the leading German singing society in New York, and served as its president for fourteen years. Under his guidance, Steinway Hall was opened in 1866 to provide New York with a handsome concert hall where outstanding musical groups performed. Charles Dickens lectured there in 1867, and political groups, such as Victoria Woodhull's Equal Rights party, met in it.

William Steinway raised thousands of dollars for charities, including $112,000 for the German (later Lenox Hill) Hospital. He and the firm established, in the early 1870s, the factory and company village of Steinway in Astoria, Long Island. Proud of the village, he often noted its advantages over city living for the workers: light and air, good housing, public baths, a public park, a free circulating library, and, in the public schools, a teacher of German and music. In connection with this operation, he set up a land company, a streetcar line, and a ferry from Manhattan to Long Island. He was the original promoter of the East River tunnel (now used by the IRT) and, under his chairmanship, in 1891 the Rapid Transit Commission drew up plans for the first subway in New York. Active in Democratic politics and a lifelong friend of Grover Cleveland, he served as a delegate to the Democratic Convention in 1888 and presided over the New York presidential electors in 1893.

His civic pride, business acumen, and knowledge of high-quality musical instruments made Steinway a celebrity in the worlds of art and finance. In 1883 he appeared before a U.S. Senate hearing on the relations between labor and capital. In his testimony he insisted that America was a land of opportunity for those with high standards and the willingness to work. In earlier letters to Germany from William's brother Charles the report had not been so thoroughly sanguine:

I cannot advise you to come here if you are able, by diligence and thrift, to make a living in Germany. . . . The worst thing for the Germans is that few of them can stand the climate; almost all have chest pains. . . . of course America is a haven for anyone willing to work, who had no employment in Germany and had to contend with hardships and worries; but nothing is perfect, not even human happiness in America.

Still, in 1883, no stranger to unhappiness—with an unsuccessful first marriage and the deaths of his father and brothers behind him—William Steinway was optimistic for his adopted America. In his view, a skilled artisan was better off in this country than in Europe: he had better clothing, better food, and (perhaps most important of all) a chance to move in better society. But Steinway felt that America was wasting her potential. America needed a law for compulsory education from ages six to fourteen; after that, there should be a two-year industrial school where boys could go to "find for what business they have aptitude and talent." Following that should be a five-year apprenticeship to develop a skilled artisan, one who would know all the branches of a trade and, because of his knowledge, would find employment through panics and depressions. In reply to questions about the possibilities for advancement of the American working man, Steinway said: " . . . under the institutions of our country, if an individual has the talent, the energy, and the industry he has as good a chance as ever to work himself up. . . . I think in this country a young man has a better chance to work up in the world than anywhere else that I have seen."

*Although "Steinway" had been the company name from the beginning, the family name "Steinweg" did not change in legal contracts until 1866.

210

Furniture Making—
Immigrant Hands and Yankee Machines

Steinway's observation that American craftsmen showed a natural aptitude for invention was similarly expressed by nearly every foreign observer who reported on the trades, the factories, and the commerce of the United States. Adaptability and accommodation were singled out, as well as the Yankee aptitude for mechanization. C. L. Fleischmann's report (1852) was emphatic. To tinsmiths thinking about a voyage to America, he advised: "The German tinsmith may be more skilled in making objects requiring great dexterity, but when he comes to this country he must learn to work quickly and with machines, . . ." To blacksmiths, wagonmakers, trunk manufacturers, ropemakers, and other craftsmen, the same scene was described:

The American does not let himself be constrained by the accepted way of manufacturing a thing. He uses a new method that seems suitable to him, and thereby endeavors to gain an advantage over the other workers in his field. Water or steam power drives his machines which supplant human hands, and he is thereby able to supply many articles so cheaply that they are accessible to the affluent and poor alike; that is why even in the remotest part of the Union in stores set up in primeval forest, articles can be found which in Europe are available only in large cities.

The variables in transplanting any skill or craft from one continent to another were more numerous and complex than most craftsmen could have imagined. No guidebook or anecdote that circulated in European villages could have remained abreast of the changes in the United States. The growth was hectic. Nothing was fixed—only change was certain.

Surely Fleischmann, writing to a German audience in 1852, had this in mind when he warned prospective emigrants that success in America demanded perseverance. "It is necessary to grow gradually, together with the place, to expand one's business gradually and to try to make the most of one's local knowledge and the opportunities that arise." Any immigrant seeking to enter the mainstream of an American trade or business had to learn about raw materials, credit practices, local business laws, and salesmanship. Many unwittingly did follow Fleischmann's advice because they simply had no choice. Beginning with tiny shops or sales stands in the French Market of New Orleans [148], the Polish fairs of New York [149], or any of the other ethnic zones of trade [150], the luckier or the more talented newcomers gradually established viable firms. Others became peddlers [151]. The Italians and the Jews of Eastern Europe were the stereotypical immigrant peddlers in America [152], but real knowledge of which groups did fill the role, and in what proportion, has not become available.

Old practices coexisted with new ones, hand with machine, and foreign workers of diverse skills had to weave themselves into whatever was the current American design. A particular pattern was developed in the furniture-making trade.

Old World methods of furniture production were adopted in North America from the time of the first settlements until well into the nineteenth century. Along the eastern coast, British styles dominated. They were transmitted by craftsmen from Great Britain, by imported furniture, and beginning in the eighteenth century, by designs published in London. Cabinetmakers and chair makers found that foreign training was an asset with the American clientele: the simple phrase "from London"— or Dublin or Edinburgh—in newspaper advertisements conveyed an assumed skill and familiarity with the most recent designs. A majority of immigrant furniture makers from the European continent (few in number by comparison with those from the British Isles during the colonial and federal periods) accommodated quickly to the prevailing fashion, although some—especially the Dutch and Germans in rural communities—retained for a time forms, styles, and decorative motifs peculiar to their cultures.

Two developments in the nineteenth century, however, had profound effects on the furniture industry. First, an influx of European artisans provided an abundance of eager laborers (see tables 1 and 2) and transplanted styles directly from the Continent—particularly France—to America [**153**]. Second, production processes were mechanized, which resulted in the availability of more and more furniture at a wide range of prices for the rapidly growing population. These factors changed patterns that had prevailed for more than two hundred years.

At the first two international exhibitions held in the United States, the work of some immigrant craftsmen was sufficiently notable to draw the attention of commentators. The superiority of these furniture makers was emphasized in a review of the 1853 New York Crystal Palace Exhibition edited by Benjamin Silliman, Jr., and C. R. Goodrich:

We have often had occasion to remark that the ornamental parts, at least, of articles exhibited in the American Department, were the work of foreigners who have become citizens by adoption. So far as we can ascertain, all the specimens of sculpture in wood worthy of notice are of such origin. While our native mechanics exhibit an unequalled constructive skill and versatility, they are not often gifted by nature with artistic cleverness, and their attempts of this sort are usually far inferior to the productions of European workmen, who, in many cases, have received an artistic education, and always have been surrounded by good models, and stimulated to imitate their excellencies. The mention of the deficiency points out the remedy, and we are confident that our quick-witted artisans will not hesitate to instruct themselves by the examples furnished by the Exhibition.

Elaborate furniture produced by Frenchmen and Germans active in New York, Philadelphia, and Boston prompted this observation.

It was noted again at the 1876 Philadelphia Centennial Exhibition that "our best furniture is not American at all except that it is made here; the designers and workmen are generally foreigners." The Marquis de Rochambeau wrote a report on the American furniture displays in which he acknowledged that they were "truly remarkable; only permit us to observe that the firms of New York which are distinguished most by their good taste and their purity of style are of French origin and that, in many American establishments, a number of foremen and workmen are of that nationality." He was particularly impressed by the New York furniture-making establishment of Auguste Pottier and William Pierre Stymus:

Its founder, Monsieur Pottier, is a French worker who arrived in America some thirty years ago with hardly any baggage; he has succeeded, aided only by his intelligence and his talent, in founding a manufactory which is, of its kind, the most important in New York. . . .

To speed of execution, the firm of Pottier and Stymus joins superiority of work; its directors have neglected nothing in order to assure superiority of performance. For a long time, they have noticed that certain people furnish better workers for this or that trade; they have enrolled workers of those different nationalities according to the needs of their industry.

Thus, among the draftsmen [dessinateurs], *the proportion is 3 French to 15 Germans; cabinetmakers, 3 French to 100 Germans; chairmakers, 3 French to 20 Germans; carvers, 5 French to 30 Germans; varnishers, 8 Irish to 30 Germans; gilders, 8 English to 4 Americans; upholsterers, 3 French to 5 Americans and 30 Germans; workers in bronze, 10 French to 2 Americans.*

All the ornamental painters are French or Italian; the salesmen in the store are American; finally, the men who operate the mechanical equipment are in the proportion of 6 Americans for about 40 Germans. Thanks to this workers' Tower of Babel which only the United States can produce, each detail of a piece of furniture is dealt with by the hand of a master.

Table 1

Nativity of cabinetmakers and upholsterers in the United States and its territories and in specific states and cities having more than 1,000 employed in these occupations (numbers taken from the U.S. Census of 1870).

PLACE OF BIRTH	United States	Germany	England & Wales	Scotland	Ireland	Sweden, Norway & Denmark	France	Other North of Europe	Italy	Other South of Europe	British America	China & Japan	Other & Unknown	TOTAL
United States & Territories	28,125	13,481	1,333	310	2,032	731	618	359	46	475	945	11	105	48,571
Illinois	996	944	86	30	73	162	35	8	2	65	34	—	—	2,437
Indiana	1,584	560	25	7	20	20	19	2	2	19	9	—	—	2,269
Iowa	650	262	24	8	22	18	13	20	—	22	12	—	—	1,062
Kentucky	644	407	13	4	16	—	9	1	—	9	3	—	—	1,110
Maryland	680	501	18	4	16	—	6	1	—	4	2	—	—	1,235
Massachusetts	4,245	265	142	58	601	86	32	25	12	28	376	—	—	5,880
Michigan	788	285	61	18	110	6	8	18	—	56	90	—	—	1,442
Missouri	695	542	37	4	36	27	10	24	—	22	8	—	—	1,409
New Jersey	558	376	74	6	39	1	24	11	1	9	2	—	—	1,105
New York	3,891	4,583	406	93	609	161	211	86	20	63	199	—	—	10,344
Ohio	3,110	1,760	96	20	114	4	59	56	—	46	28	—	—	5,297
Pennsylvania	4,060	1,406	108	12	154	34	57	31	2	16	8	—	—	5,894
Wisconsin	365	434	44	7	13	53	7	45	—	46	31	—	—	1,049
Boston	794	159	48	18	163	50	20	13	7	7	113	—	2	1,394
Chicago	274	562	36	12	48	114	14	7	2	49	16	—	—	1,134
Cincinnati	779	1,070	13	7	51	1	28	50	—	3	7	—	2	2,011
New York	1,069	3,103	167	45	359	41	143	50	14	53	18	—	—	5,071
Philadelphia	884	966	64	9	107	10	34	19	2	11	4	—	5	2,115

Although the Census of 1870 combines cabinetmakers and upholsterers when analyzing country of birth within occupations, by state and city, it is possible to deduce that upholsterers account for 10 percent or less of the total figures in eight of the thirteen states; their numbers range from 39 in Iowa to 1,959 in New York. Therefore, cabinetmakers represent the large majority of individuals reported in this table.

Table 2

Nativity of cabinetmakers and upholsterers in the United States and its territories and in specific states and cities having more than 1,000 employed in these occupations (numbers taken from the U.S. Census of 1880).

PLACE OF BIRTH	United States	Germany	Great Britain	Ireland	Sweden & Norway	British America	Other Countries	TOTAL
United States & Territories	35,995	15,371	1,976	1,735	1,468	1,629	2,923	61,097
California	573	410	70	73	43	43	166	1,378
Illinois	1,822	1,664	157	90	616	137	355	4,841
Indiana	2,802	751	39	21	16	17	97	3,743
Kentucky	740	387	19	15	2	8	28	1,199
Maryland	855	482	13	20	2	3	27	1,402
Massachusetts	4,327	312	274	364	107	565	151	6,100
Michigan	1,524	540	134	47	41	203	431	2,920
Missouri	1,229	736	53	22	40	34	85	2,199
New Jersey	782	438	64	142	13	9	62	1,510
New York	5,262	4,583	457	537	234	233	618	11,924
Ohio	3,421	1,768	103	54	5	60	204	5,615
Pennsylvania	4,832	1,412	195	150	31	19	227	6,866
Wisconsin	450	593	43	22	68	29	83	1,288
Baltimore	594	449	9	18	2	3	27	1,102
Boston	1,243	187	134	195	68	189	85	2,101
Brooklyn	566	743	98	99	37	24	75	1,642
Chicago	909	1,204	99	75	466	90	306	3,149
Cincinnati	960	985	21	26	2	11	86	2,091
New York	1,712	2,833	166	313	62	32	423	5,541
Philadelphia	1,981	935	140	101	16	8	145	3,326
St. Louis	698	591	36	16	14	17	54	1,426

As in Table 1, the vast majority of individuals noted here were cabinetmakers.

148

149

148
A scene of the French Market in New Orleans.

149
A Polish market area in New York City.

150
Vendors and housewives of the Italian colony of Mulberry Bend, New York City, c. 1890.

151
This handsome 7' red cart served a New England peddler after the Civil War, when a variety of factory goods extended household conveniences to an ever-widening public. This shift from hand- to machine-made goods did not, however, disguise the time-honored activity of the peddler. First appearing in the Middle Ages, European peddlers in time became urbanized, hawking their wares in village streets. Some still preferred the open road and continued to serve remote settlements.

The account books of peddlers of tinware, textiles, or brooms list numerous sales but do not reveal the ingenuity with which a "fair" price was reached. With his winter-made wares loaded on his back, pack mule, or cart, the peddler set out in the springtime. From New England, New York, and Pennsylvania, whitesmiths (tinsmiths) set forth to sell or swap their lightweight, painted vessels. In the same regions and into the South, local potters moved their heavier goods along primitive roads. Whether he provided a single stock or a mobile country store, the peddler brought products directly to the farm gate.

152
Typical stereotype of an immigrant Jewish peddler, from *Puck* (October 3, 1894).

150

NEW CUSTOMERS.

ITINERANT GENTS' FURNISHING GOODS DEALER. — Suspenders!
Gollar puttons, Negties!

151   152

FROM
ALEXANDER ROUX,
827 & 829 BROADWAY,
NEW-YORK,
French Cabinet Maker,
AND IMPORTER OF
FANCY & MOSAIC FURNITURE.
ESTABLISHED 1836.

The French shared prominence with the British in establishing fashions in American furniture beginning in the second quarter of the century. Contemporary designations applied to styles give proof of this: Louis XIII, Louis XIV, and Louis XVI, French Modern, French Antique, Elizabethan, Jacobean, Early English, Old English, Henry II, Queen Anne, and Eastlake. In the shops, however, German workers often far outnumbered the French and British [**154, 155**]. It was the Germans, in fact, to whom blame was given in the 1840s for the significant decrease in cabinetmakers' wages in New York City, then the center of furniture manufacture. While journeymen—the backbone of the labor force—earned twelve to fifteen dollars a week in 1836, this amount had dropped by 1845 to five dollars for the majority and to eight dollars for "smart hands" working in firms producing the finest furniture. According to the New York *Daily Tribune* (November 11, 1845):

The cause of the great decrease in the wages of Cabinet Makers is in a great measure the immense amount of poor Furniture manufactured for the Auction-Stores. This is mostly made by Germans, who work rapidly, badly and for almost nothing. There are persons who are constantly on the watch for German emigrants who can work at Cabinet-Making—going on board the ships before the emigrants have landed and engaging them for a year at $20 and $30 and their board, or on the best terms they can make. The emigrants of course know nothing of the state of the Trade, prices, regulations, &c. &c. and become willing victims to anyone who offers them immediate and permanent employment. This it is which has ruined the Cabinet-Making business, and the complaints on the part of the Journeymen are incessant. There is, however, no remedy for the evil as we see. So pervading is the idea among the great purchasing classes, the housekeepers, that it must of course be good economy to buy cheap things, that good work and good prices must of necessity go a-begging.

Regardless of whether the disparaging remarks about their skills were accurate, it is true that German cabinetmakers and carvers had flooded the New York labor market by the middle of the century.

154
U.S. patent model by John Henry Belter, 1858. Belter was a
cabinetmaker and carver trained in Württemberg, Germany,
who worked in New York from at least 1844 until his death in
1863. The method he devised of laminating wood by means
of a steam process, patented in 1858, was particularly
suited to the rococo revival style introduced in America in
the 1840s. It allowed ornate piercing and carving of curved
surfaces. At the time, this style was known as "antique
French," "modern French," and, mistakenly, "Louis
Quatorze," as well as "Louis Quinze." Belter became one of
the best known of the nineteenth-century German furniture
makers in America. His prominence was such that his contemporaries referred to furniture of this type as "Belter furniture," a designation that is still used. H 11¹⁵/₁₆".

155
Center table, inlaid by Peter Glass. Center tables were common in the balanced spatial arrangement of neoclassical parlors. The scrolled base and baluster post came from an early-1800s design. The form, however, continued in popularity into the American Victorian era. This example was made about 1864 by an immigrant from Germany, Peter Glass, of Sheboygan County, Wisconsin. The octagonal tilt-up top is inlaid with 30,000 pieces of wood in patriotic images (four generals, eagles, and flags), bowls of fruit and flowers, American song birds, chevron and vine designs. Demonstrating the strength of his thorough foreign apprenticeship, Glass won special recognition for himself with the table at the Universal Exposition in Paris in 1867. W 37½".

Ernest Hagen witnessed the coming of one wave of these artisans to his own neighborhood in New York. The displacement of the residents, to which he refers in his recollections written in 1908, reflects a pattern occurring time and time again as immigrants invaded American communities.

Being born in the City of Hamburg in Germany on September 8, 1830, we came to New York June 22, 1844, after a passage of 47 days in a small German sailing vessel. A year later, 1845, father indentured me to a party of German cabinet makers (Krieg & Dohrmann) located at #106 Norfolk Street, near the present terminal of the Delancy Street Bridge. That part of the town was at that time very different from what it is now, there were but few Jews there then. Although we had only cobble stone pavement with brick sidewalks, no sewers, whale street lamps, and had to go to the next corner pump for drinking water, there were nice American familys living there in 2 story and attic brick houses, some of which were quite ornate with carved brownstone lintels over their windows and very ornamental front door entrances with carved collums and circular transoms with leaded sash at the top and sides and all had gardens. . . . Some people which became quite prominent in Society lived right near us. . . . With the incoming of the large German immigration about 1849–50, all those old residents moved away and a Colony of German mechanics took their place. There were cabinet makers shops, saw mills and marble mills everywhere.

155

221

During the nineteenth century furniture production evolved from a handcraft to a mechanized industry. The change was radical. Machines were developed to saw, plane, turn, shape panels, and rough-out forms, to make grooves, mortises, tenons, and dovetails, as well as to execute decorative detailing. In the establishment of Pottier and Stymus, the Marquis de Rochambeau observed in 1876 the maximum use of mechanization.

Everything is moved by steam. The perfection of these machines is such that they do work equivalent to two-thirds of the labor, and permit, with personnel which varies according to the season from 400 to 600 individuals, to complete in a very short time an order no matter how extensive. This factor is of great importance in a country where time is money.

It has already been noted that this firm employed Americans and Germans in the ratio of six to about forty to operate the machinery.

While man and machine were brought together in the workshops of Pottier and Stymus, mass production of chairs, tables, and other household essentials was growing rapidly in the Midwest. In fact, Ernest Hagen recalled that by about 1870 the impact of furniture factories ''and especially the Western factory work'' was felt in New York City (and doubtless in the East in general). As a result, ''all the smaller cabinet makers were simply wiped out.'' As early as 1854, the British traveler William Chambers was astounded by the scale and methods of production in Cincinnati:

When one thinks of a carpenter's shop, he has probably in his mind two or three rude-looking apartments, with at the most a dozen men in paper-caps working at benches with planes and chisels, or leaning over a plank with a hand-saw; or with experience a little more extended, he may perhaps get the length of fancying a cabinet-making establishment with fifty picked hands turning out several handsome pieces of furniture daily. The idea of a factory as large as a Lancashire cotton-mill for making chairs, tables, or bedsteads by machinery, would hardly present itself to his imagination. Yet, it is on this factory-mill system that we find house-furniture produced in Cincinnati. Curious to see such places, I spent a day in rambling about the outskirts of the city, where manufactories of various kinds are conducted upon a scale that went very far beyond my previous notion of what can be done by machinery.

The first establishment I visited was a furniture-factory–a huge brick building, five stories in height, with a long frontage at the corner of two streets, and in which 250 hands are employed in different departments. Many of these are occupied merely in guiding and superintending machines moved by shafts and belts from a large steam-engine on the ground-floor. Every article receives its shape in the rough, by means of saws; and these move with such rapidity, that their teeth are invisible to the eye. The articles are next planed, or turned, and morticed, in the same inconceivably rapid manner. In the planing operations, some surprising effects are produced. A rough deal, or other piece of wood, being arranged on a bench under the action of a plane which revolved horizontally, was in a few instants smoothed as if by the finest hand-labour. Chairs of a common class, but neatly turned and painted, were the principal article of manufacture. The number produced almost goes beyond belief. I was informed that the average quantity was 200 dozen every week, or at the rate of 124,800 chairs per annum, worth from five to twenty-four dollars per dozen. Among these, a large number are rockers. The machinery for scooping out and shaping the seats was exceedingly ingenious. . . . My attention was called towards the process of ornamental hand-turning, chiefly executed by Germans. One of these clever mechanics went through his work with astonishing speed and precision; his keen eye never being for one instant raised from the whirling lathe before him. This person, I was told, made eighteen dollars per week, and being a sober, well-behaved man, he had already realised property to the value of 5000 dollars (£ 1000 sterling). Many other workmen in the establishment were spoken of as having accumulated property by their industry and economical mode of living. The most steady hands were stated to be native Americans or Germans. ''English and Scotch were good workmen, but not usually well educated, or of sober habits.'' I heard the same thing said elsewhere.

The next establishment I looked in upon was a bedstead factory, in which similarly improved machinery was employed to cut out and finish various parts of the articles required. As many as 1000 bedsteads are turned out every week, . . . In the fabrication of iron stoves, locks, and hinges, holstery, firearms, hats, boots and shoes, machinery, axes and other edge-tools, carriages and numerous other things—the operations were on a similarly gigantic scale. . . . On hearing facts of this kind, the question continually occurs: Where do all these manufactures go? Of course the explanation is found in the perpetual demand over the vast regions of which, as has been said, Cincinnati is the centre. Every day, thousands of fresh families are making a settlement in the wilderness, and each needs bedsteads, tables, chairs, and other articles of domestic use. On the quay at Cincinnati, therefore, you see vast piles of new furniture, iron stoves, tinware, cases of boots and shoes, and everything else needed by settlers, preparing to be despatched a thousand miles by steamers on the Mississippi and its tributaries. One manufacturer of cabinet-work told me he had received an order to make the whole furniture of a hotel in California!

Mechanization did not make the skilled artisan obsolete. His trained hands were essential, and for carved detailing there was no substitute for the craftsman. This facet of the operation captured the attention of a reporter for the Detroit *Free Press*, who described the furniture factories in Grand Rapids, Michigan, in 1877. There he watched Scottish carvers who had been trained to fashion figureheads as well as stem, stern, and cabin decorations in the ship-building center of Glasgow. ''This apprenticeship stood them in good stead. There is no style of carving too intricate for their deft chisels. . . . It is an interesting sight to behold a force of thirty or forty of these handicraftsmen employed in one large room, and to inspect the wonderful variety of work executed there.''

While American cabinetmakers established most of the early shops in Grand Rapids, the immigrant craftsmen and mechanics were essential to the industry's growth during the second half of the nineteenth century. For example, the Berkey and Gay Furniture Company, a major firm in 1886, employed 255 workers, of which only 82 were native born; among the remaining 173 were 97 Dutchmen, 31 Germans, 13 Canadians, 9 Swedes, 8 Englishmen, 6 Norwegians and Danes, 3 Irishmen, 1 Scotsman, 1 Welshman, 1 Belgian, and 1 Russian.

There is no better source to establish the continuing reliance on foreign workmen in Grand Rapids than the study of furniture manufacturing undertaken by the Immigration Commission and published in 1911 as part of *Immigrants in Industries,* now referred to as the Dillingham Report. In discussing Grand Rapids, this report stated:

The names of its shops are known in every part of the United States, but to a very small number of the thousands of persons who regard the city as a center of the furniture industry is it known that more than 85 per cent of the employees in its shops are aliens. The specimens of the wood-carver's art which are offered for sale in the stores of the larger cities of the United States and the plain kitchen chairs found in the homes of the laboring classes are both the production of the furniture plants of Grand Rapids. Dutch, German, Swedish, Polish, and Lithuanian immigrants have developed these shops and have given the city its present industrial recognition.

And in the same report, Rockford, Illinois, was cited as another example of a furniture-producing city indebted to the foreign-born: ''with the close of the [Civil] war, and the arrival of a large number of Swedes, the industry began a development which during the past twenty years [1890–1910] has placed Rockford among the leading furniture manufacturing centers in the United States.'' Swedish immigrants were credited with having ''practically given the city its furniture industry, for they have supplied the labor, skill, and in most instances, the money for conducting the several plants.''

With regard to the United States as a whole, the number of employees involved in furniture production more than doubled between 1880 and 1905, and in states such as Michigan and Indiana, it quadrupled. The demand for workers ''was largely met by the employment of immigrants,'' according to *Immigrants in Industries.* Mechanization and foreign workers were key factors in the phenomenal expansion of this industry. Yet, as pervasive as the immigrant furniture maker was in nineteenth-century America, the details of his history remain to be written.

156A

The Czechs and Mother-of-Pearl

The law of change and progressive mechanization, and the resulting Americanization that followed a step or two behind, did not preclude the transfer of purely ethnic trades. The Dutch, for example, brought the diamond-cutting craft to New York during the second part of the nineteenth century. And for several decades of the early twentieth century the Jews of Eastern Europe and Russia dominated the garment industry of New York [**156A, 156B, 157, 158**]. On a smaller scale, Czechoslovaks established the mother-of-pearl industry in the mid-Atlantic states.

Zirovnice, a small town in southeastern Bohemia, was a center of mother-of-pearl industries, famous for its buttons, buckles, and clasps. In the course of the nineteenth century the United States had become its best customer. In 1890, when Congress passed the McKinley tariff bill, designed to protect American industry by restricting foreign imports, the buttonmakers of Zirovnice saw their livelihood jeopardized. Their response was bold: emigration to America. Within a few years, the manufacture of mother-of-pearl buttons (made from ocean shells, in contrast to the much cheaper freshwater shells) in America became a distinctly Czech industry. In 1921, there were in the U.S. sixty-seven independent manufacturers of Czech origin employing some 1,500 workers. Located almost exclusively in New York, New Jersey, and Connecticut, they constituted three-fourths of the entire mother-of-pearl industry of the United States.

Some of the buttonmakers from Zirovnice struck it rich. Benedict Schwanda, for example, who emigrated in 1892 with his family, two workmen, and three foot-powered lathes (the essential tool in the craft), built a large button manufacturing and importing business that flourished for generations. For others, like Frank Ranuska, buttonmaking was a home industry carried out with the help of family members. The lathe that Frank Ranuska brought with him in 1905 was already old, perhaps a hundred years or more [**159**]. Getting the bulky antique across continental Europe and, in steerage, over the Atlantic Ocean was no small task. His readiness to undertake it bespeaks the craftsman's attachment to the time-honored tool and his dependence upon it as a means of livelihood.

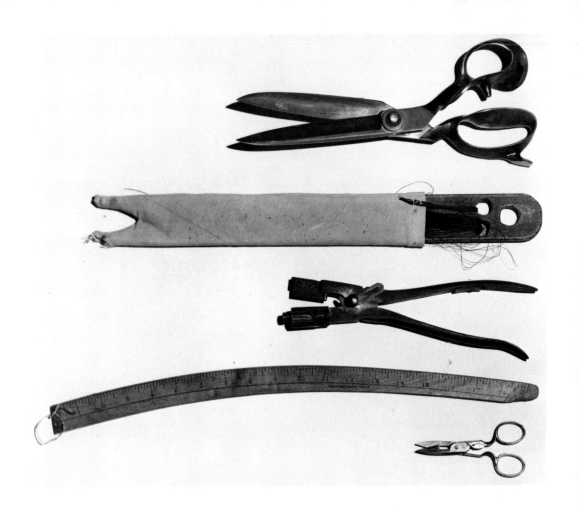

156B

156A
Glass sign of Russian-born
Bainet Rudin. L 30″.

156B
Tailor's tools belonging to
Bainet Rudin (1881–1959),
who was born in Minsk, Russia, emigrated to New York
City in 1899, and worked in
Rochester until his death.
From the top: tailor shears,
pressing board for seams,
buttonhole cutter, curved rule
for making patterns, and buttonhole scissors. Similar tools
can be seen in 157.

157
Immigrant sweatshop in Ludlow Street tenement, photographed by Jacob Riis.

158

158
A clothing worker in New York City carrying work to be sewn at home (1910).

227

159
Bohemian buttonmaker's lathe used in Little Ferry, New Jersey. This lathe was brought to America in steerage in 1905 by Frank Ranuska, an immigrant from Zirovnice in Austria-Hungary (now Czechoslovakia). H 52″.

While the mother-of-pearl business was a curious example of craft transfer, the much larger and more influential world of printing and the manufacture of printing equipment was an immigrant domain for many years. With patriotic pride tinged with apology, the publisher of *Story and Humphrey's Pennsylvania Mercury* announced to his readers on April 7, 1775, the debut of American-made type:

The printers beg leave to acquaint their Subscribers and the Public that the Types with which this Paper is printed are of American manufacture, and should it by this means fail of giving such entire satisfaction to the judicious and accurate eye, they hope every patriotic allowance will be made in its favour, and that an attempt to introduce so valuable an art into these colonies, will meet with an indulgent countenance from every lover of his country.

The type probably came from the Germantown foundry of Jacob Bay, a Swiss silk weaver who, in the belief that type founding held more promise, had taught himself the art. Bay had a mechanical genius of many facets: he had a weaving partnership and an interest in stone quarrying as well as his foundry. But his business did not succeed, and in 1793 the foundry was sold, at about the same time that Bay went into bankruptcy.

Adam Mappa was a Dutch type founder who had to leave his hometown of Delft after taking part in the unsuccessful revolution of 1787. He arrived in New York two years later. The type founding equipment he brought with him included matrices for Hebrew, Greek, Samaritan, Arabic, and Saxon type—not the best selection for a foundry in the United States. Mappa's first effort was announced in 1791 with sentiments similar to the *Mercury*'s: "The Types are not so perfectly Regular as those from the London Foundaries, which have been improving for centuries—but, no Cash went to London for them—and our infant Manufactures ought to be encouraged, so that they also may improve." Mappa advertised for journeymen skilled in type founding, but apparently he ended as his own workman. A few years later he gave up the struggle and put his foundry up for sale.

The next attempt to establish type founding in this country was made by the Scots Archibald Binny and James Ronaldson, type founder and baker, who set up their foundry in Philadelphia in 1796. Business was not easy at first, but the partners were able to profit from the failures of their predecessors: over the years they acquired type and equipment from Mappa's defunct foundry as well as material from the Philadelphia foundry of the Scot John Baine, the French founding equipment that had been imported by Benjamin Franklin for his grandson Benjamin Franklin Bache in 1786, and the foundry of another Scot, Robert Lothian, whose enterprise had failed about 1810. Binny and Ronaldson prospered, and type founding proved a viable American industry.

Eighteenth-century printing-press builders in America faced the same difficulties as the early type founders: inadequate skills and equipment and too strong competition from Europe. The first to get rich was Adam Ramage, a Scot who had a shop in Philadelphia in the first half of the nineteenth century. While the early 1800s in Europe already saw the tradtional wooden press yielding to the new and faster iron presses, Ramage specialized in an improved form of the old wooden press, giving it an extension of life and perhaps holding back acceptance of iron presses in this country for a few years.

Two of Ramage's contemporaries in the printing trade were Robert Hoe, an English immigrant, and George Bruce from Scotland, both of whom founded more forward-looking enterprises. Hoe's press-building factory eventually eclipsed Ramage's and reversed the direction of trade across the Atlantic; after 1850, Hoe presses were used by many European newspapers. George Bruce, with his brother David, set up a type foundry in 1815, and the business flourished until 1892, when competition from the new Linotype machine forced Bruce to merge with other founders and form the American Type Founders Company.

Ottmar Mergenthaler, whose Linotype had brought about the type founders' amalgamation, was cut of another cloth. His genius was invention, not business. Mergenthaler arrived in Baltimore from Germany in 1872 at the age of eighteen and, while working at his cousin's instrument shop, applied himself to any puzzling mechanical problems that came his way. Among these was the matter of a machine to set printer's type. This was not a new idea: various devices had been proposed in the preceding fifty years and some were on the market, but none had done serious damage to the hand compositor's trade. The most promising approach seemed to be a dual apparatus, with one machine to cast a supply of specially nicked type and a second with a keyboard to set this type in lines and pages and later return it to storage compartments for reuse. Mergenthaler took a different approach from the start—he used no type. "I knew the direction in which others had attempted to solve the problem, and was careful not to fall into the same rut which had led every previous effort into failure and ruin."

His first machine punched letters into a papier-mâché mold in which a stereotype plate was to be cast. The second one used bands of brass in which letters were stamped. The bands were arranged by keyboard action and lines of letters cast from them. Over the next fifteen years Mergenthaler doggedly pursued his idea through patent and legal action, illness and dispute. In 1885, his backers suggested that he might now stop improving the machine and concentrate on production, but Mergenthaler was already back at the drawing board. The following year a syndicate of newspaper publishers, men with the greatest interest in the success of the invention, was formed to oversee the business end of the operation. But while they eventually brought success to the Linotype, there was only more discord and bitterness for Mergenthaler. In 1892 Bruce and twenty-four other type founders were forced into their protective alliance because Linotype was stealing away their most important customers, the newspapers. By 1895 it was estimated that there were four thousand Linotypes around the world. Four years later Mergenthaler died, a sick and unhappy man, still seeking redress from the syndicate that had, he thought, taken his name and his invention from him.

The art of wood engraving—another area of printing in which the immigrant reigned—was imported from England in the 1790s and by the 1820s had evolved into the most common form of picture seen by Americans until the start of the twentieth century. *Harper's Weekly* and *Frank Leslie's Illustrated Newspaper,* both inaugurated in the 1850s, employed numerous Europeans in their wood-engraving shops. Today these pictures are reproduced repeatedly as historical windows to nineteenth-century life, and they seem so "American" that it takes almost a scholastic discipline to recognize them as products of immigrant hands. The same is true of lithography. While wood engravings appeared in books, magazines, and other bound periodicals, the lithographs—for technical reasons—dominated the market for single-sheet pictures. Everything from fine art reproduction to insurance company calendars and political blurbs was lithographed. The most famous firm was Currier and Ives, but there were many others. In nearly every large American lithographic company Germans, French, Swiss, Russians, or English could be found, and in several firms all these nationalities were present. When color lithography became a practical reality in America in the 1850s, it was due to the contributions of an Englishman, William Sharp, the four Rosenthal brothers from Russia, two German refugees from the revolution of 1848 (Louis Prang and Julius Bien [**160**]), a Frenchman named P. S. Duval, several Canadians, and one Philadelphian born in the Orkney Islands (Thomas S. Sinclair). Each brought a skill from abroad and shaped it in such a way as to please American customers. The story echoes repeatedly in nearly every craft and trade.

160
A chromolithograph by German-born printer Julius Bien of John James Audubon's "Dusty Duck" (1859). This was one of the earliest full-color lithographs printed in America.

In the exploration and settlement of the North American continent, firearms were the indispensable companions of the explorers and settlers. They provided both sustenance—game was a staple of the early American's diet—and protection from constant conflict. For over two hundred years the European powers were contending among themselves for control of the New World, while also battling the Indians, who fought a losing fight against those who encroached on their lands.

In the beginning the arms came from Europe. The Spanish, English, Germans, Dutch, French, and Scandinavians brought their weapons with them and depended on their homelands to keep them supplied [161A–161C]. It has been estimated that during the seventeenth and eighteenth centuries over 320,000 firearms were sent to America by European governments for their troops and settlers. In spite of laws prohibiting the selling of arms to the Indians, the white man's desire for furs and the Indian's for firearms resulted in a brisk trade [162, 164]. A typical transaction between the Dutch settlers and their Indian neighbors was to exchange twenty Indian beaver pelts for one firearm.

The demand for firearms made the gunsmith one of the most important craftsmen in America. It has been estimated, based on the census of 1850, that in the preceding two hundred years over seven thousand men and their apprentices were engaged in the making and repairing of firearms. Although these gunsmiths could be found in almost every settlement, they tended to locate in the large communities. The largest group was in New England, concentrated about Boston, Hartford, and Springfield. The next largest was in eastern Pennsylvania, particularly in Lancaster. From these two regions distinct types of weapons emerged which reflected the European origins of the American gunsmiths.

Most of the New England gunsmiths were from the British Isles. They produced smooth-bore fowling pieces of the patterns they had used or made previously. In eastern Pennsylvania the German and Swiss settlers introduced in the late seventeenth century their native rifles, which they modified over a period of fifty years until a new pattern emerged that was to become respected throughout the world as the American long rifle. The distinctive feature of the original Central European firearm was that the bore was cut with spiral grooves to engage the bullet and give it a spinning motion in flight, thereby increasing its accuracy and range. It was a short, heavy arm, ideally suited to hunting conditions in its place of origin. But it was inadequate for the needs of the American settlers and hunters, who encountered a wider variety of game and did not have a ready supply of powder and lead.

By the first half of the eighteenth century these immigrants from Central Europe and their descendants had developed a rifle with a long, slender barrel of reduced caliber which permitted the complete and effective combustion of a smaller charge of powder and reduced the amount of lead needed to bring down game. For over one hundred years this American long rifle was regarded as the most accurate long-range rifle in the world. Although this arm originated in Pennsylvania, we know it today as the Kentucky rifle because of its extensive use in the eighteenth and nineteenth centuries in that area west of the Cumberland known then as the Kentucky Territory [163A–163F].

The long rifle in turn was modified to meet new conditions of hunting and different varieties of game as the American frontier moved westward across the Great Plains and over the Rocky Mountains. By 1830 gunsmiths had altered the basic Kentucky design to produce a shorter rifle for use on horseback. It had a thick barrel and a large bore which fired a heavy charge at long range. During the course of its development it was known by many names: plains rifle, mountain rifle, buffalo rifle, Missouri rifle, and Hawken rifle [165A–165C]. The latter was made in St. Louis by the brothers Jacob and Samuel Hawken, sons of Christian Hawken, a Kentucky riflemaker of Hagerstown, Maryland. Other gunmakers on the Missouri who were either immigrants or their descendants were Adolphus Meir, John Gemmer, Meyer Friede, Frederick Schwarz, and John Blickensdorfer.

These firearms were made in small one- and two-man shops staffed with apprentices who worked with simple hand tools fabricating and assembling all the component parts. In some of the larger communities there was a small degree of specialization; that is, some artisans would make locks, barrels, or roughed-out stocks to be assembled and finished by others. Labor-saving machine tools followed late in the eighteenth century. In Lancaster, as early as 1719, a boring mill for smoothing out gun barrels was in use. In New England it was not until the beginning of the nineteenth century that an arms industry, based on labor-saving machinery, began to develop.

Following the American Revolution, the need for guns accelerated as increasing numbers of settlers moved west and were protected by the army and the militia. The young Republic could no longer depend on European imports to supplement the inadequate production of local gunmakers. To meet its military needs, the U.S. government in 1795 established two national armories to make small arms: one in Springfield, Massachusetts, and the other in Harper's Ferry, Virginia. It soon became evident that these were not sufficient, and contracts were made with private gunmakers. Provided with liberal cash advances, the contractors were able to invest the necessary capital and time in the development of machine tools that could produce quality arms in quantity.

By 1842, the national armories, working with their government-subsidized contractors, developed machinery with which they produced arms made of completely interchangeable parts. The "American system of manufacturing," as it became known in Europe, was extended to other fields, and the age of mass production was born.

The gun, however available, however well made, and however interchangeable its parts, could not perform effectively with low-grade gunpowder. During the colonial period American powder was notoriously poor. Once again, an immigrant stepped into the breach.

161A

161A
English flintlock military carbine bearing the cipher of James II (1685–1688). OAL 45½".

161B
German matchlock military musket, c. 1640. OAL 58½".

161C
French wheel-lock fowling piece, 1625. OAL 64".

161B

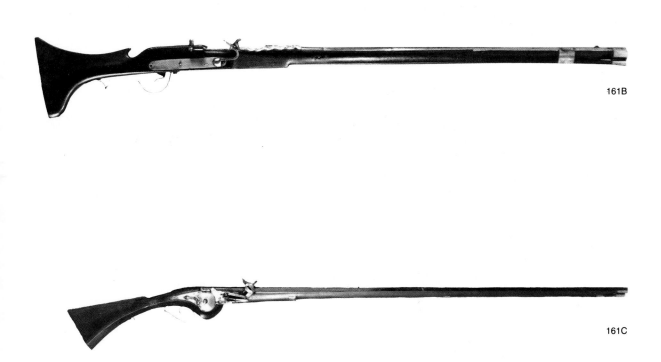

161C

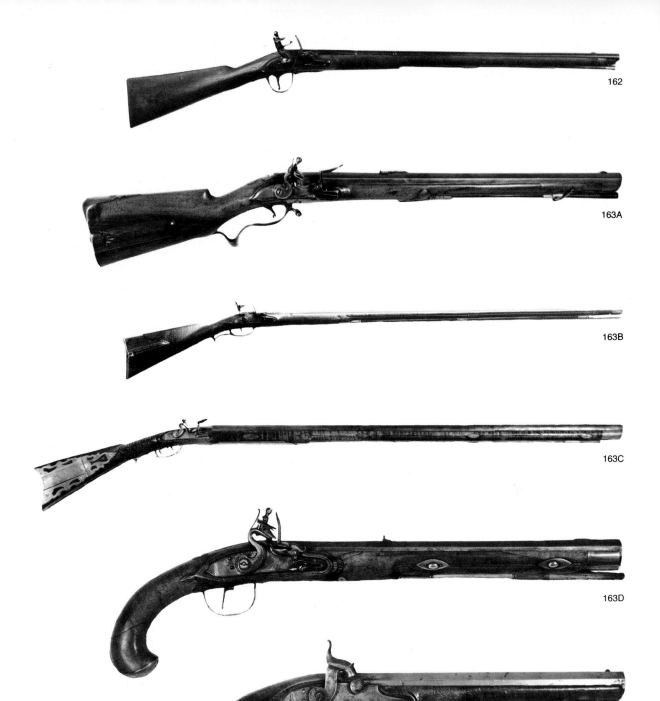

162
Northwest trade gun made by Parker Field and Co. of London for the Hudson Bay Company. OAL 45½".

163A
German flintlock hunting rifle, c. 1725. OAL 37½".

163B
Kentucky flintlock rifle, c. 1780. OAL 44½".

163C
Kentucky rifle, made in 1817 by Nathan Kile, Jackson County, Ohio. OAL 58".

163D
Kentucky flintlock pistol by J. Bellah, c. 1814. OAL 17¾".

163E
Kentucky flintlock pistol, by S. Lauck, converted to percussion system (c. 1815). OAL 15".

163F
Kentucky flintlock rifle made by Henry Deringer in 1830. OAL 58½".

164
Mezzotint of Sa Ga Yeath Tow, a Mohawk chief, made in England in 1710 on the occasion of his visit to Queen Anne. He is holding a flintlock fowler of the pattern often presented to Indian chieftains by the British government.

162

163A

163B

163C

163D

163E

163F

SA GA YEATH QUA PIETH Tow, King of the Maquas.
Printed for Jac. Bowles & Son, at the Black Horse in Cornhill London.

I Verelst Pinx.ᵗ

I Simon fe

165A
Plains percussion rifle by
Samuel Hawken of St. Louis,
c. 1835. OAL 53½".

165B
Plains percussion rifle by
Tryon Company of Philadel-
phia, c. 1850. OAL 53".

165C
Sharps breech-loading "Old
Reliable" buffalo rifle, c. 1876.
The Sharps rifle was the most
widely used breech-loading,
single-shot rifle in the American West. OAL 45".

165A

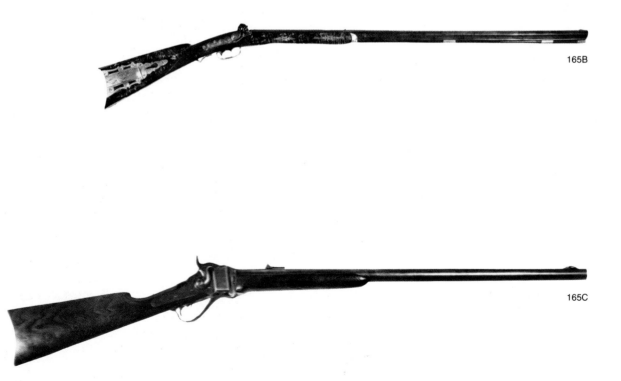

165B

165C

Éleuthère Irénée du Pont de Nemours and the American Gunpowder Trade

The immigrant guidebooks of the nineteenth century echoed a common refrain: "The rich stay in Europe; it is only the middling and the poor that emigrate." America was a place for those who had nothing to lose. Aristocrats, landed gentry, and privileged clergy were advised to stay at home. The same was true for scholars and university professors, particularly in the early part of the nineteenth century, before overproduction of well-trained academics filled American schools with foreign-born instructors. The idea that a family of the French nobility with scientific and intellectual status would emigrate to America in 1800 suggests unusual circumstances—and this was the case of Éleuthère Irénée du Pont de Nemours.

Irénée was born in 1771. His family owned an estate south of Paris, and his father, Pierre (1739–1817), who was elevated to the nobility in 1783, was part of an intellectual economic and political reform group known as the physiocrats. Irénée's godfather was one of the most important men in France—Anne Robert Jacques Turgot (1727–1781), the philosophe—and his most influential teacher was the renowned Antoine Lavoisier (1743–1794).

Lavoisier is justly celebrated as the father of modern chemistry, but from 1775 on he was helping the government of France establish a viable gunpowder industry. One of his assistants was Éleuthère Irénée du Pont. As a member of the Gunpowder Commission, Lavoisier showed a genius for planning and organizing that was on a par with his scientific abilities. The systems for producing saltpeter were reviewed, revised, and standardized in print, and in relatively short order France achieved a stable and adequate supply of gunpowder. Working at the arsenal, young Du Pont learned the best in chemistry, for Lavoisier was just in the process of codifying the chemical revolution, as it has come to be called. Moreover, Irénée undoubtedly learned the latest science-based technology as well, for Lavoisier produced more than two score works which dealt with saltpeter and gunpowder. For anyone who would later be employed in making gunpowder, there simply was no better place to learn the trade.

The three years spent with Lavoisier were no happy idyll. The French Revolution was beginning, and soon the political and financial fortunes of Irénée's father, Pierre, waned. In 1791, with the adjournment of the Constituent Assembly, of which he had been a member, Pierre embarked on a career in the printing trade. Capital was supplied by Lavoisier in return for a mortgage on the Du Pont lands. In late September 1791 Lavoisier was removed from the Gunpowder Commission and, though briefly reinstated, he was forced to leave the arsenal in early 1792.

Although gunpowder-making operations continued at the arsenal, Irénée had no wish to stay after Lavoisier's removal. Moreover, he wished to marry, and to support himself and his bride he assumed an active role in the management of his father's printing company. In spite of the difficult times and the competition from the older houses, the venture did well in its first year, involved mostly with printing the pamphlets and short tracts that abounded during the revolution. Ironically, Du Pont also obtained several contracts to print assignats, the revolutionary currency he had earlier denounced before the Constituent Assembly.

Pierre du Pont's political ventures during this time were less successful. In 1792 he organized a small militia, which took part in the defense of the king at the Tuileries during the riot of August 10. When the defense collapsed, Pierre and his small band escaped through the simple but clever maneuver of marching in formation as though they were victor instead of vanquished. But Pierre's presence on the king's side had been noted, though Irénée's had not, and he was forced to go into hiding. In September Pierre slipped out of the city, leaving Irénée to print books, bonds, and still more money. Somehow Irénée found time to help set up a saltpeter refinery, to establish a newspaper, and to double the work of the printing business.

In May 1794 Lavoisier went to the guillotine. In July Pierre was arrested and taken to La Force prison. Luckily, it was late in that important month, and within the week the architect of the Terror, Robespierre, was overthrown and Pierre was saved. But the end of the Terror did not bring an end to trouble for the Du Ponts. Pierre involved himself in the affairs of the new government: first elected a deputy from Nemours to the upper house, then elected its president by his fellow deputies, he clashed with the ruling directors and was again arrested, as was Irénée, on September 5, 1797. Although quickly freed, Pierre du Pont submitted his resignation to the government and along with Irénée decided to go to America.

The choice was not unexpected. Irénée's brother, Victor Marie (1767–1827), had entered the diplomatic service in 1787 and served in the French legation in America the same year. By 1798 he was on his third tour and had been appointed French consul general, but President John Adams refused to accept him because of the current serious deterioration in French-American relations, and he returned to France.

Despite this unhappy period, Victor du Pont had enjoyed his life in America. His positive reactions played a strong role in the all-too-optimistic picture that Pierre described shortly before leaving France: "The temperate, moderate, judicious and republican government of the United States offers almost the only asylum where persecuted men can find safety, where fortunes can be rebuilt through work." In 1797, after a talk with Robert Fulton, Irénée called it the "promised land" in a letter to his wife. The repellent effect of their experiences during the Terror and the Directorate was greatly intensified by the attraction of apparent opportunity in the new land.

In late 1799, after two years of seemingly interminable preparations by Pierre du Pont, most of the family sailed aboard the *American Eagle*. Never was a vessel more inaptly named. Far from soaring majestically across the Atlantic, the *American Eagle,* overloaded and inadequately provisioned, took a month longer than Columbus to reach the New World. Only the indomitable Pierre retained anything approaching good spirits. On New Year's Day, 1800, in the midst of an extremely harsh winter, the family arrived at Newport, Rhode Island. Several days later they made their way by packet boat to the New York area.

The original intent of Pierre du Pont and his sons Irénée and Victor was to set up a company "chiefly to buy and sell land and incidentally to organize any commercial and industrial establishments that may contribute to the improvement of the estates and increase their value." Although a number of important Frenchmen bought shares in the new company, there were more promises than payments, and sufficient capital was lacking to begin a large enterprise. After getting some opinions, including a letter from Pierre's old friend Thomas Jefferson about the dangers of land speculation, the du Ponts decided to abandon the land schemes.

With Victor as its acting head, the family next attempted to set up a company that would act as a broker for commercial ventures between France and America. This was more effective, but the strained French-American relationship meant that the ventures were limited and the profits correspondingly small. A number of new schemes which they hoped would bring better returns were considered toward the end of 1800. One of these was Irénée's proposal for a gunpowder manufactory.

It is believed that the idea came to Irénée during one or more hunting expeditions with a Frenchman who had fought in the American Revolution, Colonel Louis de Tousard. When forced to buy powder at local stores, Du Pont had noticed its poor quality, and Tousard and others assured him that this was usual. Further investigation, including visits to American powder mills, convinced Irénée that profit could be made from a well-run mill producing powder of the quality he had come to know when working under Lavoisier.

In January 1801 Victor and Irénée sailed for France to raise capital for the new venture. Irénée was completely successful, and in addition was able to obtain drawings for necessary machinery as well as some of the machinery itself. He returned to America in July to find a good location for the new enterprise. After trying in vain to buy existing mills at Frankfurt, Pennsylvania, he toured the area from Washington to New York. A local investor, French émigré Peter Bauduy, of Wilmington, wanted Irénée to locate the mills in Delaware, and eventually Irénée purchased the farm of one Jacob Broom on the banks of the Brandywine River near Wilmington.

Irénée immediately set about building the manufactory. Drawing upon both his experience and his fresh ideas, he produced an innovative arrangement: the several processes required to produce powder were to be performed in a number of small buildings spaced well apart instead of in a single large facility. Thus an explosion at one stage would not set off the entire mill. Each building had three strong sides and one relatively flimsy wall facing the river. The roof, too, was of very light construction. Thus any explosion would be "released" in a relatively controlled fashion and in a direction away from the other buildings to avoid heavy "shrapnel."

To make the plant operational took two years, but by the end of the first year the facility was able to process saltpeter, and it soon received an order from the secretary of war to refine some saltpeter for gunpowder for the army. For every step of the process, Irénée had introduced the best methods and machinery he could in order to bring the product up to French standards as established by Lavoisier. This paid off in more than one way. Not only did the new company receive a gratifying number of orders for new powder, but on many occasions it was sent saltpeter to refine and even powder to "remake."

The years of early growth were not without blemish. The most severe problems, perhaps, came from Peter Bauduy, whose personality and outlook were so different from those of Irénée du Pont that clashes were inevitable. Bauduy had invested heavily in the project, and he was anxious to see rapid and maximum profits. Du Pont saw Bauduy's role as that of a "silent" partner and resented the intrusions. Du Pont attributed, probably rightly, the plant's first major explosion to Bauduy's "economy" of burning charcoal and drying powder under the same roof.

There were additional problems, mainly financial, but on the whole the performance of the young company was impressive. There is disagreement about the sales figures, but those in 1805 were clearly almost triple those of 1804. In the first year they had produced well over 40,000 pounds of powder; by 1808, their capacity had increased to about 300,000 pounds. It was a period of rising prosperity and rising tensions with Britain. By February 1808 Irénée could write to his father, then in France: "I do not know yet whether we will have war or not, but at any rate I am ready, and our reputation is now so well established and our market so extended that even in time of peace we will have a larger demand than we can fill."

Although war did come, and with it orders from the government, it brought new problems. Irénée had to borrow all he could in order to increase the capacity of the plants. This situation was aggravated by his father's successful campaign to convince the French shareholders of his son's great success: they were clamoring for payment of dividends and threatening to dissolve the company just when Irénée needed as much credit as he could obtain. Eventually Du Pont provided some 750,000 pounds of powder to the army and, through local dealers in the principal seaports, an unaccountable amount to the navy. The War of 1812 did not bring the Du Ponts immense profits, but it consolidated the company's position as the largest of the American powder mills.

In 1815 Irénée's father returned to Delaware. He landed in the midst of the final disagreement between Bauduy and Irénée, and the partnership was dissolved that spring. It did not end the trouble with Bauduy, for he went into the powder business for himself, building a rival mill nearby and coaxing away Du Pont workers. In addition, he started a lawsuit which dragged on eight years before judgment was given in favor of the Du Pont family.

On the night of July 16, 1817, misfortune struck in the form of a fire in the charcoal house. Indefatigable as ever, Pierre placed himself in the midst of the fire fighting. The next day he was unable to rise, and a month later, on August 17, he died, at the age of seventy-seven.

In spite of another disaster on March 19, 1818, when some 85,000 pounds of powder exploded in the space of a few minutes, with the loss of many lives, Irénée Du Pont had the satisfaction of receiving numerous honors during his remaining years. He was consulted on problems in manufacturing and on an interest he had shared with his father and Lavoisier—agriculture. He gradually added other chemical product lines to the company, and although several of his ventures failed, they set a precedent for American product diversification.

Irénée died on October 31, 1834. His American odyssey had involved the transfer of certain gunpowder-making processes from France to America. Like Samuel Slater and the Crompton brothers, who played an important part in placing American textile mills on sound technological and business foundations, this son of a French nobleman brought the discipline of Lavoisier's chemistry to a trade which—for better or worse—has played an essential role in the history of the United States.

The stereotype of the working immigrant in America is too often a picture of sweatshops, labor gangs, and mass poverty. Yet, as we have seen with the Steinways and the Du Ponts, the printing trades and the furniture industry, the story was often one of the success of individual talent and initiative. The annals of American mining also contain the names—often unfamiliar to our ears—of individual immigrants whose enterprise and venturesome spirit helped to change the course of American industrial history.

In 1835 Johann August Suter, a thirty-five-year-old Swiss army officer, landed in New York. Suter, who had been born in the German Black Forest of an immigrant family of Swiss papermakers, had attended the military academy at Neuchâtel, practiced papermaking, returned to the army in the post-Napoleonic depression, and developed a wanderlust which finally carried him to America.

He soon headed west, to St. Louis, and then to Independence, the takeoff point for the western adventure. With a companion, he joined the Santa Fe traders. On one of his trips, "Indian troubles" diverted him northward as far as Vancouver, and to avoid wintering there he took passage to Hawaii. His objective was California, and he finally made it after another detour to Russian America (Sitka) in 1839.

Interior California was still a wilderness on which Mexicans and Russians were gradually encroaching. Suter, acquainted with both, became a Mexican citizen and induced the governor at Monterey to authorize him to establish a colony on the northern frontier. Here he founded Nueva Helvetia (which included the site of the subsequent capital, Sacramento), of which he became the virtual sovereign. In 1841, when the Russians gave up the contest, their southernmost settlement, Rossya (Fort Ross), was sold to Suter, who hauled most of it off to Nueva Helvetia. He constructed a fort which became a rallying point for others who drifted in from the East.

The conquest of California by the United States so little disturbed Sutter, as he now called himself, that he was a candidate for the governorship in the first election. But he was disturbed by something else. On January 24, 1848, when he was away on business, gold had been found on his estate. While he was running for governor his workmen were deserting him, and his herds disappeared to be replaced by gold-seeking squatters. The estate was never to be put together again.

The year 1848 was also decisive for the family of Emanuel Sutro, a prosperous cloth manufacturer in Aachen, the legendary seat of Charlemagne. Sutro was killed in that year in a freak carriage accident, and within a few months his business collapsed in the disorders of the revolution of 1848. His eighteen-year-old son, Adolph, one of eleven children, responded with the energy to be expected of a young man who at sixteen had wanted to join a rebellion in Poland. He left school, engaged himself to construct a cloth factory like his father's for a friendly capitalist in Memel, Lithuania; and when war, and especially conscription, closed in, he departed for America. His mother followed with the family, settling in Baltimore with yet another plan for a textile business. But Adolph caught gold fever, and after two weeks in New York he departed, via Panama, for San Francisco, where he arrived in November 1851.

Bad luck—or a prudence residual from his mercantile background—led Sutro to forgo the goldfields in favor of business in general merchandise, especially tobacco. After a decade of moderately successful trading and shrewd observation of the travails of the miners, Sutro was in a position to capitalize on his interest in the newly discovered silver bonanza in Nevada. The decade since the discovery of gold on Sutter's estate had seen the decline of the solitary prospector and the rise of the entrepreneur, and also the replacement of the "pan" by more complex machinery capable of processing larger quantities of material. Sutro is said to have had two overriding interests not often found together: books and machinery. He recognized the primitive and wasteful methods practiced in the Nevada mines, and established at East Dayton a mill capable of extracting valuable ore from the tailings (residues) of other mills. He then conceived the unprecedented idea of driving a large tunnel three miles into the source of the Comstock Lode—Mount Davidson. He obtained a charter from the state for a Sutro Tunnel Company in 1865 and set about raising money.

By the 1870s the uproarious competition among the obstreperous "mining interests" of the West had exceeded the governing powers of the states and had become a matter of continuous concern to the federal government. Sutro was soon engaged in a struggle with his California backers over control of the tunnel company and went to Europe to seek counterbalancing financial support. By 1872 Congress, which had authorized the company to carry the tunnel through public lands in 1866, was investigating the project.

The country celebrated its hundredth birthday in 1876 with a great fair at Philadelphia which was probably attended by our third immigrant, Hermann Frasch, who was completing a decade of work and study at the Philadelphia College of Pharmacy. Frasch had less the aspect of a refugee, being the son of the *Bürgermeister* of the town of Gaildorf in Württemberg. Whatever wanderlust brought him to America in 1868, at the age of seventeen, found an antidote—at least to the lure of California—at the Philadelphia College of Pharmacy. But by 1876 neither the colonial metropolis nor the new El Dorado was the center of gravity of the United States; it had settled, almost imperceptibly, on the often ridiculed town in the swamps of the Potomac, "Washington City." Here the fates of Sutter and Sutro were settled in the 1870s, in very different ways.

Sutter had fallen into bankruptcy in the 1850s, despite some monetary restitution and the bestowal of a commission as general by the state. In 1866 he moved to Lititz, Lancaster County, Pennsylvania, for a number of reasons, not least to be near Washington, where another bill for his relief was pending. He came almost every summer and must have crossed paths with Sutro, who occasionally visited Washington in connection with the seemingly endless investigation of the tunnel project. When the tunnel was completed in 1877 (at a cost of six and one-half million dollars), Sutro was still in control; but his control was not firm, and in the early months of 1880 he sold off his stock and returned to California. He had no need to be in Washington in the summer of that year when Sutter, summering in the hot city while his "bill" was brought up for the sixteenth time, died in a Washington hotel room.

Sutro turned to a new and less uncertain bonanza—real estate. At one time he is said to have owned one-eighth of San Francisco, and he repaid the city with such ornaments as the famous Cliff House and the spectacular Sutro Baths, the finest bathing pavilion then in existence. He was also able to indulge his other enthusiasm, books, and he assembled a library of rarities which remains (less the substantial part destroyed in the earthquake and fire) a cultural monument of the city. In 1894–1895 he was mayor of San Francisco.

Frasch had also fallen on a new bonanza—petroleum. He had left the Philadelphia College of Pharmacy in 1877 to open a private laboratory in the current oil capital, Cleveland. He proved to be an ingenious and successful inventor and revolutionized the industry with a process for removing sulfur from the low-grade petroleums of the Great Lakes area, increasing the value of these oils sevenfold. By 1885 he had established his own oil company in London, Ontario, an enterprise he later abandoned profitably to the Rockefeller interests.

Our fourth immigrant arrived in 1879, while Frasch was revolutionizing the petroleum industry, Sutro was enjoying his brief victory in the tunnel contest, and Sutter was nearing the end of his quest for restitution. This was Anthony F. Luchich, an Austrian naval officer and son of a Dalmatian ship-builder of Montenegrin stock. "Slavs" were not well placed in the Austrian navy, and Luchich, who had come on a visit to an uncle in Saginaw, Michigan, decided to stay. He resigned his commission, changed his name to Lucas, and entered the lumber business in Michigan. He was twenty-four years old, a graduate of the polytechnic school at Graz, as well as of the naval academy at Fiume and Pola, and hence overtrained for the lumber business. By 1888 he appears as a consulting engineer in Washington, D.C.

The West had not altogether lost its appeal, nor yielded all its secrets. About 1890 Frasch turned his attention to the problem of Gulf Coast sulfur. Deposits were known to exist there, but deeply buried in unstable ground and virtually inaccessible to mining. The world continued to depend, as it had through the century, on Sicilian sulfur, controlled by a monopoly which became increasingly troublesome as the growing sulfuric acid industry bolstered the demand for the material. By 1891 Frasch had devised a method for extracting sulfur from deposits in Louisiana. It consisted of a system of three concentric pipes, driven down to the level of the mineral. Hot water was pumped through one pipe, air through another, the former to melt the sulfur and the latter to force it to rise, in the form of foam, through the third pipe. After several years of experimentation Frasch again found himself with a company, and the United States, which had produced almost no sulfur, became the world's principal exporter.

One element of the success of the Frasch process was the local availability of petroleum, which provided the cheap fuel needed by this extravagantly energy-consuming process. It had been remarked for a generation that the peculiar "islands" of the Gulf Coast—low, domelike elevations in the coastal swamps—seemed to contain salt, sulfur, and petroleum, sometimes all three. Salt, until the late nineteenth century esteemed the most important of the three, had been mined sporadically on Petit Anse "island" since the Civil War, the intermittent character of the mines being a consequence of the instability of the ground. Although the oil craze in the United States was in its second generation, hardly anyone believed that petroleum existed in sufficient quantity to serve large-scale energy requirements. The oil that oozed from some of the coastal "islands" was found to be both cheap and adequate for local uses, including the firing of the boilers for the Frasch process.

Lucas, who had not only gained some acquaintance with the West but had indulged in unsuccessful gold prospecting in Colorado, found his bonanza in the Gulf Coast "islands." In 1893, while Frasch was perfecting his process for extracting sulfur, Lucas arrived at Petit Anse, having been engaged by the salt company to revive its ever-precarious mines. As the mines were periodically flooded, drilling for better sites was more or less continuous. It was thought that the Petit Anse deposit was near the surface over a relatively small, circular area beyond which the deepest drillings seemed to find no salt. Lucas became an expert driller and soon a contributor to the theory that the salt existed in the form of a plug or dome thrust up from some extreme depth.

He also became interested in the frequent accompaniment of the salt by petroleum and sulfur. Many of the easily identifiable domes on the Gulf Coast had become targets for oil prospectors. One of the domes was Big Hill near Beaumont, Texas, where Otillio Higgins had been drilling for years and had succeeded in extracting enough petroleum to fire his own boiler. In 1899 he was joined by Lucas, who saw the problem to be technological, the difficulty of drilling in sand. He adopted a type of drill that rotated (most oil wells were drilled by percussion bits) and flushed out the material cut away by water carried down the drilling tube. Such drills had been used for artesian wells and for a few oil wells. Lucas improved on them, at a cost that necessitated frequent visits to eastern capitalists. Finally, with the resources of J. M. Guffy and the Mellon interests of Pittsburgh behind him, he began the new century with his drill below a thousand feet. On January 10, 1901, the drill hole erupted with oil at 1,139 feet and flooded the fields around. Lucas had "brought in" Spindletop gusher, still by far the most productive oil well discovered in the United States.

A new century and a new age had also been brought in. Lucas's profits were modest, for he had mortgaged them to his backers, and his connection with the Spindletop oil field lasted only eight months. He returned to his consulting business in Washington, where he died in 1921, the last of our group of immigrants to survive. Sutro had died in 1898, full of honors and repute as one of the most colorful of the San Francisco gentry. Frasch, publicly honored in 1912 as "one of our greatest industrial chemists and chemical engineers," returned in spirit to the Old World, endowing his birthplace with a "hall" and dying in Paris on the eve of World War I. It was the end of an era.

Chapter 14

The Sights and Sounds of Ethnic Identity

A Foot in Two Worlds

"Green one" or "greenhorn" is one of the many English words and phrases which my mother-tongue has appropriated in England and America. Thanks to the many millions of letters that pass annually between the Jews of Russia and their relatives in the United States, a number of these words have by now come to be generally known among our people at home as well as here. . . . I understand the phrase at once, and as a contemptuous quizzical appellation for a newly arrived, inexperienced immigrant it stung me cruelly.

As I went along I heard it again and again. Some of the passers-by would call me "greenhorn" in a tone of blighting gaiety, but these were an exception. For the most part it was "green one" and in a spirit of sympathetic interest. It hurt me, all the same. Even those glances that offered me a cordial welcome and good wishes had something self-complacent and condescending in them. "Poor fellow! he is a green one," these people seemed to say. "We are not, of course. We are Americanized."

The setting is the lower East Side, on an immigrant's first day in New York City. It is from Abraham Cahan's *The Rise of David Levinsky* (1917), the classic tale of the young Jewish immigrant who climbs the financial ladder only to find isolation and loneliness in a rootless American existence.

The sense of dislocation, of cultural shock, of having lost part of an Old World identity without becoming fully American, are themes that permeate Cahan's short novels, as well as those of other Jewish-American authors, such as Bruno Lessing and Mary Antin, writing in 1890–1920. Cahan was born in Vilna, Russia, in 1860, emigrated to America in 1882, and became the editor of the Jewish *Daily Forward* in 1886. A socialist by philosophy and a forceful orator by personality, he was better known as a journalist than as a novelist, yet he wrote many poignant stories, including *Yekl,* in which Cahan captures the essence of the cultural tension experienced by immigrant families who crossed the sea one at a time. Yekl—Jake—has been Americanized. He is waiting for his wife and daughter, whom he has not seen in several years, to be processed at Ellis Island. "The prospect of meeting his dear wife and child, and incidentally, of showing off his swell attire to her, had thrown him into a fever of impatience." The newly made American was ready for reunion:

But on entering the big shed he had caught a distant glimpse of Gitl and Yosselé through the railing separating the detained immigrants from their visitors, and his heart sunk at the sight of his wife's uncouth and un-American appearance. She was slovenly dressed in a brown jacket and skirt of grotesque cut, and her hair was concealed under a voluminous wig of a pitch-black hue. This she had put on just before leaving the steamer, both "in honor of the Sabbath" and by way of sprucing herself up for the great event. Since Yekl had left home she had gained considerably in the measure of her waist. The wig, however, made her seem stouter and shorter than she would have appeared without it. It also added at least five years to her looks. But she was aware neither of this nor of the fact that in New York even a Jewess of station and orthodox breeding is accustomed to blink at the wickedness of displaying her natural hair, and that none but an elderly matron may wear a wig without being the occasional target for snowballs or stones. She was naturally dark of complexion, and the nine or ten days spent at sea had covered her face with a deep bronze, which combined with her prominent cheek bones, inky little eyes, and above all, the smooth black wig, to lend her resemblance to a squaw.

The immense social pressure to conform, which innumerable observers criticized in America, simply made the Americanizing process seem more important to any immigrant looking for a new beginning.

While there was no one "typical" immigrant experience, on one basic point immigrants did agree: for better or worse, life in America required personal adjustment. There was a chorus of protest against mistreatment by immigration officials. Cahan called them "not a whit better then the Cossacks of Russia." The native Americans were accused of being unfriendly and materialistic. Work conditions were often condemned and cultural practices so different that many immigrants never adjusted to the American way. The foods, the common courtesies of opening doors and shaking hands, the commingling of sexes on public beaches and railroad trains, the use of cosmetics, the loss of Old World status, and the practice of choosing a marriage partner were but a few of the facets of cultural shock.

Those newcomers who came in groups and proceeded to rural areas seemed the most secure. Reverend D. R. Thomason wrote in his *Hints to Emigrants* (1848):

It is a striking fact . . . that the Germans, Dutch, and Swiss succeed much better than those of any other country. This is not so much owing to any greater industry or economy, as to the more judicious mode they adopt in settling. In general, before these people emigrate, they form associations, lay down their plans, and when all necessary arrangements are made, they move over in a body.

Even those who came singly often sought security in a well-defined group identity—in Irish Boston or German Cincinnati, Scandinavian Minneapolis, or Polish Chicago. For virtually every group there were immigrant banks, mutual aid societies, nationalistic associations, cooperative stores, and foreign-language churches and synagogues [166, 167]. In every case the mission was clear: to help each immigrant group maintain a sense of ethnic identity and adjust to the new social conditions of America. There were many other immigrant institutions, which filled diverse roles: to get the newcomer across the sea, to help him find lodging, to give him basic language training, to locate a job for his particular skills, or to supply moral support. Some were informal, such as the Chinese *tong* or the Italian *padrone* system; others were public and institutional. The Hebrew Sheltering and Immigrant Aid Society stated as its purpose:

To facilitate the landing of Jewish immigrants at Ellis Island; to provide for them temporary shelter, aid as may be deemed necessary; to guide them to their destination; to prevent them from becoming public charges and help them to obtain employment; to discourage their settling in congested cities; to maintain bureaus of information and publish literature on the industrial, agricultural, and commercial status of the country.

Many of these agencies have long ago disappeared, the results of their work existing in the form of thousands of linear feet of reports and leaflets on forgotten library shelves throughout the nation.

It is virtually impossible to determine when a "greenhorn" lost his Old World manner and learned the "American way." In dress, in work habits, indeed in all he did in America, the greenhorn struggled to establish himself in society, but the problem of identity remained. In part this was caused by a lack of knowledge about America, and language, of course, was an obvious barrier. The non-English-speaking newcomer had to learn a basic vocabulary almost instantly. We know too little about the history of how millions learned to speak a single tongue, but as early as 1810 a Jesuit visitor from Europe observed:

About nine-tenths speak precisely the same language, which is a national unity probably not to be found, without source variation of dialect, among the same number, so largely diffused, in any other quarter of the world. The German is the only tongue spoken, that forms an exception to this unity of language. That is gradually losing ground, and unless some unforeseen calamity should check the progress of natural increase, it is probable that in one century, there will be 100 millions of people in America, to whom English speech, in its purity, will be vernacular.

While many immigrant women who found themselves locked to housework failed to learn to speak English, the previous observation was usually seconded. In fact, for many who commented on the immigrants' status, the process was too successful: the original languages were left unused or were bastardized by infusions of Americanisms; the essence of the immigrant's Old Worldness—his words—was too often discarded. One Norwegian visitor to America in 1847 lamented:

They do not bother about keeping the two languages separate, so that they may speak Norwegian to their own countrymen and English to others; instead they eliminate one word after the other from their Norwegian and substitute English words in such a way that the Norwegian will soon be completely forgotten.

Such a practice, to be sure, is rather common among uneducated people who emigrate to a foreign country, but the Norwegians seem to have a special knack at it. The first words they forget are "ja" and "nei," and, even if everything else about them, from top to toe, is Norwegian, you may be sure they will answer "yes" or "no" if you ask them any questions. Gradually other English words, pertaining to their daily environment, are added. They have a "faens" about their farm and have probably "digget" a well near the house so that they need not go so far even if there is a "laek" or a "river" in the vicinity, because such water is generally too warm. Near the houses there is frequently a little garden, where they grow "pompuser" (pumpkins) among other things, and a little beyond is "fila" (the English word "field" with the genuine Norwegian feminine article "a").

The ease with which the Norwegians learn the English language has attracted the attention of the Americans, all the more because they are altogether too ready to consider them entirely raw when they come here. "Never," one of them told me a few days ago, "have I known people to become civilized so rapidly as your countrymen; they come here in motley crowds, dressed up with all kinds of dingle-dangle just like the Indians. But just look at them a year later: they speak English perfectly, and, as far as dress, manners, and ability are concerned, they are quite above reproach.

166
The offertory cup or chalice is essential to the Roman Catholic ritual of the Mass. In its gilded, medieval form, the chalice holds wine that symbolizes the blood of Jesus. This chalice was used from 1916 in a Slovene-American church in Connecticut. H 8¾".

167
The Ten Commandments, or Decalogue, delivered by Moses to the ancient Hebrews, appears in synagogues today. This carved walnut and painted example was used in Philadelphia before 1900. H 36¾".

166

There are no fewer then eleven Athenses, eight Frankforts, ten Genevas, eight Moscows, and seven Waterloos in the United States. "It takes three log houses to make a city in Kansas," wrote Horace Greeley in 1866, "but they begin calling it a city as soon as they stake out the lots." Some of these instant cities were presented with ancient and exotic names, like Carthage, in the hope of enhancing their appeal to settlers. John Regan, in *The Emigrant's Guide to the Western States of America* (c. 1852), discussed the naming procedure:

During the palmy days of Land Speculation in Illinois, it was customary to project a city in some favourable looking spot on the banks of some river or creek, without any specific or distinct title. Call the river "Tiber," "Thames," "Tay," or whatever other name appeared most taking. Lay off the ground into streets, blocks, and building lots, and throw the whole into the market by the name of "Mount Vernon," "Troy," "Palmyra," "Bagdad," "Thebes," "Paris," or whatever suited the fancy of the projector.

The German historian Karl Theodor Griesinger (1809–1884) even warned in his *Lebende Bilder aus Amerika* (1858) that many schemes were aimed at particular language groups, with plots of land "given a properly German name like Hermann or Germania."

While many names on the American landscape do reflect a Yankee land shark's attempt to lure the newcomer, many were simply the product of immigrant settlement. Amsterdam, Idaho, was christened by Dutch settlers, as were Holland, Michigan; Holland, Nebraska; and Holland, Minnesota. The story is repeated endlessly in London, Texas; Moscow, Idaho [168]; and Stockholm, South Dakota. One nineteenth-century observer wrote: "On a board in front of a stage-office in Buffalo, I once read, 'stages start from this house for China, Sardinia, Holland, Hamburg, Java, Sweden, Cuba, Havre, Italy, and Penn-Yan.' "

The incongruity and confusion of American geographic nomenclature caused some Americans to call for order. But not one nineteenth-century New York City newspaper disagreed:

The names of towns, cities, and streets in America are standing historical monuments; they tell us from what country, whether England, Holland, Germany, or France, the first settlers came, and the names of King and Queen street tell us we were once subject to a foreign monarch. This, so far from being a reason for abolishing the names, should be a reason for preserving them.

But what do these names mean besides a point of origin? In many cases, they reflect the hope for identity, the immigrant's wish that his American community—while full of opportunity—will not be *disturbingly* different from his home. Somehow, by naming a little piece of Iowa Pella, after the free city in Palestine that served as a refuge, a group of Dutch immigrants hoped to practice their religion in peace. To thousands of others, the various place names symbolized the immigrant's reasons for coming and his future hopes, in addition to his belief in his Old World heritage.

Names of places were but a single sign. We noted in Chapter 13 how numerous Europeans practiced crafts that appeared to be stamped with peculiar ethnic strains. This was by no means limited to the white immigrants. Blacks, first as slaves, then as free men, were found in all the trades before 1800. Their craft patterns in textile designs [169, 170], basket weaving, iron and wood, musicmaking, and food preparation preserved a unique cultural expression.

The same is true for the American Indian. Although there are notable differences in the customs of Indian subgroups, distinguished by tribe, culture, and region, these peoples share common traits in long-practiced hunting and agricultural habits because of their closeness to nature. Their compatibility with the land and the efficient use of its natural products distinguished the Indian people of America. In addition, the crafts of weaving and pottery that developed centuries before any contact with Europeans remained a distinctive feature of the work patterns of our native population [171, 172]. Extraterritorial contact, in time, affected the materials and designs of Indian crafts but did little to alter their traditional techniques.

168
Moscow, Idaho, is one of the thousands of places in America named by immigrant settlers.

169
Harriet Powers, a Negro woman, made this Bible quilt sometime around 1886, when she was about forty-nine years of age. Measuring 88½″ in length and 73¾″ in width, it records this farm woman's affection for the Bible. *From top left:* (1) Adam and Eve in the Garden of Eden; (2) Paradise continued, but Eve has conceived and borne a son; (3) Satan; (4) Cain killing Abel; (5) Cain going into the land of Nod to get a wife; (6) Jacob's dream; (7) the baptism of Christ; (8) the Crucifixion; (9) Judas Iscariot and the thirty pieces of silver; (10) the Last Supper; (11) the Holy Family.

250

171
Bowl made by Zuñi Indians,
1884. H 9¾".

172
Zuñi owl bowl, late nineteenth
century. H 9½".

171

172

173
Gate-leg table with drop
leaves, invented by the
Chinese. This particular table,
of turned and painted wood,
was used in San Francisco,
1850–1900. L 52¼".

174
A pair of bamboo baskets on a
thin pole was used to carry
fish and vegetables and often
served as a display bin for direct sales in San Francisco's
Chinatown. L 60½".

173

The immigrants from Asia, particularly the Chinese, after 1850 established reputations as industrious workers on railroad gangs, and in mining
camps, laundries, restaurants, and pharmacies
[**173, 174, 175A, 175B**]. The objects native to
their Asian culture, when transported to America
in body or in design, added another dimension to
the multifaceted American civilization [**176**].

Within the community boundary line the immigrant women—more isolated and less acculturated
than the men—were influential in preserving their
cultural heritage, often through the crafts they
worked on in the home. Numerous samplers [**177,
178**] and quilts attest to foreign birth or racial
distinction, as do the tools and products of hand
spinning. The European spinning wheel, introduced to America with the flow of immigration,
was both an essential household tool and a symbol
of Old World cultural practices in a New World
environment.

In its simplest form, the spinning wheel had
reached Europe by the thirteenth century. Several
technical improvements were made by the fifteenth
century, and in the sixteenth, a Saxony stonemason
and carver added the foot treadle to the hand-turned
"Dutch wheel" (the name "Saxony" was given to
this treadle spinning wheel). Even with these improvements, it remained primarily a "hand" or
home implement [**179**]. Unlike the loom, which
was used mainly by professional craftsmen, the
spinning wheel was found in almost every household. Even after the machine spinning of cotton
was perfected late in the eighteenth century, wool
and flax continued to be spun at home and the yarns
used for the numerous humble articles needed by
the household: tapes, drawstrings, mittens, socks.
The spinning task always fell to the women of the
family and usually to the unmarried girls, the
"spinsters." Their spinning wheels, from England, Sweden, France, and Italy, all differed in
design and occasionally in operation; each was
unique to its local origin. Thus the spinning
wheel—as much as or perhaps even more than any
other single item—reflects the rich multiple heritage of the immigrants [**180A–180G**].

Spinning was only part of a vast multiethnic folk
art tradition within America. German glazed
ceramics, documents illuminated with medieval
"broken" script (*Fraktur*), *Fachwerk* buildings
with exposed wall timbers, appeared across
America by 1850. Musical instruments such as the
courting flute [**181**], the zither [**182**], the mandolin
[**183A, 183B**], the barrel organ [**184**], the dulcimer
[**185**], the shofar [**186**], the concertina [**187**], and
even the jawbone [**188**] were immigrant contributions to American musicmaking. The immigrant
and second-generation bands and orchestras, organized around a particular foreign nationality,
were common during the period 1875–1940 [**189**].
At the same time, the descendants of Spanish
settlers along the Rio Grande produced a distinctive type of religious imagery of saints (*santos*), of
embroidery (*colcha*), and of mud-brick (*adobe*)
architecture. The traditional arts of other rural
European groups, dominated by the English from
Connecticut to California and best expressed in
furniture forms, pewter, music, and textiles,
joined with African and Oriental motifs and with
native artistic forms to enrich our heritage and to
provide for the immigrants and their descendants
objects that were links to the Old World.

174

175A
Chinese-American apothe-
cary cabinet. Painted wood
with paper labels in ink.
Philadelphia, 1875–1900. H
73″.

175B
Detail: Apothecary cabinet.

175A

176
Lion masks, male and female, represent natural forces for the Chinese, who use them in New Year's processions of social and religious significance. This pair, measuring 16″ across the face, from the Chinese-American community in Philadelphia, dates before 1900.

177
This 13″-square sampler was embroidered in 1850 by Dorothea Seestädt. Samplers were made by young girls as a way of practicing various embroidery stitches. In design and subject they often reflect Old World origins.

176

A
B C D
E F G H I
K L M N O P Q
R S T U V W X Y Z.
a b c d e f g h i k l m n
o p q r ſ ß s t u v w x y z.
1 2 3 4 5 6 7 8 9 0 12.

A B C D E F G H I K L M N
O P Q R S T U V W X Z.

Dorothea Seeſtädt.
1850.

177

178
Sampler made by Catalina
Mason in 1836 at the
Academy of Puerto Rico.
L 17″.

179
Illustration of a two-spindle
flax spinning wheel similar to
the one in 180A. This is
taken from T. Firmin, *Some
Proposals for the Employ-
ment of the Poor* (England,
1681).

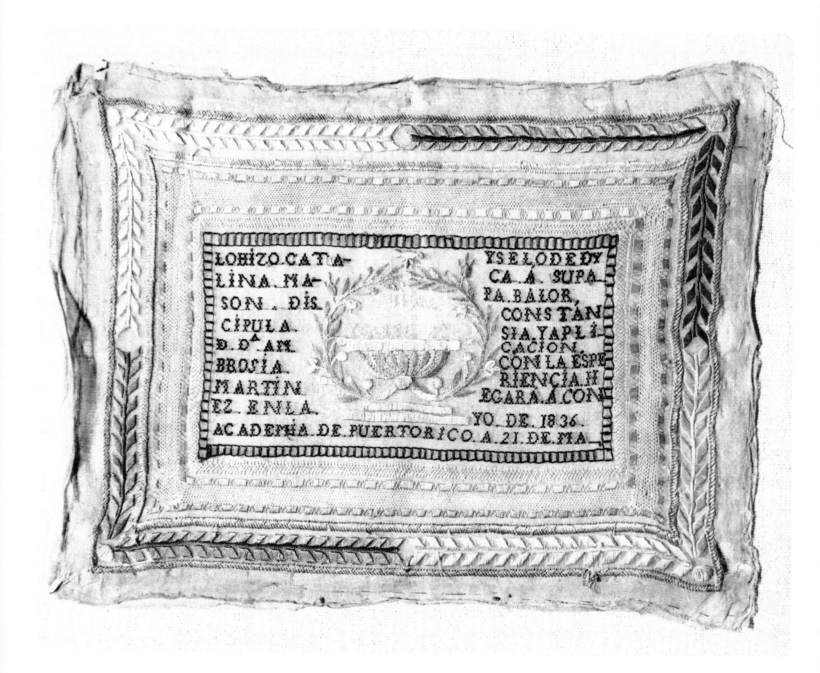

178

179

180A
English spinning wheel used to spin two yarns at once. The style was known in England in the late seventeenth century and was introduced into America by the New England settlers. It remained popular in the eighteenth century until the vast commercial production of cotton yarns replaced the need for the two-treadle wheel. This one was recorded as being owned by the Beach family of Stratford, Connecticut, c. 1735. H 54″.

180B
Spinning wheels with the wheel and spindle-bobbin assembly in a horizontal plane are classified as Tyrolese, as they developed in the several European countries of this region. Several examples have been found in the Shenandoah region of Virginia. H 43¾″.

180A

180B

180C
The Saxony-type spinning wheel is the one most easily recognized. This "linen or foot wheel" had spread throughout Northern Europe until, in the second quarter of the seventeenth century, it was introduced into Ireland, where it became known as the low Irish wheel. The Scots who went to Ireland and then on to New Hampshire in the second decade of the eighteenth century brought it to America. The symbol of this type of spinning wheel was used to denote a spinning-wheel maker and eventually any business relating to yarns or cloth (see 180D). The sample shown was made in Massachusetts, c. 1800; it was owned by Rachel Burr Corwin and is marked "RC." H (approx.) 49".

180D
Typical American newspaper advertisement of the late eighteenth century using the Saxony-type spinning wheel as a generic symbol.

William Scott,
At the Sign of the SPIN-
NING WHEEL,
In Marlborough Street
(Resolving to quit Trade in
the Fall)
WILL sell all his
GOODS on hand
at the STERLING COST
and CHARGES. Among
which are,
Some elegant Merfailles Bed-Quilts,
Merfailles Quilting in pieces, Irifh Linens,
Gauzes, Shawls and Luteftrings of a fuperiour
quality, &c. &c.
A large quantity of filk Gloves,
Mitts and Fans.
CASH for POT-ASHES.

180D

180C

180E
One of several types of "German" spinning wheels. Beautifully made with ivory finials, it exemplifies a type considered to be the English interpretation of a German form. This one was made in Edinburgh, Scotland, however, and brought to the United States in the nineteenth century by Mrs. Euphemia Hill Johnstone. H 53".

180F
When the wheel is centrally placed over the tripod base with the spindle unit above, the spinning wheel is the type that originated in southern Germany. The example shown here was made in Alsace-Lorraine; it was brought to the United States in 1822 by Mrs. Philip Beck and used in Ohio. H 46".

180G
Saxony-type spinning wheel, whose ornate turnings and minor details show it was made in Sweden, c. 1830. It was owned by Lisa Karin Johnson, who was still using it when she migrated to Hannibal, Missouri, in 1890. H 46".

180E

180F

180G

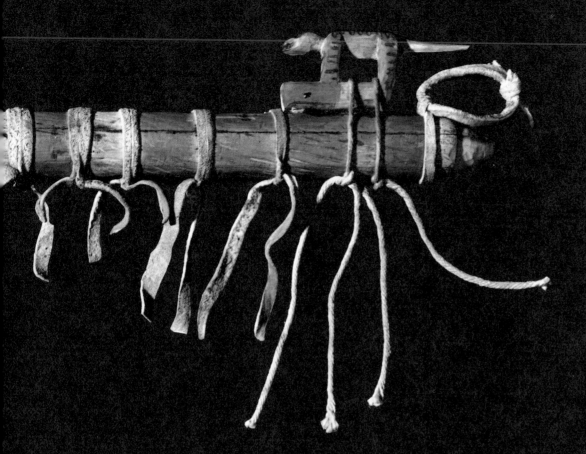

181
Courting flute made of tanned hide, feathers, and painted wood by the Ute Indians. Late nineteenth century. L 21½″.

Zither made by Franz Schwarzer c. 1890, Washington, Missouri. L 23¾". The son of an Austrian building contractor and musical-instrument maker, Franz Schwarzer emigrated to Missouri in 1864, having purchased a farm sight unseen. According to family tradition, this was a result of glowing reports he had read of the idyllic life and potential fortunes to be made in America, written by Gottfried Duden, a German who had settled in Missouri. But by 1867 Schwarzer had given up his farm and moved to the nearby town of Washington, where he worked as a cabinetmaker and soon began making zithers.

After Schwarzer won the highest Gold Medal for zither-making at the 1873 Vienna International Exhibition over a field of more than thirty entrants, his business prospered and he even exported instruments to Europe and South America. Schwarzer's zithers were admired for their inventive structural improvements as well as for their skillful inlay work and their tone.

183A
Tho mandolin, a traditional Italian instrument, became increasingly popular in the United States during the last decades of the nineteenth century. This exceptionally fine example was made in New York City in 1900 by Gene Trusiewicz. L 24¾″. At about the same time, Orville Gibson of Kalamazoo, Michigan, developed a flat-backed version of the mandolin which gradually replaced the traditional design in this country. First used in the hundreds of amateur "plectrum orchestras" which flourished in the first quarter of this century, it was later adopted as a lead instrument in southern "Bluegrass" bands by performers such as Bill Monroe. American Bluegrass music and its associated instruments have recently enjoyed a surge of popularity in a number of countries, including Japan.

183B
Side view of 183A.

183A

183B

184
Organ grinder and his wife,
New York City, c. 1895. The
Italian organ grinder, sometimes accompanied by a
monkey with a tin cup, was a
familiar sight on many American streets during the late
nineteenth and early twentieth centuries. The frequently
out-of-tune music was not always welcome, and increasingly strict city regulations
have made these sights and
sounds rare.

Italy remains a center of barrel organ manufacture, and
Boston's Haymarket Square
on the edge of the Italian
North End has for many years
been a good place to hear one
of this country's few remaining organ grinders.

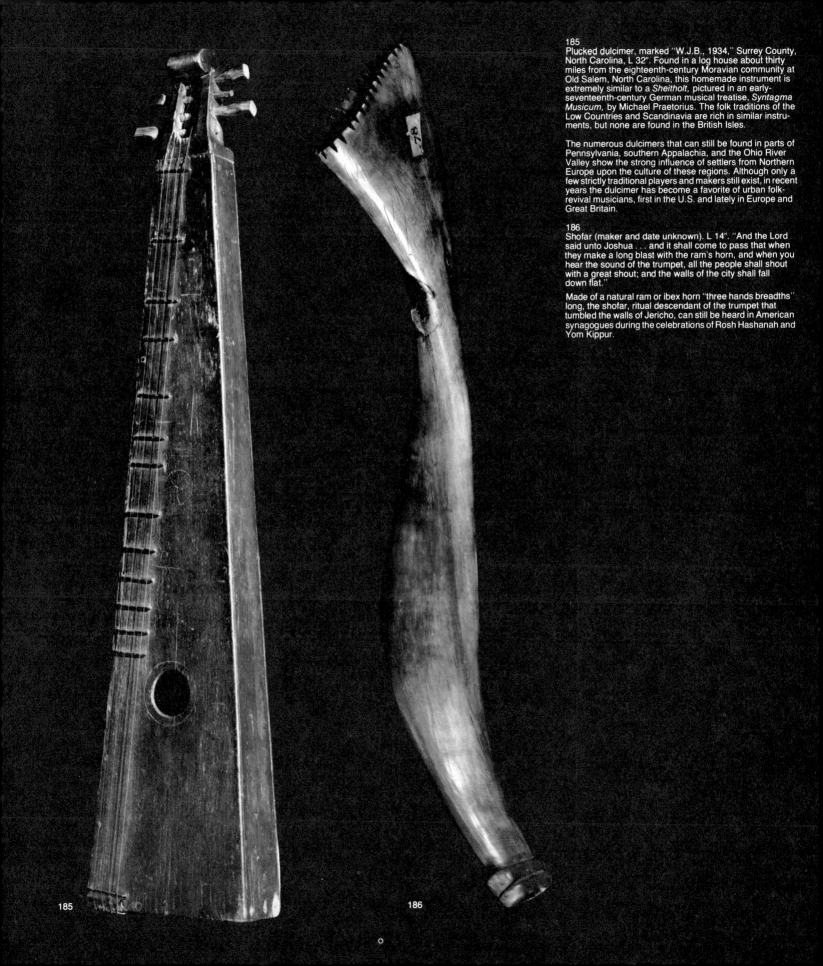

185
Plucked dulcimer, marked "W.J.B., 1934," Surrey County, North Carolina, L 32". Found in a log house about thirty miles from the eighteenth-century Moravian community at Old Salem, North Carolina, this homemade instrument is extremely similar to a *Sheitholt*, pictured in an early-seventeenth-century German musical treatise, *Syntagma Musicum*, by Michael Praetorius. The folk traditions of the Low Countries and Scandinavia are rich in similar instruments, but none are found in the British Isles.

The numerous dulcimers that can still be found in parts of Pennsylvania, southern Appalachia, and the Ohio River Valley show the strong influence of settlers from Northern Europe upon the culture of these regions. Although only a few strictly traditional players and makers still exist, in recent years the dulcimer has become a favorite of urban folk-revival musicians, first in the U.S. and lately in Europe and Great Britain.

186
Shofar (maker and date unknown). L 14". "And the Lord said unto Joshua . . . and it shall come to pass that when they make a long blast with the ram's horn, and when you hear the sound of the trumpet, all the people shall shout with a great shout; and the walls of the city shall fall down flat."

Made of a natural ram or ibex horn "three hands breadths" long, the shofar, ritual descendant of the trumpet that tumbled the walls of Jericho, can still be heard in American synagogues during the celebrations of Rosh Hashanah and Yom Kippur.

185   186

187

Concertina, made by Louis Lachenal, late nineteenth century (London). H 6¼″. First designed by the English inventor Charles Wheatstone and patented by him in 1844, the concertina is a keyed instrument whose tones are produced by freely vibrating reeds similar to those in harmonicas and accordians. Said to have been played by Prince Albert, the concertina was originally an expensive instrument used primarily by the well-to-do. But by the late nineteenth century mass production and competition from other makers, such as Wheatstone's former foreman Louis Lachenal, had brought its price within reach of the working classes. A fad for the instrument developed, especially in the north of England, and uniformed marching concertina bands competed annually for prizes.

The Chicago musical merchandise house of Lyon and Healy were optimistic in their 1898–1899 catalogue: "These instruments fill a niche peculiarly their own. The favor that invariably greets Concertina playing upon the vaudeville stage makes it not unlikely that Concertinas will continue to grow in popularity." However, in the United States the concertina was most commonly used by Salvation Army musicians.

188

Jawbone. L 18″. Used throughout the New World by slaves from West Africa and their descendants, the jawbone of a horse or mule was beaten and scraped with a stick to provide a rhythmic accompaniment to music and dance. During the nineteenth-century vogue for blackface minstrel-show parodies of Negro music and culture, troupes such as Dan Emmett's Virginia Minstrels presented Negro instruments such as the jawbone and banjo to audiences throughout the U.S., England, and Europe.

189

Knights of St. Casimir, Polish uniformed group, Cleveland, Ohio, standing in front of St. Stanislaus Church, c. 1900.

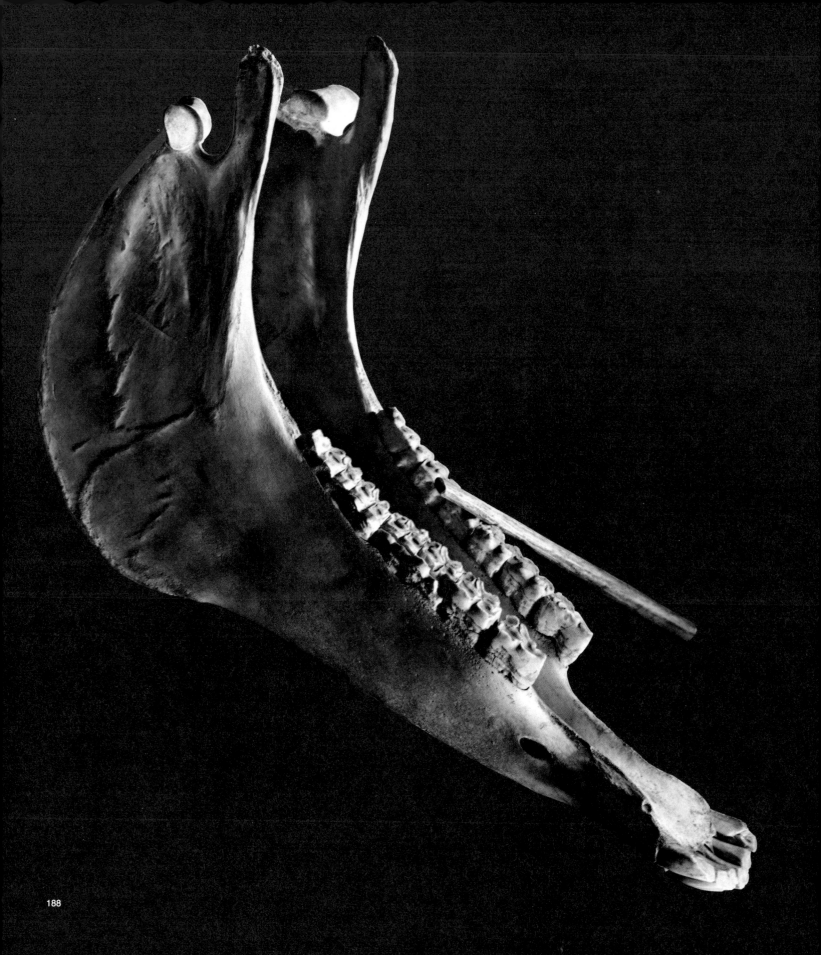

Chapter 15

Status and Prejudice—
A Pictorial Essay

There is society *in America, as good as in any part of the world. But notwithstanding all the theoretical notions of Republican equality, society there has its* grades, *and everyone must expect to take his own proper rank.*

CALVIN COLTON
Manual for Emigrants to America, 1832

The urban immigrant and his rural brethren faced an inner turmoil which historians have only begun to perceive. True, home crafts such as spinning gave some outlet for expression and a link with the past. The ethnic musical societies, the churches, and the foreign-language press all gave the newcomers something to relate to. But these were not the heart of the immigrant's life; what was, was his relationship to American society as a whole. His position in and his acceptance by that society were dominant issues in his identity. The ultimate dilemma was inescapable: how could the immigrant retain his Old World identity and still fit into the mainstream of American life?

Among intellectual members of most ethnic groups there arose a philosophy of the middle ground—a belief that somehow the newcomers and their descendants should stand between the Yankee and the newly arrived foreigner, that indeed, through some unexplained process, the hyphenated American would be composed of the best of both. The danger of this position was that the middle ground might prove to be a no-man's-land: the immigrant could very well lose his Old World status without gaining a new one. The Baron von Hübner, a career officer in the Austrian foreign service, illustrated the dilemma in his two-volume account of a trip around the world, *Promenade autour du monde, 1871* (1873):

I met some Italian peddlers once in the Pacific States. They had just returned from Turin. One of them said to me: "There are upwards of four hundred of us in Nevada and California, all more or less doing well. Twenty-four, with their boxes full of gold, returned a short time ago to their native village. But only three could stand the life there; the others came back to California. This is easily explained. You see, in Europe we can't associate with the gentry and we can't live with our equals above whom we have unconsciously raised ourselves. We feel therefore like fish out of water, and so, we give up the dream of living in our native land and return to America."

A Bulgarian immigrant, Stoyan Christowe, expressed this classic predicament more than fifty years afterward in an article titled "Half an American" (1919):

While I am not a whole American, neither am I what I was when I first landed here; that is a Bulgarian. Still retaining some inherited native traits, enough to bar me forever from complete assimilation, I have outwardly and inwardly deviated so much from a Bulgarian that when recently visiting in that country I felt like a foreigner and was so regarded. . . . In Bulgaria I am not wholly a Bulgarian; in the United States not wholly an American.

The immigrants who found wealth often used it to define their places in their adopted homeland. At one level, the Irishwoman's lace curtains became a symbol that her family was on its way. In rural areas, the symbols of status seeking were just as evident. One critic wrote in 1835: "The German farmer loves his farm sometimes to the disadvantage of his own family. In some parts of Pennsylvania, the love of the farm has degenerated, it might be said, into a kind of mania. You can find there barns as large as well-sized chapels, with glass windows and blinds."

Here was a country that had rejected hereditary aristocracy. The British consul for the state of Massachusetts observed the coarseness of Americans in 1859 but explained in his patronizing manner that "Everyone knows that it takes three generations to make a gentleman." But most Americans, both native and foreign-born, disagreed: rank did not depend on genealogical distinction. Rather, acquired wealth provided the base that enabled status to be expressed in many ways, all of which were expensive.

This, in a way, was the immigrants' salvation. Of course, this is not to say that some men of letters, divines, entertainers, pugilists, soldiers, and even criminals acquired status without wealth. But it was the material accouterments of the rich that were so visible and titillating to the hoi polloi—great houses, splendid matched teams and shiny carriages, beautiful clothes and rare jewels, entertainment on a grand scale. Later in the century new symbols were added to the contest. In 1884 an observer noted that "French cooks preside over the destinies of the houses of the Vanderbilts, Astors, Goulds, Lorillards, Schuylers, and the Havemeyers." By the last quarter of the century, yachts, private railroad cars, and Newport "cottages" enabled the superrich to differentiate themselves from the merely rich.

There was a blatancy to all this that was both vulgar and naïve. Mrs. Trollope, no admirer of the Americans, complained as early as 1832 about New York society women: "to show half their revenue in silks and satins, seems to be the chief object they have in these parties."

Within various ethnic communities, rigid class rankings gradually replaced the initial one-level social structure. In a capitalist system this was natural, but it had a curious effect upon the ethnic consciousness of the people involved. For example, within the local German churches—Lutheran, Reformed, and Catholic—schisms often developed which followed class lines. The wealthier members often demanded that English, not just German, be used in the services, and the issue was sometimes resolved only with the creation of a new church. One German visitor, Dr. Ernst Ludwig Brauns, who was surveying the status of the German language in America, wrote in 1829: "Some Germans who had become rich thought that they were superior to their less wealthy associates, and their children began to be ashamed of the German language of the rabble. They demanded that in addition to German, the English language should be introduced into the German churches." The outcome of this kind of status seeking, in Dr. Brauns's view, was inevitable: "Experience had already taught that the two languages could not be united in one church, since in such cases German gradually disappeared." Every major immigrant religion in America faced this dilemma.

Whether the immigrant climbed the economic ladder to the heights achieved by the foreign-born Andrew Carnegie or simply earned enough to build his own home, he still faced the problem of prejudice. This negative social force was the inevitable result of the newcomer's attempt to identify himself. To many Yankees of the post-Civil War era, the immigrants who assimilated were barely tolerable; but those alien peoples with strange languages, customs, and values who did not fit into the existing pattern of life were the objects of scorn and ostracism. Natives pressed the newcomers to abandon their funny ways and accept the American way, but the ridicule made such adjustment even more difficult. The immigrant was expected to conform; to change his language, his dress, his customs, his values, and his personality traits. Some newcomers even changed their names, Americanizing them so that they would be more readily accepted.

Through the years ethnic stereotypes developed which expressed the ideas of the natives regarding the nature and habits of the different groups. For example, Germans were fun-loving and boisterous, prone to beer drinking and unacceptable behavior on the Sabbath as well as possessing radical, anarchistic ideas; Irish were rowdy, drunken, quarrelsome ne'er-do-wells; Jews were cunning Shylocks, prone to greed, vulgarity, and ostentation; Italians were excessively passionate and inclined to crime and violence; immigrants from Southern and Eastern Europe were degraded, illiterate paupers unfit for democratic society; blacks and Orientals were dismissed as creatures of inferior races, not quite human. These stereotypes are found in the writings, cartoons, and theater of both the nineteenth and twentieth centuries.

In upstate New York, numerous towns inhabited by Europeans were well established by the second decade of the nineteenth century. Often isolated from one another, they drew the concern of observers who feared that each group of Scottish, Irish, German, English, and French would fragment the nation. Yet even the blueblood Timothy Dwight, writing in his *Travels in New England and New York* (1822), marveled at these immigrants. Never had he "seen so large a tract changed so suddenly from a wilderness into a well-inhabited and well-cultivated country as that which extends on the great Western road from the German Flats to the Genesee River." He predicted a time when all these people would be "so entirely amalgamated with those from New England as to be undistinguishable."

If it were not for a little-known fact in American history, the fragmentation and isolation of immigrants both as individuals and in groups would have been far greater than it was. In 1818, several Irish societies for social welfare in Philadelphia and New York petitioned the Congress for a grant of land somewhere in the West to be used as settlement colonies for pauper immigrants. The government refused on the grounds that it would damage the nation's unity if it encouraged aliens to remain in geographic clusters. The Congress feared a checkered nation of Irish, German, Italian, and other alien states within the national boundaries and gave not a single acre for this purpose.

To the German immigrant intellectual and social reformer Francis Lieber the government's decision was sound. While he favored the retention of foreign languages through the public school instruction, he denounced the utopian or isolationist schemes of various groups, for two reasons: (1) they hurt the nation by splitting it into cultural atoms, and (2) the settlers who clung together suffered from "mental stagnation" or "ossification." Writing in *The Stranger in America* (1825), Lieber observed:

Whenever colonists settle among a different nation, in such numbers and so closely together that they may live on among themselves, without intermixture with the original inhabitants, a variety of inconveniences will necessarily arise. Living in an isolated state, the current of civilization of the country in which they live does not reach them; and they are cut off from that of their mother country: mental stagnation is the consequence. They remain a foreign element, an ill-joined part of the great machinery of which they still form, and needs must form, a part.

277

Throughout the nineteenth and early twentieth centuries, the social and economic consequences of immigration were discussed ad infinitum, often by the recently assimilated immigrants themselves. For every argument in favor of immigration, there was one or more against it. On the negative side, it was argued that immigrants competed for jobs, which drove down wages and led to unemployment; they tended to settle in cities, causing overcrowding, crime, and poverty-ridden slums; they caused corruption in politics; they increased the illiteracy of the population; and, in general, they lowered the standard of living of the entire country. The evils blamed on the immigrants became particularly acute toward the end of the nineteenth century, at a time when the arriving foreigners were more unlike the native Americans and therefore more repugnant to them. Even educated men, such as the Progressive Party leader Edward A. Ross, were among those who felt that the new immigrants with their "pigsty mode of life" and their "brawls" and "animal pleasures" lowered the moral tone of society. They were unhygienic and alcoholic, they raised the insanity and illiteracy rates, and they weakened the position of women with their "coarse peasant philosophy of sex." But worst of all, they bred in such numbers that they threatened to overwhelm the "American blood of the native stock and debase American civilization."

In addition to the general xenophobia produced by dissimilar customs and ways of life, which has been a psychological reality in many countries, there were three other forces operating against immigrants in America: anti-Catholicism, antiradicalism, and racism. Since the 1790s, one or more of these prejudices have worked to the disfavor of newcomers and to the dishonor of the nation. Fear of foreign political extremists, fear of Catholics, fear of cheap foreign labor, fear of Jews, fear of Chinese and later Japanese, and at times a pervasive fear of all foreigners—America has known them all in recurring waves through the years.

Many foreigners encountered yet another prejudice, the belief that the white race is superior to other races. The belief that Negroes were members of an inferior race was used to justify slavery and later the low status of the free Negro. This idea also excused the white man's poor treatment of the "inferior" Indian. In the 1880s the argument was used against Oriental immigrants.

An expanded theory of racism was used in the early twentieth century by native Americans and "old" immigrants against the "new" immigrants from Southern and Eastern Europe, who were regarded as so different from native Americans and so inferior as to be unassimilable.

In the early years of the nineteenth century, the idea that the Anglo-Saxon "race" was superior to all others had already begun to take shape in America. It gradually expanded to encompass the Teutonics or Nordics, the blond Northern Europeans. These people, according to this theory, were particularly suited to advance civilization and they possessed a special gift for self-government and a mission to spread its blessings. Many biological and sociological arguments were advanced in support of the theory. At first the Anglo-Saxon racists in America were very optimistic, feeling that other white races who came to America could be assimilated and strengthened by contact with the superior native stock, but as the number of foreigners increased and their ethnic character changed, the racists began to worry. They feared that instead of the Teutonic blood improving the inferior races, the inferior races would weaken and overwhelm the Teutonics.

As Madison Grant wrote in his popular work *The Passing of the Great Race* (1916): "the whole tone of American life, social, moral and political has been lowered and vulgarized" by what he called "this human flotsam." He even struck out at the new immigrants' attempts to become American, saying that they "adopt the language of the native American, they wear his clothes, they steal his name and they are beginning to take his women, but they seldom adopt his religion or understand his ideals. . . ."

The Ku Klux Klan, formed in 1915 and modeled after the anti-Negro Klan of the 1860s, exhibited all the anti-foreign sentiments of the day as well as the idea of white supremacy. Anti-Semitism and anti-Catholicism were particularly strong in the Klan. Jews were regarded as members of an international conspiracy to control America, an idea given much support by Henry Ford. The Klan in its period of greatest activity, in the early 1920s, attempted to impose on American society its own idea of social morality as well as its views regarding foreigners.

Prejudice, of course, was not reserved exclusively for the foreign-born, nor is it a thing of the past. Many native-born blacks, Jews, Orientals, hyphenated Americans, and even various segments of the Anglo-Saxon population have been subjected to the feeling of not belonging. Economic discrimination is the most blatant and the most damaging because it hampers the means of earning a living, but it has never been the sole manifestation of prejudice. Discrimination in the social sphere is more subtle, ranging from the exclusion of Jews, blacks, Orientals, and various other groups from country clubs and summer resorts to the ostracizing of such people from all sorts of social functions. Educationally, discrimination has produced quota systems to restrict, for example, the number of Jews in some of the prestigious universities, as well as providing inferior facilities for the education of inner-city "ghetto" children, usually comprising blacks and the most recent foreign arrivals. Discrimination also includes the refusal of merchants to serve certain peoples and the secret covenants not to sell or rent homes to members of particular races or ethnic groups. Many forms of discrimination can and have been legislated against, but the subtle feeling of not being completely accepted lingers on for many Americans.

The ethnic stereotypes and racial slurs in the following illustrations come primarily from post-Civil War America. They testify to the deep and not so quiet stream of fear that runs through American society. They attack such a bewildering array of outsiders who eventually have become insiders that it appears a period of prejudice is a painful requirement for every group that knocks at the golden door.

"They Would Close to the New-Comer the Bridge that Carried Them and Their Fathers Over."

The descendants of the old immigrants faced the dilemma caricatured here. In advocating restriction of immigration, they were denying to the new immigrant that which had benefited them or their fathers. (*Puck,* January 11, 1893.)

The tavern and the German or
Irish or Dutch bartender became symbols of prejudice for
many Yankees. The
stereotype of a "drunken immigrant" remained constant
throughout the nineteenth
and twentieth centuries. This
piece of sheet music ap-
peared in 1875.

192
The German love of beer is
parodied in this undated
lithograph, "The Effects of the
New Liquor Law," by Kimmel
and Forster (second half of
the nineteenth century).

193
Nineteenth-century sheet-
music cover depicting the
course of an Irishman's pursuit of "fun." The Emerson
Drug Co., which published the
work, may have specialized in
remedies for hangovers.

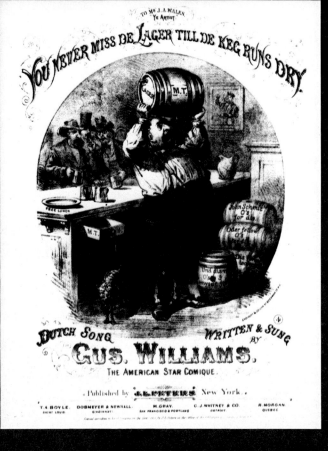

191

192

194
In the late nineteenth century
the Irish were increasingly
portrayed as ape-faced men,
at times wearing a battered
hat with a clay pipe stuck in
the hatband. This is the cover
of *Muldoon's Jokes: A Select
Collection of the Sayings and
Doings of Terrance Muldoon*
(New York: Frank Tousey,
1902).

194

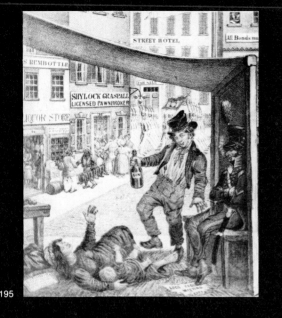

195

195
Detail from the lithograph "The Times," drawn by E. W. Clay, published by H. R. Robinson, 1837. This detail from a political caricature published during the depression of 1837 shows the active business enjoyed by "Shylock Graspall, Licensed Pawnbroker" as a result of the hard times. It is typical of the belief that the cunning Jewish "Shylock" profited by the adversity of others.

196
The "new" immigrants were attacked as illiterate paupers, criminals, and advocates of anarchy and socialism. In this cartoon from *Judge,* the Judge says to Uncle Sam as they view the arrival of "Polish Vagabonds," "Russian Anarchists," "Italian Brigands," and "English Convicts": "If Immigration was properly Restricted you would no longer be troubled with Anarchy, Socialism, the Mafia and such kindred evils!"

196

"Their New Jerusalem." By 1892 a large number of Jewish immigrants had settled in New York. This cartoon illustrates the fear that the Jews would overwhelm the rest of the population, especially driving out the "first families" (shown here with exclusively Dutch names). (*Judge*, January 23, 1892.)

ASK FOR
ROUGH ON RATS
THEY
MUST
GO!
ROUGH ON RATS
CLEARS OUT
RATS MICE.
BED BUGS
FLIES
15 CTS
PER BOX

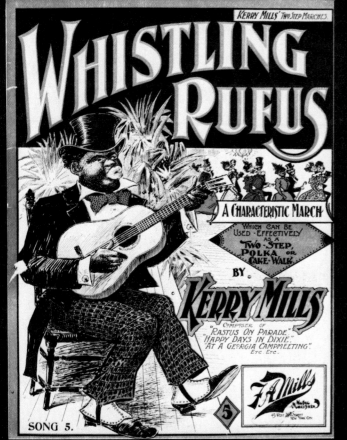

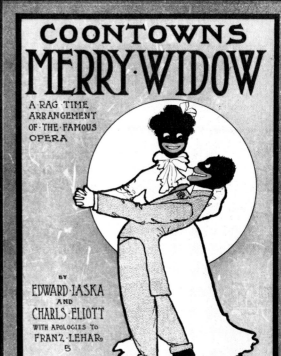

KN

QUICK STEP

DEDICATED TO THE

KNOW NOTHINGS.

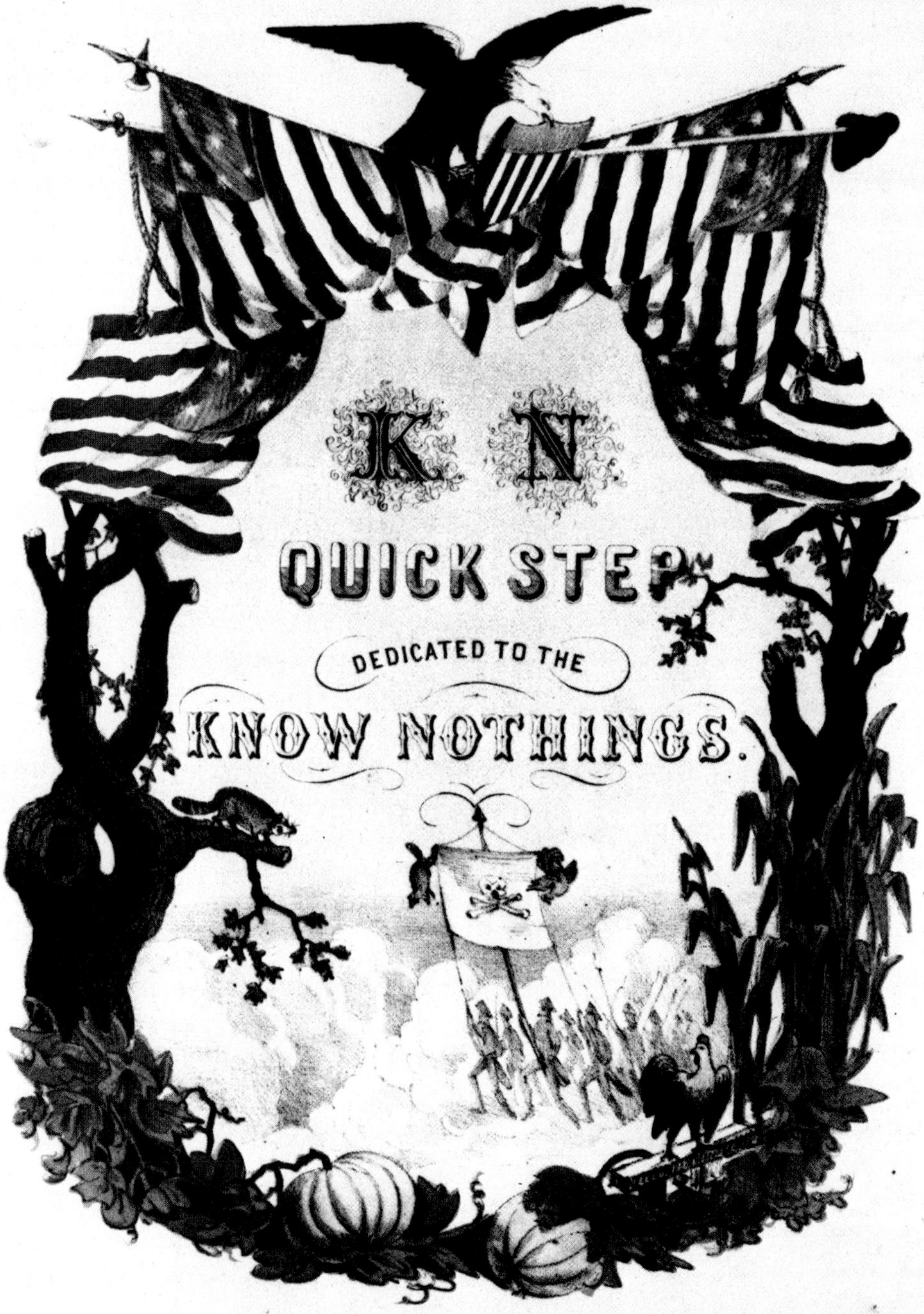

Price 38 cts.

Philad.ª Published by **WINNER & SHUSTER**, *110. North Eighth St.*

NEW YORK   **BOSTON**   **INDIANAPOLIS**   **CINCINNATI**
Firth. Pond & C.º   *G.P. Reed & C.º*   *A.B. Jones & C.º*   *W.C.Peters & Son.*

PUCK.

THE ANTI-CHINESE WALL.
The American Wall Goes Up as the Chinese Original Goes Down.

204

204
"Every Dog (No Distinction of Color) Has His Day. Red Gentleman to Yellow Gentleman: 'Pale face 'fraid you crowd him out, as he did me.' " (*Harper's Weekly*, February 8, 1879.)

205
"The Great Fear of the Period." Three illustrations from the 1870s showing Uncle Sam being consumed by an Irishman and a Chinese, and the Irishman, in turn, being swallowed by the Chinese.

205

206
Trade card, late nineteenth century. Chinese laundries were common on the West Coast as well as in other areas of the country. In this trade card the popular anti-Chinese slogan "The Chinese Must Go" is used in advertising a new steam washer.

207
Cap pistol, late nineteenth century. Anti-Oriental agitation was at first confined to the West Coast but soon spread as Chinese began settling in the East. The competition of their cheap labor was the motivating force of the exclusion campaign. The Chinese were attacked as members of an inferior race with debased living habits.

207

The Pests of Our Pacific and Atlantic Coasts.... Uncle Sam—"There shall be no discrimination. I will shut you both out.' " The "pauper immigrant" of the Atlantic coast carries baggage containing "pauperism," "disease," "anarchy," and "socialism," out of which rises the specter of "cholera." The "pauper laborer" of the Pacific coast brings "opium" with him. (*Judge,* late nineteenth century.)

AMERICAN FARMER
JAPS OR HINDUS NOT WANTED
Anti-Alien Ass'n

210
Prejudice against blacks extended to such measures as exclusion from white businesses and the establishment of separate facilities and sections for them in public places and on public transportation.

211
A burlap-wrapped wooden cross that was burned, as a symbol of "pure" Christianity and as a means of intimidating blacks, by members of the Ku Klux Klan. H 6'.

210

211

Part Three

Shared Experiences

A Nation announcing itself...
I reject none, accept all,
then reproduce all in my own forms...

Walt Whitman

Chapter 16

Becoming American

Citizenship

In response to strong emotional, economic, and political pressures, the qualifications for citizenship have evolved spasmodically over two and a half centuries of colonial and national experience. The issue first appeared in 1709 when the British conferred citizenship on Palatine Germans who emigrated to New York to set up a naval stores industry. Although the industry failed, the Germans remained as citizens of British America.

The first general naturalization law for America, passed by Parliament in 1740, provided that after a seven-year residence in the colonies an immigrant could take the necessary oaths and become a citizen of British America—but not of England. Individual colonies used liberal immigration and citizenship policies to encourage settlers: South Carolina offered immigrants exemptions from taxes, and Massachusetts required only a one-year residency.

Following the French and Indian War, British policy, particularly the Proclamation Act of 1763, limited both immigration and mobility. Such restrictions gave rise to one of the colonists' grievances against King George III, stated in the Declaration of Independence: "He has endeavoured to prevent the population of these States; for that purpose, obstructing the laws for naturalization of foreigners, refusing to pass others to encourage their migration hither. . . ."

Under the Constitution, Congress was given the power to grant citizenship, but dissension appeared immediately between restrictionists and those who wanted freer immigration. The first naturalization act, passed in 1790, required only a two-year residency and limited citizenship to "free white persons." But in 1795, fearing an influx of refugees from the French Revolution, Congress required a five-year residency and insisted that applicants renounce their former allegiances and any titles of nobility. In 1798 Federalist party members of Congress took advantage of the anti-French hysteria to raise the residency requirement to fourteen years. This same Congress passed the unpopular Alien and Sedition Laws, enabling the President to deport any alien he believed to be dangerous to the United States.

In spite of such efforts and partly because of the immigrant vote, the Jeffersonian Republicans were swept into power in 1800, and in 1802 Congress passed a naturalization act restoring the five-year residency rule. The general requirements established by this law form the basis for citizenship to this day: a five-year residency, good moral character, attachment to the U.S. Constitution, declaration of intention, and witnesses who will affirm loyalty, character, and residency.

For most of the nineteenth century, easy naturalization was the rule. Such a policy benefited the country and its rapidly expanding economy. During periods of recurring economic crisis in the 1870s, 1880s, and 1890s, however, nativist movements sought to limit the flow of immigrants and access to citizenship. At the time, naturalization practices administered by state and local government had little uniformity and were frequently corrupt. After male suffrage went into effect in New York in 1827, Tammany Hall developed a system of recruiting aliens as instruments of its urban machine. In one instance, during the twenty-three days preceding an election, two New York City judges naturalized 1,147 persons a day, thus qualifying them to vote. Immigrant groups, by using their collective ethnic power, were able to exert a strong influence in city halls, city councils, and state legislatures.

This situation increased tensions between native and foreign-born Americans and finally resulted in more restrictive policies. State legislatures in New York and Massachusetts began to regulate immigrants through health and livelihood requirements. In 1882 Congress passed the first general immigration restriction. It excluded certain undesirable persons, such as convicts and "idiots," and suspended immigration from China—the earliest discrimination against a particular nationality. In addition, a modest head tax of fifty cents was introduced (and later gradually increased) to act as a barrier to the destitute.

One of the chief causes of friction between native Americans and immigrants was the fear that cheap foreign labor would replace native workers and depress the labor market. As a result, the first contract labor law was adopted in 1885 to end the practice of importing large numbers of cheap laborers.

In 1891 another general immigration law was adopted that provided for medical inspection and listed certain contagious diseases as reasons for exclusion. The following year the newly created Office of the Superintendent of Immigration opened the Ellis Island station to determine who was eligible to land. In cases of uncertainty, immigrants were interviewed by a Board of Special Inquiry and, if found ineligible, could be deported.

The general immigration law of 1903, largely in response to the assassination by Leon Czolgosz of President McKinley eighteen months earlier, added anarchists to the excludable classes list.

The phenomenal tide of immigrants in the early twentieth century—1,026,000 were admitted in 1905 alone—coincided in part with a time of widespread economic hardship. American workers feared for their jobs, and nativists asserted that the new arrivals, primarily from Southern and Eastern Europe, would be difficult to assimilate. Again there was a call for more standardized and restrictive legislation. In 1906 federal officials were put in complete charge of naturalization, and jurisdiction to grant or deny naturalization was shifted from lower to higher state and district courts. In addition, the law set uniform fees and required naturalization papers to be filed in Washington. The applicant had to sign the papers in his own handwriting and be able to speak English.

Restrictionists took advantage of the extreme nationalism fostered by World War I to agitate for their cause and to coercively Americanize immigrants. Night schools and extension courses offering English and civics were funded both publicly and privately. In 1917 Congress, overriding President Wilson's veto, voted to require a literacy test for all immigrants. In addition, a certain geographical zone, encompassing most of Asia and the Pacific islands, was automatically excluded. The immediate postwar period also saw the mass deportation of "undesirable" aliens for the first time as a result of anti-radical, anti-foreign hysteria.

Not until the 1920s, however, were attempts made to limit the actual number of aliens admitted. A combination of influences—the postwar isolationist impulse, an expanding wave of immigrants, and unsettling social and economic changes—worked to end free immigration. The Johnson Act of 1921, signed by President Harding after a similar law had been vetoed by President Wilson, limited annual immigration to 3 percent of those of each nationality in the United States in 1910. The total number of new arrivals was set at about 355,000 each year: 200,000 from Northern European countries and 155,000 from Southern and Eastern Europe.

Restrictions were further strengthened in 1924 by the "national origins" quota rule. This system allowed annual entry to only 2 percent of the number of persons of each nationality in the United States in 1890, a year prior to the wave of Southern and Eastern European immigrants. A further provision of the 1924 act, which did not go into effect until 1929, fixed the total annual quota at 150,000: 130,000 from Northern Europe and only 20,000 from Southern and Eastern Europe. The count was made of white inhabitants only, to keep Africans from having any quota. The law of 1924 also required advance procurement of immigration visas by aliens. This visa provided a preliminary test for citizenship, since the prospective immigrant had to establish his eligibility with respect to quota, character, lack of communist or anarchist affiliations, and unlikelihood of becoming a public charge.

As legislation gradually closed the door to immigrants, worldwide depression in the 1930s also lessened the desire to move. In 1933 only 23,068 immigrants arrived from Europe—the smallest number since 1831. Conditions even motivated a significant number of foreign-born Americans to return to Europe. Using the clause in the immigration acts forbidding entry to anyone "likely to become a public charge," American consuls issued few immigration visas and the United States government deported thousands of unemployed aliens. The Alien Registration Act of 1940 extended the deportable classes to include certain criminal and subversive groups.

With Hitler's takeover of Germany, thousands of Jews and political enemies of Nazism were left homeless. In response, the United States from 1934 to 1940 absorbed some 250,000 Germans, though the national origins quota system remained intact. World War II continued to produce millions of displaced Europeans. After prolonged congressional debate, the United States assumed its traditional role as an asylum for the persecuted and allowed nearly 400,000 refugees to enter as immigrants. Other special rules have permitted the absorption of refugees from Eastern Europe, from Hungary after the uprising of 1956, and from Castro's Cuba.

The McCarran-Walter Act of 1952 survived President Truman's veto and further strengthened the national origins formula. Reflecting cold war tensions, heavy limitations were put on the entry of those suspected of being security risks or of holding anti-American views. Immigration was no longer barred on racial grounds, however, partially due to the effectiveness of previous quota restrictions. Since 1940 all racial bars to naturalization have also been removed.

In 1965 legislation was passed setting the annual quota for immigration on a worldwide basis. The number of immigrants from any one country was limited, and unused quotas were distributed to other nationalities. However, a quantitative limit of 170,000 newcomers was maintained. Although not entirely dead, nativism has receded since the 1920s, and its antithesis—ethnic pride—now flourishes among many national groups within the country.

Albert Einstein (1879–1955)

On October 1, 1940, Albert Einstein, standing in the Federal District Court in Trenton, New Jersey, with raised right hand, took the oath of allegiance to the Constitution and became a naturalized American citizen [212]. In so doing he was representative, indeed he was the very symbol, of some hundreds of "illustrious immigrants," those of outstanding accomplishment in the arts and sciences who had emigrated to the United States in the 1930s from Germany, Italy, Austria, Russia, and Spain, where totalitarian political regimes had deprived them of the conditions for a fruitful life and creative work. Einstein's odyssey of national loyalty, which here ended in swearing allegiance to these United States, is unusual but nonetheless symbolic of America as a place not only where so many emigrant craftsmen and laborers found a new life, but also where men of genius found ultimate asylum from totalitarianism.

For Einstein citizenship was a serious matter. He felt that it constituted a personal endorsement of and branding by the social and political system of the country he thus identified himself with. This extreme ethical sensibility was manifest in his youth. While still a high school student in Munich, Einstein had resolved to renounce citizenship in the country in which he—like his parents, grandparents, and greatgrandparents—had been born and raised. Apparently the single most important factor behind this resolve was a dread of the compulsory service in the German army, which Einstein saw as the severest expression of the general coerciveness of the German social system. Renouncing German citizenship would release him from this terrible obligation as well as from an oppressive sense of responsibility and restraint.

The opportunity for this radical step presented itself early in 1894 with his parents' decision to move to northern Italy in a search for better business prospects. But Einstein's father refused his son permission to drop his German citizenship, and continued to do so even after Albert had fled his high school in Germany to join the family in Milan. Only in January 1896, two months before the end of Einstein's sixteenth year—the statutory limit for emigration with dispensation from military service—did his father give in and file the necessary petition.

For the next five years, until shortly before his twenty-second birthday, Einstein was "stateless." His constant aim, however, was to become Swiss. During his four years at the Zurich Polytechnic, from which he emerged in August 1900 as a qualified teacher of high school physics and mathematics, he was satisfying the residence requirement. During this same period at considerable personal sacrifice he put aside twenty of his one-hundred francs of monthly allowance in order to be able to pay the high cost of Swiss naturalization. In October 1899 Einstein formally applied to the authorities of the city of Zurich for civic rights, the conferral of which also carried Swiss citizenship. The consideration of Einstein's application dragged on for more than a year. Not until his father had again given his permission, and Einstein had submitted himself to an interrogation by the city fathers—"Was he inclined to drink, had his grandfather been syphilitic, did he himself lead a proper life?"—was this coveted political identity finally obtained in February 1901.

Even though in possession of Swiss citizenship papers and a diploma from the world's most renowned technical institute, Einstein had the greatest difficulty finding employment appropriate to his education and his inclinations—not to mention his talents. After a series of temporary jobs, he finally obtained a position as an examiner (technical expert, third class) in the Swiss patent office in Bern. There, from 1902 to 1909, at his desk covertly and after working hours overtly, he developed and published conceptions which were to transform physics and our view of physical reality.

212
Albert Einstein and his stepdaughter, Margot, taking the oath of citizenship in a Trenton, New Jersey, court, October 1, 1940.

Recognition began to come shortly after his first paper on relativity appeared in 1905. Four years later Einstein took up his first appointment as a university professor, a subordinate position at the University of Zurich. But now his stock was rising very fast. He was called to a full professorship in Prague in 1911, then to one at his alma mater in Zurich the following year. In 1913 the leading physicists in Berlin put together an extremely attractive package in order to lure Einstein to the capital of Germany and thereby ensure its position as the world capital of theoretical physics. But the research professorship they offered, like every German professorship, carried with it civil servant status and thus German citizenship.

Einstein was ready to accept this exceptionally prestigious and advantageous research position, but only on the condition that he not be required to become a citizen of Germany once again. In the spring of 1914, when Einstein took up his appointment at the Prussian Academy of Sciences, he believed that this condition had been fulfilled. In fact it had not. At least there was nothing in the records of the Education Ministry to this effect ten years later when it became an issue, and the German nationality law was quite explicit that German citizenship followed automatically upon employment by the Prussian state.

Only a few months after Einstein's arrival in Berlin World War I broke out, and he found himself as thoroughly out of tune with his German environment and colleagues as he had feared. He remained in Berlin, however, taking the fullest possible advantage of his research post to immerse himself in his work. Five years later, the coincidence of Einstein's enormous international fame with the establishment of a republican regime in Germany caused Einstein to feel that he could not deprive the prostrate democracy of his prestige. "German science is the one thing for which the world still envies us" could be heard left and right in the German parliament. Traveling abroad, accompanied everywhere by his great notoriety, Einstein always let himself appear a German scientist, though he traveled on a Swiss passport. But behind the appearance, and notwithstanding his obligatory oaths of allegiance to the constitutions of Germany and Prussia, Einstein continued to regard himself as a citizen of Switzerland only.

The issue was forced by the announcement in November 1922 of the award of a Nobel Prize to Einstein, who was then en route to Japan. It was customary for the ambassador to Sweden from the recipient's native country to participate in the award ceremony and in the absence of the recipient to represent him. Now both the Swiss and the German ambassadors stepped forward to claim this privilege. The German ambassador, to whose nation the matter was of considerably greater importance, immediately asked for clarification and received a wire from the Prussian Academy stating that Einstein was a German national. The Swiss ambassador thereupon withdrew his claims, remarking that Einstein was generally regarded as German and probably wanted to be counted as such. The ambassador was wrong. Einstein was unwilling to be counted as a German citizen—as he made very clear to the Prussian Academy and the Nobel Foundation as soon as he returned to Germany at the end of March 1923. His legal situation, however, was inarguable. A year later Einstein was obliged to declare that he had "no objection to make" to the view that he had acquired German citizenship—in addition to his Swiss—through his position at the Prussian Academy.

Even in the summertime of the German republic, Einstein was not entirely comfortable with his German citizenship. As the economic and political situation began to deteriorate in the late 1920s and early 1930s (in Germany the depression came earlier and hit much harder than in the United States), Einstein again felt his German citizenship to be incompatible with his need for independence. He took no action, however, until the Nazi seizure of power early in 1933. Einstein was in the United States at the time; he returned only as far as Belgium, where he surrendered his German passport and once again applied for nullification of his German citizenship. The Nazi regime was in no hurry to accept Einstein's resignation, if only because it was unwilling to be deprived of the pleasure of expelling him. This it did early in 1934 when Einstein, along with thirty-six other notable anti-Nazis, was formally deprived of his German citizenship. One year later, his own application was approved.

Einstein did not turn immediately to the United States. Although over the previous four years he had come to spend an increasingly larger part of his time at American universities and research institutes, he at first inclined toward England. In the summer of 1933 a private bill to confer British citizenship upon Einstein was introduced into the House of Commons—while Einstein looked on from the visitors' gallery—and for some months he looked forward to its passage. By contrast, when in the spring of 1934 a United States congressman introduced in the House of Representatives a joint resolution ''That Albert Einstein is hereby unconditionally admitted to the character and privileges of a citizen of the United States,'' Einstein himself wrote requesting that the motion be withdrawn. A year later, however, he had changed his mind. It was clear to him that physically and emotionally he was not, and probably never again would be, well able to face the stresses of a return to Europe. He resolved to remain in Princeton at the Institute for Advanced Study, where he enjoyed seclusion and independence.

It is uncertain, however, whether Einstein had by the spring of 1935 already made up his mind to obtain U.S. citizenship. It was not merely a question of feeling persuaded that this, too, was ''a country where political liberty, toleration and equality of all citizens before the law is the rule,'' but of identifying himself so fully with this nation as to forgo his treasured Swiss nationality. The United States is a jealous nation; it demands that aliens renounce all other political allegiances before admission to its citizenship. By the summer of 1938, in any case, the decision had been taken: the naturalization law of 1906, which continued in force through 1940, required a Declaration of Intention, the so-called first papers, at least two years prior to the citizenship test. That quizzing of Professor Einstein took place in the Federal District Court in Trenton on June 22, 1940, and was the occasion for a broadcast sponsored by the United States Immigration and Naturalization Service. Then, after the statutory ninety-day hiatus, the admission ceremony followed on October 1. It was anticlimactic. *The New York Times* reported:

Dr. Einstein was smiling broadly when he entered the court room, but he became grave as the proceedings got under way. Standing at the head of the class of new citizens, he toyed with a fountain pen throughout the taking of the oath and Judge Forman's speech. After the ceremony, Dr. Einstein talked briefly with newspaper men in an adjoining room. To requests for a statement, he said: ''I do not feel that I should say anything.'' . . . Finally Dr. Einstein said: ''I feel it is an important moment in my life,'' and said that he had given up his Swiss citizenship.

Chapter 17

Educating Everyone

A Pictorial Essay

I have always had a great desire for education, but in the ole countre I didn't have no opportunity. But in the contre United States of America we all have the privilege to learn and educate ourselves as far as our ability allows us to. Therefore, I have all the reasons to like this contre, America, for all this from the botton of my heart. I thank the American people for their kindness in taking an interest in educating us, strangers, and making men of us.

A NEWCOMER

Public education has been a major contributor to the blending of the population of the United States, as well as the catalytic agent for other "Americanizing" social forces. So obtrusive is the role of literacy alone in the unification of diverse peoples that reformer Horace Mann declared in 1848: "Without under-valuing any other human agency, it may be safely affirmed that the common school, improved and energized as it can easily be, may become the most effective and benignant of all forces of civilization." Interest in the particular use of education as a means of aiding the immigrant in his adjustment and involvement in America did "energize" schooling as progressive programs, legislation, and controversy developed.

Recognition of the intrinsic value of education had resulted in the provision of organized tax-supported schooling as early as 1649 in New England settlements, where public schooling already had a strong foothold because of the Puritan belief in a literate church membership. Both the Boston Latin School and Harvard College had been founded in 1636, but it was the Massachusetts School Laws of 1642 and 1647 that dictated the establishment of public schools according to town population. Other New England colonies similarly provided for schools, while in the middle and southern regions education remained limited and mostly private until the start of the Revolution. Soon after the war, however, realization of the role of education in a national union inspired leaders to focus on schools. For instance, while the Senate in 1789 expressed the belief that "Literature and Science are essential to the preservation of a free constitution," the first President even more strongly extolled education on various occasions. In proposing a national university to the fourth Congress in 1796, George Washington commented:

The assembly to which I address myself is too enlightened not to be fully sensible to how much a flourishing state of the arts and sciences contributes to national prosperity and reputation. . . . Among the motives to such an institution, the assimilation of principles, opinions, and manners of our countrymen, by the common education of a portion of our youth from every quarter, well deserves attention.

The more homogeneous our citizens can be made in these particulars, the greater will be our prospect of permanent union; and a primary object of such an institution should be the science of government.

The belief that education was essential to assimilation of the culture made the state school systems the choice institutions through which the immigrant could be absorbed. Many felt that the security of the United States depended upon education of aliens to ensure that newcomers could play a responsible part in a democratic society. Again, Congressman Horace Mann warned that "if we do not prepare children to become good citizens, if we do not enrich their minds with knowledge—then our republic must go down to destruction as others have gone before it." Social worker Jane Addams perceived a mutual need:

I wish I had the power to place before you what it seems to me is the opportunity that the immigrant colonies present to the public school: the most endearing occupation of leading the little child, who will in turn lead his family, and bring them with him into the brotherhood for which they are longing. The immigrant child cannot make this demand upon the school because he does not know how to formulate it; it is for the teacher both to perceive it and to fulfill it.

The extent to which educational programming went to fulfill the needs of the immigrant is illustrated by an order of the Commission of Immigration and Housing in California. An Americanization Committee in each county was to cooperate with existing educational agencies to encourage compulsory school attendance for foreign-born children, evening classes for adult immigrants, factory classes, home teaching of domestic arts, naturalization centers, library extensions in foreign quarters, and neighborhood schools.

The most concentrated effort, however, was in the teaching of the English language. Noah Webster, a proponent of standardized American English, defined goals for nineteenth- and twentieth-century reformers: "To refine and establish our language, to facilitate the acquisition of grammatical knowledge, and diffuse the principles of virtue and patriotism is the task I have belabored to perform." To achieve such goals, educators worked in two directions: increased enrollment and improved teaching methods tailored to given needs. Legislation was one route to widespread enrollment. Laws establishing compulsory attendance of children between given ages, longer school terms, and provisions for mandatory increase in night school opportunities were enacted. In Indiana, for example, by 1914 night schools had to be established in cities of three thousand residents upon the petition of twenty residents with children between fourteen and twenty-one years of age who were necessarily employed during the day. Publicity, too, was utilized to draw immigrants into schools. H. H. Wheaton, Specialist in Immigrant Education, Bureau of Education, described some common methods such as posters, placards, handbills, and announcements in foreign newspapers. Slides shown in theaters and circular letters to employers, labor organizations, civic clubs, and ethnic social clubs were popular techniques in several cities. He further explained an effort made by the Bureau of Education to attract foreigners into night schools by the distribution of over 150,000 posters. The "America First" posters listed in seven languages the advantages of learning English. The experiment resulted in a definite increase in enrollment. A demand for facilities came from the communities and interest in the Americanization movement grew.

Word-picture games, globes, maps, penmanship copy books, flash cards, stereographs, phonographs, as well as standardized textbooks and routines were used to overcome language barriers and thus open the way for further learning. Scrupulous attention was paid to phonetic drills and reading classes as the means by which both children and adults could be taught to function as American citizens. Charles F. Towne, the Director of Immigrant Education in Massachusetts, outlined an approach:

Consequently our teaching procedure should place oral instruction and practice in speaking ahead of instruction in reading. Pupils should first be taught the meaning of the theme through the devices of action, gesture, play of features, inflection of the voice, together with the use of objects and pictures. They should learn to voice each sentence through imitation and repetition until they are able to repeat the complete theme or that portion of the theme that serves for the lesson.

The method prescribed in private evening classes was often no less structured than that endorsed by state-supported schools. The description below comes from "The Education of the Immigrant," published by a spokesman for the San Francisco Y.M.C.A in 1916.

First of all the teacher must not forget that his primary function is to teach English and not geography, mathematics or chemistry. He usually commences the evening's work with conversation. The subject of conversation should be based upon the foreigner's experience. It should be about his work, his home, his country or his business relations. What the teacher must do is give the pupils English equivalents for what they already know in their own language. He must teach them to express these words in such a way that they will be understood. Thus conversation will be made the basis of instruction. A drill in phonetics, concert reading and individual reading will lead up to conversation. The unaccustomed ear must be made accustomed to the sounds of our words and phrases. . . . Dry, formal technique will fail to hold the interest of any group. . . .

307

Vocational education, like evening and English classes, was further developed to fulfill immigrant needs. Sociologist Peter Roberts was one who urged that children of foreign-born mine workers be "taught some manual labor or service whereby they could earn a competency when they leave home. . . . Ignorance and discontent lead to confusion, knowledge and social utility bring order and stability." To complement education in English with a trade skill was to furnish the immigrant with adequate means to survive in the United States. Vocational programs offered courses similar to the Tuskegee Institute curriculum, which included agriculture, basketry, blacksmithing, brickmasonry, carpentry, cooking, dairying, dressmaking, electrical engineering, harness making, laundering, millinery, nursing, painting, printing, and tailoring.

"To diffuse the principles of virtue and patriotism" was an intention of educators from the mid-nineteenth to the mid-twentieth century. In Horace Mann's opinion, "Moral education is a primal necessity of social existence. The unrestrained passions of men are not only homicidal, but suicidal; and a community without a conscience would soon extinguish itself." As well as morality and virtue, practical standards of behavior were of concern. Some reformers, like Booker T. Washington, established school environments for teaching values in addition to academic lessons: "We wanted to teach the students how to bathe; how to care for their teeth and clothing. We wanted to teach them what to eat . . . to give them such a practical knowledge . . . together with the spirit of industry, thrift, and economy . . . We wanted to teach them to study actual things instead of mere books alone." Here again, the precedent for use of the school as a pulpit can be found in the early New England catechism classes of dame schools, in which early lessons were conducted in the home of a literate townswoman, and in the Puritan discipline and philosophy of the grammar schools.

Education's patriotic purpose was to "Americanize" the foreigner, a process that could be mutually beneficial, as explained by Philander P. Claxton, U.S. Commissioner of Education at a Conference of Americanization Specialists held in Washington D.C., May 1919:

These new people are coming now with much the same spirit that brought our earliest settlers to America, from the great middle classes as we are, all of us, and we have confidence in their ability and in the strength of their good right arms. In making them into Americans, we shall ourselves learn more of the spirit of America and broaden our own ideals and enrich our own material and aesthetic lives.

Theodore Roosevelt had a more extreme vision in 1915:

There is no room in this country for hyphenated Americanism. When I refer to hyphenated Americans, I do not refer to naturalized Americans. . . . But a hyphenated American is not an American at all. This is just as true of the man who puts "native" before the hyphen as of the man who puts German or Irish or English or French before the hyphen. Americanism is a matter of the spirit and of the soul. Our allegiance must be purely to the United States. We must unsparingly condemn any man who holds any other allegiance. But if he is heartily and singly loyal to this Republic, then no matter where he was born, he is just as good an American as anyone else.

Teaching patriotism, however, proved easier in theory than in practice. Patriotic themes could be incorporated into English classes, civics courses could be introduced, and children could be influenced by pictures, stories, songs and assemblies, and holidays. Still, Frank V. Thompson, Superintendent of Boston Public Schools, noted that "a curious paradox" existed because "to democratize our newer brethren we must resort to autocratic procedure; the democratic method does not democratize. But the democratic method has at least permitted the foreigner to Americanize himself." Speaking for his own jurisdiction, he reflected that the schools should be given considerable credit for the "degree of amalgamation" that had taken place despite the fact that Americanization was "an un-conscious by-product" in most cases.

The patriotic fervor of cultural assimilation in school inevitably led to misunderstandings and alienation within the immigrant family.

Too often we find that the cause of disrupted immigrant homes is due to the fact that the parents do not understand nor sympathize with their children who have been remoulded in our public schools. Children become ashamed of their parents' ways and lose the proper respect for them. Quarrels ensue and the older boys and girls leave home to work in the mill or factory.

Convinced of the superiority of American ways, the child characteristically shunned his heritage—the language, customs, and sometimes even the religion of his parents. Known as the "second-generation phenomenon," this estrangement aroused awareness of the need for improved understanding in handling family relationships and for greater interchange between the immigrant population and American society. Jane Addams's Hull House, a community center in Chicago, included an ethnic museum. She argued that ignorant teachers forced rejection of non-American culture rather than welcoming diversity in order to give the child an ever-broadening perspective of the world. She insisted:

The children long that the school teacher should know something about the lives their parents lead and should be able to reprove the hooting children who make fun of the Italian mother because she wears a kerchief on her head, not only because they are rude but also because they are stupid. We send young people to Europe to see Italy, but we do not utilize Italy when it lies about the schoolhouse. If the body of teachers . . . could take hold of the immigrant colonies, could bring out of them their handicrafts and occupations, their traditions, their folk songs . . . could get the children to bring these things into the school as the material from which culture is made . . . they would discover by comparison that which they give them now is a poor . . . and vulgar thing.

213A
Entrance to the public elementary school in the Dundalk
section of Baltimore, Maryland. "I consider it the paramount
duty of our public schools, apart from the educational knowledge to be instilled into our pupils, to form American citizens
of them, to take up and gather together all the heterogeneous elements of this cosmopolitan population, and through
the crucible of the public school to fuse and weld them into
one homogeneous mass, obliterating from the very earliest
moment all the distinguishing foreign characteristics and
traits, which the beginners may bring with them, as obstruc-
tive, warring, and irritating elements." Commissioner of
Common Schools in New York City, 1896.

214A

213B
Saluting the flag in a New York City public school, early twentieth century.

214A
A comical nineteenth-century version of chaos in the common school. "The Commercial tone prevalent in the city tends to develop, in its schools, quick, alert habits and readiness to combine with others in their tasks. Military precision is required in the maneuvering of classes. Great stress is laid upon (1) punctuality, (2) regularity, (3) attention and (4) silence, as habits necessary through life for successful combination with one's fellow-men in an industrial and commercial civilization." "A Statement of the Theory of Education in the United States of America, as Approved by Many Leading Educators" (Washington, 1874).

214B
Eighth-grade students at work in Hough School classroom, Cleveland, Ohio.

215A
Teaching a standardized writing style was common in nineteenth-century schools. This page of script letters shows the effort of one scholar trying to conform.

214B

215A

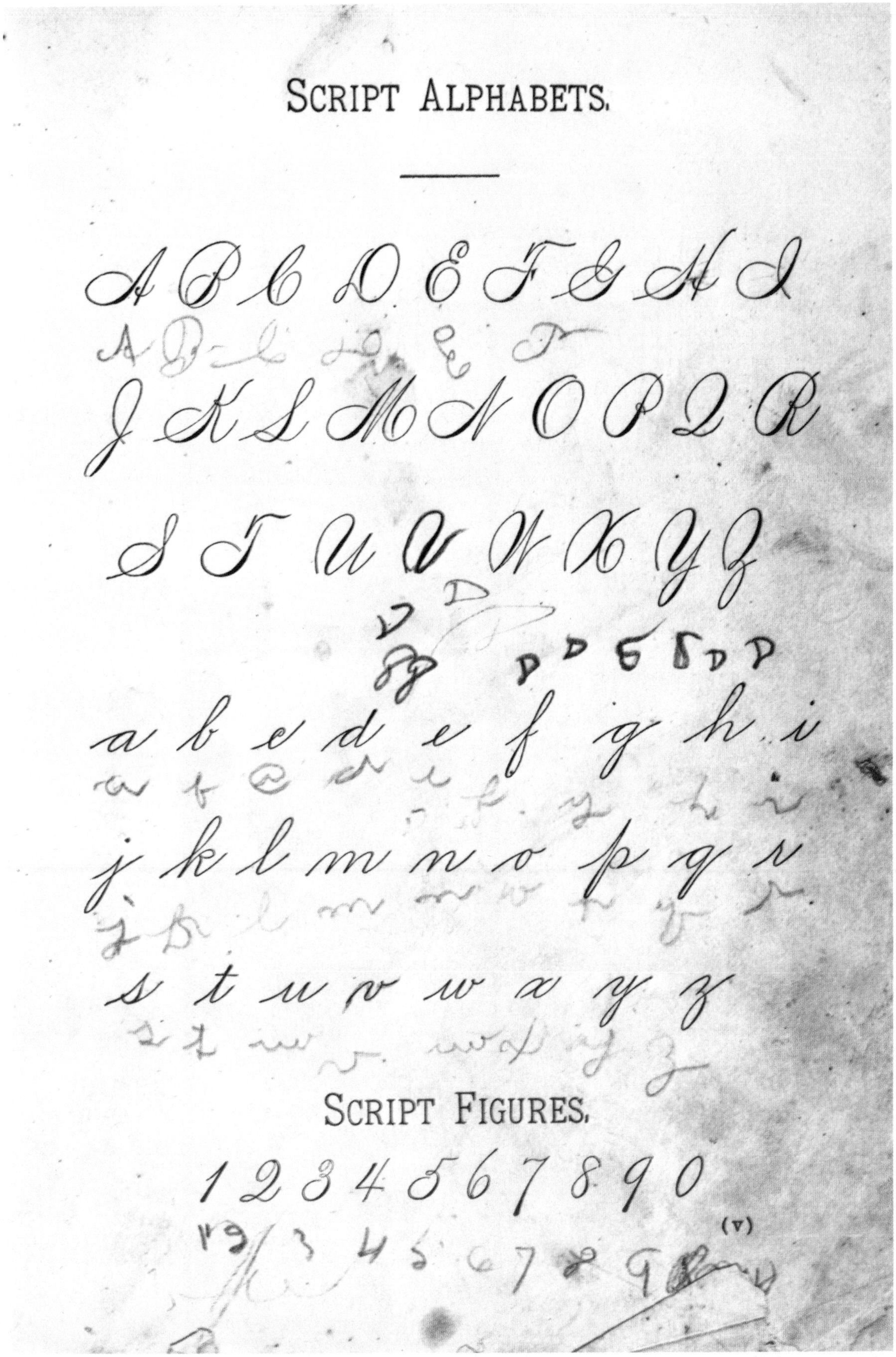

SCRIPT ALPHABETS.

A B C D E F G H I

J K L M N O P Q R

S T U V W X Y Z

a b c d e f g h i

j k l m n o p q r

s t u v w x y z

SCRIPT FIGURES.

1 2 3 4 5 6 7 8 9 0

215B
Page from the *New England Primer,* eighteenth century. "Nothing but the establishment of schools and some uniformity in the use of books, can annihilate differences in speaking and preserve the purity of the American tongue. A sameness of pronunciation is of considerable consequence in a political view; for provincial accents are disagreeable to strangers and sometimes have an unhappy effect upon the social affections. All men have local attachments, which lead them to believe their own practice to be the least exceptionable. Pride and prejudice incline men to treat the practice of their neighbors with some degree of contempt. Thus small differences in pronunciation at first excite ridicule—a habit of laughing at the singularities of strangers is followed by disrespect—and without respect friendship is a name, and social intercourse a mere ceremony." Noah Webster, *Dissertations on the English Language* (Boston, 1789).

216
Reading lesson for Czech students, New York City, 1942. "The child must be made to feel from the beginning that he is learning something which fits him for his new surroundings. There must be an abundance of pictures and objects on hand in order to hold the child's attention. . . . The teacher will secure toys representing a cow, a chicken . . . cups, saucers, plates, knives, forks; duck, baby, boy, girl. . . . The children know the names of these objects and pictures in their native tongue and are very anxious to learn the English word for the same." Frank B. Lenz, "The Education of the Immigrant" (*Educational Review, 51,* 1916).

217
Students using school library, Cleveland, Ohio. "The influence of a library in school is second only to that of the teacher, and, in many instances, the information self-gleaned by the pupils from books, is the most valuable part of their common school education. Books will give them a taste for reading, make them *alive* to knowledge, and start them on a plan of self-culture through life. A teacher may fail in the discharge of his duty, but the influence of good books is sure and lasting." John Sewett, Superintendent of Public Instruction of the State of California, 1867.

"The children's room in the public library is beginning to fill a need in the lives of the immigrant children. Special books and games are provided which aim to enfold the child's interest in the book world. The story-telling hour keeps the children's interest centered on thoughts that are clean and wholesome. It also keeps them off the street and away from evil companions and surroundings." Frank B. Lenz, 1916.

In Adam's Fall
We sinned all.

Thy Life to mend,
God's Book attend.

The Cat doth play,
And after slay.

A Dog will bite
A Thief at Night.

The Eagle's Flight
Is out of Sight.

The idle Fool
Is whipt at School

216

217

218A   218B

218A
Children at play in a
schoolyard. Cleveland, Ohio.

"Home, playground, school,
should be the golden path-
ways to a higher culture."
Francis W. Parker, Report of
the School Committee of the
Town of Quincy, Mas-
sachusetts, for the School
Year 1875–1876.

218B
Mid-nineteenth-century wood
engraving of playground activity.

219

Sewing class. Boston, 1909. "Now the leaders of the new education for girls recommend training them for self-support, assuming that, if wifehood and motherhood come, those who have received such a training can best take care of themselves. This assumption is radically wrong and vicious, and should be reversed. Every girl should be educated primarily to become a wife and mother, and, if this is done wisely and broadly, the small minority who remain single will, with this training, be best able to care for themselves." G. Stanley Hall, "The Ideal School as Based on Child Study" (National Education Association, *Journal of Proceedings and Addresses,* 1901).

220

Young basket peddlers, photographed by Lewis Hine. "From the point of view of one kind of reformer, the immigrant family exploited its children. . . . The reformer thus had to fight the 'bad' family by getting the child off the streets or out of the factory, and into institutions such as the school . . . they pushed compulsory education as a way to fight exploitation by parents. This reform attitude fitted in nicely with the goal of Americanization: the schools that children were forced to attend were supposed to teach them an efficient, standardized way of adjusting to cultural and commercial patterns outside the home." Daniel Calhoun, *The Educating of Americans: a Documentary History* (Boston, 1969).

219

220

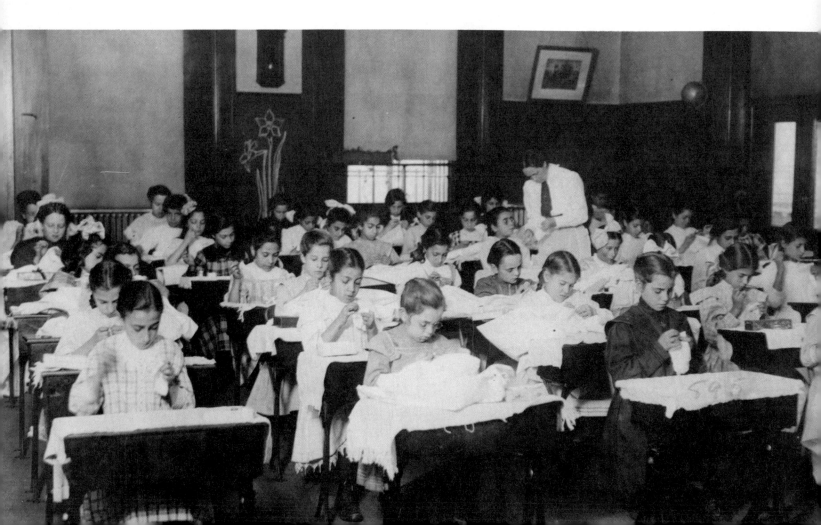

221
A fourth-grade class in Cleveland, Ohio. "And yet in spite of the fact that the public school is the great savior of the immigrant district, and the one agency which inducts the children into the changed conditions of American life, there is a certain indictment which may justly be brought, in that the public school too often separates the child from his parents and widens that old gulf between fathers and sons which is never so cruel and so wide as it is between the immigrants who come to this country and their children who have gone to the public school and feel that they have there learned it all. The parents are thereafter subjected to certain judgment, the judgment of the young which is always harsh and in this instance founded upon the most superficial standard of Americanism." Jane Addams, "The Public School and the Immigrant Child" (National Education Association, *Journal of Proceedings and Addresses,* 1908).

222
Class picture, probably San Francisco, early twentieth century. "For the immigrant children the public schools are the sluiceways into Americanism. When the stream of alien childhood flows through them, it will issue into the reservoirs of national life with the Old World taints filtered out, and the qualities retained that make for loyalty and good citizenship." Howard B. Grose, *Aliens or Americans?* (New York/ Toronto: Young People's Missionary Movement, 1906).

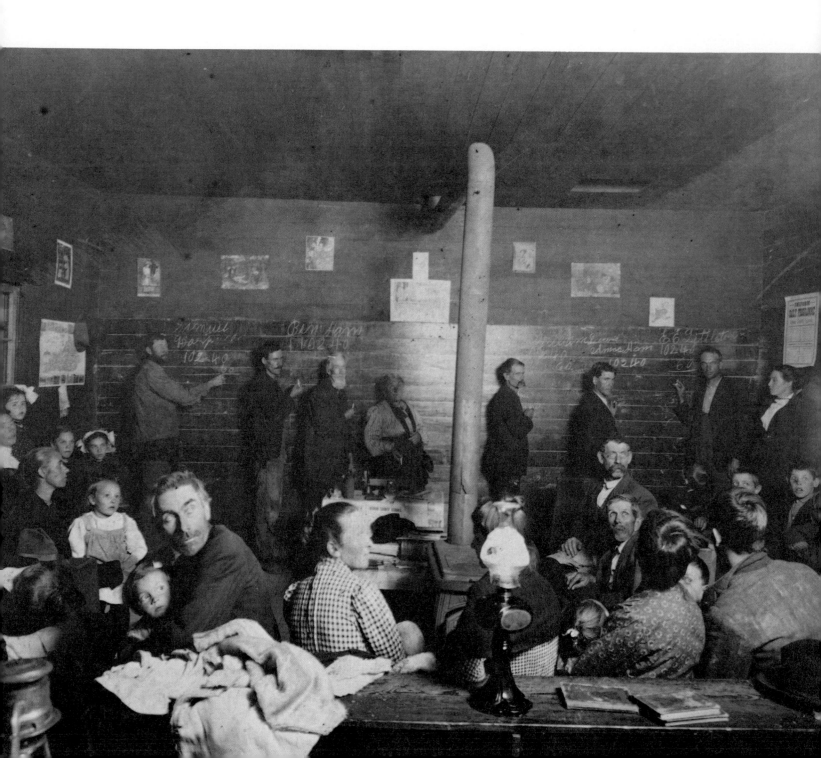

223B
Americanization class in English, c. 1919. "Why is it necessary or even desirable to educate the immigrant adult? For two reasons: for our own protection and for the immigrant's benefit. Today the majority of the immigrants coming to this country come to better their economic condition. Therefore it is our first business to teach him English—the colloquial English that will enable him to get on in life; to get a job, to keep it and then to get a better one; to find his way about the streets and to familiarize himself with American life." Frank B. Lenz, "The Education of the Immigrant," (*Educational Review, 51*, 1916).

Following passage of the Morrill Act in 1862, land-grant colleges sprouted everywhere during the last third of the nineteenth century. These institutions generally emphasized the diffusion of knowledge rather than basic research or the discovery of new information. Even the venerable private universities had seldom emphasized research and publication, although these became increasingly important functions later in the century. But the mission of teaching was also encouraged, and it became clear that imaginative teaching was a resource quite as important as research. The career of Louis Agassiz at Harvard University is illustrative of this.

Jean Louis Rodolphe Agassiz (1807–1873) was the most illustrious European scientist to settle in America prior to the twentieth century. The only conceivable rival would be the English chemist Joseph Priestley, who lived his last ten years at Northumberland, Pennsylvania. But the circumstances of Priestley's emigration and Agassiz's were vastly different. While Priestley conversed with Americans abroad throughout the Revolutionary period—his notable *History of Electricity* (1767) was written at the urging of Franklin, and Jefferson had often sought his advice—by the time he crossed the Atlantic in 1794 he was in his sixties and long since displaced from the scientific vanguard. Moreover, he left his homeland simply because he could no longer cope with abusive retaliation to his antiestablishment preachments; he was "pushed" to America, not "pulled."

With Louis Agassiz it was quite otherwise. When Agassiz embarked for Boston in September 1846 he was in his very prime. Though not yet forty, he was an honored professor at Neuchâtel, a brilliant naturalist patronized by the King of Prussia, an intimate of giants such as Baron von Humboldt, a genuine celebrity lionized everywhere. He was clearly "pulled" to America. For many years he had anticipated a grand field trip through the New World, the great *terra incognita* of natural history. Though not predisposed to remaining permanently, he did envision a productive sojourn. "There is something intoxicating in the prodigious activity of the Americans which makes me enthusiastic," he wrote to Benjamin Silliman, proprietor of the *American Journal of Science* in New Haven. "I already feel young through the anticipated contact with the men of your young and glorious republic."

Agassiz had an immediate purpose in coming to Boston when he did—a series of lectures at the Lowell Institute. But far more important, he was at that crucial psychological moment men often face at his age, when a radical personal reorientation becomes peculiarly attractive. His ultimate decision was to adopt America. It was a decision, hindsight suggests, that had an air of inevitability from the minute he set foot on these shores. As with Agassiz personally, American science was at a crucial juncture. "I thought myself tolerably familiar with all that is doing in science in the United States," he wrote to his mother, "but I was far from anticipating so much that is interesting and important. What is wanting to all these men is neither zeal nor knowledge. In both, they seem to compete with us, and in ardor and activity they even surpass most of our savants."

About the state of European science Agassiz could speak with unquestionable authority. The son of a Swiss Protestant minister, he had studied at Zurich, Heidelberg, Erlangen, and Munich, earning both a Ph.D. and an M.D. In 1829, at the age of twenty-one, he had published an important treatise on the fish life of Brazil. Although his subsequent researches ranged broadly, it was in ichthyology that he most solidly established himself. After a stint in the Paris laboratory of Baron Georges Cuvier, architect of the science of paleontology, he plunged into an extraordinarily ambitious study that eventually yielded five massive volumes on fossil fishes. He also published on the fishes of Central Europe, Russia, and Scotland, on fossil and living echinoderms, and on fossil mollusks. This work provided the basic underpinning for his reputation as a zoologist, while his investigation of glaciation—his "icy researches"—helped fix what William James called "the Agassiz legend."

The Agassiz legend derived from an image of the great romantic naturalist, handsome and engaging yet selflessly devoted to the pursuit of truth. "Since Benjamin Franklin, we had never had among us a person of more popularly impressive type," James observed. A legend, by definition, cannot precisely fit the facts of history, yet the image of Agassiz was essentially accurate. And it was this Agassiz—an irresistible personification of dash and depth—who captivated a nation in 1846. The feeling was mutual. It was a magic moment.

And it was a propitious moment. Agassiz arrived just as a group of Boston Brahmins was laying the groundwork for the first professional scientific school in America at Harvard, just as Joseph Henry was taking in hand the infant Smithsonian Institution and steering it toward basic research, and just as Alexander Dallas Bache was transforming the United States Coast Survey into a unique organization aimed both at increasing and applying scientific knowledge. American science had capable leaders such as Henry and Bache, but Agassiz had something no American scientist had in like measure—charisma. Before long, it was clear in his own mind that he had "a scientific mission to fulfill."

Agassiz's Lowell Lectures were a huge success, and he was immediately besieged with requests to speak elsewhere. In less than six months he earned more than six thousand dollars. Thoughts of returning to Europe receded rapidly. He began sending for former associates and assistants; at one point nearly two dozen of them gathered around him in Boston and Cambridge. (Some, such as Count François Pourtalès, went on to achieve major rank on their own.) American scientists everywhere were eager to help propel Agassiz into new researches. Bache, for instance, put at his disposal a ship assigned to the Coast Survey, so that he might make a scientific excursion off Cape Cod. That ship, it happened, was commanded by Lieutenant Charles Henry Davis, a major figure in American science, who immediately became Agassiz's close friend. So did others, in Washington and especially in Cambridge, and these alliances comprised the genesis of a fraternity that soon dominated the politics of American science.

In the fall of 1847 Agassiz, wise to the subtleties of such matters, played the key role in founding the American Association for the Advancement of Science. He had moved naturally to the forefront of the American scientific community. After his friends arranged to have a professorship at the new Lawrence Scientific School precisely tailored to fit him, his decision to stay was sealed. Thenceforth Agassiz was an American. Only once did he return to Europe. And if his scientific accomplishments in America never measured up to his grand visions, if his "mania for rushing full gallop into the future" far outdistanced his actual capacities, his impact on American science was nonetheless momentous. First, there was his voracity as a collector and his prodigious talent for raising funds. Then there was his founding of the Museum of Comparative Zoology at Harvard, an institution he nurtured into a major research center where he trained an eminent group of natural scientists. But most important were his efforts on behalf of the whole of American science.

Even had he not had his unique flair for organization, Agassiz's very presence proclaimed that American science could hold its own in any implicit competition with Europe. But Agassiz was indeed a peerless organizer, and he took to himself the task of establishing in America a milieu properly conducive to scientific research and receptive to science as a profession. So single-mindedly did he pursue that goal that he declined bids from several of the great universities of Europe, even a truly spectacular offer from Emperor Louis Napoleon to direct the National Museum of Natural History in Paris. "I prefer to build anew here," he replied.

And build he did. In 1851 he was chosen president of the American Association for the Advancement of Science, an organization he had largely shaped, but one that was not and could not become an elite body with power to make public policy in scientific matters. To the establishment of such an organization as this Agassiz dedicated himself. In concert with a handful of associates, including Bache in Washington but mostly Harvard men, he succeeded in setting up the National Academy of Science in 1863. This was not done without stirring deep suspicions about the true motives of "the Coast Survey and Agassiz Clique." Such suspicions were not unfounded; to some of his peers grown skeptical with time, Agassiz seemed to adhere to the lofty ideals of professionalism only when it personally suited him, and to diverge when *that* suited him. He insisted, for example, that a scientist's professional competence must be judged only by his equals, never by popular opinion. Yet, when compelled by his teleological precepts to stand in adamant opposition to Darwinism, he did not hesitate to take his case to the public—to "talk to the rabble" as his chief adversary, the botanist Asa Gray, put it.

As every great man embodies a complexity that is bound to foster paradox, so it was with Louis Agassiz. Whatever his flaws of egotism and inflexibility, Agassiz gave immeasurable riches to his adopted country. He stirred popular enthusiasm for science as never before. Many significant institutions felt his catalytic power. He established America's first distinguished research museum. He set the stage for the scientific pursuit of zoology in America and stimulated its development everywhere. He helped create a great university. Indeed, it was as a teacher that he made his most profound impact. Henry Adams remarked in his *Education* that his studies with Agassiz at Harvard "had more influence on his curiosity than the rest of the college instruction together." And when James Russell Lowell, visiting Italy in 1874, heard the news of his death, he penned an epitaph which students of Agassiz's career find irresistible:

We have not lost him all; he is not gone . . .
The beauty of his better self lives on
In Minds he touched with fire, in many an eye . . .
He was a Teacher . . .
Whose living word still stimulates the air . . .

Chapter 18

Military Uniformity— A Pictorial Essay

On Columbus Day, 1915, former President Theodore Roosevelt urged an audience in Philadelphia to support a universal draft for military service. He was obviously arguing for military preparedness in the face of the war being fought in Europe; but his appeal went beyond guns and ships, into society itself, where in Roosevelt's mind the man who has received military training is "a better citizen, is more self-respecting, more orderly, better able to hold his own, and more willing to respect the rights of others." As for foreign-born Americans, Roosevelt was an adamant proponent of assimilation and unity: "It is our duty from the standpoint of self-defense to secure the complete Americanization of our people,—to make of the many peoples of this country a united nation, one in speech and feeling, and all, so far as possible, share in the best that each has brought to our shores." Military service for all would obviate "older racial types, . . . maintain a new American type," and give everyone a feeling that he had a stake in American society.

Whether Roosevelt really believed in the Americanizing influence of the military or simply floated the idea past the crowd like a flag bearer carrying the Stars and Stripes is difficult to say. Modern historians such as Marcus Lee Hansen have seen the military—particularly in wartime—as binding even the most recent arrivals to the American mainstream. In addition to forming bonds among fighting men, wars have also given the economy periodic boosts, and immigrants both on the farms and in industrial towns have benefited. And when a community of young men marched away to war, those left at home paid closer attention to battle accounts and to death notices. The years of anxiety in the Civil War and in the two world wars made the emotions, the fortunes, and the futures of the immigrant family one with those of the nation.

Even in peacetime the military system of rank, dress, personal appearance, discipline, and behavior continuously reinforced a uniform code of conduct and a sense of national loyalty. From the beginning of America's military history the emphasis was on standardization of thought and behavior, and—appropriately enough for a nation of immigrants—the first standard training manual was written by a foreign volunteer, Major General Friedrich Wilhelm von Steuben, in 1779.

Historically, ethnic diversity has been a fact of military life. As early as 1775, the polyglot make-up of the Continental forces was a continual source of anxiety for General Washington and his staff. Early in the war only "native born" Americans were enlisted, but with a growing need for recruits, all men were eventually accepted. Some regiments mixed in a few free Negroes, but Christopher Greene's Rhode Island Regiment was exceptional in that the noncommissioned officers and enlisted men were predominantly black. This regiment fought in numerous campaigns throughout the war. Southern Negroes, mostly slaves, also served in the Revolution, as did Indians. Of the latter, a few worked alone as scouts or guides, but most fought along with their tribes. Certain Algonquin tribes, for example, allied with the patriots against their traditional enemy the Iroquois, many of whom supported the British.

From the very outset the armed forces have been composed of heterogeneous peoples who somehow, in Theodore Roosevelt's words, had to be Americanized. From the War of 1812 to the Mexican War in 1846, the army regulations stated that enlistees had to be "free white male persons, above eighteen and under thirty-five years, who are able bodied, active, and free from disease." An 1825 amendment stipulated that no foreigner could be enlisted "without special permission from general headquarters." This was changed in 1834 to read: "All free white male persons . . . who are 'effective ablebodied citizens of the United States,' native or naturalized, sober, free from disease, and who speak and understand the English language, may be enlisted." By 1857 regulations no longer made any mention of citizenship but did require "a competent knowledge of the English language."

The navy's experience was somewhat different. From the very beginning foreign-born sailors were found in abundance on United States navy and merchant ships. This contributed to difficulties with Great Britain prior to the War of 1812, for it was known that natural-born American sailors sold their names and papers to foreigners. For much of the nineteenth century it was a source of concern to U.S. navy and merchant officers that a large portion of the sailor population was foreign-born. They feared that some men might not be entirely reliable in the event of foreign wars. But it was not until the early years of the twentieth century that there was a specific ban on the enlistment of aliens in the navy.

The military, particularly during the Civil War, appeared to be in a contradictory situation. On the one hand it was composed of people from many races and many nations, all theoretically following uniform codes and rules and all fighting for a common cause: all were becoming an "American type." Yet this same armed force was anything but a mixing bowl, for many regiments and companies were ethnically homogeneous, even commanded by bilingual officers because the enlisted men often spoke only their own native tongue. One of the reasons was that the war closely followed large-scale migrations from Ireland and Germany. Irishmen and Germans thus predominated among the foreigners fighting for the Union, although other nationalities were heavily represented, too. Indeed, there was a definite element of competition among ethnic groups to top each other in enlistments. Individual units adopted such names as the British Volunteers, Cameron Swiss Rifles, Gardes Lafayette, Highlanders, Polish Legion, and Scandinavian Regiment. The legions of Germans and Irish included the German Rangers, German Turners, German Heavy Artillery, and the Hibernian Guard, Hibernian Target Company, and Irish Dragoons.

In the North the initial response to the call for volunteers was overwhelming, exceeding requirements. However, as the Civil War dragged on and casualties mounted, enlistments slowed. The Draft Act of March 3, 1863, shifted an individual's militia obligation from the states to the federal government. It applied to all white male citizens, and to those aliens who had declared their intention to become citizens, who were between twenty and forty-five. A draftee could provide a substitute or fulfill his obligation by paying the sum of three hundred dollars. The immediate reaction to the draft law was rioting in the streets of New York City, Boston, and elsewhere. Immigrants who had responded so eagerly to the initial call for volunteers were now violently against the draft. One cause was resentment by workingmen against the three-hundred-dollar escape clause.

Ultimately, foreign-born troops accounted for nearly one-fourth of the total manpower of the Union army. After Appomattox the war hero became a symbol of prestige for every nationality, and veterans' organizations perpetuated the memory of conflict and sacrifice which wedded the foreign-born community to America. The standing army was cut to an authorized strength of 54,641, which included four Negro infantry and two cavalry regiments. This marked the first inclusion of Negro units in the regular army, though they were commanded by white officers. These Negro units fought throughout the Indian wars, the Spanish-American War, and during both world wars; not until the Korean War were they completely desegregated.

Indians presented a special case: while they were obviously native-born, they were not citizens. Before the Civil War they were hired as scouts, and during the war companies of Indians acted as home guards in the trans-Mississippi South. Some saw action in Texas. After the war, Indian scouts were assigned to units throughout the West. By 1890 scouts were serving lengthy terms of enlistment, wearing special uniforms. After 1902 they were issued regular uniforms, distinguished only by the letters USS for United States Scouts.

From the Civil War up to World War I, various immigrant groups were represented in the peacetime army roughly in proportion to their representation in the overall population. Immigrants enlisted for a variety of reasons. One was economic security: the services afforded a regular income, food, clothing, shelter, and medical care. For the immigrant attracted by the West and its promise of free land, the army offered a way to get there. And all the while, it provided instruction in American customs and modes of behavior.

The National Guard Act of 1903 had special significance for immigrants. The Spanish-American War had shown existing measures to be inadequate for mobilizing large numbers of volunteers, and this precipitated adoption of a nationwide system for maintaining a pool of civilians more or less ready for combat. The foreign-born were eligible to serve in National Guard units.

Nothing that had ever happened in American military history affected the immigrant as World War I did. In May 1917, shortly after America's formal declaration of war, Congress passed the Selective Service Act. With the unhappy experience of the Civil War draft law in mind, the legislators framed this act to preclude substitutions and purchase of exemptions. There were no bounties for enlistment. Instead, male citizens and "friendly aliens" who had declared their intention of becoming citizens were required to register. At first the age limits were twenty-one to thirty, later eighteen through thirty-five. As the war progressed, nobody eligible for the draft was permitted to enlist. Ultimately, conscription supplied 67 percent of those who served in the armed forces, as opposed to 6 percent during the Civil War.

A law passed in 1918 adjusted quotas in favor of states that had large numbers of aliens not required to register for conscription because they had not declared intent of becoming citizens. Subsequent draft laws were passed; the 1951 law was significantly titled "The Universal Military Training and Service Act." Every male was now explicitly subject to conscription.

The draft has had a profound impact. Men from every social, economic, and ethnic background have been subject to the same requirements. Basic training entails the closest relationship between inductees and the most rigid imposition of uniformity. All garments are alike, all haircuts the same, all eat the same meals, all march to the same cadence. Every new experience is shared, including combat and the reality of death. The markers in a military cemetery are identical. Out of 3,216 Congressional Medals of Honor conferred in the century between the Civil War and Vietnam, more than one-sixth went to men born beyond American shores, men born in thirty-two different nations.

224
Civil War draft lottery box. The Draft Act of March 3, 1863, was the first in this nation's history. This particular lottery box was used by Chester Pike for drawing names of those to be drafted in the western part of New Hampshire during the Civil War. L 24″.

225
U.S. troops, Civil War.

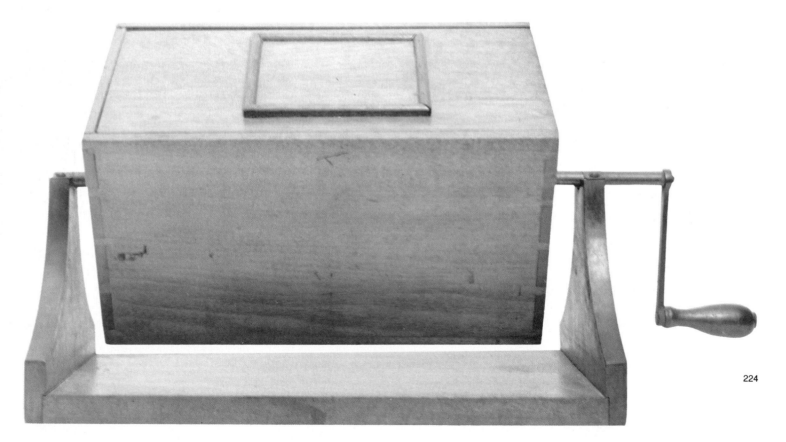

224

1829

225

226A
Apache Indian Scouts of the
U.S. Army, c. 1880. These
men are wearing official clothing together with their own
choice of footwear. While Indian scouts had been used by
the Army prior to the Civil
War, by 1890 they received
their own distinctive dress
uniform in addition to the
campaign garments seen
above.

226B
Indian Scout campaign hat
adopted in 1890 and used
through 1902.

226A

226B

227
Drawing of the first draft
number during World War I.

228
One of the few surviving announcements for registration
for the draft in World War I. It
is particularly rare since it is
written in Hawaiian.

227

228

229

230A

TELL THAT TO THE MARINES!
AT 371 MARKET STREET

230B

231
Battery A, 330th Field Artillery, World War I.

LRY A. 330TH FIELD ARTILLERY

#286
PHOTO DIV.
POST EXCHANGE
CAMP MILLS, L.I.

233A

COHEN, STANLEY
US52464532
B

JEWISH

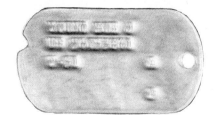
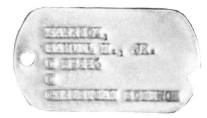

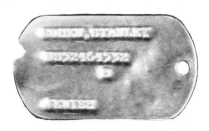

340

340

233B
Identification tags used by the U.S. armed forces from World War I through the present. The elongated rectangular tags with the rounded corners are from the Army; the slightly oval tags are from the Navy or Marine Corps. The Army tags from World War I and earlier were circular. Each individual wore two of these tags. They all contain the person's name, religious preference, and, since World War II, the blood type and dates of specific inoculations. The Army dog tags prior to 1918 did not bear a serial number and often included the name and address of the next of kin.

234
Examples of footwear used by the U.S. armed forces.
Foreground: hobnailed shoes, often termed boots, used by
the U.S. Army and Marine Corps during World War I; *left to
right:* service or garrison shoe of the "Munson Last" type
adopted c. 1913 and used through the 1930s; jungle boot of
canvas and rubber used during the 1960s and 1970s; "shoe
pac," a rubber boot adopted for use in cold, wet areas during
World War II; cavalry boot used from 1876 to 1884; combat
boot adopted c. 1944 and used during the Korean War
period; "paratrooper" or "jump boot" used during World War
II; combat boot used by the entire Army, 1950s to date;
garrison shoe of World War II.

A typical interior of a U.S. Army barracks during World War II. Note the precise location of each and every object according to strict regulations. This photograph was taken at Fort Sam Houston, Texas, in 1942.

WE ARE NOW IN THIS WAR

We are all in it all the way

Every single man, woman and child is a partner in the most tremendous undertaking of our American history. We must share together the bad news and the good news, the defeats and the victories — the changing fortunes of war.

(President Roosevelt, Address to the Nation, December 9, 1941)

DIVISION OF INFORMATION
OFFICE FOR EMERGENCY MANAGEMENT
WASHINGTON, D.C.

U. S. GOVERNMENT PRINTING OFFICE

236B

236A
This poster is based upon an appeal from President Roosevelt at the outbreak of World War II.

236B
U.S. Navy recruiting poster from World War II.

237
Battery E, 211 Coast Artillery, U.S. Army.

237

238
Company 54, U.S. Naval
Training Station, Newport,
Rhode Island, 1950s.

AMERICANS ALL!

HONOR ROLL

Du Bois
Smith
O'Brien
Cejka
Haucke
Pappandrikopolous
Andrassi
Villotto
Levy
Turovich
Kowalski
Chriczanevicz
Knutson
Gonzales

Victory Liberty Loan

239A
U.S. government poster designed to encourage the new immigrants to purchase Liberty Loan bonds during World War I.

239B
World War I Victory Loan poster aimed at the diverse ethnic groups in the U.S.

240A
U.S. Military Cemetery at Lorraine, St. Avold, France. Note the Star of David markers in the near foreground.

240B
Polish-American cemetery on German Hill Road in Baltimore.

Chapter 19

Working Together

Work in America functioned as a magnet, drawing millions of immigrants to the New World [241]. For most newcomers, employment, not streets paved with gold, or political liberty, was the chief goal in migrating to the United States. The aim of finding work was reinforced by swarms of agents in Europe representing steamship companies, American railroads and industries, and state governments. Working and economic prosperity were themes of thousands of "American letters" written by immigrants in the United States to their relatives back home. A Welsh coal miner wrote home from Ohio in 1864: "We work very hard here while we are working but we leave every day about three to four o'clock. I like it here very much; it is so much better than being a fireman in Wales. I feel healthy and strong...." A Norwegian settler wrote with great feeling about the advantages available in his new home:

Hardly a day passes without my reflecting on how richly God blesses this country every year; and then my heart is moved to pity when my thoughts go back to Norway and I recall the poor people in cities and in the country who had to beg for the bare necessities of life with tears in their eyes. How happy the poor and landless would consider themselves if they were here, especially those who are honest in purpose and cheerful.

Working immigrants were part of a massive process of economic development in the United States during which the American economy of the nineteenth and early twentieth centuries expanded, industrialized, and built, although in an uneven manner. Growth varied from time to time and from region to region, but the tendency was dramatically upward. Comparing the United States and Great Britain, in 1870 this country produced one-third as much coal and about one-quarter as much steel as Britain. In 1890 it produced slightly more steel and nearly as much coal. In 1910 it produced almost twice as much coal and more than four times as much steel. Immigrant labor was an essential ingredient of this great expansion.

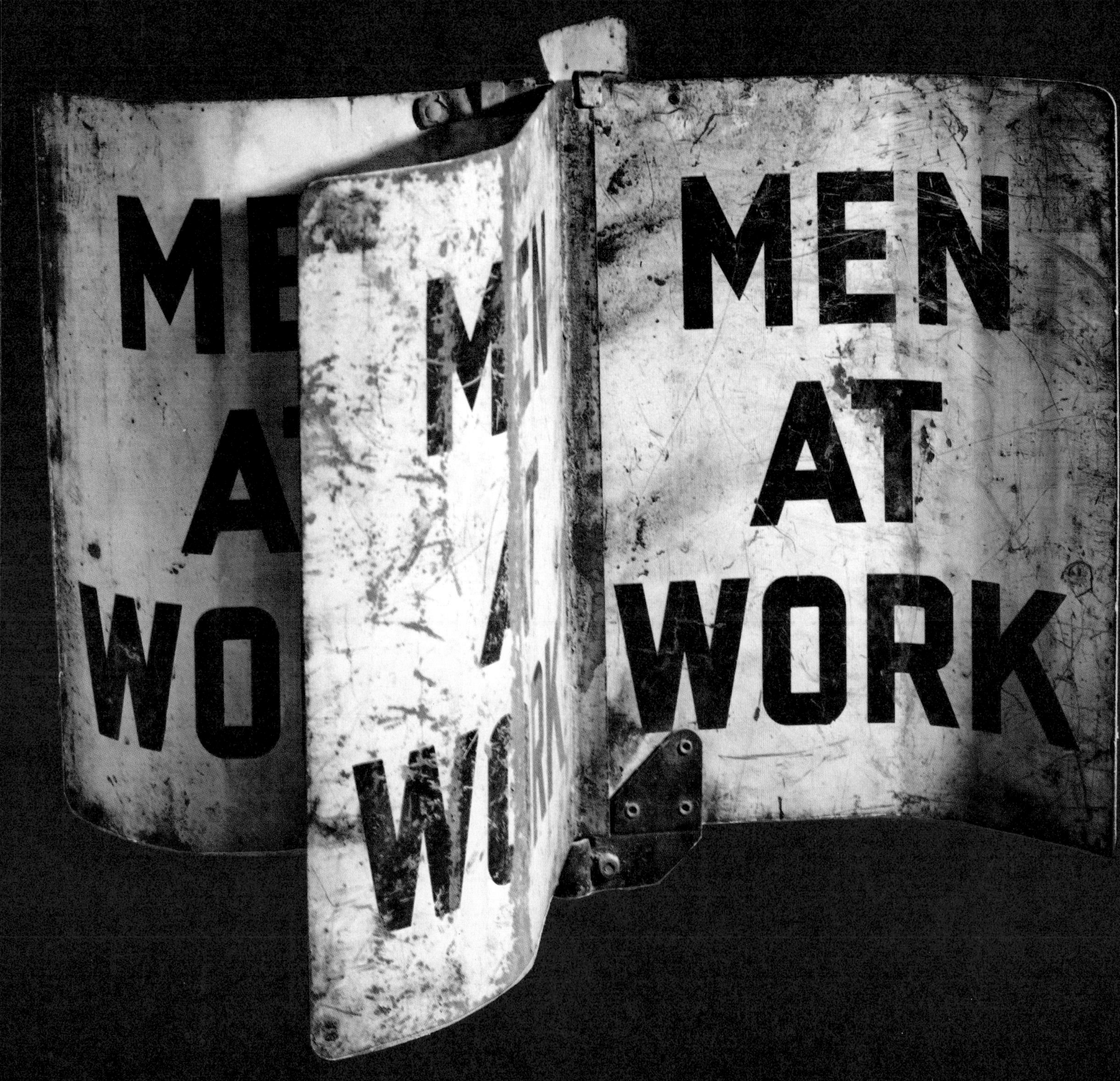
MEN
AT
WORK

There was no exact formula or pattern for immigrant employment, although certain general trends existed. The variations between working experience can be illustrated by comparing nationality groups. Two prominent groups of the mid-nineteenth century (1850–1860), the British and the Irish, had contrasting work histories. Of all newcomers to the United States, the British seem to have been more generally employed at trades they had practiced in the homeland. They were especially prominent in three basic industries: textiles, mining, and metalworking. Roughly 40 percent of British immigrants had experience in skilled industrial trades. In textiles they were for many years the chief technicians and most highly skilled operatives, presiding over the introduction of several new and complex processes between 1820 and 1870 (see Chapter 12). They worked in cotton, woolens, carpetmaking, silk, hosiery, lace, and thread production. As skilled artisans, they commanded the best wages and had the greatest mobility of any textile workers. Only when the application of new machinery late in the century eliminated the bulk of the highly skilled jobs did British craftsmen lose their position as the aristocrats of textiles.

Substantial mining of American coal did not begin until the 1830s, and few natives had skills necessary to do the job. From this time onward British miners emigrated, knowing they would find work. Welsh pitmen were most in demand in the anthracite regions because of their experience, while English and Scottish miners best understood bituminous mining. When skilled men were short, the immigrants could earn good wages, but over-production in the mines, and periodic depressions and strikes, often reduced income below British levels, leading some miners to reverse the direction of their migration. As late as 1888, one anthracite corporation employed more than one thousand Welshmen and more than four hundred Englishmen as "inside workers," totaling nearly half of its mining crew. British workers were the vanguard of mining, teaching native Americans and other immigrants the basic skills and introducing innovations into mine procedures. More than any other group, they worked their way into positions as foremen. The British, especially the Cornish, also contributed mightily to the development of ore mining in lead, iron, and copper country. British leadership in mining, as in textiles, tended to diminish as the mines became increasingly mechanized. When pick and shovel work was replaced by blasting and undercutting machines beneath the ground, the cheaper labor and brute strength of Slavic and Italian workers could do the job for less money [242].

The iron industry also used British skills and British artisans who carried techniques of metallurgy to the New World, where they had previously been unknown. The earliest American blast furnaces, iron rolling and puddling mills, and coke processes were inaugurated by Englishmen. Not only the technicians, but many of the skilled iron craftsmen were immigrants. Welsh ironmakers were prominent in Pittsburgh and Johnstown, Pennsylvania, Pueblo, Colorado, and elsewhere, and they performed much of the highly skilled work. In 1890, 10 percent of the iron and steel industry's fifteen thousand workers were natives of Britain, but employment patterns were changing rapidly. New steel mills with new processes reduced the need for skilled labor, and after 1900, instead of British artisans, mill operators hired workers from Poland, Hungary, and Italy [243].

Although not all British immigrants were skilled artisans, a substantial number were, and they had a special role in American industrial development. Functioning as an elite group, they could command higher wages than the norm because their skills were so much in demand during the early phases of our industrialization. Indeed, they made critical contributions to American technical growth. Thousands of other British immigrants were farmers, potters, clerks, carpenters, and businessmen. An elite, too, in cultural terms, British immigrants (except for some Welshmen) generally knew the English language and assimilated better to American ways than most other alien groups.

242

243

242
Coal and iron workers pause for their photograph with a Pennsylvania Railroad engine, c. 1890. As of 1910, more than 60 percent of the iron miners in America were foreign-born.

243
The Bowler and Company foundry, Cleveland, c. 1910.

In contrast to the British, Irish newcomers at mid-century had few advantages. Victims of terrible overpopulation, cultural and political oppression, and finally of the tragic potato famine in the late 1840s, Irish natives arrived in increasing numbers during the 1830s, and constituted a flood in the 1840s. They totaled more than 1.6 million by 1860. Accustomed to eking out a precarious existence on the land at home, they became city dwellers in the New World. Without capital to take up land or purchase tools, or even to travel beyond the point of entry, the Irish came to occupy the lowest rung in American cities, that of unskilled, irregularly employed labor. While the majority remained in cities such as Boston and New York, some becoming the typical "Irish cop" [244], many thousands of Irish were herded inland by contractors to labor in construction or in textile mills, which required heavy concentrations of unskilled workers. They built canals—the Erie and others—they built the growing network of railroads [245, 246], they began in the 1840s to replace native workers, including the famous Yankee mill girls in Lowell, Massachusetts.

In several cities the Irish dominated the ranks of day laborers and domestic servants. The New York Association for Improving the Condition of the Poor in 1852 described the condition of the city's Irish: "During the busy season, the men work about the wharves, or as diggers, hodmen, &c., and the women as rough washers, house cleaners, course sewers, or in any other rude work they can find to do." It was held that the Irish would never become good workers: "Of the large number of Irish immigrants, it may be said that they are but little disposed to change their thriftless habits with a change of country. They are prone to stay where another race furnishes them with food, clothing and labor." The phrase "No Irish need apply" was a rule of thumb for most occupations demanding skills or having prestige.

As time went on, manufacturers saw in the supply of cheap Irish labor opportunities to expand their profitable businesses. In Boston the ready-made clothing industry increased its workers from fewer than five hundred in 1845 to more than three thousand in 1860, making Boston a major center of clothing manufacture. Although pay of $4.50 to $5.50 per week was low for this semiskilled work, it was more reliable than day labor. Numerous other industries, both heavy and light, took advantage of the Irish labor supply, workers who would accept wages that natives would not touch. Women worked prodigiously in household labor, needle work, and textile mills. It was common labor, but these destitute, unskilled people had no choice. Their situation changed slowly with time, but even in 1910 more than 20 percent of foreign-born Irish were laborers. Succeeding generations of Irish Americans expanded their roles in the labor force and gained higher levels of status [247, 248].

Why the disparity between British and Irish? Skills and capital are key factors, although not the only reason, for the British advantages. Their industrial experience favored the British. Prejudice and numbers were undoubtedly other critical elements. British artisans arrived over a longer period of time, were distributed more generally through the country, and came often in response to quite specific needs. The Irish came in greater numbers, concentrated over less time, and settled in more restricted areas. Without much skill, culturally "backward," and Roman Catholic to boot, the Irish triggered negative responses among native Americans.

244
"The Greatest Freak on Record. . . . The Wonder of the Age. An American Policeman. . . . The Only Policeman Ever Born in America." A reference to the fact that during the nineteenth and early twentieth centuries American policemen were predominantly recent immigrants, primarily Irish. (*Judge*, 1891.)

THE GREATEST FREAK ON RECORD.

245
Construction gang of immigrant laborers working on the
Cleveland Belt Line Railroad,
c. 1910. As of that date, one-
half of the laborers on steam
railways were foreign-born.

246
Special train of the Philadelphia & Reading Railroad for
quartering and moving company policemen to quell labor
disturbances in the coal and
iron regions of eastern
Pennsylvania. Photographed
by George N. Bretz at Gordon, Pennsylvania, on February 23, 1888.

245

GEO. M. BRETZ, Photographer, Pottsville, Pa.

Negatives Nos. 27409—27410.

Philadelphia & Reading R. R. and Coal & Iron Police Quarters,

Gordon, Pa., Feb'y 23rd, 1888.

1—LIEUT. JOHN HARRIS,	6—GEO. CAMPBELL.	11—FRANK GRAEFF,	16—WM. W. FAUST.
2—C. T. LYON,	7—MAHLON ALLENBACH,	12—SEB. DANIEL,	17—CHAS. W. CRAMER,
3—H. C. MILLER,	8—WM. SHRAGEN,	13—CHARLES BECKLEY,	18—M. P. STUTZMAN,
4—LEE BERRY,	9—W. S. GROFF,	14—JOHN J. SIMMET,	19—WM. SCHNEIDER,
5—GEO. BUCHANNAN,	10—K. C. LEE,	15—WM. R. PYLE,	20—W. H. LEIB,
21—HENRY KAUFMAN,		JOHN A. STIEF.	

Engine Company No. 21,
Chicago Fire Department,
1874. The Irish as well as
numerous other groups made
up many of the professional
and the volunteer fire companies in America.

248
Fire helmet used in the Far
Rockaway, New York, Fire
Department, c. 1894. H 8½".

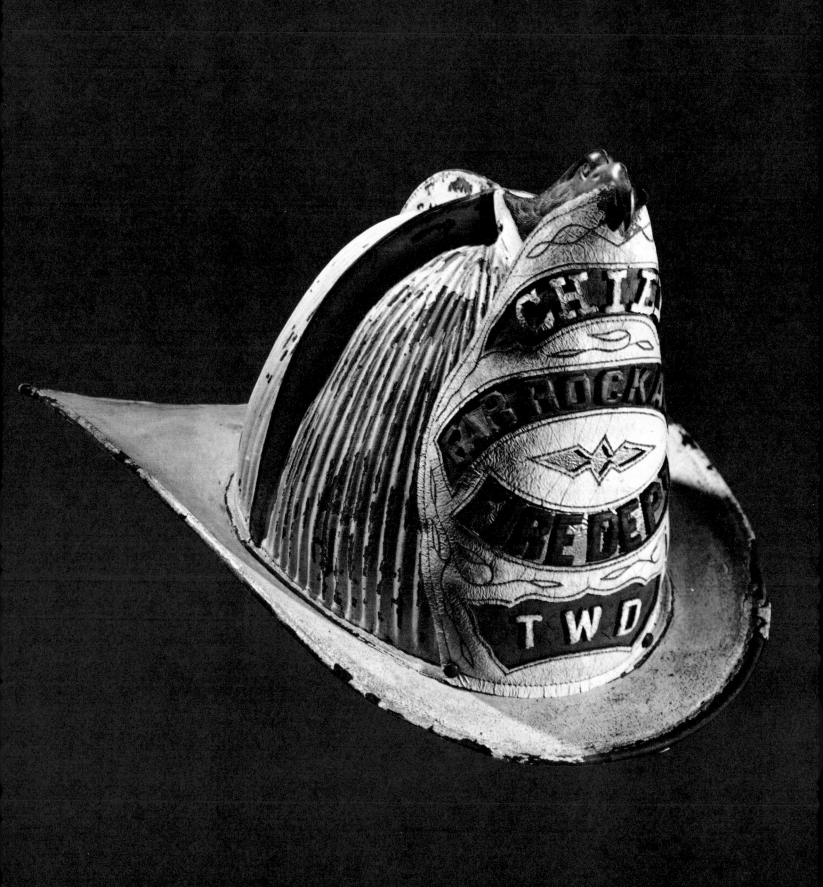

Another contrast, fifty years later, illustrates the diversity of experiences among nationalities. Between 1880 and 1920, more than 1.5 million Jews poured out of Eastern Europe, driven by persecution, pogroms, and murder. Arriving in the United States from Russia, Poland, Lithuania, and Hungary, these newcomers seemed more clannish and alien than many other immigrants. They brought with them traditions of the ghetto—the separate sections of the Eastern European cities where Jews were confined—and a more distinct urban experience than other immigrants. Their working lives in the New World reflected their experience in the old. Concentrating in the cities, especially New York, Jewish immigrants became prominent in two occupations—retail trade and the garment industry [see **156A, 156B, 157, 158** in Chapter 13].

Trade was an established Jewish occupation in Europe. Many Jews had been shopkeepers, wholesalers, merchants, or simple peddlers. Not surprisingly, they sought to continue in a familiar occupation. Streets in American Jewish neighborhoods represented this pattern, crowded with pushcarts of vegetables, shoes, clothing, jewelry, foodstuffs, and other goods, the sidewalks lined by small shops of every variety. Yiddish, the language of European Jews, dominated trading and haggling. Beginning on a small scale, some of these peddlers and petty merchants accumulated capital that permitted them to expand into substantial businesses such as department stores, to purchase real estate, to move into more luxurious neighborhoods, and to educate their children.

Less easy to explain is Jewish involvement in the garment trade. Between 1890 and 1920 the ready-made garment industry was dominated by Jewish immigrants, yet only about 10 percent of the newcomers had experience as tailors. Two aspects of the business may help to explain Jewish prominence.

First, the garment trade was largely organized by the sweating system, described as follows by the Illinois Bureau of Labor Statistics: "... sweating consists of the farming out by competing manufacturers to competing contractors of the material for garments, which in turn is distributed among competing men and women to be made up." Thus, the industry was divided into hundreds of small units, each operated by a separate contractor who employed his own workers. Such a system apparently attracted Jewish immigrants, accustomed to doing business independently. Small shops could be established with a minimum of capital, yet the contractors were like traders in the Old World. Naturally the garment-industry labor force became Jewish—people who shared the language and culture of the contractors. "Greenhorn" newcomers quickly found work in sweatshops in the immigrant neighborhood because the garment trade centered in small, localized shops.

Second, because of developments in the clothing industry, it became more suitable for semiskilled immigrant labor. In the late nineteenth and early twentieth centuries, ready-made apparel largely replaced custom-made garments; new sewing machines, cutting tools, and pressing irons made skills less crucial, and a minute division of labor encouraged the employment of less skilled workers. Thus, tens of thousands of Jewish immigrants labored in the sweatshops of New York, Chicago, and other cities. Later, as factory production replaced sweatshops, the immigrants worked for large manufacturers.

Jewish immigrants carried from the Old World two other significant characteristics, social and cultural, that influenced their working lives. Socially, they arrived in family groups to a greater extent than other newcomers. Often consisting of two or three generations, Jewish families were less mobile territorially than most new arrivals. Culturally, they brought a unique attitude toward intellectual endeavor and learning. Based on religious traditions extending centuries into the past, Jewish respect for learning gave the group a positive response to educational achievement. Because of these characteristics, fewer Jewish immigrants lived or worked outside family structures, or joined the throngs of single wandering workers so typical of immigrant labor. Jewish immigrant children spent more time in school and more of them grew up to be professional and business men, artists, or entertainers than children of other nationalities. Jewish Americans contributed in a distinctive way to the labor movement and a variety of political and humanitarian reforms.

Italian immigrants who arrived during the same period offer a contrast to the Jewish newcomers. In terms of numbers, nearly twice as many Italians as Jews came to the United States—more than three million between 1900 and 1920. Until 1900 Italians came chiefly from northern Italy, the largest number of them, before 1870, heading for California, where they discovered regions reminiscent of their homeland and where they founded the California wine industry. After 1900 southern Italians dominated the immigrant mass, fleeing poverty, overpopulation, and economic oppression. They came almost entirely from rural peasant communities and, for the most part, they settled in American cities where opportunities for work existed. They concentrated in the northeastern United States, replacing the Irish as laborers in construction and industry. Arriving first as single men, they were relatively free to go where opportunities called, but when they could afford it they sent for wives and sweethearts to establish families, or returned to the Old Country to find wives.

Italians were most numerously employed in construction—the pick and shovel trades [249]. They built the subways and street railways of New York; they rebuilt, added to, and maintained many miles of railroad throughout the country; they worked on streets and highways; they helped to construct thousands of office buildings, factories, and houses in growing cities and towns. In time some of their number accumulated capital and became building contractors. Italian workers could also be found in New England textile towns, in the woolen mills of Lawrence, Massachusetts, for example, where they did the least skilled labor. Next to Jewish immigrants, they became the most prevalent needle workers in the garment trade. In some coal fields they worked in the mines, whereas in cities many Italians went into service occupations such as barbering, peddling, and the restaurant business. A minority of Italian natives went into agriculture, where they achieved some success in truck gardening near major cities. Entire families worked the land, doing the careful, intensive cultivation required to grow vegetables for the urban tables. Willing laborers that they were, they filled the need for millions of unskilled hands.

One feature of Italian working patterns set them apart from most other immigrants—the padrone or boss system. Originally used to describe men who recruited bands of children and adults, paid their fares to America, found work for them, and extracted a profit, padrones later came to mean contractors who controlled gangs of Italian workmen in the United States, negotiated for their services with builders and other employers, and profited handsomely from the transactions. Still later, padrones were chiefly employment agents who could be said to assist the immigrants by finding them jobs and helping to overcome the language barrier. Once the Italian immigrants became well established, their need for padrones disappeared.

Turn-of-the-century Jewish and Italian immigrants, like the British and Irish of fifty years earlier, had quite different patterns of employment. For Jewish and British newcomers, their experience in certain Old World trades and industries prepared them to follow specific lines of work in the New World. For Italian and Irish immigrants, native experience was less important. Both these nationality groups came out of rural peasant traditions and were accustomed to hard outdoor labor, but for the most part they avoided agriculture, entering instead construction and industrial work.

Diversity characterized the working lives of other immigrant groups in the United States. Germans, the largest immigrant population from any single European background, probably had the most complicated employment patterns. They dominated the brewing industry and carried on other Old World occupations, such as cabinetmaking, baking, watchmaking, bookbinding, printing, machine and metal trades, and piano making. A great many Germans became midwestern farmers. Immigrants from Scandinavia were prominent in agriculture but also entered into occupations such as metallurgy and machining, in which they had special skills. Some Scandinavians, with a seafaring tradition, became fishermen and mariners. Finnish immigrants were drawn to the iron and copper mines of Michigan and Minnesota as well as to the timber lands farther west and north [250].

Immigrants arriving in the United States after 1890 found changing employment opportunities. The end of the great rush to settle open agricultural lands removed farming as an alternative for the great mass of newcomers and made industrial work the goal of most groups. Among the early immigrants to concentrate in industry were the French Canadians, who entered the New England states in large numbers after 1870 to work in the textile mills. The rapid development of American heavy industry in the late nineteenth century and the first years of the twentieth gave employment to several nationality groups. Slavic immigrants did much of the heavy labor that enabled iron and steel mills and coal mines to expand in this period [251]. Newcomers from Poland, probably more than two million in number, flowed into the industrial cities. The largest single Polish community appeared in Chicago, where immigrants worked in the stockyards and meat-packing plants, in steel mills, and on the railroads. A large Polish settlement in Detroit was attracted by the growth of automobile manufacturing and other heavy industries. In Buffalo, New York, metals industries and transportation brought substantial numbers of Poles. In the coal fields of Pennsylvania, Polish, Hungarian, and Italian laborers replaced native, British, Welsh, and German miners. Many Poles also came to New England, where they competed with French Canadians, Irish, and Italians for textile mill jobs. Growing industrial cities such as Cleveland, Akron, Toledo, Milwaukee, and Detroit were largely populated by immigrants from Hungary, Slovenia, Rumania, Lithuania, Bohemia, and other European countries—sturdy peasants who did the heaviest kind of work and lived in distinct ethnic neighborhoods [252A–252C]. Greek and other Mediterranean immigrants came during the same period, entered service occupations such as peddling, shoe shining, and restaurant work, and worked in light industries.

354

250
Lumbermen with axes and
springboards ready to cut a fir
tree in the Northwest, about
1907.

251
"Forging the Shaft: A Welding
Heat." Painting by John Ferguson Weir (1841–1926). By
1910 one-half of the laborers
working with blast furnaces
were immigrants.

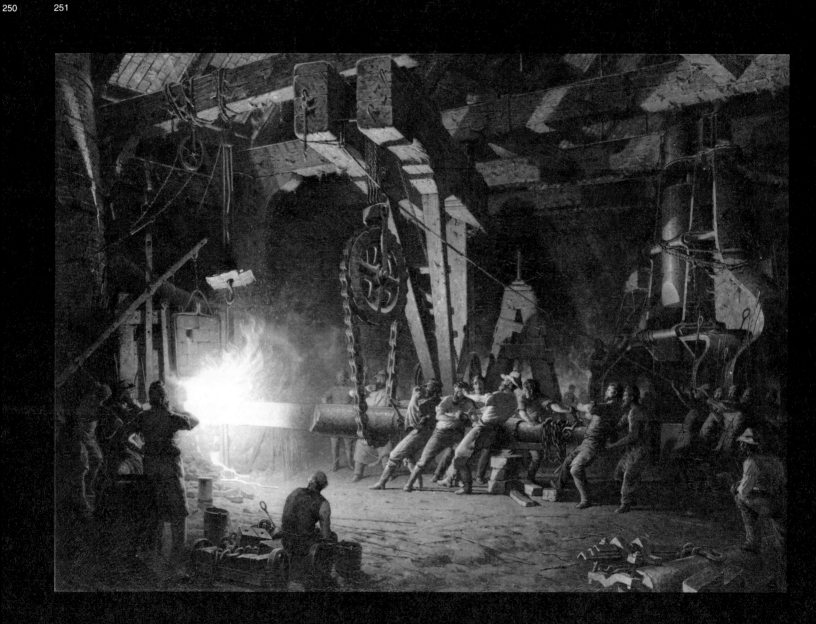

252A
Dey Time Register of about
1900. Six slots are provided
for workers to punch in and
out. To a European from a
rural village, a factory time
clock was a symbol of deper-
sonalization and regimenta-
tion. H 29½".

252B
International Time Recorder
of about 1915, used for
punching workers' time cards.
H 46⅝".

252C
Dey Register, patented in
1889. An unusual time clock
with 23"-diameter ring for
punching workers' time cards.
H 31".

252A

252B

252C

Outright prejudice seriously affected the working lives of several groups of nonwhite immigrants: the Afro-Americans, Chinese [253], Japanese, and Hispano-Americans. Again, however, the experience of each group was unique, reflecting its background and circumstances in the United States. For Afro-Americans or blacks, the circumstances have been tragic. Brought to the New World involuntarily and enslaved, they became a major laboring force in the southern states during the plantation era. Following the Civil War and the abolition of slavery, blacks were nominally free, but they continued to suffer from vicious discrimination in education and employment. The sharecropping system or other forms of farm tenantry gave southern blacks their chief employment, except for a tiny minority who served as professionals in the segregated black society.

Migrating north throughout the twentieth century, blacks continued to suffer the effects of discrimination, unemployment, and underemployment. Blacks have performed a disproportionate share of the menial, dead-end jobs in the American economy, working in low-paying service jobs in laundries and restaurants, in custodial, domestic, and other marginal occupations. Although their status and working lives are improving, and black Americans are increasingly entering the middle class, more than 350 years since their first arrival on this continent Afro-Americans have inferior opportunities in comparison with those available to other ethnic groups.

Oriental immigrants, chiefly Chinese and Japanese, also suffered from discrimination. Chinese laborers were brought to California after 1850 to work in the gold mines and on the railroads. They had a major role in building the Central Pacific railroad line and later worked in light industry, as domestics and laundrymen, and as agricultural laborers. After a great deal of agitation, including violence and murders, Chinese immigrant laborers were excluded from the United States in 1882. Since then prejudice has abated and the American Chinese occupy respected yet distinct positions in many of our cities.

Between 1890 and 1920, about 100,000 Japanese arrived in the United States, settling on the Pacific coast, to work as farmers, in domestic and personal services, and in canning and other industries. Anti-Japanese sentiment resulted in serious occupational discrimination and prohibition of additional Japanese immigration after 1924. Hispano-Americans, chiefly from Mexico and Puerto Rico, today still occupy some of the lowest rungs of the American occupational ladder, working as agricultural laborers, migrant workers, employees in low-paid service jobs, and laborers. Their status is likely to improve, however, just as the condition of earlier immigrant groups has improved.

From the massive, confused picture of immigrant employment in America, several generalizations may be offered. First, as noted earlier, each group had an occupational history somewhat different from that of others. British and Irish, Jewish and Italian, German and Slavic, black and Japanese— all had diverse experiences. Second, the employment of each group depended on two factors—the fund of knowledge they brought to the new land, and industrial conditions prevailing when they arrived. Thus, artisans and skilled workers from Britain and Germany before 1880 were often able to practice their trades, while unskilled Italians and Poles, arriving during the expansion of heavy industry, found construction jobs or did heavy work in mines and mills. Third, there was a tendency—with many exceptions—for nationality groups to cluster in the same occupations. To some extent this pattern arose simply because immigrants of one nationality attracted others who spoke the same language and shared cultural interests.

Although each group's experience was different, all shared some common patterns of working. Exploitation of labor characterized American industry until well into the twentieth century. Immigrant workers labored for long hours—a seventy-two-hour work week was not uncommon, and the seven-day week prevailed in many steel mills. Wages were often pitifully low—after deductions for rent, purchases at the company store, and other fees, the take-home pay for coal miners might amount to pennies per day. Many observers of labor in the late nineteenth century calculated that working-class families existed at or beneath a bare subsistence level, a hardship even more distressing in times of economic collapse when work was not available for many. Working conditions were often deplorable and accidents commonplace, although no workers who lost a limb or an eye on the job had any claim on the employer. Unfit for further service, the worker would simply be dismissed. An inhumane pace of labor, with piecework and the "speed-up" introduced to reduce costs, often dominated the working environment.

Despite its exploitative quality, the employment scene was not entirely bleak. Evidence suggests that real wages for workers rose by at least one-third between the Civil War and World War I. Other evidence indicates that when they remained settled and fairly steadily employed, thrifty immigrant families could accumulate modest holdings of property.

253

THE ARGUMENT OF NATIONALITY.

EXCITED MOB—"*We don't want any cheap-labor foreigners intruding upon us native-born citizens.*"

254A

Another process common to nineteenth- and early-twentieth-century immigrant workers was what one writer has called the "immigrant cycle"—successive waves of new arrivals replacing those at the bottom of the economic ladder. Although this process worked very imperfectly in the first generation—the majority of newcomers apparently spent their lives just about where they began in the labor force—it enabled many immigrants' children to surpass their parents' economic condition. Thus, Irish laborers replaced native Yankee operatives in the New England textile industry, the Irish in turn were replaced by French Canadians, who might be succeeded by Italian and Polish workers in the lowest-level textile occupations. At each point a few of the older immigrant groups might graduate into positions as foremen or might obtain more skilled, better-paying work. Similarly in the coal industry, skilled British and Welsh miners often graduated into technical and managerial positions as masses of Slavic immigrants took over menial jobs in the mines. Seldom did any immigrant undergo the famous—and infrequent—"rags to riches" occupational rise. But as industries grew, the economy expanded, and "greenhorn" immigrants appeared to fill unskilled positions, earlier arrivals sometimes found more rewarding jobs.

In their working lives immigrants were subject to a variety of pressures, including the drive to become Americanized. Factory discipline, the need to understand English, the contact with fellow workers of differing background—all these relationships should have encouraged newcomers to cast off their old ways. Surprisingly, many immigrants were strongly resistant to Americanization.

A number of industries sponsored programs to teach English and citizenship to foreign-born employees. Of all the industrial Americanization programs, that set up by the Ford Motor Company in 1914 was probably the most rigorous. Henry Ford had an almost pathological desire to Americanize his workers. Ford's spokesman declared: "Our one great aim is to impress these men that they are, or should be, Americans, and that former racial, national, and linguistic differences are to be forgotten." The Ford classes were compulsory; workers had the choice of taking the course or leaving the company. Graduation ceremonies held at the end of each class were intended to illustrate the transformation of immigrant workers: men entered a huge melting pot on the auditorium stage as aliens in their national costumes and emerged from the pot dressed alike in standard conservative working clothes! [**254A, 254B**] The assembly line had done its magic. Ford's Sociological Department investigated the home lives of immigrant workers to evaluate their habits and determine whether they were worthy of receiving the generous five-dollar daily wage offered in 1914. American habits, naturally, were those desired of everyone.

For all their efforts at education, and in Ford's case coercion, the industrial Americanizers met powerful resistance from foreign-born laborers. The traditions of centuries and the habits of lifetimes could hardly, after all, be shucked off like worn-out clothing. First-generation immigrants had to compromise in the factory, learning enough English to get by, but at home they spoke the old-country dialects. Most of their associates outside work were the same nationality, their nonworking activities being centered in the ethnic community.

The experience of one group illustrates the failure of Ford's patriotic force-feeding. The Ford Sociological Department investigated a group of Armenian workers, consisting of 437 men, and found it well on the way to practicing good American habits of thrift and upright conduct. What the Ford investigators apparently did not realize was the Armenian workers saved their money in order to establish an *Armenian* community in Detroit— to bring Armenian girls from abroad to become wives, to establish households and businesses that would form the basis of an ethnic neighborhood. Working at the Ford plant, in spite of its aggressive Americanism, did little to make these workers forget their "former racial, national, and linguistic differences." The fact that ethnicity remains today such a potent force in American life should suggest how inadequate were the forced denationalization efforts of American companies.

254A
The shared experiences of
working together are reflected
in this sea of workers outside
a Ford Motor Company.

254B
Graduating class of the Ford
English School, emerging
from the "Melting Pot."
Teachers were recruited from
the Ford staff and trained in
Americanization before being
assigned to a class.

254B

The working lives of immigrants were closely bound up with their social lives and living conditions. For the early immigrants, two essential living conditions had to be met: they required cheap lodgings and they needed to live close to their places of employment. In the early textile mill cities these conditions were met by the mill owners, who built rooming houses and lodgings near their factories. Similarly, in the coal fields, "company towns" were constructed with dreary barrackslike houses for the miners. In the teeming cities such as Boston, New York, and Chicago the problems were different. Here older neighborhoods located in proximity to the waterfront or workshop areas consisted of single dwellings which were subdivided, sometimes again and again, into multifamily tenements.

In Boston, a state commission described the process of slum growth:

. . . houses . . . long inhabited by the well-to-do class of people, are vacated by them for others in more fashionable quarters . . . and then a less fortunate class of folk occupy for a while,–they, in their turn, to make room for another class on the descending scale . . . till houses, once fashionable . . . become neglected, dreary tenement houses into which the families of the low-paid and poverty smitten . . . crowd by the dozens. . . .

Irish immigrants jammed into two Boston neighborhoods, the North End and Fort Hill, where they occupied hastily erected shanties and court dwellings, remodeled mansions, factories and warehouses and cellars. Sanitary facilities were primitive, leading to a prevalence of filth, odors, and disease. Conditions, in short, were miserable, creating a sense of demoralization among many immigrants. Similar overcrowded living situations developed in smaller Massachusetts cities such as Lowell, Newburyport, and Lawrence. In the latter place, each new wave of immigrants created additional tenements in the central city until no open space aside from streets and alleys existed. In 1910 central Lawrence contained 268 four-story buildings, mostly tenements, and population density was 119 persons to the acre.

New York City, virtually a hive of immigrants, contained some of the most intense congestion in the United States. Jacob Riis, the immigrant reporter from Denmark, wrote vividly of slum tenements in *How the Other Half Lives*:

Bottle Alley is around the corner in Baxter Street; but it is a fair specimen of its kind, wherever found. Look into any of these houses, everywhere the same piles of rags, of malodorous bones and musty paper. . . . Here is a "flat" of "parlor" and two pitch-dark coops called bedrooms. Truly, the bed is all there is room for. The family tea-kettle is on the stove, doing duty for the time being as a washboiler. By night it will have returned to its proper use again. . . . One, two, three beds are there, if the old boxes and heaps of foul straw can be called by that name; a broken stove with crazy pipe from which smoke leaks at every joint, a table of rough boards propped up on boxes, piles of rubbish in the corner. The closeness and smell are appalling.

Eleven people occupied that dismal "flat." Thousands of similar dwellings in New York filled the immigrants' needs: cheap housing close to the docks, shops, and factories where men and women worked.

The pattern of immigrant settlements occurred throughout the country, as Jane Addams described it in Chicago:

Between Halsted Street and the river live about ten thousand Italians—Neapolitans, Sicilians, and Calabrians, with an occasional Lombard or Venetian. To the south on Twelfth Street are many Germans, and side streets are given over almost entirely to Polish and Russian Jews. Still farther south, these Jewish colonies merge into a huge Bohemian colony, so vast that Chicago ranks as the third Bohemian city in the world. To the Northwest are many Canadian-French, clannish in spite of their long residence in America, and to the north are Irish and first-generation Americans.

Neighborhoods might change completely in the course of a decade, earlier settlers being replaced by newcomers. As Addams related: "The older and richer inhabitants seem anxious to move away as rapidly as they can afford it. They make room for newly arrived immigrants who are densely ignorant of civic duties." As urban transportation improved, with horsecars, electric streetcars, elevated railways, and subways, the need to be physically close to work lessened, and the concentrated ethnic community tended to disperse. But this was substantially a development affecting the native-born children of first-generation immigrants. The foreign-born most often preferred to remain in the immigrant neighborhood, among familiar landmarks, institutions, and people.

In addition to contributing energetically to America's industrial development, immigrant workers became involved in a by-product of economic growth—the labor movement. Foreign-born workers supplied many of the leaders, a large proportion of the membership, and major sources of ideology for trade unions in the United States in the late nineteenth and early twentieth centuries. And immigrants were active in all wings of the union movement. Labor leaders envisioned two major contrary roles for organized labor: (1) the path of craft organization and acceptance of the capitalist economic system, which would bargain for better conditions, shorter hours, higher wages, and would limit political action; (2) following a reformist direction, the other path would organize politically to change the structure of government and the economy, bringing a utopia of cooperation or some form of socialism.

British immigrants helped to make the craft union America's dominant style of labor organization. Believing that they had alternatives to industrial labor, American workers were not so eager to organize along craft lines as the British, who remembered the class consciousness and solidarity of their homeland. British craftsmen already belonged to unions when they arrived in the New World. Two crafts actually imported their unions, the Amalgamated Society of Engineers and the Amalgamated Society of Carpenters and Joiners, which set up American branches in the 1860s. A vigorous British miners' union gave many immigrant coal miners experience in union organization, which soon translated into efforts to unionize in the New World. An Englishman, John Bates, organized the first union and led the first strike in Pennsylvania's anthracite coal fields in 1849. Other English miners developed the sporadic miners' unions that came and went between 1850 and 1873. John Siney and John Hinchcliffe were among the leading figures in coal unions of the period.

During the 1870s it was the turn of another immigrant group, the Irish, to achieve fame in the labor history of the coal fields. Much of the decade was a time of depression and the mine operators were resolved to strangle any vestige of unionism. During a prolonged strike in 1875, open warfare broke out between workers and company police, who protected strikebreakers. Accustomed in Ireland to direct action and intimidation, a group of men formed the "Molly Maguires," an offshoot of the Ancient Order of Hibernians, to frighten miners into remaining away from the mines. They threatened foremen and officials and probably assassinated some persons. An undercover agent of the mine owners infiltrated the "Molly Maguires" and secured or fabricated enough evidence to send ten "Mollies" to the gallows and others to prison. Unions thus disappeared from the anthracite region. Whatever its ethnic origin, violence among unions and operators had become a standard practice in the mine fields.

British craftsmen were also active in forming unions in the textile industry. In Fall River and New Bedford, Massachusetts, where English cotton weavers and spinners were substantially employed, a strike was said to be "as natural as a day's rest on Sunday." Enthusiastic in defense of their rights and eloquent, the British unionists kept up steady agitation against the mill owners and would not leave other immigrant workers—Irish and French—in peace. In 1875 Lancashire weavers struck the Fall River mills twice but failed to reverse wage reductions. George Gunton, a British immigrant, led the 1875 strikes, published the *Labor Standard in Fall River,* mounted a mass demonstration against wage cuts in 1878, and led another strike in 1879. Another Fall River Englishman active at this time, John Howard, formed the National Mule Spinners' Union in 1885. These British immigrants came out of an established craft-oriented, job-centered union structure which they brought to the United States.

Britain's most significant contribution to the American labor movement was Samuel Gompers, organizer of the American Federation of Labor in 1886 and its president for thirty-seven years. Not by inheritance an Englishman, Gompers was the son of Jewish immigrants from Holland, but his view of labor was strongly conditioned by his youth in London and his apprenticeship in cigarmaking. Emigrating to America with his family in 1863, thirteen-year-old Gompers took up his trade and in 1864 joined the Cigarmakers' Union. Discussions with his fellow cigarmakers stimulated his interests in social, economic, and labor issues, including Marxism. Socialist idealism appealed to Gompers, but he was more fully committed to the pragmatic concerns of craft unionism, its concentration on job issues and bargaining power.

Reorganizing the Cigarmakers' Union in the late 1870s, Gompers established principles of centralized control and sound financing that were models for other unions. The AFL depended on this conservative program plus opposition to "dual unions"—only one national union could exist for each trade. United in the AFL, national craft unions had two basic problems: they fragmented jurisdiction in industries organized for mass production, such as automobiles, steel, mining, and others; and they discriminated in favor of the more skilled elite industrial workers against the more numerous unskilled laborers. Over and over, Gompers resisted the drive for industrial unions, adhering to the British craft union pattern. The official head of American organized labor until his death in 1924, Gompers led the labor movement through periods of trial and of growth. He was a national figure, enjoying the respect of presidents of the United States and leading businessmen, but by the end of his life he had become something of an anachronism. For the most part he opposed any alliance between partisan politics and organized labor and he repudiated socialist and communist influences in labor unions.

For labor the ultimate weapon was the strike, and the United States witnessed thousands of walkouts between the Civil War and World War I. Employers fought strikes with a number of weapons, including some that would not be considered respectable today, such as armed attacks on peaceful picket lines or demonstrations. A favorite tactic was the replacement of striking workers by strikebreakers, or "scabs," often newly arrived immigrants [255]. Setting one nationality against another, employers tried to take advantage of ethnic differences and prejudice to prevent unified action by labor. Sentiments expressed by a Carnegie steel mill superintendent in 1875 illustrate this view:

We must steer clear as far as we can of Englishmen, who are great sticklers for high wages, small production and strikes. My experience has shown that Germans and Irish, Swedes and what I denominate "Buckwheats"—young American country boys, judiciously mixed, make the most effective and tractable force you can find.

By the turn of the century company managers in the mining, iron and steel, and meat-packing industries practiced the mixing of Polish, Hungarian, and Italian laborers to produce a docile anti-union working force. In some cases the practice succeeded; in others it did not.

Immigrant workers participated in a great variety of strikes, despite employers' efforts to exploit them. Union activities were largely eliminated in the anthracite coal fields after 1875, but periodic unsuccessful strikes occurred against the terrible conditions of mining. Finally in 1900 the United Mine Workers union succeeded in organizing the polyglot mining population in a massive strike of more than 100,000 workers. John Mitchell, president of the United Mine Workers, followed a conciliatory nonviolent policy and eventually won a partial victory for the workers and the union, which had gone into the strike with about 8,000 members and emerged from it with more than 100,000. The fact that a national election campaign was in progress undoubtedly helped the union. Two years later, thousands of foreign-born miners united in a five-month strike which ended only after intervention by President Theodore Roosevelt. The miners won some, though not all, of their demands. Slavic and Italian miners, who had been brought in as an anti-union device, demonstrated in these great coal walkouts that they were not mere tools of the mine operators.

255
Puck, October 3, 1888. This Democratic periodical argued that the very businessmen who wanted high tariffs also called for unrestricted immigration. The result, according to *Puck,* would be low wages, high prices, and depression for the American workingman.

THE REPUBLICAN IDEA OF PROTECTION—
A High Tariff on the Monopolist's Wares, Free Entrance for Pauper Labor, and a Lock-Out for the American Workingman

Three other significant examples of ethnic cooperation in labor disputes are worthy of mention. At Lawrence, Massachusetts, in 1912 unskilled immigrant workers struck against the woolen mills, responding to a wage reduction. Initially the strikers were Italian, but other workers—French Canadian, Irish, Belgian, Polish—quickly joined the strike after some of the strikers ran through mill buildings disabling machinery. Within a few days more than 25,000 mill hands were out. Joseph Ettor, an Italian organizer for the Industrial Workers of the World, arrived in Lawrence and took charge of the strike, avoiding violence and managing with great skill. Understanding the strength of ethnic ties, Ettor reorganized the strike along nationality-group lines, giving each group reason to be proud of its contribution. Efforts by company officials and local politicans to divide the strikers proved fruitless, and after eight weeks the woolen mill owners came to terms, offering a pay raise and other concessions. Eventually more than 250,000 New England textile workers gained better pay as a result of the strike. Although the Lawrence dispute could have been an advantage to the IWW, this union, a rival of the AFL, did not follow up on its opportunity, and no durable organization remained. But here again a group of diverse nationalities had been able to cooperate to win the fight against entrenched corporate leadership.

Two other stories of ethnic cooperation during labor trouble had unhappy endings. In 1912 the silk industry of Paterson, New Jersey, began installing machinery that operated at a higher rate than former machines, thus creating a speed-up. In the next year the IWW demanded a return to the old rate of work. Eight thousand weavers and dyers, including many immigrants, walked out immediately, and within a few weeks the strike shut down the entire industry, putting more than twenty thousand people out of work. In attempting to break the strike, police were notoriously brutal and free-swinging with their clubs. Union leaders suffered constant harassment, finding that their rights to free speech and assembly were null and void in Paterson. Five months of increasing hardships broke the spirits and emptied the pocketbooks of strikers, until there was no choice but to accept defeat and return to work.

A similar fate met 350,000 men, largely foreign-born, who walked off their steel mill jobs in 1919. Determined to eradicate unionism in the steel industry, the managers would not discuss grievances, but instead employed strikebreakers, manhandled the strikers, and accused unionists of being "reds" and traitors. After more than three months without work, the strikers, their funds exhausted, returned to the mill, not having achieved a single objective. Despite their failure, these two massive strikes demonstrated that the old management technique of dividing the immigrants because of their ethnic differences would not work. Economic hardship, not immigrant rivalries, broke these strikes.

A happier outcome resulted from union organizing in the garment trades. The International Ladies Garment Workers Union, founded in 1900, its small membership made up largely of immigrant Jewish women, was an industrial union that did not distinguish workers according to their crafts. Its first important strike, in 1909–1910, resulted from wage disputes and working conditions in the chaotic shirtwaist industry. More than twenty thousand workers, chiefly young Jewish and Italian women, struck after hearing an impassioned speech in Yiddish from a woman who had received a beating from hired guards. Brutality continued, creating widespread sympathy for the workers. Finally the union worked out a settlement, the strike was largely won, and the ILGWU went on to become one of the most progressive and successful labor organizations in America. Much of its strength derived from the powerful bonds of loyalty among the predominantly Jewish membership.

The growth of unionism among male clothing workers similarly had a favorable outcome. After jurisdictional rivalry and turmoil in the men's garment trade, the Amalgamated Clothing Workers of America was founded in 1914 as a rival of the ineffective United Garment Workers, affiliated with the AFL. The ACWA conducted its first great strike in Chicago in 1915, achieving a number of concessions, although it was not recognized as the workers' bargaining agent. The ILGWU and ACWA were unusual for the time in being industrial unions, dominated by Jewish immigrants, idealistic in their aims [256]. Although strongly influenced by socialist ideology, they were highly practical in achieving a cooperative relationship with management in the disorganized garment industry. They illustrate another side to the immigrant labor movement.

Foreign-born labor leaders came in all shapes and sizes. Andrew Furuseth, a native of Norway, became secretary of the Pacific Coast sailors' union in 1887 and was thereafter single-minded in his devotion to the rights of seamen. After more than twenty years of lobbying in Congress. Furuseth's efforts bore fruit in a seamen's protective bill sponsored by Senator Robert M. La Follette and passed finally in 1915. Under this bill the federal government regulated conditions aboard ships trading in America and gave seamen the freedom to quit oppressive masters.

Quite different was the career of Mary Harris Jones, known as "Mother Jones." Born in Cork, Ireland, in 1830, she came to the United States as a child. After the death of her husband and children in an epidemic, she worked as a dressmaker and gained a strong consciousness of workers' grievances. From 1880 onward she aided striking workers in many fields of labor, but especially in coal mining. She became a familiar figure at the most bitter labor conflicts, leading demonstrations, speaking, encouraging strikers, and winning favorable publicity for them. She lived to see her hundredth birthday, a labor heroine.

Still another vision of labor's role was represented in Sidney Hillman, a Jewish immigrant who arrived here from Lithuania in 1907. A veteran of the Russian labor movement at the age of twenty, Hillman brought the idealistic and socialistic enthusiasm which infected the Russian empire in the early twentieth century. Settling in Chicago, Hillman did various kinds of work until he found a job at the huge Hart, Schaffner and Marx clothing firm in 1909. During the next year about eight thousand workers struck against the firm and Hillman was one of the strike leaders. From this experience he rose rapidly in the garment workers' union, he led in organizing the Amalgamated Clothing Workers in 1914, and he established good relations with Hart, Schaffner and Marx and other garment manufacturers.

Hillman held progressive views quite distinct from those of Samuel Gompers: he favored militant industrial unionism over craft organizations, he wanted labor to be politically involved, and he incessantly promoted welfare-state programs and labor legislation. In Hillman Jewish idealism combined with earthy practicality to make a labor leader perceptive of the needs of his times. During the New Deal under Franklin D. Roosevelt, Hillman vigorously supported the federal government's expansion and economic programs. At the same time he led the movement for industrial unionism that emerged in the Committee for Industrial Organization of the AFL, later the independent Congress of Industrial Organizations. During World War II Hillman headed the CIO Political Action Committee, carrying forward his belief in the need for labor's direct influence in politics.

Numerous other immigrant labor leaders represented the radical fringe—men who had little or no sympathy with the existing social and economic structure and little or no following among American workers, native or foreign-born. The Haymarket bomb explosion of 1886 in Chicago was falsely blamed on a group of seven anarchist labor leaders, most of them aliens. More significant was the radicalism of Daniel DeLeon, a native of Curaçao in the Dutch West Indies, former student at the University of Leyden, organizer in 1895 of the Socialist Trade and Labor Alliance, and later of the Socialist Labor Party. DeLeon was absolutely doctrinaire and denunciatory; he called the AFL " a cross between a windbag and rope of sand," and Samuel Gompers a "labor faker." DeLeon exposed American workers to a type of extreme socialist dogma that probably opened their minds to more moderate economic views. But because of vociferous characters like DeLeon, immigrants were wrongly accused of originating and fostering the "un-American" left wing in this country.

Immigrants, it is clear, had a significant and lasting impact on the labor movement, but it is appropriate to ask whether the unions had any important effects on the immigrants. Carroll D. Wright, first commissioner of the Bureau of Labor, addressed this question in a report to the President in 1904 and found that the union was indeed a positive influence on the immigrant: "It is the first, and for a time the only, point at which he touches any influences outside his clan." To fulfill its purpose the union had to meet the immigrant and begin the process of Americanization:

The trade union, however, must deal with the immigrant himself, and the immigrant, when he learns that the union wants to raise his wages, decrease his hours of labor, etc., begins to see the necessity of learning the English language, of understanding the institutions he hears talked about in the union meetings, and other matters which interest him.

Wright's report was submitted as part of a study of labor troubles in the Chicago stockyards, where, after a series of disputes in the 1880s and 1890s, the working force had become predominantly Central and Eastern European in origin—Polish, Bohemian, Lithuanian, Slovakian, with smaller numbers of other groups. Each nationality formed its own community geographically and culturally and had little contact with outsiders. Wright called this pattern the "clan spirit." Nationalities even fought one another from time to time. It was one function of the unions to reduce the clannishness and tensions of the nationality groups. Discussing the pork butchers' union, made up of five or more immigrant groups, Wright described the union procedures:

This union recently elected a Pole as president of the local. In their business meetings the motions made, resolutions read, and speeches delivered are usually interpreted in five languages, though in some locals in only three. All business, however, is transacted primarily in English, although any member may speak to any motion in the language he best understands. . . . It is here that the practical utility of learning English is first brought home forcibly to the immigrant.

Associating together in union activities brought many benefits to the immigrants. Union members found their prejudices and hostilities breaking down and mutual respect increasing as they mingled and participated in joint discussions. Unions also taught elementary lessons in civics and self-government. Eastern European peasants, suspicious of government, were entirely unprepared to accept the American system, much less to participate in it. But in union meetings the immigrants slowly came to grasp what it meant to cast a ballot, how the process of discussion and decision making could relate directly to the worker's self-interest, his wages and working conditions. Because of its emphasis on bettering the position of working people, the union encouraged the immigrant to "think American" in terms of his own expectations: "The union point of view is that for a Lithuanian peasant to be contented, satisfied, and happy with the Lithuanian standard of living in America is a crime, a crime not only against himself but against America and everyone who wishes to make individual and social development possible in America. . . ." Thus, the union sought to undermine the peasant's former traditionalism, replacing it with discontent, optimism, the desire for a better future. Wright concluded that organized labor was the most potent unifying and Americanizing influence in the immigrant's American experience.

This may be overstating the case. Some unions emphasized and exploited ethnicity, taking advantage of national rivalries. For the most part, however, unions seem to have had a practical Americanizing influence on working people. Perhaps a European visitor's description of a union meeting in 1901 sums up the meaning of unionism for the immigrants:

For a European, this was a memorable occasion. A report was made in English, but the very next speaker spoke in Italian, naturally and as if it seemed natural to his predecessor. The Italian spoke vehemently, long and loud. . . . He was followed by two orators who used Yiddish. Then came a report, in remarkable English, by a Greek. . . . So I heard here in New York, out of the mouths of poor needle workers, the language of the Divine Comedy, seconded by that of the Odyssey, and commented on by that of the Nibelungenlied—the old German that is Yiddish.

At its best the labor union respected the immigrant's own language and institutions, yet it encouraged him to subordinate the interest of nationality to broader issues of American self-government and economic improvement [**257, 258**].

258

257
United Packing House workers demonstrate in 1952 against the wage freeze.

258
Banner of Cesar Chavez's United Farm Workers Union (*huelga* = strike).

Given the deep and continuing relationship between immigrants and the labor movement, organized labor's attitude toward the problem of immigration was curiously ambivalent. Conflicting demands pulled labor first in one direction, then in another, until a pattern evolved. Dictating a positive attitude toward immigration were the foreign backgrounds of so many of labor's leaders and its union members. On the other hand, the fear of competition from cheap, foreign ''greenhorn'' workers led labor to doubt the policy of unlimited immigration. Early unions favored various restrictions and opposed the admission of contract labor—workers imported with their fares paid to take prearranged jobs. Samuel Gompers along with most union men supported the Chinese exclusion act of 1882. But the issue of more generalized immigration control arose with the growth of nativism in the late nineteenth century. Would labor continue to support free immigration?

During the 1890s the AFL debated the issue and formulated a hesitant policy of restriction. Labor's attitude reflected the anxieties originating in the depression of 1893–1896, the fear of foreign-born workers and the use of such men as ''scab'' labor, and the changing, more alien character of the Eastern and Southern European immigrants themselves. Gompers proposed that the AFL take a stand on restriction in 1891, but nothing came of his recommendations. Debates continued until in 1897 the AFL convention endorsed restriction by means of the literacy test. Gompers continued to support literacy tests through their tortuous legislative career and presidential vetoes, until restriction of entry to those able to read became law in 1917.

World War I with its violent Americanization campaign and anti-foreign hysteria was bound to affect attitudes toward immigration restriction. One of the first major organizations to react in the postwar period was the AFL, which, in December 1918, called for a two-year ban on immigration in order that men in the armed forces could be reabsorbed into the civilian economy and the whole problem of restriction could be thoroughly studied. Again organized labor feared that immigrant workers would flood into American job markets to reduce wages and wipe out the advances made by labor during the preceding decade [259]. Significantly, the AFL also for the first time expressed doubts about the Americanization process. Eastern and Southern Europeans, the unions argued, seemed not to be assimilating. Perhaps there were already too many aliens in the country. During the early 1920s the AFL pressured for outright exclusion of newcomers and when this alternative proved hopeless, the organization supported the quota laws of 1921 and 1924. It was commonplace to favor restrictions during the 1920s—a great number of influential Americans did so. Yet there is an irony in the fact that of all American institutions, none had been so influenced by immigrants as organized labor, and the unions were now rushing to close the gates of entry.

Immigrants and their children have continued to play a role in the labor movement since restriction. John L. Lewis, the son of Welsh immigrants, David Dubinsky from Poland, Sidney Hillman, a native of Lithuania, and Philip Murray, born in Glasgow, Scotland, in an Irish family, all led in the great industrial unionization drive of the 1930s. A. Philip Randolph and Cesar Chavez, leaders respectively of predominantly black and Chicano union organizations, have fought for the fair treatment of American minority workers—among the most downtrodden of America's labor force. But the germ of American labor power was and remains the craft-oriented trade union. To the early immigrant union members who brought the craft organization from England, Wales, Scotland, and Ireland we owe this major institution.

WORKINGMEN!

WHICH DO YOU WANT?

AMERICAN OR EUROPEAN WAGES!

POTTERIES.

	English.	Trenton, N. J.
Plate makers,	$ 7 75	$20 40
Dish makers,	9 67	19 43
Cup makers,	9 97	18 50
Saucer makers,	7 97	18 50
Wash bowl makers,	9 71	25 64
Pressers,	8 18	17 12
Printers,	6 59	13 56
Kilnmen,	6 59	12 00
Saggur makers,	8 50	17 00
Mould makers,	10 29	20 00
Turners,	8 05	18 00
Handlers,	8 43	19 00

WINDOW GLASS.

	Ohio Valley Average, per Week.	Belgium Average, per W'k
Blowers,	$40 09	$20 00
Gatherers,	23 03	6 25
Flatners,	34 45	6 25
Cutters,	27 59	5 00

COAL MINERS AND COKE MAKERS.

TIME, TEN HOURS PER DAY.

Occupation.	W. Va. Wages, per Day.	English Wages, per Day
Blacksmiths,	$2 00	$1 14
Blacksmiths' helpers,	1 25	72
Coal cleaner,	1 25	60
Drivers,	1 60	50
Engineers,	1 75	1 12
Furnacemen,	1 25	72
Laborers,	1 25	72
Miners,	1 40 to 1 87	1 12
Mine boss,	2 50	1 68
Track layer,	1 80	90
Trappers,	50	22
Weighers,	1 80	90

BLAST FURNACES.

	Ohio Valley per Day.	Cumberland, Eng., per Day
Keepers,	$2 25	$1 41
Helpers,	1 65	85
Top fillers,	1 65	1 13
Bottom fillers,	1 65	1 13
Cinder loaders,	1 55	85
Blast engineer,	2 25	1 00
Cindermen,	1 65	1 11
General labor,	1 40	77

The wages of Blast Furnaces here denominated as Ohio Valley wages are the smallest west of the Allegheny Mountains. Those paid in Joliet, Ill., and even in Pittsburgh, are higher than those given here.

ROLLING MILL.

	West of Allegheny M'tn's, per Ton.	England, per Ton.
Puddling,	$5 50	$1 57
Muck rolling,	68¾	24
Bar rolling and catching,	1 13¾	73
Bar heating,	70	34
Hoop rolling and heating 1½" and No. 17,	3 50	1 80
Cotton tie rolling and heating,	4 10	2 37

BESSEMER STEEL WORKS.

	United States, per Day.	England, per Day
Converter men,	$4 35, 12 h'rs.	$1 45
Steel works pit men,	4 00, 8 "	1 15 to 1 25
Steel works ladle men,	3 98, 12 "	1 00 to 1 15
Rail heaters,	5 00, 12 "	1 60
Rail rollers,	7 00, 12 "	2 50
Common laborers,	1 34, 10 "	62

(June, 1888.)

FLINT GLASS WORKERS.

	WEST VIRGINIA WAGES, PER DAY.	GREAT BRITAIN WAGES, PER DAY
Glass blowers, Pressers and Finishers,	$3 25 to 4 25	$ 96 to 1 20
First-class Castor place Workmen,	4 50 to 6 00	1 25 to 2 40
Punch Tumbler Blowers,	1 50 to 3 75	65 to 96

The hours of work in Europe are longer than in America for the same amount of work.

Chapter 20

Immigrant Politics

The Politics of Survival

"Stand together," Tamanend, the Delaware Indian chief who was later to become the patron saint of Tammany Hall, purportedly told his tribe. "Support each other and you will be a mountain." It is doubtful that many immigrants ever heard of this exhortation, but as members of various national groups arrived in America, they banded together, isolated, lonely, and often destitute, against a strange environment, with group cohesion initially their sole strength.

To many Americans New York City's infamous Tammany Hall symbolizes political corruption at its worst, yet to thousands of immigrants it represented a helping hand in the new country as well as a ladder to success. Tammany was intimately tied to the tumultuous rise of each successive group of immigrants in New York City and in many ways set the stage for immigrant politics throughout America. Other groups either followed the political example set by the Irish or reacted against it.

Most early immigrants—the Norwegians, Swedes, Germans, Dutch, Swiss, and British—arrived when land was cheap or free, and they settled in rural areas, coming together in ethnic communities. Those communities that survived gradually prospered and developed a middle class—a source of both leadership and financial backing for future politicians [**260, 261**].

By the time of the later arrivals—the Irish, Italians, and Slavs—capital was necessary for farming, and the nationwide economic shift from country to city was already beginning. Even the earlier Irish, however, tended to avoid rural America: land for them had come to represent oppression and insecurity. Like the Slavs and Italians who followed, they were used to a gregarious community life, dominated by the Catholic Church, and the harsh isolation of the American frontier had little appeal. A whimsical ditty from the 1830s advised the Irish:

I tell you not to leave the city
Because ye know t'would be a pity
To see men digging farms and doating
Who should be in the city voting.

The Irish congregated in cities a generation before other immigrant groups and found political opportunities there dramatically different from those in rural areas. Even before the Civil War they had risen from ward bosses to aldermen to state legislators. Mike Walsh, who eventually became a U.S. congressman, was a product of New York's neighborhood Irish gangs. These gangs had semiofficial status as ward committees and they, along with saloons, volunteer fire departments, and the boxing ring, were the proving grounds for many a Tammany politician.

The heyday of the Irish political machine was the half-century beginning in 1870. "Honest John" Kelly, Richard Croker, and Charles F. Murphy learned their political lessons well from the infamous native American bosses Fernando Wood and William Marcy Tweed, and they ruled in turn over Tammany Hall [**262**].

Tammany and politics to these men and the immigrant community from which they came did not represent corruption, but justice for the poor and a chance at success. Boss Croker once reminisced about what politics had offered him at the age of twenty-one. "I felt that the Democratic Party was the young man's party; that the young blood of the nation must naturally be drawn toward Democracy, which made a ready place for the newcomers, and welcomed them to a share in the management of the affairs, even into the councils, of the nation." So enamored was he with participating in the democratic process that the following year he voted seventeen times for a constable in Brooklyn—William Lyman. As Jimmy "The Famous" O'Brien, a Tammany alderman, said: "Show me a boy that hustles for the organization on election day and I'll show you a comin' statesman" [**263–265**]. Jimmy himself encouraged such youngsters at his annual election-day breakfast, held for voting "repeaters," whom he supplied with the identification papers of opposition voters not expected to turn out. These same aspiring politicians often appeared as witnesses at naturalization proceedings when election day was nearing, sometimes as often as twenty-five times a night under different names. As for motivation, John Theofil, a Queens boss, explained it when he said that politics was jobs and jobs was politics and jobs went to men who served the organization. What other reason was there to work for the party?

It was "Honest John" Kelly who turned Tammany into an efficient, tightly hierarchical Irish organization. Tammany's sage, George Washington Plunkitt, called it "a great big machine, with every part adjusted delicate to do its own particular work. . . . Every district leader is fitted to the district he runs and couldn't exactly fit any other district." Paternalistic and strictly disciplined, Kelly's design had an Old World flavor and was strongly inspired by the Roman Catholic Church. Kelly's charge and basis of his power were the city's immigrants.

Alone and frightened in the urban setting, often destitute and unskilled, most immigrants were not concerned with political ideas but with survival: a job, a room, food, and clothing [266]. "Mr. Dooley," the Irish-American character created by the journalist Finley Peter Dunne, put it this way:

Congress has got to wurruk again, an' manny things that seems important to a Congressman'll be brought up befure them. 'Tis sthrange that what's a big thing to a man in Wash'nton, Hinissey, don't seem much account to me. Divvle a bit do I care whether they dig th' Nicaragoon Canal or cross th' Insthmis in a balloon; . . . What we want to know is, ar-re we goin' to have coal enough in th' hod whin th' cold snap comes; will th' plumbin' hold out, an' will th' job last.

In such an alien world, the boss and his cronies stood by, trustworthy allies, ready to dispense jobs, rent, coal, clothes, or a Christmas turkey in return for a simple vote. A day in the *Life of George Washington Plunkitt* typifies how city machines perfected their system of dependency. Plunkitt writes that he began this average day at 2 A.M., bailing a bartender out of jail. Awakened again at 6 A.M. by fire engine sirens, he dashed to the scene to find his election district captains already there, helping the burned-out tenants. ("If a family is burned out, I don't ask whether they are Republicans or Democrats. . . . I just get quarters for them, buy clothes for them if their clothes were burned up. . . . It's philanthropy, but it's politics too— mighty good politics.") At 8:30 A.M. he arrived at the police court, to find six drunk constituents; four were released "by a timely word with the judge," and for the two others he paid fines. From 11 A.M. to 3 P.M. he made the rounds of funerals (Italian and Jewish), church fairs, and clubhouses, ending his day at a Jewish wedding reception. Small wonder "The poor look up to G. W. Plunkitt as a father and don't forget him on election day."

Of course, rich from graft, the bosses could afford to be generous. More important, however, they attempted to look at the world from the immigrant's viewpoint and to supply his needs. As Plunkitt philosophized: "You must study human nature and act accordin'." If his ultimate goal was to hold the district, he did not fail to satisfy the immigrant's more immediate goal of a job or food. Because the political boss could manipulate the American environment, he became a bridge between immigrants and the new country. As Boss Croker said:

We have thousands of men who are alien born. They are alone, ignorant strangers, a prey to all manner of anarchical and wild notions. Tammany looks after them for the sake of their vote, grafts them upon the Republic . . . and although you may not like our motives or our methods, what other agency is there by which so long a row could have been hoed so quickly or so well?

By the 1890s Irish political machines dominated most major U.S. cities. In East Boston a saloonkeeper, Patrick Kennedy, became first a friend and counselor to his Irish-American customers, then a ward committeeman, and finally its chairman. His growing access to jobs and favors confirmed the loyalties of his constituents and gave him power to command votes. Between 1880 and 1910, although he held few public offices, he was one of the strong men in Boston's political machine as well as a business success. Politics for him was a ladder to power and economic gain. It also established a family tradition: his grandson, John F. Kennedy, was elected the first Catholic President of Irish descent.

Irish machines controlled not only city politics but also police forces, fire departments, and other public organizations. Monopolizing local government, they became increasingly corrupted by power and graft. Yet they initially retained their power by appealing to ethnic voters, including the non-Irish, as they reached the city. Immigrants arriving in New York came under the immediate care of Tammany barkeeps, who provided the faithful with quick naturalization, public jobs and contracts, assistance and counseling, and a bucket of coal or pitcher of beer, depending on the season. As with the Irish, Bronx boss Ed Flynn noted that "Ninety-nine out of a hundred want jobs first and political theorizing afterward."

While in politics the Irish are most famous for their "perfection" of the Tammany Hall machine, it is important to note that not all Irish politicians were corrupt or indulged in "clean graft." Thomas J. Walsh, a second-generation Irish Catholic, as senator from Montana exposed the Teapot Dome scandal in the 1920s. And Alfred E. Smith, although a product of the machine, typifies the coming of age of the Irish-American politician as he rose above the machine's parochial interests.

Born in 1873, Al Smith was reared in a solidly Irish neighborhood in New York's lower East Side. Forced by poverty to begin working when he was twelve, he overcame a meager education with a sense of drama and driving ambition. Before he was twenty-one he did political errands that led to a patronage job with the city. In 1903 Tammany Hall rewarded his loyalty by sending him to the New York State Assembly, where he rose to be majority leader and then speaker. Popular with the working people, he waged a successful campaign for governor in 1918. He served for eight years and was the first effective bridge between the idealism of the reformers and the humanity of the bosses.

In 1928 he was nominated the Democratic candidate for President [267A, 267B]. Swamped by a combination of Coolidge prosperity and prejudice against his origins, he was defeated, but he had nevertheless shown the ability of an Irishman to become a political power in his own right with a personal following in the state and the nation. While the political machine had used Al Smith to advance its power and interests, he had used the machine to rise socially, economically, and politically. In the end, he rose above the machine to work for a wider constituency, whose interests were not dictated by the machine's limited goals.

Continued Irish dominance of city government and the Democratic party had political implications for other immigrant groups. Most of the later arrivals followed the Irish example and worked their way up in the urban machine and the Democratic party. By 1947, for example, the Italians had displaced the Irish as masters of Tammany.

260

260
"County Election," by George
Caleb Bingham, 1852, from
engraving on steel by John
Sartain.

261
A Czechoslovakian-born artist's view of American politics, 1893.

261

262
Protest against the Irish-run Tammany Hall and the alleged "deals" with Thomas C. Platt, a long-time power in the politics of the state of New York. (*Judge,* April 7, 1894.)

263
Political cartoon, 1857.

Judge

THE SLAVE OF THE GREEK
New York—" Will emancipation never come?"

AT THE POLLS.

264
Political cartoon on election of 1864.

265
Sign used in the District of Columbia elections of 1974.

266
An immigrant, possibly Irish, selling his vote as cartooned by H. R. Robinson, one of the most brilliant satirists to work before the Civil War.

265

NO ELECTIONEERING
WITHIN 100 FEET OF THE
ENTRANCE TO THE POLLS

266

A DEMOCRATIC VOTER

267A

267B

Other groups, however, because of ethnic rivalries with the Irish, gravitated toward the Republican or minority parties [268]. Protestant Germans, Scandinavians, and the Dutch did so in part because of their anti-Catholicism. In the upper Midwest, Knute Nelson, a native of Norway, had become governor of Minnesota by 1893 and served in the U.S. Senate from 1895 to 1923 as a conservative Republican. Floyd Olson, also of Norwegian ancestry, helped to organize Minnesota's Farmer-Labor party in the 1920s. Governor of the state in 1930, he was known for his progressive (radical) views on social programs, labor legislation, and conservation.

One of the most notable nineteenth-century leaders of German birth, Carl Schurz, emigrated because of the failure of the 1848 revolution in Germany. He settled in Wisconsin and by 1856 had become an active Republican. In 1860 his support of Abraham Lincoln (he delivered hundreds of addresses to German audiences) helped to turn out much of the German vote. During the corrupt Grant era, Schurz split with the Republicans and joined the Liberal Republican movement, bringing many German voters with him.

In New England, French Canadians, in direct competition with the Irish for jobs and control of local Catholic churches, initially gravitated into the Republican party, which presented a greater chance at upward mobility than the Irish-dominated Democratic machines. By 1908 Aram J. Pothier was elected governor of Rhode Island—the first French Canadian governor in the United States.

Perhaps no one better typifies the power of ethnic voting or the rise of later immigrant groups than Fiorello La Guardia [269]. With an Italian father, a Jewish mother, and a Protestant wife, he balanced the ticket single-handedly. As a young man without funds for an education, he worked days and attended law school at night. In 1910 he hung out his attorney's shingle and the same year joined the Republican party, which offered him a better chance to work into politics than did the still Irish-dominated Tammany Hall. After serving in petty offices, he won election to the U.S. House of Representatives—the first Italian American to serve in Congress. La Guardia brought incredible flamboyance, political skill, and energy to his political efforts. Acting on his own convictions and responding to pressure from Socialist and Progressive rivals, he became one of the most aggressive liberal reformers in Congress.

Between 1934 and 1945 he served as mayor of New York, establishing issue-oriented politics and helping the city to weather the Depression. A master linguist, he would speak Yiddish in one ghetto, Italian in the next. In achieving office he had to beat the city machine at its own game, invigorate an unsympathetic Republican party, and inspire an inert Italian electorate. And inspire them he did. As an editorial in the *Sons of Italy* magazine proclaimed during his candidacy:

> *In helping to elevate one of our race to an important public office it must be remembered that we are helping ourselves and our individual aspirations for future realization because in almost each case the occupancy of a public office by an Italo-American establishes a precedent for the office which then receives permanent consideration. What is important, then, is to win some of these offices for the first time.*

It was a classic situation in American politics: a dominant early immigrant group was being displaced by a struggling newer group.

If the Irish loom large in the myths of American political history for machine politics and corruption, then the Germans and Jews do so for radicalism. In both cases only a small part of the story is true and only a minority of each immigrant group was involved. Yet, like the Irish political machine, the generalizations about German and Jewish radicalism has some basis in fact, for Germans virtually founded socialism in the United States. Of seventeen socialist newspapers in the country in 1876, ten were German, three Bohemian, and one Swedish. The Socialist Labor party, founded in 1878, was largely composed of German immigrants, as was the anarchist movement in Chicago in the 1880s. Milwaukee, the most German of American cities, was the citadel of American socialism. In 1916 twenty-one of its twenty-five councilmen were socialists, as was its mayor. Victor Berger, who arrived in Milwaukee from Austria in 1881, edited the German-language socialist newspaper *Vorwarts* there. He became the first socialist elected to the U.S. Congress (1911–1913, 1923–1929).

At the other extreme was the notorious and effective anarchist Emma Goldman, a Russian Jew who arrived in America in 1885. Her life was typical of those of the more violent radicals of the time. From 1890 onward she was continuously persecuted for attacking the government, fighting economic oppression, and speaking in favor of women's freedom and birth control. A magnetic, violent agitator, she was finally deported from the United States in 1919.

While anarchists, communists, and the Socialist Labor party derived much initial support from the foreign-born, especially the Russians, their members represented only a small fraction of the total number of immigrants. And the sympathy they evoked within their own ethnic groups lay in common bonds from the fatherland: German radicals were primarily products of the 1848 German revolution—an event of pride for all Germans; East European Jewish radicals were against the Czar and were later anti-fascist—causes that struck a responsive chord within their whole community.

The vast majority of German, Austrian, and Jewish "radicals" in America were peaceful socialists. Their radicalism was influenced by the Marxist idea that the government should own and control industry, and it was centered on the issues of social welfare and the organization of unions. For the most part these groups have become liberals in their "middle age," as their political ideas have entered the American mainstream and the labor movement has become a fixture of the establishment. Similarly (with the exception of the Jews), their more conservative brethren who started out as Democrats have tended to become Republicans as they rose on the socioeconomic ladder.

Contributions of immigrant groups to American politics depended on their background, the period and pattern of their settlement, and the possibilities open to them in their new environment. At first immigrants had their primary political effect at the local level, but as they increased in numbers and influence, they produced shifts in state and national voting patterns. As of 1974, more than 430 of them had been elected to the House and Senate [270A–270L]. The impact on cities of an ethnic electorate, oriented toward the Democratic party, helped to transform the United States from a normally Republican majority to a Democratic one. While in 1920 Republicans had a plurality of more than 1.5 million votes in America's twelve largest cities, by 1936 the Democratic plurality in these areas was more than 3.5 million.

Ironically, the master of this new voting coalition was Franklin D. Roosevelt, a Hudson Valley blueblood of early Dutch ancestry [271]. Contributing to his success were the Great Depression, support from big-city machines, his appeal to distressed people from almost every background, and his administration's sympathy to social and economic change. During the Democratic era from 1932 until 1952, ethnic voters exercised decisive power in national elections. Since then the ethnic coalition has been fragmented, with both major parties seeking support of the various groups [272–276].

Ethnic influence has also affected foreign-policy making. The rapidity with which President Truman recognized Israel's independence in 1948 was undoubtedly influenced by strong Jewish American sentiments. At Yalta in 1944 Roosevelt asked Stalin not to publicize his agreement that the eastern third of Poland would go to Russia until after the American elections so he would not lose the Polish vote.

Even though mass immigration has stopped, ethnic politics still persists [277]—most dramatically now in groups such as the blacks, Indians, and Spanish Americans, who only recently have begun banding together in a politically conscious effort to achieve group success [278]. These ethnic political organizations tend to center not on a formal political machine but on an individual—a Martin Luther King or a Cesar Chavez—who represents the group's aspirations and interests.

Even beyond the first and second generations of immigrants, ethnic politics persists as later generations have accumulated sufficient political clout to make their influence felt. The effect of this phenomenon has been mixed: while it assures the recognition of a variety of interests, ethnic politics can also play on ethnic biases to exaggerate group tensions and lead to divisiveness in government and society. Ethnic consciousness in politics has been an important means in the immigrant's efforts to enter the American mainstream. Yet as Harold Cruse, a noted writer on ethnic communities, said: "Every four years the great fiction of the assimilated American (white and/or Protestant) ideal is put aside to deal with the pluralistic reality of the hyphenated-American vote."

GARFIELD · ARTHUR

269

268
Rare political banner from the election of 1880 with "Pennsylvania Dutch" markings. Throughout the second half of the nineteenth century the German vote was generally described as Republican.

269
Fiorello H. La Guardia.

270A–270L
Sampler of foreign-born congressmen. More than 430 foreign-born citizens have been elected to the Senate and the House of Representatives. An overwhelming percentage have come from England, Ireland, and Canada, where English is the native tongue; yet, as shown in this small sampling, the variety of nationalities has been another sign of American pluralism and of the ability of American democracy to accommodate a variety of opinions.

270A
Timothy Campbell. Ireland. 1840–1904.

270B
Dow H. Drukher. Holland. 1872–1963.

270C
Victor L. Berger. Austria-Hungary. 1860–1929.

270D
Albert Gallatin. Switzerland. 1761–1849.

270E
Richard William Guenther. Prussia. 1845–1913.

270F
Thomas Baldwin Peddie. Scotland. 1808–1889.

270G
Knute Nelson. Norway. 1843–1923.

270H
Octaviano Ambrosia Larrazolo. Mexico. 1859–1930.

270I
Judah Philip Benjamin. St. Croix, Virgin Islands. 1811–1884.

270J
Karl Stefan. Bohemia. 1884–1954.

270K
Jacob Johnson. Denmark. 1847–1925.

270L
Joseph Pulitzer. Hungary. 1847–1911.

A

B

C

D

E

F

G

H

L

Joseph Pulitzer

I

J

K

WE WANT ROOSEVELT
MASSACHUSETTS
MASSACHUSETTS
GIVE US ROOSEVELT
WE WANT ROOSEVELT
WE WANT ROOSEVELT

271
Franklin D. Roosevelt was a master at creating a national ethnic coalition. His political rallies seemed to bring together a bewildering array of foreign-born and second-generation supporters from nearly every part of the world. In speaking to the Daughters of the American Revolution on April 21, 1938, he made his feelings clear: "All of us, and you and I especially, are descended from immigrants and revolutionists." Later the same day, at a press conference, he said:

I am not going to ask any questions but I am going to tell you what I said to the D.A.R. today. [Laughter] I am going to preach the same sermon to you that I preached to them. It is a perfectly good text. I said that I probably had a more American ancestry than nine out of ten of the D.A.R. I had various ancestors who came over in the Mayflower and similar ships—one that carried the cargo of furniture—and furthermore that I did not have a single ancestor who came to this country after the Revolutionary War; they were all here before the Revolution. And, out of the whole thirty-two or sixty-four of them, whichever it was, there was only one Tory. [Laughter] Well, they began to wonder if they ought to applaud that or not. And, I said, now I will come down to the text. It is just as good for you in the same category. [Laughter] I said, Here is the text: Keep in the front of your heads all of the time, dear ladies, first, that you are the descendants of immigrants. And they did not know whether to applaud that or not. So there is the text and I won't expound on it any further.

272
Eisenhower election poster, 1952.

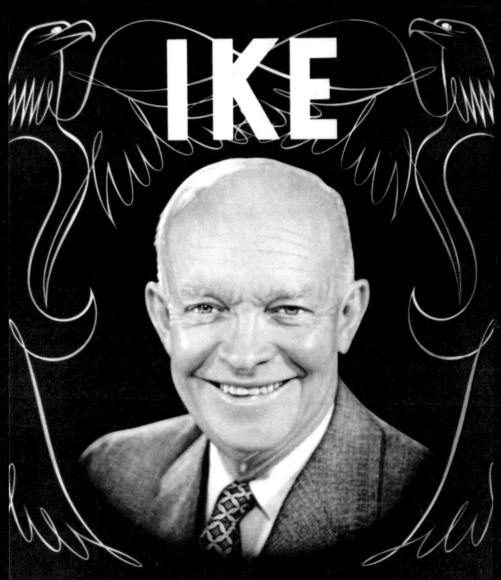

IKE

HERÓI DA GUERRA
E DA PAZ

273
Automobile bumper stickers
from the unsuccessful Re-
publican campaign of 1964.

274
Rockefeller campaign poster,
1968.

275
Democratic National Convention, 1972.

276
Poster displayed at the Cleveland Airport in the 1972 presidential campaign.

273

404

SCANDINAVIAN-AMERICANS
FOR ROCKEFELLER

275

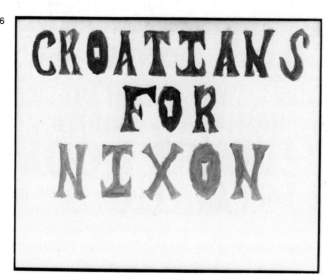

276

278

277
Billboard in front of the Lower Manhattan Republican Club, Market Street between Monroe and Cherry Streets, 1950. The ethnic pluralism of New York State is clearly seen in the names of the candidates.

278
A random selection of campaign buttons from numerous elections. Pluralism—ethnic and racial variety—is vividly portrayed.

Politics, of course, spawned the political cartoon, and an immigrant observer, Thomas Nast, carried the art to its highest expression. Nast (1840–1902) was a German-born cartoonist who invented or helped to popularize some of the common symbols of American life: the Democratic donkey, the Republican elephant, Santa Claus, Uncle Sam, and Columbia.

He was born in Landau, Germany, and emigrated with his parents to the United States in 1846. He studied fine arts for a time and at age fifteen joined the staff of *Frank Leslie's Illustrated Newspaper* (a periodical begun in 1855 by Henry Carter, an Englishman). In 1859 he left this job, free-lanced in Europe and America, and joined *Leslie's* competitor, *Harper's Weekly,* in 1862. For the next twenty years his cartoons were a star feature, earning both Nast and *Harper's* generous incomes.

Nast detested slavery, and he fought against anything that suggested that blacks were second-class citizens. He also hated Tammany Hall and the corrupt Irish Catholics who ran it. With an intense scorn, he focused his wrath on the Tammany leader, William Marcy Tweed [279]. Two of his cartoons, "The Tammany Tiger Loose" (November 11, 1871) and "Who Stole the People's Money" (August 19, 1871), are classics. "Boss" Tweed himself was contemptuous of the common man, particularly in a nation made up of people from the rest of the world. He observed one time:. "This population is too hopelessly split into races and factions to govern it under universal suffrage, except by bribery of patronage, or corruption."

Tweed, of course, practiced what he preached—and it was bribery that Nast attacked. Tweed was sensitive to the barbs of the German-born cartoonist, for if his constituents were too dumb to read, they nevertheless could understand "them damn pictures." Prison was Tweed's final destination, and Nast's cartoons were credited with helping to put him there. When Tweed died in New York City's Ludlow Street Jail in 1878, all of Nast's cartoons that contained caricatures of Tweed were found with his belongings.

But Nast did more than smash the myth of invincibility that enveloped Tammany Hall; he added the donkey and the elephant to our political symbols, and even Santa Claus was a contribution from this immigrant's pen [280].

Santa Claus had had a long history and a variety of countenances, beginning as far back as the fourth century in Asia Minor and coming up to the Dutch version, which was introduced into America: Sancte Klaas, complete with short jacket and pantaloons. Nast remembered the German Santa of his childhood—Pelz-Nicol or Sankt Nikolaus—and he remembered the German Christmases with fondness and sensitivity. In 1862 he drew his own version, based in part on Professor Clement Clarke Moore's recently published poem. " 'Twas the Night Before Christmas." Nast's drawings from that time on—culminating with the publication of his book, *Christmas Drawings for the Human Race* (1890)—helped to make Santa Claus what he is today: the jovial fat man who works in the neutral zone of the North Pole, free from political pressure and busily employed in the manufacture of good will.

Christmas itself, as it evolved in America, became a composite of traditions from the numerous immigrant groups. The indoor Christmas tree is said to have come from seventeenth-century Germany, while the practice of decorating it with baubles and candles was developed a century later. The religious crêche, as a symbol of Christmas, developed in France and Italy. The practice of leaving shoes or stockings for Santa to fill appeared in Holland, and the exchange of gifts goes back to the Roman Empire. The commercial Christmas card is generally attributed to another German-American, Louis Prang.

Nast, by 1890, captured all these customs in his Christmas cartoons. He drew them with warmth and human compassion, almost as though he was attempting to show his "other side" to an audience who knew him as a ruthless crusader, punishing men who violated the public trust.

279
"What are you laughing at?
To the victor belong the
spoils." Thomas Nast,
November 25, 1871.

280
"Merry Christmas to all, and
to all a good-night." Thomas
Nast, *Christmas Drawings for
the Human Race* (1890; also
Harper & Row, 1971).

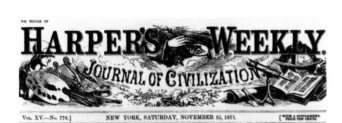

279

280

Chapter 21

American Entertainment— An Immigrant Domain

American entertainment! Flowing from the wellsprings of Broadway and Hollywood and a thousand tank towns in between, it has inundated the country and has spread abroad, to be imported and imitated by the very nations that provided its unique ingredients. For, paradoxically, the peculiarly American character of much of our entertainment is the product of creative contributions from the uprooted of other countries, the non-native, the offspring of those who came from somewhere else.

Two qualities, nevertheless, are distinctly American in our peculiar assortment of theatrical environments. The first is the remarkable mingling of talents provided on an extraordinary scale by artists and performers of diverse origins. The second factor is the rather generous measure of freedom that was available within the American theater, especially after the Civil War. One among several reasons for this comparatively liberal setting has been the receptivity of the American audience. On one hand, their heterogeneous constitution provided a broad spectrum of interests. On the other, the circumstances of geographic isolation contributed to the attitude of exceptional responsiveness so often exhibited by early American audiences. Whether Americans were separated from the Old World by the oceans or isolated in widely scattered inland communities, the effect was the same.

Elements of "native American" humor, dance, and song—well rooted in the old homelands—were perpetuated consciously and with great tenacity for many years before the professional European entertainers descended on the larger towns and before itinerant troupers reached the interior settlements of the young nation. On the surface, the spectrum of the performing arts in pre-Revolutionary America may seem paltry by present standards. However, strong improvisational drives were given rather free play among an isolated people who valued their artistic heritage, limited though its basic ingredients may seem to us. Improvisation has become characteristic of American storytelling, humor, dance, jazz, and rural music. At the same time, traditional forms of music and drama were fostered, eventually giving the large body of American entertainment its great variety of forms. This variety made it unique. And the survival of traditional and improvisational forces side by side attest to the high place accorded entertainment by those who otherwise were preoccupied with hard work.

281
Joseph Jefferson the first,
born in England.

282
Joseph Jefferson III (1829–
1905).

In 1655 a play was acted in Accomac County, Virginia, an extremely early example of theatrical enterprise which remains on record because three players were brought before the court on criminal charges for participating in the performance. They were acquitted. Seventeenth-century theatrical productions were rare, however, and it was not until the eighteenth century that organized, commercial entertainment was established. Apparently the first theater built in America was the one that opened in Williamsburg, Virginia, in 1718. It was run by a merchant, William Levingston, and Charles and Mary Stagg, a husband-and-wife team who taught social dancing. In Charleston, South Carolina, dramatic productions enjoyed such popularity that government officials made the courthouse available as a substitute theater before the first playhouse was opened in 1736. Quaker opposition to the drama gradually lost its force in Philadelphia, and in 1749 the traveling company of Thomas Kean and Walter Murray staged Addison's *Tragedy of Cato*. The same troupe performed works by Shakespeare, Congreve, Addison, Farquhar, Dryden, and Lillo in New York, Williamsburg, Annapolis, and other towns during 1751 and 1752. New York City—which for the past two centuries has been regarded as the entertainment capital of the nation—embarked upon its destiny in 1732 at the New Theatre, owned by Rip Van Dam, an early "impresario" of Dutch stock.

The earliest professional performers were from England. Despite a later influx of talent from other countries and a gradual swelling of the troupers' ranks from the native-born population, the American legitimate stage was unquestionably dominated by British talent for well over a hundred years. Among the early arrivals were the members of the Sully family. Their artistic contribution may have been less than their numerical impact, since there were eleven Sullys—father, mother, and nine children—who descended on the Charleston stage at one time in 1792. The first Joseph Jefferson [**281**] created a more lasting impression on the American stage. Not only talented in his own right, Jefferson founded an acting family whose leading figure was Joseph Jefferson III [**282**], the well-remembered actor who specialized in the role of Rip Van Winkle. The elder Jefferson, however, was a comedian of more versatility. The son of an actor in David Garrick's London troupe, he performed in New York for the first time in 1796, two years after emigrating from England. Curiously, he found one of his greatest successes in portraying the humorous Yankee character of Brother Jonathan, the prototype of our Uncle Sam.

281

282

Perhaps the best-known American theater family in the nineteenth century was founded by yet another English immigrant, Junius Brutus Booth [283], who arrived in 1821. His first performance in Richmond was well received. Booth's American career—overwhelmingly involved in the presentation of Shakespeare—spanned thirty years. Successful in the East, he also toured the western mining camps with his son, Edwin, who at an early age entertained the miners as a blackface banjo player. By the 1860s, the Booth family's theatrical reputation was solidly established. In November 1864, three of Booth's sons appeared together in *Julius Caesar* at the New York Winter Garden.

The theater family founded by James O'Neill (1847–1920), father of the Nobel Prize-winning playwright Eugene and grandfather of Oona, who married Charles Chaplin, spanned both the nineteenth and the twentieth centuries. James was born in Ireland and emigrated to America in 1854 at the age of seven. A player of talent who enjoyed great popularity, he is primarily remembered as the man who made the role of Edmund Dantes in *The Count of Monte Cristo* his exclusive property.

One of the most brilliant immigrants associated with the stage was Dion Boucicault (1820–1890), the Dublin-born actor and playwright [284]. Boucicault's pieces not only enjoyed popularity in his own time but have been revived or rewritten as musical comedies and contemporary dramas. His adaptation of Washington Irving's *Rip Van Winkle* rivaled the success of the staged *Uncle Tom's Cabin*. More important, Boucicault recognized the advantage of being topical. In *The Poor of New York*, for example, he played upon the public mood growing out of the economic panic of 1857 and contrasted the lavishly furnished homes of the rich with the filthy tenements of the poor in immigrant neighborhoods. In *The Octoroon*, which opened in December 1859, Boucicault drew a sensitive portrait of Zoë, the much-put-upon heroine. The scenario included a slave auction, a riverboat conflagration, a plantation sale, and a part for an idealized Indian. Although Boucicault's works contained a good measure of exaggeration and melodramatic effect, which he frankly added for entertainment value, his themes were frequently based on situations of considerable social significance. Two of his more successful works, *The Colleen Bawn* and *The Shaughran*, owed much of their popularity to the sympathetic treatment of themes of current interest to his large Irish-American audience.

Richard Mansfield (1854–1907) also cut a wide theatrical swath in America [285]. An actor of difficult temperament, he was born in Helgoland, Germany, of mixed ancestry, his father being English and his mother a Russian prima donna. Mansfield starred memorably as Cyrano de Bergerac in addition to numerous other roles and had the distinction of appearing in the first play by George Bernard Shaw to be produced in the United States, *The Devil's Disciple* (1894).

Helena Modjeska (1840?–1909), born in Poland, was an actress of charm and superior abilities who overcame the hurdle of learning English quite late in life. After emigrating to America, she went on to play leading roles, appearing in the first performance of an Ibsen play in America, *A Doll's House* (Louisville, 1883). If Ibsen's message was mystifying to the audience in Kentucky, so was Modjeska's accent; nevertheless, the Louisville audience was captivated [286]. The audience in Boston was similarly enthusiastic in their approval of Fanny Janauschek, who played Lady Macbeth in German opposite an English-speaking Edwin Booth.

283

283
Junius Brutus Booth (1796–1852), born in England.

284
Dion Boucicault (1820–1890), born in Dublin.

285
Richard Mansfield (1854–1907), born in Germany.

286
Helena Modjeska (1840–1909), born in Poland.

285

284

286

Although the traditional drama in America was long under the spell of its British counterpart, musical developments were far more variegated. From the earliest days of settlement, songs could be heard. Even the Pilgrims and Puritans countenanced singing, so long as the songs contributed to religious worship. An outgrowth of the effort to preserve the traditional forms of religious music was the appearance of singing schools. The American itinerant singing master thus came into being, traveling from town to town with songbook and pitch pipe. By the beginning of the nineteenth century, singing schools were flourishing from New England to the southern states and as far west as Cincinnati. Frankly, their popularity rested squarely on the entertainment value and only incidentally on their original religious purpose. A result of the singing-school movement was the introduction of choirs in American churches, a popular innovation which was wholly out of favor with the minority of hidebound traditionalists. Moreover, the movement provided the greatest stimulus for the writing and publishing of music in America for many years.

The ballad opera of the London stage enjoyed a great vogue in America during the second half of the eighteenth century. Many of the professional dramatic companies performed ballad operas as afterpieces to plays, demonstrating a versatility that would be lost with specialization in the following centuries. *The Beggar's Opera,* for example, was first performed in America in 1750 by a company that offered both dramatic and musical programs. With the arrival of Hallam's London Company of Comedians in 1752, the American musical theater was considerably advanced. In addition to legitimate drama, Hallam's players provided a full range of musical programs in towns such as New York, Williamsburg, Annapolis, and Charleston, and in many smaller communities. The hospitality of American audiences was remarkable, and the group was impelled to change its name to the American Company.

Not surprisingly, after the Revolution the London ballad opera no longer held the attraction it had commanded before the war. Soon professional French musicians were enjoying a popularity superior to that of their English and German colleagues. At the same time, independence gave birth to a patriotic musical outburst which, in the hands of zestful Americans like Francis Hopkinson (1737–1791), contributed a small but important number of works to the national body of music. Innovative forces gradually found strength over the years, and the native strains—always decidedly ethnic in their origins and vigor—developed in close conjunction with a body of musical work that was nurtured by immigrants and natives alike.

The native, innovative trends, however, were not always valued by those who professed to speak from a position of good taste. Mrs. Trollope, the British novelist who visited the United States during the years 1827–1830, established her literary reputation by writing a biting account of her experiences in *Domestic Manners of the Americans.* She thought American musical appetites were barbaric. Josef Gungl, the leader of a German orchestra who toured the United States in the 1840s, found that Americans preferred vulgar circuses and crude minstrel shows to his more sophisticated offering. Ole Bull, the Norwegian violinist who toured the States in 1843 and 1844, soon discovered that his popularity increased when he resorted to tricky playing and rendered a few choruses of "The Arkansas Traveler" in the best backwoods foot-stomping tradition of the frontier fiddler.

Of all the numerous visitors from Europe, none received more adulation and success than Jenny Lind (1820–1887), the Swedish songstress of whom Mendelssohn said: "She is as great an artist as ever lived and the greatest I have known." Under her American manager, P. T. Barnum, Lind opened at Castle Garden, New York, on September 11, 1850, then traveled across America to record one of the greatest successes in the early musical theater, netting a profit of $100,000. If Barnum's publicity techniques were brash, they were also effective. And if Lind's musical selections were subject to criticism for their "simple," unchallenging quality, her American audiences at least had an opportunity to hear one of the most exquisite voices of the time and an artistry that none could fault. As the nineteenth century unfolded, American audiences steadily developed their artistic appreciation and appetites, creating a favorable environment in the New World which eventually rivaled that of any part of Europe.

Traditional orchestral music was slow to take hold before the Civil War, despite well-intentioned efforts in Boston and New York. Subscription concerts and philharmonic societies failed to gain widespread public support. The efforts of two immigrants, however, gradually bore fruit. Theodore Thomas (1835–1905), the man who must receive the greatest credit for establishing symphonic music on a firm basis in America, emigrated with his family from Germany in 1845. Basically a violinist, Thomas received his musical training in Europe and in 1854 was elected to membership in the Philharmonic Society of New York, shortly emerging as a conductor of superior talent. Starting with his first New York concert in 1862, he created what was to become the Theodore Thomas Orchestra, which traveled to most of the major cities in the United States and Canada. His musical success was brilliant, but financial stability eluded his grasp until the last fifteen years of his life, when his Chicago Symphony Orchestra found permanent acceptance.

Thomas's rival, Leopold Damrosch (1832–1885), had a similar career in America [**287**]. Born in Posen, Poland, Damrosch made his musical reputation in Europe as violinist, conductor, and composer, becoming concertmaster of the Grand Ducal Opera of Weimar. In 1871 he was invited to become conductor of the Arion Society of New York. After founding the New York Symphony Society, which replaced Thomas's orchestra at Steinway Hall, Damrosch also pursued an energetic career in popularizing traditional orchestral music, making a notable tour of the West in 1883. Largely because of the efforts of Thomas, Damrosch, and Damrosch's son, Walter, symphonic music was a permanent part of the American musical scene by World War I, with a number of major cities providing a home for excellent orchestras.

The slowness of the public to accept opera was similar to the early reluctance exhibited toward symphonic music. In the first years of the nineteenth century, however, New Orleans, with its multiethnic traditions, gave opera its earliest permanent home in America. John Davis, an immigrant from Santo Domingo, opened the first opera house there in 1813. Although the New Orleans house also hosted French plays and ballets, traditional opera was the main staple. Well supported by local patronage, the New Orleans company ventured on the road in 1827, sending touring companies to New York and Philadelphia. New York had heard its first opera in 1825, when Manuel Garcia opened a series of performances with Rossini's *Barber of Seville*. Despite these early successes, there was a deep-seated resistance to opera which persisted until late in the century. Opera retained an aloof character for many Americans who objected, perhaps, to the theatrical pomp and the foreign languages in which the arias were rendered.

The opera did have tremendous snob appeal for the wealthy, nevertheless, and the old patrician families were able to support a small body of foreign performers in theaters such as New York's Academy of Music on Fourteenth Street. With the swelling of the ranks of the rich after the Civil War, opera was significantly boosted by the construction of the Metropolitan Opera House in New York in 1883. The Met, which would eventually dominate all phases of opera in America, was created by a new breed of fabulously wealthy American industrialists and financiers, who found themselves excluded from the charmed circle of socialites whose fortunes often dated from colonial times. The result of this upper-crust rivalry was a definite boon to the opera. Leopold Damrosch launched a series of German operas for the Met in 1884 which made a lasting—if controversial—contribution to American musical standards.

Traveling companies of operatic performers traversed the land and attracted a loyal if small following among the working classes in every part of the country. Nevertheless, support in such communities as Chicago, San Francisco, and Central City, Colorado, still sprang essentially from the newly rich who wished to dabble in high culture. The value of this largely superficial effort was the fact that many hundreds of ordinary folk had the opportunity to hear some of the finest voices in the world, including Lilli Lehmann, Adelina Patti, and Marcella Sembrich.

In the early part of the twentieth century, opera enjoyed a further increase in popularity through the production of phonograph records, which carried arias into the homes of millions of Americans. The immigrants—many of whom had never attended an operatic performance in their homeland—found a new source of pride in the records of the Russian Feodor Chaliapin, the Italian Amelita Galli-Curci, and the Irishman John McCormack. America became so hospitable to the opera during the generation of World War I that numerous stars, such as Enrico Caruso of Italy (1873–1921) and Ernestine Schumann-Heink of Germany (1861–1936), made the United States their permanent residence. (The patriotism of Schumann-Heink during World War I became legendary, rivaling the best public displays of George M. Cohan.)

The impact of foreign entertainment in America was given a new dimension by the immediate popularity of Gilbert and Sullivan's operetta *H.M.S. Pinafore,* a work that was brought to Boston in 1878, only six months after its London opening. It was not covered by an American copyright, and hundreds of performances were given in every part of the country before enthusiastic audiences. *Pinafore* was followed by *Pirates of Penzance*—this time protected by copyright and introduced by a British company in New York in 1879.

The success of Gilbert and Sullivan inspired an interest in the stage musical on the part of American audiences and composers alike. Indeed, there was a veritable rush toward operetta by composers who normally worked in more traditional musical forms. John Philip Sousa (1854–1932) tried his hand at operetta, with *El Capitan* incorporating the march that bore the same name. If Sousa was not ultimately at home in the new form, others were, such as the European-trained Reginald De Koven (1859–1920), whose ''Oh, Promise Me'' survives from *Robin Hood,* and the Bohemian-born Karl Hoschna (1877–1911), perhaps best remembered for ''Cuddle Up a Little Closer,'' the hit song of *The Three Twins* (1908).

287

Among the best composers who contributed to
popular American musical productions was Victor
Herbert (1859–1924), born in Dublin, the grandson of the Irish poet and novelist Samuel Lover
[**288**]. Herbert was first taken to the opera when
he was seven. Years later, after an across-the-
footlights romance, he married the Stuttgart Opera
star Therese Foerster. Walter Damrosch signed
Herbert's wife to a contract with the New York
Metropolitan Opera on her condition that her
husband be hired as the Met's cellist. Despite
Therese's so-so success in New York and her early
retirement from the stage, Herbert's career progressed with all the drama of a Broadway-musical
scenario. He became a close associate of Anton
Seidl, the great Wagnerian conductor at the Met,
and then moved on for a six-year stint as conductor
of the Pittsburgh Symphony Orchestra. While in
Pittsburgh, Herbert, then approaching middle age,
began writing operettas more or less on the side.
Herbert's sound training and superior talent distinguished his work from most of his contemporaries.
Sigmund Spaeth contended that Herbert "never
wrote a technically bad piece." His first success
was *The Wizard of the Nile* (1895), but more notable were *Babes in Toyland* (1903), *The Red Mill*
(1906), and *Naughty Marietta* (1910), perhaps his
best achievement. Herbert's *Mlle. Modiste*, however, the tremendous hit of 1905, not only included
the song "Kiss Me Again," but the beautiful
Austrian-born singer Fritzi Scheff (1879–1954).
Scheff, who had performed sixteen roles with the
Met, was catapulted to fame in that show, replacing the Iowa-born Lillian Russell as America's
darling before the outbreak of World War I [**289**].

Operettas and musical comedy productions were in
the mainstream of American entertainment. The
language was in the vernacular and the plots were
invariably light and refreshing. Equally important,
the music was popular in a very basic sense, and
the multituned productions provided American
composers, musicians, and performers with opportunities in addition to the customary channels of
Tin Pan Alley. Among such later writers would be
George Gershwin, Jerome Kern, and Cole Porter.
Composers such as Sousa, De Koven, and
Hoschna had already included hybridized elements of a musical form that was termed ragtime, a
syncopated approach to music credited to the
American Negro.

Ragtime had surfaced, albeit in various disguises,
long before *H.M.S. Pinafore* had taken the United
States by storm. The music of the American Negro, whether in the mode of spirituals, rags, blues,
or jazz, had been heard for many decades and had
changed the character of popular music not only
within the United States but beyond its borders.
American musicals had gradually assumed a national character, especially when the German or
Austrian operetta fell from favor during World
War I. If syncopation was evident in Hoschna's
"Cuddle Up a Little Closer," it was strongly
present in the music of Kern's *Show Boat* (1927)
and Leonard Bernstein's *West Side Story* (1957).

Kurt Weill (1900–1950) had taken American
music to heart long before fleeing to the United
States from Germany in 1939, and his song "Mack
the Knife" became a favorite of Louis Armstrong's [**290**]. American musical idioms—
essentially ragtime, jazz, and the blues—had been
making an impact on Old World composers such as
Stravinsky, Debussy, and Dvořák for many years,
but their influence was even more evident in more
ephemeral music. Indeed, by the mid-twentieth
century, the musical comedy itself had become the
exclusive province of the United States. Curiously,
the operetta and musical comedy blossomed during
the years that saw the decline of the American
minstrel show.

288

Schott

289

If any form of stage musical entertainment could be termed "strictly American," it was the minstrel show. By 1842, after nearly twenty years of development, the various elements of the minstrel show were fairly well defined [**291A, 291B**]. Foreign visitors were completely baffled by the shows. And when some of them learned that the minstrels were usually better box-office attractions than visiting musicians, they often expressed resentment by criticizing American musical taste. Josef Gungl exhibited such sentiments in the 1840s: "The so-called Minstrels have the best business here. . . . They paint their faces black, sing negro songs, dance and jump about as if possessed, change their costumes three or four times each evening, beat each other to the great delight of the art-appreciating public, and then earn not only well-deserved fame but enormous sums of money."

The minstrel show was the product of many forces. In the first place, it played up to the appetites of the "middling" Americans. Immigrant actors and playwrights catered to middle America through vehicles such as Brother Jonathan (Uncle Sam), Rip Van Winkle, Monte Cristo, *The Poor of New York, The Octoroon,* and *H.M.S. Pinafore.* These audiences of the early and mid-nineteenth century were largely unsophisticated and liked raw humor, which stood in sharp contrast to the drawing-room tastes of Europe. They loved exaggeration in melodramas such as *Uncle Tom's Cabin;* they enjoyed fast-stepping dance routines, brassy bands, ballads that fairly dripped with sentiment, and the lively, often syncopated songs played on southern or frontier fiddles and banjos. Moreover, Americans were keenly alive to their unique position on the western fringe of European civilization. Their peoples were heterogeneous, and their environment encouraged innovation. They turned the character of Brother Jonathan to their own advantage, creating the image of the Yankee in the guise of a shrewd wisenheimer who valued the basic qualities of European society without the trappings of pretension, deceit, or decadence. The primary vehicle was humor; the style was exaggeration. And entertainers who succeeded best on the popular stage drew heavily on either the most exotic subject matter that imagination and folklore could supply or, at the other end, the familiar features of American life.

Minstrel show melodies were great favorites, widely distributed by published sheet music. The "Christy's Melodies," published in the third quarter of the nineteenth century, included "Carry Me Back to Old Virginny," but did not give credit to the great black composer James Bland.

291B
The book of *Minstrel Songs and Negro Melodies from the Sunny South* was published in 1884.

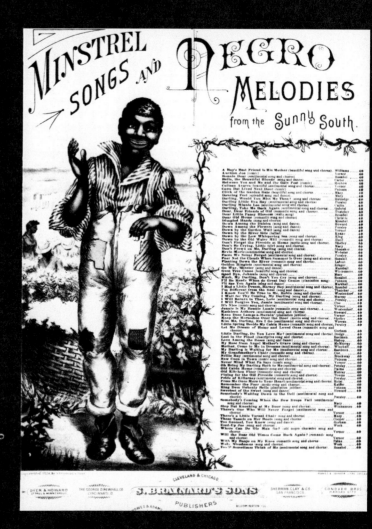

Negroes, of course, made up a very large portion of the American population in the South and near Southwest before the Civil War. They were never far from the center of national attention—slavery was a major issue in American life. In addition, blacks had the distinction of being somewhat exotic, especially in the eyes of the European immigrants and northern settlers. These factors alone probably made it inevitable that the Negro would become a subject for exploitation in the American popular theater.

White actors in black faces had appeared on the American stage before the Revolution, but the English actor Charles Mathews was apparently the first white man to incorporate a Negro song in an act. This was "Possum up a Gum Tree," a tune Mathews picked up in 1822 from a performance at New York's African Theater Company, a resident Negro dramatic troupe which primarily offered legitimate productions such as Shakespeare's plays. Within a short time, many white performers in blackface were rendering hybridized Negro songs and dances as interludes during dramatic plays or as novelty circus acts. These early specialists included Thomas D. Rice, who presented productions like *O Hush* and *Bone Squash,* which Rice billed as "Ethiopian Opera."

Under the leadership of men such as Dan Emmett, a performer of Irish descent from the backwoods who would be assured of a permanent place in the nation's memory as the author of "Dixie," the American minstrel show moved toward its classic form in the 1840s. The early shows soon included exchanges of witty dialogue between the interlocutor and end men, massed singing and banjo playing, choral and competitive solo dancing, and full-company walk-arounds. The Negro dialect was exaggerated, and the tunes were loosely based on both Negro and European models. The stand-up blackface comedians at first wore the red striped trousers and the long-tailed blue frock coat of Brother Jonathan. The amalgamation of the exaggerated Yankee folk hero—Uncle Sam—and the rural Negro remains a striking image.

For the most part slaves, the Negroes were definitely outsiders, set apart to a far greater degree than even the "greenhorn" immigrants. The blacks were the butt of caricatures broadly drawn by those middling Americans who were in turn the butt of the European's put-down. The exploitation of the Negro in the minstrel show became a target of the abolitionists, while they in turn did much to foster the impression that Negroes lacked a sense of humor. Yet the minstrel stage acted to freeze and stultify the popular image of the Negro. By the end of the Civil War the show had become a stylized art form, owing much of its popularity to its predictability.

Through it all, nevertheless, curious elements of American Negro culture penetrated. There were, in certain songs and routines, for example, evidences of the field holler and response. The jaybird and other animals that frequently appeared in Negro fables often were mentioned in minstrel songs. African antecedents for the form of the banjo and the playing of bones have been recognized. If much of the Negro's music was drawn from European models, rhythmic and innovative melodic variations which were distinctly Negro in origin were transcribed or further hybridized by white performers. There was a constant interplay and borrowing—frequently indirect—but it was no accident that the same melodic southern folk strains appeared in the works of both Louis Moreau Gottschalk (1829–1869)—the New Orleans-born pianist-composer who drew freely upon Creole melodies for his flashy compositions—and Stephen Collins Foster (1826–1864), the Pennsylvania-born composer whose musical works for minstrel troupes are among his best remembered.

The stylized form of Negro imagery reflected in Foster's songs is more remarkable in its long-lived impact when it is recalled that only about thirty of his songs were based on the Negro-on-the-plantation theme and that some 150 pieces were solidly in the British-American ballad tradition. This pervasiveness of pseudo-Negro music in antebellum America is perhaps more easily grasped if it is also remembered that Foster probably never traveled more than a few miles south of the Ohio River in his entire life.

In addition to minstrel songs, the dance—both choral and solo—figured prominently in the program. In this the minstrel show may have more effectively mirrored the Negro's proficient and innovative interpretations of Irish reels, jigs, and lilts. The backwoodsman and Negro both claimed the breakdown.

Some elements originally delineated in the minstrel shows remained with the popular American theater for many decades. A large place was given to the humorous banter between the end men and the interlocutor, with puns, riddles, and one- and twoliners perpetual sources of laughter for American audiences everywhere. The exaggerated dialect—the value of which had been keenly appreciated for a long time by American comedians—set a model which was freely adapted to the Irish, German, Swedish, and Yiddish comic images developed somewhat later on the American vaudeville stage. The blackface makeup itself was appropriated by entertainers who had only a minimal relationship with the classic minstrel shows—Al Jolson, Eddie Cantor, and Frank Tinney. Bert Williams, the great Negro entertainer who achieved universal stardom on the white vaudeville and musical stage in the early years of the twentieth century, always worked in blackface [292A–292E]. Moreover, the folk-based nonsense that was abundantly seen and heard in the minstrel shows must certainly be included among the more lasting contributions of this important form of American entertainment. And the American minstrel show provided yet one more contribution to entertainment: the opportunity for black performers to enter the profession in considerable numbers.

Negroes, of course, had been entertainers during the colonial period, enjoying their greatest success as musicians and singers. Working under the tremendous disadvantage of being considered inferior outsiders, a few talented blacks nevertheless had achieved theatrical success and a limited measure of mobility even before the Civil War. Frank Johnson (1792–1844) was a composer and violinist who, as a band and orchestra leader, became one of the most sought-after musicians for dances by the white society of the eastern seaboard.

The earliest appearance of all-black minstrel troupes occurred in 1855, but it was not until after the Civil War that Negro minstrelsy enjoyed a sense of permanency. The billing for these groups emphasized the fact that they were "the real thing"—authentic Negroes of slave background (even though many entertainers had been free blacks before the war). Although the format of the minstrel show had become established by 1865, the advent of a considerable number of Negroes into the field made a significant impact. In addition to the introduction of original dance styles and "plantation" songs, the content of even more conventional material was altered. In Negro minstrel songs, for example, there was no reference to white masters. The lyrics expressed antislavery feelings and often focused on the importance of freedom.

The black companies—not surprisingly—became extremely popular with black audiences and inspired many talented black youngsters to enter entertainment, thereby enriching the theatrical and musical heritage of American popular culture. One of these was William C. Handy (1873–1958), the author of "St. Louis Blues" (1914), "Beale Street Blues" (1917), and other important compositions that contain Afro-American musical elements. James Bland, who had become a minstrel in the 1870s and starred in his own troupe on a tour to England and Europe, was perhaps the most prolific of the black composers. He wrote "Carry Me Back to Old Virginny," "In the Evening by the Moonlight," "Dem Golden Slippers," and several hundred other songs. Talented blacks were attracted to minstrelsy because it was among the few opportunities in the nineteenth century open to them. It held the promise of financial success, geographic mobility, and social esteem and prestige among the whites and especially among the blacks.

The career of Sam Lucas exemplifies the frustration experienced by blacks who wanted to break the bounds of prejudice and convention in post-Civil War America. Lucas became a minstrel in 1869. Determined to free himself from the stereotypes imposed by minstrelsy, by 1873 he had earned recognition as an accomplished singer, actor, and composer, largely because of the leading role he had taken with the Hyer Sisters in *Out of Bondage,* a musical comedy that hailed the virtues of freedom for the blacks and, by extension, for other "outsiders" in American society. He became the first Negro to play the title role in *Uncle Tom's Cabin,* in 1878. Despite such successes, he was forced to return to minstrelsy more than once during his long career, for the American dramatic stage was less than hospitable to blacks, reflecting fluctuating public attitudes and the fears of timid or prejudiced impresarios. Lucas moved instinctively into all-black musical productions: Sam T. Jack's Creole Shows in 1890 and Cole and Johnson's *Shoo Fly Regiment* and *Red Moon*. He was a member of the cast of *A Trip to Coontown* during 1898–1899, the first black-written and black-produced musical that broke with the minstrel tradition. Between appearances in musical comedy, the dramatic stage, and minstrel shows, Lucas and his wife enjoyed success on the newly developing variety and vaudeville circuits. Lucas's remarkable career was capped in 1915 when he played the title role in the motion picture version of *Uncle Tom's Cabin.*

By the time Lucas had played Uncle Tom, minstrelsy was a theatrical relic. Only a few thin shadows of its multidimensional past would survive in the resurrections performed on the Hollywood sound stages of the 1930s and 1940s and in the amateur productions of city school children or church groups, which, incidentally, drew upon the earliest stereotyped images.

If the once vigorous minstrel show no longer attracted the curiosity of the nation's audiences and no longer served as an adequate platform for the talents of performers, the circus enjoyed a more durable and flexible life. For nearly the full two centuries of the nation's existence, the circus has retained a loyal following.

Bert Williams (1877–1922),
born in Nassau, Bahama Islands. Portrait in blackface.

292B
Frank Tinney (1887–1940).

292C
Al Jolson (1888–1950), born
in Srednicke, Russian
Lithuania.

292D
Eddie Cantor (1892–1964).

292E
Eddie Cantor's blackface
makeup, lent by Museum of
the City of New York.

292A

292B

292C

292D

292E

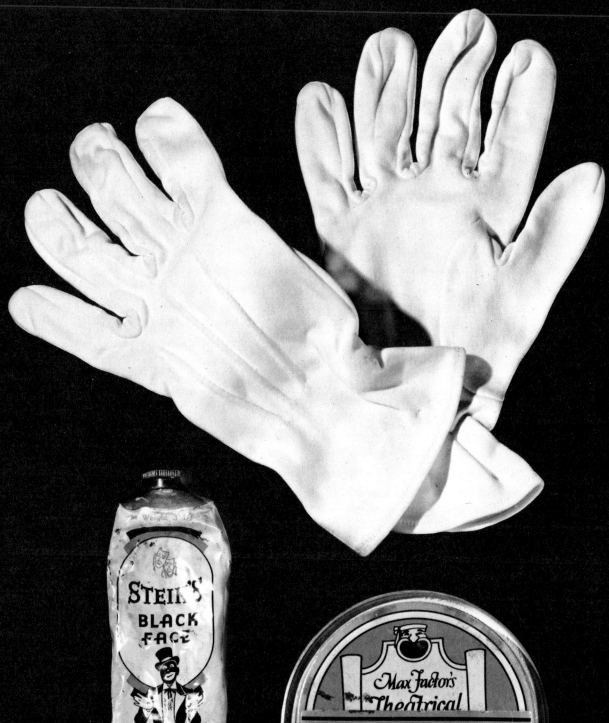

The circus that Americans came to know had its origins in England, and it is generally conceded that Philip Astley's one-ring equestrian circus of London, which opened in 1770, was the model for the earliest versions brought to America. Within one year, in 1771, a certain Faulk introduced an equestrian show in Philadelphia, and, from 1792 to 1799, John Ricketts, an Englishman, toured the young United States with his circus. One of Ricketts's productions featured a dramatization of the Whiskey Rebellion, a curiously un-English stunt which some recognize as a precursor for Buffalo Bill's Wild West productions of a century later.

With Hachaliah Bailey's importation of an elephant to the United States in 1808, the American circus began to assume its familiar form, and very soon trick-riding acts, trained animal routines, freak exhibits, menageries, rope-walking and trapeze acts, tumbling performances and clowns were combined into one large show. Clowns, of course, claimed a direct lineage with their medieval European predecessors. When mid-nineteenth-century circuses began to incorporate chariot races on a hippodrome track, a connection—-contrived—with the Roman *circus maximus* was reestablished. The hippodrome track resulted in the enlargement of the size of the main arena tent which both suggested and necessitated the incorporation of two or three rings instead of one. The one-ring circus, meanwhile, remained the European standard.

The circus at first traveled from town to town in wagons, and the entrance into each community was usually staged in the form of a spectacular parade which started early in the morning for maximum effect on the waking townspeople [**293**]. The wagons became elaborate works of the wood-carver's art, frequently produced by immigrant craftsmen in such firms as the Sebastian Wagon Works of New York, the Bode Wagon Works of Cincinnati, or the Moeller Brothers of Baraboo, Wisconsin. Parade wagons were covered with intricate and imaginative decorations, with carved and guilded figures and scrolls and cartouches, with sunburst wheels, mirrors, and painted murals. Music was supplied by a brass band and a steam calliope, and most of the performers and animals would parade down the main street.

The circus's gigantic size, the exotic qualities of the performers and animals gathered from every corner of the earth, and the unusual people exhibited in the side shows were among the elements that perpetually fascinated people. Hollywood would have it that the rural dwellers were most taken with the circus, but it is equally true that the millions of immigrants residing in America had never seen the like of such circuses in the old country. When P. T. Barnum distributed advance publicity—as he did in 1872—he made a point of translating the highlights of his ballyhoo into German.

Barnum's traveling show of 1872 required six tents: the National Museum, the Menagerie, the Caravan, the Hippodrome (or main arena), the Polytechnic Institute, and the International Zoological Garden. The hippodrome tent, which covered two rings and a track, had a seating capacity for fifteen thousand (comparable hippodrome tents of the day seated five thousand). Barnum featured three automatons that year—mechanically animated life-sized figures of a dying Zouave, a "Sleeping Beauty," and a trumpeter. He had scores of animals, including 120 performing horses, six live sea lions in water tanks, camels, elephants, Rocky Mountain sheep, gnus, lions, tigers, ostriches, a black leopard, a yak, a zebra, and other strange beasts. In addition to trick and bareback riders, rope walkers, and jugglers, there was a little girl with a beard, the only Digger Indian on exhibition, an African whistling snake charmer, a few "Wild Fiji Cannibals," Admiral Dot (the California dwarf), the armless Anna E. Leake, and a troupe of glassblowers.

Dan Costello's circus traveled across the newly opened transcontinental railroad to the West Coast in 1869, the same year that the rails had been joined by the Golden Spike. More enterprising circuses had traveled to California some twenty years earlier via the steamship route around Cape Horn. And Gilbert Spalding and Charles Rogers even constructed a theater barge, the *Floating Palace*, for staging circus productions in 1852. It toured the inland river system and provided seating for 2,500, one of the nation's larger theaters at that time. By 1872, Barnum's show required three locomotives to move his circus in two or three sections of trains. In 1885 circuses reached a numerical peak, with at least fifty road shows traveling across the country. A number of American circuses successfully toured Europe, and the best European performers were lured to the United States for nearly two centuries.

In the early one-ring circus, the single clown was a stand-up comedian who used the ringmaster as his straight man. Clowns were also singers who helped popularize countless songs across the country, selling printed songbooks to the audience between acts. Early blackface comedians flourished in circuses and moved freely between the tent shows and minstrel stages. With the appearance of multi-ring circuses, the conversational banter became impractical, and clowns became specialists in pantomime. When immigrants arrived in great numbers in the nineteenth century, clowns were among the pioneer entertainers who caricatured the Irish, Germans, Swedes, and Jews, paralleling the trends in white minstrel shows and early vaudeville.

William F. ''Buffalo Bill'' Cody (1846?–1917), army scout, railroad meat supplier, and actor in western melodramas, gave the circus a peculiar twist when he launched Buffalo Bill's Wild West in 1883 [**294**]. The Wild West (Cody never liked the word *show*) was an outdoor spectacle featuring sharpshooting, steer riding and roping, mock battles between Indians and Pony Express riders, lariat exhibitions, and spectacular horsemanship. Cody signed up well-known figures of the western frontier—ex-army officers, scouts, marksmen, and famous Indians—to lend additional luster to the exaggerated dramatization, creating an attraction that pulled in huge crowds until World War I. Cody's success tempted many imitators; as many as 116 Wild West shows have been recorded. Buffalo Bill made a successful four-year tour of Europe following a brilliant season at the World's Columbian Exposition in Chicago in 1893. The Wild West literally overwhelmed the Europeans and, along with translated dime novels and the later cowboy-and-Indian motion pictures, greatly distorted their image of America.

Taking a page from the circus's book, Cody imparted a strong if somewhat incongruous international flavor to his Congress of Rough Riders, or, variously, his World's Rough Riders, In addition to U.S. cavalry and cowboy horsemen, he included English-Irish lancers or dragoons, French chasseurs, German uhlans, Hungarian ''Magyars,'' ''Bedouin Arabs,'' Russian Cossacks, South American gauchos, ''Tartars'' of Asia, Mexican rurales, American Indians, and, significantly, ''Afro-American Jockeys.'' Only American show business would hit upon such an idea, for only in America would the actual mixture of the foreign-born stimulate the idea in the first place. If the foreign troops seemed incongruous in the Wild West, the notion was not at all incongruous in an American show.

Vaudeville or variety holds a particularly important place in the history of American popular entertainment. When viewed in relationship to the immigrant entertainer and the audiences of a nation of immigrants, vaudeville is especially significant [**295**]. It was a form of entertainment that offered numerous opportunities to many thousands of entertainers. Because vaudeville was mainly unstructured, simply a succession of acts, it accommodated nearly any kind of a performance that was interesting, and was thus open to almost anyone who could put his act across. Finally, it was important because it reached its height at a time when mechanized and electronic developments revolutionized American entertainment, making it possible for the most talented variety specialists to help shape radio and motion pictures as they developed. Vaudeville shared common elements with the circus, the minstrel show, musicals such as *The Black Crook* [**296**], and the British music hall. As early as the 1870s acts were being imported from England at a fairly steady pace for performances in bar-theaters such as Koster and Bial's Music Hall in New York. Basically, vaudeville was an outgrowth of variety, the ''blue'' side of entertainment. While variety survived as burlesque, vaudeville remained family entertainment.

BUFFALO BILL'S WILD WEST AND

AN ASSEMBLAGE OF THE WORLD'S ROUGH RIDERS

SELECTED FROM AMONG
THE MOST CELEBRATED OF THE UNIVERSE OF ALL RACES,
ALL MEN WHO RIDE, INCLUDING

A GRAND INTERNATIONAL MILITARY TOURNAMENT
INTRODUCING FOR THE
FIRST TIME ON EARTH AND ON HORSEBACK, AND IN ONE ARENA TOGETHER,

GENERAL NELSON A. MILES AND "BUFFALO BILL."

CONGRESS OF ROUGH RIDERS OF THE WORLD

ACTUAL, GENUINE, NATIVE EXPERTS
REARED IN THE SCHOOL NECESSITATED BY
THE PRIMITIVE LIFE NOW PASSING AWAY, THE LAST LINGERING DISCIPLES
OF
AN ART ALLIED WITH HISTORY'S HEROES
Men, Veterans in the Tented Fields of War! Graduates from the Tests of the March!
THE RAID! THE BIVOUAC! THE CHARGE!

THE LARGEST ARENIC EXHIBITION KNOWN IN HISTORY

BUFFALO BILL

Anthropological Congress, Paris.

THE AMERICAN COWBOY—THE MODERN CENTAUR

From Every Section, Every Latitude of the Vast West, from

The Roving Ranchero and Ranger of the Mustang-Land of the Rio Grande, to the Broncho Busting Buck Rider from the Cayuse Ranges near the British Border.

THE SCOUT, THE GUIDE, THE TRAPPER, THE FRONTIERSMAN, AND

The United States Cavalry Man,	The Hungarian Magyar,	The Tartar of Asia,
The French Chasseur,	The Bedouin Arab,	The Mexican Ruralie,
The English-Irish Lancer,	The Russian Cossack,	The American Indian,
The German Cuirassier,	The South America Gaucho,	The Afro-American Jockey.

Born Hereditary "Princes of the Saddle."

COL. W. F. CODY—"BUFFALO BILL."

THE INDIAN—Late Terror of the Plains

CAMPED IN PEACE WITH THE CONQUERING FOE. NOW IN FRIENDLY INTERCOURSE, FRATERNALLY FRATERNIZING

The Star Spangled Banner, The Cross of St. George, The Tri-Color of France, AND The Black Eagle of Germany

IN HARMONIOUS UNITY.

THE ARAB OF THE DESERT and THE GAUCHO OF THE PAMPAS viewed in open-eyed wonder by those learning the wonderful story of man; THE CAUCASIAN COSSACK and MEXICAN CAVALIER verifying their dim traditions by associated facts with the Afro-American; THE SCOUT, RANGER, FRONTIERSMAN and the PROUD PRODUCT OF THE PRAIRIE LAND—THE COWBOY, adding interest to this picture of man's brotherhood. A lesson of the fact of the passing of racial prejudice; a garden for the cultivation of general amity in

THE FIRST CAMP OF UNIVERSAL ARBITRATION SINCE THE DELUGE.

Vaudeville's preoccupation with—or exploitation of—the multiethnic composition of the American population is exhibited in this late-nineteenth-century poster for Howorth's Double Show, which apparently featured German, Irish, Negro, Dutch, British, and Scandinavian comics. The humor was often rough and frequently loaded with prejudice.

296
The Black Crook, which opened in New York City in 1866, is regarded as the first American musical comedy. If the story line was thin, the audiences were thrilled by the chorus line of Parisian can-can girls in tights.

BLACK CROOK

Many new Americans who gravitated to urban settlements sought the convivial atmosphere of beer gardens—introduced by the Germans during the 1850s—the "stall" saloons, gambling dens, "low" music halls, and houses of prostitution. These well-patronized places existed in every large town, and efforts to close them down only drove them underground for a brief time. Such houses were not merely places of common amusement; they served as incubators for some of the most vital strains of American theatrical and musical creativity. A sizable group of Negroes, for example, found their opportunities for musical expression through the idioms of ragtime, jazz, and blues. They first performed in the saloons, barrel houses, clubs, and front parlors of brothels in New Orleans, Sedalia, Kansas City, and other towns of the Mississippi Basin. Their act traveled on excursion boats upriver to St. Louis, Davenport, and Chicago and overland to Detroit, Washington, and New York. The "low" music halls of the cities fostered the rise of social dancing in the 1880s and 1890s, a vigorous development which enlarged the demand for danceable tunes and the services of countless musicians until well after World War II. The second- and third-rate music halls—built by the hundreds—were often utilized on Sundays by immigrant organizations which produced traditional Old World plays or pageants and musical programs put on by orchestras and the "singing societies" of scores of nationality groups.

Philadelphia boasted at least three variety houses that had originally served as churches. One of the converted churches—at Eleventh and Wood streets—was the scene of the first hootchy-kootchy dance in an American theater. It was a genuine Turkish act with three male musicians using Turkish instruments and two dancing girls wearing only very short skirts and silk scarfs around their breasts. The little troupe had been imported for the Turkish Theatre on the midway of the Centennial Exposition in 1876, but the Turkish pavilion had a poor location and soon closed. American stag audiences were unimpressed by the generous exposure of flesh; the men preferred the French-type can-can girls in full costume. It was not until 1893 that the cooch became a hit, with its sensational introduction at the World's Columbian Exposition in Chicago and its subsequent presentation at Coney Island by Little Egypt.

The creation of an absolutely clean version of variety and the launching of vaudeville as a "puritanical," non-blue form of entertainment is credited to Tony (Antonio) Pastor (1837–1908), a New York-born showman-impresario. When he was six, Pastor sang duets with Christian B. Woodruff, a New York state senator, in Dey Street Church for meetings of the Hand-in-Hand Temperance Society. Somewhat later, Pastor's father got his son a job as a child prodigy in Barnum's Museum, and when Tony was ten, the lad joined the minstrel show in Raymond and Waring's Menagerie as a solo blackface singer and dancer as well as the tambourine end man. Pastor became a circus ringmaster when he was fourteen and, as such, had to perform as a singer, dancer, and participant in the afterpieces. In 1861 he returned to New York and opened his first theater, a typical lower-Broadway show bar known simply by its address, "444." His second theater, Tony Pastor's Opera House, became the forum for early heroine-villain melodramatic pieces. Pastor himself, in the early 1870s, also originated one of the first touring variety companies. Although players had always traveled as singles, Pastor put together a complete company, with acts stressing comedy, songs, dancing, and skits. This essential format provided the basis for the subsequent form of vaudeville.

Apparently Pastor's genuine concern over the excessive blue material in vaudeville led him to launch the cleaned-up variety program presented in a conventional American theater. It was an immediate success. Pastor's opening bill included Frank McNish's eccentric acrobatic act; Ferguson and Mack's Irish "rough" act, a comic skit full of pratfalls and slaps which finished with a hatchet buried in Ferguson's trick wig; a song-and-dance act by the Leland Sisters; the blackface eccentric song-and-dance team of Lester and Allen; another singing duo billed as the French Twins; Lillie Western's trick musical instrument act; Ella Wesner's male impersonations, which she had perfected in English music halls; British songs by Dan Collyer; and popular songs rendered by Pastor himself. The bill is significant for reflecting the importance of music and the presence of ethnic material.

In the 1880s the so-called racial comics achieved prominence on the popular American stage as a direct result of the numerous immigrants in northern cities. Like the Negro before them, the immigrants were just "different" enough to be singled out as objects of raw humor. Needham and Kelly were among the early Irish teams, and in many respects were typical, although they had a reputation for having perhaps the roughest act. They featured the song "The Gas House Terriers," a musical ode to the Saturday-night brawl. Irish songs, arguments, sparring matches, and dancing were also the ingredients of Kelly and Ryan's Irish act, often given the setting of the hard-coal mining areas of Pennsylvania. Bradford and Delaney opened their skits dressed as Irish washerwomen and used urban immigrant settings to gain immediate rapport with their audiences. Pat Rooney's outstanding single act included frequent references to hard work and the virtues of unionism, the Democratic party, baseball, and the immigrant's success in the American theater. The chorus of Rooney's version of "Is That Mr. Riley?"—an extremely popular vaudeville song, to which numerous entertainers laid claim to ownership—contained a summary of the Irish immigrant's dream:

I'd have nothing but Irishmen on the police;
Patrick's day would be Fourth of July.
I'd get me a thousand infernal machines
To teach the Chinese how to die.
Help the working man's cause, manufacture the
*   laws;*
New York would be swimming in wine.
A hundred a day would be very small pay,
If the White House and Capital were mine.

The Jewish comics became prominent in vaudeville after Frank Bush's huge success during the 1890s, although the distinction of the first Yiddish presentation was claimed by the team of Burt and Leon, who developed their act as early as 1878. The Dutch (German) acts, which became popular in the 1880s, characterized the German immigrants as beer drinkers, yodelers, and dancers, freely mixing German words into accented guttural English and emphasizing an image of foxy stupidity. Joseph Weber (1867–1942) and Lew Fields (1867–1941), sons of Jewish immigrant parents, were New York comics who were both born over a saloon and grew up in the immigrant-dominated section of the city [297].

Ed Gallagher (1873–1929) and Al Shean (1868–1949, born in Dornum, Germany) combined the Irish and Yiddish comic images in one act, reaching their height of popularity in the Ziegfeld Follies of 1922 [298]. The career of the great popular singer Nora Bayes (Leonora Goldberg, 1880–1928), also had origins in vaudeville. Another daughter of Jewish immigrants, Fanny Brice (Fannie Borach, 1892–1951), found stardom in the musical vaudeville productions of Ziegfeld, phonograph records, radio, and motion pictures. Similarly, Eddie Cantor (Israel Iskowitz, 1892–1964), traveled the route from a humble immigrant family to fame and substantial fortune.

The headliners of vaudeville also included a substantial number of foreign-born who did much to give entertainment its distinct "American" flavor. The free-wheeling, hedonistic quality of the American vamp or theatrical floozy owes much to the remarkable talents of Eva Tanguay (1878–1947), the Canadian-born daughter of a Parisian physician and French Canadian mother [299]. Tanguay's theatrical life style objectified the image of her torrid song "I Don't Care," when few other entertainers dared to project such blatant irreverence in public. The success of Yvette Guilbert (1868–1944) was more remarkable, because most of her songs were in French. Although she was sophisticated and stately, Guilbert's unerring style and rapport with audiences not only helped her put over her songs but enlarged the American appreciation for European material [300]. The British star Albert Chevalier enjoyed great success presenting unaltered his London Music Hall monologues and songs. Other British imports to vaudeville included Vesta Victoria, whose specialty, "Waiting at the Church," is still performed; Olga Petrova (Muriel Harding); Lillie Langtry, the "Jersey Lily," who made a number of trips to America between 1882 and 1915 for both legitimate and popular performances; and Vernon Castle (Vernon Blythe, 1887–1918), who, together with his American-born partner, Irene, did more than any other team of dancers to launch America on a craze for dancing which spanned two generations.

Hungarian immigrants were well represented in American vaudeville by the Dolly Sisters, Jennie (1892–1941) and Rosika (1892–1970), the song-and-dance team who set a four-week record engagement for sister acts at the New York Palace. Budapest-born Harry Houdini (Harry Weiss, 1874–1926), was among the most spectacular performers on the vaudeville stage [301]. Houdini began his career as a card-trick magician in a dime museum and as a sharper in medicine shows. He tried vaudeville initially as a handcuff-escape artist but flopped until he developed his legendary escapes.

Among the foreign-born singers who were closely identified with American vaudeville are Sophie Tucker (Sophie Abuza, 1884–1966) and Harry Lauder (1870–1950). Tucker, of Russian birth, belted out such songs as "Some of These Days" in her own nightclub as well as on stage, radio, and phonograph records. She took pleasure in being billed as "the last of the red-hot mamas," but owed a great deal in her style of singing to black entertainers such as Bessie Smith and Ethel Waters. Conversely, the style of Tucker and her rival, Nora Bayes, influenced the phrasing of some lesser Negro blues shouters. This constant borrowing back and forth did much to entrench the ragtime- and jazz-oriented qualities in popular American song.

297

298

299

300

301

The popularity of Harry Lauder [**302A, 302B**] represents the continuing attraction exercised by British and European influences in American entertainment and, in several dimensions, is consistent with the popularity enjoyed by Gilbert and Sullivan in earlier times and the Beatles or Marcel Marceau more recently. The basis of Lauder's programs was straightforward Scottish folk songs which he modified only slightly for the benefit of London music hall audiences, who had some difficulty with Lauder's purest burr. In a number of American tours Lauder never changed the content of his London act. His recording of ''I Love a Lassie'' was a top-selling number in the Victor catalogue. Between songs he recounted homely episodes he claimed to have experienced in Scottish villages. The multiethnic audiences in America packed the theaters to hear him.

While a relatively few performers reached supreme stardom and wealth, thousands of performers less fortunate were locked into a ruthless commercial system which put a lid on their potential earnings. As a result, they formed a powerful union in 1913—Actors Equity—and in 1919 called a successful strike which won the right for the union to negotiate for better working conditions and pay scales for all performers. A ''closed shop'' had been established, with nearly every professional performer a union member with the singular exception of George M. Cohan, the famous grandson of an Irish immigrant. Cohan—the self-styled superpatriot of the boards, who was born on the third (not the fourth) of July—was the only entertainer without a union card permitted to perform in professional houses.

The Irish-born Patrick Gilmore helped to develop band concerts into one of America's favorite pastimes in the 1870s and 1880s. Even Gilmore's popularity was surpassed after 1893 by John Philip Sousa (1854–1932), the son of a Portuguese immigrant, who had a distinguished career with the U.S. Marine Band. (Sousa's father emigrated with the name of So, and, in a burst of superpatriotism, is said to have changed his name by adding the letters u, s, and a.) Bandstands were built in public parks in thousands of towns, and cities like New York, Philadelphia, and Baltimore maintained permanent bands, paying the musicians from city treasuries. In the summer people heard band music in parks, at the beach, and in specially constructed outdoor amphitheaters; in the winter the bands played in armories or drill halls, opera houses, and auditoriums constructed by ethnic associations, often playing music which itself reflected the ethnic variety of the American people [**303A– 303G**].

302A

302A
Harry Lauder (1070-1950),
born in Scotland.

302B
Harry Lauder's famous cane.
H 31¼".

302B

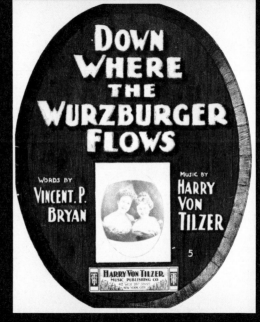

303A

303D

303E

America's multiethnic, multinational character was always mirrored by the sheet music that was played on parlor pianos and sung, whistled, and hummed in streets and shops. "Min Heimathstrand," by Carl von Wegern for Adolph Philipp's *Corner Grocer* (nineteenth century), had lyrics in a Low German dialect; Harry von Tilzer's "Down Where the Wurzburger Flows" of 1902 was a German-American tune that swept the country; the romanticized notion of the American Indian was reflected in such songs as "Pawnee" (1906) by Silvio Hein; Richard A. Whiting's "It's Tulip Time in Holland" of 1915 and Hoagy Carmichael's "Hong Kong Blues" of 1939 used exotic places for settings; the "Spaghetti Rag" (1909) relates to the presence of Italian immigrants and to the syncopated music of the American Negro; "Where the River Shannon Flows" (1910) was in the mainstream of "Irish" songs that were written, published, and performed by the thousands in America.

303F

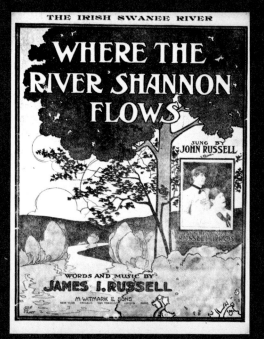

303G

The music of the American blacks had been evident throughout the history of the United States, but the piano and the phonograph became unmatched agents for popularizing Afro-American music at every level of society. Ragtime took the country by storm at the turn of the century, and its popularity held until the mechanical piano was replaced by the phonograph record and radio performances of orchestral jazz in the 1920s and 1930s. The better ragtime numbers were usually the work of black composers who, as already noted, were sometimes employed as piano players in barrel houses and brothels. The leading composers of rags were also employed to "cut" recordings for player-piano-roll companies. The foremost black composer of this group was Scott Joplin, born in Texarkana in 1868. Joplin's musical instincts were as sympathetic to the traditional music of Europe as they were responsive to strongly Afro-American idioms. Few surpassed Joplin, however, in creating some of the most beautiful musical Afro-Americanisms and giving ragtime its four-square foundation. Joplin was also among the most prolific of black composers, producing waltzes, marches, ballads, arrangements, a musical instruction book, and two operas in addition to about forty rags written strictly for piano.

The Negro James Scott was nearly as prolific; his "Grace and Beauty" and "Hilarity Rag," both written in 1910, are still heard. The white composers Joseph Lamb and Percy Wenrich wrote ragtime numbers solidly in the best traditions of their black counterparts. Wenrich, born in Joplin, Missouri, could impress equally with such tunes as "The Smiler—A Joplin Rag" (1907) or "Put on Your Old Gray Bonnet" (1909) and "When You Wore a Tulip and I Wore a Big Red Rose" (1913), both of which owe as much to ragtime as they do to the traditional balladry of Europe. The black minstrel and bandleader William C. Handy worked not only in the ragtime format but in the blues as well, and fellow black writers such as Ferdinand "Jelly Roll" Morton ("Kansas City Stomps" and "Milenberg Joys") also stand midway between ragtime and jazz.

Of all the European-born composers who were completely at home in the musical and theatrical environment of America, few can compare with Irving Berlin (Israel Baline), born in Temun, Russia in 1888. He grew up in the immigrant neighborhood of the lower East Side of New York and, after only two years of formal schooling, became a song plugger, a saloon entertainer, and a songwriter who dominated American popular music for half a century [**304A, 304B**]. His first composition, "Marie from Sunny Italy," reflected an immigrant orientation and so did his first hit, "Sadie Salome, Go Home." Berlin joined the ranks of those who churned out simplified ragtime pieces before World War I, and in 1911 he wrote what has become the most symbolic popular song of the prewar generation, "Alexander's Ragtime Band." Berlin remains the most prolific producer of popular music and the undisputed leader in the sale of sheet music. If his ragtime was not true ragtime and his "jazz" not truly jazz, his melodies nevertheless remained danceable, singable, and topical. His "Easter Parade" did much to lend that venerable Christian holiday a new dimension; his "White Christmas," as sung by the Irish-American Bing (Harry Lillis) Crosby during World War II, broke all popularity records. Berlin's "God Bless America" became the nation's popular anthem during World War II, and his Jewish-Russian origins never seemed to have caused the raising of a single nativistic American eyebrow.

304A

04B

304A
Irving Berlin, born in Rus
1888.

304B
Irving Berlin's piano, spe
constructed with a mov
transposing keyboard. l
60½".

WESER BROS.
NEW YORK

MADE EXPRESSLY FOR
IRVING BERLIN

In many ways as thoroughly American are the works of George Gershwin (1898–1937), the son of Jewish-Russian immigrants and also a resident of teeming immigrant neighborhoods in New York. Gershwin was a writer of popular songs who in the 1920s diverged into the more ambitious and demanding field of classical composition. His serious music shows Gershwin's fascination with Afro-American syncopated music.

Jazz, during the years before World War II but particularly during the 1920s, was not given a high place in the opinions of a number of influential critics. For one thing, the music was stigmatized by its early creation by blacks and its association with "low" places of entertainment. Gershwin and a few others—notably Joplin before them—sensed the potential of ragtime, jazz, and blues as a new force in the world's music. Gershwin's immigrant family had instilled in him a sound appreciation for Old World values, and it is clear that Gershwin took it upon himself to invest jazz with a new "respectability." If his music did not mirror the purest strains of black jazz (Gershwin was apparently never completely immersed in the idiom), his music was by the same token not thoroughly European either.

Gershwin's first ambitious musical composition of extended length, his "Rhapsody in Blue," was performed with Paul Whiteman's dance orchestra in New York on February 12, 1924, in a brilliant arrangement by Ferde Grofé, one of Whiteman's pianists and arrangers since 1920. Whiteman, rather inappropriately known as the "King of Jazz," was, like Gershwin, determined to elevate the status of the products of Tin Pan Alley. In addition to the "Rhapsody," the program included Rudolph Friml's "Chansonette" and Victor Herbert's new "Suite of Serenades."

Many white jazz musicians took a turn on the Whiteman bandstand. If Whiteman's all-time roster did not read like the Who's Who of pre-World War II jazz, it did read like pages from a telephone book representing the immigrant neighborhoods of a large American city. There were Italian-American instrumentalists, such as Salvatore Massaro, better remembered as Eddie Lang (guitar); Giuseppe "Joe" Venuti (violin), born on an ocean liner bearing his immigrant parents to America in 1903; and Mario Perry (accordion). Among the German Americans were the outstanding jazz musicians Leon Bismarck "Bix" Beiderbecke (cornet) and Frank Trumbauer (saxophone, oboe, and bassoon). The Irish Americans who performed for Whiteman included Tommy and Jimmy Dorsey (trombone and reed instruments) and singer Bing Crosby.

The jazz musicians in Whiteman's orchestra were seldom able to demonstrate their improvisational techniques, for Whiteman favored heavily orchestrated sequences and rather tightly written arrangements, termed "symphonic jazz," which anticipated a trend toward written arrangements later evident in the big "swing" bands of the 1930s. Jazz instrumentalists preferred the freedom provided in smaller bands or orchestras. Although the Negro instrumentalists and composers had the best apparent ethnic claim to jazz, it was not their exclusive domain. Significantly, many jazz musicians were either German or Italian. In addition to those already mentioned, there were Frank Teschemacher and George Brunies, Milton "Mezz" Mezzrow and Joseph "Wingy" Manone. Among the giants of jazz was Benny Goodman, the son of Russian-Jewish immigrants who had settled in a ghetto on the West Side of Chicago.

It is appropriate to draw a distinction between white and black jazz musicians, but it is also useful to recognize the alliance between the blacks and the large number of white musicians of immigrant backgrounds. The American Negro found that the universal popularity of jazz soon created job opportunities in the American and European entertainment industries. The "new" music of the post-World War I years gave the prosperous decade of the 1920s the apt name of the "Jazz Age." And the Negro by no means surrendered leadership, though he did not always receive acclaim.

Among the hundreds of black musicians who shaped the popular music of half a century was Sidney Bechet, clarinetist and soprano saxophonist, who was an internationally acclaimed musician before the 1930s. There was Jelly Roll Morton, the legendary piano player who started his musical career in New Orleans. His works rank among the best jazz compositions, and his recordings as a band leader for Victor, on the Red Hot Peppers sessions of the late 1920s, remain among the best of "traditional" jazz. There were trumpeter John "Dizzy" Gillespie and his early companion the innovative alto saxophonist Charlie Parker; the jazz pianists Earl "Fatha" Hines, Art Tatum, and Earl "Bud" Powell; the leaders and arrangers Edward Kennedy "Duke" Ellington (who has been called our country's greatest composer), Fletcher Henderson, and Jimmy Lunceford. There were Jimmy Noone (clarinet), Coleman Hawkins (saxophone), Charlie Christian and Wes Montgomery (guitar), Lester Young and John Coltrane (saxophone), Joseph "King" Oliver (cornet), and Louis "Satchmo" Armstrong (cornet and trumpet).

Daniel Louis Armstrong was undoubtedly one of the most important musicians in American history. Although he was a topflight jazzman from the time of his first appearance with King Oliver's Creole Jazz Band in 1923, his work did not immediately catapult him to fame. By the time he had achieved a good measure of success with a large "swing" road band during the 1930s, he had already exercised considerable influence on the playing styles of virtually every jazz musician and popular entertainer, besides working more subtle changes in music around the world. His appearances in a number of motion pictures, especially those with Bing Crosby, added to his acceptance by a wide public. With the end of the "big band" era in 1947, Armstrong reorganized his career with a smaller band, and enjoyed a swift resurgence of popularity. By 1957, George Avakian could write that Armstrong had become "the strongest single international symbol of jazz." By the time of his death in 1971 it could be said that Armstrong—whose formal musical education was administered in the Waifs Home for Boys near New Orleans—had become the strongest single personification of what the international community regarded as "best" in America.

Armstrong was perhaps the first of a succession of American trumpeters—Roy Eldridge, John "Dizzy" Gillespie, Clifford Brown, and others—whose work has permanently contributed to the development of brass music throughout the world. And on this point it is best to make an important distinction. Jazz musicians function in the milieu of popular entertainment, but both their intentions and their achievements are of a different sort. What they do is usually both more personal in nature and higher in art. Duke Ellington started with a more or less conventional dance band, used it as a means of both personal and cooperative expression, and went on to become perhaps the greatest instrumental composer (as opposed to songwriter) America has produced. Both the intentions and the achievements of, say Glenn Miller, Guy Lombardo, or Irving Berlin are quite different. Paul Whiteman's intentions were much the same as Ellington's, but his artistic achievements less.

The unmatched career of Louis Armstrong—born in the first year of this century—was fortunately helped along by significant technological and sociological developments which were unavailable to the performers before 1900. It seems that a rather impartial technology exercised more positive influence than some of the prevailing social conditions on behalf of talented artists outside the pale of white Anglo-America. Armstrong and Ellington and some others ignored or escaped the most severe social hardships imposed on their fellow outsiders. To the less fortunate, however—Billie "Lady Day" Holiday among them—social oppression could be fatal. Yet it was largely through the technological innovations which burgeoned in the field of entertainment that so many performers of diverse origin attained a fuller measure of success, acceptance, and esteem from a greatly enlarged audience.

The phonograph, radio, motion picture, and television—technologies superficially so cold and full of gimmickry—actually made the performers more human through the intimacy of the darkened movie theater and the private home, as well as through the familiarity of repetition. It may even be suggested that the constant exposure of talented individuals over the acoustical and visual media for a period of half a century contributed greatly to a fuller understanding and appreciation of all Americans from whatever ethnic sources and, indeed, to the ultimate successes of the civil rights movement of the 1950s and 1960s.

The phonograph was the invention of a Yankee, Thomas A. Edison. In its original form—that is, a machine utilizing records in the form of cylinders—it was available to the public many years before the turn of the century. But it was an immigrant, Emile Berliner from Germany, who modified the phonograph and introduced the disc recording. Shortly after 1900, techniques were developed to duplicate original wax "master" recordings from molds on a mass-production basis. By World War I, phonographs and records were in millions of homes, and musical offerings of all types were being mass-marketed. It was the phonograph, more than the stage, that made Enrico Caruso a household name, a veritable front-room champion. Caruso had made his first recording in Italy in March 1902, but it was his Victor recordings made at Camden, New Jersey, that ensured his immortality [305A, 305B].

305A
Enrico Caruso (1873–1921),
born in Italy.

305B
Stage personalities were
often featured in popular
music. Italian-born Caruso's
self-portrait became the cover
of "My Cousin Caruso," a Gus
Edwards tune of 1909 in Ziegfeld's production *Miss Inno-
cence*, starring French-born
Anna Held.

305A

305B

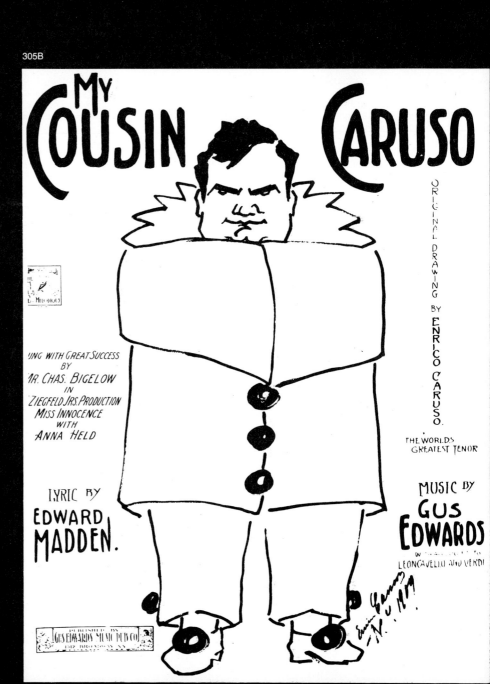

And there was Al Jolson, a singer who related primarily to live audiences yet who won a wide following through numerous phonograph recordings and motion pictures [306]. Jolson was born Asa Yoelson in Russian Lithuania, in 1888. He was the son of a cantor, Moses, who emigrated alone to New York City in 1890 and, after saving enough money from menial tasks, brought his family to Washington, D.C. Jolson's career began when he and his brother sang for pennies on the street in front of the Raleigh Hotel; when he died, in 1950, he left an estate worth four million dollars. He graduated from the streets to the bars, then to circuses and burlesque, and experienced his first success in 1911 in *La Belle Paree* at the New York Winter Garden. His love for the audience was legendary, and his techniques anticipated Judy Garland's intimate style by more than a generation. He would have the stage crew turn up the houselights, he would loosen his collar, move across the footlights, and sing to the audience while sitting on the edge of the stage.

Jolson's singing style went back to the ragtime and coon-song years—styles which later were only slightly transformed into the "mammy" songs of the 1920s. As Henry Pleasants has observed: "he could sound a lot like Ethel Waters. And Ethel Waters could, and often did, sound a lot like him. Neither of them was a grass-roots-primitive musical genius. They were at once products and representatives of that process of imitation and counterimitation—black imitating white, and white imitating black imitating white. . . ." Jolson's phrasing, rubato technique, slurring, and dynamics—approaches that were often derivative—were in turn copied by other singers. His vocal techniques included devices derived from both Jewish cantorial and Afro-American sources.

If Jolson and Ethel Waters did not represent grass-roots Afro-American music, Bessie Smith (1894–1937) did. The musical contributions of the "Empress of the Blues" can be precisely traced from her first recording, made in early 1923. Her 160 recordings and a two-reel motion picture have preserved the essential qualities of her art. She was not the first blues singer to record a song, but she was the most powerful, most original, and most artful. Her first record sold 780,000 copies within half a year of its release. Although she had always played tent shows and theaters, she was soon able to sign for appearances on the black entertainment circuits at $2,500 per week. Within six years, recordings by Bessie Smith sold between five and ten million copies, and it was rumored—with good reason—that the sale of her records alone were primarily responsible for keeping the Columbia company in the recording business during the slump years immediately preceding the introduction of commercial electrical recording in 1925.

The phonograph has fortunately preserved the contributions of other great early Negro blues singers, such as Mamie Smith, Gertrude "Ma" Rainey, Ida Cox, Alberta Hunter, Sippie Wallace, Trixie Smith, Victoria Spivey, Margaret Johnson, Monette Moore, Bertha "Chippie" Hill, Clara Smith, Addi "Sweet Peas" Spivey, and Lizzie Miles. The male blues singers seemed to gain favor on recordings slightly later, toward the end of the 1920s, with influential work being recorded by blacks close to grass-roots jazz, such as Blind Lemon Jefferson (1897–1930), Robert Johnson (?–1937), Leroy Carr (1899–1935), Big Bill Broonzy (William Lee Conley, 1893–1958), Blind Willie Johnson (1899–1949), and many more.

It is essentially through performances recorded by the phonograph that we can still enjoy the songs of the influential Irish-American singers such as Chauncey Olcott (1860–1932), the author or coauthor of "When Irish Eyes Are Smiling" and "My Wild Irish Rose" [307]; Henry Burr (1882–1941), a greatly esteemed Canadian-born singer in the Irish-American tradition, who was heard on more American recordings than any other vocalist before Bing Crosby; Irving and Jack Kaufman, Jewish-American brothers who recorded hundreds of hits in a lively vaudeville style before the Depression. The great Negro voice of Paul Robeson has been heard on folk spirituals, operatic selections, and popular songs on many recordings since 1925.

In 1916 David Sarnoff had already anticipated the success that music would enjoy over commercial radio, but it was not verified until 1920, when Dr. Frank Conrad, associated with Westinghouse, began regularly to broadcast recorded music. The response from his audience was immediately favorable and, from the first commercial broadcast of KDKA in Pittsburgh, in November 1920, music became a mainstay. Before the end of the year, Paul Specht's orchestra was broadcasting "live" from Detroit, and within the next few years bandleaders such as Vincent Lopez, Paul Whiteman, Ted Lewis, Isham Jones, Ben Bernie, Rudy Vallee, Fred Waring, Guy Lombardo, Ted Weems, and Phil Spitalny became household companions. In 1922 there were sixty thousand radio sets in American homes; by 1928 the American radio audience had grown to twenty million.

The impact of radio was evident in every sector of entertainment [308]. In 1928 Walter Damrosch introduced his "Music Appreciation Hour" over NBC, and two years later CBS aired the Philharmonic-Symphony Society of New York. The Metropolitan Opera—which at first resisted radio—decided to allow its first broadcast in 1931, and in 1933 it introduced its weekly nationwide series. In addition to obtaining a substantial income from the broadcasts, the Met profited from a greatly expanded base of public support within a decade. American audiences in every community listened to the offerings of Danish-born Lauritz Melchior, Norwegian-born Kirsten Flagstad, French-born Lily Pons, Polish-born Elisabeth Schwarzkopf, Italian-born Renata Tebaldi, and such Negro stars as Marian Anderson (who became the first Negro to sing at the Met, in 1955), Leontyne Price, and Shirley Verrett.

The radio also enabled immigrant groups in the larger cities to enjoy their native music over many "nationality" hours. On Saturday and Sunday afternoons in some cities certain stations aired nothing but foreign music, both imported recordings and many made in America by immigrant musicians or their offspring. Some of the tunes introduced over the nationality hours were converted into national hits, such as Jolly Jack Robel's recording of the "Beer Barrel Polka." Between the spot on the radio dial that carried Milton Cross's Metropolitan Opera program and that relaying the afternoon baseball game, one could find a nationality station broadcasting Joseph Snaga's Gramophone Orchestra's "Trink, Trink, Brüderlein, Trink," or Cuarteto Caney's "Perfidia," or the Maloof Oriental Orchestra's "Fatima."

443

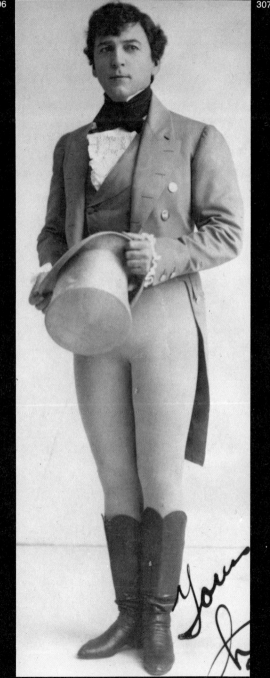

306
Russian-born Al Jolson
handsomely graced the cover
of "My Mammy," a latter-day
pseudo-plantation song from
Broadway's *Sinbad* of 1921.

307
Chauncey Olcott (1860–
1932).

308
Radiola 20 receiver (H 11½"),
manufactured by RCA in
1925 and a Radiola 103
loudspeaker of 1927.

308

In addition to music, radio carried an incredible variety of live broadcasts: the serialized melodramas called "soap operas" (because many were sponsored by laundry-soap companies), sports casts and newscasts, quiz shows, comedy programs, dramas, mystery and detective programs. For thirty-two years the most popular show—a nightly fifteen-minute program which began in 1928—was a comedy series written and acted by Freeman F. Gosden and Charles Correll—"Amos 'n' Andy." In the minstrel and vaudeville tradition, the white comedians Gosden and Correll created a cast of make-believe Negro characters: Amos, Andrew H. Brown, Kingfish George Stevens, Madame Queen, Sapphire, Lightnin', Miss Blue, and more. The lines were spoken in exaggerated dialect and were loaded with malapropisms; there was, however, good comedy and, during their peak years, it was often said that one could take a walk at six in the evening and not miss a word of their program because the show was heard through every open window in the United States. Al Smith said after losing his campaign for the presidency in 1928: "A large part of the American people is far more interested in the Kingfish, the beauty parlor, and the Fresh Air Taxicab Co. than in the affairs of this country." And George Bernard Shaw said: "Three things I'll never forget about America are the Rocky Mountains, Niagara Falls and 'Amos and Andy'!" The show was so popular that numerous motion picture theaters would stop the picture in midreel to allow the audiences to listen to the evening episode. But the traditional blackface humor eventually brought protests from the NAACP and the show folded in 1960.

There were other ethnic and dialect comedies on radio: "Life with Luigi," whose main character was played by un-Italian Allan Reed; "Meet Me at Parky's," a situation comedy built around a restaurant owned by the Greek Parkyakarkis, played by Harry Einstein; "The Goldbergs," started in 1929, which was written, produced, and directed by its female star, Gertrude Berg, giving the show its authenticity in reflecting the trials and hopes of a Jewish family living in the Bronx; "Abie's Irish Rose," converted from a Broadway hit into a radio series that probed the ups and downs of newly wed Jewish Abie (Richard Coogan) and Irish Catholic Rose (Mercedes McCambridge), which provided a good opportunity for the talents of Yiddish theater stars Anna Appell and Menasha Skulnik in supporting roles.

The rapid-fire radio gags of London-born Leslie Town "Bob" Hope were sensational and just the right sort of morale booster for those going off to World War II. He made a number of "Road" pictures with Bing Crosby and Dorothy Lamour (Dorothy Kaumeyer), which were box office hits. Hope easily moved into television and, during World War II and the Korean and Vietnam wars, made numerous personal appearances for fighting men behind the lines. He became one of those entertainers who, like George M. Cohan, John Wayne, and Ronald Reagan, used his public position gained through theatrical success for the purpose of bolstering right-wing patriotism.

Jack Benny (Benjamin Kubelsky, 1894–1975), the Waukegan-born Jewish American, became one of the most beloved comedians who had started in vaudeville but "made it big" in radio. Benny's comedy was not ethnic. It was spun out of spontaneous situations which arose in scenarios that had little, if any, story line. Gilbert Seldes has commented: ". . . Jack Benny has with infinite pains created for himself the character of the ineffectual, the truly undistinguished human being. He is the comedian who does not say funny things and who gets laughs only as they ricochet off him. . . . He is the most skillful comedian I have ever seen work before the public."

Like Jack Benny, Eddie Cantor was an American Jewish star who had started in other areas of entertainment before making a principal career in radio. Cantor, though essentially a comedian in radio, was also a song-and-dance man, with a few hit songs, such as "Whoopee," from the Broadway musical *Whoopee* of 1928–1929, and "(Potatoes are Cheaper—Tomatoes are Cheaper) Now's the Time to Fall in Love," a solid hit in 1931 with those trying to make it through that Depression year. If Benny epitomized the unruffled average man, Cantor often carried on like a nervous wreck, hopping about, making circular gestures with his white-gloved hands, rolling his big "banjo" eyes, which appeared even larger when he worked in blackface. Like nearly every other star comedian of his generation, Cantor worked in motion pictures, appearing in fifteen films between 1929 and 1953, the last of which was *The Eddie Cantor Story*. Hollywood had found it profitable to make a number of films based on the careers of leading entertainers, bandleaders, and a few composers, such as George Gershwin. Among the most successful was *The Jolson Story* of 1946.

The Jolson Story is interesting for several reasons. In the first place, it was a huge success, even though Al Jolson himself never appeared in it. Jolson's voice was dubbed into the sound track while Larry Parks acted in Jolson's place, and the same technique was used three years later for the filming of *Jolson Sings Again*. These films revived Jolson's sagging career, and he recorded a large number of new versions of old songs and a few others which were probably among the best he ever did, like the recording of Berlin's "Alexander's Ragtime Band" with Bing Crosby. The revitalization of the Russian-born Jolson recalled to many that he had made the first feature-length sound motion picture (really a "part talkie") in 1927—*The Jazz Singer*.

Of all the various forms of make-believe entertainment that have flourished, the greatest is probably the movies. Hollywood became a magnet for thousands of aspiring actors from every part of the world. So much of what seemed to be "American" in the motion pictures made in Hollywood was created by immigrants, by talented or glamorous actors and actresses, by directors who molded the film into a medium unlike the stage, unlike the Wild West show, unlike anything that had ever been done in entertainment. There were immigrant directors by the dozens in Hollywood, men such as Ludwig Berger from Germany, who worked with Emil Jannings in *The Sins of the Fathers* (1928); James Stuart Blackstone from England, who directed *Womanhood* and *Safe for Democracy,* both in 1917; Mack Sennett, the Canadian-born director who created a type of film comedy that inspired Charles Chaplin and provided the English-born comedian with his earliest opportunities in Hollywood; Victor Sjöström, the Swedish-born director who filmed *The Scarlet Letter* in 1926; Josef von Sternberg, a native of Vienna who directed *The Last Command* (1928) and Marlene Dietrich's first English-language film, *The Blue Angel* (1930). Ernst Lubitsch, born in Berlin, set a new tone in the motion picture's approach to sex in *The Marriage Circle* (1924), which viewed marriage in a sophisticated, frivolous way that mirrored the changing attitudes of the public in the 1920s. Alexander Korda and Michael Curtiz were successful as Hollywood directors after emigrating from Hungary. Lewis Milestone, who directed the masterful *All Quiet on the Western Front* in 1930, was born in Kishmev, Ukraine. Alfred Hitchcock was a native of London; Elia Kazan was an immigrant from Constantinople; and Frank Capra, who directed *It Happened One Night* (1934), *Mr. Deeds Goes to Town* (1936), and *You Can't Take It with You* (1938), was born in Palermo, Italy, emigrating with his parents from Sicily in 1900 to the orange groves of California.

It was the stars, however, who were immediately apparent to the motion picture audiences. The foreign birth of so many stars never caused Americans to like them less; in fact, it often enhanced their popularity. Of the five most worshiped film stars of the 1920s, four were foreign-born—Mary Pickford, Charles Chaplin [309], Rudolph Valentino [310], and Greta Garbo [311]. The fifth was Douglas Fairbanks. Moreover, the romanticism was heightened by the fact that the early stars were not heard, a difficult thing for many now to comprehend, but as David Robinson has explained: "The silent stars had a magic that could never quite be recaptured in days of talking pictures. The lack of voices did not constitute a deficiency in a specific human attribute. On the contrary, distancing them from ordinary human normality, it added to the mystery and romance and remoteness of the image...."

In the earliest years of film entertainment, the public did not know the names of the performers; the producers attempted to avoid the star system in order to keep the performers from demanding high salaries. But Carl Laemmle, the German-born producer who established Universal Pictures, broke with that young tradition and heralded his signing of Florence Lawrence. By 1915 Theda Bara was being ballyhooed by Fox, and by the end of World War I Canadian-born Mary Pickford was getting $350,000 for each picture and Chaplin was placed under contract for eight two-reelers at one million dollars.

Mary Pickford (Gladys Smith) had started life as a child actress, and her greatest successes were roles that echoed her own hard life as a child who was forced to earn her way after the death of her father. She became "America's Sweetheart" in films such as *Rebecca of Sunnybrook Farm* (1917) and *Little Annie Rooney* (1925), but was a disappointment to her fans in more mature roles such as *Dorothy Vernon of Haddon Hall* (1924). Truly talented, Pickford nevertheless found it personally distasteful to continue playing the role of a child while approaching her middle thirties and retired after appearing in four sound films.

Rudolph Valentino (Rodolpho d'Antonguolla, 1895–1926) reached a pinnacle in American entertainment that no other performer has attained. He emigrated from his native Italy to America in 1913, became a professional ballroom dancer, and played in his first film in 1918. He danced or played Italian villains until June Mathis recognized his potential as a romantic heavy, and Valentino was cast in the starring role of *The Four Horsemen of the Apocalypse* in 1921. His intense sincerity on the screen elevated the seriousness of Valentino's romantic appeal beyond anything attainable by non-Latin lovers. When Valentino's body was placed on view in a Broadway funeral parlor, more than thirty thousand fans crowded past for a farewell glance.

The actor-director-producer Charlie Chaplin was born in London in 1889. With a father who performed in music halls and an actress mother, Chaplin grew up in the slums and spent a long time as a music hall entertainer himself, viewing life much as his tramp clown viewed life in the movies. Even in his two-reelers, Chaplin packed in vital encounters with nearly every human experience and emotion, playing with the effects of love, hate, cruelty, poverty, authority—all handled brilliantly with grace, innovation, rhythm, and superb timing. He was a master at mime and preferred to work in his own anachronistic silent films long after talkies had arrived. With his reputation already established in Hollywood, Chaplin's first hit was *The Kid* (1921), which launched the child actor Jackie Coogan into stardom. Chaplin's work in *The Immigrant* mirrored great sympathy for the greenhorn, and his film *The Gold Rush* (1925) exhibits a profound sensitivity toward victims of privation and greed. His international following was overwhelming, but his political views largely caused him to fall from favor in America after World War II.

309
Charles Chaplin (b. 1889) and
''The Kid,'' Jackie Coogan (b.
1914). Chaplin is a native of
London, England; Coogan
was born in Los Angeles.

310
Rudolph Valentino (1895–
1926), born in Castellaneta,
Italy.

311
Greta Garbo, born in 1905 in
Stockholm, Sweden.

309

310

311

Hundreds of other actors of foreign birth have enriched the American film. Among those who received top billing in silent motion pictures, Gilbert Roland, Ramon Novarro, and Dolores Del Rio were natives of Mexico; May Robson and Leon Errol were born in Australia; Pola Negri was born in Poland [**312**]; Vilma Banky, who had starred with Valentino in *The Eagle* (1925) and *Son of the Sheik* (1926), was a native of Hungary; Claudette Colbert (Lily Chauchoin), who would become an even greater star in the talkies, was born in France [**313**]; Erich von Stroheim, who had no legitimate claim to the "von," was also a director of considerable talent who had emigrated from Austria; Ronald Colman, a leading man who enjoyed a long career in America, was born in Switzerland; Sessue Hayakawa, another actor of great durability in America, was a native of Japan; Greta Garbo was born in Sweden; and Alla Nazimova [**314**], who played opposite Valentino in *Camille* (1921) and starred on stage in O'Neill's *Mourning Becomes Electra*, was born in Yalta, Russia.

Nor were foreign-born actors a phenomenon merely of the silent films. As on the legitimate stage, England sent the most to America to work in the talkies, with Charles Laughton, Cary Grant, Boris Karloff, Elizabeth Taylor, Stanley Laurel, Victor McLaglen, and Sydney Greenstreet ranking among the stars. From Hungary came Paul Lukas (Paul Lugacs), Bela Lugosi (Bela Blasko), and Peter Lorre; from Germany, Marlene Dietrich and Lilli Palmer; from Ireland, Barry Fitzgerald, Greer Garson, Brian Donlevy, and Maureen O'Hara; from France, Simone Simon, Maurice Chevalier, and Charles Boyer; from Mexico, Anthony Quinn and Lupé Velez, the "Mexican Spitfire"; from Sweden, Ingrid Bergman and Viveca Lindfors; and from Austria, Walter Slezak and Hedy Lamarr (Hedwig Eva Maria Kiesler). And there were José Ferrer from Puerto Rico, Laurence Harvey from Lithuania, Maria Montez from the Dominican Republic, Omar Sharif from Egypt, Sabu Mysore, the actor-elephant boy, from India, the highly gifted Paul Muni, a former star of the Yiddish theater, from Lemberg, Poland; Basil Rathbone, who played Sherlock Holmes, from South Africa; Errol Flynn from Tasmania; and Keye Luke from Canton, China.

The entire industry of film making in Hollywood was largely dominated by immigrants. The powerful producers and producer-directors had, by the time the talkies were introduced, developed the business of making motion pictures into the nation's fourth largest industry. The origins of the powerful film magnates fascinated David Robinson, writing about *Hollywood in the Twenties:*

Adolph Zukor was born in Hungary and emigrated to America in 1888, with forty dollars sewn in the lining of his suit. Carl Laemmle came to the States from Germany four years before Zukor and worked for years in menial jobs. William Fox, born in Hungary, was brought to America as a child and before he was seven was helping to support his impoverished family by peddling blacking. Louis B. Mayer, the son of Polish Jews, was born in Minsk and started his life in the new world as a beachcomber and scrap dealer. Sam Goldfish (later Goldwyn) was born in 1884 in Poland, and emigrated at the age of eleven. Harry, Abe, Sam and Jack Warner were the sons of a Polish immigrant cobbler. The eldest boys, Sam and Abe, did all kinds of menial work before they encountered the Edison Kinetoscope while working in an amusement arcade.

The talented beachcombers and spirited waifs of the world, the white minstrels and black jazzmen, ringmasters and bandleaders, composers and comedians, have found that two centuries of avid American audiences have given them identity, mobility, and celebrity [**315**].

312

313
Po a Negri, born in 1899 in
Lip o, Poland.

31
French-born Maurice
Chevalier and Claudette Col-
be t were romantically paired
on the cover of "You Brought
a New Kind of Love to Me," a
hit une of 1930 from the talkie
The Big Pond.

31
Alla Nazimova (1879–1945),
bo n in Yalta, Russia.

313

314

TWICE DAILY 8.45
Matinees 3. P. M.
WARNERS'
AL JOLSON
"THE JAZZ SINGER"
WORLD
MATINEE
FLETCHER
LINGERIE HOSIERY

Baseball—
A Shared
Excitement

Entertainment was a viable means for getting ahead; it was open to the immigrant's talents and, with some luck, yielded handsome returns. Sports, particularly at the professional level, were a different matter. As spectator events they brought thousands of people together from every walk of life and gave them the joy of sharing a common experience. Photographs of crowds of the 1910s, 1920s, and 1930s show seas of heads, mostly male, complete with hat and tie, all absorbed in watching a ball game or a boxing match, a horse race or a football contest. Sports gave immigrants a chance to be part of the ''American'' crowd, to escape—for a time—the ''little Italy'' or ''little Poland'' that was their home.

In the role of participants, however, the foreign-born did not do as spectacularly as they did in entertainment. To be sure, many immigrant groups brought their own sports with them to America and perpetuated them through clubs, fairs, and other clannish get-togethers [316]. And a few sports, such as ice skating [317], which was imported by the Dutch, or skiing, from the Scandinavian countries, have become immensely popular. On rare occasions the unique skill of one sport has served another. The use of soccer-style place kickers in American football is a vivid example. Generally, however, by the time an immigrant arrived he was already in his late teens or early twenties, too old to learn the skills of such American sports as baseball or basketball. For him, the crowd was his arena of participation.

His son, however, had a different opportunity. The superstars of horse racing [318], boxing [319, 320], football [321], and particularly baseball have often been the children of the immigrants in the crowd. And indeed, many of the stars rose above any particular immigrant identity, to become the focal points of a sport, the reasons for the big crowds in the first place.

317
Ice skating, Jamaica Pond,
West Roxbury, Mas-
sachusetts.

318
"The False Start," Jerome
Park, New York, 1868.

318

THE FALSE START   JEROME PARK N.Y.

319
Jack Johnson (right) gains an
easy victory over Jim Jeffries
at Reno, Nevada, in 1910.

320
Thousands of fans paid more
than a million dollars to see
Jack Dempsey knock out the
French fighter Georges Carpentier at Boyle's Thirty Acres
in New Jersey in 1921.

320

In 1876, the nation's centennial year, America's "national game" or "national pastime"—baseball—was set upon a course that eventually carried it to the forefront of commercial sporting activity. In that year, through the establishment of the National League, organized baseball was endowed with an effective if rudimentary commercial framework such as would subsequently characterize other sporting enterprises in which athletes would compete professionally, while investors would derive enormous profits and the public would lavish billions of dollars for vicarious, ephemeral, and memorable pleasures. In 1876 baseball was already approaching what many described as a "national craze." It had not yet assumed its present, refined form, although its essential features had been established. Its origins, as a game requiring a stick or bat and a ball, were ancient, but in America its immediate antecedents were the English games of cricket and rounders. Brought to America by British colonists, rounders had also been called "feeder" in some places in England, and a form of the game had already been known as "baseball" as early as 1744. Oliver Wendell Holmes, who graduated from Harvard in 1829, played baseball there as a student, years before the "invention" later ascribed to General Abner Doubleday (in 1839) supposedly took place.

Baseball gained its initial following in New England, spread to the Midwest in the 1850s, and achieved national popularity during the Civil War, when the northern soldiers taught it to anyone with a few spare hours to pass [322]. In 1858, in Jamaica, New York, admission was charged for the first time and team sponsors immediately sensed the potential for profits that could be derived from spectators. Competition between teams representing different cities soon led to professionalism among the better players, and Alfred J. Reach, an English immigrant who would later derive great profits from his sporting goods business, in 1865 became the first ballplayer to sign a contract to play for money. In 1869 the Cincinnati Red Stockings became the first baseball team to pay all its players. The Reds went on tour and compiled a record of sixty-eight wins, one tie, and no losses. Other clubs soon converted to professional status, and the first professional league—the National Association of Professional Baseball Players—was formed in 1871.

The establishment of the National League in 1876 and the formation of the American Association as a second "major" league in 1882 gave organized baseball its modern business structure, and in 1884 an agreement was reached which ended competition over "territory" rights in cities and competition for players. Each team in these leagues eventually reserved the right to negotiate contracts solely with their own players or with newly discovered talented youngsters. The American Association folded in 1890, but the American League was formed in 1900 in competition with the National. The usual pattern of player "raids" followed for three years, but in 1903 an inter-league agreement was reached which included the reserve clause. Thereafter, new attempts to form competing leagues have failed, and players have been virtually "owned" by the holders of team franchises. This form of organization has been widely copied by other commercially organized team sports.

In 1900 restrictive laws prevented Sunday games except for those clubs in Chicago, Cincinnati, and St. Louis—cities with a heavy German and mid-European immigrant population. By World War I, only Detroit, Cleveland, and Washington had liberalized the "blue laws" and allowed Sunday baseball. It was not until fifteen years after World War I that the other major league cities were all free from the Sunday ban, but baseball, nevertheless, proved to be a primary force behind the campaign to liberalize these laws.

The nation's preoccupation with the sport was reinforced by the emergence of sportswriters as popular figures—writers such as Damon Runyon, Grantland Rice, Ring Lardner, Paul Gallico, Westbrook Pegler, John Keiran, and Gordon Cobbledick. During the 1920s, play-by-play radio broadcasts further stimulated public interest. The mania was fueled by adulation of stars such as Cy Young, Ty Cobb, Honus Wagner, Babe Ruth, and Joe DiMaggio, and amateur activity flourished across the country. Every back alley and vacant lot became a playing field, each with its special "ground rules." At the same time, the regular rules, as established by the professional leagues, were passionately imbibed by youngsters with an enthusiasm that surpassed any comparable effort demanded for learning routine school lessons. Although only a few youngsters made it from the sandlots to the big leagues—like the German Americans George Uhle and Urban Shocker (Schockeor) and the Bohemian American Joe Vosmik—boyhood passion for the game usually remained.

In the large cities interest in amateur clubs often equaled and sometimes surpassed that shown for the local professionals. The game between the Telling Strollers and the Hanna Street Cleaners in Cleveland's Brookside Park for the city championship of 1914 attracted 80,000 fans, and a year later, in the same park (a natural amphitheater with a grass-covered sloping hillside for "stands" on three sides of the playing field), a crowd in excess of 100,000 watched the Cleveland White Autos defeat the Omaha Luxus for the world amateur championship. At one time shortly before World War II, the greater Pittsburgh area supported nineteen amateur baseball leagues.

Fan interest in professional baseball stimulated the construction of giant stadiums. The combined attendance of both major leagues grew from 3.5 million in 1901 to 7 million by 1908 [**323**]. In 1920, the New York Yankees alone drew 1,289,422 spectators, largely the result of Babe Ruth, who had just been "purchased" from the Boston Red Sox. Between 1910 and 1920 new baseball stadiums of concrete and steel construction replaced the older wood stands, the new, modern plants including the Polo Grounds in New York, Comisky Park in Chicago, Ebbets Field in Brooklyn, and League Park in Cleveland [**324, 325**]. Yankee Stadium—"The House that Ruth Built" —was opened in 1923, with a seating capacity of 65,000. In the Depression year of 1931, Cleveland's Municipal Stadium was completed, with more than 78,000 permanent seats. Although the automobile—which enabled many additional fans to drive to the ball parks after World War I—enlarged people's recreational horizons, thus cutting into baseball attendance, it has been estimated that some 100 million fans still witness baseball games, either in person or on TV, every year.

In its popularity, baseball has attracted a great number of talented players from a variety of social and ethnic backgrounds. Millions of immigrant parents became baseball fans and encouraged their offspring to pursue the game, knowing that the "work" was easier than being a factory hand and that the rewards could be great. The universal belief that baseball was a "clean" and noble activity—despite the open gambling at some of the parks and occasional scandals such as the Black Sox affair of 1919—also stimulated faith in the game. Yet a peculiar feature of organized baseball was its policy of excluding Negro players until 1946, when John Roosevelt "Jackie" Robinson was signed to play in 1947 with the Brooklyn Dodgers [**326**]. The American League also followed an anti-black policy until 1947, when Larry Doby was signed by the Cleveland Indians.

The prevailing national mood and the prejudices of a few influential players and executives—men like Adrian Constantine "Cap" Anson—lay at the bottom of the anti-Negro policy, although exclusivity was not at first universally observed, and the Toledo team of the American Association employed the Walker brothers, Moses and Weldy, during the season of 1884. Frank Ulysses Grant, a second baseman in the 1880s, was regarded as the best black player of the nineteenth century.

By 1890, however, the few Negroes who had played on white teams were dropped from minor league franchises. On the other hand, all-black teams, such as the Cuban Giants of Trenton and the New York Gothams, were quite successful and, during the 1890s, became members of minor league circuits essentially composed of white teams. Leagues of mixed composition, however, did not survive into the twentieth century. In 1907 the International League of Colored Baseball Clubs was formed, and by 1910 segregation within organized baseball was nearly complete. Black teams opposed white teams only in the off season or off days, on barnstorming tours, or in Cuba during the winter.

The Negro National League was organized in 1920 in Kansas City, and in 1921 the International became the Eastern Colored League. Between 1924 and 1932, when the Depression ended both leagues, the pennant-winning black teams met in an annual World Series. A few years after the collapse, black baseball was again revived in a two-league system. Some of the great black players of the period were Joe "Cyclone" Williams, Dick Redding, Home Run Johnson, and Josh Gibson [**327**]. Leroy "Satchel" Paige [**328**], the great pitcher whose active career spanned the years from 1926 to 1965, was the only established veteran black player to move into the white major leagues. Paige was among the top-money players of his day in black baseball, earning as much as $35,000 in a single season. Jackie Robinson, Larry Doby, Roy Campanella, Sam Jethroe, and Monte Irvin all had youthful experience in the Negro leagues before the all-white policy was reformed—virtually single-handed—by Branch Rickey.

With the exception of the Negro, organized baseball was an open road to social and economic advancement to the outsider and the uprooted. Louis Sockalexis, a full-blooded Penobscot Indian, became a major league outfielder before the end of the nineteenth century [**329**]. Among other Indians was Charles "Chief" Bender, a pitcher for fourteen years with the Philadelphia Athletics, who ranked with the best [**330**]. Bender was a Chippewa who had graduated from the Carlisle Indian School. John "Chief" Meyers played for John McGraw in the New York Giants and the Boston Braves between 1909 and 1917. There were also Moses Yellowstone, a Pawnee, George Johnson, a Winnebago, and Ben Tincup. The most outstanding all-round Indian athlete was Jim Thorpe, a Sac and Fox, who also graduated from Carlisle. After Thorpe had won an impressive number of medals in the 1912 Olympics, John McGraw succeeded in signing him for the Giants, where he played for seven years.

Players of Jewish origin were tolerated on ball teams, though somewhat grudgingly. It is claimed that of the eight Cohens to play in the majors, seven changed their names. The New York Giants, on the other hand, made numerous attempts to sign good Jewish-American players to increase their neighborhood patronage in the Bronx. They brought in Benny Kauff, Moses Solomon, and Andy Cohen, but these players never achieved the superstardom the management hoped for. Hank Greenberg, born in New York, played for Detroit, hit fifty-eight home runs in 1938 and again in 1947, and was elected to the Hall of Fame [**331**]. Morris "Moe" Berg was a catcher for most of his playing days between 1925 and 1939, mainly spent in the American League. His Jewish parents emigrated from the Ukraine and settled in New York. Berg was admitted to the New York bar in 1929, was a world traveler who spoke seven languages, and acted as spy for the United States during World War II. Morris "Snooker" Arnovich played his best days in the outfield for the Philadelphia Phillies between 1936 and 1940, and Sanford "Sandy" Koufax, the great pitcher of the Dodgers in both Brooklyn and Los Angeles, compiled an incredible record of 165 wins and 87 losses in twelve seasons. His best season, 1966, was his last (because of arm trouble): a record of 27-9, with 317 strikeouts.

Latin Americans, numerous in the majors since World War II, had been imported sporadically since 1882. Rafael Almeida, a third baseman, and Armando Marsans, an outfielder, were signed by Cincinnati in 1911. Other Cubans reached the American leagues in the following years and included Jacinto Calvo, Balmadero Acosta, Angel Aragon, Emilio Palmero, José Rodriquez, Eusebio Gonzales, Oscar Tuero, Miguel Gonzalez, and Adolfo Luque. Cuban players, however, were often subjected to abuse by fans and fellow players who suspected that they were part Negro. The great Cuban pitcher José Mendez was not signed by an American team because his features were thought to be "too Negroid."

The Puerto Rican Roberto Walker Clemente]332], as Smith's offical history of the Baseball Hall of Fame acknowledges, was

... one of organized baseball's true heroes. Unlike too many of the men who performed miraculous feats on the diamond, Clemente devoted much of his time, energy and income to improving the lot of his poorer friends and neighbors. A man of wide ranging intellect, Clemente involved himself in all sorts of causes far removed from professional athletics. ...

The Hall of Fame waived its five-year waiting period in order to honor this great man. But actually Roberto Clemente honors the Hall of Fame by his presence there.

Clemente had been killed in a plane crash off Puerto Rico in 1972 while en route to aid the victims of a severe earthquake in Nicaragua.

Among a number of outstanding Polish-American players was Aloysius Harry Simmons, whose real name was Szymanski. Simmons won the batting championship twice, compiling a lifetime average of .334 in twenty-one seasons in both major leagues. Stanley Anthony Coveleski, whose brother Harry was also a major league player, was a pitcher who starred at Cleveland and compiled a record of 215 wins and 141 losses over a career of fourteen seasons in the American League. In the 1920 World Series, Coveleski accomplished the rare feat of winning three games, working nine full innings of each of the three. Stanley Frank "Stan the Man" Musial, from the mill town of Donora, Pennsylvania, had a lifetime batting average of .331 in twenty-two summers as an outfielder and first baseman with the St. Louis Cardinals. Musial became one of the few players to appear in more than 3,000 games and was second only to Ty Cobb in total lifetime major league hits—3,630. Casimir "Cass" Michaels (Kwietniewski), from Detroit, spent twelve seasons on the infields of the American League, from 1943 to 1954; George "Whitey" Kurowski played third base for the Cardinals and hit more than .300 in four of his nine summers; Frankie Pytlak spent twelve years as a catcher with the Indians and Red Sox; William Urbanski, from Linoleumville, New York, played shortstop for the Boston National League team in the 1930s; and William "Glue Glove" Mazeroski starred as a second baseman for the Pittsburgh Pirates.

Several French-American players stood out in the majors, but Napoleon Lajoie and Louis Boudreau, both members of the Hall of Fame, topped the list. Lajoie, a second baseman who played twenty-one seasons in Philadelphia and Cleveland between 1896 and 1916, attained a lifetime average of .339. As a fielder, Lajoie was rated with Honus Wagner and was regarded as one of the most graceful players ever to appear on a diamond [**333**]. Oldsters, such as Roger Angell's father, never lost the visual memory of Lajoie in action:

A great broad-shouldered fellow, but a beautiful fielder. He was a rough customer, If he didn't like an umpire's call, he'd give him a faceful of tobacco juice. The shortstop was Terry Turner—a smaller man, and blond. I can still see Lajoie picking up a grounder and wheeling and floating the ball over to Turner. Oh, he was quick on his feet!

It was French-American Boudreau and German-American Ken Keltner who teamed up to stop Italian-American Joe DiMaggio's incredible hitting streak of fifty-six games before 67,468 fans under the lights in Cleveland on July 17, 1941. Franklin A. Lewis described the action in *The Cleveland Indians:*

Joe sent a screaming grounder over the third base bag. Ken Keltner backhanded the ball with his glove hand, straightened up, and shipped the ball to first. In a later inning, DiMaggio again pulled the ball down the third-base line. And again Keltner made the play "after the ball was past him," as observers later said, to throw out the sweating Californian. In the ninth, DiMaggio made his final bid. Bagby had replaced Smith [on the mound]. Joe sent a terrific smash to shortstop. The ball was hit so hard that Boudreau barely got his hand on the ball, but scooped it up and started a double play.

Since the 1920s, baseball has been enriched by the superior playing abilities of Italian Americans. Joseph Paul "Joltin' Joe" DiMaggio and his brothers, Dom and Vince, were California-born sons of Sicilian immigrants. In the great shadow cast by Joe, it has been easy to lose sight of Dom's successful career in the Boston Red Sox outfield from 1940 to 1953, playing in 1,399 games, hitting over .300 in four full seasons, and reaching a .298 lifetime batting average. Vince also played the outfield, but in the National League from 1937 to 1946, in 1,110 major league games.

Joe DiMaggio [**334**], who played his first full season with the New York Yankees in 1936, was a star from the beginning, arriving in the season that followed the retirement of Babe Ruth. A "pull" hitter, who specialized in long drives, Joe hit in 1,736 games for a lifetime average of .325. DiMaggio's most famous record was his hitting safely in fifty-six consecutive games from May 15 through July 16, 1941—for a .408 average. He had exceeded records set by Rogers Hornsby, George Sisler, and Willie Keeler—all giants of the game. He won the league batting championship twice. As an outfielder, he was among the fastest and most graceful. DiMaggio's marriage to Marilyn Monroe in 1954, after his retirement but at the height of her career, caused a sensation.

The Yankees seemed to evolve into a special haven for Italian Americans, and most of them were superior players—Anthony "Poosh 'Em Up" Lazzeri, Frank "Crow" Crosetti, Phil "Scooter" Rizzuto, Lawrence "Yogi" Berra, and hot-tempered Alfred Manuel "Billy" Martin (real name, Pesano) among them. Elsewhere and at different times, fans enjoyed the skills of Ralph Arthur "Babe" Pinelli (Rinaldo Angelo Paolinelli), a steady, productive infielder who spent most of the 1920s with Cincinnati; Harry "Cookie" Lavagetto, another good National League infielder; the fine pitcher Salvatore Anthony Maglie, who won most of his 119 victories with the New York Giants; and Joseph Henry Garagiola, the catcher who appeared in 676 National League games between 1946 and 1954 and went on to become a television personality, revealing the multitalented character so often exhibited by others who started in baseball.

It is well known that English and Irish Americans have always been present in baseball in great numbers. Cecil Travis, a .313 hitter for Washington; Harry Bartholomew Hooper, the outfielder; Ted "Teddy Ballgame" Williams of Boston are easily recalled. There were Cornelius "Connie Mack" McGillicuddy; Steve O'Neill and Arnold "Mickey" Owen, the catchers; the Delahanty brothers—five of them—Edward, Frank ("Pudgie"), James, Joseph, and Thomas. Big Ed Delahanty was the most famous, playing from 1888 until 1903, batting .400 or better in two seasons and .345 for an amazing lifetime average.

The baseball "ethnics" were not all second-generation. In addition to the imported Cuban players, there was Melo Baldomero "Mel" Almada, one of the relatively few players of Mexican birth. Patrick Joseph Donovan [**335**], an outfielder from 1890 to 1907, who also managed five major league teams, was born in County Cork, Ireland. John Joseph Doyle, born in Killorglin, Ireland, played for seventeen seasons (1889–1905) in the majors, mainly at first base, and compiled a lifetime average of .302. Charles Joseph "Curry" Foley, who played as a pitcher, first baseman, and outfielder from 1879 to 1885, was born in Milltown, Ireland. The great Roger Patrick Bresnahan (1880–1944), the hard-hitting catcher who invented shin guards, was born in Tralee. James H. Hallinan (1849–1879), Andrew Jackson Leonard (1846–1903), and Henry Cooke "Irish" McIlveen (1880–1960) were among a number of players who emigrated from Ireland. Alexander John Schauer Dimitrihoff, who pitched from 1913 to 1917 in both leagues, was born in Odessa, Russia. Jacob Charles "Chick" Fraser was a native of Switzerland, Edward "Parson" Lewis was born in Wales, and Arndt Jorgens was from Norway. Marino Paul "Chick" Pieretti, an American League relief pitcher from 1945 to 1950, was an immigrant from Marlia, Italy. Elmer Valo, the durable outfielder who played on numerous teams in both leagues from 1940 to 1961, compiling a lifetime average of .282 and topping .300 in five full seasons, was born in Ribnik, Czechoslovakia.

Frederick "Dutch" Schliebner, a first baseman with the St. Louis Browns in 1923, was born in Germany, as was William J. Kuehne (Knelme), a third baseman from 1883 to 1892. The players of German descent have given baseball some of its most memorable and zaniest moments. Among the all-time greats the German Americans contributed are Babe Ruth, Honus Wagner, Lou Gehrig, Frank Frisch, Rube Waddell, Heinie Groh, Bob Meusel, Heinie Manush, and Ray Schalk.

Babe Ruth stories have been retold for decades, and his feats have become legendary [336]. Ruth attracted fans to ball parks in unheard-of numbers in the 1920s. The money that poured in at the gate did much to transform baseball into the lucrative monopolistic business it has remained. The appeal of Ruth was not in a little way grounded in his rags-to-riches career, rising as he did from the poor immigrant neighborhoods of Baltimore's South Side and the friendly confines of St. Mary's Industrial School for Boys of the City of Baltimore. Contrary to popular myth, Ruth was not an orphan. His mother, Katie, was a German-Catholic immigrant and his father, a Lutheran from Pennsylvania, was of mixed German and Irish descent. The Babe was given his father's name—George Herman Ruth. Ruth's parents lived over his father's saloon in a rough district. The day after a shooting that followed an argument in the saloon, Ruth was placed in St. Mary's by his father, apparently at the urging of the court. Babe entered St. Mary's in 1902, when he was seven. Although he seldom spoke of his parents, he did maintain contact with them. German was spoken in his home, and sportswriter Fred Lieb, who would occasionally chat with Lou Gehrig [337] in German, was surprised when Ruth joined the conversation one day, speaking German "surprisingly well."

Ruth's exploits on the diamond surpassed anything that had been done before. He was at first an excellent pitcher for the Boston Red Sox (1914–1919) and then an unmatched slugger and graceful outfielder for the New York Yankees from 1920 until 1934. He played a few games for Boston in the National League before retiring in 1935. Ruth's records are still committed to memory by fans, even though some of the marks have been topped. His lifetime batting average of .342, his pitching record of 93 wins and 44 losses, his good home run years of 54 in 1920, 59 in 1921, and 60 in 1927, remain part of the Ruth magic. Ruth was voted, in one poll, along with English-born Charlie Chaplin, the most popular American of his day. He undoubtedly ranked with Charles Lindbergh and Sergeant York in public esteem, despite his well-known gargantuan appetite and unquenchable thirst for bootleg hooch and beer, despite arrests for traffic violations, and despite publicly circulated rumors of marital unhappiness with his first wife. He was constantly followed by reporters, and when he was hospitalized for a stomach ache newspapers carried bulletins about his health on the front page until the crisis passed. As the New York Yankees traveled across the country, crowds would gather at station platforms along the way to steal a glance at the Babe sitting at the window, eating, drinking, or playing cards.

He earned the highest baseball salaries ever paid. During the Depression a reporter noted that Ruth's salary was higher than the President's. Ruth retorted, "Hell, I had a better year than Hoover." Another reporter observed that "The poor could wrap their dreams around him." Although fabulously rich by the factory worker's standard, Ruth was at the same time the epitome of American democracy.

John Peter "Honus" Wagner (1874–1955), born in Carnegie, Pennsylvania, was another German American with a flock of nicknames, such as "the Flying Dutchman," "Jay," and "Old Bowlegs" [338]. Wagner is still regarded as one of the best players of all time, never having batted under .300 in three seasons in the minors and seventeen in the majors with Louisville and Pittsburgh. He played until the age of forty, compiling a lifetime batting average of .329, and led the National League hitters in eight seasons. Rube Marquard, the superb pitcher for the Giants, recalled that Wagner

. . . was a wonderful fielder, you know, terrific arm, very quick, all over the place grabbing sure hits. . . . You'd never think it to look at him, of course. He looked so awkward, bowlegged, barrel-chested, about 200 pounds. And yet he could run like a scared rabbit. He had enormous hands and when he scooped up the ball at shortstop, he'd grab half the infield with it. . . . Talk about speed. That bowlegged guy stole over 700 bases in the 21 years he played in the big leagues. A good team man, too, and the sweetest disposition in the world. The greatest ballplayer who ever lived, in my book.

And then there was George Edward "Rube" Waddell, another German American from Pennsylvania, who compiled a pitching record of 197–138 in thirteen seasons in both leagues between 1897 and 1910 [**339**]. His appearances and absences from the ball park were unpredictable: he had a penchant for "epic beer benders" and fishing trips. Sam Crawford, who played for Detroit, remembered that Waddell's arrival at the park was often cause for excitement in the grandstand. There would be a roar: "Here comes Rube!" Waddell would come racing through the stands and then "he'd jump down onto the field, cut across the infield to the clubhouse, taking off his shirt as he went. In about three minutes—he never wore any underwear—he'd run back out on the field in uniform all ready to pitch." In 1903, Rube climbed into the stands during a game and beat up a heckling gambler. On another day, in the middle of a game, Waddell jumped the center field fence to chase a fire engine. The Columbus *Dispatch* called him "thoughtless about married life," because "he took frequent wives and led an exciting life with them and with their relatives, being in and out of jail for non-support and occasionally varying the monotony by shying a flat-iron or other missile at one of his parents-in-law."

But the Rube was lovable. He saved the life of a drowning man in icy water. He also saved the life of his teammate Danny Hoffman when he was knocked to the ground by a fast pitch. While others stood and looked at the unconscious player, Waddell lifted him gently to his shoulders, ran out of the stadium to the street, and hailed a carriage to get Hoffman to the hospital. Still wearing his uniform, Waddell stayed at Hoffman's bedside until the next day, holding ice bags on Danny's head all night. Waddell died at thirty-seven.

For sheer nonsense, however, probably nobody topped Herman A. "Germany" Schaefer (1878–1919), a second baseman who spent more than fifteen years in the big leagues. In the off seasons, he appeared as a comedian in vaudeville with Charles O'Leary; on the field, he kept everyone howling. Perhaps his zaniest antic occurred in a 1908 game between Detroit and Cleveland. With Crawford at bat and Schaefer on first and Davy Jones on third, Schaefer gave the sign for a double steal. The Cleveland catcher held the ball while Schaefer stole second, holding Jones on third. On the next pitch, with Schaefer on second and Jones on third, Jones recalled:

Schaefer yelled, "Let's try it again!" And with a blood-curdling shout he took off like a wild Indian back to first base, *and dove in headfirst in a cloud of dust. He figured the catcher might throw to first since he evidently wouldn't throw to second—and then I could come home same as before.*

But nothing happened. Nothing at all. Everybody just stood there and watched Schaefer with their mouths open . . .

So there we were, back where we started, with Schaefer on first and me on third. And on the next pitch darned if he didn't let out another war whoop and take off again *for second base. By this time the Cleveland catcher evidently had enough, because he threw to second to get Schaefer, and when he did I took off for home, and both of us were safe.*

The incident precipitated an emergency meeting of league officials and a new rule, requiring base runners to run counterclockwise, was solemnly promulgated.

Henry Louis "Hank" Aaron was born in Mobile, Alabama, in 1934, the last year Babe Ruth played in a Yankee uniform. On the evening of April 8, 1974, before 35 million television viewers and 53,000 fans perched in Atlanta Stadium, Aaron hit his 715th regular-season home run, breaking Ruth's record, which had stood since 1935. It was in every way a remarkable achievement and, in many respects, not a mere feat of baseball skill and endurance. That home run demonstrated that baseball was still the avenue to upward social and economic mobility it had always seemed to be, yet it also threw into sharp relief the advances that not only baseball but all America had made since the days of Cap Anson and John McGraw. The words of *The Sporting News* publisher, J. G. Taylor Spink, crystallized the image:

Baseball is the American success story. It is the only avenue of escape for thousands of boys born into a dreary environment of poverty. It is, moreover, a great common ground on which bartenders and bishops, clergymen and bosses, bankers and laborers meet with true equality and understanding. The game has proved in everyday language that democracy works. [**340**]

322
Early baseball scene, 1863.
"Union prisoners at Salis-
bury, N.C."

323
The grandstands in Boston,
late nineteenth century.

324
Fans at the Polo Grounds in
New York during the 1920s.

324

Fans of the Brooklyn Dodgers
in Ebbets Field in 1930.

325
Fans of the Brooklyn Dodgers
in Ebbets Field in 1930.

326
Jackie Robinson, an out-
standing infielder and .311 hitter with the Brooklyn Dodgers
from 1947 to 1956.

471

471

328

327

329

ENDER, P.
ADELPHIA ATHLETICS, A. L.

330

331

327
Josh Gibson was regarded by
many as the greatest slugger
in baseball history, hitting 75
home runs in 1931, 67 in
1932, 72 in 1933, and 69 in
1934. He is shown playing for
the Homestead Grays
c. 1944.

328
Leroy "Satchel" Paige (b.
1906) was one of the fastest
and most effective pitchers to
play the game. After a long
career in the Negro leagues,
he was brought to Cleveland
in 1948 at the age of forty-two
and won six games to help
gain the American League
pennant.

329
The American Indian baseball
outfielder Louis Francis
"Chief" Sockalexis (1873–
1913) was a sensation at Holy
Cross and in his first year with
a major league team in 1897,
batting .331, playing the outfield superbly, and stealing
bases as though he owned
them.

330
Charles "Chief" Bender
(1883–1954) pitched in 482
major league games, winning
204 and losing 129. Bender
was one of several Indians
who achieved stardom in the
majors.

331
Henry Benjamin "Hank"
Greenberg (b. 1911), the
most successful Jewish-
American major league star,
spent eleven seasons with
the Detroit Tigers, hitting 58
home runs in 1938 and finishing with a .313 lifetime batting
average.

332
Robert Walker Clemente (1934–1972), born in Carolina, Puerto Rico, starred with the Pittsburgh Pirates for seventeen seasons, compiling a lifetime batting average of .318.

333
French-American Napoleon "Larry" Lojoie (1875–1959), peerless second baseman and .339 hitter in the big leagues from 1896 to 1916.

334
Italian-American Joe DiMaggio (b. 1914), star slugger with a .325 average for the New York Yankees from 1936 through 1951.

627 NAPOLEON L
CLEVELA

333

334

332

335

336

337

338

339

340

335
Patrick Joseph Donovan (1865–1953), starred in the outfield and at bat with a number of baseball teams between 1890 and 1907. He batted over .300 in twelve seasons and managed major league teams during eleven seasons, eight of them while he was still active as a player.

336
German-American George Herman "Babe" Ruth (1895–1948), star pitcher and master of the home run in the major leagues from 1914 to 1935 and holder of a lifetime .342 batting average.

337
German-American Henry Louis "Lou" Gehrig (1903–1941), the Iron Man of the New York Yankees from 1923 to 1939, a .340 lifetime hitter who played in 2,130 consecutive games between 1925 and 1939.

338
German-American John Peter "Honus" Wagner (1874–1955), the .329 hitter for Louisville and Pittsburgh, regarded as the best shortstop of his day.

339
German-American George Edward "Rube" Waddell, one of the greatest clowns of the diamond, was also a great left-handed pitcher in both major leagues between 1897 and 1910, playing more than twenty games in four consecutive seasons for Connie Mack's Philadelphia Athletics.

340
If the big leagues discriminated against Negro baseball players, such exclusion was not necessarily practiced in vacant lots in the poor neighborhoods of large cities. Youngsters take time out from softball in a Cleveland neighborhood game for their photograph c. 1925.

Chapter 23

At Home

The American Dream

To enter the American middle class and to own a home filled with the latest household conveniences was a dream common to innumerable immigrants. The road to achieving that dream, however, was often long and disappointing.

Like everything else in America, the new residence and its contents were usually sufficiently unlike Old World counterparts to keep the newcomers aware that they were in an alien land. Those who settled in rural areas were most able to replicate some familiar features of the architecture of the old country [**341**]. More often, American practice in house and barn construction prevailed, with mass-produced building components and locally available materials frequently dictating the form and composition of the shelter. The majority of immigrants who settled in a city—and even many who took up farming—moved into living quarters that were typically American.

To the newcomers, who had customarily known but one place of residence, Americans seemed to be forever moving somewhere else; even within the cities there was a constant shifting about. In northern industrial and commercial centers, where millions of poor immigrants settled, the oldest and most dilapidated housing was the initial home for the "greenhorn" [**342, 343**]. But as savings accumulated or a better-paying job became available, the immigrant's first residence was often abandoned for better quarters. In most northern cities, the streetcar lines obviated the need to live close to one's place of employment.

The houses in the poorest sections of the northern cities often sheltered immigrants in a cyclical pattern reflecting the waves of arrivals at Castle Garden and Ellis Island [**344**]. The house occupied by Anna Maria Gavin Egan, a native of Ireland who spent the latter part of her life in the Point district of Brooklyn, seems typical for early twentieth century:

The city house she rented for eighteen dollars a month was an abandoned mansion, let to her because my dead grandfather had "done favors at the Hall" [Tammany Hall] to someone dead even longer than he. [Winston] Churchill's mother was born five minutes' walk from it. The Protestants, for that was what she called native-born Americans, moved out as the immigrants moved in. The first wave of immigrants must have been German and Scandinavian: there were still a few families of them left in my day [the 1920s]. Then from the backyard tenement houses on the other side of Court Street in Brooklyn, the Irish began to move in. They were succeeded by the Italians, with whom they lived in uncertain amity.

Her house was a narrow brownstone, two windows to every floor except the ground, where the place of one window was taken by a double door of solid walnut plated with layers of dust-pocked cheap black enamel. Its shallow stoop, with ornate, Gothic-arched wrought-iron railings eaten away by rust, was fronted by a long area (pronounced "airy").

A stationery store had nibbled into the basement of the brownstone. . . . It was run by the Wechslers, the only Jews in the neighborhood. They were beloved by Irish and Italians alike, because of their kindness to children, and because they had the only phone on the block, and would walk the block's length to call a person to it.

What semblance there was of urban permanence was often the result of the immigrant's desire to reside among people who spoke his native tongue and shared his religion or other cultural customs. But after the Civil War many of the urban German neighborhoods began to break up, and somewhat later many of the original "Irishtowns" as well. Today, within the memory of those born before World War II, most Little Russias, Little Italies, and a host of other enclaves within the nation's cities have either disappeared or dwindled to a fraction of their former size. Despite the desire of many European-born to set down roots and reestablish a sense of place, the second and third generations have scattered widely, helping to make impermanence of residence one of the more commonly shared experiences in America.

Though the immigrants found a new and sometimes tempting mobility in America, they encountered too a peculiar and depressing quality of sameness no matter where they moved. Their very shelter usually confronted them with machine-produced uniformity and drabness [345]. In the building trades, especially house construction, the structures were assembled on the site by hand, but the materials and the thousands of components of the house were mass-produced in standardized forms. In the cities after the Civil War, nearly all the lumber for housing was cut and shaped at mills to nationwide standards of width and thickness; even the lengths of stock lumber became standardized on two-foot modules, usually starting with eight-foot lengths and progressing up to fourteen-foot and longer pieces. This standardization as a rule determined the height, length, and width of rooms and, indeed, the average sizes of dwellings in more general ways.

Standardization in housing did not stop there, of course. Window sashes and frames and casings, doors, newel posts, fireplace mantels, and eventually kitchen and bathroom cabinets were prefabricated in shops miles from the building site. Glass, pipe and fittings, wire, porch and staircase spindles, bricks, tile, hardware, and numerous other components were manufactured perhaps hundreds or even thousands of miles from the house. Basic building materials had become so standardized by the close of the nineteenth century and the methods of assembling the parts so systematized that most urban homes of low or average price assumed the look-alike appearance that characterizes American housing to the present day. Even the charming and capricious decorations applied by the Victorian carpenter-builders ultimately failed to relieve the drabness that underlay gingerbread camouflage. Indeed, the various components of the gingerbread itself were, for the most part, mass-produced.

The arrangement of the living spaces was also predictable. The living room became the "front room." The kitchen and bathroom—or water closet, after indoor plumbing became more common during the early part of this century—were generally located side by side, certainly not an ideal arrangement, but it was economical and less laborious for plumbers to run the pipes and drains through a common wall. In many detached houses and the more generous tenements, a dining room was usually positioned between front room and kitchen, which was invariably located at the back of the quarters. The arrangement is so commonplace that it hardly merits description. Yet an immigrant carpenter who had the rare opportunity to design and build his own house in a midwestern city during the late 1890s chose to place the principal entrance to the house in the kitchen. He was plagued for the rest of his thirty-four years with hearing the same remark from strangers entering the front door: "A *kitchen* . . . how novel!"

In broad terms, there were limited forms of housing available to the majority of immigrants. In the crowded port cities of the East, the traditional row houses for many years dominated the neighborhoods, for the simple reason that land values were high [346, 347]. While horse-car street railways in the 1850s enabled investors to construct new residences beyond the old city confines, an adequate economic return from row houses perpetuated that type of housing in Philadelphia and Baltimore. With horse-car routes limited by the difficult terrain in interior cities such as Pittsburgh and Cincinnati, row houses were also favored there. The form was modified in other places—Newark and Boston, for example—where four-story flats appeared before the Civil War. For the most part these structures were clapboard or brick veneer applied over a basic wood frame. On busy streets the ground floors of multistory tenements were often converted to commercial quarters, which increased the owner's returns and provided numerous immigrants with the opportunity to become shopkeepers. Immigrants living in the single-family row houses in cities like Baltimore also found that there was a good chance of eventually owning one of the units. The multidecked dwellings elsewhere held less promise.

341
The sod house built (1887) by
Isadore Haumont, an immi-
grant from Belgium, in an area
of Nebraska known as the
French Table. Although it was
common American practice to
construct sod buildings west
of the Mississippi, immigrants
such as Haumont occasion-
ally followed European architectural forms as an expression of sentiment for the
old country, even though the
addition of essentially decorative elements required extra
labor and materials.

342
Laundry drying over a back
court of New York City tenements, c. 1910. The balconies
are crammed with flower pots,
vegetable bins (for potatoes),
flats of small plants (perhaps
herbs, carrots, or radishes), a
stalk of bananas, and a bread
box or two. (Photograph by
Jacob A. Riis.)

341

344

343

343
Teeming with immigrants in about 1905, Mulberry Street was typical of the high-density tenement neighborhoods of New York City. Pushcarts with peppers, eggplants, apples, potatoes, string beans, rhubarb line the gutter of the street, which carries both pedestrian and wagon traffic. Horse manure remains unswept. Shops, offering shoes and boots, ready-made clothing, yard goods, blankets, and trunks, occupy the ground floor of nearly every tenement and commercial bank. Business signs show a range of ethnicity, even in this Italian-dominated block: Rizzo and Foglia, Brokers; Banca Malzone; Welz & Zerweck, Beer; Beneke Bros. The real estate (and rental) office sells used furniture, haphazardly stacked on the sidewalk. Drying laundry hangs from balconies which, in most buildings visible here, are provided with fire escapes. Street lighting is by gas lamp.

344
The tenement flat of an immigrant couple and at least five youngsters in New York City, 1910. The crudely plastered room is illuminated by a single open gas jet overhead. Only a fragment of linoleum remains on the floor beneath the father's feet. The small room behind the father contains an iron-framed, brass-trimmed bed, a variety of shabby clothing hung from nails driven into the walls and woodwork, a child's buggy tipped on end, and other possessions wrapped in paper next to lard can and a solitary Mason jar on a shelf. A cheap washboard leans against the foot of the bed. The interior glass window, with the lower sash partly raised, admits some light and a bit of air to the inner bedroom. The kitchen includes a second but simpler iron-framed bed and a sagging iron-framed crib. On the floor, to the left of the crib, are a dishpan and wine bottle. The girl in the foreground sits on a chair but the father sits on an upturned wooden crate. The girl and boy at left are well dressed, but the father has worn a hole at the knee of his right trouser leg. The glass-doored cupboard displays a few dishes on shelves lined and decorated with napkins. The original wood-burning stove is temporarily unused—probably because of summer heat—and covered with newspapers, on which rests the portable double gas burner, connected to the exposed gas pipe by a kinked rubber hose. The enameled kettle and pot are chipped and encrusted with carbon. A water-cooled smoking pipe—a hookah—rests on the shelf over the stove and is the only possession that seems to give evidence of the family's Old World origins. Newspapers cover the wall under the cupboard, probably hiding broken plaster. An improvised curtain covers the window of the door, providing privacy for the family circle.

483

345
Balloon-frame brick-veneer houses of identical pattern in the mill town of Bethlehem, Pennsylvania. Although inexpensively constructed perhaps twenty to thirty years before World War I, such brick dwellings survived quite well, as this photograph of 1935 indicates. Only a few wooden porch posts have been replaced by brick piers.

346
The row houses of Baltimore, with their famous white steps, were home to thousands of immigrants. Babe Ruth, the son of a German immigrant mother and a father of German-Irish origins, spent his earliest years in an immigrant neighborhood of Baltimore.

347
These row-house tenements on Chicago's South Side were well constructed of stone. Such dwellings were often occupied successively by middle-class natives, immigrants, and Negroes.

347

The true apartment house evolved from the multidecked row house. The Stuyvesant (New York City, 1869) is generally recognized as the first apartment house constructed in the United States. It became somewhat of a model for simplified imitations across the country, and within a short time there was a remarkable proliferation of similar cheaply constructed multifamily dwellings. Overcrowding, small rooms, and the resulting filth and threat of disease inspired Alfred T. White of Brooklyn to energetically advance the "model tenement movement," attracting the support of well-intentioned civic leaders and a small number of industrialists, such as George M. Pullman.

To the concerned it seemed self-evident that urban congestion, dirt, crime, prostitution, and the corner saloon impaired the morality, health, and productive capacity of workers, and that better housing—offering more space, better sanitary conditions, properly lighted and ventilated rooms—would cure most of the urban evils and incidentally sustain the vigor of the workers. White was among the relatively few to test the theory. His Homes Building (1877) and Tower Building (1878) in Brooklyn and New York were well constructed and designed to provide tenants with improved living conditions. For all this, White was content with a 7 percent return on his investment in exchange for prompt advance payment of rent and strict adherence to rules of occupancy and behavior.

Unfortunately, only a small number of investors followed White's noble example. Most landlords expected more monetary gain and seemed determined to pack as many immigrants into their apartments as possible. Even in old houses and mansions originally constructed for a single family, the rooms were commonly divided by partitions consisting of nothing more than boards or simple curtains to accommodate immigrants and uprooted drifters, with some single houses in Chicago sheltering as many as twelve families.

New York City, of course, was severely afflicted with tenement blight. Fifteen thousand tenements were recorded in the late 1870s, and within ten years the number of these dreary and stench-filled places multiplied to more than thirty thousand. A million people—the vast majority immigrants—lived in them. In the later part of the nineteenth century the most popular form of multistory construction became the "dumb-bell tenement," named after the shape of the floor plan, with living quarters located in the wide end portions, front and back, and stairways and the meager plumbing facilities located off the narrow central, connecting passageway. The court or air shaft on either side of the central passageway was not only narrow but inadequate for admitting daylight and fresh air. In many structures there were in fact rooms without window openings. Basements were also divided into living quarters when not converted to commercial purposes such as bakeries.

Cheaply constructed, occupied by wave after wave of poor immigrants, and owned by tightfisted landlords, these buildings fell into disrepair. Despite the abuse and neglect, the basic structural elements were so durable that these buildings survived a remarkably long time, too long in the opinion of vocal social workers such as Jane Addams, Lewis W. Hine, and Jacob A. Riis. Despite valiant efforts toward reform, only a meager number of the most blighted tenement areas had been removed before World War I. Many of the worst survived until replaced by the better housing projects of the public works programs of the 1930s.

The New York Tenement House Commission of 1884 succeeded in outlawing privy vaults and requiring fire escapes (1887). Other commissions made better headway and in 1901, under the leadership of Robert W. DeForest, obtained a much improved housing law. The so-called New Law Tenements offered better sanitation, enlarged air shafts and room sizes, and bathrooms for each apartment. Individual bathrooms, in fact, were required in older buildings.

However, the new law did not eliminate high-density construction; if anything, it encouraged urban congestion. New building codes, eventually termed "high density codes," were modeled after the 1901 New York code by cities such as Newark, Jersey City, and, surprisingly, the inland industrial center of Rochester, New York. Moreover, there was nothing to prevent immigrant families from doubling up in single apartments, and this practice remained the rule for a long time.

The old mill-town dormitories of New England found little favor in other parts of the country after the Civil War. The new "company towns" of single-industry communities more frequently adopted a low-cost single or semidetached style of home construction [348]. Individual family quarters, closely packed along streets that abruptly climbed the hill slopes, were reproduced from a single plan in steplike monotony, providing immigrant housing in many mining and steel towns in Pennsylvania, southeastern Ohio, and neighboring West Virginia [349].

348
Balloon-frame construction was freely employed for semi-detached and conventional apartment house dwellings, as indicated in this 1938 photograph of housing in Ambridge, Pennsylvania. These buildings were occupied by Greek immigrants who were employed by the American Bridge Company, the buildings of which are seen at the end of the street. While screen doors are seen at the entrances, the residents had to insert flimsy adjustable screens when a window sash was partly raised for ventilation. The modest luxury of the Depression decade is shown by one parked car—at least ten years old—and a jerry-rigged radio aerial suspended from the stick nailed to the underside of the eave of the building in the foreground. The clapboard siding shows signs of weathering because the buildings had not been painted for many years.

349
The houses of the steelworkers in the company town of Aliquippa, Pennsylvania, were separated into "plans," according to race or nationality. At least four such groups of balloon-frame houses are seen in this 1938 photograph.

After the decade of the Civil War, the need for larger expanses of low-priced undeveloped land forced numerous manufacturers to seek new factory sites on the fringes of such cities as Chicago and Cleveland. The managers of most manufacturing firms assumed that the unskilled workers would follow the job and secure housing haphazardly provided by speculators and contractors, an assumption that proved to be correct.

A few of the larger manufacturers, however, supplied not only new housing but community business centers, entertainment facilities, schools, and shopping districts. George M. Pullman's company town, Pullman, Illinois, is perhaps the best known. Pullman even provided his workers with a community church which hosted various denominations on a prearranged schedule in a manner not unlike many military chapels. Open to its first residents early in 1881, the town offered several types of housing; approximately two thirds consisted of tenements and the remainder was single-family residences. All housing was rented; ownership was prohibited. By 1885 more than 53 percent of Pullman residents were foreign-born. The constant turnover of house occupancy can be largely attributed to the worker's opportunity to obtain more spacious housing in neighboring towns for comparable rents and especially to his consuming desire to own a home outright. It was, after all, the dream that had inspired so many to journey to America in the first place. The workers in the company town at the McCormick Reaper Works at least had the benefit of living in detached cottages which were inexpensive to rent or, more important, to purchase.

Realization of the dream of home ownership was aided substantially by the balloon-frame house, the cheapest to construct and to buy. It was built easily, and by the millions, by workers with a minimum of carpentry skills in a nation where low-cost timber abounded. Even in thinly settled areas, heavy-timbered framing and log construction gave way to the new form. Dugout houses were regarded as temporary, and the adobe structures of the plains were frequently sheathed with a clapboard veneer to improve durability.

The earliest known example of balloon-frame construction—also known as basket-frame or Chicago construction—is the first St. Mary's Church of Chicago, built by Augustine D. Taylor in 1833. Modifying the New England heavy-timber frame, Taylor reduced the wall framing to a simple system of vertical studs nailed to the bottom sill and the horizontal upper plate, with studs generally being spiked in place on sixteen-inch centers [**350A, 350B**]. In single story buildings, the upper ribbon or plate supported the roof rafters. Floor joists were nailed to the foundation plate or sill. In two-story buildings, another row of studs and the second-floor joists were nailed to the first-floor top plate, with the roof rafters resting on the uppermost plate. Flooring was nailed directly to the joists. The stud-and-plate frames of the wall were covered by rough board sheathing which, in turn, was covered by the outside clapboard siding or a veneer of brick.

By 1834 an average balloon-frame house could be finished in about a week. Any worker who could competently handle saw, hammer, and spikes could put up a frame. The older heavy-timber frames had required the skillful cutting and fitting of mortises and tenons to form the critical joints. The rapid spread of balloon-frame construction in the 1830s was phenomenal, and today nearly three-quarters of all houses in this country are of this type [**351, 352**].

Even in neighborhoods where the houses were built close to lot lines, constructed as doubles or duplexes, or where two were shoehorned onto lots in a front-and-back arrangement, the house dweller was better off than the tenement dweller.

The front or side porches of these cheap houses became summer parlors for social interchange or fair-weather theaters which transformed the sidewalk and street into a stage. The porch—its introduction in America is credited to the Dutch—developed a mystique of its own. It spawned special devices for comfort or delight, such as swings, flower planters, and all-weather rockers [**353**]. Before the introduction of television and home air conditioning on a wide scale after World War II, city residents spent much of their time outside the house in warm weather, and if there was no true front porch, the family would crowd onto the outside landing and steps, even those at the rear of the house. Summer evenings on the porch or stoop (the word has Dutch origins) were cheap but first-rate entertainment and enabled the mill hand or laborer to enjoy a breath of air or a growler of beer after spending ten to fourteen or more hours at the job.

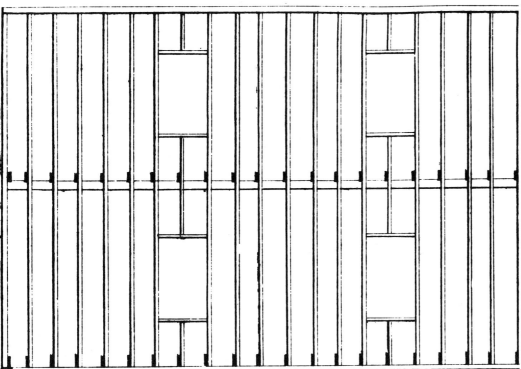

350A

350A, 350B
The balloon-frame method of house construction shown in elevation (1858) and perspective (1898). The basic framing method has remained unchanged to the present. Elevation drawing from William E. Bell, *Carpentry Made Easy* . . . (Philadelphia, 1858), plate 6; perspective drawing from T. E. Kidder, *Building Construction and Superintendence* (New York, 1898), p. 49.

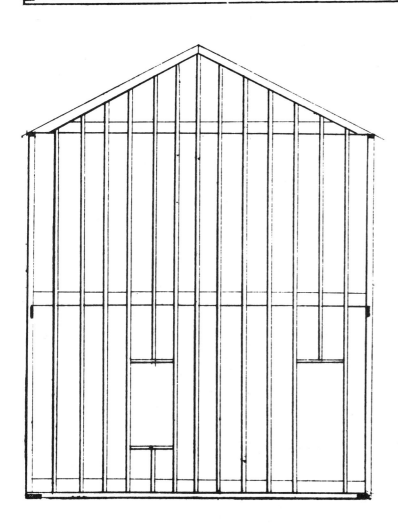

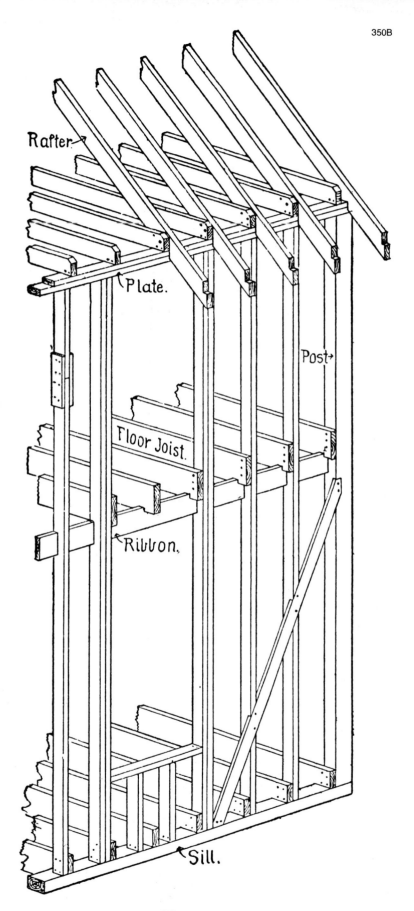

Rafter.

Plate.

Post→

Floor Joist.

Ribbon.

Sill.

351
Immigrants from Germany
and a few from Ireland lived in
balloon-frame houses built
from the same plan on Cleveland's "Dutch Hill" (lower
Holmden Avenue). At the
lower end of the unpaved
street were the B & O Railroad
yards and, across from there,
the steel mills.

352
Houses in the poor immigrant
neighborhood near Orange
Avenue, Cleveland, Ohio, already in a state of neglect
even when relatively new in
1910. The unpaved alley,
parked peddler's cart, and
trash fitted well with the slapdash siding and crumbling
roofing of the cheaply built
dwellings. This neighborhood
was occupied by numerous
immigrants from Italy.

351

352

The interiors of American houses, in countless ways so similar, were at the same time continually changing. While Old World counterparts also changed during the years 1860–1940, the rate of change in the average American household was more rapid than elsewhere. And it evolved in a standardized form, with mass-produced furnishings and consumer items which made each home less special, to the point where a sense of uniqueness could hardly be created. This domestic environment made it difficult for the newcomers to reproduce the old patterns of domestic life, and the effect was especially evident in the lives and aspirations of their offspring. If such new American influences—stemming from a material rather than a spiritual base—seem at first glance subtle or superficial, they were actually quite powerful.

The American kitchen provides a good example. It began to assume its present form only after the Civil War—after American industry entered its advanced stage of development. The transformation of the kitchen in the United States was gradual and by no means fully delineated until the 1920s.

The well-planned environment of work areas which reduced unnecessary motion in the kitchen was suggested as early as 1869 by Catherine Beecher. She recognized the value of organizing and storing kitchen implements in proximity to their area of work and of arranging working surfaces at a continuous level, using the series of counters along the walls instead of a kitchen table, food safes, and scattered cabinets. Shelves above the counters stored the utensils, and drawers or bins below contained various flours and containers for sugar and molasses. Towels and cleaning articles were stored at the sink. The stove remained in a separate area, but she suggested storage space there for the pots and pans. It is perhaps surprising that someone would have to suggest something so sensible.

Miss Beecher's early kitchen plan remained an ideal for the better part of the nineteenth century but contributed nevertheless to the form of certain types of portable kitchen furniture. Kitchen work cabinets—selling for less than five dollars in 1902—provided a table-height (a standardized thirty inches) working surface of about twenty-eight by forty-eight in area, with drawers for small utensils and two hinged bins underneath—one holding up to sixty pounds of flour and the other with a divider to provide space for sugar and a second type of flour. These storage bins were advertised as "dirt and mouse proof," a feature, if true, of considerable value to tenement dwellers. A second type of cabinet, very similar to the first, had a cupboard toward the back of the working surface which rose to about seven feet. The cupboard was divided into various compartments to hold additional utensils, spices, and other cooking ingredients. These cabinets—known variously as the "Organized Cupboard" or the "Hoosier Cabinet"—sold for less than ten dollars in 1902 and were advertised as "very valuable . . . especially where people want to economize in space and cannot have a kitchen safe and table in the same room." Such cabinets became so popular that many housewives incorporated them into kitchens that already had built-in cupboards and pantries.

The built-in cupboards of the late nineteenth and early twentieth centuries were often equipped with glass doors to provide visibility and also the chance to display the family china. In many photographs from the period 1890–1915, the immigrant homemakers' dishes, cups, and serving bowls are neatly stacked on cupboard shelves lined with doilies, die-cut paper napkins, or fancy-edged shelf paper. Although it is assumed that most of the dishes were purchased at reasonable prices or acquired secondhand, the cupboard contents are often arranged tastefully and carefully.

Just as Catherine Beecher's efficient kitchen was patterned after a ship's galley, some house builders by the 1920s had grasped the value of the compactness provided by the Pullman kitchen in railroad dining cars. Continuous work counters, the "Organized Cupboard," indoor plumbing, iceboxes, and the increasing use of gas ranges made it possible by the 1920s to combine the storage-preservation area, the cleaning-preparation area, and the cooking-serving area into one architectural space.

Kitchen stoves underwent a slow but important transition in America. Throughout the second half of the nineteenth century the cast-iron coal-(and wood-) burning range was the most dominant form of kitchen stove in America. It survived, in fact, well into the next century, even in the most heavily populated urban centers and especially in the older dwellings and apartments, which housed millions of immigrants. Cast-iron stoves were produced in great numbers and in a great variety of forms. They were so characteristic of American kitchens that many European observers, such as Charles Dickens, took special note of them. European immigrants were usually more at home with tile or brick ovens, which, contrary to developing American patterns, had to be individually constructed by special craftsmen. By the late 1860s the mass-produced iron ranges had largely displaced the brick oven in the United States [354], and many an immigrant housewife had to adjust her culinary talents to the idiosyncrasies of these unfamiliar "red-hot monsters."

The gas range—apparently a British innovation dating from about 1850—slowly gained favor in America after 1880. There was a lingering uneasiness about using gas as a heating fuel in the house, despite its widespread use as an illuminating agent. By 1910, however, half the gas produced in the United States was consumed in heating and cooking devices [355]. Following closely the design of late-nineteenth-century coal ranges, the most common forms of American gas ranges were constructed with the oven and broiler at levels higher than the cooking surface. Not until after 1930 were the majority of American stoves produced with ovens and broilers below waist level.

Immigrants who encountered a distinctly American kitchen environment [356] were also confronted with a rapidly emerging technology in domestic plumbing. During the latter decades of the nineteenth century, the form and quality of fixtures such as bathtubs, toilets, basins, and water heaters varied greatly, but by 1915 these elements had been largely standardized. The rapid development of American plumbing was distinct and in advance of Old World parallels. If, as recent clichés imply, the multiplicity of American toilets did not promote the standard of American morality, the steady advances in sanitation in congested districts gave the average American home environment an added advantage over Old World counterparts.

354
A cast-iron wood- or coal-burning kitchen stove, 1872.

355
By 1912 the gas range had become a standard American household appliance, taking the general form of this Diamond Gas Range manufactured by the Lindemann firm. This black-enameled, nickel-plated model, which retailed for $57, had four burners, a broiler, and a shoulder-high oven. A. J. Lindemann & Hoverson Co., *The Lindemann Stoves and Ranges* (Milwaukee, 1912).

356
An average kitchen in 1905 was spartan by later standards. The cast-iron sink was supported by cast-iron legs; paper kept the top of the work table clean. Glass cupboard doors and patterned linoleum were standard. The die-cut shelf paper, calendar, and die-cut fold-out wall pocket added a few decorative notes. If the overhead gas jet failed, this housewife had two kerosene lamps in reserve.

354

355   356

494

In many respects hotels provided the nation's sanitary ideal. In Cape May, New Jersey, the Mount Vernon Hotel boasted running water and baths in each room as early as 1853. In 1877 a hotel in Boston piped hot and cold water into each wash basin, and hotels in Kansas City (1877) and Boston (1894) installed bathrooms in the larger suites. By 1908, Statler's Buffalo hotel offered a bath with each room for $1.50 a day—a previously unheard-of bargain that was an immediate success.

The great number of apartment houses in American cities during the last quarter of the nineteenth century stimulated—albeit inadequately, in the opinion of reformers—the development of indoor plumbing. At first, piped but unheated water was supplied to basins located in the public areas of the central hallways of each floor. The single tap was shared by all residents, an arrangement reminiscent of the old village well or pump. Although, as already noted, plumbing techniques and basic fixtures had become commonly available at costs low enough to permit the New Tenement Law to require baths for each New York apartment by 1901, it was in Chicago that residential plumbing made more notable early advances. During the 1890s, newly constructed Chicago apartments provided flush toilets, wash basins with taps, and tubs for each family unit. There were also hot water heaters for kitchen and laundry sinks and drains to carry the waste. But in most parts of the country, and in older dwellings of Chicago as well, piped hot water was introduced slowly. By the 1880s separate coke-fired heaters were being marketed, and the more familiar gas-fired heaters became available by 1898 [357A–357C]. The installation of these conveniences was by no means universal, and until after World War I, much of the water used in the average city home was heated on the kitchen stove and carried to the basins or bathtubs in buckets or kettles.

The standard American compact bathroom had made its debut by 1908, when the cast-iron enameled tub was essentially standardized at a length of five feet [358]. Mass-produced and low in cost, this readily available convenience was soon placed in its standard position in the bathroom—along the short wall of the room. The width of the average bathroom in the United States assumed its rigidly predictable narrow dimensions at that time—a width that barely accommodated the five-foot tub. The two remaining fixtures, toilet and basin, were most frequently positioned on a common long wall for the convenience of the plumbers [359A, 359B, 360A, 360B]. The one-piece double-shelled enameled tub was first mass-produced about 1920, gradually replacing the four-legged type, to become the familiar American standard. The sale of enameled bathroom fixtures in America doubled between 1921 and 1923, marking rather precisely the introduction of water heaters and hot-water pipes in the majority of American homes.

The immigrant housewife even met a new standard of home refrigeration in America. When the traveler Thomas Cook visited the United States in 1876, he was singularly impressed with the amount of ice consumed in New York households—two million tons per year. Cook calculated that the city's domestic consumption of ice required the full-time services of ten thousand men and four thousand horses, formidable numbers even by today's standards. Conventional insulated iceboxes remained common until the 1930s. By 1936, however, mass-production techniques had made it possible for householders to own some two million low-cost mechanical refrigerators powered by lightweight electrical motors.

Other household conveniences and labor-saving devices were introduced more slowly. Home laundry, for example, was largely a matter of hand labor until the early part of the twentieth century, despite the many patents that were taken out on laundering devices and the comparable advancement in the mechanization of commercial laundries. Manually powered wringers and mechanical washers became more common after 1900, but the cost of power-driven washing machines remained high throughout the 1920s, with less than a million units being sold in the prosperous year of 1926 [361]. Westinghouse, in an advertisement of 1906 for electric irons, noted that the housewife could do the ironing on the porch to escape the heat of the kitchen; but it was not until the 1920s that electrical irons were commonly used in the home [362]. Similarly, the familiar form of electric vacuum cleaner evolved about 1908, but not until 1917 was it offered by a national mail-order house at reasonable prices.

All the forces that slowly evolved for the advancement of the American home—from light construction techniques to low-cost mass production—gained enormous momentum in the 1920s, stalled during the 1930s and 1940s, then moved at top speed until the present day. The magic words were *modern, new, progress,* and *easy terms.* Indeed, who could argue against the indoor convenience? Only now are sociologists en masse taking a second look. Lost in the aggressive pursuit of the "middle-class-new" was much of the individuality each immigrant possessed.

The great majority of immigrants landed in America with a trunk or a bundle of the barest necessities—some clothing, bedding, and perhaps a few pots or tools. To the many newcomers who had little money or were forced into unskilled occupations, the process of equipping a new household was slow and difficult. The apparent cheapness of mass-produced consumer goods was often an illusion. Even though the last heavy waves of immigration came during a time of high employment—that is, the period 1901–1915, when some 11.5 million immigrants arrived—it was also a period of rising prices. Wages barely kept pace with the increased cost of living. And while the general economic trend was favorable for native and greenhorn alike, there were periods of unemployment, such as 1908–1909 and 1914, which severely pinched the purses of millions of workers.

Consumer goods, while not luxurious, were generally durable. The common iron bedsteads and frames, for example, often went through a succession of generations until they were tossed out by the more affluent or style-conscious offspring [**363**]. Many articles of furniture produced during the period 1890–1920 were made of oak, a wood that can withstand considerable wear and abuse. The gauge of metal used for buckets, pans, stoves, and household tools was heavier than is seen in today's household objects. Wool for carpeting and clothing was common and relatively inexpensive. Long-wearing leather was a part of many objects—particularly low-priced upholstered furniture—and household hardware was usually hefty iron or brass instead of the present light-gauge steel stampings, extruded aluminum, or cast plastic. In many ways the immigrant homemakers received a good product for their hard-won dollar.

Fundamentally, household furniture during the last years of the nineteenth century and the first third of the twentieth was massive, indelicately proportioned, and boringly common. Undistinguished by a craft tradition, it failed to evoke the sentimental attachment that grows out of many generations of family possession. The immigrants who were able to scrape together enough cash to buy a new living room or bedroom suite found but a limited choice of styles and functional pieces. Low-cost bedroom suites for many years before World War I were three-piece outfits consisting of the bed, a dresser, and a washstand, or commode. Chiffoniers were available but were frequently offered as separate items. Iron beds, popular for a long time, could be purchased new for less than five dollars in 1902, and in the same year a mail-order firm advertised a five-piece fully upholstered living room suite for less than fifteen dollars. Even the wallpaper of the American home had been mass-produced since the 1840s and was made cheaply available after the introduction of wood-pulp paper in the 1880s.

357A
A richly decorated coal-burning stove of "handsome silver nickel," manufactured by the Keeley Stove Company.

357B
Cast-iron kitchen stoves were adapted to heat household water and warm the room in cold weather. This model, the Columbian Newport, was available for $32.25 without the hot water tank in 1898.

357C
Coal-fueled hot-air furnaces for central heating systems in the home were well developed by 1898, as indicated in these illustrations of furnaces manufactured by the Keeley Stove Company. When home owners found they could afford such furnaces, they frequently had to excavate a full or part cellar under their homes, which usually had been constructed without basements. During the 1930s, some middle-class families were able to purchase automatic coal stokers for this type of heating system. From Keeley Stove Company, *Stoves, Ranges, Furnaces and Hot Water Specialties* (Columbia, Pa., 1898–1899).

357A

357B

357C

The new-found American sameness was not without a small measure of relief. There were three American household articles—in addition to the front-porch swing—that especially captured the domestic fancies of the immigrants. The first, and in many respects the most traditional to the United States, was the rocking chair. Whether it was "invented" by Benjamin Franklin or derived from a prototype first fabricated about 1750 in Lancashire, England, is of less importance than its supreme popularity in the average American household since the eighteenth century. Rockers were cheap and ubiquitous. "The American farmer, at the end of the day, will instinctively move to the rocker on his porch. The European peasant sits immovable through the twilight as if nailed to the bench before his cottage."

The second mass-produced article that stimulated the acquisitive desires of many immigrants was the piano. To the immigrant's family, especially in such teeming urban centers as lower New York, the possession of a piano became "a symbol of relative affluence." It mattered little if it was secondhand. George Gershwin, the son of Jewish parents who had emigrated from St. Petersburg, Russia, recalled when a hand-me-down piano was hoisted through the window of his family's downtown tenement window: "No sooner had it come through the window and been backed up against the wall than I was at the keys. I must have crowded out [my brother] Ira very soon, for the plan originally had been to start him off on the instrument."

The piano seemed to be everywhere in the United States. It has been estimated that by 1887, 800,000 pianos existed here. In 1890, one person out of every 252 bought a piano. Even this remarkable rate of sales increased, especially after the Depression ended toward the close of the decade, by which time the upright, which had become the American standard, was being mass-produced at prices that steadily dropped, in contrast to the upward trend of prices for daily necessities. In 1909 264,545 pianos were manufactured in the United States, and by the following year they were selling at the rate of 1,200 per working day (that is, six days out of seven). For those who could not buy a new piano outright, the installment plan was available in the last quarter of the nineteenth century, although its true vogue came only in the 1920s.

Between 1890 and 1910 music lessons were offered at an increasing scale as well, not only by private teachers, but by public schools and city settlement houses. Moreover, the newly perfected and mass-produced mechanical player piano began invading the American home. By 1915 these devices—usually termed "pianolas" after the originally patented Pianola of the Aeolian Company—accounted for one out of every four American pianos. By 1919 there were more pianolas than conventional instruments, and between 1900 and 1930 they were found in at least two and a half million American homes.

It can hardly be argued, as some have done, that the American piano was never the possession of the "masses." For one thing, single titles of sheet music, created in phenomenal quantities by composers of New York's Tin Pan Alley, frequently sold in the millions at five cents a song. This would not have been possible without the existence of millions of home pianos, providing diversion, comfort, and in many cases a key to social and economic mobility.

Negroes—the native-born who shared a seemingly perpetual "newcomer" existence with (or, more aptly, apart from) the foreign-born—often developed an attachment to the piano which paved the way to genuine success through creative achievement. Earl Hines, whose mother played the organ and piano, studied with a German-born music teacher who used the well-known Czerny books, a foundation that Hines said provided the groundwork for his piano technique. Thomas "Fats" Waller, self-taught, gained his first recognition by playing the piano in New York's Public School 89. Frank Signorelli, of Italian heritage, rose to considerable fame as a jazz piano musician, and Adrian Rollini—best remembered for his exquisite creative passages on the bass and baritone saxophones and xylophones—for many years "cut" piano solos for pianola rolls. The piano work in the American jazz idiom of Arthur Schutt and Bix Beiderbecke—both of Germanic extraction—is still appreciated widely through recordings originally made in the 1920s and early 1930s.

The American piano literally greeted millions of newcomers at Ellis Island—at least those who had to stay overnight in the dormitories. Its strains invaded the apartment windows of the lower East Side, often accompanied by the sound of the mechanical street piano, a modified upright on wheels, invented in the nineteenth century and generally cranked by Italian immigrants, sometimes a man and wife. In the dead of winter, when windows were closed to the sound of this "hurdy-gurdy," a new American might instead put a copy of Victor's record number 18328 on the hand-wound phonograph and hear a medley of "Italian Airs," played, of course, by a street piano.

The phonograph was the third household object that animated many otherwise somber interiors. There were two types available until after World War I: the cylinder-playing machine originally invented by Edison in 1877 and the gramophone, which played a flat disc, an invention of Emile Berliner, an immigrant from Germany. After some years of legal skirmishing and hard work to perfect mass-production techniques, Edison and others began full-scale commercial sales of cylinder recordings in 1890, and, four years later, the Berliner interests began producing gramophones and disc records on a large scale as well. By 1901 there were three leaders in the phonograph industry—Edison, Victor, and Columbia—with mass production bringing the price of their machines down steadily. The Edison "Gem" cylinder phonograph sold for only $7.50 in 1912.

In 1914—an outstanding year for piano sales—some 500,000 phonograph machines were produced in the United States. By 1919 annual production of home machines had reached 2,225,000 and individual disc and cylinder record production reached 100 million copies. In 1903 Victor had brought out its famed but high-priced Red Seal series, and one year later it signed Enrico Caruso to an exclusive contract. The expensive celebrity or prestige recordings, which lent an aura of relative affluence and culture to households in which they could be heard, were not nearly as numerous as the lower-priced "popular" series. While recordings produced for the immigrant trade have not held much appeal for researchers, it is clear that a considerable number of both American-made and imported record-molding matrices were always in production in America after 1901.

358
Enameled cast-iron tubs with four feet were popular as late as World War II. Although the standard size remained 5 feet, sizes as short as 4 feet were produced to fit into bathrooms that had been created by converting pantries, back porches, and sections of kitchens in thousands of houses. *Kohler of Kohler Planned Plumbing and Heating Catalogue K-39* (Kohler, Wis., 1939).

359A
This flush toilet of 1893 would have been a luxury in the average home. A pull on the chain released the water through a 2″ pipe and activated a valve to supply new water; a float automatically shut off the water when the tank was refilled. This model cost $65—without the marble floor slab. Standard Manufacturing Company, *Illustrated Catalogue of Sanitary Plumbing Goods* (Pittsburgh, 1893).

359B
The standard household flush toilet has changed very little in more than fifty years. This model, manufactured by Kohler in 1939, was a low-profile version, 30″ high, with a "close-coupled" tank that eliminated the pipe connection.

358

KOHLER of KOHLER

359A

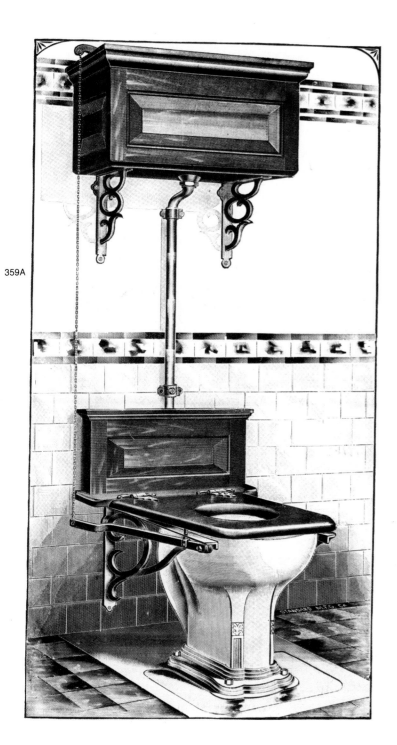

359B

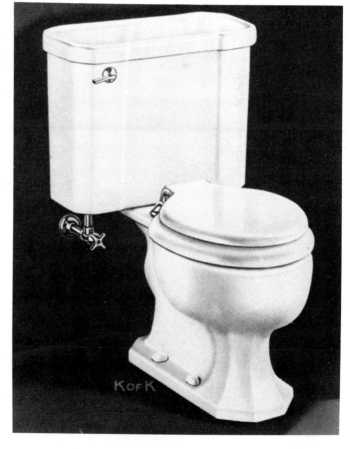

360A
Bathroom sinks were generous in size and constructed of durable materials, with polished marble splash boards, nickel-plated brass taps, and iron brackets. This sink, with faucets for hot and cold water, was manufactured by the Standard firm in 1893.

360B
Kitchen sinks for many years were generally simple in design and most frequently sold without the prefabricated cupboards or closets that have become standard since World War II. This Kohler sink of 1939 was offered in two sizes, 42″ or 52″ in length.

361
The installation of electricity in urban residences was rapid and virtually complete by the beginning of the Depression. Of all the labor-saving household devices, none was probably so greatly valued by housewives as the electric washing machine. By the time this ABC Companion was introduced in 1928, rubber wringer rollers had become a standard and "necessary" supplementary device. *The Remarkable Development of Altofer Brothers Company* (Peoria, Ill., 1928), p. 7.

362
Electric iron, c. 1920s. L 6⅜″.

360A

360B

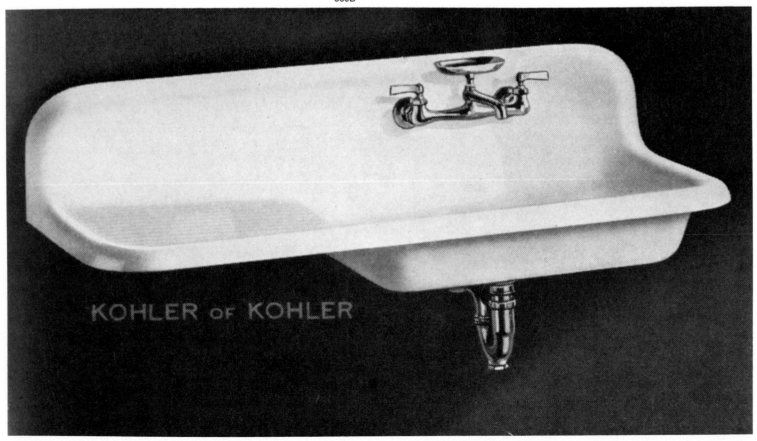

361

362

363
The ubiquitous iron-frame bed, a kerosene lamp, a cheap alarm clock, and a cast-iron cook stove are household landmarks typical of the United States in this shack occupied by a Mexican sugar-beet worker in the vicinity of East Grand Forks, Minnesota, in 1937. The bed is possibly forty years old.

Moreover, the home record "libraries" of immigrants were not restricted to songs or artists of the same ethnic origin. The recordings of the band directed by John Philip Sousa—who had the audacity to criticize "canned" music in an article for *Appleton's Magazine* in 1906—were best sellers and constant favorites in workingmens' homes, especially Sousa's "Stars and Stripes Forever." Other popular records were Chauncey Olcott's "My Wild Irish Rose" and Henry Burr's "I'll Take You Home Again, Kathleen," tunes not by any means limited to the Irish trade. More than a few immigrants could quote snatches of monologue from Joe Hayman's tremendously popular talking record "Cohen on the Phone," a witty vaudeville routine built on an immigrant's frustration in trying to make his thickly accented English understood over the then-crude telephone. The same immigrant household would also likely have a copy of Bert Williams's superb "Nobody." Williams, a great Negro singer and vaudeville star who broke the color barrier on the popular stage early in the twentieth century, broke a more intimate barrier when he invaded millions of white homes via the phonograph.

In 1911 one could enter a store and select these discs from the same Victor popular Black Label series: "The Watch on the Rhine" by Reinhold Werenrath, "Roll Jordon Roll" by the Fisk University Jubilee Quartet, "Maria Mari" by Vessella's Italian Band, and "Alexander's Ragtime Band" by Collins and Harlan. In fact, those four recordings could very well constitute a typical day's purchase by anybody, native-born or greenhorn.

Jacob Riis—The Other Half

The purchase, however inexpensive, often came at some sacrifice. Seldom did the wages of an immigrant worker allow for "spending money." To supplement the husband's salary, wives and children worked at home, and one tool seemed ever present: the sewing machine. It was reasonably priced, highly valued, and openly cherished. In 1860 it was estimated that 111,000 sewing machines were being produced each year in the United States. By 1900 the rate of sales had reached 747,587 units and by 1912, some 1,250,000. These products, all made by domestic firms, were among the more indestructible of the American household devices available to the immigrant; a working life span of sixty years was not uncommon.

James Parton summarized the social impact of the sewing machine as early as 1867: "The sewing machine is one of the means by which the industrious laborer is as well clad as any millionaire need be...." The immigrant wife and daughter of the lower East Side of New York City and neighborhoods of the garment districts of other eastern and midwestern cities frequently used the machine for earning a large part of the family income. Elsewhere a good seamstress could supplement the family income by doing custom dressmaking. Sewing machines, for whatever reason, were much in demand by immigrant wives, and all the larger settlement houses and evening adult educational programs offered courses in dressmaking.

What many Americans may not have known was that the sewing machine, particularly the Singer, was destined to become not just a tool of immigrant survival, but a mass-produced symbol of America throughout the world.

Despite the enormous strides in the housing industry, thousands of immigrants found themselves in hovels at the turn of the century. One immigrant reformer brought this to the nation's attention. Jacob August Riis (1849–1914), born in Ribe, Denmark, emigrated to this country in 1870 and became a leading crusader for social reform. He sought to eliminate abuse of the poor through newspaper reporting, magazine articles, books, and photographs. He fought against the horrors of slums, against sweatshops, child labor, inadequate schooling, and governmental neglect.

His father, a Latin teacher in Ribe, had hoped his son would follow a literary career, but Jacob apprenticed as a carpenter and became a member of that guild. At the age of twenty-one, spurned in love, he came to America seeking his fortune, with little more than forty dollars in his pocket. He tried many jobs, including carpentry, mining, crop picking, door-to-door sales work, and newspaper reporting, but in the first years he earned barely enough to keep himself fed. It was during this time that Riis obtained firsthand knowledge of the conditions that existed in police lodging houses. Destitute and desperate for a place to sleep, he had turned to one of these houses, where he was robbed and then thrown out when he complained; outside, a police attendant seized his pet dog and killed it. This indelible experience helped to crystallize Riis's resolve to improve conditions for the poor.

He briefly owned a one-man newspaper, which he sold a year later for more than two thousand dollars profit. In 1877 he was hired as a reporter for the New York *Tribune,* where he remained ten years, transferring then to the *Evening Sun.* His newspaper work provided ready access to the slums and sweatshops as well as to the public, whose support was crucial in getting corrective legislation passed, programs enforced, and governmental corruption exposed. As his reputation grew, the time spent writing for newspapers diminished. After 1900, most of his ideas appeared in magazine articles and books.

Riis also fought against the "reign of rum." He wrote that "turn and twist as we may . . . the saloon projects its colossal shadow, omen of evil wherever it falls into the lives of the poor." He felt that drink subjugated the poor and that the "growler"—beer pitcher—stands "at the cradle of the tough . . . bosses him through his boyhood . . . and leaves him . . . at the door of the jail . . . to finish his training . . . [as] a thief."

It was in the 1880s that Riis first read about the use of flash powder in photography, and he realized how dramatically this medium could reinforce and extend his written message: flash photographs could expose and document the darkness of tenement life. The camera and flash pan became his constant companions. At this time, however, the printing industry had not perfected the techniques necessary to reproduce photographs on newsprint. As an alternative, Riis went on the road with a lecture tour illustrated by lantern slides, and New York's deplorable conditions were seen by audiences all across the country. (An example of his photography is **157** in Chapter 13.)

It was these slide shows that eventually led to the writing of *How the Other Half Lives,* published in 1890. The book was so successful that it appeared in eleven editions within five years, making Riis a leading exponent of social reform and resulting in his friendship with Theodore Roosevelt, who had entered political life.

Riis wrote twelve more books, but when talking of reform his message remained the same: if immigrants were moved from the slums and given the opportunity to have a decent home, they would assimilate easily into American society and become valuable citizens. To be sure, Riis alerted many Americans at the turn of the century to the dangers of poverty, but his own solutions to the problem were often naïve and romantic.

Part Four

A Nation
Among Nations

*Pleas'd with the native
and pleas'd with the foreign,
pleas'd with the new and the old…*

Walt Whitman

Chapter 24

Mass Production—An Example of Global Give-and-Take

From the earliest Indian migrations until the present day, America has continued to receive the people of the world. Immigration is so much a part of America that one of the country's senior historians, Oscar Handlin, has noted that to write a history of the immigrant is to write a history of the nation. But America is even more than a nation of nations; it is a nation *among* nations, constantly interacting in virtually every phase of human endeavor with most countries of the world. In the nineteenth and twentieth centuries it helped to create and to disseminate two of the most potent forces in the world—mass production and mass communications. One by-product of this creative energy has been a worldwide interest in American culture and, in turn, an increasing interest by Americans in other cultures of the world. The key to this exchange has been trade.

Of all the social forces that determine the relationships between communities, none is more basic and universal than the need to trade. Trade is a quiet force and it is enduring; wars, revolutions, and mass migrations may disrupt its workings, but only temporarily. The basic motivation to trade is sheer need; but that is not the only incentive. From the beginnings of civilization trade has also meant wealth, adventurous travel, exotic luxuries, fabulous stories, battles of wits, and the command of languages.

At any moment in history, however, trade flourished only to the extent that the available means of transportation and communication permitted. From the earliest beginnings up to the nineteenth century, these means were very restricted. Messages and goods traveled only as fast as the horse or the sailing ship. As a consequence, many early communities were self-sufficient, and their members lived in cultural isolation. Villages only miles apart could maintain different dialects, folk customs, eating habits.

What a contrast is the world of today. Any place on the globe can be reached within hours, for the price of a few hundred dollars; the greatest remaining hardship is jet lag. News and messages travel around the world instantaneously. The result is a fading of regional differentiation and a spreading of international uniformity. Foreigners seem less foreign. The world's people increasingly dress alike, consume goods that are internationally standardized, and lead similar lives.

Responsible for this transformation is the wedding of the age-old custom of trade with modern technology. By producing goods in huge quantities, technology can make them inexpensive, affordable for vast numbers of people; conversely, this technology is affordable itself only if its products are indeed bought in vast numbers. The result is a disregard for national and continental boundaries in marketing. Moreover, technology has created the means of transportation to deliver the harvests of mass production around the globe; it has provided the communications systems that regulate and direct his worldwide commerce, that stimulate demand among the buyers.

Behind this technological revolution are ancient commercial motives, rooted in the concept of acquiring wealth by satisfying other people's needs in return for a share of their surplus. Fundamental to this exchange is the principle of give-and-take: a deal can be made only when the terms have been accepted by both partners through the process of bargaining, negotiating, compromising. This process, which constitutes the only rational resolution of conflict situations, is the basis of all civilized existence; in addition, the process itself is civilizing, for it promotes attitudes of flexibility and open-mindedness.

Trading is by nature peaceful. It cannot flourish without a minimum of mutual trust and respect of laws. At the beginning of this century, just at the time when America's industry was approaching a position of world dominance [364], President Taft enunciated an American point of view which rang with business's approval: "The diplomacy of the present administration . . . has been characterized as substituting dollars for bullets. It is one that appeals alike to idealistic humanitarian sentiments, to the dictates of sound policy and strategy, and to legitimate commercial aims." In short, to governments there is not a more practical incentive to keeping the peace than their interest in a prospering trade, for trade is, directly and indirectly, their chief source of revenue. Yet, as an agent of peace and happiness among men, trade has peculiar limitations. By its nature, it works best among equal partners and becomes problematic between the rich and the poor. What can nations threatened by overpopulation, starvation, and epidemics offer in return for their rescue?

Among the modern industrial nations, however, give-and-take is the dominant feature of life. It is institutionalized in countless multinational firms and supranational organizations. But it is by no means limited to the exchange of goods. Equally important and far-reaching is the exchange of ideas and values in all areas of political, social, and cultural life. The world is wrapped in a dense network of communication lines of the most diverse forms, as visible as telephone wires and as invisible as radio waves. International interchange, interaction, and interdependence continue to increase, at the expense of regional and national individuality and independence.

To say that our world had been transformed by the automobile and the airplane, the radio and the television set, is to repeat a truism. It is probably equally well known that we owe these glamorous machines to a process that is pervasive as well as deeply ambiguous in its effects: mass production. Mass production makes possible international commerce on a gigantic scale, but it also makes life more uniform; it is praised for raising our standard of living, but blamed for threatening the quality of life; it provides jobs for millions, but such jobs tend to be degradingly monotonous.

Mass production is neither an invention nor a technology; it is a business philosophy. Based on the premise that any article can be offered at a low price if it is produced in large enough quantities, it means the application of all the technological devices, principles, and processes that make production efficient and economical, combined with the systematic study—and sometimes manipulation—of the needs of the public who will consume the article.

The ingredients of mass production are diverse:

Division of labor: a principle demanding that a given production process be divided into its distinctive components, which are assigned to separate workers, machines, or shops with specialized skills.

The factory: an institution providing overall direction as well as the physical facilities (power, transportation) necessary for the production process.

"Dedicated" machines: single-purpose machine tools designed to perform a single production operation.

Interchangeability: A mass-produced article is interchangeable if any one of its parts can be replaced by a corresponding part from another specimen without the need of fitting, i.e., without special adaptation of the new part to the whole. Interchangeability is obviously beneficial in permitting repair through the replacement of a faulty element in a mechanism by a spare part [365A–365C]. Its significance, however, goes far beyond this: interchangeable-parts manufacture is crucial for the mass production of complex products in a cooperative effort. It permits an article to be assembled, without hand fitting, from components produced at different locations. It is safeguarded by precision measurement, quality control, and standardization.

Scientific management: the mechanical as well as psychological analysis of the individual manipulations, procedures, and processes of manufacturing with the purpose of saving time and energy while eliminating fatigue and accidents.

The continuous production line: the entire plant is organized around, and subordinated to, a conveyor system that moves the product in a continuous flow from raw material to the finished article.

Mass production is popularly identified with American technology. A commission of English technologists who in 1853 visited America to study the revolutionary methods of mass-producing firearms with interchangeable parts coined the phrase "American system of manufacture." Yet the roots of that system lay in the Old World. One ingredient, the division of labor, had been practiced in the manufacture of vases in classical Athens, where some enterprises employed thirty and forty workmen. European writers, from Jean Rodolphe Perronet (1762) and Adam Smith (1776) to Charles Babbage (1832), pointed to the example of the manufacture of pins [366] and extolled the economies achieved by division of labor. The new institution of the factory as a large workshop where all suitable production methods as well as mechanical power are subordinated to a central management was also born in Europe. It was occasionally employed in the eighteenth century by the absolutist governments of continental Europe (e.g., the factory for woolen cloth of the Counts of Waldstein in Oberleutensdorf, Bohemia, 1715), and consistently used (especially in textile manufacture) by the independent entrepreneurs of the industrial revolution in Britain. Single-purpose machine tools demonstrated their effectiveness in the famous block-making machinery of Portsmouth, England (1803), where a sequence of forty-four special machines manufactured 130,000 pulley blocks per year. Used in the rigging of sails, they were in large demand by the English navy, which was expanding to fight Napoleon. The idea of manufacturing firearms with interchangeable parts had repeatedly been suggested in eighteenth-century France; indeed, Thomas Jefferson, when ambassador to France, reported home about these attempts.

It was early-nineteenth-century America, however, where mass production reached maturity. Leaders in the development were armories under government contract which, with varying success, attempted to produce muskets with interchangeable parts. Arms manufacture became a proving ground for the skills and techniques required in mass production. Here the milling machine (commonly but incorrectly attributed to Eli Whitney) and Thomas Blanchard's gunstock-copying lathe [367] were born. Here were developed superlative machine tools that Europeans soon came to regard as indispensable requisites of high-quality manufacturing facilities. In 1855, for example, the British government equipped its Enfield Royal Small Arms Factory with a set of 157 machines (mostly milling machines, turret lathes, and Blanchard lathes) from the Robbins and Lawrence Company in Windsor, Vermont, and the Ames Manufacturing Company in Chicopee, Massachusetts. A milestone was reached in 1848 when the Robbins and Lawrence Company produced, strictly by machine and without the expedient of hand fitting, an order of fifteen thousand rifles that were unconditionally interchangeable.

Although the "American system of manufacture" developed and matured around one particular product—firearms—other articles were mass-produced just as well. Early in the nineteenth century, New England entrepreneurs applied this system to the manufacture of clocks and achieved sensational economies. Arms manufacturers themselves discovered that the facilities and techniques of their plants could be profitably employed to mass-produce other products. The firm of E. Remington and Sons, for example, which had grown large in the Civil War mass-producing a famous rifle, in its efforts to convert its capacity to a suitable peacetime production branched out into sewing machines and agricultural equipment before concentrating upon typewriters.

The general trend in the historical development of mass production was the elimination of the human operator. In 1856, when Samuel Colt had completed his new armory in Hartford, Connecticut, he boasted that all manufacturing operations were performed by some 1,400 machines [368]; handwork was required only in assembly (his revolvers' parts were not interchangeable). Factories like those of Robbins and Lawrence and Colt were, of course, exceptional achievements. Other industries continued to rely heavily on human labor, and compared with the rationally designed machine, man appeared distressingly inefficient. Later in the century, a new concept was added to the philosophy of mass production under the name "scientific management," with the goal of rationalizing the human operator. Time-and-motion studies of individual factory jobs helped to reduce fatigue and increase productivity, but they also tended to make the pace of factory work more relentless, more monotonous.

Rather than turning man into a machine, it seemed more human, as well as more efficient, to eliminate him from mass production entirely. The first step was the introduction of the moving assembly line. Its antecedents reach far. Oliver Evans in the 1780s had devised an automatic flour mill that employed endless belts, bucket chains, and conveyor screws to transport the grain in its continuous transformation into flour [369]. Next conveyor belts and chains were used in large foundries and bakeries and in the stockyards of Chicago [370].

The most dramatic demonstration of a whole factory functioning to the rhythm of a continuous production line was Henry Ford's Highland Park plant (1913), designed exclusively for the production of Model T's [371A–371C]. The Model T production line had a revolutionary impact, both in the hypnotic speed of its actual functioning and in the unheard-of economies that it achieved. The actual Model T production operations were still performed by men, but the assembly line not only transported the product; more importantly, it set the pace. It took away from the human operator the initiative of his actions. The final goal of technology—the elimination of the operator entirely from the mass production process—is today largely achieved; if justified economically, it is possible to design automated plants that can produce a complex article from its raw components without once being touched by human hands.

The "American system of manufacture" proved adaptable to a multitude of products. Countless inventions that are now everyday articles owe their survival, their very shape, and their worldwide dissemination to mass production. Typical inventions are the revolver, the sewing machine, the typewriter, the camera, and the automobile.

365A
Interchangeable parts, 1882.

365B
Spare parts list for Champion Harvester.

365C
Interchangeable parts, 1965.
Disassembled Volkswagen.

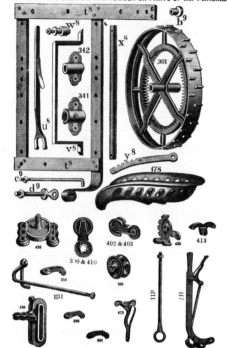

365A

PRICE LIST OF EXTRA PARTS
—FOR—
CHAMPION NO. 4
Mowers, Self-Rakers and Droppers, 4 1-2 and 5 feet cut.
Also, certain Parts used in Light Mowers, Single and Light Reapers.

Tel. Cipher. NO.		NAMES OF PARTS.	YEARS USED.	PLATE.	PRICE.
(Emigrant)		For **Number Four Machines.**			
(Eagle)	30	Small Bevel Pinion	1871 to 82	27	$ 75
	69	Double Tree Plate, (also for Single Reaper)	1871 to 81	28	50
	72	Tongue Hinges, (each)	1871	28	30
	75	Casting for Track Clearer	1871 to 74	27	1 00
	78	Cast Bracket for Driver's Foot Board and Arm	1871 to 82		40
	95	Double Tree Plate for No. 4, Single Reaper, Light Reaper and Light Mower for 1882, also for New Mower	1878 to 82	39	50
	145	Knuckle for Grain Wheel Arm, (4½ feet)	1871	23	50
	149	Head for Rake Arms, (cast)	1871 to 77	25	2 50
	149½	Head for Rake Arms, (M)	1878 to 82		2 50
	A161	Cast Head for Reel Arms	1871 to 79	23	1 25
	178	Cast Seat, (old style)	1871 to 74	28	1 50
(Ear)	182	Malleable Iron Rake Hinge without Roller	1871 to 82	25	1 00
(Easter)		Malleable Iron Rake Hinge with Malleable Roller	1871 to 81		2 00
(Early)		Malleable Iron Rake Hinge with Cast Chilled Roller	1882		2 00
(Easel)	225	Pinion Coupling, (right side)	1871 to 82	27	1 50
(Easy)	226	Pinion Coupling, (left side)	1871 to 82	27	1 50
(Eager)	233	Master Wheel Pinion, (right side)	1871 to 82	27	1 50
(Earth)	244	Master Wheel Pinion, (left side)	1871 to 82	27	1 50
	301	Master Wheel, (4½ and 5 feet)	1871 to 82	28	7 50
	305	Chain Wheel for Reel Shaft	1873 to 79	26	1 00
	310	Hinge for Slatted Platform, (5 feet), (M)	1871 to 82	26	25
(Ebony)	312	Front Rake Switch (M)	1871 to 81	25	1 00
(Echo)	315	Small Outer Shoe, (5 feet), (M)	1871 to 77	24	2 50
	316	Grain Wheel, (5 feet)	1871 to 77	24	1 75
	317	Grain Wheel Arm, (5 feet)	1871	24	1 25
	318	Grain Wheel Knuckle, (5 feet)	1871	24	75
	319	Grain Wheel Plate on Divider, (5 feet)	1871 to 77	24	1 00
(Eckert)	320	Small Outer Shoe for Cutter Bar, (4½ feet)	1871 to 77	27	2 25
(Eclipse)	322	Divider Point, (M), (also for Single and Light Reapers)	1871 to 82	23	50
	323	Chain Wheel for Master Wheel Hub	1871 to 72	23	1 50
	324	Chain Wheel for Reel Shaft	1871 to 72	23	1 50
	328	Dropping Platform Lifter	1871 to 79	23	1 25
	330	Casting for Hoisting Lever	1871 to 74	28	1 00
(Economy)	331	Plate over Heel of Knife, (4½ feet), (M)	1871 to 82	27	75
	333	Grain Wheel, (4½ feet)	1871 to 73	23	1 50
	334	Grain Wheel Arm, (4½ feet)	1871	23	1 00
	336	Bevel Wheel Shield	1871 to 77	28	1 00
(Editor)	337	Fly Wheel Shaft Box and Shield	1871 to 77	27	3 00
	338	Grain Wheel Plate, (4½ feet)	1871 to 77	23	1 00
	339	Cast Seat Slide	1871 to 74	28	1 25
(Edifice)	340	Sliding Stop, (M)	1871 to 82	27	35
	341	Master Wheel Shaft Box	1871 to 82	28	1 00

365B

365C

366

366
Division of labor in pin manufacture. From "Art de
l'épinglier," *Descriptions des
Arts et Métiers,* vol. 8 (Paris,
1762).

367
Butt-stock turning machine
(1850s) based on Thomas
Blanchard's invention of
1818, made by the Ames
Manufacturing Co.,
Chicopee, Mass. From
Charles H. Fitch, "Report on
the Manufactures of Interchangeable Mechanism," in
*Report on the Manufactures
of the United States at the
Tenth Census (June 1, 1880),*
vol. 2 (Washington, D.C.,
1883).

368
Interior of one of Colt's armory
shops, showing horizontal
slotting machines (*fore-
ground*), small lathes (*front
row, left*), and a row of Root
profiling machines with vertical shafts (*behind*). From
Charles H. Fitch, "Report on
the Manufactures of Interchangeable Mechanism."

367

368

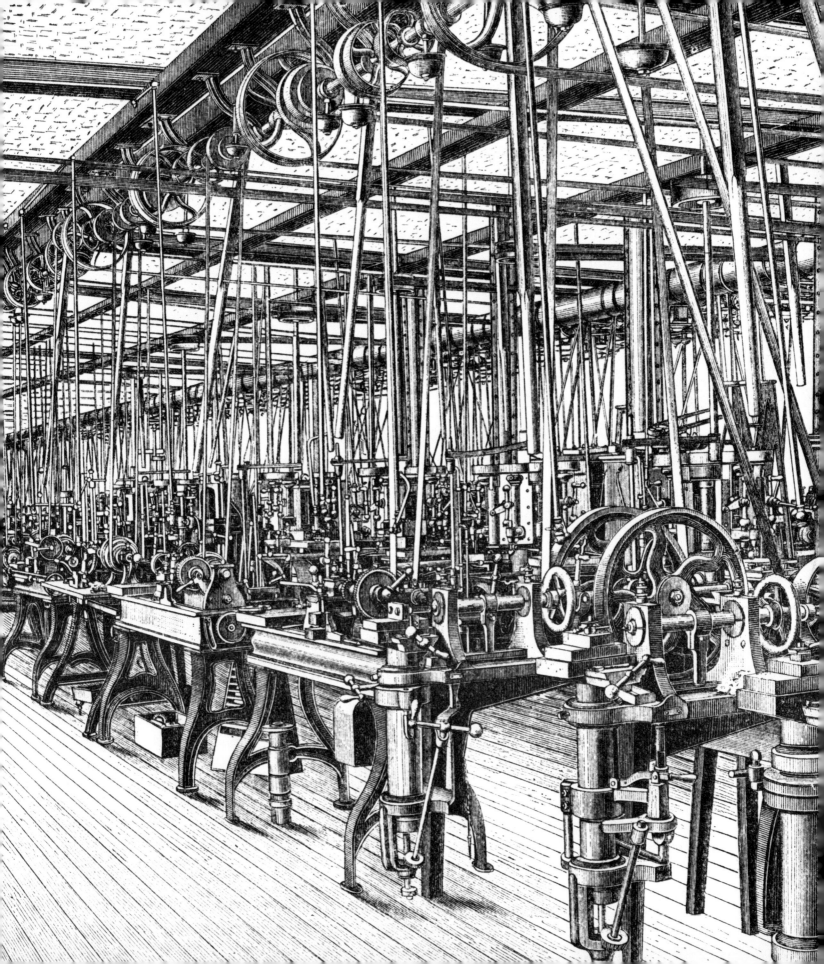

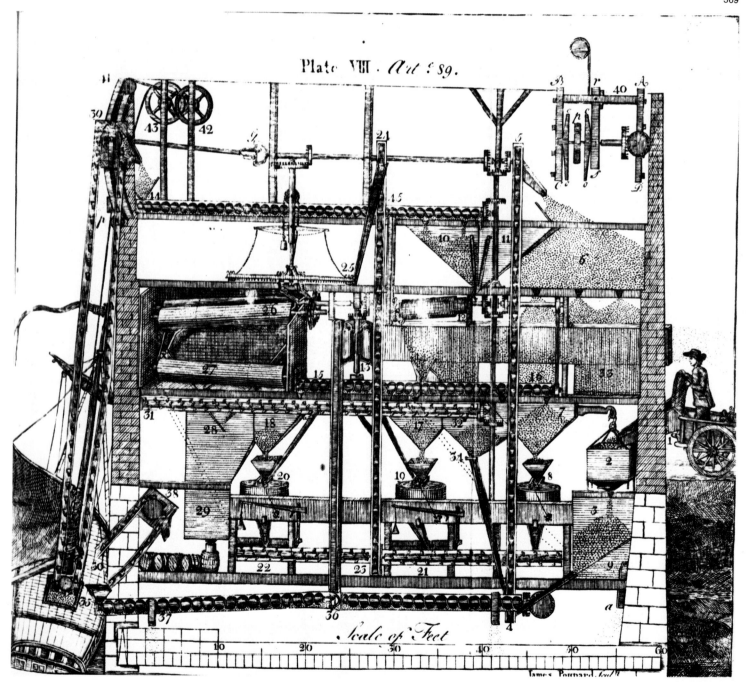

Plate VIII. Art: 89.

Scale of Feet

10   20   30   40   50   60

James Poupard sculpt

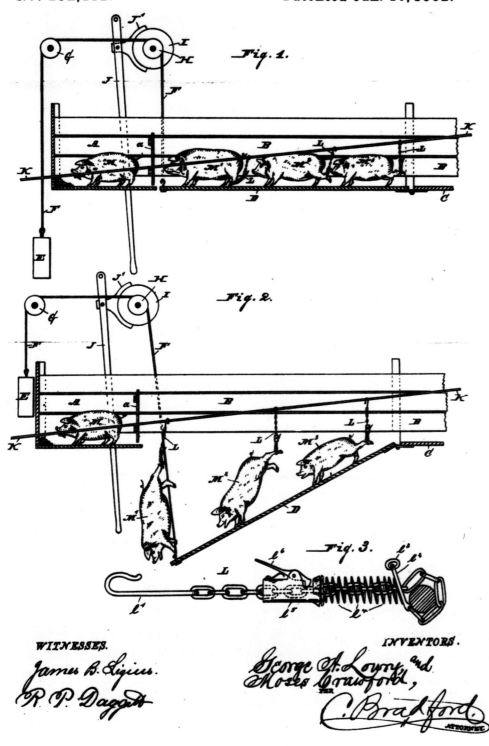

(No Model.)

G. A. LOWRY & M. CRAWFORD.
APPARATUS FOR CATCHING AND SUSPENDING HOGS.

No. 252,112.   Patented Jan. 10, 1882.

Fig. 1.

Fig. 2.

Fig. 3.

WITNESSES.
James B. Ligius.
R. P. Daggit

INVENTORS.
George A. Lowry and
Moses Crawford,
C. Bradford.
ATTORNEY.

N. PETERS, Photo-Lithographer, Washington, D. C.

370

369
The first automatic production
line: Oliver Evans'
mechanized flour mill, 1780s.
From Oliver Evans, *The
Young Millwright and Miller's
Guide* (Philadelphia, 1795).

370
Apparatus for catching and
suspending hogs. U.S. patent,
January 10, 1882.

517

371A
The magneto line, Ford's first moving assembly line (1914) served as a pilot operation and testing ground for the concept that soon became the basis of automobile mass production.

371B
Body chute: Ford Model T bodies are mounted on chassis, c. 1914.

371C
Fifty years after—body drop of Volkswagen Beetles.

371A

371B

371C

Chapter 25

From Guns to Cars— Products for Mass Consumption

The Revolver Before, By, and After Samuel Colt

If a small mechanical device capable of shooting well-aimed bullets at distant and most probably human targets was considered a good thing, even more desirable was one that could do the same in rapid succession. One way to achieve this was to mount on a handgun several barrels in a circular arrangement so they could be rotated into action and fired consecutively. Over the centuries the idea of such a handgun occurred independently to many inventors. Although the concept was difficult to realize with the flint-, wheel-, and snaphance locks of early firearms, a remarkable number of revolving guns were built from the times of King Henry VIII on. Samples of such weapons dating from the late sixteenth and early seventeenth centuries are still preserved in numerous European and American museums and private collections.

In the eighteenth century two basic types of revolving arms emerged. One of them was called the "pepperbox" and had four, six, or more complete barrels bundled together and rotating about a central axis [372A–372C]. The other type consisted of a single barrel and a concentric arrangement of breach chambers that could be rotated into alignment with the barrel [373]. In the eighteenth and early nineteenth centuries the "pepperbox" enjoyed considerable popularity on both sides of the Atlantic. Among the single-barrel revolvers, a modest amount of success was achieved by the complex and costly flintlock revolvers of Elisha Collier, an American who operated in London [374].

The design of handguns was revolutionized in the 1820s by the introduction of the percussion cap. This replaced the uncertain and inconvenient ignition systems based upon flint, steel, and flash pan, and led to a lock that was vastly superior in terms of simplicity, ruggedness, and dependability. It was shortly thereafter that Samuel Colt (1814–1862) made his appearance [375]. In 1835 he took out English and French patents (a U.S. patent followed in 1836) on a revolver that combined the new percussion lock with parts of previous flintlock revolvers [376]. The features patented were relatively minor; the chief asset of his revolver was that it offered, at precisely the right moment, a synthesis of the best existing design elements. Within two decades the Colt revolver was to be the world's prototype, but this, it turned out, was less a result of its mechanical qualities than of Colt's prodigious talents as an entrepreneur.

Colt's first enterprise ended in failure. He established a factory, on a somewhat shaky financial basis, in 1836 in Paterson, New Jersey, which produced a few thousand revolving arms, among them a large order for the government of Texas, but it went bankrupt in 1841. The Mexican War offered a second chance. In 1846 Colt received a U.S. government contract to produce one thousand pieces of improved design, and other orders soon followed. Colt had no factory of his own and was forced to subcontract for the manufacture of the parts, but he retained ownership of the special machinery developed. On the basis of this equipment, the profits earned from the contracts, and the improvements in revolver design and in production techniques, Colt founded an arms factory in Hartford, Connecticut. Colt and his capable plant superintendent, Elisha Root, planned the new factory on a large scale, according to the latest principles of mass production and mechanized to the point that Colt could claim that some 1,400 machines did all the work—the only hand labor was in assembly. In 1856, when the new plant was completed, it employed some five hundred men and produced one hundred fifty to two hundred pistols a day.

Successful as Colt was in matters of design and production, his real genius lay in salesmanship [377A–377C]. He realized that the military was his most important potential customer, and he was indefatigable in making presents of his pistols to high officers, especially those likely to testify before Congress. He solicited military advice on arms design and employed former officers as salesmen. An experienced showman (once he had raised money by giving, under the name Dr. Coult, public demonstrations of laughing gas), he appreciated the power of appearances and went to great lengths to obtain some form of officer's commission. When he did receive an appointment as honorary lieutenant colonel in the entourage of a friendly governor of Connecticut, he forever after styled himself Colonel Colt.

From the start, Colt had aimed at the world market. After 1849, when his American position was securely established, he traveled to Europe with increasing frequency. He acquired additional patents in all major countries, arranged marketing organizations and license agreements, and continued his policy of making presents of expensively decorated Colts wherever they would do the most good. (Typical recipients were the czar of Russia, the prime minister of Great Britain, the kings of Sardinia and of Sweden, and the sultans of Turkey and of Muscat.) After a successful showing at the Great Exhibition of London in 1851, Colt established an affiliate factory in London which, although not overly successful (he disbanded it in 1857), was visited and vividly described by Charles Dickens.

The demand for revolvers grew rapidly [**378, 379**]. In America, Colt had a virtual monopoly, defended ruthlessly in court, until the expiration of his original patents in 1857. Abroad, however, competition sprang up early, partly in the form of rival designs that escaped the umbrella of his patents (in England, for example, the revolver of Robert Adams [**380**] and its subsequent versions), partly in the form of unauthorized imitations. Nevertheless, the position of the Colt revolver was unique: it had become a legend. The name Colt was used all over the world as a generic term for revolver and as a symbol for cowboys, sheriffs, and the Wild West. Indeed, as popular sayings like "God made men, Colonel Colt made them equal" indicate, Colt helped to make the Wild West what it was.

The Colt revolver became immortal also in the strictly technical sense. All its subsequent rivals were unmistakably similar [**381A–381H**]. By the 1860s, revolvers were mass-produced in every industrial country. To reconstruct, or even sketch, the historical processes by which the mass-produced revolver spread over the world would be impossible here, but we can easily demonstrate the pervasive influence by comparing the shapes of revolvers made in various foreign countries. Some superior designs, like those of Remington and of Smith and Wesson, challenged Colt's supremacy. The Colt firm responded in 1872 with its famous cartridge-loaded six-shooter, variously called the "Single Action Army," the "Peacemaker," and the "Frontier" revolver, which has remained in production, with minor changes and except for the interruption of World War II, up to the present.

The triumph of Colonel Colt's idea has its dark side. Next to another achievement of mass production, the automobile, the mass-produced handgun has become the leading cause of violent death in modern America. Chiefly responsible is a class of revolvers and "automatics" produced without consideration of quality, workmanship, or accuracy, with the single aim of cheapness—a class of guns commonly referred to as "suicide specials" or "Saturday night specials." At present, most of these guns are imported to America from abroad, manufactured there by latter-generation imitators and disciples of Samuel Colt [**382**].

372A
English six-barrel flintlock revolver made about 1800. The barrels are revolved by hand and secured in the firing position by a catch on the left side of the frame. Barrel 3".

372B
German four-barrel percussion pistol made about 1836. The barrels are revolved manually and are discharged separately by two hammers released by a single trigger. The barrels are locked in firing position by a bolt attached to the sliding trigger guard. Barrel 6½".

372C
Belgian percussion "pepperbox" revolver made about 1836 on the Marietti system. Barrel 3".

373
American seven-barrel flintlock carbine made by Artemus Wheeler, Concord, Mass., in 1817. The barrels are revolved by hand and secured in firing position by a ratchet which also permits the barrels to turn. Barrel 11".

374
Anglo-American five-shot flintlock revolver patented in England in 1818 by Elisha Hayden Collier of Boston, Mass. Collier developed his design from collaborating with Artemus Wheeler and Cornelius Coolidge of Concord and Boston. Coolidge introduced the system into France. Although the barrels of the pistols were designed to be rotated mechanically, production models were operated manually. Barrel 8".

375
Portrait of Samuel Colt, 1850s.

376
American Colt-Paterson single-action percussion revolver made about 1842. Patented by Samuel Colt of Hartford, Conn., in England in 1835 and the United States in 1836. It was the first practical revolver and the beginning of the famous Colt revolvers. Colt combined the ancient revolving-cylinder principle with the percussion cap and provided a simple and reliable method of revolving and locking the cylinder by the cocking action of the hammer. Barrel 8¾".

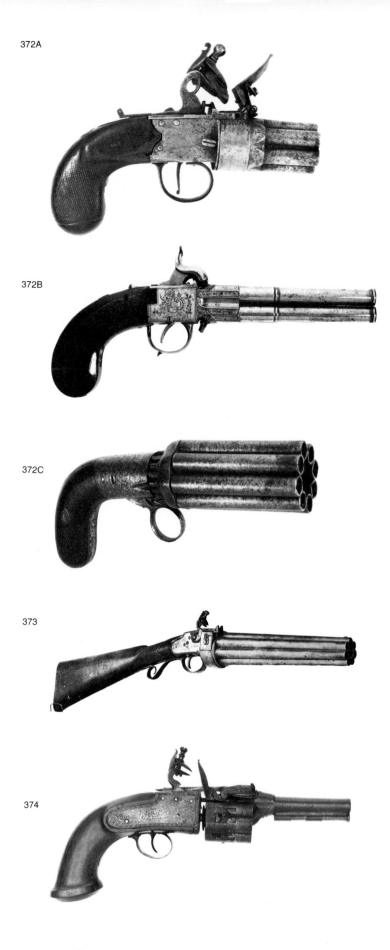

372A

372B

372C

373

374

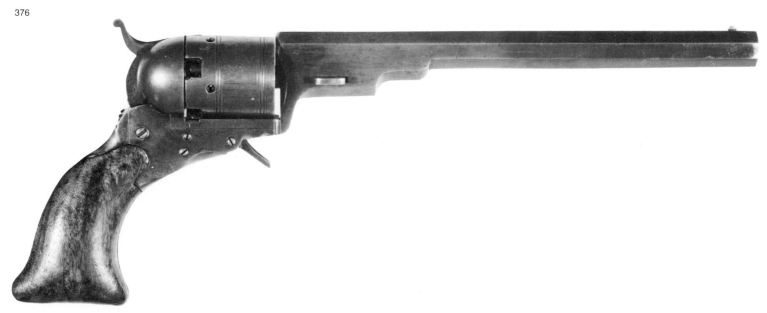

377A
Colt advertising slogan, late
1850s.

377B
An account of Colt's revolver
in a Spanish newspaper,
1852.

377C
Colt advertisement, 1859.

378
American Colt single-action
percussion revolver, model of
1860, with percussion caps
and box of six linen car-
tridges. This was the handgun
most widely used during the
American Civil War. Barrel 8″.

377A

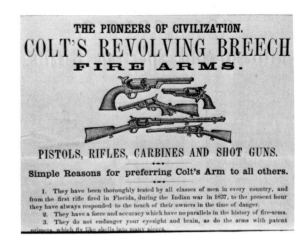

377B

377C

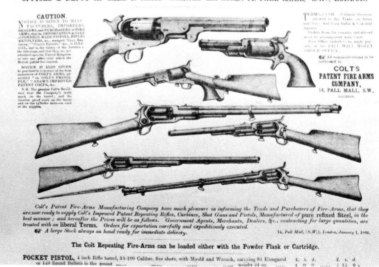

378

379
American Colt center-fire, metallic-cartridge, single-action revolver, manufactured from 1872 to 1941 and from 1955 to date. This is the most famous of all revolvers. It was adopted by the U.S. Army in 1872 and was the indispensable companion of settlers in the western frontier in the post–Civil War era. Barrel 4¾".

380
Engraved English double-action percussion revolver patented in 1851 and 1855 by Robert Adams and Frederick Beaumont. The hammer can be raised for firing either by the thumb or by squeezing the trigger. This was Colt's principal competitor in England, and its success was a contributing factor to the closing of Colt's London factory. Barrel 6¼".

381A
Prussian needle-fire revolver made about 1860 by Frederick Von Dreyse. Barrel 4¾".

381B
Dutch center-fire, metallic-cartridge, double-action revolver made about 1870. Barrel 6¼".

381C
French center-fire, double-action, military revolver, 1873 model. Made in the French National Armory at St. Etienne. Barrel 4⅕".

381D
Spanish center-fire, metallic-cartridge, double-action revolver made by Orbea Brothers c. 1880. Barrel 6".

381E
German center-fire, single-action military revolver, 1883 model, made by the firm of Sauer, Schilling, and Haenel of Suhl. Barrel 4½".

381F
Belgian center-fire, metallic-cartridge, double-action revolver made about 1900. This was a Colt imitation, marked "Texas Ranger." Barrel 5½".

381G
Russian Nagant center-fire, metallic-cartridge, double-action revolver made in 1900 in the Tula Arsenal. Barrel 4½".

381H
Italian center-fire, metallic-cartridge, double-action revolver made by Gilisenti, Brescia, in 1917. Barrel 4½".

380

381E

381A

381F

381B

381G

381C

381H

381D

The career of the Singer sewing machine has been similar to that of the revolver and other mass-produced articles. But more clearly than the others, it demonstrates how long the distance is from the individual invention to the commercially successful product. Sewing machines were invented early and independently at many places. In 1790, an English cabinetmaker, Thomas Saint, received a British patent covering, among other things, a machine for sewing (which was unworkable, as historians have since discovered, unless modified). Sewing machine patents were also awarded in France to Thomas Stone and James Henderson in 1804, and in England to John Duncan (1804) and William Chapman (1807). Before long, sewing machines were actually being produced. Balthasar Krems, of Mayen, Germany, built one in 1810 [**383A**], as did Josef Madersberger, a Viennese tailor, first in 1814 [**383B**], and the Frenchman Barthélemy Thimonnier, in about 1830 [**383C**]. Specimens of all these have survived, but all three failed in practice. The machine of Krems fell into oblivion with the inventor's death; Thimonnier's machines, employed in stitching army uniforms, were smashed by a mob of tailors who felt threatened by them. Both Madersberger and Thimonnier died in poverty.

The first American known to have built a sewing machine (c. 1834) was Walter Hunt, a versatile New York inventor, who had no faith in it and sold it without patenting it. No authentic picture of his machine has survived. The first U.S. patent for a sewing machine was granted in 1842 to J. J. Greenough. By 1855 there were seventy such patents; between 1855 and 1867 the number climbed to 843; and from then to the end of the century there were roughly two thousand per decade. No single patent sufficed to make a truly practical sewing machine; the essential elements eventually were contributed by several different inventors. Elias Howe, who in 1846 patented a machine producing the lock stitch [**383D**], was in one sense the most important contributor, but the patents of C. Morey and J. Johnson (1849), J. Bachelder (1849), A. B. Wilson (1850), and I. M. Singer (1851) were equally indispensable.

Isaac M. Singer (1811–1875) was an outsider. A cabinetmaker and mechanic who had made occasional inventions with indifferent success, Singer had enjoyed a second career as an actor and theater director. When he first encountered, by chance, the sewing machine in 1850, its essential elements had been invented; indeed, several models were already being produced in quantity. Singer combined the most promising design features into a single machine and arranged them in a new shape [**384**]. Singer's first machine had little resemblance to its predecessors and in fact looked rather like the sewing machine of today [**385**].

From the start the sewing machine business was incredibly lucrative. Patents served as devices for blocking competitors and for extorting tributes from the successful. Since the individual patents crucial for a practical machine were in different hands, the leading sewing machine makers were destined to have continuous litigation against each other until they joined in a patent pool in 1856 (after which date all makers began to imitate Singer's general design). Singer's lawyer in the court battles, Edward Clark, became his partner in sewing machine manufacture. Clark, an educated New Englander, was a cool, farsighted businessman who ideally complemented the dynamic, fun-loving, self-made Singer. Both Singer and Clark understood that the secret to success in their enterprise was aggressive and imaginative salesmanship. Mindful of the sensitivities of his chief customer, the Victorian matron, Singer installed large, lavishly decorated showrooms. To make the machines affordable (at $125 each, they at first were not cheap), Clark invented the installment plan. By the late 1850s, I. M. Singer and Company was producing ten thousand machines per year, and ten years later—by now the leading American manufacturer—it turned out one hundred thousand.

Almost from the start Singer aimed at the international market [**386**]. A Singer machine received a prize at the Universal Exposition of Paris in 1855, and even before the Civil War more machines were sold abroad than within the United States. The first foreign manufacturing plant was established in Glasgow, Scotland, in 1867. Notable among the many that followed was the Singer plant in Podolsk near Moscow. After World War I, when all Singer holdings in Russia were nationalized by the Soviet government, their value was estimated at $115 million.

From the Civil War to the end of the nineteenth century, the volume of sewing machines exported by the U.S. averaged $2–$3 million per year [**387**]. It did not rise higher because other countries established sewing machine manufactures of their own, for domestic consumption as well as for export. Leading these foreign competitors was Britain and later Germany, which in the 1920s boasted of outproducing both the U.S. and England. Today a large share of the home sewing machines sold in the U.S. are imports from Europe and the Far East. The only remaining domestic manufacturer is the Singer Company, but sewing machines and related products make up less than one-third their total business. Apart from their American production facilities, they operate factories and assembly plants in twenty-two countries, notably Brazil and Scotland.

383A

383C
The original sewing machine of Barthélemy Thimonnier, France, 1830. Museum Thimmonier, Lyon. H (approx.) 38″.

383D
Sewing machine (patent model) by Elias Howe, U.S.A., 1846. H (approx.) 11″.

384
As a patent model for his first sewing machine, 1850, Isaac Singer submitted a specimen from his regular production line. The first Singer sewing machine was a heavy machine for commercial use. Even after the introduction of the "Family Sewing Machine" in 1858, it continued, with various improvements, to be produced into the twentieth century. H 18¼″.

383C

383D

384

386

385
In Singer's "New Family" sewing machine, manufactured from 1865 to about 1883, the mechanical sewing machine has found its definitive shape. H 38½".

386
Singer on all continents. The title page of sheet music used for advertising the Singer sewing machine.

JAPAN.

OVER

HUNGARY. AUSTRIA - HUNGARY.

OVER

NETHERLANDS (ISLAND MARKEN)

OVER

PORTUGAL (VIANNA)

OVER

MANILA.

COPYRIGHT 1892 BY THE SINGER MANUFACTURING CO.

OVER

ZULULAND

COPYRIGHT 1892 BY THE SINGER MANUFACTURING CO.

OVER

CEYLON

COPYRIGHT 1892 BY THE SINGER MANUFACTURING CO.

OVER

Singer sewing machines for the peoples of the world. A series of advertising postcards published by the Singer company in 1892. The making of intricately ornamented folk costumes such as those shown here was enormously facilitated by the sewing machine.

The origins of the idea of writing by machine are widely scattered in space and time. In 1714 an Englishman, Henry Mill, received a patent on a machine capable of writing "letters . . one after another"; a blind English mathematician claimed to have built, in 1730, a writing machine for the blind; in 1745 a German, J. F. Unger, described the invention of a machine for transcribing music, and in 1749 a Frenchman, Pierre Carmin, is said to have built a writing machine with a piano keyboard. A peculiar breed of writing machines were the automata of the German Freidrich von Knauss and the Swiss Pierre Jacquet-Droz (in the 1770s and 1780s). They were mechanical human figures that could write, with pen in hand, a few preprogrammed words—impressive showpieces but entirely impractical as devices for writing. More than a dozen other claims exist to the invention of some form of writing machine before the year 1800, inventions that were described vaguely, documented poorly, and possibly never built.

In the nineteenth century the rate at which writing machines were invented increased considerably. From the evidence of dated typed letters, the first practical machine actually built was that of Pellegrino Turri (1808), followed by that of his fellow Italian Pietro Conti in 1823. In 1827 the Frenchman Gonod built a machine for writing shorthand. The first American writing machine was patented and built in 1829 by William Burt [**388A**] and the first German one, by the Baron Drais von Sauerbronn (the inventor of the bicycle) in 1831. The first British machine actually built, as opposed to merely patented, was the musical typewriter of Miles Berry, in 1836. Before the year 1867 the number of claims amounted to over one hundred. Almost every country participated, and the inventions proposed were incredibly diverse [**388B, 388C**].

In a few cases, writing machines were even manufactured in quantity, namely Foucauld's 1849 "Clavier Imprimeur" [**388D**], the "Typograph" of the Englishman G. A. Hughes (1850), and the "Mechanical Typographer" of John Jones of New York, who in 1852 tooled up to produce a batch of 130. The first writing machine to achieve a measure of commercial success was the "writing ball" of the Danish pastor J. R. Malling Hansen, invented in 1865 and put into production in 1870 [**388E**]. One feature that all the machines prior to 1867 shared is this: none of them looked or worked like the modern typewriter.

The modern typewriter was the result of a peculiar chain of events. In 1867 Christopher L. Sholes, a Milwaukee newspaperman and politician, and some associates invented a writing machine, and they persuaded a Pennsylvania oilman. James Densmore, to promote and finance its manufacture. The resulting collaboration between Sholes and Densmore led to many experimental models and eventually to a prototype christened "Type-Writer" (1872). It comprised the essential features of the machine that we know now by that name, including the keyboard with its characteristic QWERTY arrangement. What was needed next was a factory with the latest methods of mass production and the willingness to venture into the manufacture of typewriters.

The firm of E. Remington and Sons in Ilion, New York, decided to risk it. They had grown to considerable size as arms manufacturers during the Civil War and had then diversified by adding to their line sewing machines and agricultural equipment. Notable characteristics of this firm were high mechanical expertise and an energetic and imaginative sales force. First, the Remington engineers redesigned the crude prototype. The result, while retaining the original principles of operation and basic shape, was a professionally engineered mechanism, designed with the specific requirements of mass production in mind [**389**]. Production began in early 1874, and by the end of the year four hundred machines were sold at a price of $125 each [**390**].

The fortunes of the "typewriter" and its manufacturers—the Remington Company and its various offshoots and rivals—are too complex to relate here; it is enough to say that the model of 1874, later known as the Remington No. 1, was only moderately successful. In 1878 it was replaced by an improved design, the No. 2, still a "blind writer" (the impression being made on the underside of the carriage) but capable of typing both capital and lower-case letters. With minor modification this machine remained in production for about thirty years and became the model for all successful typewriters in the world.

In spite of the typewriter's obvious promise, commercial success came only when an effective sales organization was built up. By the end of the 1880s sales offices for Remington were established in most European countries, and, since the typewriter was easily equipped with keyboards for the various non-Latin alphabets—from Greek, Russian, and Arabic to the various phonetic scripts of the Far East—before long it reached the most remote corners of the earth. By the end of the century the house organ of the typewriter factory in Ilion was full of news from distant sales offices and of pictures of typewriters in exotic settings [**391, 392**].

Competition for Remington arose soon, and a vast variety of models and designs appeared on the world market. The process of natural selection that followed led to a remarkable result: by the end of the century all the successful typewriters looked very much like the Remington machine; conceptions that differed had fallen by the wayside.

The typewriter's acceptance was symbolized by its use by such celebrities as Mark Twain, Leo Tolstoy (who dictated to his daughter) [**393**], and Lloyd George, but they did not constitute the kind of market needed to make a mass-produced appliance economical. The manufacturers had to generate their own market, which they did by starting hundreds of typewriting schools to train office personnel. When it became apparent that most pupils were women, the firms included in their campaigns a powerful new inducement: they offered the typewriter as the key to women's economic independence. Soon their advertisements showed typewriters operated only by women, and the work of secretaries, stenographers, and typists in the formerly strictly male world of business became the domain of women. For this the typewriter industry claimed credit and posed as agents of women's emancipation, but one observer detected a trace of irony in a situation where "women, after declaring their independence from domestic tyranny, went out and took dictation."

Today an estimated eight or nine million typewriters are produced every year by a surprisingly small number of manufacturers, perhaps no more than twenty-five, whose operations cross all national and continental boundaries. A variety of constantly changing corporate arrangements can be observed. Some firms, like IBM or Remington Rand, operate factories in Europe, South America, and India; others market foreign-made machines under their own label; still others have joined in international mergers (Olivetti-Underwood) or have been absorbed by conglomerates (for example, the American Royal, the German Adler and Triumph, and the British Imperial, by Litton Industries). All this has led to a curious result: not a single mechanical typewriter is produced in the country where that machine was born. Remington, IBM, and Smith-Corona manufacture only electrical machines in America; the market for the mechanical typewriters has been relinquished, for economic reasons, entirely to imports. Foreign producers include not only the industrial nations of Western Europe and Japan; typewriters are also made in various Eastern bloc countries; the People's Republic of China produces a machine of standard Western appearance with an English keyboard, designed specifically for export.

The QWERTY keyboard arrangement of Sholes and Densmore, although by no means optimal, is used universally for all languages written in the Latin script (there are some 130 versions of it, differing slightly according to the special needs of different languages). Comparable standard keyboards are also available for the non-Latin scripts as long as they are phonetic. Only picto- or logographic scripts present difficulties, for which two kinds of solutions have been found. The Japanese use a selection of symbols from their Katakana syllabary as phonetic characters, and Katakana can be directly applied to the conventional keyboard, matching the QWERTY arrangement letter by letter. For a purely logographic script like Chinese, however, with its thousands of different characters, the traditional Western typewriter with a keyboard of only forty to fifty keys is totally unsuited and a fresh solution had to be found. A typical Chinese typewriter consists of a large type bed with some three thousand characters and a single key with which the character is selected, brought to the proper place and printed; the paper is held on the familiar typewriter drum. The process of typing with such a machine is, of course, slower than in a phonetic alphabet, but this is countered by the fact that a single character represents a whole word or phrase.

388A
A reconstruction of the "Typographer" of William Burt, 1829. (The original was destroyed in 1836 in a fire at the U.S. Patent Office.) L 17½".

388B
The "Plume Ktypographique" of Xavier Progin, French patent, September 6, 1833.

388C
Writing machine, made of whittled wood and bent wire, by Peter Mitterhofer, Austria, 1864. Technisches Museum, Vienna. L 12".

388D
The "Printing Piano" or "Clavier Imprimeur" of Pierre Foucauld, France, 1849.

388E
The "Writing Ball" machine of Pastor J. R. Malling Hansen, Denmark, 1870.

389
The first "Type-Writer" of Sholes and Densmore manufactured by E. Remington and Sons, 1874–1876, later designated as Remington No. 1. H 14".

388A

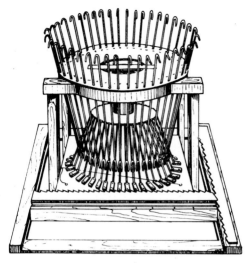

388B

388C

388D

388E

THE
TYPE-WRITER!

A Machine to Supersede the Pen.

MANUFACTURED BY

E. REMINGTON & SONS,
ILION, N. Y.

SOLD BY

Remington Sewing Machine Co.

Price, $125

Ministers, lawyers, authors, and all who desire to escape the drudgery of the pen, are cordially invited to call at our office, and learn to use the Type-Writer. Use of machines, paper and instructions,
FREE!

THE TYPE-WRITER.

COPYING.

A special department has been set apart for this purpose, and we are now prepared to do all kinds of copying, in the best manner, on the TYPE-WRITER.

Any number of copies—from one to twenty—of any document, can be taken AT THE SAME TIME; ensuring *exact duplicates*, and obviating the necessity of more than a single comparison with the original.

The Work is Plain as the Plainest Print.

No pen-writing can compete with Type-Writing, either in

SPEED, LEGIBILITY, OR PRICE,

STENOGRAPHERS

Can come to our office and dictate to operators, *from their short-hand notes*, and thus save the labor of transcription.

AUTHORS,

Who do not desire their manuscripts to go out of hand, can also dictate directly to operator; which saves the labor of revising and preparing a legible first copy for copyist, as such revision can be made when dictating to operator.

DRAMATIC WRITERS

Will see the benefit of our *manifold copying*, in the fact that we can furnish *at the one writing* a COMPLETE CAST for every actor.

Any person, within the city limits of our territory, having copying to do, may notify us of the same by postal card or otherwise, and we will promptly dispatch a competent person to the office or residence. designated, who will give full particulars, estimates, prices, &c.

392
"The Remington Salesman in
Beluchistan," a typical picture
in the Remington house organ (*The Remington Item,*
1907–1908, *5*).

393
Russian novelist Count Leo
Tolstoy dictating to his daugh-
ter.

392

393

Photography is much less a specifically American achievement than, say, the revolver, the sewing machine, or the typewriter. However, the outstanding American contribution to its development—the Kodak system of producing, marketing, and processing photographic materials—dramatically exhibits the characteristic features of the "American system."

The first photograph was taken by the Frenchman Joseph Necéphore Niepce in 1826, long before the development of the Kodak system. Another method was developed independently in the 1830s by Louis Jacques Mandé Daguerre; in the resulting daguerreotype, a positive image was produced *directly* on a specially prepared silver-plated sheet of copper. At the same time, a different photographic process was invented independently in England by W. H. Fox Talbot; his photogenic drawing (later calotype or talbotype) process was based on a negative which could be used to produce an unlimited number of positives. This arrangement became the model for the system universally used today.

For these pioneers, as for photography through the entire nineteenth century, the chief problems were chemical, not optical. The crucial element was not the camera but the light-sensitive material from which the photographs were made. Photography was a complex mixture of science and art. The early wet-plate process required from its practitioners formidable skills and elaborate equipment [**394**]. Before and after taking a photograph, the artist had to perform complicated chemical operations. The darkroom had to accompany him wherever he wanted to work. As a result, early photography was an exclusive form of art reserved for the professional and the strongly committed amateur. The products of this art reflected these difficulties: early photographs combine high artistic quality with an air of deliberate planning, formality, and immobility [**395**].

The invention in 1871 of the gelatin dry-plate process with its simplified procedures opened up the field to a larger circle of participants. George Eastman (1854–1932), a young bank clerk and amateur photographer in Rochester, New York, began to produce gelatin dry plates, first for his own use, then for his friends, and eventually (1880) commercially in a factory of his own. Eastman's success did not rest on his skill as an inventor (although he made a number of minor inventions) but on his ability as an entrepreneur who could foresee and create new markets. Most of the patents, the technical and scientific expertise that his enterprises demanded, he would obtain from others. Eastman's own contributions were five business principles, which he formulated at the start:
1. Production in large quantities by machinery.
2. Low prices.
3. Foreign as well as domestic distribution.
4. Extensive advertising.
5. "Control of the alternative" (that is, he would make sure to always "control" at least one alternative to each invention or process that he was using).

He combined these principles with a general business attitude that is best summed up in his own words: "Peace extends only to private life. In business it is war all the time. . . . We do not always win, but when we lose, the victory does not seem to have much attraction for the enemy."

Recognizing the limitations of glass-plate photography, Eastman and his associates set out to market an old idea that nobody had been able to bring to success: mounting the photographic layer not on glass but on some flexible carrier. By 1885 he introduced a kind of film [**396**] having paper as its base, supported on rolls in the manner now universal, which could be used in existing cameras by means of a simple attachment, the roll holder.

Now the stage was set for his big coup—the device that was to introduce photography into the lives of ordinary people. In 1888 he put on the market a small box camera [**397A, 397B**] of simple lines, designed expressly for roll film and requiring no adjustments. Named "The Kodak" (a word invented for its sound), this camera was more than a novel piece of apparatus. What it represented was an entire system, and it included, for a fixed price, all the equipment, materials, and services needed for successful photography. The price of twenty-five dollars covered the camera plus the purchase and developing of a roll of film with one hundred exposures [**398**]. As the advertising slogan "You press the button—we do the rest" said, all the owner had to do, after finishing a roll of film, was to take his camera to the dealer, or mail it directly to the factory. There the film would be developed, printed, and for another ten dollars, replaced by a fresh one.

The subsequent history of the Kodak system can be described simply in terms of the implementation of Eastman's five business principles. The system was mass-produced and therefore cheap. Massive nationwide advertising stimulated the necessary demand, and commercial success followed quickly. What previously had been a difficult and exclusive technique became an eminently democratic pastime. And the products of this new photography were no longer works of high art but . . . snapshots [**399**].

Eastman assembled a staff of professional engineers and chemists who continuously perfected the system and developed new products. Numerous additional patents were purchased from outsiders. Important photographic innovations followed in quick succession: transparent film (1889), a daylight-loading camera (1891), a pocket camera (1895), and the one-dollar Brownie camera (1900).

Eastman almost immediately entered the international market. In 1889 he founded a subsidiary plant in England, which was to produce for the markets of Europe, Asia, and Australia. Eastman's products were advertised abroad just as aggressively as in the United States, and by the mid-1890s the Kodak sign appeared on the buses of Paris and on billboards above the squares of other European capitals. Subsidiaries were opened in Paris and Berlin and sales headquarters in virtually every European country. Acceptance of the system followed quickly. Early British users of the Kodak were Rudyard Kipling and George Bernard Shaw; Lord Kelvin was a director of the Kodak Company; a Kodak even appeared in *Utopia,* an operetta by Gilbert and Sullivan.

In the history of photography, the introduction of the Kodak system is only an episode. Its essence was the application of mass-production techniques and, like mass production itself, the system was characteristically American. Subsequent chapters in the story—which would have such headings "Cinematography," "Color Photography," "High-Speed Photography," and "X-Ray Photography"—deal with actions and events that are thoroughly international, where the significant technical breakthroughs were brought about cumulatively through contributions from many different countries, in the way that photography itself was born. Nevertheless, the Kodak system has not only survived, it has become virtually universal. Today industrial countries like Japan, America, and Germany outdo each other to produce photographic products that combine high performance with simplicity of operation. The photographic material universally used is the roll of film introduced (although not invented) by George Eastman. Equally universal is the system of processing pioneered by Eastman, by which the individual sends his film to a processing center which has the expertise and the specialized automatic equipment necessary to produce photographs in sufficient quantities to ensure low cost.

394

395

396

397A

THE
KODAK
CAMERA.

Silver Medal at Minneapolis Convention F. A. of A. for most important invention of the year.

PHOTOGRAPHY REDUCED TO THREE MOTIONS.

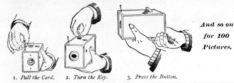

And so on
for 100
Pictures.

1. *Pull the Cord.*   2. *Turn the Key.*   3. *Press the Button.*

ANYBODY CAN USE IT.

Size of Camera, 3¼ x 3¾ x 6½ inches.

Weight, 1 lb. 10 oz.

Size of Picture, 2½ in. diameter.

PRICE, - - - $25.00

Price includes hand-sewed sole leather Carrying Case, with shoulder strap and film for 100 exposures.

Amateurs can finish their own negatives or send the roll of exposed films to the factory by mail to have them developed and printed.

Price for developing, printing and mounting 100 Pictures, including spool 100 films for

reloading Camera, - - - $10 00

Spool for reloading only, - - - 2 00

Uncapping for Time Exposures.

THE EASTMAN DRY PLATE AND FILM CO.,

15 Oxford Street, London. | ROCHESTER. N. Y.

Send for Descriptive Circulars.

XX

398

397B

396
Eastman's "American" stripping film, c. 1885. This early form of roll film was used primarily before the advent of the Kodak in former plate cameras converted by the Eastman-Walker "roll holder." H 5½".

397A
The original version of the Kodak No. 1 camera, 1888, with its characteristic barrel shutter. H 4".

397B
Kodak No. 1, second model, c. 1892, with sector shutter. The opened case shows the arrangement of the roll film.

398
One of Eastman's first advertisements for the Kodak system, 1888. From *Anthony's Photographic Bulletin*, 19 (Dec. 8, 1888).

The snapshot. The informality, spontaneity, and playfulness of this early Kodak photograph illustrate the transformation of the art of photography through George Eastman's system. The characteristic circular format of early Kodak photographs maximized the effective picture area.

379

Mass Production Carried to Extremes—Henry Ford and the Model T

The question "Who invented the automobile?" can only be answered meaningfully after first establishing "what kind of automobile." At the turn of this century, of all the automobiles in the United States, 40 percent were driven by steam engines, 38 percent by electrical batteries, and only 22 percent by internal combustion engines. Each of the three types has its own history. The steam automobile is the oldest. The first one, built in 1769 by the Frenchman Nicolas-Joseph Cugnot, was soon followed by others, in France as well as America. Indeed, in England steam coaches achieved considerable popularity in the 1830s [**400A**] before they disappeared in the face of adverse legislation and the competition of the railroad. Electrical vehicles first appeared in the early 1880s in France and England and shortly after in America [**400B**].

Among the first vehicles powered by internal combustion engines were those of the Frenchman J. J. E. Lenoir in the 1860s and the Austrian S. Marcus, in the 1870s, but both remained without influence. For practical purposes the development of the road vehicle powered by an internal combustion engine began with the Germans Gottlieb Daimler and Carl Benz, who, working some fifty miles apart, without knowing of each other, both road-tested such vehicles in 1885 [**400C**]. Their perfected designs were commercially successful and became the prototypes for subsequent developments [**400D**] (although the American George B. Selden succeeded in defending the validity of his 1879 patent). The companies that Daimler and Benz had started merged in 1926; the two men, however, never met.

By 1900 the contest among the three sources of power was by no means decided. In some ways steam and electricity were superior. The electric car was the first (1899) to exceed a speed of 60 miles per hour and to win the French hill-climbing contest (1898); in 1906 a steamer set a speed record at 127.66 miles per hour. What finally tipped the scale in favor of the internal combustion engine was its fuel economy and its convenience. The early automobiles of all types, however, had one characteristic in common: they were produced in small numbers and hence were expensive. Operating under the prevailing unfavorable traffic and road conditions, they were essentially playthings for wealthy sportsmen.

Mass production of automobiles started before Henry Ford. Benz began to build cars in series in 1894, and by the end of the century he was producing over five hundred a year. Ransom E. Olds built ten times as many Oldsmobiles in 1904. In America in the first decade of the twentieth century the market for automobiles seemed potentially unlimited.

Henry Ford, whose Ford Motor Company (incorporated in 1903) was one of the larger ones among the great number of competing automobile manufacturers, conceived the idea of manufacturing a simple and rugged "universal car" at low cost by means of the single-minded application of the latest mass-production techniques. In 1905 he concentrated his plant on the production of one single model (first his "Model N"); in 1908 he put his "Model T" on the market, and in 1910 he built the sixty-acre Highland Park plant, devoted exclusively to the Model T. Production at this new plant was to be geared to one controlling principle: the concept of the moving assembly line. When, in 1913, the assembly line was put into full-scale operation, the results were sensational. In 1913–1914 the annual production was one-quarter of a million cars, and the profits were such that in January 1914 Ford announced to his workers the "five-dollar day," approximately doubling their wages. When the 300,000-cars-per-year mark was passed in 1915, Ford paid back fifty dollars to each of the previous year's purchasers. As the Model T's production rate increased (1.7 million in 1923), its price dropped; a minimum was reached in 1925, when the "Runabout" model [**401A, 401B**] cost no more than $260. The Model T remained in production virtually unchanged for almost twenty years. Only in 1927, after the fifteen millionth had rolled off the assembly line, was the Ford plant shut down for the painful conversion to a more up-to-date Model A [**402A–402G, 403**].

In many ways, with his production of the Model T, Henry Ford was but following in the footsteps of Samuel Colt, Isaac Singer, George Eastman, and all the other pioneers of the "American system of manufacture." Like them, he appreciated the power of public opinion, which he took care to cultivate by means of advertising as well as by impressive public gestures. He also thought internationally, quickly organizing a worldwide network of distribution offices and manufacturing facilities [**404A–404G**]. The Ford house organ was just as fond of presenting the company's product in exotic surroundings as were the publications of the Remington and Singer companies. But Ford's eagerness to span the globe [**405**] with his products may have had motives that went beyond the purely commerical: his naïve and often ridiculed attempt in 1915 to stop World War I by his personal mediation was born out of a belief that the experience of modern technology and the engineer's approach to problem solving had something new to contribute to international affairs.

Henry Ford's innovations in production technology had more effect on the modern world, however, than his idealism. The introduction of the moving assembly line at the Highland Park plant was taken as the beginning of a new era (in Aldous Huxley's novel *Brave New World* the years were counted not A.D., but A.F.—"After Ford"). Technologists from afar visited the plant as they would a shrine, and Ford's *My Life and Work* (1922) became the gospel of his disciples. Followers and competitors appeared soon. General Motors brought out the Chevrolet, which in the course of the 1920s surpassed the Model T in sales. Austin, Fiat, and Citroën in Europe applied Ford's philosophy of the small mass-produced popular automobile with success.

The Model T's most famous offspring was the Volkswagen. Its history has two parts. The first began in 1923, when Hitler, already a fanatical automobile enthusiast, read Henry Ford's memoirs while in prison. The idea of a "people's car" was planted in his mind, and in 1934, when he was firmly in power, he summoned Dr. Ferdinand Porsche and gave him orders to design such an automobile. Prototypes of the future Beetle were tested in late 1936, and in 1937 Hitler publicly announced his decision to manufacture, in government-owned factories, the Volkswagen, to be sold at just under 1,000 marks (then $250). Construction of a factory, started in 1938, was unfinished when World War II began. In war production the factory's role was insignificant: only sixty or seventy thousand of its best-known product—a Volkswagen converted into a kind of jeep—were produced, and eventually the factory was thoroughly bombed.

In 1945 the car inspired by Hitler and designed by Porsche started its second career under entirely different circumstances. With the support of the British occupation authorities, the workers of the VW factory started to repair their plant and to produce an automobile almost exactly like the 1938 prototype. The beginning was slow: the fifty thousandth postwar Beetle was produced only in 1949, but when Germany's economic recovery gathered momentum, both the demand for and the production of Volkswagens rose rapidly. The one million mark was reached in 1955, five million in 1961, and in 1972 VW surpassed the fifteen million record set in 1927 by the Model T Ford.

An automobile production of such size could, of course, not be sold in Germany alone. In time the VW organization has built up not only an international network of sales and maintenance establishments; it also operates entire factories in Australia, Brazil, and South Africa and assembly plants in European and Latin American countries, the Philippines, and New Zealand.

The story of the Volkswagen is representative of the success of automobile mass production in many countries; Datsun, Fiat, Renault, Toyota, and Volvo have had similar careers. In the early 1970s the world production of automobiles ranged from twenty-five to thirty million per year, with the U.S.A., Japan, and West Germany as leaders. These manufacturing countries export large shares of their automobile production, except for the American firms, who have preferred to acquire automobile factories in foreign countries to supply the local markets (General Motors owns Vauxhall in Britain, Opel in Germany, and Holden in Australia; Chrysler controls Simca in France and Rootes in England; Ford operates relatively autonomous factories under its own name in Great Britain, Germany, France, and other countries).

The total number of motor vehicles today may be estimated at a quarter billion. This is obviously too many. To be sure, for millions of people, the advent of the inexpensive mass-produced automobile has been the fulfillment of a dream. As a result, the automobile has gained power over men's lives as no machine before. Societies have willingly sacrificed to it cherished traditions, adjusting their settling patterns, roads, and public transportation systems to accommodate this gift from technology. In turn they have accepted grave disadvantages: traffic congestion, air pollution, defaced cities and landscapes, high rates of fatal accidents, and a rapid depletion of the world's energy supplies.

An expedient solution for these problems would be to limit the use and production of the automobile. Such a solution, however, risks new problems, for automobile production has become the basis of the world's strongest national economies. Countries like the United States, Japan, Germany, France, Italy, and Sweden depend to a critical degree upon their automobile industries. To them, a declining market for automobiles means unemployment, unfavorable foreign trade balances, weakening currencies. Quickly the problem becomes a political one of international dimensions, made difficult not only by its own inherent complexity but also by the political influence of the powerful industries whose future, and perhaps survival, is linked to the automobile.

Nevertheless, the limits of the mass-produced automobile have doubtless been reached. Emerging in the 1960s, a number of social and economic forces have come into play counteracting the automobile's previously irresistible appeal. Steadily growing portions of the population refuse to accept the high accident rates, the air pollution, and the energy waste associated with a ''nation on wheels.'' In the end, perhaps, a balance will be achieved between the manifold incentives of mass-producing an immensely desirable article and social responsibility, where the fruits of technology will be enjoyed with a newly discovered moderation.

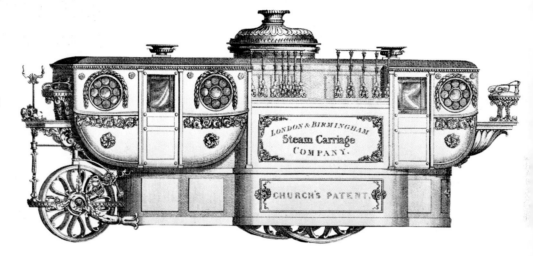

400B

400C

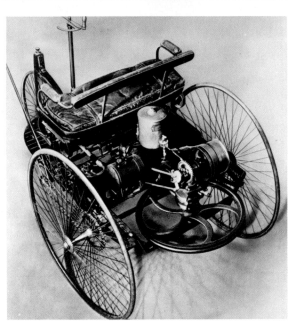

400D

400B
Electric automobile manufactured in 1899 by the Riker Motor Vehicle Company, Elizabethport, N.J. L 10'10".

400C
Carl Benz built and road-tested his first automobile, a gas-powered tricycle, in 1885 in Mannheim, Germany.

400D
Gas-powered automobile designed and built by Charles and Frank Duryea, Springfield, Mass., 1893–1894. L 97".

401A
Advertisement for the 1924 Ford Model T Runabout. The all-time lowest price for any Model T was reached with $260 for the Runabout of the following year.

Ford
RUNABOUT

$265
F.O.B. DETROIT

Starter and Demountable Rims $85 extra

Order Your Ford Runabout Now!

Each spring the demand for Ford Runabouts is far in excess of the immediate supply.

Fast in traffic, easy to park and fitted with ample luggage space, the Ford Runabout is especially adapted for the work of salesmen and others who must conserve time and energy in making their daily calls.

If you do not wish to pay cash for your car, you can arrange for a small payment down and easy terms on the balance. Or you can buy on the Ford Weekly Purchase Plan.

Ford Motor Company
Detroit, Michigan

See the Nearest Authorized Ford Dealer

Ford
CARS · TRUCKS · TRACTORS

402A

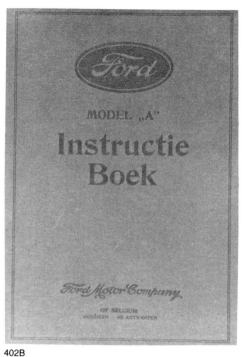

402B

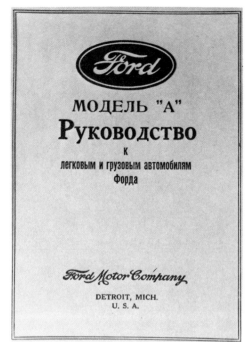

402C

402D

402E

402F

402G

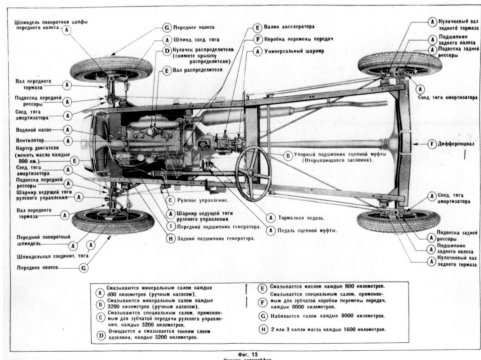

403

559

404 A

404B

404C

404D

404E

404F

404G

405
Ford Times cover emphasizing the enormous success of the Model T. The total mileage of all the Ts on the road in 1915 was supposedly equal to three trips around the world.

The American System of Manufacture— A Second Look

Looking back on these case histories of five classic mass-produced consumer products, it is impossible not to notice their similarity. They all follow the same three-stage pattern.

1. The first stage has an international character: the "original inventor" might have come from any country. Usually the origins of the invention were obscure. Versions of the same idea might appear at different times in history, or simultaneously in different countries. The inventions might differ wildly in conception and shape. One thing, however, they had in common: they were commercially unsuccessful at this stage. For reasons economical or technical, at best the article invented was produced in small quantities for an exclusive market.

2. The second stage was characteristically American. A Yankee inventor, after surveying the range of available solutions, would succeed in inventing a new version of the article that was simple, rugged, practical, and, above all, suitable for mass production. He would at once proceed to mass-produce it, either by himself or with the help of a willing entrepreneur. As soon as the design of the product was mature and its production successful, the next task was to find a market. This meant creating a sales organization, hiring and training salesmen, investing in advertising. The more successful American manufacturers did not confine themselves to their national boundaries; for them the natural market was the whole world. With amazing energy, they introduced their products to remote parts of the globe, and their international acceptance was proudly displayed in their home advertising. In many foreign languages, Colt, Singer, Remington, and Ford, originally names of individual Americans and then of specific commercial products, in time became generic terms for "revolver," "sewing machine," "typewriter," and "automobile."

Commercial success has had a curious effect upon the technical characteristics of a mass-produced article. Seemingly as soon as it has been accepted by the masses, its design freezes. The similarity of today's typewriters, sewing machines, and revolvers to the original Remingtons, Singers, and Colts of more than a century ago is almost touching; all the more so when we compare them with the wild diversity of their original rivals.

Do mass-produced products cease to change because they have reached perfection? There are examples to the contrary. To mention only one, our typewriter still features the keyboard selected about 1870 by Christopher L. Sholes, the inventor; it is adequate but, as has often been shown, far from optimal. The reasons for such conservatism must lie in the huge financial, institutional, and psychological momentum of an industry dedicated to mass production.

3. The last stage in the history of mass production completes the circle. The mass-produced articles America has marketed abroad present challenges for other countries to adopt mass production and capture export markets of their own. Often they have responded by studying the American philosophy of mass production, copying its techniques, and adapting it to local conditions. Today it is no longer an American domain. Mass-produced goods are exchanged among all continents, and the countries of North America, East Asia, and Europe compete as equal partners. In some areas, the American industry has ceded entire domestic markets to foreign suppliers. For example, mechanical typewriters are no longer manufactured in the United States. Those sold here—even those with American brand names—come from abroad.

Chapter 26

A Taste for Foreign Things at Home

Motels to Chewing Gum—A Pictorial Essay

The Ford Model T and the Colt handgun were known for their reliability, low price, and serviceability, but utility was not their sole attraction. They were also exotic machines when placed in distant lands, American machines as new as spring flowers, as enthralling as a cobra swaying to the tune of a flute.

Singer sewing machines, Remington typewriters, and all the other children of mass production became commercial ambassadors of the "American system of manufacture." As numerous foreign observers wrote, nearly every phase of life in America appeared subject to mass production and standardization. And not just "hardware" items, to be sure. Food production and food processing, clothing, even the accouterments of travel, such as restaurants, motels, and credit cards, carried the stamp of automation. The end product appeared to be a life style that, if not formed by mass production and computerization, at least represented a way of doing things that accepted mechanization as a necessity.

In the present century, as mass production has continued to increase the supply of goods, America has needed the world for a marketplace. While military hardware, scientific knowledge, and even abstract art have received the attention of those concerned with America's influence on the world, it may well be that the less essential consumables and services—fast food, cigarettes, chewing gum, soft drinks, credit cards, jeans, and motels—more accurately reflect the American style abroad. The primary elements in the production and marketing of these items are standardized product identity, "predictable" product performance, and an atmosphere of something indefinable called "American." This last factor is essential. Whatever is foreign to a person's normal life style often becomes a magnet to his curiosity. And when—as in the case of American goods—this strangeness is institutionalized, mass-produced, and mass-marketed, the products appear to become irresistible to vast numbers of people everywhere.

The historical roots of modern American products and services are diverse. Some, like the motel, are purely American in origin, and others—the cola drinks, for example—have come from somewhere else.

The "American" standard of comfort for travelers is one of the unique exports that are purely American. It is used by numerous hotel and motel chains to lure the world traveler no matter where he may be. In advertisements published in Asia, Europe, and South America in 1974–1975, Holiday Inn, a pioneer in the post-World War II motel boom, promised to provide the "ten things" clients want the most: "cleanliness," "comfort . . . big comfortable beds and cozy furniture," "quiet—thick walls," "food . . . in a pleasant atmosphere," "good service," "private bathroom—every room has one," "parking . . . free," "temperature control," "telephone," and a less definable but most typically American ingredient called "know what to expect." The "guarantee" that one Holiday Inn will be essentially the same as every other Holiday Inn (as of May 1975 there were more than 1,700 throughout the world) is backed up by a training center in Mississippi called Holiday Inn University, a rigid code of sign regulations, a furniture supply service, a giant printing press, and a world-wide inspection program. Just as mass production provided Americans with reliable, affordable, look-alike appliances which eventually caught the fancy of the world, the standardized motel environment, too, is an American product for world consumption.

This pursuit of a standard of comfort for travelers did not begin with the rise of motels in the 1940s; the imaginative historian of mechanization, Sigfried Giedion, traced it back to the Pullman Sleeping Car shortly after the Civil War. By devising a swing-down upper berth and a lower berth that served for seating during the day, George Pullman (1831–1897) built cars for middle-class travelers that remained unchanged in their basic design until after World War II [see **133**]. Sleeping comfortably on a long-distance trip became a reality in America in the 1870s.

European observers saw the Pullman as purely American, and they described the "Pullman style" as an effort "to democratize aristocratic luxury." Shortly after the first Pullman cars were rolling on American rails, eighteen of them were shipped to England in 1873. The style was then transplanted to the Continent, where it remained a unique symbol of American influence abroad. From the Pullman to the modern motel, the style of sleeping on the road is consistently American. And, to be sure, the selling of the predictable (what Holiday Inn calls "know what to expect") spills over into numerous other American products and services that enjoy an international market.

While the cola soft-drink industry followed the path of standardized product identity similar to the motel chains, the product itself evolved not from earlier American forms but from foreign sources. Cola drinks were a fad in Europe in the final quarter of the nineteenth century, a decade or more before they arrived in America. They were based on the extract of the cola nut, which is native to Africa and the West Indies and was known for centuries by Europeans. Interest in the cola nut grew in the nineteenth century. In 1883 *The American Journal of Pharmacy* observed: "The nuts are used to form a refreshing and invigorating drink throughout a large portion of tropical Africa. . . . Moreover, if once introduced as a beverage in civilized countries, the demand for it would soon become enormous." Four years later the first cola beverage was registered in the United States Patent Office: its name was Coca-Cola. Yet even into the 1890s the cola drinks seemed most popular in Europe. The *National Bottlers' Gazette* (London, 1894) gibed: "Kola is a new drink which seems to take over here. . . . Where is your American enterprise?" By the second decade of this century American enterprise had indeed taken hold and promoted cola drinks almost as if they were basically American.

In the case both of the native motel and the imported cola beverages the one message is clear: the "American style" helps to sell the American goods. Today, for numerous products, the image of the American cowboy is ubiquitous in sales campaigns. He sells Marlboro cigarettes in Ethiopia and Levi's pants in Italy. He means "American." America's football heroes promote Wrigley's chewing gum in Japan and American Express Travel Service in Paris and Rome. McDonald's and Colonel Sanders, whether in Denmark or England, provide a "fast food" service which seems as American as the Rocky Mountains. (Indeed the history of the "quick lunch" dates back to the ten-minute whistle stop of the American railroad before the advent of the dining car.) Most of these products are not sold to fill basic human needs; their appeal is in their style, their foreignness. They add variety and choice to foreign cultures, just as styles and tastes from abroad enrich American culture.

The illustrations that follow show American products and services advertised in eighteen different languages. At times they seem incongruous, almost comical, but they represent America's image abroad in a way that is seldom seen by Americans themselves.

406
Cartoon by Jeff MacNelly, Richmond *News Leader*,
March 18, 1975. In the process of visualizing a typical
American street after the commercial takeover by oil-
wealthy countries, the cartoonist has included American
trademarks familiar the world over.

407A
Holiday Inn ad for French magazines (1974).

407B
Holiday Inn ad reflecting the ultimate in the standardization
of comfort (1974). Used in Asian hotels.

407C
Holiday Inn ad, Germany, 1974.

407D
Holiday Inn ad, Japan, 1974.

407E
Holiday Inn ad, Spanish-language countries, 1974.

Standardized signage, which more and more American
firms appear to find increasingly desirable, reflects the growing trend to market what Holiday Inn calls "know what to
expect." McDonald's in Tokyo wants to look, to taste, and to
feel just like McDonald's in Stockholm. And credit card
companies as well as travel services work more and more
on consistency and instant recognizability. The languages
change but the message and the "look" remain the same.
And these standardized signs in the form of billboards,
magazine ads, and packaging materials are becoming part
of the world's landscape. While in the mid-twentieth century
a Coca-Cola sign in Italy attracted notice, today the presence of a soft drink such as Pepsi in Russia is still newswor-
thy but not surprising.

406

407B

407C

407D

407E

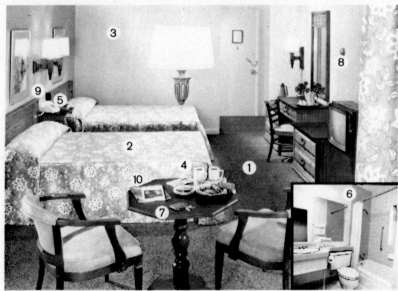

407A

408

Cantilevered Sign
German
Stripe A

Cantilevered Sign
Russian
Stripe B

Cantilevered Sign
Arabic
Stripe B

Cantilevered Sign
Japanese
Stripe B

Cantilevered Sign
Chinese
Stripe B

Cantilevered Sign
Norwegian
Stripe A

Cantilevered Sign
Hebrew
Stripe A

Cantilevered Sign
French
Stripe B

Cantilevered Sign
Greek
Stripe B

409A

409B

410A

410B

411A

411B

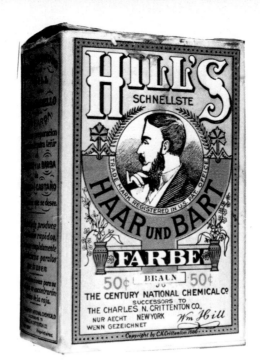

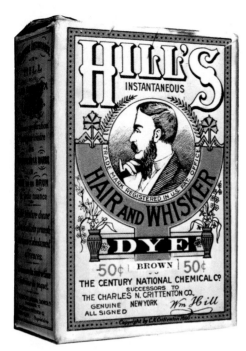

412

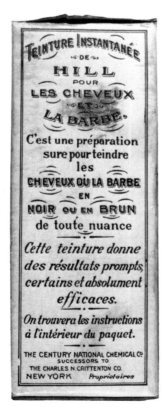

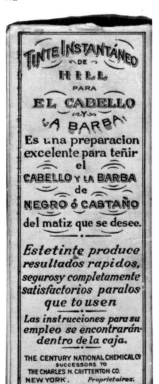

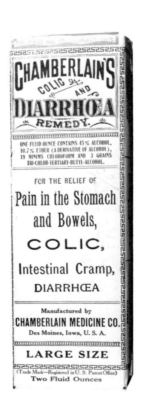

413

411A
Levi's clothing ad used in Mexico and South America.

411B
Levi's clothing ad used in several countries, including Italy. The Levi's jeans ad that uses Michelangelo's "David" as a model for a pair of "cut-offs" is a study in cultural incongruity. It symbolizes the meeting of two cultures and makes one point quite clear: the American style is abroad.

412
Hill's hair and whisker dye. Hair dyes were a common patent medicine produced in the nineteenth century. Hill's dye was copyrighted in 1880 and sold until about 1910. German was a dominant language for patent medicines produced in New York City and Milwaukee. The use of French, Spanish, and English enabled the product to be sold nationally as well as to be exported.

413
Chamberlain's started manufacturing patent medicines in 1920 and sold internationally up to 1965. It produced a cough syrup and other preparations in multilingual format, which opened the various ethnic markets in the United States to Chamberlain salesmen.

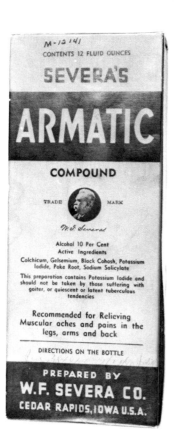

M-12 141
CONTENTS 12 FLUID OUNCES

SEVERA'S

ARMATIC

COMPOUND

TRADE MARK

W. F. Severa

Alcohol 10 Per Cent
Active Ingredients
Colchicum, Gelsemium, Black Cohosh, Potassium
Iodide, Poke Root, Sodium Salicylate

This preparation contains Potassium Iodide and
should not be taken by those suffering with
goiter, or quiescent or latent tuberculous
tendencies

Recommended for Relieving
Muscular aches and pains in the
legs, arms and back

DIRECTIONS ON THE BOTTLE

PREPARED BY

W. F. SEVERA CO.

CEDAR RAPIDS, IOWA U.S.A.

Spanish   Contenido 12 onzas flúidas

COMPUESTO ARMATIC SEVERA

Alcohol 10 Per Cent

Ingredientes Activos: Cólquico, Jazmín silvestre, Lechera, Yoduro de potasio, Fitolaca, Salicilate de sodio.

Esta preparación contiene Yoduro de potasio y no deben tomarla squéllos que sufren de papera o que tengan tendencia a la tuberculosis, ya sea en estado inactivo o latente.

Se recomienda para aliviar los dolores en los músculos y en las piernas, los brazos y la espalda.

Preparado por W. F. SEVERA CO., Cedar Rapids, Iowa, U.S.A.

414

Czech   Obsah 12 tekutých uncí

SEVEROVA ARMATICKÁ SMĚS

Alcohol 10 Per Cent

činné přísady: Ocún jesenní, Gelsemium, Black Cohosh, Jodid draselnatý, Poke Root, Sodík Salicylový.

Tato přípravka obsahuje Jodid draselnatý a neměla by býti brána těmi, kdož trpí na vole, anebo tajenými tuberkulosními sklony.

Doporučená na úlevu svalových bolestí, bolestí v nohách, pažích a v zádech.

Připravený W. F. SEVERA CO., Cedar Rapids, Iowa, U.S.A.

Polish   Zawartość 12 płynnych uncyj

SEVERY ARMATIC COMPOUND

Alcohol 10 Per Cent

Aktywne składniki: Zimowit, Gelsemium, Czarny cohosh, Potas jodowy, Coakum, Sodium salicylate.

Ten preparat zawiera Potas jodowy i nie powinien być zażywany przez osoby cierpiące na wole u gardła albo osoby mające spoczywające lub ukryte skłonności gruźlicze.

Polecany na ulżenie muszkularnych bólów i bólów w nogach, ramieniach i krzyżach.

Spreparowany przez W. F. SEVERA CO., Cedar Rapids, Iowa, U.S.A.

Croatian   Sadržina 12 unce

SEVEROVA ARMATICNA SPOJINA

Alcohol 10 Per Cent

Djelotvorni sastavci: Kolčijum, Jasmin, Crni cohoš, Kalijumov jodid, Elabora, Sódijumov salicylit.

Ova preparacija sadržava kalijumov jodid i nesmiju je upotrebljavati oni koi pate od gušobolje, angine ili ranih tuberkuloznih započetaka.

Priporačljiva v odpomoč obolenega mišičevja in vbodljajev v nogach, rokah in hrbtu.

Priredjeno W. F. SEVERA CO., Cedar Rapids, Iowa, U.S.A.

WRIGLEY'S

"After Every Meal"
Everywhere

All over the world people use this goody for its **benefits,** as well as **pleasure.**

Keeps teeth clean, breath sweet

CHICAGO

CALCUTTA

Aids appetite and digestion

PARIS

STILL 5c

CATALINA ISLAND

WRIGLEY'S DOUBLEMINT CHEWING GUM
PEPPERMINT

WRIGLEY'S JUICY FRUIT CHEWING GUM
THE FLAVOR LASTS

WRIGLEY'S SPEARMINT THE PERFECT GUM
THE FLAVOR LASTS
MINT LEAF FLAVOR

B 1

UNITED PROFIT SHARING COUPONS

Sealed Tight—Kept Right

415A

Hermétiquement
cachetée

La gomme

WRIGLEY

TOUS ces trois aromes sont vendus en paquets
cachetés imperméables à l'air, à l'épreuve des
impuretés. Soyez sûr d'acheter **WRIGLEY'S**

*Après
Chaque
Repas*

Faite au
Canada

*SA
SAVEUR
DURE!*

76

415C
415D

416A
Japanese Pepsi bottle.

416B
Pepsi ad used in Tunisia in
1959.

416C
Russian Pepsi-Cola.

416A

416B

يــوم الاحد 29 نونمبر 1959 على الساعة الوحدة

جائزة العرشى العاشرة الكبرى
لسباق الدراجات

ينظمها التحاد الفتح الرياضى لفائدة التعاون الوطنى

تحت رئاسة صاحب السمو الملكى ولى عهد المملكة

المغربية ورئيس اركان الحرب العامة للقوات الملكية

المسلحة الامير الجليل

مولانا الحسن

LA BOISSON
des Sportifs

PEPSI-COLA

Imp. de l'Espérance - Tél. 281-11

576

417A
McDonald's ad in Swedish.

417B
McDonald's ad in Japanese.

418
Kentucky Fried Chicken ad in
Japanese.

417A

417B

418

419
McCormick Spice, an
American firm, advertising its
"French dressing" in Japan
(1974).

As our Republic is made up from the people of all lands, so I have gathered the best receipts from the Domestic Economy of the different nations of the Old World. Emigrants from each country will, in this "New Cook Book," find the method of preparing their favorite dishes.

Mrs. Hale's New Cook Book, 1857

The most striking aspect of American cuisine is the extent to which it reflects the cuisine of other nations. American markets, restaurants, cooking schools, and cookbooks display a remarkable diversity of national foods—adapted, blended, diluted, intensified, simplified, improved. There are pure ethnic pockets in the country where original customs in eating are carefully preserved, and there are also localities where indigenous American specialties, such as New England clam chowder, have developed. There are dishes with foreign names that are strictly American inventions, such as chop suey and chili con carne. There are Old World specialties, like pizza, which in the process of becoming Americanized have been perfected. The indebtedness of the American diet to the diverse peoples who have settled this country has been apparent from the beginning.

Many of the earliest settlers starved to death, and they all might have perished had it not been for the assistance of the native Indians who showed them how to make use of the unfamiliar foods they found. Of the three native crops—the "Indian triad," corn, beans, and squash—corn, which the early settlers had never seen before, was to become all-important. Ground, it was the basic ingredient for breads, cakes, and puddings; combined with beans and cooked in bear grease, it was succotash (the Narragansett Indians' *misickquatash*); with potatoes, onions, salt pork, and milk, it became corn chowder.

Over the years corn recipes, as well as Thanksgiving pageants and historical textbooks, have endlessly repeated the story of the Indian Squanto, who in 1621 taught the Plymouth settlers how to grow corn and how to fertilize their crops with fish. A letter from one of the pilgrims that year commented: "according to the manner of the Indians, we manured our ground with herrings, or rather shad, which we have in great abundance." The latest documentary and cultural analysis, however, reveals that the centuries-old assumption—which has become a solid part of the botanical and anthropological literature—that this was a native North American practice is probably wrong. Evidence from seventeenth-century documents shows instead that Indians were not observed to use fertilizer and in fact seem to have been culturally resistant to the practice, which had a long tradition in Europe. Before Squanto appeared in Plymouth, he had lived in European settlements both in the Old World (he was captured and then sold into slavery at Málaga, Spain) and the New World (in Newfoundland). This famous Indian thus appears to have been transmitting a European technological concept to the Plymouth pilgrims.

Once settled on the American continent, learning to grow and prepare new foods, the colonists also began to cook as many of their traditional foods as possible. British preferences (mainly English) prevailed in the early colonial period, reflecting the predominance of the English. For over one hundred years no cookbooks were published; the early colonists relied on tradition and handwritten recipes, or on what cookbooks they had brought with them or imported. This reliance of new arrivals on their own cooking traditions has continued throughout American history.

In 1742, William Parks of Williamsburg, Virginia, published the first cookbook in this country. Not surprisingly, it was merely an American printing of an English work, *The Compleat Housewife,* by E. Smith. A truly American cookbook did not appear until 1796 in Hartford, Connecticut. *American Cookery,* by Amelia Simmons, "An American Orphan," was the first cookbook to use *American* in its title and, more important, to have been written by an American. Even this, however, is largely a compilation of English recipes with a few notable additions using the native American corn: these are recipes for Indian pudding [**420A, 420B**], johnny cake, hoecake, and Indian slapjacks. The English settlers, used to leavened bread, had quickly learned that dough made from corn flour refuses to rise. They therefore devised or borrowed from the Indians other methods of making bread from the plentiful corn. For instance, johnnycakes (or jonnycakes, perhaps originally Shawnee cakes or journey cakes) were in their simplest form a batter of white corn meal, boiling water, and salt, fried on a hot griddle. Hoecakes included melted lard and were baked on a hoe over an open fire.

Amelia Simmons also included instructions for preparing cookies and slaw, indications that the blending of the foods of different nationalities, so evident in the modern American cookbook, was beginning. Both words are borrowed from the Dutch who settled New Amsterdam: cookie from *koekje,* "little cake," and slaw from *sla,* or "salad." *American Cookery* is a small book in which recipes for pies, puddings, custards, and preserves predominate. It was much copied and imitated in the early decades of the nineteenth century.

A little more variety is apparent in Mary Randolph's *The Virginia House-wife,* published in 1824. Regionalism as a factor in American cooking reflects available crops and climate as well as the traditions of the settlers in the area. Like New England, Virginia and the surrounding southern states were settled primarily by the British, but here there is a noticeable French, African, and Spanish influence. Okra, a vegetable commonly used in the Southern and particularly in the distinctive Creole cooking of Louisiana (a blending of French, Spanish, American Indian, and African cooking), is believed to have been introduced to this country by the blacks from Africa, who were responsible for so much of the cooking in the South. Mrs. Randolph lists recipes for okra soup, "ocra and tomatas," and gumbo, which she says is a "West Indian dish." The term *gumbo* is actually a corruption of the West African name for okra. Olla, ropa vieja, and gazpacho, all Spanish dishes, also appear in *The Virginia House-wife* [**421A, 421B**], as does curry, which probably came from India by way of England, and two Italian pastas, macaroni and vermicelli.

By the 1820s and 1830s, French cooking had a definite effect on American cookery. The French influence was felt not only through settlers from France but also through a conscious American effort to adopt French cuisine, generally accepted as superior. French-trained chefs in the homes of wealthy Americans and the establishment of French restaurants in the growing American cities did much to popularize French cooking, although not without opposition from those who looked upon such tastes as snobbery.

In the 1830s and 1840s, translations of French cookbooks were published, and French-trained chefs in the United States started cooking schools and began writing cookbooks aimed at the American housewife. Pierre Blot, a former editor of the *Almanach gastronomique* of Paris, lectured extensively, founded the New York Cooking Academy, and produced cookbooks. His *Hand-Book of Practical Cookery* (1869) covers many of the dishes the American writers offered but gives them a French subtlety by the use of sauces, herbs, and spices [**422A–422E**]. His statement that "no one need be afraid of using garlics in cooking" is the opposite of Miss Simmons's view that "Garlicks, tho' used by the French, are better adapted to the uses of medicine than cookery."

The ambitious culinary attempts of Americans were not always well received, as can be seen by the comments of T. C. Grattan, a British consul in America during 1839–1846:

At hotels, with a few exceptions in the large cities, it [American cooking] is detestable; in private houses, very indifferent. The great evils are the odious attempts at la cuisine française, *and the bad butter [which he describes as "impregnated with salt to an almost incredible excess"] used in the sauces. Every broken-down barber, or disappointed dancing-master, French, German, or Italian, sets up as cook with about as much knowledge of cookery as a cow has of cowcumbers. In a word, the science of the table is at the earliest stage of infancy in the United States. In all the doubts and fears expressed as to their future fate, nothing sounds so terribly ominous as that aphorism in the "Physiologie du Gout," which solemnly says, "La destinée des Nations depend de la manière dont elles se nourissent."*

Although classic French dishes never became commonplace on the American table, the French influence is pervasive. Even in Mrs. Randolph's book we find "Beef-a-la-Mode," and "Eggs-a-la-creme." *Hors d'oeuvres, soufflé, consommé,* and *croquettes* are only a few of the French terms in constant use in American cookbooks throughout the nineteenth century.

In the early part of the century, the majority of recipes were for plain, simple fare similar to that of Miss Simmons's book. They show heavy English influence in such dishes as pies, puddings, boiled dinners, chowders, Sally Lunn (a teacake, probably from the French *soleil-lune,* "sun-moon"), and trifle. Corned beef, which was a common dish throughout the English colonies, became closely associated with the Irish, who arrived in ever-increasing numbers in midcentury. Irish stew made its appearance in American cookbooks at this time. Doughnuts, crullers, and waffles (all Dutch), and sauerkraut, scrapple, and sausages (German), are common in the cookbooks of the day.

The eating habits of modern Americans have been greatly affected by changes that began in the mid-nineteenth century. Increasing industrialization spurred the development of many kitchen aids, including new utensils, stoves, and ranges. Produce formerly unknown to many or limited in distribution now became readily available to the general public as a result of new methods of transportation and the introduction of refrigeration. With the growth of cities, the number of restaurants multiplied and more and more cookbooks were published. Most significantly, immigration swelled, and the traditional dishes immigrants brought steadily enriched American cookery. The newcomers tended to settle in groups and to grow or, if necessary, import the ingredients needed to make their native dishes. Some immigrants established restaurants to cater to their fellow countrymen's culinary desires [423A–423C]. Gradually Americans of diverse backgrounds became aware of each other's foods.

The 1870s witnessed the establishment of many cooking schools to improve standards of cooking and nutrition. Miss Maria Parloa, an early principal of the Boston Cooking School, the most famous of these schools, formed in 1879, was the author of a multitude of cookbooks, both large and small. In *Miss Parloa's New Cook Book and Marketing Guide,* first published in 1880, we find recipes for mulligatawny soup (an East Indian recipe also found in some earlier works), Scotch broth, potage à la reine, Irish stew, pâté de foie gras, Polish sauce, Flemish sauce, French-fried potatoes, and strawberry Bavarian cream, to give an idea of the variety of the recipes [424A–424E].

The most well-known of the cooking school cookbooks are those of Fannie Merritt Farmer. Her 1896 *Boston Cooking-School Cook Book* was soon to become known in its many editions and revisions as the "Fannie Farmer Cook Book." The first version is still heavily English- and French-influenced, with the German and Dutch touches mentioned earlier and an increasing Italian flavor. There are recipes for German coffee bread, sweet French rolls, Turkish pilaf, spaghetti, eggs à la finnoise, and gnocchi à la romaine, for example. The Turkish pilaf shows the acceptance of a dish popular in the South. Pilaf or pilau, a combination of rice and vegetables with meat or seafood, shows a Near Eastern or North African influence in Southern cooking.

The appearance in 1896 of the *Boston Cook Book* marked the beginning of a distinctly American preference for precise measurements in the kitchen. This practice—a boon to the novice cook—has never been successfully imported to Europe, where traditional "pinches" and "glassfuls" are still used in recipes. Fannie Farmer was very specific: "To measure tea or table spoonfuls, dip the spoon in the ingredient, fill, lift, and level with a knife, the sharp edge of the knife being toward tip of spoon." She even taught the American cook how to boil water, cautioning her not "to wood" the fire to make water boil vigorously, for "Slowly boiling water has the same temperature as rapidly boiling water, consequently is able to do the same work."

Many foods that were unknown or little used before the arrival of the new immigrants started to appear with regularity in cookbooks. Tomatoes, peppers, eggplant, and zucchini—all with origins in the New World—are a few vegetables that gained popularity through use in immigrant cooking. The artichoke that appears in Miss Simmons's cookbook is the Jerusalem artichoke, a tuber from a plant related to the sunflower, not the globe or French artichoke. The globe artichoke is mentioned by Miss Randolph in 1824 and is usually at least listed in most cookbooks afterward. Pierre Blot remarks (1869) that the artichoke is a "native of Sicily" and is an "excellent and delectable vegetable." Miss Parloa says that the globe artichoke is "much used in France, but we have so many vegetables with so much more to recommend them, that this will probably never be common in this country." The artichokes used in America at that period were imported from France, according to Fannie Farmer, who includes four recipes using artichokes in her 1896 cookbook. It was the Italian immigrants who introduced the cultivation of artichokes to the West Coast and brought about their popular acceptance. (The city of Castroville in California now proclaims itself "The Artichoke Center of the World.")

The "Irish" potato has had a strange history, having become part of the American diet only after crossing the Atlantic four times. Originating in myriad varieties among the Peruvian Incas, it was carried to Spain and cultivated there soon after the conquest of Peru in the sixteenth century. Spanish colonists brought it back to the New World, where it was picked up by the British (probably Sir Francis Drake) and carried to England. The unusual plant became fashionable in some European circles, but in others was considered unfit for human consumption. Suspected of causing leprosy, it was banned in Burgundy in 1619. In Switzerland, where it was popular, it was blamed for scrofula. It was finally introduced into America by the Virginia colonists.

As late as 1819, these thoughts were expressed by William Cobbett (in *A Year's Residence in the United States of America*):

What I laugh at is, the idea of the use of them [potatoes] being a saving; of their going further than bread; of the cultivation of them in lieu of wheat adding to the human sustenance of a country . . . but of this I have said enough before; and therefore, I now dismiss the Potatoe with the hope, that I shall never again have to write the word, or see the thing.

The initial resistance to the potato was especially strong in Germany. As late as 1795, the Germans were rejecting the efforts of the American scientist Benjamin Thompson (Count Rumford, who had fled to England during the Revolutionary War) to persuade the starving poor of Munich to add potatoes to their diet.

The Irish, however, accepted and began cultivating the potato in the late sixteenth century. It was discovered to have many advantages, including its ability—underground—to withstand the ravages of battle. Soon the Irish economy became dependent upon it, and the disastrous potato blight in 1845 and subsequent famine had such far-reaching consequences that floods of Irish left their homeland, many thousands emigrating to America.

Macaroni, though mentioned in early cookbooks, was used primarily for soups and later in puddings and baked with cheese [425A–425C]. By 1964 the *Joy of Cooking* extravagantly announced that spaghetti, macaroni, and noodles were so popular that "there are over 500 kinds and shapes to choose from." According to Fannie Farmer, in 1896, "Macaroni is manufactured to some extent in this country, but the best come from Italy." In addition to macaroni and vermicelli, she included spaghetti, which she said "may be cooked in any way in which macaroni is cooked, but is usually served with tomato sauce" [426]. Soon spaghetti appeared as a common dish in American cookbooks and was paired with meatballs, apparently an American innovation.

The foods of the Southwest—where Spanish and Mexican influences are noticeable in the mixtures of tomatoes, peppers, red beans, and onions and in the use of the avocado and the garbanzo—do not appear in the national cookbooks until well into the present century. But by the turn of the century a German in New Braunfels, Texas, had found a means of extracting the pulp from chili pods and mixing it with spices to produce chili powder. Soon he was canning and marketing chili con carne.

The 1945 edition of *American Woman's Cook Book* includes a recipe for chili con carne, as well as jambalaya shrimp, sauerbraten, beef goulash [427A–427C], and Wiener schnitzel. Some of these are dishes that had appeared in regional cookbooks for years, while others were more newly adopted. Still more recently, Jewish foods, such as blintzes, knishes, chopped liver, and bagels; Chinese foods, such as egg foo yong and stir-fried vegetables; and Japanese foods, such as sukiyaki, tempura, and teriyaki, have started to become commonplace in the general American cookbooks.

Every year Americans become more intrepid in exploring and adopting cuisines from the far reaches of the world. Not only Japanese Americans, but enthusiastic non-Japanese, relish sashimi and sushi (both based on raw fish). North African couscous, Indonesian-Dutch rijstaffel, Thai curries, Vietnamese spring rolls, and Spanish paella are enjoyed in restaurants and prepared authentically at home with the aid of numerous highly sophisticated cookbooks.

In their enthusiasm, affluent Americans are ironically discovering and duplicating hearty Old World peasant dishes originally developed to sustain men working long hours in the fields (the unfortunate effect is often obesity, a serious national health problem). Often the only field work done by these Americans is tending a home vegetable garden. The increasing interest in growing food at home has many sources. The main one is probably a resentment of the commercial farmer, who has enlisted the advances of agricultural science to produce symmetrical, brightly colored, visually appealing, expensive fruits and vegetables with long storage lives and little flavor. There is also an antipathy toward the American food-processing industry and its penchant for adding preservatives, emulsifiers, bleaching agents, artificial colors, improvers, anti-caking agents, and sequestrants to everything edible. So, after years of demanding increasingly efficient galley kitchens, labor-saving appliances, and canned, frozen, precooked, instant foods, the American cook is back in the kitchen (perhaps redesigned as an Old World "country kitchen"), baking bread, drying home-grown herbs, making mayonnaise, pickling and preserving home-grown fruits and vegetables, and chopping, mincing, grating, simmering, and stir-frying with great delight.

But not all Americans are enthusiastic about the kitchen or adventurous about what they eat. There are many who have demanded that hot dogs, hamburgers, French fries, fried chicken, and malts be comfortably predictable—i.e., taste the same—from one end of the country to the other. Most of these foods are not included in cookbooks, nor can much be written about the preparation of the most popular dinner in American-style restaurants: a tossed green salad (served as a first course and often arranged by the patron himself from a "salad bar"), a charcoal-broiled steak, and a baked potato wrapped in aluminum foil and served with sour cream. This combination of simple foods is ubiquitous and reliably reproduced across the land, affording solace to those who consider even spaghetti exotic.

The European visitor who is merely puzzled to see an American put ketchup on his French-fried potatoes, as well as his hamburger, is apt to be horrified to watch him drink hot coffee with his steak dinner. But then there are many Americans who take pleasure in drinking wine and beer with their meals.

AMERICAN COOKERY:

OR, THE ART OF DRESSING

VIANDS, FISH, POULTRY, AND VEGETABLES.

AND THE BEST MODE OF MIXING

PUFF-PASTES, PIES, TARTS, PUD-DINGS, CUSTARDS, AND PRESERVES.

AND ALL KINDS OF

CAKES,

FROM THE IMPERIAL PLUMB, TO. PLAIN CAKE.

ADAPTED TO THIS COUNTRY AND ALL GRADES OF LIFE.

———

BY AN AMERICAN ORPHAN.

———※———

BRATTLEBOROUGH, VT.
PUBLISHED BY WILLIAM FESSENDEN.
1814.

420B
The influence of the native American corn on the diet of the early settlers is evident in this recipe from the 1814 *American Cookery*.

421A, 421B
Two recipes from Mary Randolph's *The Virginia House-Wife* (1824).

422A
Tin of cocoa manufactured by Huyler's Manufacturing Co. of New York, c. 1890.

422B
Side view of 422A.

422C
One-pound tin of crystallized ginger manufactured by E.C. Rich, Inc., of New York, c. 1920s.

422D
Tin shaker of pepper manufactured by Utright & Gillies of New York, late 1800s. Black pepper (*Piper nigrum*), a native of India, is the oldest known and the most popular of spices. It has had a spectacular impact on man's history, from the days when the early Romans began to by-pass the Arabs, who controlled the trade routes to Asia, and built ships capable of sailing from the Red Sea coast directly to India, returning from the dangerous voyage with pepper which sold for as much as $125 a Roman pound (12 ounces). The medieval cities of Europe became so dependent on pepper to brighten the monotony of their salted and dried winter diets that pepper became a negotiable currency. The fifteenth-century Europeans were determined to find at last a direct sea route from the Atlantic coast to the Indies, and black pepper was itself one of Columbus's objectives when he set sail. By the end of the sixteenth century, the English concern over the price of pepper was a main reason for their setting up the East India Company—and thus the British Indian Empire.

A tasty Indian Pudding.

No. 1. Three pints scalded milk, seven spoons fine indian meal, stir well together while hot, let stand till cooled; add four eggs, half pound butter, spice and sugar—bake four hours.

No. 2. Three pints scalded milk to one pint meal salted; cool, add two eggs, four ounces butter, sugar or molasses, and spice sufficient: it will require two and half hours baking.

No. 3. Salt a pint meal, wet with one quart milk, sweeten and put into a strong cloth, brass or bell metal vessel, stone or earthen pot, secure from wet and boil twelve hours.

420B

421A

GUMBO—A WEST INDIA DISH.

Gather young pods of ochra, wash them clean, and put them in a pan with a little water, salt and pepper, stew them till tender, and serve them with melted butter. They are very nutritious, and easy of digestion.

421B

TO MAKE AN OLLO—A SPANISH DISH.

Take two pounds beef, one pound mutton, a chicken, or half a pullet, and a small piece of pork; put them into a pot with very little water, and set it on the fire at ten o'clock, to stew gently; you must sprinkle over it an onion chopped small, some pepper and salt, before you pour in the water; at half after twelve, put into the pot two or three apples or pears, peeled and cut in two, tomatas with the skin taken off, cimblins cut in pieces, a handful of mint chopped, lima beans, snaps, and any kind of vegetable you like; let them all stew together till three o'clock; some cellery tops cut small, and added at half after two, will improve it much.

422A

422B

422D

422C

422E
Ad from the early twentieth century.

423A
Chinese restaurant in New York City, photographed in 1975. The Chinese food in a German Rathskeller atmosphere complete with cocktails (generally considered an American type of drink) is an example of acculturation and ethnic blending, which has occurred continually throughout American history.

423A

422E

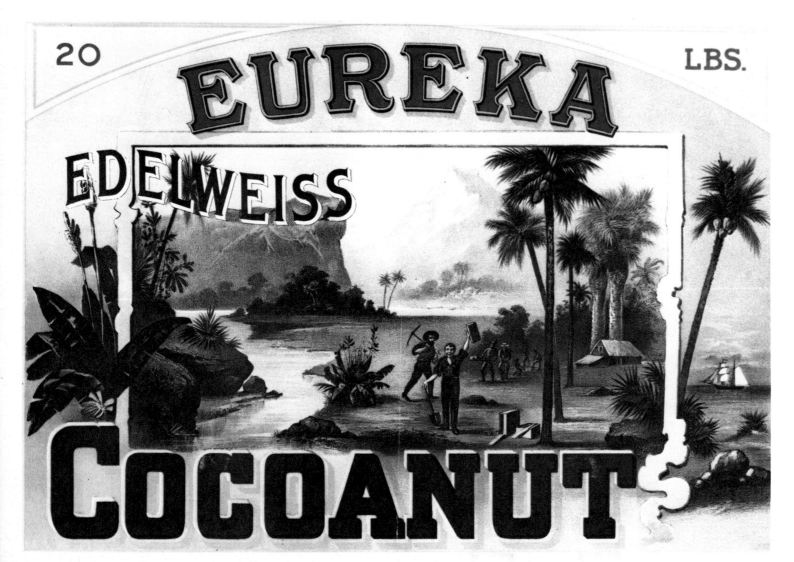

WARSAW
FOOT LONG

423B

423C

Florio's **ITALIAN RESTAURANT**
PIZZERIA

192

DOUGH-NUTS.

Three pounds of sifted flour.
A pound of powdered sugar.
Three quarters of a pound of butter.
Four eggs.
Half a large tea-cup full of best brewer's yeast.
A pint and a half of milk.
A tea-spoonful of powdered cinnamon.
A grated nutmeg.
A table-spoonful of rose-water.

Cut up the butter in the flour. Add the sugar, spice, and rose-water. Beat the eggs very light, and pour them into the mixture. Add the yeast, (half a tea-cup or two wine-glasses full,) and then stir in the milk by degrees, so as to make it a soft dough. Cover it, and set it to rise.

When quite light, cut it in diamonds with a jagging-iron or a sharp knife, and fry them in lard. Grate loaf sugar over them when done.

424A

423B
Neon Polish food sign from Cleveland, Ohio, c. 1950.

423C
Pizzeria in New York City, photographed in 1975. It is one of thousands of similar Italian restaurants throughout America.

424A
From Eliza Leslie, *Seventy-five Receipts for Pastry, Cakes, and Sweetmeats* (1832).

424B
From *Miss Parloa's New Cook Book and Marketing Guide* (1908).

424C
From Elizabeth F. Lea, *Domestic Cookery, Useful Receipts, and Hints to Young Housekeepers* (1878).

424D
From Sarah J. Hale, *Mrs. Hale's New Cook Book* (1857).

424E
From Sarah J. Hale, *Mrs. Hale's New Cook Book* (1857).

Polish Sauce.

One pint of stock, two table-spoonfuls of butter, four of grated horseradish, one of flour, one of chopped parsley, the juice of one lemon, one teaspoonful of sugar, salt, pepper. Cook the butter and flour together until smooth, but not brown. Add the stock; and when it boils, add all the other ingredients except the parsley. Boil up once, and add the parsley. This sauce is for roast veal.

424B

An Egyptian Method of dressing Meats and Poultry.—Prepare a proper soup, or properly seasoned water; cut the fowl in quarters, or the meat into steaks, and let it simmer till sufficiently done upon a hot hearth; then take out the meat, and put in as much rice as will thicken the liquor into a pillau; in the meantime, fry some onions and the meat; dish the rice, strew over the onions, and lay meat over it.

424D

424C

Irish Stew.

Take five thick mutton chops, or two pounds of the neck or loin, two pounds of potatoes, peel them and cut them in halves, six onions or half a pound of onions, peel and slice them also. First put a layer of potatoes at the bottom of your stew-pan, then a couple of chops and some onions, then again potatoes, and so on till the pan is quite full; season with pepper and salt, and three gills of broth or gravy, and two tea-spoonsful of mushroom catsup; cover it very close to prevent the escape of steam, and stew on a slow fire for an hour and a half; a slice of ham is an addition Great care should be taken not to let it brown.

424E

French Hare Soup.—Skin and wash perfectly clean 2 young hares, cut them into small pieces, and put them into a stew-pan, with 2 or 3 glasses of Port wine, 2 onions stuck with 2 cloves each, a bunch of parsley; a bay leaf; of thyme, sweet basil, and marjoram, 2 sprigs each, and a few blades of mace; let the whole simmer upon a stove for an hour. Add as much boiling broth as will entirely cover the meat, simmer till it be soft enough to pulp through a sieve, then strain it and soak the crumb of a small loaf in the strained liquor; separate the bones from the meat, pound the meat in a mortar, and rub it along with the liquor through a sieve; season with pepper and salt, and heat the soup thoroughly, but do not let it boil.

Early-twentieth-century macaroni label. *Macaroni* was for centuries the common name for pasta, including spaghetti. According to records, the Chinese have eaten such noodles since 5000 B.C., but not so certain is the popular fable that Marco Polo introduced them to Italy from China. He most likely enjoyed eating pasta in China, but historians have shown that Indians and Arabs were eating noodles fifty years before Marco Polo left Venice, and they had probably introduced pasta to Italy long before. The first published references to pasta in Italy are in a cookbook dated c. 1290, five years before Marco Polo returned from China.

The introduction of macaroni—and spaghetti—into America is credited to Thomas Jefferson, who as Minister Plenipotentiary to the Court of Louis XVI traveled about Europe, keenly enjoying the various cuisines. After he left France in 1789, he had his confidential secretary, William Short, make a special trip to Naples to pick up a "maccaroni mould." This proved to be a mold of a small diameter—that is, it produced spaghetti. As President, Jefferson subsequently helped to popularize "macaroni" at his daily informal 4 P.M. dinner parties.

Now a definite part of the American diet, this pasta is composed of water and semolina, which is made from durum wheat, the hardiest variety known, grown in the U.S. principally in a triangular area of thirteen counties in North Dakota.

425C
Macaroni label, probably 1930s.

425B
From *Juliet Carson's New Family Cook Book,* 1885. Recipes for macaroni dishes appear in many early-nineteenth-century American cookbooks, but it was not until late in the century that its "importance," as Miss Carson calls it, was realized and the number of recipes increased.

225A

425C

425B

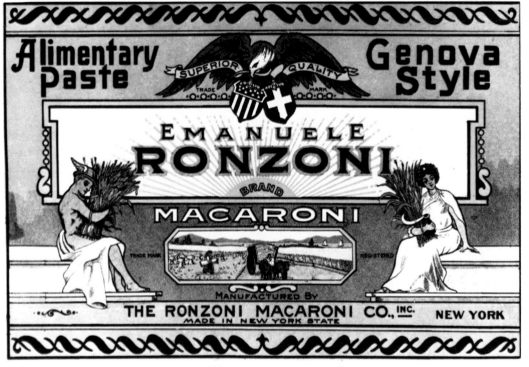

MACARONI WITH CHEESE.

The importance of this article of food is beginning to be realized in this country, and now it remains only to learn how to cook it palatably. Carefully follow the directions given, and you can not fail to produce a delicious dish of macaroni, fit for the most finished epicure's taste.

First of all, remember that good macaroni is always of a yellowish color. That which has a white, blanched appearance is decidedly inferior. You can buy the genuine Italian macaroni at the Italian stores generally to be

426

Early-twentieth-century tomato sauce label. Many experts consider Italian (not French) cooking to be the "mother cuisine" of Europe and date the birth to 1533, when Caterina de' Medici went to France to marry the future King Henri II, bringing with her the world's most sophisticated cooks. Yet at that time the hallmark of Italian cooking—the tomato— was unknown in Europe, for Cortés had not yet conquered Mexico. Tomatoes seem to have first appeared as weeds in maize fields in Mexico and were cultivated by the time the Spaniards arrived. Introduced into Spain and Europe, a small yellow variety was first described in Italy in 1554 as *pomi d'oro* (apple of gold). The tomato was only gradually recognized as a food in Europe in the 1700s, and it often appeared as a curiosity in botanical gardens, as *pomme d'amour,* supposedly having aphrodisiacal properties. Many also considered it poisonous because of its affiliation with the nightshade family, so even though Thomas Jefferson grew it in 1781—the first record of its culture in America—it was not thoroughly accepted here until about 1900. It had an interesting passage from the New World to the Old World and back again.

GULYAS, HUNGARIAN STYLE.

Take three pounds lean beef without sinew or fat, and cut it in small square pieces ; then take three good-sized onions, and cut them in very small squares ; put the onions, with a quarter pound of butter, in an **Agate** saucepan, and fry light yellow ; then put the beef with it, and cover up the saucepan close, and let it simmer one hour and a half ; then put a half ounce of caraway seed into it, and a spoonful of flour and a half bottle of Hungarian white wine, and salt to taste, one teaspoon of paprika (Hungarian red pepper), and about ten raw potatoes cut into quarters ; stew for about twenty minutes more ; serve hot.

427A

427B

427A
This recipe from *The Agate Cook Book,* published by the Agate Iron Ware Manufacturing Company in the last quarter of the nineteenth century, calls for paprika (Hungarian red pepper) in a dish described as Hungarian. Many manufacturers of cooking utensils and products published cookbooks which promoted the use of their products.

427B
Ten-ounce can of paprika manufactured by the R. T. French Company of Rochester, N.Y. (c. 1930s). Irrevocably associated with the cooking of Hungary, paprika is not at all native to that country. Its origins remain mysterious, but there is considerable agreement that this piquant, somewhat sweet spice was not known in Europe before the voyages of Columbus. Its genus, *Capsicum* (which includes many peppers, including cayenne), is part of the nightshade family, which includes tomatoes and potatoes, native to the New World. Hungary had exactly the right climate and soil for the pepper plant to flourish, and a robust paprika industry developed. At the time the recipe (427A) was published, it was sufficiently exotic in America to warrant a definition.

Gulyás, spelled *goulash* now in the United States, is one of the four main types of Hungarian paprika stews. This peasant dish can be traced at least to the ninth century. The dried ingredients were carried by nomadic shepherds, who added water to make a stew or soup over the campfire (today's backpackers probably have a freeze-dried version of goulash). The special touch—paprika—seems to be an eighteenth-century addition.

427C
Top-lid from 427B.

428A
Tin of "Tetley's Teas" manufactured by Hudson, Scott & Sons of New York (c. 1914).

428B
Tin of "Pure Indian Tea" manufactured in England and sold in America (early 1900s). The first shipment of tea to England, in 1658, was advertised as the "*China* drink" and was regarded as a medicine. But Catherine of Braganza, who married Charles II in 1662, soon introduced the fashionable Lisbon custom of tea drinking to the English court, and its popularity spread immediately. By the eighteenth century, when it made its first appearance in the American colonies, it was rivaling beer as the national drink in England. Until the 1830s tea still came from China, but soon the British were planting tea in Darjeeling—in the foothills of the Himalayas—and in the cool central highlands of Ceylon.

428A

428B

In 1788, Thomas Jefferson, who considered wine "a necessity of life," traveled through the vineyards of France and Germany, buying vines and cuttings to bring back to America. One hundred years later, these vineyards of Europe, celebrated for centuries, were on the verge of annihilation. The denouement of this critical chapter in agricultural history is that the vines—and the wine industry—were saved, but only by being literally grafted upon grape rootstocks from the eastern United States. This dramatic reversal of the usual process by which America became populated by the rootstocks of the world came about through a combination of events.

Sometime in 1870, English and French botanical gardens received some eastern American grape plants that happened to be carrying the root louse phylloxera. The American vines were immune to the louse, but it quickly infested the European vines. Between 1870 and 1900 most of the vineyards of France were destroyed by phylloxera, along with those of Austria and Germany, Rumania and Hungary, Spain and South Africa. Nearly every vineyard in the world was threatened that was not on unusually sandy soil, as were some in Portugal, or geographically isolated, like those of Chile and Cyprus. The vineyards of California, which had imported the noble European wine grape *Vitis vinifera,* were also being systematically destroyed.

The French, by exploration and experimentation, determined that the resistant strain, *Vitis labrusca* from eastern America, could be used as a hardy rootstock on which to graft their own surviving grapevines. This practice succeeded dramatically throughout the world, including California, which imported the resistant eastern rootstocks indirectly via France. (The French had first made sure that the characteristic taste and aroma of *Vitis labrusca*—strong, wild, and "foxy"—which many connoisseurs find unpleasant, was not at all transmitted through the rootstock.) Very soon, almost all the grapevines of the world were sprouting from American roots and continue to do so, as phylloxera remains a danger. The initial destruction by phylloxera was also responsible for a migration of grape growers from France and Italy to America and other parts of the world.

The hardy native American "foxy" grape has never received much acclaim, but California wines of the classic *Vitis vinifera* grape are enjoying some success, especially the products of the northern counties of California, which are similar in climate and soil to the outstanding vine-growing areas of the world. The early 1830s saw importation of noble grapes—from France to Boston, then around Cape Horn to California. With the Gold Rush came a fabulous character, a Hungarian count who gave himself the title of colonel, Agoston Haraszthy. He has received most of the credit for seeing California's potential and establishing the industry by introducing large amounts of vines and cuttings from famous European vineyards in 1861.

The subsequent success of California vineyards attracted scheming entrepreneurs, whose unsavory winemaking practices necessitated a California Pure Wine Law in 1880. Then came the disaster of phylloxera, countered by eastern rootstocks, and by about 1900 excellent wines were being produced in California. Soon, however, the industry was decimated by yet another event—thirteen years of Prohibition. From the time of repeal in 1933, it has taken the industry several decades to become vital.

These years have also seen a great increase in the popularity of wine in the United States. In 1832, Mrs. Trollope, writing about *Domestic Manners of the Americans,* noted that "Almost everyone drinks water at table, and by a strange contradiction, in the country where hard drinking is more prevalent than in any other, there is less wine taken at dinner." But by now a wide variety of Americans have learned—through their heritage, their travels, or their inclinations—to enjoy wine as a "necessity of life."

Beer

429A

429A
At least three lager beer breweries were established in Brooklyn by the 1850s, soon after the American debut of lager in the 1840s. This ad, by one of the Brooklyn firms, probably dates from the 1870s.

429B
The annual picnic of the Brewers' Union at River Park, Seattle, on August 12, 1894. Only two men sitting on the ground, near the center, are drinking beer.

Beer—the quintessential symbol of the American working classes—has, perhaps appropriately, been around forever. Sumerian farmers were planting barley and washing down their meals with beer in 2500 B.C. By the seventeenth century beer was the universal beverage of Englishman and European alike, who considered it a healthful drink and thought water unwholesome—with good reason then. All the ships of the first settlers carried beer along with their passengers, but the supplies soon gave out and the emigrants had to resort unhappily to water.

Very shortly after the third settlement on the American coast was established—the Massachusetts Bay Colony—brewing began, and one of the first licensed commercial brewers was Captain Robert Sedgwick, of Charlestown. At first malt (sprouted barley) had to be shipped from England, as barley had not been grown extensively enough. But by 1649, when a pamphlet was published in London attempting to make Virginia appear irresistible to prospective colonists, it commented: "That they have plenty of barley, make excellent malt. . . . That they have six publick brew-houses, and most brew their own beer, strong and good."

Some modest commercial enterprises were actively in production, but colonial beer was brewed mainly in the home for daily use by the entire family, including the women and children, although some of the more prosperous families still imported their beer from England. Beer was so much a part of the colonists' life that the Harvard College laws in the seventeenth century officially allotted students a provision of beer, and many Harvard students paid for their board with wheat or malt.

This beer of the seventeenth century was brewed intuitively, almost completely without the benefits of technology and chemistry. Even simple measuring devices such as the thermometer and hydrometer were not used widely until the late eighteenth century, and the mysteries of yeast were not unraveled until Pasteur's work in the 1870s. The beer of the first colonists was strong, unpredictable, and probably occasionally unpalatable.

Starting in Philadelphia, there was a movement to encourage brewing, with the aims of promoting agriculture and discouraging distilled liquors, considered injurious to the health and morals of Americans. Laws were enacted to free breweries from taxes and to impose heavy taxes on distilleries (hostility to these laws in western Pennsylvania resulted in the "Whiskey Rebellion"). But in the eighteenth century beer was no longer the universal beverage. Cider became a substitute, especially in rural areas; coffee and tea made their appearance [**428A, 428B**]; and wines such as claret, madeira, and sherry became fashionable. Rum made the greatest inroads in popularity, becoming especially cheap as molasses was easily shipped from the West Indies and turned into rum in New England (rum in turn was exchanged in Africa for slaves, who were brought back to cultivate sugar cane in the West Indies for molasses).

At a time when beer-making had declined to a low point, Thomas Jefferson, a great lover of European wines, was enthusiastically promoting the brewing of beer. He believed it could be socially and economically advantageous to the country. He himself brewed a good beer at Monticello from 1813 until his death on July 4, 1826.

429B

So far in the country's drinking history, British tastes in beer—porter, ales, and stout—had prevailed. When the time was ripe and the tide of German immigrants high, the brewing of lager beer, known in Germany since the thirteenth century, was first attempted in America. This was in the 1840s, and along with the steam engine, which mechanized manufacturing processes, *lager bier* brought the industry triumphantly out of the shadows.

Lager differed from other beer in requiring cooler temperatures for an important storage period (difficult at a time when artificial ice and refrigeration were unknown); it also required yeast for fermentation. Yeast seemed to be an especially critical factor in lager's American debut, for the proper type was unknown in this country, and living yeasts imported from Germany did not survive the long voyage. One author, writing in *Frank Leslie's Popular Monthly* in 1882, suggested: "it was only when the Baltimore clipperships made the voyage in three weeks that yeast was imported, and thus lager was first produced in America."

So with a bit of the right kind of yeast that managed an Atlantic crossing along with vast numbers of German immigrants, the German monopoly of the American brewing industry began. From its beginnings in Philadelphia, lager was popular, as recorded by the early Wolf and Engel brewery: "the Germans of Philadelphia . . . more than once drank the brewery dry; and often we were compelled to display the placard that beer would again be dispensed after a certain date."

By the 1870s American beer drinkers had decided upon their preferred brew—a preference that continues today—a Pilsen-type lager instead of a Munich lager or English beers. This is a pale, light, fizzy beer with a low alcoholic content compared with the earlier strong beers. The demand for beer increased dramatically, and brewers became prosperous and organized, forming the United States Brewers Association in 1862 [**429A, 429B**].

One of the subtler reasons for the soaring demand was undoubtedly the effect of such temperance groups as the Anti-Saloon League, whose campaigns caused many to switch from demon rum to beer. But finally the prohibitionists trounced even the brewers, and in 1919 the Volstead Act was passed over President Wilson's veto. Franklin Roosevelt ran for election strongly in favor of repeal, but even before that came about, a "beer bill" was passed which once again set the industry in motion. Since the Volstead Act allowed Congress to determine what an "intoxicating beverage" was, by the end of 1932 they accepted 3.2 percent alcohol, and on April 7, 1933, the bill was passed, allowing 3.2 beer on the market. The *New York Times* headline on the crucial day of the bill's passage read:

BEER FLOWS IN 19 STATES AT MIDNIGHT

The industry was not only off to a running start; it had obviously somewhat illegally jumped the gun. With optimism the brewers set about making America's national beverage, not suspecting that the infant soft-drink industry would soon give them a mighty race and would end up affixing Coca-Cola and Pepsi-Cola signs to the remote corners of the world.

Chapter 27

American Comic Art

The comic strip, in its major development as purely an American art form as jazz, may be defined as an episodic, open-ended dramatic narrative, or series of linked anecdotes, about recurrent identified characters, told in successive drawings enclosing ballooned dialogue and/or a narrative text, and published serially in newspapers. American cartoon art is part of an obvious and extensive mainstream of European comic drawing, including the development of the broadsheet. Also, it is as much a literary as a graphic medium and belongs in the tradition of narrative art, with fiction, drama, and film as creative companions.

Clearly the comic strip develops and delineates its characters far beyond the capacity or purpose of the individual caricature or graphic cartoon. By supplying them with a versatile and adaptable vehicle for dialogue in the form of a balloon, the comic strip artist enables his visible dramatis personae to speak their minds as freely as characters in a novel or play. Thus it is arguable that such prominent and typical comic strip figures as Dick Tracy, Moon Mullins, Barney Google, Popeye, Krazy Kat, Pogo, and Charlie Brown are not, as some have suggested, as close to the stock figures of Hogarth and Daumier as they are to Commodore Trunnion (of Tobias Smollett's *Peregrine Pickle*), Dr. Syntax, Gulliver, Don Quixote, Micawber, Sut Lovingood (of the yarns by George W. Harris), Huckleberry Finn, and other larger-than-life fictional heroes of illustrated eighteenth- and nineteenth-century fiction.

That such heroes were pictured is a vital factor, for the majority of the novel illustrations of the last century, particularly in England, were highly grotesque or comically rendered, from the stunningly effective drawings of Phiz (H. K. Browne) and George Cruikshank for the narratives of Dickens (first published serially), through the self-illustrated works of Thackeray and Lover, to the nominal realism (perhaps even surrealism) of the illustrators of Jules Verne, Rider Haggard, and Arthur Conan Doyle. It is in the area of nineteenth-century novel and magazine fiction illustration, then, that we find more clearly the sympathetic origins of the comic strip.

The wedding of comic illustrative art and narrative text appears to have occurred in England in 1812 with the publication of Dr. William Combe's *Tour of Dr. Syntax in Search of the Picturesque,* with line illustrations in color by Thomas Rowlandson. The considerable success of this volume, with its highly relished combination of rakish story and luridly unforgettable art, made the illustrated narrative popular with the general reader in a way that the cheaply illustrated sporting stories of the time had not been. Readers were delighted to see the characters they followed so avidly in Combe's text lit up as if by a Satanic satirical light every fifteen pages or so, and they "saw" the characters as rendered by the artist, even when they did not quite jibe with the author's words.

Before collaborating on the Combe book, Rowlandson had worked primarily with posters, chapbooks, and broadsides. Now, instead of making a political or social statement in a single panel or a short series with one or more static character symbols, Rowlandson helped to delineate fully rounded characters through prolonged narrative and illustration. He liked the result so much that he worked with Combe on three successive volumes about Dr. Syntax and his foundling son between 1820 and 1822. By now, he and others were beginning to realize that here lay a major path of development for the nineteenth-century comic artist.

Among the others was Robert Cruikshank, who urged his talented brother, George, to join him in illustrating Pierce Egan's roistering *Life in London; or, The Day and Night Scenes of Jerry Hawthorn, Esq., and His Elegant Friend, Corinthian Tom,* in 1821. This book proved an enormous publishing success and went into many printings, and with it the future of the humorously illustrated novel was assured. George Cruikshank went on to illustrate two of Dickens's early works: *Sketches by Boz* (1836) and *Oliver Twist* (1838), as well as many popular novels by such writers as Harrison Ainsworth and Frank Smedley. Cruikshank's chief rival for popularity among novel illustrators was Hablot Knight Browne (Phiz), who achieved fame through his drawings for *Pickwick Papers* (1837) and went on to illustrate over half of Dickens's later novels. John Leech, Charles Keene, and Richard Doyle were notable among the numerous cartoonist-illustrators of that time, and neither the novelists nor the public seemed to find exaggerated graphic character and background at all out of keeping with tragedy or realism in narrative, unlike a prevalent modern view of comic drawing as essentially frivolous.

This illustrated vogue in fiction was marked in France by the works of such gifted caricaturists, fantasists, and comic artists as Jean-Ignace-Isadore Gerard (Grandville) in his *La Vie privée et publique des animaux* (1842) Gustave Doré with his illustrations for Balzac's *Les Cent contes drolatiques* (1837), and C. H. Brabant in his drawings for Jules Verne's *L'lle mystérieuse* (1875). In Germany Rodolphe Töpffer's hand-lettered picture narratives such as *Monsieur Crepin* (1837) were praised by leading writers of his time, though they were not popular successes, while the gifted Wilhelm Busch combined extended character exposition in rhyme with matched drawings in book after book, most notably *Max und Moritz* (1865), *Plisch und Plum* (1882), and *Balduin Bählamm* (1883). Through Busch this tradition directly touched hands with the American comic strip, for *Max und Moritz* was the inspiration for the 1897 creation of Rudolph Dirk's *Katzenjammer Kids* [430].

In America, many of the English illustrated novels were reprinted, sold widely, and almost immediately imitated. American illustrative talent, however, was not at the European level for most of the nineteenth century, and much of the best remained simply imitative of English models, as in the technically skillful but only adequate illustrations by John McLenan for the T. B. Peterson American edition of Dickens's *Great Expectations* in 1860. By the late 1860s, however, the first great wave of genuinely American graphic humorists and novel illustrators had begun to appear in print with artists like Frederick Burr Opper, Edward Windsor Kemble, and Arthur Burdett Frost. Kemble, of course, was the classic illustrator of Mark Twain's *Adventures of Huckleberry Finn* (1884); Opper was noted for his illustrations for Edward Eggleston's popular *The Hoosier School-Master* (1871) and Marietta Holley's *Samantha at Saratoga* (1887); and Frost achieved fame through his comic illustrations in the Joel Chandler Harris volumes of the Uncle Remus stories, which began appearing in 1880 and to which Kemble also contributed. The fact that two of these artists, Opper and Kemble, also did early comic strips for the Hearst newspapers is another direct link between comic illustration and the new comic strip narrative form.

With the establishment by the Hearst papers of what many consider to be the earliest definitive comic strip (the 1896 New York *American* Sunday episodes of Richard Feldon Outcault's *Yellow Kid*), the pressure grew for other large metropolitan newspapers to find comic strip artists of their own. Most sought American talent, but the Chicago *Tribune* in 1905 turned to Germany and acquired the services of several notable German cartoonists for its four-page Sunday comic section, most prominently Lyonel Feininger, whose stunning pair of strips, *The Kin-Der-Kids* and *Wee Willie Winkie's World*, were surpassed in their time only by Windsor McCay's brilliant *Little Nemo in Slumberland*. Though born in the United States, Feininger settled in Germany before the turn of the century and achieved distinction through his affiliation with the Bauhaus school of design founded at Weimar in 1919 to promote the artistic doctrine of functionalism. Difficulties in transmission, payment, and circulation led the *Tribune* to drop its group of German artists within a year and return to American sources.

The comic strip developed rapidly in America from the 1890s on, reaching its now standard form in a very few years and exhibiting wide varieties of content and mood, from satire and family humor to adventure and melodrama, moving between stylistic extremes of explicit realism and pure fantasy.

Because comic strips touch such a popular chord in the American psyche and are created to appeal to such a broad spectrum of people, they inevitably reveal a good deal about national attitudes toward politics, society, and culture. To understand the laissez-faire philosophy of typical American conservatives, who generally believe in independence, self-sufficiency and initiative, one has but to read the late Harold Gray's *Little Orphan Annie*, Al Capp's *Li'l Abner*, or Chester Gould's *Dick Tracy*. The usual liberal point of view, with its faith in human nature and distrust of authority, is found in the late Walt Kelly's *Pogo* and G. B. Trudeau's *Doonesbury*. These tend not to be the most popular strips for foreign readers, however, who prefer those based on the common frailties of mankind and universal philosophical attitudes, such as Charles Schulz's *Peanuts*, Johnny Hart's *B.C.*, and Brant Parker and Johnny Hart's *The Wizard of Id*. In that all American comic strips are carefully monitored by the syndicates and tailored to appear in newspapers for family consumption, they inevitably tend to support average American mores and beliefs, from the family unity reflected in the late Chic Young's *Blondie*, to the busybody common sense of Ken Ernst and Allen Saunders's *Mary Worth* (the Ann Landers of the funnies), to the cold war politics of Milton Caniff's *Steve Canyon*.

Because they have proved to be effective circulation builders, daily comic strips are published by nearly every newspaper in the United States, and it has been estimated that more than 110 million Americans read the comics. According to data supplied by the King Features Syndicate, *Blondie*, created in 1930, appears in over 1,600 newspapers; Mort Walker's 1950 creation, *Beetle Bailey*, is circulated to 1,100 newspapers; and *The Phantom*, originated in 1936 by writer Lee Falk, is published in nearly 600 daily papers. United Feature's *Peanuts*; Newspaper Enterprise Association's *Alley Oop*, created by V. T. Hamlin; Field Enterprise's *B.C.* and *Steve Canyon*; and the Chicago *Tribune*–New York *News* Syndicate's *Dick Tracy* and *Li'l Abner* are distributed as widely in other papers.

Beyond the boundaries of the United States, American comic strips and their characters appear in various formats—newspaper strips, television programs, comic books, paperback and hard-cover books, on novelty items, and in conjunction with advertising campaigns—in almost twenty nations, including Argentina, Australia, Belgium, Brazil, England, France, Germany, Greece, India, Israel, Italy, Japan, Mexico, the Netherlands, Portugal, Spain, South Africa, and Sweden. King Features, in particular, has promoted its strip characters abroad. Thus the Phantom [431A, 431B] is especially popular throughout all of Europe and is the subject of a series of novels, with a narrative text only, published in ten languages. Mandrake is used in France to promote Renault automobiles, Blondie helps sell margarine in Norway, and the first superhero, Popeye, is used in the promotion of a fast-food restaurant chain in Canada [432A–432C]. Popeye also appears in theater festivals and bazaars in Israel. Mickey Mouse and other creations of the Walt Disney studios are among the most world-renowned figures from the American comics [433]. Through thousands of publications in all major countries of the world, and the distribution of Disney animated films, semblances of Mickey, Donald Duck, and Scrooge McDuck are likely to be found anywhere one might travel. One theater in Buenos Aires is entirely dedicated to screening Walt Disney motion pictures. Curiously, some comic strips are much more widely printed abroad than at home. Notable among these are United Features's *Tarzan* by Russ Manning, a forceful adventure feature apparently too untamed for most American newspapers but read in millions of copies overseas [434A–434I]. During the 1930s the Editors Press Service was organized to meet a substantial demand for translated American comics in South America, and thirty years later the company had twenty-two representatives throughout the world supplying more than 1,500 publications in some sixty countries in twenty different languages.

At first, to European eyes, the comic strip seemed irremediably linked to newspaper entertainment supplements, which were eschewed as demeaning to the dignity of the press. The English introduced the strip format into an uninspired series of comic weeklies for children, such as *Comic Cuts* and *Chuckles,* where it remained unchanged for three decades, but they refrained from adding many daily comics to newspapers until the 1930s, when one of the best British strips, *Just Jake* by Bernard Graddon (1938–1951), was introduced in the *Daily Mirror.* French developments were similar, and while much of the rest of Europe showed little interest during the early decades, in Italy American comic strips were reprinted in a magazine format from the beginning of the century. During the years before World War II, Mussolini feared the influence of American comics on the Fascist state, so beginning with *Flash Gordon* he systematically banned all imported titles until just one remained—his personal favorite, *Mickey Mouse.* A public outcry forced the reinstatement of *Popeye,* however. Some Latin American countries, notably Argentina, Brazil, and Mexico, added their own local comic strips to imported American work in newspaper supplements in the 1930s. The Asiatic nations appeared generally uninterested, aside from Japan, where primitive comic books emerged in the 1930s.

A few European and South American strips reached notable North American newspaper circulation through judicious syndicate importation in the 1920s and 1930s, most memorably J. Millar Watts's English strip *Pop* (1928–1940), *Adamson's Adventures* by O. Jacobsson of Denmark (1922–1928), and *Patoruzo* by a beloved Argentine cartoonist who used the pseudonym Dante Quinterno (1941–1948). World War II brought American comic strips to widespread attention through the wide circulation of *Stars and Stripes,* which included a daily comic page, and American strip reprint books. A demand for good native strips arose in the postwar years, and as a result a number of daily English newspapers added some highly imaginative and innovative strips of their own by the 1950s, a few of which were widely circulated in this country, Reginald Smythe's *Andy Capp* being the most obvious example. A list of several of the other best English strips might include *The Perishers* by Dennis Collins, *The Fosdyke Saga* by Bill Tidy, *Colonel Pewter* by Arthur Horner, *Flook* by Wally Fawkes, and *Willy Biggelow* by Frank Dickens.

The most notable developments in European comic art during the postwar years took place in France and Belgium. Here the comic strips had rarely been incorporated into the newspaper medium. Rather, many of the best American strips were reprinted in weekly full-color magazines for children, primarily during the 1930s and after, while early French strips appeared in similar magazines, later to be collected into annual volumes. Excellent titles of the 1920s and 1930s were *Zig et Puce* by Alain Saint-Ogan, *Tintin* by Georges Rémi (Hergé), and *Spirou* by Robert Velter. During the 1950s, concurrent with a French ban on the importation of the American superhero comic books, French and Belgian publishers began a well-planned program for supplying young readers of both countries with sizable quantities of imaginative comic strips by major cartoonists and writers, working largely in the American narrative strip traditions of the 1930s. Such magazines as *Tintin, Spirou,* and *Pilote,* appearing weekly with many pages of full-color strips continuing from one issue to the next (with the completed stories about each of the several characters appearing in a separate series of volumes later), produced such mature and superbly written strips that adults across both France and Belgium read them as avidly as the children they were supposedly published for. Some of the major comic strip works created in these publications, aside from the *Tintin* and *Spirou* strips already mentioned, were *Asterix* by Albert Uderzo and René Goscinny, *Les Schtroumpfs* by Pierre Culliford (Peyo), *Chlorophylle* by Raymond Macherot, *Lucky Luke* by Maurice de Bévère (Morris), *Gaston Layaffe* by "Franquin," and *Valerian* by J.-C. Mezières and P. Christin. By almost any standards, these French and Belgian strips constitute the finest sustained body of comic strip work in the world today, equal in their range and style, their imaginative narrative and inspired character creation, and their dignity and quality of production, to the great American comic strip developments of the 1920s and 1930s.

430
Max und Moritz (1865) by Wilhelm Busch, a German artist whose work influenced the evolution of the America cartoon and the comic strip.

The American comic book is a direct by-product of the daily comic strip, and facsimile reprint collections of such favorites as *Yellow Yid, Mutt and Jeff,* and *Buster Brown* constitute, in a sense, the earliest "comic books." What we now know as comic books, however, came into being when two salesmen conceived the idea of reprinting color comics in a folded and stapled booklet about seven and one-half inches wide and ten inches high, and persuading commercial product and manufacturers to give them away as premiums and promotional gifts. When one of the reprint collections was placed on the newsstands for sale, its popularity brought about the establishment of the first monthly comic book, *Famous Funnies,* in 1934. Within a year comic books began to include original material, and with the publication of *Action Comics* No. 1 and the first appearance of Superman by Jerry Siegel and Joe Shuster, the success of the comic book was assured. Soon there were hundreds of superheroes competing for the expanding market, most notably Batman and Robin, Wonder Woman, and Captain Marvel.

Comic books were carried into many parts of the world by American soldiers during World War II, and wherever they were seen, they attracted attention. After the war, a considerable market for comic books, in English and other languages, developed. The *Superman* and *Batman* comic books are translated into all the major languages of the world. In the Arabic nations alone, 2.6 million copies of translated American titles are published annually by one firm. The superhero comic books are not the only ones sought and enjoyed by foreign readers. Archie Comic Publications, which specializes in teen-age subject matter, distributes its several series throughout the world in English as well as Spanish, French, German, and Swedish.

Max und Moritz

Schnupdiwup! there goes, O Jeminy!
One hen dangling up the chimney.

Schnupdiwup! da wird nach oben
Schon ein Huhn heraufgehoben.

431A
The Phantom as distributed in India.

431B
The Phantom in German.

432A
Blondie in Japanese.

432B
Blondie in Spanish (here Blondie is called Pepita and Dagwood is Lorenzo).

432C
Blondie in Finnish.

431A

CHIC YOUNG

LORENZO y PEPITA

Con TABLA
Bingo PEPSI

MEJORES REVISTAS
$2.00
M.N.

432B

432A

¥240.

BLONDIE,
THE CHARMING

チャーミングなブロンディ

by CHIC YOUNG

深尾凱子・上野一磨 共訳

TSURU COMIC

432C

BLONDIE
-hela familjens skämttidning!

NR 11 • 1971 • PRIS 1:75
(Inkl. moms) I Finland MK 2:15

VINN EN RESA FÖR
HELA FAMILJEN!

While it may concern some of the guardians of high culture, it seems obvious that comic art is a most viable and effective ambassador of popular American culture, second only perhaps to motion pictures. It is doubtful that the American way of life, however, is what the foreign reader seeks in our comics, or that he assumes all marriages in this country are of the Blondie and Dagwood type, any more than we assume Andy Capp and Flo represent the average British couple. What he does see is a creative and original face of our popular culture showing through. Nearly every other form of modern popular culture, be it film, drama, literature, or music, is pretty much modeled after European patterns and standards, and the practitioners have worked under the influence of foreign masters—Eisenstein, Ibsen, Joyce, and the Beatles, for example. Only in the comic strip and comic book have Americans defined the forms, expanded their aesthetic dimensions, and become the first masters of their unique possibilities. While the American intelligentsia have not yet accorded comic art the respect it deserves, this is not true abroad. Major exhibitions of American comic art have been held in Italy, Canada, France, Belgium, Sweden, Finland, Germany, England, Brazil, and Japan;

courses in the aesthetics of the comics are taught at the Sorbonne and the University of Brasília; and several major critical studies have been published in Spanish, French, German, and Portuguese. Organizations have been established for the advancement of the comic arts, such as Socerlid, founded in Paris in 1967, and ICON, founded in Brazil in 1970, and special publications are devoted to the reprinting and study of classic American comic strips, such as *Phenix* in France, *Linus* in Italy, and *Bang!* in Spain. Slowly these activities are having their influence as we witness the development of university courses and the establishment of research centers in the United States. American comic art is a neglected but obvious example of the way this nation has absorbed a part of world culture and reshaped it into a new and powerful instrument of international visual communication.

434A

434B

434C

434D

434E

434F

434G

434H

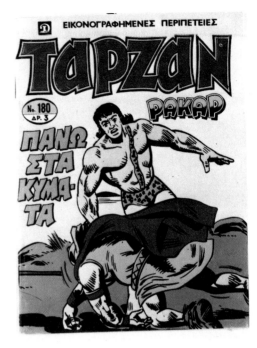

434I

434A
Tarzan in Finnish.

434B
Tarzan in Dutch.

434C
Tarzan in French.

434D
Tarzan in Czech.

434E
Tarzan in Hebrew.

434F
Tarzan in Norwegian.

434G
Tarzan in Danish.

434H
Tarzan in Japanese.

434I
Tarzan in Greek.

Everywhere Is Here and Now

A Scot's Contribution

The immigrants' success in nearly every phase of American life testifies to the strength of those who came and to the riches of the land that welcomed them. Farmer, scientist, merchant, musician, laborer, or statesman—the new American often became a distinguished presence. In the realm of invention, no one rose above the man who gave us a device which became the symbol of America's almost fanatical need for up-to-the-minute information and instant communication.

The invention was the telephone. The inventor, Alexander Graham Bell, was born in Edinburgh, Scotland, on March 3, 1847. Both his father and his grandfather were well established as elocution teachers. His father shared with many others a desire to develop a universal alphabet by which any vocal sound could be expressed, and by 1864 he was the first to achieve a practical solution. In demonstrations he would have skeptics utter a variety of words and noises, which he would then put on paper in his "visible speech." His son Alexander would be called in from another room and would read from the paper, exactly reproducing the original sounds and often dumbfounding the audience.

Young Alexander Bell had already begun his own teaching career, while continuing his studies, when first his younger brother (in 1867) and then his older brother (in 1870) died of tuberculosis. This hastened his parents' decision to emigrate to Canada, which they did in July of 1870, settling in Brantford, Ontario. With his father's help Alexander obtained a job teaching in Boston the following year. It was in Boston that he developed an interest in electricity and began to imagine that he might make an important breakthrough in a fundamental problem in telegraphy—how to send several messages over a single wire at the same time. His teaching suffered as a result, and during the early 1870s he was barely supporting himself. Still he persisted, returning to Brantford in the summers for rest and rejuvenation and occasionally a few experiments.

One of Bell's characteristics—which he himself freely described—was the difficulty he had in keeping to one line of experimentation. It is partly because of this that his telephone was produced. For in 1875, when success with the multiple telegraph seemed to be in sight, he began to spend more and more time pursuing the development of a device that might transmit speech. This was quite contrary to the wishes of the two financial backers he had acquired, who could see no practical use for such an instrument even if it could be made to work.

When Bell's patent on the telephone was issued, March 7, 1876, he had still not achieved successful voice transmission over any of his experimental models. It was three days later that his assistant, Thomas Watson, heard the now famous words: "Watson, come here, I want to see you." But the device was still far from perfect. Further experiments and demonstrations were performed, most notably one at the Centennial Exposition in Philadelphia in June. By the end of the year sufficient improvements had been made so that a commercial telephone could be introduced in 1877.

Bell became famous as the inventor of the telephone and amassed a fortune under the broad interpretation that the U.S. Supreme Court gave his patent. But it is important to note that his success was due in large part to his persistent belief that he was not playing around with a gadget, that his work would ultimately have practical value. This was an enthusiasm not shared by his most important competitors—his predecessor in Germany, Philip Reis, or his contemporary in America, Elisha Gray. Each pursued a line of investigation that could have led to a commercial telephone; neither had the vision or imagination or faith to see that as a realistic goal.

The wealth Bell derived from the telephone led him to pursue a number of scientific researches of his own and to support the work of others. He published several articles on hereditary deafness, which led him to studies on longevity and eventually to a long-term series of experiments breeding sheep with multiple nipples (which correlated with the economically desirable characteristic of multiple offspring). After twenty years he succeeded in developing a flock that consisted solely of six-nippled sheep. He conducted a number of experiments in medical electricity, and developed an induction probe that could detect pieces of metal under the skin. One of these was used in 1881 in an unsuccessful attempt to locate the bullet with which President Garfield had been shot and which subsequently caused his death.

Bell's support of the work of others took various forms. In 1880 he took the fifty thousand francs of the Volta prize which the French government had given him in recognition of his telephone invention and established the Volta Laboratory Association (later the Volta Bureau) in Washington. Activities were to be largely devoted to work for the deaf, but in the early years Bell experimented with his photophone (transmitting sounds by means of light rays), and associates did important work on the phonograph. In 1882 Bell conceived the idea of publishing the journal *Science,* and the first issues appeared the following year. During the next eight years Bell and G. G. Hubbard, his father-in-law, spent about $100,000 in support of the journal. Bell was a long-time supporter of activities at the Smithsonian, dating back to 1875, when Joseph Henry, secretary of the institution, had encouraged him. Bell contributed to S. P. Langley's personal researches when he took over as secretary, and in 1891 gave five thousand dollars to support Langley's flight experiments. Encouraged by work he had been doing with kites, Bell organized the Aerial Experimental Association, which was financed by his wife, and in the period 1907–1909 he and four asssociates (including Glenn Curtiss) spent $35,000 constructing airplanes and making experimental flights. Bell also helped to organize and finance the National Geographic Society; he served as its president from 1898 to 1903.

Soon after the invention of the telephone, Bell took up residence in Washington, D.C., and in 1882 he became an American citizen—a fact of which he was immensely proud. But the place he loved most was his estate, Beinn Bhreagh, near Baddeck in Nova Scotia, where he spent his summers and pursued his experiments on sheep breeding, flight, and tetrahedral kites. He died there on August 2, 1922. He was buried on the property, in a grave marked with a simple stone inscribed with his name, his dates, his profession of "inventor," and in accord with his wishes the words: "Died a citizen of the United States."

"Bell" is now an institutional name, a corporate identity which means "communication." But instantaneous communication—even across the ocean—predates the first successful telephone. The transatlantic instantaneous sharing of experience is a little more than a century old. It first occurred on August 5, 1858, when the final splice was made in the first Atlantic cable and operators in Ireland and Newfoundland exchanged messages. This was, of course, a very limited form of sharing—especially since the cable failed after a month and was never opened to commercial traffic; but the reaction of the public indicates that the importance of the event was deeply felt. In the newspapers it was called "the last and greatest achievement of the human genius," "the boldest and perhaps the greatest engineering work that ever was attempted," and one stated: "Since the discovery of Columbus nothing has been done in any degree comparable to the vast enlargement which has thus been given to the sphere of human activity" [**435**]. With a similar display of enthusiasm. Tiffany's in New York purchased the excess cable from one of the ships and had it cut up into umbrella handles, canes, medallions, and short souvenir samples. The samples, about four inches long, were accompanied by a certificate and signed by Cyrus Field, the American promoter of the first cable; they sold for fifty cents.

It is worth noting that the Victorian engineers were·straining at the limits of available technology when these early submarine cables were laid. The first successful line stretched across the English Channel in 1851. This was less than a decade after practical telegraphy had been introduced on land. Other essential ingredients were similarly quite recent: techniques of manufacturing wire rope, used to protect the cable, were first patented in Britain in 1840; and guttapercha, a natural plastic substance that was to be the principal insulating material for cables for a hundred years, was first introduced to the West in 1843. Finally, to lay ocean cables steamships were needed large enough to carry a thousand miles or more of cable; by the mid-1850s only a half-dozen such ships existed, two of which were pressed into duty in the attempt to span the Atlantic (the cable ends were spliced halfway across and the ships proceeded in opposite directions). By 1866, when the first completely successful link was accomplished between the Old World and the New, a single ship—the *Great Eastern*—was available which could carry the entire two thousand miles of cable [**436**].

The cable acted like a large electrical capacitor (or Leyden jar), with the central copper wire acting as one conductor and the sea water on the outside acting as the second conductor. A signal introduced at one end would first charge up the entire length of cable, and then it could be discharged at the other end, producing a relatively long smeared-out pulse. If signals were transmitted too close to each other they would overlap at the receiving end and therefore be indistinguishable. The result was that at first the 1866 cable was operated at a slow twelve words per minute [**437A, 437B**]. Improved techniques over the succeeding decades brought the capacity up to several hundred words per minute. But the demands placed on the cables by a public thirsty for information also increased.

The Atlantic was crossed and recrossed numerous times by cable ships, until by the twentieth century more than a dozen cables were in continuous operation. Links between Britain and the world were also quickly made—to Hong Kong and Australia by 1871 and to South America by 1874. Except for a few short lines along the coasts, however, the depths of the Pacific remained undisturbed. The reason for this was simple economics: Pacific cables would be very expensive, and the amount of business expected would not be sufficient to pay for them. Finally, in 1903 the British completed a line from Vancouver via Fanning Island and Fiji to Australia and New Zealand, more for political than for economic reasons. At the same time an American cable was being laid from San Francisco to the newly acquired possessions of Hawaii and the Philippines [**438**].

The initial enthusiastic reaction to the cables gave way quickly to casual acceptance. But the original response can be considered the more appropriate, for over a period of time the cables permanently altered the political and economic world. Foreign policy could now be run from a central location, allowing swift responses to local crises (sometimes also precluding a healthy cooling-off period). The financial centers of London, Paris, and New York were linked. For the public the cables were most visible through the daily press, which carried information from around the globe that was only hours old, giving an unprecedented sense of immediacy and involvement [**439**]. And for half a century all of this was transmitted through thin strands of copper, guttapercha, and iron, stretched across the ocean bottoms.

435

A commonly held—if certainly unconfirmed—view is that improved communications lead to understanding, and understanding is the cornerstone of peace. This cartoon, taken from a wood engraving (1858), expresses that hope as it was kindled by the momentary success of the first Atlantic cable.

436

Telegraph cable design remained remarkably constant for almost a hundred years. A stranded copper wire in the center was surrounded by the plastic insulator guttapercha (which comes from the sap of certain trees in southeast Asia). There was a protective wrapping of tarred jute or hemp and then iron wires. For the deep-sea portions these outer wires could be relatively small, since their purpose was merely to provide sufficient strength so that the cable would not break when being laid or picked up. But near the shore much heavier wires were used to provide protection from the effects of tides, anchors, and trawling equipment. H 13¾″.

436

435

THE LAYING OF THE CABLE---JOHN AND JONATHAN JOINING HANDS.

437A

437B

437A

The electric signal that emerged from 2,000 miles of cable was quite feeble, and special techniques were devised to detect it. For several years the sole instrument used was the mirror galvanometer, designed by British scientist William Thomson. A very lightweight mirror with small needle magnets glued to its back was suspended at the center of a coil of wire. The fluctuating current from the cable was led through the coil, producing a fluctuating magnetic field inside and causing the mirror to twist accordingly. A light shining on the mirror was then reflected on a scale—one direction for dots, the other for dashes—which the operator would read. Beginning in the 1870s, recording instruments were developed (the first one also by Thomson), but the mirror galvanometer has remained in use up to the present day for testing purposes. Thomson was knighted for his contributions to the Atlantic cable in 1886, and in 1894 he became the baron Lord Kelvin.

437B

Engraving of the Thomson mirror galvanometer system from W. H. Preece and J. Sivewright, *Telegraphy* (New York, 1876).

438

The high point of the telegraph cable industry occurred in the 1920s, when almost 400,000 miles of wire joined the world's land masses. Competition from radio and the effects of the Depression then combined to produce a decline. Cable map, 1920.

438

"Via Eastern" THE EASTERN AND ASSOCIATED TELEGRAPH COMPANIES' CABLE SYSTEM. "Via Eastern"
(INDICATED IN RED.)

439
Postal telegraph messengers
photographed by Lewis Hine
early in the twentieth century.

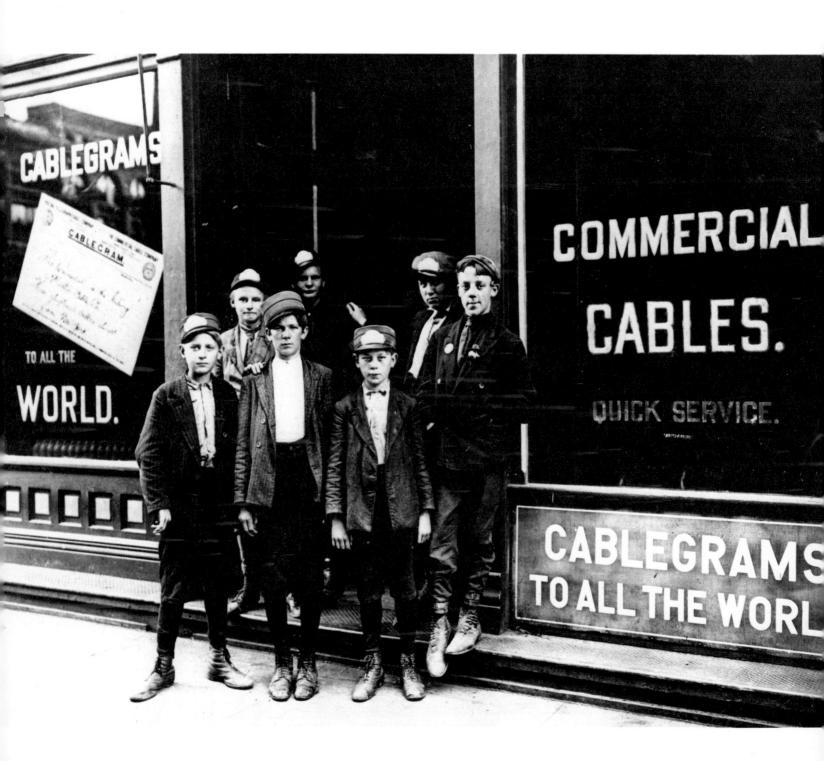

The first evidence that the cable monopoly might be broken occurred on December 12, 1902, when a twenty-seven-year-old Italian, Guglielmo Marconi, stood on Signal Hill, Newfoundland, and using a four-hundred-foot kite line for an antenna, received the repeated message . . . . from a transmitter in Poldhu, Cornwall, England. Actual commercial competition over these long distances, however, was still two decades away. The most important use of wireless communication in the early twentieth century was for ships. The U.S. Congress in 1910 passed an act requiring that all American ships carrying more than fifty persons install wireless apparatus with a fifty-mile range. The value of such legislation was proven in several disasters, but the sinking of the *Titanic* in 1912 dramatically exhibited the need for adequate international controls. The *Titanic*, equipped with appropriate equipment, sent out an SOS after colliding with an iceberg [440]. The *Californian* was well within range for rescue operations and even saw the flares that were sent up, judging them to be fireworks for a big party. The *Californian* was equipped with wireless, and indeed had tried to warn the *Titanic* about the icebergs earlier in the day, but the operator was not required to be on duty and had quit for the evening. Considerably farther away, the *Carpathia* did hear the call for help and steamed to the rescue. David Sarnoff, as an operator for the Marconi Wireless Telegraph Company in New York, happened to be on duty as the first wireless messages were relayed from the *Carpathia,* giving details about survivors. Interference from other stations was reduced by presidential order, and for three days, until the *Carpathia* reached port, the world was made aware, through Sarnoff's station, of the magnitude of the tragedy that had taken place [441].

The sinking of the *Titanic* was one of several incidents that prompted increased efforts to equip ships with wireless and to have them manned continuously. At the same time, new equipment began to come into service, replacing the inefficient spark transmitters which could not be tuned to narrow frequency bands and therefore constantly interfered with each other. After 1913 continuous-wave arc transmitters invented by the Dane Valdemar Poulsen backed up spark transmitters in the major U.S. coastal stations and were installed on substantial numbers of ships [442]. A radio-frequency alternator, developed by the Swedish immigrant Ernst Alexanderson at General Electric, was the mainstay of the most powerful American transmitting stations in the 1920s [443]. But the future belonged to vacuum tubes, which were cheaper, could be more easily controlled, and could be taken to higher frequencies. Tube transmitters were used in 1928 when the first transatlantic telephone circuits were established and members of the public for the first time were able to talk across the ocean. They experienced an immediacy and sharing which we still feel in our ability to communicate personally from one continent to another.

The availability and reliability of telephone communications increased dramatically in 1956 with the laying of the first transatlantic telephone cable. Key elements in this new cable were the repeaters (amplifiers) which were spaced twenty miles apart and buried with the cable in the sea. The problem had been to construct repeaters out of equipment that could be trusted to operate over long periods of time without servicing. TAT-1 [444], which was a joint venture of the American Telephone and Telegraph Company and the British General Post Office, originally was capable of carrying thirty-six 4-kilohertz telephone channels (later changed to forty-eight 3-kilohertz channels, with additional conversations possible through special techniques). Once the technical possibility was proved, however, the need turned out to be explosive. Additional cables have been laid, with increasing information capabilities: TAT-5, laid in 1969, was capable of eight hundred 3-kilohertz channels, and CANTAT-2 in 1974 carried 1,840. In addition there have been the satellites, beginning with Telstar in 1962, and an ordinary telephone conversation is as likely to be carried up through space as down through a cable. Not all such conversations are between people, of course. More and more "talking" is done between computers, exchanging and processing information. For them, too, the immediacy of the contact is of fundamental importance.

440
Radio room of the S.S. *Olympic,* sister ship of the *Titanic.* The multiple tuner (center of desk) and magnetic detector (mounted on the wall above) were significant innovations by Marconi to early wireless receiving systems.

441
David Sarnoff. On April 15, 1912, the world's largest ocean passenger liner, the *Titanic,* on its maiden voyage, collided with an iceberg. Thanks to wireless, some 504 passengers and 201 crew members were rescued by the Cunard liner *Carpathia.* The messages from the *Carpathia* were picked up by the *Olympic* and sent in toward shore, where they were picked up by Sarnoff, wireless operator for the Marconi Company's Wanamaker Station in New York, who stayed on duty many long hours relaying messages to anxious relatives and the press.

440

441

442
Until 1910 most commercial radio work was carried on with various types of spark transmitters employing transmission techniques not much different from those of the late 1890s. In 1909 a "continuous wave generator," termed a high-frequency arc, was brought to the U.S. and developed commercially by the Federal Telegraph Company. The original design was that of Valdemar Poulsen of Denmark. The device became crucial for long-distance communication at low frequencies, and shore stations employing such equipment were still operating in the early 1930s.

443
The Poulsen Arc, though available in small sizes for shipboard use, did not radiate a "clean" signal and had certain other intrinsic limitations. The high-frequency alternator was often preferred for reliable transoceanic communication. First designed for wireless work by Reginald Fessenden, these devices were brought to a high state of engineering design by General Electric Company engineer E. F. W. Alexanderson. In 1918 President Wilson's "fourteen points" were sent abroad via the station at New Brunswick, New Jersey.

444
The old-style telegraph cables (436) have now disappeared, made obsolete by the development of repeaters (amplifiers) which could be buried at sea with the cable. This means that the signal does not deteriorate, for it is boosted every few miles along the route, making it possible to use cables with considerably more information capacity. The new cables are coaxial, the two concentric conductors being separated by polyethylene. The sample shown is part of the first transatlantic telephone cable (TAT-1), laid in 1956. Later designs have a central steel strand for strength; the central conductor is then a tube around the steel. H 9".

443

444

442

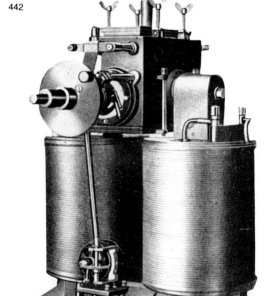

619

445
Amateur radio began virtually with the inception of wireless technology in the 1890s, but call letters were not issued officially in the U.S. until 1912. Shown here is a typical amateur station c. 1916, with audion (tube) receiver and spark transmitter.

446
QSL cards verifying a two-way radio contact between amateur shortwave stations throughout the world. Those pictured here were received by WIAW, headquarter station of the American Radio Relay League, Newington, Connecticut.

From the beginning the amateur has played an important role in the use of radio waves over long distances. Relegated by the Radio Act of 1912 to wavelengths less than two hundred meters—which at the time were thought to be almost useless—amateur radio operators helped to pioneer the shortwave area of the spectrum and discovered that these waves were peculiarly suited to long-distance communications [**445**]. Over the years the amateurs (or ''hams'') have developed a world-wide network which today numbers on the order of half a million individuals, more than half of them in the United States. They form an international community in constant communication with each other—by Morse code, by voice, and even by television [**446**]. Special techniques have to be adopted for television transmission by an amateur in the standard shortwave spectrum since the band width allowed is not large enough to accommodate an ordinary TV signal. Instead, a coarser picture is used (128 lines) and a complete scan takes a little over eight seconds. With a persistent phosphor on the receiving tube, however, a reasonable picture can be transmitted and viewed successfully. In addition, the amateurs have satellite capability through the orbiting Oscar VI and VII communications systems [**447**].

Aside from contributing to world understanding through interactions within their own groups, the hams have been of major assistance in numerous disasters, where their radios are often the only means of outside communication. An example of this occurred in the Honduras earthquake of 1973. For two weeks all contact with the outside was handled through the ham network. Polar expeditions have traditionally relied on ham circuits for communications. This is obviously important for receiving and sending information essential to the expedition, but it is at least equally important to the members for providing them with a direct link home.

KHARKOV, UKRAINE
UY500
YURI ANISHENKO
RADIO W1AW CONFIRMING OUR 2-WAY SSB
of 7 JULY 1973 at 2251 GMT ON 14 mc
YOUR SIGS 59 73 Yuri □ PSE QSL TNX
TNX TEST QSO ALAN.

JOSÉ A. RODRIGUES FONTE SANTA
EVORA - PORTUGAL
n: 2160
To Radio W1AW QSA 5 R 8
Ur Pom Wkd hr 30/1 QRI 9 QSB —
1950 at 20,45 GMT Band 14 MC.
XMTR Fa 87 Receiver MC-81X
Watts 40 Aerial Zeppelin Aerial Zeppelin
RemarksGlad with the qso Tom Operator
Tnx QSL Om. direct or via R.E.P.
CT1PM

SV0WR
AΘHNAI | ATHENS
EΛΛAΣ | GREECE
IS PLEASED TO CONFIRM RADIO CONTACT
WITH W1AW ON 17 SEPT. 1958 1715 GMT
ON 28 MCS RST 589 OPR Ole
HOWARD J. OLSON
VIA SV - BUREAU USASG
P.O. BOX 564 OR APO 223,
ATHENS NEW YORK, N.Y.
THRILLED TO DX ARRL HQ 1ST TIME. V73

6 HILLSIDE PARADE, BOX HILL, VICTORIA, 3128
AUSTRALIA
AX3ZT
RADIO W1AW CFMG CW. QSO 5-7-70 RST 599 AT 0530 G.M.T.
XMTR 807PA 50 WATTS HRO RX G.P. ANT
REMARKS TNX FoR FB 14 MHZ QSO JOHN (WA1CQW)
PSE QSL. alf.
73 ALF. MATTHEWS

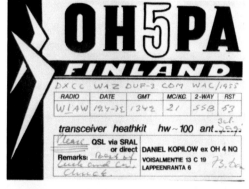

OH5PA
FINLAND
DXCC WAZ DUF-3 COM WAC/1955

RADIO	DATE	GMT	MC/KC	2-WAY	RST
W1AW	19-4-73	1342	21	SSB	53

transceiver heathkit hw-100 ant.
Please QSL via SRAL
or direct DANIEL KOPILOW ex OH4NQ
Remarks: VOISALMENTIE 13 C 19
LAPPEENRANTA 6 73.

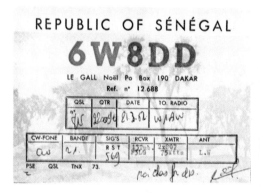

REPUBLIC OF SÉNÉGAL
6W8DD
LE GALL Noël Po Box 190 DAKAR
Ref. n° 12.688

QSL	QTR	DATE	TO. RADIO
	12.00	21.3.72	W1AW

CW-FONE	BANDE	SIG'S	RCVR	XMTR	ANT
CW	21	RST 569		75watts	L.W

PSE QSL TNX 73.

COLOMBIA
QTC
QRG 21 mc
Trx HT-39
Recv. NC-303
Ant. YAGI
DXCC 226 217
WAS WAC DUF/4 W4OQ-U TPH
Date 2-I-63
QTR 2025 GMT
RST 579
QSB Yes QRM some
Remks: Very prou to make this QSO Gud luck
HK3LX
Confirming QSO with radio W1AW
Edmundo Quiñones P.
73/DX QTH: BOGOTA

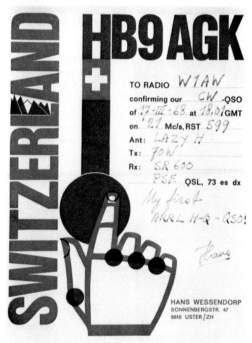

SWITZERLAND
HB9AGK
TO RADIO W1AW
confirming our CW-QSO
of 17-III-68 at 18.01 GMT
on 21 Mc/s, RST 599
Ant: LAZY H
Tx: 70W
Rx: SR 600
PSE QSL, 73 es dx
My first ARRL H-Q - QSO!
HANS WESSENDORP
SONNENBERGSTR. 47
8610 USTER/ZH

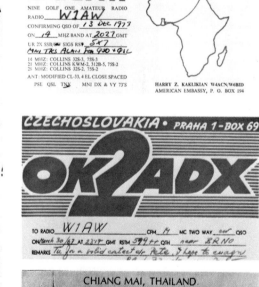

9G1AR ACCRA GHANA
NINE GOLF ONE AMATEUR RADIO
RADIO W1AW
CONFIRMING QSO OF 13 Dec 1973
ON 14 MHZ BAND AT 2027 GMT
UR 2X SSB/CW SIGS RST 5x7
MNI TKS ALAN Fer QSO + QSL
14 MHZ: COLLINS 32S-3, 75S-3
21 MHZ: COLLINS KWM-2, 312B-5, 75S-2
28 MHZ: COLLINS 32S-2, 75S-2
ANT: MODIFIED CL-33, 4 EL CLOSE SPACED
PSE QSL TNX MNI DX & VY 73'S
HARRY Z. KAKLIKIAN W4ACN/W6BID
AMERICAN EMBASSY, P.O. BOX 194

CZECHOSLOVAKIA • PRAHA 1-BOX 69
OK2ADX
TO RADIO W1AW CFM 14 MC TWO WAY QSO
ON March 30/67 AT 2314 GMT RSTM 599 ++ near BRNO
REMARKS Tu for a solid contact dr Pete, I hope to work

LUXEMBOURG LX1DO
CQ DX
LX1DO
TO RADIO W1AW
Many thanks for our AM-SSB-RTTY Mcs
QSO on the 13.5.66 MEZ. Ur were
RST 57 Best 73 es DX
Operator: ROGER GEHLEN
QRA: Esch s/Alzette Bech-Kleinmacher
Post Box 26, Esch s/Alzette

CHIANG MAI, THAILAND.
HS5ABD
"FRED" LAUN
ALSO W9SZR EX-HI8XAL HS3AL
T4XB - NCL2000 1KW - R4B - 14AVQ DIPOLE QUAD

CONFIRMING QSO WITH	1970	GMT	REPORT	BAND	FONE
W1AW	5 AUG	1731	589	21	2XSSB CW

QSL VIA:
PHILIP J GOETZ W6DQX
P.O. BOX 5491
LOS ANGELES, CAL. 90055 U.S.A.
แอลเฟรด เอ.ลอน
ถนนเจริญราษฎร์ 352 ฟ้าฮ่าม
เชียงใหม่ ประเทศไทย

447
Amateur radio techniques have always incorporated the latest in telecommunications devices. The Smithsonian station includes a radioteletype installation and slow-scan television in addition to the traditional Morse code and radiotelephone modes of transmission. The SSTV television operation permits contact with some 4,000 operators worldwide using this medium on the high-frequency bands. Speaker, L 10½".

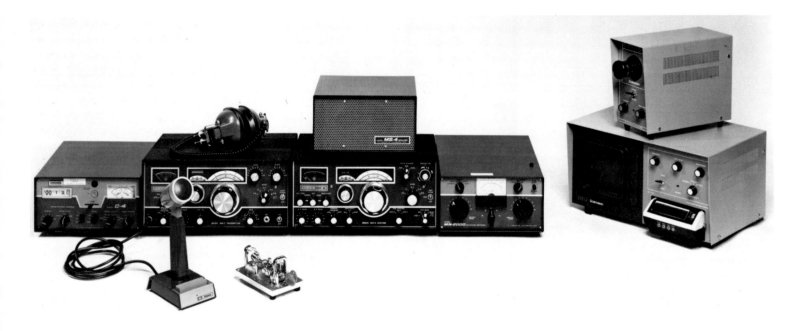

Thus far we have been discussing point-to-point communications, with one person or one machine conversing with another. This is only part of the story of instantaneous communication. The impact of broadcasting—where information from a single source is transmitted to many receivers—has also been enormous. Domestic radio broadcasting had its practical origins in the 1920s. It was discovered that shortwaves could be reflected from the ionosphere and therefore transmitted over long distances [**448**], and since the late 1930s shortwave broadcasting has been a reality sponsored mainly by governments for political purposes.

Outside the United States shortwave is easily the most important medium for international broadcasting. Because shortwave transmitters are cheap compared with the amount of territory they can cover, most of the newly established and underdeveloped countries have been quick to set up at least one station for domestic use. This has given an incentive for the marketing of receivers capable of receiving shortwave, and these in turn have been ready receptors for international broadcasting. The result is that approximately one hundred countries maintain international broadcasting services, using close to one thousand individual transmitters. The number of receivers in the hands of individuals is more difficult to estimate. In the United States the number is relatively small—three or four million out of a total of perhaps three hundred million radios. But in the rest of the world approximately one-third of the half-billion radios in use can receive shortwave [**449**], and there is evidence that they find a great deal of use. Fifty million different radios, for instance, are estimated to be tuned to Voice of America broadcasts in a typical week, and in times of crisis the numbers are far greater.

For many countries, the United States included, shortwave radio broadcasting is a major means of national propaganda. It leaps over international boundaries as if they did not exist and reaches directly into the individual home. The message is often flagrant, sometimes subtle; but the basic aim is almost always to get the point of view of the transmitting country across to the people of other countries without the middleman interpretation of their governments. There are many forms that this can take: from Axis Sally and Tokyo Rose to rock music and "objective" newscasts, from exhortations by governments in exile to religious services. The impact is difficult to measure. Does the immediacy and universality of such contacts help to bring the world together by creating an awareness of shared problems? Or does it serve to rend us apart by revealing our many differences? The purpose behind most of the broadcasts seems to be centered on the latter purpose; one can only hope that the actual effect is more the former.

448
The Westinghouse Electric Corporation conducted experimental work in shortwave communication techniques as early as 1922. By the early 1930s station W8XK (Saxon, Pa.) operated an extensive programming schedule, with broadcasts on 13.93 meters (21540 kHz) from 7 A.M. to 2 P.M. daily. This photo was taken in 1936.

449
The extension of electric power and communications to rural areas is a continuing process even in today's advanced technology. Some remote farm areas still operate with portable energy systems. A unique device developed in the U.S.S.R. in the mid-1950s incorporated a thermoelectric generator, with kerosene lamp as the heater, to power a radio receiver. The frequency bands include two shortwave ranges and two medium-wave bands. Radio, H 12″.

448

449

It is worth noting that the cheap transmitter is only half the story of the proliferation of shortwave broadcasting. Equally important has been the availability of inexpensive receivers, and this has been possible because of the transistor. Discovered at the Bell Laboratories in 1948, the transistor and its possibilities were quickly examined here and abroad. The first transistor radios were produced here and in Japan in the mid-1950s, and their effect on the world has been enormous. In this country the most obvious result often seems to be that every teen-ager has one, usually emitting loud music. In many other countries the transistor radio—especially when it can be tuned to shortwave—has wrought a different kind of revolution. It has made instantaneous communications from the outside available to millions who previously might have had their closest contact through newspapers that were several days old, and perhaps not even that if they were unable to read. Governments of these countries can therefore communicate directly and quickly with their citizens; and other governments, including the United States, can do the same.

Transmission of pictures must inevitably give a greater sense of reality than that of words; the recipient "sees for himself" and is likely to feel that he is not relying on intermediate interpretation. Photographs were first transmitted commercially across the Atlantic by electricity in the 1920s, first by radio in 1924 [**450**], and then by cable in 1927 [**451**]. As far as the viewer was concerned, the effect was not instantaneous; the photograph had to be processed and prepared for transmission, and the received image had to be transferred to a plate and printed. Nevertheless, the impact was considerable as newspapers began routinely to carry photographs of events that took place only a few hours earlier.

Real-time viewing by the public became possible with the development of communications satellites capable of carrying all the information that goes into a television signal. Telstar [**452**] was barely able to carry out this function, but in a series of experimental transmissions after its launch on July 10, 1962, until it went permanently inactive on February 22, 1963, the public was treated to a series of indications of what the future would bring. The intervals were brief—at most a little over an hour—because Telstar circled the earth at a relatively low orbit (between 600 and 3,500 miles) and was in sight of both sides of the ocean only during certain periods of time. To have had continuous transmission capabilities would have taken several satellites of the Telstar type. Another solution was to place a satellite in synchronous orbit, at an altitude of approximately 23,000 miles. At this height the period of revolution of the satellite is the same as that of the earth, or one day. If the satellite is located directly over the equator, moving in the same direction as the earth (from west to east), then it will remain stationary over the same spot on the earth's surface. The first satellite of this type, called Syncom, was launched on July 26, 1963. It was an experimental device, and its information capabilities were barely sufficient for a degraded television signal, but it proved that basic principles of a synchronous satellite were sound and laid the groundwork for future practical systems.

In 1965 Early Bird (Intelsat I) was positioned above the equator over the Atlantic, and commercial international television was a reality. It was capable of transmitting one television channel and 240 voice channels (two thousand 3-kilohertz voice channels are equivalent to one television channel). Ground stations were established in the major countries on both sides of the Atlantic, and it was now possible for people to share experiences in a manner undreamed of only a few years before. By 1974 there were four commercial Intelsat IV satellites operational in orbit—two over the Atlantic, one over the Pacific, and one over the Indian Ocean—plus two in orbit available as backups. Each was capable of handling five thousand telephone channels plus one television channel. And as of 1975 plans were being made to launch Intelsat IVa, with twenty-four television channels and nine thousand voice channels [**453**].

What does this mean? It means that people are talking to each other across the oceans of the world at an unprecedented rate. It means they are watching, together, astronauts walking on the moon and shaking hands in space; Olympic games from Mexico City and Munich and Montreal; murders under different guises and called by different names in Vietnam and Northern Ireland and New Orleans, Tokyo and the Sinai and Cyprus; a royal wedding in London; Americans celebrating their two hundredth birthday in different ways; famine in India; the heavyweight championship fight in Zaire; the United Nations General Assembly debating in New York; drought in Africa; the Watergate hearings; the Pope's Christmas message; World Cup soccer. They see and hear, together, what is news everywhere, here and now.

FIRST PHOTO OF LADY LINDY IN IRELAND—Amelia Earhart
Putnam sits, boyish fashion, in a Londonderry home as she tells two
reporters of her record 2,000-mile solo flight from Newfoundland
Picture was flown to London in special plane and radioed.

450

451

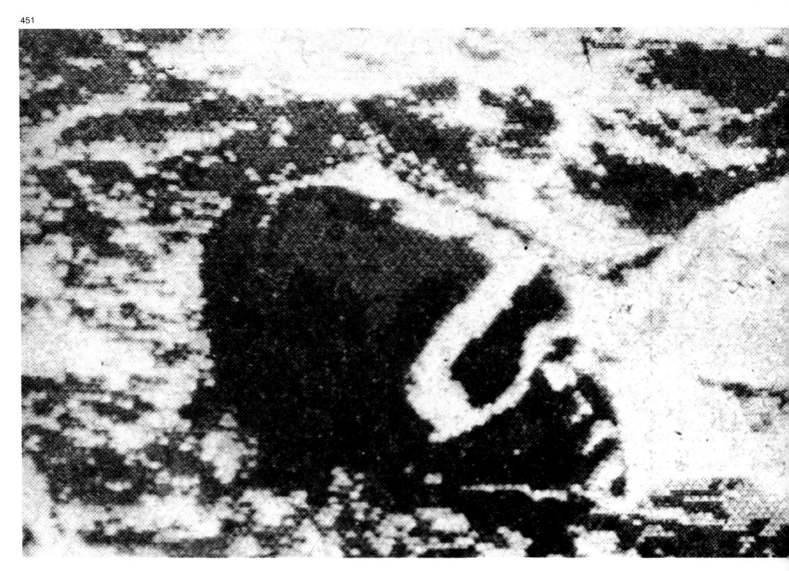

450
Photograph of Amelia Earhart
sent via radio waves from
London to America.

451
The transoceanic cables
began to carry pictures as
well as sounds in the 1920s.
For newspapers, pictures
from distant parts of the globe
became as timely as the
stories themselves. Above is
Gertrude Ederle swimming
the English Channel in 1926.

Did Trudie come across? We'll say so! Marvelous Bartlane process
brought this splendid photo of her, in midst of channel swim, to New
York for you. It was rushed from midchannel by boat, from Dover to
London by motorcycle, where Bartlane process tape was prepared,
thence to New York by cable. It shows Trudie's greased left arm raising for one of mighty sweeps which carried her to victory.

452
Satellite communications.
When the Bell System's first
Telstar I experimental communications satellite was
launched from Cape Canav-
eral on the morning of July 10,
1962, the age of satellite communications began in earnest.
For the first time an active
satellite, operated on transis-
tors and solar cells, was able
to transmit high-quality voice
communications and live television between the Bell System's Andover, Maine, ground
station and similar stations
in England and France. The
Telstar satellite and Andover
station were designed and
built by Bell Laboratories for
the American Telephone and
Telegraph Company. AT&T
also paid for the launching
of this first privately owned
communications satellite. In
the picture, a Bell Laboratories engineer inspects a
model of Telstar. The room is
lined with absorbent plastic
foam pyramids which prevent
reflections during testing of
the antenna.

453
Antenna at Tanay, Philippine
Islands, located about thirty
miles east of Manila, completed in April 1968 and designated TA-1. The system is
designed for use with the
Pacific Intelsat IV Communications Satellite. A companion antenna at the same site,
TA-2, is employed with the Indian Ocean Intelsat. The stations are a facility of the
Philippine Communication
Satellite (PHILCOMSAT).

452

We are presently in a period of revolutionary
change in international communications. It has
been greeted with less public excitement than was
the unsuccessful Atlantic cable of 1858, yet it is
probably far more important because it touches
individuals directly. Reinforced by all the other
means of cultural interaction and exchange, the
modern methods of real-time communications are
forcing individuals to share the world. Each country is a nation among nations; each individual is a
part of humanity. Intimate contact and good communications and even the sharing of experiences
do not, of course, automatically produce understanding and a sense of brotherhood. They unfortunately often produce just the opposite. But in a
world where even the most remote peasant is affected by decisions that are being made about
thermonuclear bombs, it seems necessary that as
many people as possible be aware of what is happening everywhere. Somehow this may help us to
recognize and even to appreciate our differences,
at the same time allowing us to see how very much
we have in common.

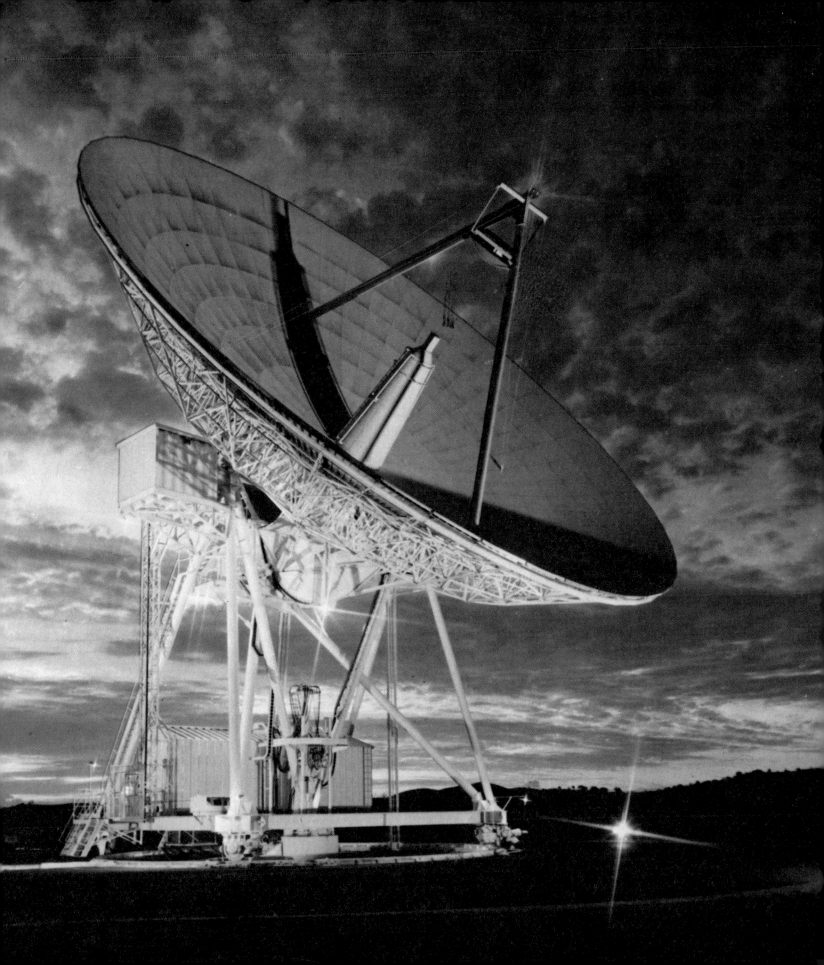

Acknowledgments

The exhibition *A Nation of Nations* was put together by a group of staff members from the National Museum of History and Technology of the Smithsonian Institution. They reached into most of the corners and reference areas of the museum, with the cooperation of the rest of the staff, to find appropriate objects and documents. They reached far beyond to acquire and to borrow large numbers of additional objects. Those primarily responsible for the exhibition have written this book. Led by Carl H. Scheele, the exhibit committee included Richard E. Ahlborn, Grace R. Cooper, Bernard S. Finn, Ellen Roney Hughes, Harold D. Langley, Otto Mayr, Richard S. Virgo, C. Malcolm Watkins, John H. White, Jr., and Peter C. Marzio. Dr. Marzio, who edited this book, is responsible for its coordination and for much of its style. The original concept of the exhibition is that of Dr. Daniel J. Boorstin, Senior Historian of the National Museum of History and Technology and its former Director.

The exhibition and this book were designed by Chermayeff & Geismar Associates of New York City. Their staff, which gave so much of its time and creativity, included:

Principal designers	John P. Grady
	Ivan Chermayeff
Design team	
Exhibit designers	Priscilla Deichmann
	Judith Ellis
Graphic and book designer	Stephan Geissbuhler
Exhibit coordinator	Pamela Smith
Construction detailing and coordination	Joseph R. Simons
	Frank Koester
	George S. Kanelba
Design assistants	Edward Broderick
	Denise Brooks
	Walter Deichmann
	Peter Felperin
	Vincent W. Gagliostro
	Ferdinand S. Paganini
	Dorcas Roehrs
	Elaine Rooney
	Louis Scrima
Consultants	
Audio-visual	Rusty Russell
	Donna Casavant
Lighting designer	Howard Brandston Lighting Design Inc.
Label script	Jane Cooper
Structural engineer	Olaf Sööt
Mechanical and electrical engineers	Cosentini Associates

Many individuals of the Smithsonian Institution provided their energy, their enthusiasm, and their expertise in the production of both the exhibition and this book.

Rita J. Adrosko
Ann Auman
Edwin A. Battison
Silvio A. Bedini
Don H. Berkebile
Kathleen Bishop
Charles Blitzer
Doris Bowman
Deborah M. Bretzfelder
Franklin R. Bruns, Jr.
Lawrence A. Bush
W. F. Cannon
Marylin Cohen
Herbert R. Collins
Kip Cordero
Audrey Davis
Katherine Dirks
Richard Drake
Jon B. Eklund
John C. Ewers
John T. Fesperman, Jr.
Shelley J. Foote
Paul Forman
Paul Gallagher
Paul Gardner
Margaret C. Gaynor
Bethune M. Gibson
Craddock R. Goins, Jr.
Anne C. Golovin
Genevieve M. Gremillion
David Haberstich
Elizabeth M. Harris
Karyn J. Harris
Michael Harris
Brooke Hindle
John H. Hoffman
Cynthia A. Hoover
Harry Hunter
Melvin H. Jackson
Undine Jones
Barbara Keville
Mary Keys
Claudia Kidwell
Sally S. Klass
Robert Klinger
Donald E. Kloster
Anton Konrad
Benjamin W. Lawless
Philip K. Lundeberg

Ulysses G. Lyon
John Matthis
Eleanor McMillan
Jean Middleton
Susan Myers
R. Stanley Nelson
Reidar Norby
Wendy O'Bert
Jay Scott Odell
Robert Organ
Eugene Ostroff
Harry Patton
George E. Phebus
Margie L. Porter
Robert Post
Diane Prior
Virginia Przystas
Beverly Robinson
Rodris Roth
Charles Rowell
John T. Schlebecker
Catherine Scott
Anne Marie Serio
George Terry Sharrer
Robert E. Sheldon
Elliot N. Sivowitch
James E. Spears
Carlene E. Stephens
Barbara Stuckenrath
William C. Sturtevant
Barbara Suit
Robert Tillotson
Lois Van
Herman J. Viola
Robert M. Vogel
Paul Walker
Robert Walther
Deborah Jean Warner
Wilcomb E. Washburn
George Watson
Sylvia A. Werner

Volunteer workers donated generously to the *Nation of Nations* project: Margaret Dong, Margaret Fahs, Olivia Feldman, Judy Goodman, Laura C. Higgins, Rolf Jacoby, Carol Kominoth, Lee Langston, Betty McIntosh, Sandy Medallis, Betty Morin, Jeanette Richoux, August Scheele, Joanne Scheele, Martha Scheele, Charlotte Taylor, Elizabeth Topp, and Lee Wheelwright. Members of the Smithsonian photographic laboratory also worked a hectic schedule: David Blume, Harold Dougherty, Alfred F. Harrell, Jr., Richard Hofmeister, Sterling Jones, Ernie Kazas, Robert Myers, and Daniel Thompson. Additional photographs which appear in these pages were made by Arthur Vitols of Helga Studio. Their high quality speaks for itself.

The professional staff of the *Nation of Nations* offices provided continuity and order which proved so essential for maintaining high museum standards: Joan P. Nicholson, Sally J. Richner, Francis D. Roche, and Craig J. Turner.

The *Nation of Nations* project would not have been possible without the generosity of numerous business firms and the many individuals who donated so much in the way of artifacts and information.

Organizations

Adler Business Machines, Inc.
Agfa-Gevaert Inc.
Albany Institute of History and Art
Allgemeiner Deutscher Automobil-Club
Alliance Internationale de Tourisme, Geneva
Amalgamated Clothing Workers of America
Amalgamated Meat Cutters and Butcher Workmen of North America, AFL-CIO
American Automobile Association
American Express Company
American Museum of Fire Fighting, Fireman's Association of the State of New York, Hudson, N.Y.
American Museum of Immigration, Statue of Liberty National Monument
American Radio Relay League
American Telephone & Telegraph Co.
Arena Stage of Washington, D.C.
Atchison, Topeka, and Santa Fe Railway Co.
Australian Automobile Association
Automobile and Touring Club of Greece (ELPA)
The Automobile Association, Great Britain
Automobile Association of Malaysia
Automobile Association of Rhodesia
Automobile Association of South Africa
Automobile Club of Madagascar
Automobile-Club de Suisse
Automobile and Touring Club of Egypt
Automobile and Touring Club of Israel
Automovel Club de Brasil
Automovil Club Argentino
Automovil Club de Chile
BankAmericard
G. Barbèra Editore, Florence
Bavarian Restaurant of Washington, D.C.
Bell Telephone Company
Bell Telephone Laboratories
Berlin Radio Station SFB
Berol Corporation
Bethlehem Steel Corporation
Board of Supervisors of Elections for Montgomery County, Md.
Bonfils Theatre of the Denver Center for the Performing Arts
British Typewriter Museum
Broadcast Pioneers Library
Canadian Automobile Association
Chicago Public Library
Chicago Historical Society
China Trade Museum
The Church of Jesus Christ of Latter-Day Saints
City of Alexandria, Virginia
Clemson University
Cleveland Board of Education

Cleveland Indians, Inc.
Cleveland Public Library
Colonial National Historical Park, Jamestown, Va.
Colt Industries
Commissioner of Streets, City of Cleveland, Ohio
Communications Satellite Corporation
Congregation Shearith Israel, New York City
Connecticut State Library
Coyne Industrial Laundries, Inc.
Cross Company
Danmarks Tekniske Museum
Department of Environmental Services, Washington, D.C.
E. I. du Pont de Nemours & Co.
Duquesne University Tamburitzans Institute of Folk Arts
Eastman Kodak Company
East Ohio Gas Company
Eberhard Faber Company
Edgar Rice Burroughs, Inc.
Edison National Historic Site
Ente Governativo per il Turismo, Sport e Spettacolo di San Marino
Facit Typewriters
Fédération Français des Clubs Automobiles
Fédération Internationale de l'Automobile, Paris
Fiat
Field Museum of Natural History, Chicago, Ill.
Film Studio, Inc.
F. M. Bodington Plumbing Co.
Foto-Quelle GmbH
Frito-Lay, Inc.
Fuji Photo Film U.S.A., Inc.
G & I Cafeteria, Washington, D.C.
General Drafting Company
General Electric Co.
General Foods Corporation
General Motors Corporation
General Telephone and Electronics
Germanisches Nationalmuseum
Gibbes Art Gallery, Charleston, S.C.
Goldberg's Pizzeria, New York City
Hanimex Pty, Limited
Harris Corp.
Harry M. Stevens, Inc.
Henry Ford Museum and Greenfield Village
Henry J. and Sons Sohio Service of Cleveland, Ohio
Hershey Food Corporation
Heublein International Ltd.
Hillerich and Bradsby Company, Inc.
Holiday Inns, Inc.
Hotel and Restaurant Employees and Bartenders International Union
I. D. Advertising, Jegenstorf
Ilford Ltd.

Illinois Labor History Society Collection
Independence National Historical Park, Philadelphia, Pa.
Institute of Jazz Studies
Insurance Company of North America
International Ladies Garment Workers Union
International Telephone & Telegraph Corp.
The Islamic Center, Washington, D.C.
Japan Automobile Federation
Kentucky Fried Chicken
King Enterprises, Inc.
Kingsbury Machine Tool Corporation
Koninklijke Nederlandse Toeristenbond ANWB
Kurtz Brothers School Supply
Kuwait International Touring and Automobile Club
Lansburg's Department Store
La Vina Restaurant, New York City
Levi Strauss and Company
Library of Congress
Lions International
Long Island Automotive Museum
Luchow's Restaurant, New York City
McCormick and Company, Inc.
McDonald's International
Magyar Auto Club
Marconi Company, Ltd.
Mercedes-Benz of North America, Inc.
Metropolitan Museum of Art
Midtown Neon Maintenance Corp.
Milwaukee Brewers Baseball Club
Milwaukee Public Museum
Monastery of St. Dominic, Newark, N.J.
Monument Service, Veterans Administration
Morris Brown College Library, Atlanta, Ga.
Motormännens Riksforbond
Museum of Mankind, British Museum, London
Museum of the City of New York
Musgrave Pencil Company
National Baseball Hall of Fame
National Beauty and Barber Manufacturing Association
National Gallery of Art
National Machine Tool Builders Association
Necchi Development Corporation
Nelco Sewing Machine Company
Georg Neumann GmbH
New Hampshire Historical Society
New Jersey Institute of Technology
New York Public Library and the Library and Museum of the Performing Arts, Lincoln Center
New York Yankees, Inc.
New Yorker, Inc.
New Zealand Automobile Association
Norges Automobil-Forbund
Oakland Museum, California
Obergassner K.G.

Old Salem, Inc., Winston-Salem, N.C.
Olivetti Corporation of America
Olympia U.S.A., Inc.
Österreichischer Automobil-, Motorrad-, und Touring Club
Oscar Mayer & Co., Inc.
Palace Theatre, New York City
Peabody Museum, Harvard University
Pencil Makers' Association, Inc.
Pepsi-Cola Company
Pfaff International Sales Corporation
Philippine Motor Association
Pilsen Butchers Benevolent Association
Polski Zwiazek Motorowy
Pro-Football Hall of Fame, Canton, Ohio
Providence, Rhode Island, Board of Elections
Radio Canada
Radio City Music Hall
Rapid City, Iowa, Public Schools
RCA Corporation
Reading Railroad
Real Automovil Club de España
Renault, Inc.
Republican Congressional Committee
Rhode Island Society for Encouragement of Domestic Industry
Riccar American Corporation
Ring Magazine
Roth Novelty Company
Royal Typewriter Company
Rutgers Institute of Jazz Studies
St. Louis National Baseball Club, Inc.
Schwinn Bicycle Company
Science Museum London
Sears, Roebuck & Co., Display Department, Washington, D.C.
Silverescent Sign Co.
Singer Company
Sony Corporation
Sperry Remington Division of Sperry Rand Corporation
Sports Illustrated Enterprises
Swedish Council of America
Swiss-Bernina, Inc.
Tacony Distributors, Inc.
Tavaro, S. A.
Touring and Automobile Club of Iran
Turkish Embassy, Washington, D.C.
United Features Syndicate
United Parcel Service
U.S. Department of Defense
U.S. Department of Justice Immigration and Naturalization Service
U.S. Patent Office
Valentine Museum
V.D.I. Verlag
Viking Sewing Machine Company

Voice of America
Volkswagen of America, Inc.
Walt Disney Archives
Walter Hampden Memorial Library, The Players
  Club, New York City
Washington Redskins Football Team
Western India Automobile Association
Western Union Telegraph Co.
White Sewing Machine Company
Wilson Sporting Goods Company
Worcester Historical Society, Mass.
Wm. Wrigley Jr. Company
Yankee Stadium, Inc.
Zenith Radio Corporation

Individuals

Mrs. Arthur F. Abt
Dorothy A. Adamson
Eva Salazar Ahlborn
Reed H. Albig
Belle Rudin Altman
Renee Altmann
Lillian T. Anthony
James M. Apple
Anne McClerkin Arneson
Memory of John C. Bacon
Alan L. Bain
Ralph M. Barnes
William F. Barnett, Jr.
Harry P. Barton
Robert Baublitz
William H. Beach
Richard H. Beahr
Charles Beck
Ralph E. Becker
Clay P. Bedford
Wilfred A Beeching
Eugene F. Behlen
Louise D. Belcher
Thomas J. Bellino
John F. Bellwoar, S.J.
Henry Berchert
Frank J. Berek
Charles G. Berger
Irving Berlin
Countess de Beughem
Surindar Singh Bimbra
Joseph Block
Thomas J. Bond
Ruth Joan Booth
Ken Bowers
Doris Bowman
E. Boyd (deceased)
Regis L. Boyle
Donald Bredernitz
Mr. & Mrs. Robert Bretzfelder
Hans Bretzner
Richard E. Briggs
J. B. Buchanan
Bill Burk
Agostino Santo Buttinelli
Janus Campbell
Ernestine Gilbreth Carey
Roxane Connick Carlisle
Elmo Celentani
Moreau Browne Chambers
Edward Charol
Linda H. Chase
Bogomir Chokel
Angelo G. Cicolani
Becky Clapp

Henry Austin Clark, Jr.
C. M. Clinkscale
Mr. & Mrs. Robert M. Clinkscale
Stanley Cohen
Ellen Cohn
M. Coletta
Meredith Colkett
Mr. & Mrs. Belisario Contreras
James A. Cooper
Stanley Cotton
Bette Craig
Mr. & Mrs. Richard D. Crawford
Alice Carr de Creeft
David R. Crippen
Maximiano Cruz
Merle Curti
Dr. & Mrs. Arcangelo D'Amore
Marguerite Darkow
Edward M. Davenport
Valerie Davis
Gregory Day
John A. Denbow
William E. Depuy
Eleanor Dickinson
Edward F. Dirks
Katherine Dirks
Frank Dobias
Adele Dobrolsky
Larry Doby
James W. Dodd
G. A. Donovan
Glorian Dorsey
Richard Drake
Mr. & Mrs. Billy R. Duerson
Ileana Dunn
E. B. Duvall Sr.
  (deceased)
Adele Earnest
Harry E. Edmunds
Aloysius J. Eftink
John C. Eiselle
Lee Elder
Charles Elliott
Frank Enten
John C. Ervern
Theodore H. Fetter
Harvey C. Fifield family
Detmar H. Finke
Frank L. Fisher
Maurice Flagg
Fred Flamenhaft
J. Howard Foote
H. A. Crosby Forbes
Audrey Fox
Margaret L. Frank
Mr. & Mrs. Max Furman
Julie Gaebe

Charles Edward Gallagher
Joseph Garagiola
Luis Garcia-Curbelo
Mrs. Daniel Gardner
Wendell Garrett
Lewis German
Natalie Giana
David Gilbreth
William M. Gilbreth
Merl P. Glaser
Nathan Glazer
Mrs. George Gleckel
Patrick E. Gorman
John Grabowski
Don Graham
Perry Green
Dr. & Mrs. Arthur M. Greenwood
  (deceased)
Jess Gregory
Genevieve M. Gren
Grace Cohen Grossman
Thomas A. Gruber
Anna Grum
Ashley B. Gurney
Charles Hacker
Sarsour Hamed
Mary Handlin
Oscar Handlin
Fred Hansen
J. Clifford Harden
Katherine Harden
H. Lincoln Harrison
Mr. & Mrs. H. M. Heckman
Jim Heddings
Mr. & Mrs. John Helm
William K. Henson
Joseph F. Herbert
Rochambeau A. Herosian
John Hintlian
B. Elder Holahan
Martin James Holohan
Judy Hora
Robert Hosler
Mark Houghstaling
Mrs. Jack R. Hovey
Edgar Howell
D. Christopher Hughes
Gary L. Hughes
Raford M. Hulan
Julie Hunter
Thomas Inge
Lawrence Isham
William Jaffe
Helen M. P. Jagodzinske
Jim R. James
Mrs. Julian James
  (deceased)

633

William J. Janes
Lawrence Janka
Donald R. Jansen
Mr. & Mrs. Frank Johnson
Mrs. John H. Jones
Mother Mary Joseph, O.P.
Joseph Juck
Samuel N. Karrick, Jr.
Robert I. Kasindorf
Roslyn Kasindorf
Robert E. Keating
Russell B. Keating
Michael J. Keefe
Kathleen M. Keegan
H. H. Kelly
Kathleen Kenyon
Isabella C. King
Joseph H. Kler
Frederick J. Kloes III
Harry W. Kluth
Ron Knappen
Peter L. Koffsky
David René Kolar
Walter W. Kolar
Mr. & Mrs. Tony P. Kominoth
Murray Kramer
Fred La Malfa
Helene A. Larkin
Jonah H. Laubhan
Peter W. Leach-Lewis
William Le Gro, Jr.
Kerry R. Lewis
Rosemary Lewis
Priscilla Winslow Watson Liggett
Edward J. Loeffler
Dorothy Logan
Charles W. W. Lohrig
Carl Long
Fern Long
Regina Longo
Richard S. Lovering, Jr.
Mr. & Mrs. Henry E. Lowenstein
Kathy L. Lutz
Mr. & Mrs. Ralph P. Lutz
George J. McDonald
Helen Dianna McGeorge
Frederick B. McIntosh
Jean S. MacKenzie
Robert McNulty
David McWilliams
James Marks II
W. E. Martin
Sara L. Marzio
Steven A. Marzio
Walter L. Mason, Jr.
Clifford G. Massoth
Joseph Matthews

Mrs. Harry G. Meem
Edith R. Meggars
Keith E. Melder
Juan Menchaca
Cynthia Merman
Mary Merrill
Al Metzger
Thomas Micro
Robert Milevy
Frederick A. Miller
Maceo Mitchell
Norman Mitchell
Set Momjian
Earl Moore
Julia Moore
William H. Moorhouse
Louis Morasco
David C. Morgan
Harold F. Moriarty
Fannie Munchmayer
John B. Murphy
Michael H. Murphy
Paul Myers
Gunter F. Nawrocki
R. Stanley Nelson
John E. Nolan
Charles E. Novel
Rt. Rev. Msgr. Novicki
Smith Hempstone Oliver
Leslie F. Orear
Mrs. Leon Orlowski
Richard H. Palange
Elias P. Pantazopoulos
Irene Paonessa
Charlene Pasco
Maryrose Vigna Patrone
Jacques Paynter
James S. Perkins
Robert P. Perkins
Mr. & Mrs. Alfred A. Perry
Mrs. Richard Peterson
Frank A. Pietropaoli
David E. Price
Lewis A. Rachow
Muhammad Abdul Rauf
John S. Reed
Arthur Reifke
Raymond Reiff
Abraham Resnitzky
Denise Restoui
Allie Reynolds
Eugene F. Richner
Mrs. Joe Ricozzi
Max Joseph Riedl
Watson R. Risher
Ethel L. Robinson
Memory of Francis A. Roche

Peter T. Roche
Ann Carroll Meem Rogers
Carley Roney
Christopher Roney
Irene Howe Roney
John M. Roney
Richard Rosenthal
Robert E. Roy
Harry C. Rubicane
Janet Coe Sandborn
Joseph J. Sandler
Michael R. Santoro
August K. Scheele
Carl A. Scheele
Frances J. Scheele
Harry G. Scheele
Joanne B. Scheele
Ralph L. Scheele
Hilda Schneider
William Schrage, Jr.
Derek Semper
Mr. & Mrs. Joseph L. Serio
James Seymour
David P. Sheridan
Mrs. Deeks Shryock
Michael H. Shelley
P. A. Simiele
James F. Simpson
Lillian Skelly
   (deceased)
Harold Skramstad, Jr.
John Slocum
Robert Ward Smith
Morton Snowhite
Arabella Sparmon
Alice B. Speizman
R. K. Steele
John Steinway
William Stephan
John N. Stine, Jr.
Elias Howe Stockwell
Emily G. Storrow
James M. Sutton
David W. Talbot
Sr. M. Therese
Gerald F. Tierney
Robert J. Toye II
Donald Troiani
Robert L. Tull
Hugh Van Dusen
James Van Stone
Roger Van Vliet
Mary Varga
Lionel Vas
Edward J. Vinnicombe, Jr.
Paul Wagoner
Alvin H. Walker

Joan Pearson Watkins
Tony Weaver
Marjorie Webb
William J. Webb
Thomas E. Weber
Paul Weinstein
Mr. & Mrs. Robert W. Welsh
Christopher White
Bessie R. Wigutoff
Barbara Wilson
H. Edward Winter
Everett S. Wyman
Robert B. Wood
the Misses Wright
Edward Yambrusic
David Yong
Joseph M. Young
John T. Zanone
Wilbur Zelinsky

References

General

Abbott, Edith

Dictionary of American Biography. 24 vols. New York, 1928–1974.

Historical Aspects of the Immigration Problem. Chicago, 1926.

Immigration: Select Documents and Case Records. Chicago, 1924.

Adamic, Louis — *A Nation of Nations*. New York, 1945.

Bowers, David F., ed. — *Foreign Influences in American Life*. Princeton, 1944.

Brown, Lawrence G. — *Immigration: Cultural Conflicts and Social Adjustments*. New York, 1969.

Davie, Maurice R. — *World Immigration with Special Reference to the United States*. New York, 1936.

Eaton, Allen H. — *Immigrant Gifts to American Life*. New York, 1970.

Glazer, Nathan, and Daniel P. Moynihan — *Beyond the Melting Pot*. Cambridge, Mass., 1963.

Handlin, Oscar — *Immigration as a Factor in American History*. Englewood Cliffs, N.J., 1959.

A Pictorial History of Immigration. New York, 1972.

Race and Nationality in American Life. Boston, 1957.

The Uprooted. Boston, 1951.

Handlin, Oscar, ed. — *Children of the Uprooted*. New York, 1966

Hansen, Marcus Lee — *The Immigrant in American History*. Cambridge, Mass., 1940.

Hughes, Langston, Milton Meltzer, and C. Eric Lincoln — *A Pictorial History of Black Americans*. 4th rev. ed. New York, 1973.

Jones, Maldwyn Allen — *American Immigration*. Chicago, 1960.

Link, Arthur S. — *American Epoch: A History of the United States Since the 1890s*. New York, 1967.

Morison, Samuel Eliot — *The Oxford History of the American People*. New York, 1965.

Morris, Richard B., William Greenleaf, and Robert H. Ferrell — *America: A History of the People*. Chicago, 1971.

Park, Robert E., and Herbert A. Miller — *Old World Traits Transplanted*. New York, 1921.

Stephenson, George M. — *A History of American Immigration, 1820–1924*. Boston, 1926.

Taft, Donald R. — *Human Migration*. New York, 1936.

Taylor, Philip — *The Distant Magnet: European Emigration to the U.S.A.* New York, 1971.

Wittke, Carl — *We Who Built America: The Saga of the Immigrant*. 1st ed., 1939. Cleveland, 1964.

Chapter 1.
The First Americans

Deloria, Vine, Jr.
Behind the Trail of Broken Treaties: An Indian Declaration of Independence. New York, 1974.

Custer Died for Your Sins: An Indian Manifesto. New York, 1969.

Driver, Harold E.
Indians of North America. 2nd ed. Chicago, 1969.

Leacock, Eleanor Burke, and Nancy Oestreich Lurie, eds.
North American Indians in Historical Perspective. New York, 1971.

McNickle, D'Arcy
They Came Here First: The Epic of the American Indian. new ed. New York, 1975.

Nash, Gary B.
Red, White and Black: The Peoples of Early America. Englewood Cliffs, N.J., 1974.

National Geographic Society, ed.
The World of the American Indian. Washington, D.C., 1974.

Oswalt, Wendell H.
This Land Was Theirs: A Study of the North American Indian. 2nd ed. New York, 1973.

Spencer, Robert F., Jesse D. Jennings, et al.
The Native Americans: Prehistory and Ethnology of the North American Indians. New York, 1965.

Spicer, Edward H.
A Short History of the Indians of the United States. New York, 1969.

Stewart, T. D.
The People of America. New York, 1973.

Sturtevant, William C., general ed.
Handbook of North American Indians. 20 vols. Washington, D.C., in press (the first vols. to appear in 1976).

Walker, Deward E., Jr., ed.
The Emergent Native Americans: A Reader in Culture Contact. Boston, 1972.

Washburn, Wilcomb E.
The Indian in America. New York, 1975.

Red Man's Land/White Man's Law: A Study of the Past and Present Status of the American Indian. New York, 1971.

Willey, Gordon R.
An Introduction to American Archaeology. vol. 1: *North and Middle America.* vol. 2: *South America.* Englewood Cliffs, N.J., 1966, 1971.

Chapter 2.
The Letter to Santángel

Bourne, Edward Gaylord, ed.
The Northmen, Columbus, and Cabot. New York, 1959.

De Voto, Bernard
The Course of Empire. Boston, 1952.

Hermann, Paul
The Great Age of Discovery. trans. Arnold J. Pomerans. New York, 1958.

Hodge, Frederick W., ed.
Spanish Explorers in the Southern United States 1528–1543. New York, 1965.

Lorant, Stefan
The New World. New York, 1946.

Morison, Samuel Eliot
The European Discovery of America: The Southern Voyages. New York, 1974.

Wright, Louis B., ed.
The Elizabethans' America. Cambridge, Mass., 1965.

Chapter 3.
The English Heritage

101 Masterpieces of American Primitive Painting from the Collection of Edgar William and Bernice Chrysler Garbisch. new ed. The American Federation of Arts, 1962.

Adams, Hannah — *An Abridgment of the History of New England, for the Use of Young Persons.* 2nd ed. Boston, 1807.

Avery, C. Louise — *American Silver of the XVII and XVIII Centuries.* New York, 1920.

Beverley, Robert — *The History and Recent State of Virginia.* Louis B. Wright, ed. Chapel Hill, N.C., 1947.

Buhler, Kathryn C., and Graham Hood — *American Silver: Garvan and Other Collections in the Yale University Art Gallery.* 2 vols. New Haven, Conn. and London, 1970.

Cotter, John L. — *Archaeological Excavations at Jamestown.* Washington, D.C., 1958.

Crèvecoeur, J. Hector St. John de — *Letters from an American Farmer.* New York, 1957.

Dow, George Francis — *The Arts and Crafts in New England 1704–1775.* Topsfield, Mass., 1927.

Earle, Alice Morse — *Home Life in Colonial Days.* New York, 1898.

Felt, Joseph B. — *History of Ipswich, Essex, and Hamilton.* Cambridge, Mass., 1834; reprinted Ipswich, Mass., 1966.

Forman, Henry Chandlee — *The Architecture of the Old South.* Cambridge, Mass., 1948.

Gottesman, Rita Susswein — *The Arts and Crafts in New York, 1726–1776.* New York, 1938.

The Arts and Crafts in New York, 1777–1799. New York, 1954.

Harrington, J. C. — *A Tryal of Glasse.* Richmond, Va., 1972.

Hewitt, Cecil A. — "Some East Anglian Prototypes for Early Timber Houses in America," *Post-Medieval Archaeology,* London, 1970, 3:100–121.

Hipkiss, Edwin J. — *The Philip Leffingwell Spalding Collection of Early American Silver.* Cambridge, Mass., 1943.

Kelly, J. Frederick — *Early Domestic Architecture of Connecticut.* New Haven, Conn., 1924.

Ludwig, Allan I. — *Graven Images: New England Stonecarving and Its Symbols, 1650–1815.* Middletown, Conn., 1966.

Nettels, Curtis P. — *The Roots of American Civilization.* New York, 1938.

Prime, Alfred Coxe, ed. — *The Arts and Crafts in Philadelphia, Maryland, and South Carolina 1721–1785.* Topsfield, Mass., 1929.

The Arts and Crafts in Philadelphia, Maryland, and South Carolina 1786–1800. 2nd ser. Topsfield, Mass., 1932.

Tryon, Rolla Milton — *Household Manufactures in the United States, 1640–1860.* Chicago, 1917.

Watkins, C. Malcolm. — *The Cultural History of Marlborough, Virginia.* U.S. National Museum Bulletin 253. Washington, D.C., 1968.

"Ceramics in the Seventeenth-Century English Colonies," in *Arts of the Anglo-American Community in the Seventeenth Century. Winterthur Conference Report 1974.* Charlottesville, Va., 1975.

Watkins, C. Malcolm, and Ivor Noël Hume — *The Poor Potter of Yorktown.* U.S. National Museum Bulletin 249. Washington, D.C., 1967.

Watkins, Lura Woodside — *Early New England Potters and Their Wares.* Cambridge, Mass., 1950.

Middleton, Massachusetts: A Cultural History. Salem, Mass., 1970.

Wertenbaker, Thomas Jefferson — *The Old South.* New York, 1942.

Wolsey, S. W., and R. W. P. Luff — *Furniture in England: The Age of the Joiner.* New York and Washington, D.C., 1969.

Wright, Louis B. — *The Cultural Life of the American Colonies 1607–1763.* New York, 1957.

Chapter 4.
A Plantation of Differences—
People from Everywhere

California: A Guide to the Golden State. New York, 1939.

Amelung, John F.　Remarks on Manufactures, Principally on the New Established Glass-house Near Fredericktown in the State of Maryland. [Printed for the Author], 1787.

Avery, C. Louise　American Silver of the XVII and XVIII Centuries. New York, 1920.

Beck, Warren A.　New Mexico: A History of Four Centuries. Norman, Okla., 1962.

Bivins, John, Jr.　The Moravian Potters in North Carolina. Chapel Hill, N.C., 1972.

Boyd, E.　Popular Arts of Spanish New Mexico. Santa Fe, N.M., 1974.

Buhler, Kathryn C., and Graham Hood　American Silver: Garvan and Other Collections in the Yale University Art Gallery. 2 vols. New Haven, Conn. and London, 1970.

Clement, Arthur W.　Our Pioneer Potters. New York, 1947.

Crèvecoeur, J. Hector St. John de　Letters from an American Farmer. New York, 1957.

Dow, George Francis　The Arts and Crafts in New England 1704–1775. Topsfield, Mass., 1927.

Epstein, Dena J.　"African Music in British and French America," The Musical Quarterly, 1973, 59:61–91.

"The Search for Black Music's African Roots," The University of Chicago Magazine, 1973, 66:18–22.

Gottesman, Rita Susswein　The Arts and Crafts in New York, 1726–1776. New York, 1938.

Greenhow, Robert　The History of Oregon and California and the Other Territories on the North-West Coast of North America. New York, 1845.

Hartley, E. N.　Ironworks on the Saugus. Norman, Okla., 1957.

Hershkowitz, L.　"Some Aspects of the New York Jewish Merchants in Colonial Trade," in Migration and Settlement, Proceedings of the Anglo-American Jewish Historical Conference. London, 1971.

Jordan, Winthrop D.　White over Black: American Attitudes Toward the Negro 1550–1812. Chapel Hill, N.C., 1968.

Kostrometinoff, George　MS letter to Theodore Roosevelt, offering gift of Alexander Baranoff's chain-mail shirt, 1906. Smithsonian Institution Accession Records, Washington, D.C.

Laughlin, Ledlie Irwin　Pewter in America. 2 vols. Boston, 1950.

McKearin, George S. and Helen　American Glass. New York, 1941.

McKearin, Helen and George S.　Two Hundred Years of American Blown Glass. New York, 1950.

Madden, Betty I.　Arts, Crafts, and Architecture in Early Illinois. Urbana, Ill., 1974.

Moore, Gay Montague　Seaport in Virginia. Richmond, Va., 1949.

Morris, R.　"The Jews, Minorities, and Dissent in the American Revolution," in Migration and Settlement, Proceedings of the Anglo-American Jewish Historical Conference. London, 1971.

Nettels, Curtis P.　The Roots of American Civilization. New York, 1938.

O'Callaghan, E. B.　Documentary History of the State of New York. Albany. 4 vols., 1849–1851 (ref. to Rev. Isaac Joques, S.J., 1643, vol. IV, pp. 21–24).

Pearce, John N.　"New York's Two-Handled Paneled Silver Bowls," Antiques, 1961, 80:341–345.

"Further Comments on the Lobate Bowl Form," Antiques, 1966, 90:524–525.

Pennsylvania Assembly *Reply to the Governor*. In *Votes and Proceedings of the House of Representatives, 1754–1755* (Philadelphia, 1755). pp. 91–92 in *The Papers of Benjamin Franklin*, Leonard W. Labaree, ed. vol. 6. New Haven, Conn. and London, 1963.

Prime, Alfred Coxe, ed. *The Arts and Crafts in Philadelphia, Maryland, and South Carolina 1721–1785*. Topsfield, Mass., 1929.

The Arts and Crafts in Philadelphia, Maryland, and South Carolina 1786–1800. 2nd ser. Topsfield, Mass., 1932.

Quynn, Dorothay Mackay "Johann Friedrich Amelung at New Bremen," *Maryland Historical Magazine*, 1948, 43:155–179.

Rice, Norman S. *Albany Silver 1657–1825*. Albany, N.Y., 1964.

Rosenbaum, Jeannette W. *Myer Myers, Goldsmith*. Philadelphia, 1954.

Southern, Eileen *The Music of Black Americans*. New York, 1971.

Stoudt, John Joseph *Early Pennsylvania Arts and Crafts*. New York, 1964.

Thompson, Robert Farris "African Influence on the Art of the United States." pp. 122–170 in *Black Studies in the University, A Symposium*. New Haven, Conn. and London, 1949.

Tryon, Rolla Milton *Household Manufactures in the United States, 1640–1860*. Chicago, 1917.

Warville, J. P. Brissot de *New Travels in the United States of America performed in M/DCC/LXXXVIII*. 2nd ed. corrected. London, 1794.

Watkins, T. H. *California: An Illustrated History*. Palo Alto, Calif., 1973.

Weld, Isaac, Jr. *Travels Through the States of North America, and the Provinces of Upper and Lower Canada During the Years 1795, 1796, and 1797*. 4th ed., 2 vols. London, 1807.

Chapters 5 and 6.
"We the People"—
The Emergence of the American Nation.
The Objects of the Revolution

Greene, Evarts Boutell *The Revolutionary Generation 1763–1790*. New York, 1943.

Greene, Jack P., ed. *Colonies to Nation, 1763–1879: A Documentary History of the American Revolution*. New York, 1975.

Jameson, J. Franklin *The American Revolution Considered as a Social Movement*. Princeton, 1926.

Kurtz, Stephen G., and James H. Hutson, eds. *Essays on the American Revolution*. Chapel Hill, N.C., 1973.

MacLeod, Duncan J. *Slavery, Race and the American Revolution*. Cambridge, Mass., 1974.

Palmer, R. R. *The Age of the Democratic Revolution: A Political History of Europe and America 1760–1800*. 2 vols. Princeton, 1959, 1964.

Williamson, Chilton *American Suffrage, from Property to Democracy, 1760–1860*. Princeton, 1960.

Wood, Gordon S. *The Creation of the American Republic, 1776–1787*. Chapel Hill, N.C., 1969.

Wood, Gordon S., ed. *The Rising Glory of America, 1760–1820*. New York, 1971.

Chapter 7.
The Ocean Voyage

Transatlantic Travel

Historical Statistics of the United States. Washington, D.C., 1945.

United States 61st Congress, 3rd Session, Senate Documents 748, 753, 758. December 5, 1910–March 3, 1911.

Davie, Maurice R.   *World Immigration.* New York, 1936.

Greenhill, Basil   *The Great Migration.* London, 1970.

Hansen, Marcus L.   *The Atlantic Migration, 1607–1860.* Cambridge, Mass., 1940.

Jones, Maldwyn A.   *American Immigration.* Chicago, 1957.

Kraus, Michael   *The Atlantic Civilization: Eighteenth Century Origins.* Ithaca, N.Y., 1947.

Lindsay, William Schaw   *History of Merchant Shipping and Ancient Commerce.* vols. 3 and 4. London, 1874–1876.

Nettels, Curtis P.   *The Roots of American Civilization.* New York, 1938.

Taylor, Philip   *The Distant Magnet: European Emigration to the U.S.A.* New York, 1971.

Castle Garden and Ellis Island

"Castle Clinton National Monument." National Park Service. New York, 1972.

Corsi, Edward   *In the Shadow of Liberty: The Chronicle of Ellis Island.* New York, 1935.

Dunne, Thomas   *Ellis Island.* New York, 1971.

Novotny, Ann   *Strangers at the Door.* Riverside, Conn., 1971.

Riis, Jacob A.   "In the Gateway of Nations" in *The New Immigration.* John J. Appel, ed. New York, 1971.

Svejda, George J.   *Castle Garden as an Immigrant Depot, 1855–1890.* National Park Service. Washington, D.C., 1968.

Weisberger, Bernard A.   *The American Heritage History of the American People.* New York, 1971.

Statue of Liberty

Grover Cleveland Papers. Manuscript Division, Library of Congress.

Handlin, Oscar   *Statue of Liberty.* New York, 1971.

Chapter 8.
Agriculture and
the Movement West

Adams, William F.   *Ireland and Irish Emigration to the New World from 1815 to the Famine.* New Haven, Conn., 1932.

Berthoff, Rowland T.   *British Immigrants in Industrial America, 1789–1950.* Cambridge, Mass., 1953.

Blegen, Theodore C.   *Norwegian Migration to America, 1825–1860.* Northfield, Minn., 1931.

Norwegian Migration to America: The American Tradition. Northfield, Minn., 1940.

Blegen, Theodore C., ed.   *Land of Their Choice: The Immigrants Write Home.* Minneapolis, 1955.

Childs, Frances S.   *French Refugee Life in the United States, 1790–1800.* Baltimore, 1940.

Conway, Alan, ed.   *The Welsh in America: Letters from the Immigrants.* Minneapolis, 1961.

Cunz, Dieter   *The Maryland Germans.* Princeton, 1948.

Faust, Albert B.   *The German Element in the United States.* 2 vols. New York, 1927.

Ford, Henry J.   *The Scotch-Irish in America*. Princeton, 1915.

Gibson, Florence E.   *The Attitudes of the New York Irish Toward State and National Affairs, 1848–1892.* New York, 1951.

Glanz, Rudolph   *Jews in Relation to the Cultural Milieu of the Germans in America up to the Eighteen Eighties.* New York, 1947.

Handlin, Oscar   *Boston's Immigrants: A Study in Acculturation.* Cambridge, Mass., 1941; rev. ed., 1959.

Hartmann, Edward G.   *Americans from Wales*. Boston, 1967.

Hawgood, John K.   *The Tragedy of German-America.* New York, 1940.

Hoglund, A. William   *Finnish Immigrants in America 1880–1920.* Madison, Wis., 1960.

Jalkanen Ralph J., ed.   *The Finns in North America: A Social Symposium.* Hancock, Mich., 1969.

Janson, Florence E.   *The Background of Swedish Immigration, 1840–1930.* Philadelphia, 1931.

Lerski, Jerzy J.   *A Polish Chapter in Jacksonian America: The United States and the Polish Exiles of 1831.* Madison, Wis., 1958.

Lucas, Henry S., ed.   *Dutch Immigrant Memoirs and Related Writings.* 2 vols. Assen, Netherlands, 1955.

Netherlanders in America: Dutch Immigration to the United States and Canada, 1789–1950. Ann Arbor, Mich., 1955.

Mulder, Arnold   *Americans from Holland*. New York, 1947.

Mulder, William   *Homeward to Zion: The Mormon Migration from Scandinavia.* Minneapolis, 1957.

Qualey, Carlton C.   *Norwegian Settlement in the United States.* Northfield, Minn., 1938.

Riis, Jacob A.   *The Making of an American*. Roy Lubove, ed. New York, 1966.

Rowse, A. L.   *The Cornish in America*. New York, 1969.

Sabbe, Philemon D., and Leon Buyse   *Belgians in America*. Lannoo, Tielt, Belgium, 1960.

Schlebecker, John T.   *Whereby We Thrive*. Ames, Iowa, 1975.

Shannon, Fred A.   *The Farmer's Last Frontier*. New York, 1961.

Shannon, William V.   *The American Irish*. New York, 1963.

Stephenson, George M.   *Religious Aspects of Swedish Immigration.* Minneapolis, 1932.

Todd, Arthur C.   *The Cornish Miner in America*. Truro, England, 1967.

Von Grueningen, John P., ed.   *The Swiss in the United States*. Madison, Wis., 1940.

Walker, Mack   *Germany and the Emigration 1816–1885.* Cambridge, Mass., 1964.

Wittke, Carl   *The Irish in America.* Baton Rouge, La., 1956.

Refugees of Revolution: The German Forty-Eighters in America. Philadelphia, 1952.

Zucker, A. E., ed.   *The Forty-Eighters*. New York, 1950.

Chapter 9.
Transportation in
Early Nineteenth-
Century America

Dunbar, Seymour   *A History of Travel in America*. Indianapolis, 1915.

Earle, Alice M.   *Stage-Coach and Tavern Days*. New York, 1900.

Eggenhofer, Nick   *Wagons, Mules and Men*. New York, 1961.

Gregg, Josiah   *Commerce of the Prairies*. New York, 1844.

Hornung, Clarence P.   *Wheels Across America*. New York, 1959.

Hulbert, Archer B.   *Historic Highways of America*. Cleveland, 1902–1905.

Meyer, Balthaser H.   *History of Transportation in the United States Before 1860*. Washington, D.C., 1917.

Rose, Albert C.   *Historic American Highways*. Washington, D.C., 1953.

Searight, Thomas B.   *The Old Pike*. Uniontown, Pa., 1894.

Stratton, Ezra M.   *The World on Wheels*. New York, 1878.

Tunis, Edwin   *Wheels: A Pictorial History*. Cleveland and New York, 1955.

Walker, Henry Pickering   *The Wagonmasters*. Norman, Okla., 1966.

Chapter 10.
Railroads and the
Westward-Bound Immigrant

Overton, Richard C.   *Burlington West*. Cambridge, Mass., 1941.

Stover, John F.   *American Railroads*. Chicago, 1961.

White, J. H., Jr.   "Provisional Railroad," *Proceedings of the 13th International Congress of the History of Science*. Moscow, August 1971.

    "The Railroad Reaches California," *California Historical Quarterly*, 1973, 52:131–144.

Chapter 11.
The Immigrant Bridge Builder

Steinman, David Barnard   *The Builders of the Bridge: The Story of John Roebling and His Son*. New York, 1972.

Chapter 12.
Importing a Revolution

    "Crompton, George," and "William Crompton," in *Dictionary of American Biography*. New York, 1930.

    "Crompton, George," and "William Crompton," in *The Twentieth Century Biographical Dictionary of Notable Americans*. Boston, 1904.

    Illustrated Catalogue of Looms, Manufactured at the Crompton Loom Works. Worcester, Mass., 1881.

Cole, Arthur Harrison   *The American Wool Manufacture*. 2 vols. Cambridge, Mass., 1926.

Coxe, Tench   *A Statement of the Arts and Manufactures of the United States of America*. Philadelphia, 1814.

Fleischmann, C. L.   *Trade, Manufacture, and Commerce in the United States of America*. trans. from the German (Stuttgart, 1852) by E. Vilim. Washington, D.C., 1970.

Greeley, Horace, et al.   "Fancy Loom Making," in *The Great Industries of the United States*. Hartford, Chicago, and Cincinnati, 1872.

Hayes, John L.   *American Textile Machinery*. Cambridge, Mass., 1879.

Leavitt, Thomas W., ed.   *The Hollingworth Letters*. Cambridge, Mass., 1969.

National Archives   Naturalization Records, George Crompton. C651.

White, George S.   *Memoir of Samuel Slater*. Philadelphia, 1836.

Chapter 13.
Crafts, Trades, and Technologies

The Steinways

	"Steinway, Christian Friedrich Theodore," "Henry Englehard Steinway," and "William Steinway," in *Dictionary of American Biography*. New York, 1935.
Dolge, Alfred	*Pianos and Their Makers*. Covina, Calif., 1911.
Spillane, Daniel	*History of the American Pianoforte*. New York, 1890.
Steinway, Theodore E.	*People and Pianos*. New York, 1953.
U.S. Senate Committee on Education and Labor	*Report of the Relations Between Labor and Capitol*. vol. 2. Washington, D.C., 1885.

Furniture Making—Immigrant Hands and Yankee Machines

Chambers, William	*Things as They Are in America*. London and Edinburgh, 1854.
Davidson, Marshall B.	*The American Heritage History of Antiques from the Civil War to World War I*. New York, 1969.
Earl, Polly Anne	"Craftsmen and Machines. The Nineteenth-Century Furniture Industry." *Technological Innovation and the Decorative Arts*. Winterthur Conference Report 1973. Ian M. G. Quimby and Polly Anne Earl, eds. Charlottesville, Va., 1974.
Hauserman, Dianne D.	"Alexander Roux and His Plain and Artistic Furniture," *Antiques,* 1968, 93:210–217.
Ingerman, Elizabeth A.	"Personal Experiences of an Old New York Cabinetmaker," *Antiques,* 1963, 84:576–580.
The Metropolitan Museum of Art	*19th-Century America: Furniture and Other Decorative Arts*. Intro. by Berry B. Tracy; furniture texts by Marilynn Johnson. New York, 1970.
Ransom, Frank Edward	*The City Built on Wood: A History of the Furniture Industry in Grand Rapids, Michigan, 1850–1950*. Ann Arbor, Mich., 1955.
Rochambeau, Eugène Achille Lacrois de Vimeur, Comte de	*Rapport sur l'ameublement et les objets d'un usage général dans les constructions et les appartements*. Paris, 1877.
Silliman, Benjamin, Jr., and C. R. Goodrich, eds.	*The World of Science, Art, and Industry Illustrated from Examples in the New-York Exhibition, 1853–1854*. New York, 1854.
U.S. Census Office	9th Census, 1870. *Statistics of the Population of the United States*. Washington, D.C., 1872.
	10th Census, 1880. *Statistics of the Population of the United States*. Washington, D.C., 1883.
U.S. Immigration Commission	*Immigrants in Industries*. vol. 15. Washington, D.C., 1911.
Vincent, Clare	"John Henry Belter, Manufacturer of All Kinds of Fine Furniture." *Technological Innovation and the Decorative Arts*. Winterthur Conference Report 1973. Ian M. G. Quimby and Polly Anne Earl, eds. Charlottesville, Va., 1974.
Ware, Norman	*The Industrial Worker, 1840–1860*. Boston and New York, 1924.

The Czechs and Mother-of-Pearl

Čapek, Thomas	*The Čech (Bohemian) Community of New York*. New York, 1921.
	The Čechs (Bohemians) in America. New York, 1920.
Luscomb, Sally C.	*The Collector's Encyclopedia of Buttons*. New York, 1967.
U.S. Tariff Commission	*The Button Industry*. Tariff Information Series No. 4. Washington, D.C., 1918.

The Printing Arts

	Biography of Ottmar Mergenthaler and History of the Linotype. Baltimore, 1898.
Peters, Harry T.	*America on Stone*. New York, 1931.
Silver, Rollo G.	*Typefounding in America 1787–1825*. Charlottesville, Va., 1965.
Thomas, Isaiah	*History of Printing in America*. Albany, N.Y., 1874.
Thompson, John S.	*History of Composing Machines*. Chicago, 1904.

Tucker, Stephen D.   "History of R. Hoe and Company, 1834–1885." Rollo G. Silver, ed. *Proceedings of the American Antiquarian Society for October 1972*. Worcester, Mass., 1972.

Wroth, Lawrence C.   *The Colonial Printer*. Portland, Me., 1938.

The Evolution of the American Rifle

Dillin, John G.   *The Kentucky Rifle*. Wilmington, Del., 1959.

Hanson, Charles E.   *The Plains Rifle*. Harrisburg, Pa., 1960.

Kauffman, Henry J.   *The Pennsylvania-Kentucky Rifle*. Harrisburg, Pa., 1960.

Peterson, Harold L.   *Arms and Armor in Colonial America, 1526–1783*. Harrisburg, Pa., 1956.

Russell, Carl P.   *Firearms, Traps, and Tools of the Mountain Men*. New York, 1967.

Guns on the Early Frontiers. Berkeley, Calif., 1962.

Éleuthère Irénée du Pont de Nemours and the American Gunpowder Trade

Dujarric de la Rivière, René   *E. I. du Pont de Nemours, élève de Lavoisier*. Paris, 1954.

Du Pont, B. G., ed. and trans.   *Life of Éleuthère Irénée du Pont from Contemporary Correspondence*. 12 vols. Newark, Del., 1923–1927.

Dutton, William S.   *Du Pont: One Hundred and Forty Years*. New York, 1942.

Loomis, Stanley   *Paris in the Terror*. Philadelphia, 1964.

McKie, Douglas   *Antoine Lavoisier: Scientist, Economist, Social Reformer*. New York, 1962.

Partington, J. R.   *A History of Chemistry*. vol. 3. London, 1962.

Saricks, Ambrose   *Pierre Samuel du Pont de Nemours*. Lawrence, Kan., 1965.

Wilkinson, Norman B.   *E. I. du Pont, botaniste*. Charlottesville, Va., 1972.

Immigrants and Minerals

Dana, Julian   *Sutter of California*. New York, 1934.

Gudde, E. W.   *Sutter's Own Story*. New York, 1936.

McBeth, R. S.   *Pioneering the Gulf Coast*. New York, 1918.

Stewart, R. E., Jr., and M. F. Stewart   *Adolph Sutro*. Berkeley, Calif., 1962.

Strenger, Elsa A.   *Herman und das gelbe Teufelzeug*. Stuttgart, 1953. (Fiction.)

Strenger, Herman   *Strom aus der Erde*. Stuttgart, 1943. (Fiction.)

Chapter 14. The Sights and Sounds of Ethnic Identity

Andersen, Arlow W.   *The Immigrant Takes His Stand: The Norwegian-American Press and Public Affairs, 1847–1872*. Northfield, Minn., 1953.

Antin, Mary   *The Promised Land*. Boston, 1969.

Earle, Alice Morse   *Home Life in Colonial Days*. New York, 1898.

Hommel, Rudolf   "About Spinning Wheels," *American-German Review*, 1943, 9:4–7.

Horner, John   *The Linen Trade of Europe During the Spinning Wheel Period*. Belfast, 1920.

Little, Frances   *Early American Textiles*. New York, 1931.

Park, Robert E.   *The Immigrant Press and Its Control*. New York, 1922.

Pennington, David A., and Michael B. Taylor   *American Spinning Wheels*. Sabbathday Lake, Me., 1975.

Wheeler, Thomas C., ed.   *The Immigrant Experience: The Anguish of Becoming American*. New York, 1971.

Wittke, Carl   *The German-Language Press in America*. Lexington, Ky., 1957.

Chapter 15.
Status and Prejudice

Appel, John J.   "The Grand Old Sport of Hating Catholics,"
                                  The Critic, Nov.–Dec. 1971, 30:50–58.

                                  "From Shanties to Lace Curtains: The Irish
                                  Image in Puck, 1876–1910," *Comparative
                                  Studies in Society and History,* 1971, 13:
                                  365–375.

Appel, John J., ed.   *The New Immigration.* New York, 1971.

Hansen, Marcus Lee   *The Atlantic Migration 1607–1860.*
                                  New York, 1961.

Higham, John   *Strangers in the Land.* New York, 1974.

Hofstadter, Richard   *The Age of Reform.* New York, 1955.

Mayo-Smith, Richmond   *Emigration and Immigration.* New York,
                                  1890.

Thomas, William I.   *Old World Traits Transplanted.* vol. 3 of
                                  *Americanization Studies: The Acculturation
                                  of Immigrant Groups into American Society.*
                                  Montclair, N.J., 1971.

Chapter 16.
Becoming American

Bernard, William S., ed.   *American Immigration Policy.* New York,
                                  1950.

Billington, Ray Allen   *The Protestant Crusade, 1800–1860: A Study
                                  of the Origins of American Nativism.*
                                  New York, 1952.

Desmond, Humphrey J.   *The A.P.A. Movement.* Washington, D.C.,
                                  1912.

Divine, Robert A.   *American Immigration Policy, 1924–1952.*
                                  New Haven, Conn., 1957.

Garis, Roy L.   *Immigration Restriction: A Study of the
                                  Opposition to and Regulation of Immigration
                                  to the United States.* New York, 1927.

Hartmann, Edward G.   *The Movement to Americanize the Immi-
                                  grant.* New York, 1948.

Solomon, Barbara M.   *Ancestors and Immigrants: A Changing New
                                  England Tradition.* Cambridge, Mass.,
                                  1956.

Albert Einstein

Clark, Ronald W.   *Einstein: The Life and Times.* New York,
                                  1971.

Einstein, Albert   *Ideas and Opinions.* S. Bargmann, ed.
                                  New York, 1954.

Herneck, Friedrich   "Über die deutsche Reichsangehörigkeit
                                  Albert Einsteins," *Forschungen und Fort-
                                  schritte,* 1963, 37:137–140.

Nathan, Otto, and Heinz   *Einstein on Peace.* New York, 1960.
Norden, eds.

Seelig, Carl   *Albert Einstein: A Documentary Biography.*
                                  London, 1956.

Chapter 17.
Educating Everyone

Boorstin, Daniel J., ed.   *An American Primer*. New York, 1968.

Calhoun, Daniel, ed.   *The Educating of Americans: A Documentary History*. Boston, 1969.

Davis, Philip, ed.   *Immigration and Americanization: Selected Readings*. Boston, 1920.

Elson, Ruth Miller   *Guardians of Tradition: American Schoolbooks of the Nineteenth Century*. Lincoln, Neb., 1964.

Johnson, Clifton   *Old-time Schools and School-books*. reprint of 1904 ed., New York, 1963.

Meyer, Adolphe E.   *An Educational History of the American People*. New York, 1957.

Rippa, S. Alexander   *Education in a Free Society: An American History*. 2nd ed. New York, 1971.

Ruddy, Willis   *Schools in an Age of Mass Culture*. Englewood Cliffs, N.J., 1965.

Wright, Louis B.   *The Cultural Life of the American Colonies, 1607–1763*. New York, 1957.

Louis Agassiz—Scientist and Teacher

Agassiz, Elizabeth Cary, ed.   *Louis Agassiz: His Life and Correspondence*. 2 vols. Boston, 1885.

Lurie, Edward   ''Jean Louis Rodolphe Agassiz.'' *Dictionary of Scientific Biography*. vol. 1. New York, 1970.

Louis Agassiz: A Life of Science. Chicago, 1960.

Nature and the American Mind: Louis Agassiz and the Culture of Science. New York, 1974.

Marcou, Jules   *Life, Letters and Works of Louis Agassiz*. 2 vols. New York, 1896.

Miller, Lillian B., ed.   *The Lazzaroni: Science and Scientists in Mid-Nineteenth Century America*. Washington, D.C., 1972.

Reingold, Nathan, ed.   *Science in Nineteenth Century America*. New York, 1964.

Chapter 18.
Military Uniformity

Cunliffe, Marcus   *Soldiers and Civilians: The Martial Spirit in America 1775–1865*. Boston and Toronto, 1968.

Heitman, Francis B.   *Historical Register and Dictionary of the United States Army, from its Organization, September 29, 1789 to March 2, 1903*. 2 vols. Washington, D.C., 1903.

Hill, Jim Dan   *The Minute Man in Peace and War: A History of the National Guard*. Harrisburg, Pa., 1964.

Matloff, Maurice, ed.   *American Military History*. Washington, D.C., 1969.

Weigley, Russell F.   *History of the United States Army*. New York and London, 1967.

Chapter 19.
Working Together

Addams, Jane — *Twenty Years at Hull House*. foreword by Henry Steele Commager. New York, 1961.

Bernstein, Irving — *The Lean Years*. Boston, 1972.

Berthoff, Rowland T. — *British Immigrants in Industrial America*. Cambridge, Mass., 1953.

Cole, Donald B. — *Immigrant City: Lawrence, Massachusetts, 1845–1926*. Chapel Hill, N.C., 1963.

Conway, Alan, ed. — *The Welsh in America: Letters from the Immigrants*. Minneapolis, 1961.

Handlin, Oscar — *Boston's Immigrants: A Study in Acculturation*. rev. ed. Cambridge, Mass., 1959.

Hansen, Marcus Lee — *The Atlantic Migration 1607–1860*. Cambridge, Mass., 1940.

Hutchinson, Edward P. — *Immigrants and Their Children, 1850–1950*. New York, 1956.

Jenks, Jeremiah W., and W. Jett Lauck — *The Immigration Problem: A Study of American Immigration Conditions and Needs*. New York, 1913.

Josephson, Matthew — *Sidney Hillman: Statesman of American Labor*. Garden City, N.Y., 1952.

Madison, Charles A. — *American Labor Leaders*. 2nd ed. New York, 1962.

Perlman, Selig, and Philip Taft — *History of Labor in the United States, 1896–1932*. New York, 1935.

Riis, Jacob — *How the Other Half Lives*. New York, 1890.

Schwartz, Jonathan — "Henry Ford's Melting Pot," in Otto Feinstein, ed. *Ethnic Groups in the City: Culture, Institutions, and Power*. Lexington, Mass., 1972.

Taft, Philip — *The A.F.L. in the Time of Gompers*. New York, 1957.

Thernstrom, Stephan — *Poverty and Progress: Social Mobility in a Nineteenth-Century City*. Cambridge, Mass., 1964.

Wright, Carroll D. — "The Influence of Trade Unions upon Immigrants," (1905), in *Makers of America— The New Immigrants 1904–1913*. New York, 1971.

Chapter 20.
Immigrant Politics

Thomas Nast's Christmas Drawings for the Human Race. New York and London, 1971.

Burma, John H. — *Spanish-Speaking Groups in the United States*. Durham, N.C., 1954.

Franklin, John Hope — *From Slavery to Freedom: A History of Negro Americans*. 3rd ed. New York, 1967.

Fuess, Claude — *Carl Schurz, Reformer*. New York, 1932.

Handlin, Oscar — *Al Smith and His America*. Boston, 1958.

Haskins, James — *Adam Clayton Powell: Portrait of a Marching Black*. New York, 1974.

Higham, John — *Strangers in the Land: Patterns of American Nativism 1860–1925*. New York, 1963.

Koskoff, David E. — *Joseph P. Kennedy: A Life and Times*. Englewood Cliffs, N.J., 1974.

Lubell, Samuel — *The Future of American Politics*. New York, 1952.

Mann, Arthur — *LaGuardia: A Fighter Against His Times*. Philadelphia, 1959.

LaGuardia Comes to Power: 1933. Philadelphia, 1965.

O'Connor, Richard — *The German-Americans: An Informal History*. Boston, 1968.

Shannon, William V. — *The American Irish*. New York, 1963.

Chapter 21.
American Entertainment—
An Immigrant Domain

Blesh, Rudi, and Harriet Hanis — *They All Played Ragtime*. rev. ed. New York, 1971.

Brownlow, Kevin — *The Parade's Gone By. . . .* 3rd ed. New York, 1970.

Ewen, David — *Men and Women Who Make Music*. New York, 1949.

Fox, Charles Philip, and Tom Parkinson — *The Circus in America*. Waukesha, Wis., 1969.

Freeland, Michael — *Jolson*. New York, 1973.

Gelatt, Roland — *The Fabulous Phonograph: From Edison to Stereo*. rev. ed. New York, 1965.

Gilbert, Douglas — *American Vaudeville: Its Life and Times*. 1st ed. 1940. reprinted New York, 1963.

Goldberg, Isaac — *George Gershwin: A Study in American Music*. 1st ed. 1931. reprinted with supplement by Edith Garson, New York, 1958.

Tin Pan Alley: A Chronicle of American Popular Music. 1st ed. 1930. reprinted with supplement by Edward Jablonski, New York, 1961.

Hamid, George A., and George A. Hamid, Jr. — *Circus*. New York, 1950.

Handy, William C. — *Father of the Blues: An Autobiography*. Arna Bontemps, ed. 1st ed. 1941. reprinted New York, 1970.

Hoover, Cynthia A. — *Music Machines—American Style*. Washington, D.C., 1971.

Josephson, Matthew — *Edison*. New York, 1959.

May, Earl Chapin — *The Circus: From Rome to Ringling*. 1st ed. 1932. reprinted New York, 1963.

Michael, Paul, and James Robert Parish, eds. — *Movie Greats: The Players, Directors, Producers*. (originally *The American Movies Reference Book: The Sound Era,* 1968.) New York, 1969.

Pleasants, Henry — *The Great American Popular Singers*. New York, 1974.

Robinson, David — *Hollywood in the Twenties*. New York, 1968.

Rourke, Constance — *American Humor: A Study of the National Character*. 1st ed. 1931. reprinted New York, 1953.

Russell, Don — *The Wild West*. Fort Worth, Texas, 1970.

Sablosky, Irving — *American Music*. Chicago, 1969.

Seldes, Gilbert — *The Public Arts*. New York, 1956.

Shapiro, Nat, and Nat Hentoff, eds. — *Hear Me Talkin' to Ya: The Story of Jazz as Told by the Men Who Made It*. 1st ed. 1955. reprinted New York, 1966.

Southern, Eileen — *The Music of Black Americans: A History*. New York, 1971.

Spaeth, Sigmund — *A History of Popular Music in America*. New York, 1948.

Stearns, Marshall W. — *The Story of Jazz*. New York, 1958.

Toll, Robert — *Blacking Up: The Minstrel Show in Nineteenth-Century America*. New York, 1974.

Chapter 22.
Baseball—
A Shared Excitement

Angell, Roger   *The Summer Game*. New York, 1972.

Chalk, Ocania   *Pioneers of Black Sport*. New York, 1975.

Graham, Frank   *The New York Yankees: An Informal History*. New York, 1948.

Lewis, Franklin A.   *The Cleveland Indians*. New York, 1949.

O'Connor, Richard   *The German-Americans: An Informal History*. Boston, 1968.

Seymour, Harold   *Baseball: The Golden Age*. New York, 1971.

Smith, Chet, and Marty Wolfson   *Pittsburgh and Western Pennsylvania Sports Hall of Fame*. Pittsburgh, 1969.

Smith, Robert   *Baseball's Hall of Fame*. rev. ed. New York, 1973.

Spink, Alfred H.   *The National Game*. St. Louis, 1910.

Turkin, Hy, and S. C. Thompson   *The Official Encyclopedia of Baseball*. 6th rev. ed. South Brunswick, N.J., 1972.

Wagenheim, Kal   *Babe Ruth: His Life and Legend*. New York, 1974.

Chapter 23.
At Home

The American Dream

Bell, William E.   *Carpentry Made Easy; or, The Science and Art of Framing, on a New and Improved System*. Philadelphia, 1858.

Boorstin, Daniel J.   *The Americans: The National Experience*. New York, 1965.

Buder, Stanley   *Pullman: An Experiment in Industrial Order and Community Planning, 1880–1930*. New York, 1967.

Condit, Carl W.   *American Building*. Chicago, 1968.

Giedion, Sigfried   *Mechanization Takes Command: A Contribution to Anonymous History*. 1st ed., 1948. reprinted New York, 1969.

Goldberg, Isaac   *George Gershwin: A Study in American Music*. 1st ed. 1931. reprinted with supplement by Edith Garson, New York, 1958.

Kidder, F. E.   *Building Construction and Superintendence*. New York, 1898.

McKelvey, Blake   *The Emergence of Metropolitan America, 1915–1966*. New Brunswick, N.J., 1968.

     The Urbanization of America, 1860–1915. New Brunswick, N.J., 1963.

Wheeler, Thomas C., ed.   *The Immigrant Experience: The Anguish of Becoming American*. New York, 1971.

Jacob Riis—The Other Half

Cordasco, Francesco, ed.   *Jacob Riis Revisited: Poverty and the Slum in Another Era*. Clifton, N.J., 1973.

Riis, Jacob A.   *How the Other Half Lives*. New York, 1891.

     The Making of an American. New York, 1901.

Chapter 24.

Mass Production—
An Example of
Global Give-and-Take

Broehl, Wayne G.   *Precision Valley: The Machine Tool Companies of Springfield, Vermont*. Englewood Cliffs, N.J., 1959.

Fitch, Charles H.   "Report on the Manufactures of Interchangeable Mechanism," *Report on the Manufactures of the United States at the Tenth Census, 1880*. Washington, D.C., 1883.

Gilbert, K. R.   *The Portsmouth Blockmaking Machinery*. London, 1965.

Hobsbawm, E. J.   "Customs, Wages, and Work-Load in Nineteenth-Century Industry," in *Essays in Labour History,* Asa Briggs and John Saville, eds. London, 1967.

Jenks, Leland H.   "Early Phases of the Management Movement," *Administrative Science Quarterly,* 1960, 5:421–477.

Roe, Joseph W.   "Interchangeable Manufacture," *Newcomen Society, Transactions,* 1937–1938, 17: 165–174.

Rosenberg, Nathan   "Technological Change in the Machine Tool Industry, 1840–1910," *Journal of Economic History,* 1963, 23:414–443.

Rosenberg, Nathan, ed.   *The American System of Manufactures: The Report of the Committee on Machinery of the United States 1855 and the Special Reports of George Wallis and Joseph Whitworth 1854.* Edinburgh, 1969.

Sawyer, John E.   "The Social Basis of the American System of Manufacturing," *Journal of Economic History,* 1954, 14:361–379.

Strasmann, W. Paul   *Risk and Technological Innovation: American Manufacturing Methods During the Nineteenth Century.* Ithaca, 1959.

Thompson, George V.   "Intercompany Technical Standardization in the Early American Automobile Business," *Journal of Economic History,* 1954, 14:1–20.

Woodbury, Robert S.   "The Legend of Eli Whitney," *Technology and Culture,* 1960, 1:235–251.

Chapter 25.

From Guns to Cars—Products for Mass Consumption

The Revolver Before, By, and After Samuel Colt

Bady, D. B.   *Colt Automatic Pistols 1896–1955.* Los Angeles, 1956.

Boothroyd, Geoffrey   *Guns Through the Ages.* New York, 1962.

Dunlap, Jack   *American, British and Continental Pepperbox Firearms.* Los Altos, Calif., 1964.

Edwards, William B.   *The Story of Colt's Revolver.* Harrisburg, Pa., 1953.

Haven, C. T., and F. A. Belden   *A History of the Colt Revolver.* New York, 1962.

Mitchell, J. L.   *Colt—The Man, the Arms, the Company.* Harrisburg, Pa., 1959.

Parsons, John E.   *The Peacemaker and Its Rivals.* New York, 1955.

Serven, James E.   *Colt Firearms, 1836–1960.* Santa Ana, Calif., 1960.

Sherrill, Robert   *The Saturday Night Special.* New York, 1973.

Webster, Donald B.   *Suicide Specials.* Harrisburg, Pa., 1958.

Winant, Lewis   *Pepperbox Firearms.* New York, 1952.

Winders, G. H.   *Sam Colt and His Guns.* New York, 1959.

"We Taught the World to Sew"

Bourne, Frederick C.   "American Sewing Machines," in Chauncey M. Depew, *One Hundred Years of American Commerce.* vol. 2. New York, 1895.

Cooper, Grace Rogers   *The Invention of the Sewing Machine.* Washington, D.C., 1968.

Gilbert, K. R.   *Sewing Machines: A Science Museum Illustrated Booklet.* London, 1970.

Mahoney, Tom   "A Century of Singer," *Reader's Digest,* February 1951.

Piantanida, S.   *La macchina per cucire.* Milan, 1962.

Renters, Wilhelm   *Praktisches Wissen von der Nähmaschine.* Langensalza, Germany, 1933.

"Remington Means Typewriter"

Adler, Michael H.   *The Writing Machine.* London, 1973.

Beeching, Wilfred A.   *Century of the Typewriter.* London, 1974.

Bliven, Bruce, Jr.   *The Wonderful Writing Machine.* New York, 1954.

Current, Richard N.   *The Typewriter and the Men Who Made It.* Urbana, Ill., 1954.

Herkimer County Historical Society   *The Story of the Typewriter, 1873–1923.* Herkimer, N.Y., 1923.

Herrl, George — *The Carl P. Dietz Collection of Typewriters.* Milwaukee, Wis., 1965.

Richards, G. Tilghman — *The History and Development of Typewriters.* London, 1964.

Photography and the Kodak System

Kodak Milestones. Rochester, N.Y., 1971.

Ackerman, Carl W. — *George Eastman.* Boston, 1930.

Eder, Josef Maria — *History of Photography.* trans. E. Epstean. New York, 1945.

Gernsheim, Helmut — *The History of Photography.* London, 1955.

Taft, Robert — *Photography and the American Scene.* New York, 1938.

Mass Production Carried to Extremes—
Henry Ford and the Model T

"Automobile" and "Automotive Industry," *Encyclopaedia Britannica.* 15th ed. *Macropaedia.* vol. 2. Chicago, 1974.

Greenleaf, William — "Henry Ford," *Dictionary of American Biography Supplement 4, 1946–1950.* New York, 1974.

Nelson, Walter Henry — *Small Wonder: The Amazing Story of the Volkswagen.* Boston, 1970.

Nevins, Allan, and Frank Ernest Hill — *Ford.* 3 vols. New York, 1954–1963.

Rae, John B. — *American Automobile Manufacturers: The First Forty Years.* Philadelphia, 1959.

Wilkins, Mira, and Frank Ernest Hill — *American Business Abroad: Ford on Six Continents.* New York, 1964.

Chapter 26.
A Taste for
Foreign Things at Home

The American Diet—
An Ethnic Mix

The American Heritage Cookbook. New York. 1964, 1969.

The Complete Family Cook Book. New York, 1969.

Amerine, M. A., and V. L. Singleton — *Wine.* Berkeley, Calif., 1965.

Aresty, Esther B. — *The Delectable Past.* New York, 1964.

Bailey, Adrian — *The Cooking of the British Isles.* New York, 1969.

Baron, Stanley — *Brewed in America.* New York, 1972.

Beard, James — *James Beard's American Cookery.* Boston, 1972.

Beecher, Catherine E. — *Miss Beecher's Domestic Receipt Book.* New York, 1846.

Berolzheimer, Ruth, ed. — *The American Woman's Cook Book.* Chicago, 1945.

Blot, Pierre — *Hand-Book of Practical Cookery.* 1st ed., 1869. reprinted, New York, 1973.

What to Eat and How to Cook It. New York, 1863.

Blumberg, R. S., and H. Hannum — *The Fine Wines of California.* Garden City, N.Y., 1971.

Ceci, Lynn — "Fish Fertilizer: A Native North American Practice?" *Science,* 1975, 188:26–30.

Cummings, Richard O. — *The American and His Food. A History of Food Habits in the United States.* Chicago, 1940.

Farmer, Fannie Merritt — *The Boston Cooking-School Cook Book.* Boston, 1922. reprint of 1st ed. (1896), New York, 1973.

Furnas, J. C. — *The Americans. A Social History of the United States 1587–1914.* New York, 1969.

Kimball, Marie | *Thomas Jefferson's Cook Book*. Richmond, Va., 1949.

Lea, Elizabeth E. | *Domestic Cookery, Useful Receipts, and Hints to Young Housekeepers*. Baltimore, 1878.

Leonard, Jonathan Norton | *The Cooking of America: New England*. New York, 1970.

Leslie, Eliza | *Miss Leslie's New Cookery Book*. Philadelphia, 1857.

Seventy-five Receipts for Pastry, Cakes, and Sweetmeats. Boston, 1834.

Lichine, Alexis | *Alexis Lichine's Encyclopedia of Wines and Spirits*. New York, 1968.

Lowenstein, Eleanor | *Bibliography of American Cookery Books 1742–1860*. Worcester, Mass., 1972.

Nevins, Allan, ed. | *American Social History as Recorded by British Travellers*. New York, 1969.

Parloa, Maria | *Miss Parloa's New Cook Book and Marketing Guide*. Boston, 1908.

Randolph, Mary | *The Virginia House-Wife*. Washington, D.C., 1824.

Rombauer, Irma S., and Marion Rombauer Becker | *The Joy of Cooking*. Indianapolis, 1964.

Root, Waverley | *The Cooking of Italy*. New York, 1968.

Simmons, Amelia | *American Cookery*. reprint of 1796 ed., New York, 1958.

Smallzried, Kathleen | *The Everlasting Pleasure*. New York, 1956.

Tannahill, Reay | *Food in History*. New York, 1973.

Trager, James | *The Foodbook*. New York, 1970.

Verrill, A. Hyatt | *Foods America Gave the World*. Boston, 1937.

Waldo, Myra | *International Encyclopedia of Cooking*. New York, 1971.

Wechsberg, Joseph | *The Cooking of Vienna's Empire*. New York, 1968.

Chapter 28.
Everywhere
Is Here and Now

Bruce, Robert V. | *Bell: Alexander Graham Bell and the Conquest of Solitude*. Boston and Toronto, 1973.

Carter, Samuel | *Cyrus Field: Man of Two Worlds*. New York, 1968.

Childs, Harwood L. | *Propaganda by Short Wave*. London, 1942.

De Soto, Clinton B. | *Two Hundred Meters and Down: The Story of Amateur Radio*. West Hartford, Conn., 1936.

Dibner, Bern | *The Atlantic Cable*. Norwalk, Conn., 1959.

Finn, Bernard S. | *Submarine Telegraphy: The Grand Victorian Technology*. London, 1973.

MacLaurin, William R. | *Invention and Innovation in the Radio Industry*. New York, 1949.

Michaelis, Anthony R. | *From Semaphore to Satellite*. Geneva, Switzerland, 1965.

Pierce, John R. | *The Beginnings of Satellite Communications*. San Francisco, 1968.

Index

Page numbers in italic indicate illustrations.

Cabinetmaking, 213, 214, 218. *See also* Furniture
Cables, *See* Roebling; Telegraph
Cabot, John, 28
Cahan, Abraham, 244
Cahokia, Illinois, 54
Cajuns, 55
Caledonian games, *455*
Calhoun, Daniel, 318
California, *7, 8, 32,* 78, 160, 240, 306, 362, 370, 597
Californian, 617
Calinda (or *Kalenda*), 74
Calvert, Sir George, 41
Calvo, Jacinto, 463
Camba, Julio, 575
Camden and Amboy Railroad, 180
Cameras. *See* Kodak system; Photography
Camille, 450
Campaign buttons, *407*
Campanella, Roy, 462
Campbell, Timothy, *400*
Canada, 54; emigrant trade, 121
Canal boat, 161
Canals, 176–177, *178,* 356
Caney, Cuarteto, 443
Caniff, Milton, 601
Cantor, Eddie, 420, *422,* 431, 446
Cape Breton, 28
Cape Canaveral, 628
Cape Cod, 38, 325
Cape May, 496
Capp, Al, 601
Capra, Frank, 447
Capsicum, 594
Carder, 197, *198, 200*
Caricatures, *280, 282, 283, 284, 285, 287, 291. See also* Stereotypes
Carmel, California, 78
Carmichael, Hoagy, 437
Carnegie, Andrew, 277
Carolinas, 27, 59, 144
Carpathia, 617, 618
Carpentier, George, *459*
Carr, Leroy, 443
Carriage, steam, *553*
"Carry Me Back to Old Virginny," 421
Cart, medieval type, *165;* peddlers', 216
Carter, Henry, 408
Cartier, Jacques, 29
Cartoons, political, *130, 283, 389, 390, 392*
Carty, Florence, 59
Caruso, Enrico, 441, *442,* 499
Casimir, 55
Cassimere, 203

Cast-iron stoves, 493
Castañeda, Pedro de, 28
Castle, Vernon and Irene, 431
Castle Clinton, 131
Castle Garden, 131–132, *133,* 134, 414, 478
Castroville, California, 583
Catholics, 29, 38, 41, 59, 386, 387
    prejudice against, 90, 278, 395
    voting rights, 92, 95
Centennial. *See* Philadelphia Centennial of 1876
Central Pacific Railroad, 181, 187, 370
Ceramics, 37, 66, 254. *See also* Pottery
Chairs, Chippendale-style, 64, *65;* German, 60; ladder-back, 39, *48, 64, 65;* plank, *61;* Queen Anne, 51, *53;* rocking, *492, 499;* side, 51; Windsor, 51, *53*
Chaliapin, Feodor, 415
Chalice, *246*
Chamberlain's medicines, *571*
Chambers, William, 222
Chambers's Encyclopedia, 74
Champion Harvester, *512*
Champlain, Samuel de, 54
Chaplin, Charles, 412, 447, *448*
Charles I, 27, 40, 41
Charles II, 55, 59
Charlestown, South Carolina, 59, 70, 140, 411, 414, 598
Charlie Brown, 600
Chavez, Cesar, 383, 384, 396
Cherokee Indians, *16*
Chesapeake Bay, 28, 29–30
Chevalier, Albert, 431
Chevalier, Maurice, 450, *451*
Chevrolet, 552
Chicago, Illinois, 148, 176, *360,* 364, 374, 380, 396, 414, 461, 462, *485, 486, 488,* 496, 511
Chicago and North Western Railway Company, *189*
Chicago *Tribune,* 601
Chicopee, Massachusetts, 511, *514*
Chili con carne, 581, 584
Chilis, 10, 594
Chinatown, San Francisco, 254
Chinese
    cooking, 584
    employment, 187, 254
    exclusion, 300, 384
    masks, *258*
    porcelain, *43*
    prejudice against, 278, *287, 289, 291, 292,* 370
    restaurant, *588*

tong, 245
    violence toward, *370*
Chinoiserie, 51
Chop suey, 581
Christ, Rudolph, 60
Christian, Charlie, 440
Christianity, 8, 26, 30
Christmas cards, 408
Christmas Drawings for the Human Race (Nast), 408
Christowe, Stoyan, 276
Chromolithograph, *231*
Chronometer, 118
Chrysler, 552
Church, William, 553
Church of England. *See* Anglican Church
Cibola, 26, 28
Cider, 598
Cigarmakers' Union, 376
Cincinnati, Ohio, 196, 222, 461, 479
Cincinnati Red Stockings, 461, 463
Circus, 421–424, *426*
Citizenship, 300–301. *See also* Naturalization; Voting
Civil War. *See* Military
Clark, Edward, 530
Clavier Imprimeur, 538
Claxton, Philander P., 307
Clay, E. W., 283
Clemente, Roberto, 463, *475*
Cleveland, Grover, 141
Cleveland, Ohio, 274, 311, 320, 364, 461, 462, 488, *491*
Cleveland Belt Line, 358
Cleveland Indians, 462, 463
Cleveland White Autos, 461
Cliff Palace, Mesa Verde, Colorado, *11*
Clinton, De Witt, 72
Clipper ships, *120*
Clocks, 40; bracket, 40; English shelf, 40; lantern, 40, *50;* time, *368*
Coaches, 161–164, *170, 172*
Coal, 352, 354. *See also* Miners
Cobb, Ty, 461, 463
Cobbett, William, 584
Cobbledick, Gordon, 461
Coca-Cola, 565, 566, 599
Cocoa, 586
Cody, W. F., 425
Cohan, George M., 415, 434
Cohen, Andy, 463
Colbert, Claudette, 450, *451*
Cole slaw, 582
Colleen Bawn, The, 412
Collier, Elisha, 522
Collyer, Dan, 430

Colman, Ronald, 450
Colt, Samuel, 511, 514, 520–521, *522,* 524
Colton, Calvin, 197, 276
Coltrane, John, 440
Colt revolver, 520–521, *524, 526,* 564; factory, 204
Columbia Broadcasting System, 443
Columbia Records, 443, 499
Columbus, Christopher, 4, 8, 10, 24
Columbus *Dispatch,* 466
Comic books, 603
Comic strips, 600–609
Comisky Park, 462
Commentaries on the Laws of England (Blackstone), 92
Commereau, Thomas, *69*
Common Sense (Paine), 196
Company towns, 486, *487,* 488
Compleat Housewife (Smith), 582
Comstock Lode, 241
Concertina, 254, *272*
Concord, Massachusetts, 522
Concord coach, *172*
Conestoga wagon, 161, *174*
Coney, John, 70
Congregation Shearith Israel, 70
Congressional Medal of Honor, 327
Congressmen, foreign-born, *400*
Congress of Industrial Organizations, 380
Connecticut, 39
Conquistadores, 26
Conrad, Frank, 443
Constitution, United States, 84, 95, 300
Construction work, 363, *365*
Consumer products, 563, 565. *See also* specific products
Continental army, 326
Continental Congress, 93
Contract labor, 208–210
Coogan, Jackie, *448*
Coogan, Richard, 446
Cook, Thomas, 496
Cookies, 582
Cooking, 581–589
Coolidge, Cornelius, 522
Cooper, James Fenimore, 142
Copeland, Joseph, 41
Copp, Jonathan, 39, 41, 48
Cordova, New Mexico, 78
Corn, 4, *7,* 10, *11,* 581, 582
Coronado, Francisco Vásques de, 26, 28
Coronelli, Vincenzo, *32*
Correll, Charles, 446
Corsi, Edward, 137
Cortés, Hernando, 25, 73

Photograph Credits

Smithsonian Institution	6, 7, 8, 9, 12, 13, 14, 22, 23, 26, 32, 36, 39, 40A, 40B, 42, 44, 52, 55, 56, 57, 58A–58E, 59, 60, 61, 62A, 62B, 63, 64, 65, 66, 67, 68, 69, 70, 71A, 71B, 72, 73, 74A, 74B, 75, 76, 77, 78, 79, 80, 81A, 81B, 82, 84A–84D, 88, 89, 90, 91, 92, 93, 100A–100D, 103A, 103B, 104A–104D, 106B, 107A, 107B, 108, 109, 111, 112, 113, 116, 117, 118, 120, 121, 122, 124, 125, 126, 127, 128, 129, 130A, 130B, 131, 132, 133, 134, 135, 136, 137, 138, 139, 141, 142, 144, 145, 146, 148, 149, 151, 152, 153, 154, 159, 160, 161A–161C, 162, 163, 164B, 169, 170, 171, 172, 177, 178, 179, 180A–180E, 180G, 190, 191, 192, 193, 194, 195, 196, 198, 199, 200, 201, 202, 203, 204, 207, 208, 209, 210, 211, 214A, 215A, 215B, 218B, 222, 224, 226B, 228, 229, 230A, 230B, 231, 233A, 233B, 234, 236A, 236B, 237, 238, 239A, 239B, 242, 244, 246, 255, 258, 259, 260, 262, 263, 264, 265, 266, 267, 268, 271, 272, 273, 274, 276, 278, 279, 280, 291A, 291B, 294, 295, 296, 303A–303G, 305B, 306, 310, 313, 315, 316, 317, 318, 321, 322, 326, 329, 333, 334, 339, 350A, 350B, 354, 355, 357A–357C, 358, 359A, 359B, 360A, 360B, 361, 362, 364, 365A–365C, 366, 367, 368, 369, 372A–372C, 373, 374, 375, 376, 377A–377C, 379, 380, 381A–381H, 383D, 385, 386, 387, 388A, 388B, 388D, 388E, 390, 391, 392, 393, 394, 395, 396, 397B, 398, 400A, 400B, 400D, 401B, 402A–402G, 406, 409A, 409B, 410A, 410B, 411A, 411B, 412, 413, 414A, 414B, 418, 419, 420A, 420B, 421A, 421B, 422A–422E, 423A–423C, 424A–424E, 425A–425C, 426, 427A–427C, 428A, 428B, 429A, 430, 431A, 431B, 432A–432C, 433, 434A–434I, 435, 436, 437B, 438, 440, 441, 442, 443, 444, 445, 446, 448, 450, 451
Amalgamated Clothing Workers of America	158, 256
American Battle Monuments Commission	240B
American Express	408A–408I
Bell Laboratories	452
Bettmann Archive, Inc.	253, 319
British Museum	51
Brown Brothers	304A, 320
Chicago Historical Society	223B, 247, 261
Cleveland Public Library	351, 352
Columbia Broadcasting Systems	275
Culver Pictures	356
Field Museum of Natural History, Chicago	11
Ford Archives, Henry Ford Museum	254A, 254B, 371A, 371B, 401A, 403, 404A–404G, 405
Gary L. Hughes for the Smithsonian Institution	213A, 240A
Heimatmuseum Mayen in der Eiffel, Germany	383A
Helga Studio for the Smithsonian Institution	1, 2, 3, 4, 5, 10, 15, 16, 17, 24, 25, 27A, 27B, 28, 29, 30, 31, 33, 34, 35, 37, 41, 43, 45, 46, 47, 48, 49A–49D, 50, 53, 54, 83, 86A–86C, 87, 97A–97C, 99, 101, 102, 105, 106A, 114, 115, 119, 123, 140A–140C, 155, 156A, 156B, 164A, 164C–164F, 165A, 165B, 166, 167, 173, 174, 175A, 175B, 176, 180F, 181, 182, 183A, 183B, 185, 186, 187, 188, 241, 248, 252A–252C, 292E, 302B, 304B, 308, 353, 378, 382, 384, 389, 397A, 437A, 447, 449
Holiday Inn	407A–407E
Illinois Labor Historical Society	257
International Museum of Photography, George Eastman House	399
Library of Congress	18, 19, 20, 21, 38, 205, 216, 269, 270A–270L, 302A, 305A, 309, 312, 343, 345, 346, 347, 348, 349, 363, 400C
McDonald's Inc.	417A, 417B
Manchester Historical Association	293
Metropolitan Museum of Art	251

Finally, special thanks must go to Diana Menkes. She has been so essential to the production of this book that it is virtually impossible to imagine its timely completion without her aid. Her blue pencil touched every page of manuscript. In double checking many of the facts and in smoothing the prose she made this book more accurate and more readable.

This book was photo-composed in film by
Composing Room of Michigan, Grand Rapids,
Michigan. The text type is Times Roman. The
display type is Helvetica.

Printed on Patina in the Duotone process and
bound by Halliday Lithograph, West Hanover,
Massachusetts.

Production and manufacturing coordination was
directed by Joseph Montebello.

Manuscript and proof coordination was handled
by William B. Monroe.

In-house design liaison by C. Linda Dingler.

Design assistance was provided by Scarlett
Richman and Ann Pomeroy.